Réunion &
Seychelles

Seychelles
p270

Madagascar

Mauritius
p46

Rodrigues
p154

Réunion
p175

THIS EDITION WRITTEN AND RESEARCHED BY
Jean-Bernard Carillet, Anthony Ham

Contents

TORTOISE, CURIEUSE
ISLAND (P299)

BOTANICAL GARDENS
(P83), PAMPLEMOUSSES

Contents

SPECIAL FEATURES

Welcome to Mauritius, Réunion & Seychelles

Prediction for your arrival: it's a sunny, 29°C in the air and water. Soon you're lazing on a white-sand beach with a tropical fruit juice in hand – the best cure for winter blues.

Life's a Beach

The Seychelles (and, to a lesser extent, Mauritius) is home to perhaps the sexiest beaches in the world. They're so consistently perfect that it's hard not to become blasé about them. There's nothing better to do than spend days under the bright tropical sun on the beach, swinging in hammocks, splashing in the sea and sipping a cocktail. Even Réunion, which doesn't fit the cliché of a sun-soaked Edenic paradise, has a few good stretches of sand.

From Beach to Adventure

Believe it or not, a day will come during your stay when you decide you've had enough with the beach lounging. Mauritius, Rodrigues, Réunion and the Seychelles aren't just about pampering and relaxation; when it comes to recharging adrenaline levels, they have big surprises up their sleeves. Hike the footpaths that criss-cross the islands, ranging from meandering trails to trudges up mountains; scuba dive in enticing warm waters, marvelling at more than 300 species of fish (and the odd shipwreck or two); catch the wind and waves on a kiteboard; take a boat tour; explore magnetic canyons; or discover the countryside on horseback.

To Luxe or Not to Luxe

It's hardly surprising that the Seychelles and Mauritius are choice destinations for honeymooners: here the world's most exclusive hotels compete with each other to attain ever-greater heights of luxury, from personal butlers and private lap pools to in-room massages and pillow menus – not to mention sensuous spas. But if this is not in your budget, don't let that dissuade you from buying a ticket to these destinations. Small, family-run hotels, bed and breakfasts and self-catering establishments offer a closer-to-the-culture experience at prices that won't require you to re-mortgage the house.

Cultural Gems

The biggest mistake anyone could make would be to assume that these islands are for beach holidays, nature and adrenaline only – there's so much more to each destination that any trip will be an unforgettable and exciting experience, whether it be exploring Mauritius' fascinating colonial past in its myriad mansions or museums, attending a music festival or a fire-walking ceremony, visiting an old sugar factory or a restored Creole villa, or simply soaking up the atmosphere of a picturesque village.

Why I Love Mauritius, Réunion & Seychelles

By Jean-Bernard Carillet, Author

On my first trip to Mauritius, I was blown away by the wealth of religious buildings and the rich Indian cultural heritage. On Rodrigues, I'll never forget the sensational dives in La Passe St François. On subsequent trips I did plenty of hiking in Réunion, including a memorable week across Cirque de Mafate. The Seychelles? After four trips there, I confess I have a soft spot for La Digue, because life is so unhurried on this tiny island, it's affordable and the beaches are just incredible. My favourite is Anse Cocos. See you there!

For more about our authors, see page 352

Above: Anse Source d'Argent (p305), Seychelles

Mauritius, Réunion & Seychelles

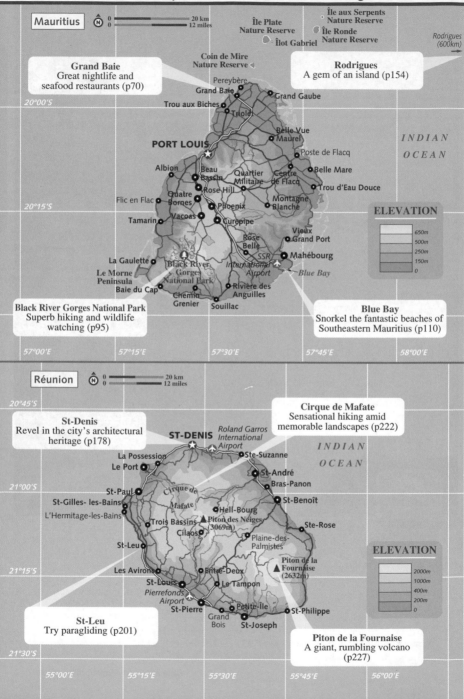

Mauritius Ⓝ 0 —— 20 km / 0 —— 12 miles

Île Plate Nature Reserve

Île aux Serpents Nature Reserve

Île Ronde Nature Reserve

Îlot Gabriel

Rodrigues (600km)

Grand Baie
Great nightlife and seafood restaurants (p70)

Rodrigues
A gem of an island (p154)

Coin de Mire Nature Reserve

20°00'S

Pereybère
Grand Baie
Trou aux Biches
Triolet
Grand Gaube

Belle Vue
Maurel

INDIAN
OCEAN

PORT LOUIS

Poste de Flacq

Albion
Beau Bassin
Quartier Militaire
Centre de Flacq
Belle Mare

Rose Hill
Trou d'Eau Douce

Flic en Flac
Quatre Bornes
Phoenix
Montagne Blanche

20°15'S

Tamarin
Vacoas
Curepipe

ELEVATION

Rose Belle
Vieux Grand Port
650m
500m
250m
150m
0

La Gaulette
Black River Gorges National Park
SSR International Airport
Mahébourg
Blue Bay

Le Morne Peninsula
Baie du Cap
Rivière des Anguilles

Chemin Grenier
Souillac

Black River Gorges National Park
Superb hiking and wildlife watching (p95)

Blue Bay
Snorkel the fantastic beaches of Southeastern Mauritius (p110)

57°00'E   57°15'E   57°30'E   57°45'E   58°00'E

Réunion Ⓝ 0 —— 20 km / 0 —— 12 miles

20°45'S

Cirque de Mafate
Sensational hiking amid memorable landscapes (p222)

St-Denis
Revel in the city's architectural heritage (p178)

ST-DENIS
Roland Garros International Airport

INDIAN
OCEAN

La Possession
Le Port
Ste-Suzanne

St-André
Bras-Panon

21°00'S

St-Paul
Cirque de Mafate
St-Benoît

St-Gilles- les-Bains
L'Hermitage-les-Bains

Trois Bassins
Hell-Bourg
Piton des Néiges (3069m)
Cilaos
Ste-Rose

Plaine-des-Palmistes

St-Leu

ELEVATION

Les Avirons
Entre-Deux
Piton de la Fournaise (2632m)
2000m
1000m
400m
200m
0

21°15'S

St-Louis
Pierrefonds Airport
Le Tampon

St-Leu
Try paragliding (p201)

St-Pierre
Grand Bois
Petite-Île
St-Philippe
St-Joseph

Piton de la Fournaise
A giant, rumbling volcano (p227)

21°30'S

55°00'E   55°15'E   55°30'E   55°45'E   56°00'E

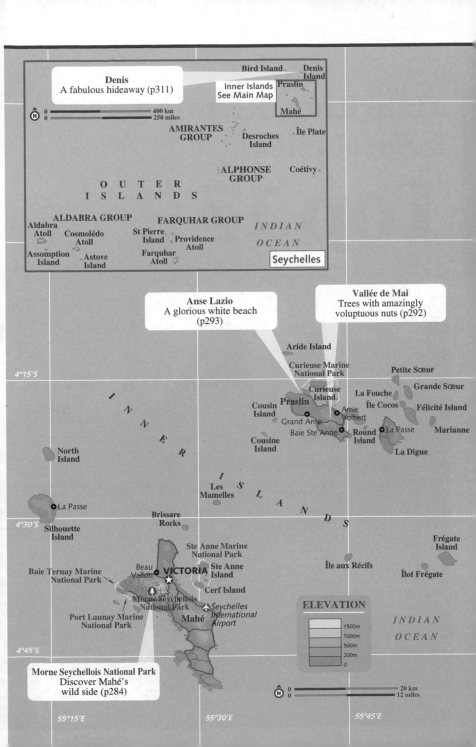

Denis
A fabulous hideaway (p311)

Bird Island Denis Island

Inner Islands
See Main Map

Praslin

Mahé

0   400 km
0   250 miles

AMIRANTES GROUP

Desroches Island

Île Plate

ALPHONSE GROUP

Coétivy

O U T E R
I S L A N D S

INDIAN

OCEAN

ALDABRA GROUP

Aldabra Atoll

Cosmolédo Atoll

Assomption Island

Astove Island

FARQUHAR GROUP

St Pierre Island

Providence Atoll

Farquhar Atoll

Seychelles

Anse Lazio
A glorious white beach (p293)

Vallée de Mai
Trees with amazingly voluptuous nuts (p292)

Aride Island

Curieuse Marine National Park

Petite Sœur

Curieuse Island

La Fouche

Grande Sœur

Cousin Island

Praslin

Île Cocos

Félicité Island

Grand Anse

Anse Volbert

Baie Ste Anne

Round Island

La Passe

Marianne

Cousine Island

La Digue

4°15'S

I N N E R

North Island

I S L A N D S

Les Mamelles

La Passe

Brissare Rocks

4°30'S

Silhouette Island

Frégate Island

Baie Ternay Marine National Park

Beau Vallon

Ste Anne Marine National Park

VICTORIA

Ste Anne Island

Île aux Récifs

Îlot Frégate

Cerf Island

Morne Seychellois National Park

Port Launay Marine National Park

Mahé

Seychelles International Airport

ELEVATION

1500m
1000m
500m
200m
0

INDIAN

OCEAN

4°45'S

Morne Seychellois National Park
Discover Mahé's wild side (p284)

0   20 km
0   12 miles

55°15'E

55°30'E

55°45'E

Mauritius, Réunion & Seychelles'
Top 17

1

Hiking Through the Cirque de Mafate (Réunion)

1 Perhaps the finest set of multiday hikes anywhere in the Indian Ocean, Cirque de Mafate (p39) feels like you're traversing the end of the earth. Wild and remote, watched over by fortress-like ridges and riven with deep valleys, this is an extraordinary experience. A four-day hike through the Haut Mafate can be combined with the four-day, even-more-secluded Bas Mafate. Best of all, these hikes take you through quiet mountain hamlets where you'll find *gîtes* (self-catering accommodation) where the welcome is warm and genuine.

Denis (Seychelles)

2 Welcome to paradise. It may be a much-abused cliché but the coral island of Denis (p311) comes as close to living up to this claim as anywhere on the planet. This is a place where warm tropical waters lap quietly upon a beach of white sand, while the lagoon offshore dazzles in magical shades of blue. The island's luxury lodge combines romance with seclusion to perfectly capture the idyll of barefoot luxury (no TV, no mobile phones), and you'll share the island with giant tortoises and gorgeous bird species.

JEAN BERNARD CARILLET

HOLGER LEUE / GETTY IMAGES ©

NARVIKK / GETTY IMAGES ©

JEAN BERNARD CARILLET / GETTY IMAGES ©

RICHARD BOUHET / GETTY IMAGES ©

Black River Gorges & Chamarel (Mauritius)

3 Some of the most dramatic scenery on Mauritius is found in the southwest. The thick forests of Black River Gorges National Park (p95) shelter fantastic and endangered birdlife that has been saved from the fate of the dodo, quite apart from the exceptional views from along the myriad hiking trails. After a morning's hiking, lunch just has to be in Chamarel (p96), home to a series of superb restaurants and a well-regarded rum distillery nestled in the hills. Black River Gorges National Park (p95)

Diving & Dolphins (Mauritius)

4 Some of the Indian Ocean's best dives are found off the west coast of Mauritius. The architecture of the underwater rock formations and the substantial schools of fish make the waters off Flic en Flac (p85) in particular a world-class dive destination. The best sites are the walls and drop-offs on the edge of the turquoise lagoon and La Cathédrale, near Flic en Flac is simply marvellous. A little to the south, off Tamarin (p92), swim with pods of dolphins out in the open water.

The Mighty Volcano (Réunion)

5 Piton de la Fournaise (p227) is Réunion's crowning glory. Seen from the viewpoint at Pas de Bellecombe, *le volcan* (as it's known to locals) broods black and beautiful, its shapely form towering over the island. But even though this is an active volcano, it's still possible to climb up to the crater rim and stare down into the abyss – one seriously memorable sight. Hiking and horse trails lead to the summit, while a scenic helicopter flight offers the ultimate birds-eye view down into the caldera.

Anse Lazio (Seychelles)

6 On the north of Praslin Island, Anse Lazio (p293) is like an apparition of just why Seychelles has become one of the most alluring destinations in the Indian Ocean. The beach here is near perfect, a stereotype come to life with golden sands, granite boulders at either end, palm trees and unbearably beautiful waters somewhere between turquoise and lapis lazuli. Ideal for hours spent lying on the beach, snorkelling or eating in one of the beachfront restaurants, Anse Lazio is the sort of place you'll never want to leave.

Gardens & Great Houses (Mauritius)

7 Mauritius' interior is, for the most part, steep and rugged, but it does shelter some exceptional sites. First on many travellers' lists are the vast botanical gardens at Pamplemousses (p83); the giant lily pads have to be seen to be believed. Not far away are two of the finest remnants of colonial plantation architecture in existence – the Chateau Labourdonnais (p83) just north of the gardens, and Eureka (p59), in the town of Moka. Sir Seewoosagur Ramgoolam Botanical Gardens (p83), Pamplemousses

PTGREENWOOD / GETTY IMAGES ©

JEAN PIERRE PIEUCHOT / GETTY IMAGES ©

Morne Seychellois National Park (Seychelles)

8 In their quest for the perfect beach, many travellers are oblivious to the fact that there's a splendid national park on Mahé, but they miss out on fantastic experiences in this lush park (p284). Take a guided hike through dense forest, coastal mangroves and rugged mountains and you'll soon believe that the world and its clamour belong to another planet. While exploring, you'll come across rare species of birds, reptiles and plants, not to mention breathtaking viewpoints.

St-Denis Architecture (Réunion)

9 The advantage of St-Denis (p178) not having a beach is that it forces you to turn your gaze inland and admire the city's architecture. The town hall, prefecture and a host of 'minor' palaces and mansions adorn the city with neoclassical columns, elaborate verandahs and *lambrequins* (ornamental window and door borders). Throw in Creole mansions, and a happy coexistence of mosque, cathedral, Chinese pagoda and Hindu temple, and the effect is at once international and quintessentially Réunionnais.

SERGIO CANOBBIO / GETTY IMAGES ©

OLIVIER CIRENDINI / GETTY IMAGES ©

Seafood by the Beach

10 The day's catch fresh to your table, with your toes buried in the sand. It's something we all dream about but it's a very real possibility on any of the islands covered by this book. Lobster, octopus, grilled fish, calamari – they're all staples of the Indian Ocean table. If you can't decide, all are regular inhabitants of your standard seafood platter; try one in Grand Baie (p75). Best of all, the rich stew of sauces and cultural influences adds flavour, from Indian curries to red Creole sauces.

Paragliding in St-Leu (Réunion)

11 Fabulous views and reliably uplifting thermals year-round make St-Leu (p201) in Réunion a brilliant place to go paragliding. Launch off and soar high above the earth surrounded by silence and an overwhelming sense of unbridled freedom. At every turn, there is some utterly dramatic natural feature – the towering volcanoes of the interior, the turquoise waters of the lagoon – and the experience will appeal as much to beginners as to those with more experience. Your touchdown on a white-sand beach is the perfect finale.

Chambres & Tables d'Hôtes (Mauritius)

12 Whether along the west coast of Mauritius or in the quiet highlands of Rodrigues, staying in *chambre d'hôte* (family-run guesthouses; p144) is a wonderful way to learn about local life. Rooms are often simple, but the warmth and personal nature of the welcome you'll receive and the nightly *table d'hôte* (meal served at a *chambre d'hôte*) where the guests and hosts gather together for a traditional meal, make for the kind of experience that you'll remember long after the luxury resorts have faded in your memory. St Aubin (p117)

Vallée de Mai (Seychelles)

13 If you can tear yourself away from the beach, Vallée de Mai (p292) is a paradise of a different kind. Inscribed by Unesco on its World Heritage List, and home to the rare and singularly beautiful coco de mer palms and a host of other endemic plants, Vallée de Mai is all about immersion in the lush tropical forest, serenaded by birdsong, and losing yourself along quiet hiking trails that meander agreeably through this verdant mini wilderness.

The Land Time Forgot (Rodrigues)

14 Marooned out in the Indian Ocean, Creole Rodrigues (p154) is the sort of place where life moves to a different beat. There's so much to do here – Port Mathurin's busy Saturday market, a boat trip out to Île aux Cocos, the coastal walk from Graviers to St François past some of the loveliest beaches we know, snorkelling off the south coast, or diving La Passe de St François. But come here first and foremost to leave the world and its noise behind. Graviers (p158)

Shark-Spotting in Seychelles

15 Discerning divers have long known of Seychelles' claims to being one of the Indian Ocean's most rewarding dive destinations (p33). We like it especially for its variety of sea life, and the unmistakeable cachet of swimming with whale sharks and massive rays off Mahé. There are wreck dives and mind-blowing fish varieties off Brissare Rocks, but nothing beats the frisson of getting up close and personal to the whale sharks who frequent the area.

Hindu & Creole Festivals

16 Hindu festivals (p20) are a wonderful way to liven up your visit to Mauritius or Réunion. The biggest festival of all, in February or March, is the 500,000-strong Hindu pilgrimage to the sacred lake of Grand Bassin on Mauritius (p100). March is also the month of colourful Holi festivities, October means Divali, and Teemeedee in December or January is all about firewalking wherever Hindus are found. For celebrations of Creole culture, October is particularly exuberant in Rodrigues, Seychelles and Réunion. Cavadee festival, Mauritius

Southeastern Mauritius

17 Choosing your favourite beach on Mauritius is like trying to pick a flavour of ice cream – they're all so good! The eastern and southeastern shores are quieter than those elsewhere, particularly the beaches at Pointe d'Esny (p110) and Belle Mare (p125), and they're close to the forests of Vallée de Ferney (p118) and the offshore Île aux Aigrettes (p110). The latter, with its endangered bird species, giant tortoises and low-slung ebony forests, is like stepping ashore on Mauritius before human beings came and tamed the landscape. Belle Mare (p125)

16

DAVID SANGER / GETTY IMAGES ©

17

WALTER BIBIKOW / JAI / CORBIS / CORBIS ©

Need to Know

For more, see p144 (Mauritius), p263 (Réunion) and p318 (Seychelles).

Currency
Mauritian rupee (Rs) in Mauritius, euro (€) in Réunion, Seychellois rupee (Rs) and euro (€) in the Seychelles

Language
French (Mauritius, Réunion, Seychelles), English (Mauritius, Seychelles), Creole (Mauritius, Réunion, Seychelles)

Visas
Generally not required for stays up to 90 days

Money
ATMs widely available in major towns

Mobile Phones
GSM mobiles phones can be set to roaming; local prepaid SIM cards are available

Time
GMT/UTC plus four hours; no daylight saving time

When to Go

• Victoria (Seychelles)
GO Apr–Dec

Madagascar

Port-Louis (Mauritius)
GO Mar–Dec

Port Mathurin (Rodrigues)
GO Mar–Dec

St-Denis (Reunion)
GO Apr–Nov

High Season
(Dec, Jan & Jul–Aug)
➡ Hindu festivals and cultural events in December/January.

➡ Whale sharks and whales visit in July and August.

➡ Hotels jack up prices during Christmas/New Year and often require minimum stays of one week.

Shoulder (Apr–May & Sep–Nov)
➡ The best time to travel – less rain, lower humidity and bluer skies.

➡ Easter is busy.

➡ Perfect for outdoor activities, especially hiking and whale-watching.

➡ Pleasant temperatures, calmer seas and fewer visitors.

Low Season
(Feb–Mar & Jun)
➡ Some resorts offer discounted packages.

➡ Cheaper airfares.

➡ Rain and cyclones (February/March) in Mauritius and Réunion can perturb travel plans.

Useful Websites

Lonely Planet (www.lonely
planet.com/mauritius, www.
lonelyplanet.com/seychelles,
www.lonelyplanet.com/reun
ion) Summaries on travel to
Mauritius, Réunion and the Seychelles, hotel bookings, traveller
forum and more.

**Mauritius Tourism Promotion
Authority** (www.tourism-mauri
tius.mu) Has a great selection of
hotels, activities and other useful information including plenty
of ecotourism suggestions.

Île de la Réunion Tourisme
(www.reunion.fr) Réunion's
official tourist website is an
encyclopedia of things to see
and do.

Seychelles Travel (www.
seychelles.travel) Official home
of the Seychelles Tourism Board,
this website overflows with great
tips and ideas.

Important Numbers

There are no area codes in Mauritius, Seychelles or Réunion.
To dial listings in this book from
abroad, dial your international
access code (⌨00), the country
code, then the number (without
the '0' in Réunion).

Mauritius country code	⌨230
Seychelles country code	⌨248
Réunion country code	⌨262
Police (Mauritius & Seychelles)	⌨999
Police (Réunion)	⌨17

Exchange Rates

For exchange rates, see p47
(Mauritius), p176 (Réunion) and
p271 (Seychelles).

Daily Costs

**Budget:
Less than €100**

➡ Bed in a *gîte* (lodge) in
Réunion: €17

➡ Double room in a
guesthouse: €40–60

➡ Takeaway meal: €3–6

➡ Bus ticket: €0.40–4

**Midrange:
€100–200**

➡ Double room in a hotel or
B&B: €60–150

➡ Lunch and dinner in local
restaurants: €20–50

➡ Ferry ride in Seychelles: €50

➡ Short taxi trip: €8–20

**Top End:
More than €200**

➡ Room in a resort
(promotional deal): from €200

➡ Top restaurant dinner:
€40–80

➡ Helicopter tour: from €150

Opening Hours

Banks 8am or 9am to 2pm,
3pm or 4pm Monday to Friday,
sometimes open on Saturday
morning

Restaurants noon to 2pm and
6pm or 7pm to 9pm (later in
tourist hubs)

Shops 8am or 9am to 5pm
Monday to Friday, 8am to noon
(to 5pm in Réunion) Saturday.
Some shops closed at lunchtime
and on Monday in Réunion.

Arriving in Mauritius, Réunion & Seychelles

**Sir Seewoosagur Ramgoolam
International Airport (Mauritius; p150)** Resorts offer pick-up

service. If not, prebook a taxi via
the hotel or guesthouse.

**Roland Garros International
Airport (Réunion; p268)**
There's a shuttle bus to central
St-Denis about once an hour between 6am and 6.15pm (€4; 20
minutes). Taxis charge around
€20 for the ride (€30 at night);
they're metered.

**Seychelles international
airport (Seychelles; p321)** A
taxi to Beau Vallon (20 minutes)
costs around Rs 600.

Getting Around

Car Outside cities, renting a
car gives unmatched flexibility
and convenience. Cars can be
hired in major towns and at
the airports. Drive on the left in
Seychelles and Mauritius; on the
right in Réunion.

Air Pricey but efficient. Most
convenient services are between
Mauritius and Rodrigues and
between Mahé and Praslin.

Boat The preferred mode of
inter-island transport in the
Seychelles. Fast, reliable but
quite expensive.

Bus Very cheap. In all three
countries, getting around by
public transport is possible but
sometimes complicated and
rather slow.

Taxi In some cases hiring a taxi
is a great way to explore an area,
especially if you can share costs
with other travellers.

For more on **get-
ting around**, see
p150 (Mauritius),
p268 (Réunion)
and p321 (Seychelles).

If You Like...

Beaches

Anse Lazio, Seychelles On the island of Praslin and simply as gorgeous as you'll find in the Indian Ocean. (p293)

Petit Anse & Anse Soleil, Seychelles On the west coast of Mahé and somewhere close to heaven. (p288)

Grand Anse, Seychelles Quieter than other Seychelles stunners and every bit as beautiful. (p305)

Trou d'Argent, Rodrigues Pick any beach on Rodrigues' east coast, but this is our favourite. (p158)

South Coast, Mauritius There's a reason that five-star resorts love this area. (p114)

Le Morne & Tamarin, Western Mauritius Pretty beaches with dramatic mountainous backdrops. (p84)

Plage de Grande Anse, Réunion Cliffs and white sand in the wild south of the island. (p236)

Étang-Salé-les-Bains, Réunion Black-sand beach with sunsets to die for. (p205)

Hiking

Piton de la Fournaise, Réunion Climb to the rim of an active volcano – a classic hike. (p228)

Tour des Cirques, Réunion Five days of mountain bliss and quite simply one of the most beautiful hikes on the planet. (p41)

Haut Mafate, Réunion Four-day hike that takes you through some of Réunion's wildest Cirques. (p39)

Bas Mafate, Réunion Another four-day trek through the roof of Réunion. (p41)

Black River Gorges National Park, Mauritius Hiking trails through bird-rich wilderness and the island's last great forest. (p95)

Lion Mountain, Mauritius Underrated hike that scales the heights with great views and good bird-watching. (p119)

Graviers to St François, Rodrigues Lovely coastal walk past Rodrigues' best beaches. (p158)

Morne Seychellois National Park, Seychelles The country's best hiking. (p284)

Wildlife

Curieuse Island, Seychelles A veritable Galapagos of giant Aldabra tortoises, the last surviving Indian Ocean species. (p299)

Cousin Island, Seychelles Hundreds of thousands of birds crammed onto one tiny island. (p299)

Bird Island, Seychelles Nesting seabirds, giant tortoises and hawksbill turtles. (p311)

Île aux Aigrettes, Mauritius An island Noah's Ark where tortoises and pink pigeons roam free as they once did everywhere on Mauritius. (p110)

Black River Gorges National Park, Mauritius Rare bird species and old-growth forest add up to Mauritius' premier wilderness experience. (p95)

Vallée de Ferney, Mauritius Go looking for the Mauritius kestrel, once the world's most endangered bird. (p118)

Le Grand Brûlé, Réunion The island's best bird-watching in the wild and beautiful south. (p245)

Spectacular Landscapes

Piton de la Fournaise, Réunion The single most dramatic landform in the Indian Ocean, bar none. (p227)

Cirque de Cilaos, Réunion Perfect hiking country amid a landscape that reaches magnificently for the sky. (p209)

Plaine des Sables, Réunion Otherworldly atmosphere atop this lava-formed plain. (p228)

Cirque de Salazie, Réunion Another beguiling mountain kingdom. (p217)

Le Morne Peninsula, Mauritius Unesco site with both stunning beauty and a tragic story to match. (p102)

Black River Gorges National Park, Mauritius Waterfalls off the high plateau, dense forest and a deep river canyon. (p95)

Silhouette, Seychelles The most dramatic island in the Seychelles archipelago. (p310)

Denis, Seychelles The coral idyll that we all imagined when thinking of a desert island. (p311)

Romantic Getaways

North Island, Seychelles A cross between heavenly paradise, James Bond glamour and the last word in luxury. (p310)

Desroches, Seychelles Remote island with a superb resort that lacks the pretentiousness of many in the genre. (p312)

Le Saint Géran, Mauritius The last word in luxury with Michelín-starred chefs, indulgent beauty treatments and glorious accommodation. (p126)

Le Prince Maurice, Mauritius There's something in the air at Belle Mar on Mauritius' east coast and this sublime complex is close to heavenly. (p127)

Le Touessrok, Mauritius More east-coast luxury with its very own island to enhance the paradise credentials. (p123)

(Top) Mauritius kestrel (p140)
(Bottom) Cilaos, seen from the trail to Piton des Neiges (p214), Réunion

Month by Month

January

January is high season for all of the islands, with warm temperatures, but rain and even cyclones are possibilities, the latter primarily in Mauritius and Réunion. Hotel prices soar over the Christmas and New Year period.

✨ Chinese New Year

Chinese New Year in Mauritius and Réunion falls in late January or early February. On New Year's Eve, homes are spring cleaned and decked in red, the colour of happiness, and firecrackers are let off to protect against evil spirits.

February

Weather-wise, February is fairly similar to January, with humid conditions and the chance of rain. However, because most of Europe and elsewhere is now back at school, crowds are generally smaller.

✨ Maha Shivaratri

This massive February or March pilgrimage sees up to 500,000 Hindu pilgrims make their way by all means possible to the holy lake of Grand Bassin, close to Black River Gorges National Park; the lake's waters are said to come from the sacred Ganges River. (p100)

March

March continues the trend of warm temperatures with possible rain. The chance of cyclones remains, but is diminished. Festivals across all islands add plenty of local colour.

✖ Fish Festival

Rodrigues lives and breathes fish, and the Fête du Poisson, held on Rodrigues in the first week of March, marks the opening of the fishing season. It's celebrated with many festivities, including fishing expeditions – and lots of eating.

✨ Holi Hindus

Holi, the festival of colours which is celebrated in Mauritius and Réunion, is known for the exuberant throwing of coloured powder and water. The festival symbolises the victory of divine power over demonic strength. On the night before Holi, bonfires are built to symbolise the destruction of the evil demon Holika.

☆ French Week

Seychelles celebrates its French heritage around the middle of March with the Semaine de la Francophonie. For almost a week, French cultural expressions (song recitals, films and art exhibitions in particular) take over Mahé.

April

The weather starts to turn around April – this is usually the last month when cyclones affect weather patterns across the region and from now on temperatures drop slightly and the rains generally ease.

✨ Tamil New Year

Wherever there are large Indian communities (Mauritius and Réunion), the Tamil New Year is marked with great gusto, with dance displays often forming the centrepiece of the celebrations. The New

Year can ensure that things grind to a halt in predominantly Tamil areas.

May

Although this can change depending on the timing of French school holidays, May is generally a great time to visit – fewer tourists, milder temperatures, with rain or wind rarely a problem.

FetAfrik

With the possible exception of Rodrigues, the Seychelles is the most African of the Indian Ocean islands, and it celebrates its African origins with FetAfrik, a weekend of music and dance in late May. (p275)

August

August is one of the driest months in the Indian Ocean, and neither temperatures nor humidity reach the heights of later in the year. European holidays often push prices upwards.

☆ Creole Music

St-Pierre on the south coast of Réunion is the island's most vibrant town, and it's the perfect setting for Sakifo, the island's premier festival of Creole music. Given that almost half of the island's population claims Creole blood, the festival is a big event. (p231)

September

An extension of the Indian Ocean winter, September remains cooler and generally dry, although in Seychelles, where temperatures are getting warmer, the rains are just around the corner and can arrive early.

✯ Christian Holy Day

The most important date for many Mauritian Christians is 9 September, Père Laval Feast Day, which marks the anniversary of the priest's death. Pilgrims from around the world come to his shrine at Ste-Croix, on the outskirts of Port Louis, to pray for miracle cures. (p58)

October

October is an excellent month to visit Seychelles, with generally dry and calm weather conditions. Elsewhere, this is the month when high season crowds arrive although you may find bargains early in the month.

✯ Festival Kreol

Late October is when Creole culture comes to the fore. On predominantly Creole Rodrigues, there's the three-day Festival Kréol, while Seychelles dedicates a week to the outpouring of Creole cuisine, theatre, art, music and dance for its own Festival Kreol. Réunion also gets into the spirit with its Semaine Créole. (p275)

✯ Divali

Both Réunion and Mauritius mark the Tamil festival of light Divali (Dipvali), in late October or early November. It celebrates the victory of Rama over the evil deity Ravana and to mark this joyous event, countless candles and lamps are lit to show Rama the way home from his period of exile. (p248)

December

The first half of December is much like November, although the rains can make an appearance to dampen things a little. As Christmas approaches, prices soar to their highest all year.

✯ Teemeedee

Teemeedee is a Hindu and Tamil fire-walking ceremony held to honour various gods. Held throughout the year, most celebrations are in December and January when participants walk over red-hot embers scattered along the ground. (p248)

✯ Remembering Slavery

The grim colonial history of slavery is a particularly poignant memory for the region's Creole communities and Réunion marks the Commémoration de l'Abolition de l'Esclavage (Abolition of Slavery Day), with much Creole music and dancing.

Itineraries

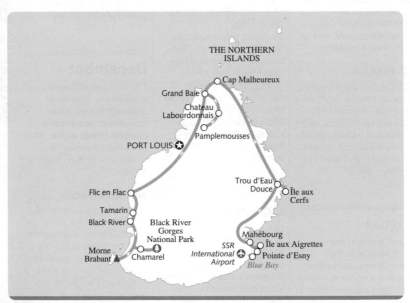

Essential Mauritius

Start near the airport along the stunning sands of **Pointe d'Esny**. Snorkel through
the sparkling azure lagoon at **Blue Bay**, eco-explore **Île aux Aigrettes**, then slip up to
sleepy **Mahébourg** for the Monday market.

Drive north along the coast. Embrace the fisherman lifestyle in **Trou d'Eau Douce**
then glide through the crystal lagoon to **Île aux Cerfs**. Pass through the endless acreage
of sky-reaching sugarcane before emerging on the north coast to take in the views at
Cap Malheureux. Hop on a catamaran bound for the scenic northern islands then treat
yourself to a round of repasts in lively **Grand Baie**. From Grand Baie, a day trip loop
could take in the botanical gardens and sugar factory at **Pamplemousses** and the lovely
Chateau Labourdonnais in Mapou.

Emerge on the west coast for a spot of diving in **Flic en Flac** then base yourself
around **Black River**. From here, there are plenty of exhilarating options to get the
blood flowing: canyoning through the **Black River Gorges National Park**, biking in
Chamarel or climbing the iconic **Morne Brabant**. Don't miss a morning of dolphin-
watching just off the coast of **Tamarin**.

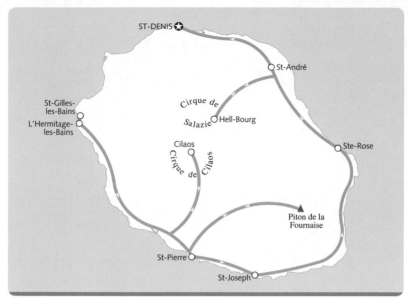

Tour of Réunion

From sophisticated beach resorts to mountain villages, art galleries to volcanoes, two weeks is perfect to sample the variety Réunion has to offer. Get hooked on the hiking and you could easily fill a month. This tour covers around 400km.

Spend a day sampling **St-Gilles-les-Bains**. This is a classic Indian Ocean resort, with all the accompanying highs and lows. We prefer to focus on the former – white sands, good surfing for beginners, diving and snorkelling and some pretty rowdy nightlife. The best beach to recover from it all is **L'Hermitage-les-Bains**. Allow three days to make the most of the area's botanical gardens, museums and water sports.

Head next to the **Cirque de Cilaos**, where you should allow at least two days to soak up the rugged mountain scenery and the laid-back atmosphere. Hiking and canyoning get you up close and personal with some of the best scenery you'll see anywhere, while there are also thermal springs, wine to taste and ecotourism possibilities thrown in for good measure.

There aren't many places in the world where you can climb an active volcano, but **Piton de la Fournaise** is one of them and in fact is one of the most accessible on earth. Base yourself at the Gîte du Volcan, ready to make a dawn ascent for stunning views.

Next make for the bright lights of **St-Pierre** – if possible, get here for the huge Saturday market and stay the night near **St-Joseph**. Don't miss **Ste-Rose**, where lava laps at the door of a church and narrowly misses the Virgin Mary. It can also serve as a return to civilisation (without the clamour of a big city) if you've been climbing volcanoes and hiking the circques.

As you head to the north of the island, go inland and stay at least two nights in **Hell-Bourg**, exploring the **Cirque de Salazie**. Finally, set off towards the capital via the Indian-influenced **St-André** and end your trip sampling cafe-culture and Creole architecture in the capital, **St-Denis**.

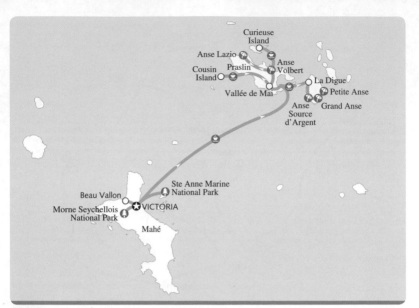

2 WEEKS Essential Seychelles

Two weeks is fine for a taster of the Seychelles' islands – allowing plenty of time for enjoying the very best of the country's superb beaches.

On the first day, tune into island life in the capital, **Victoria**, checking out the market and strolling among the palm trees in the botanical gardens. Move on to **Beau Vallon**, where three days can easily be spent messing around in and on the water – schedule in a day's diving or a boat trip to **Ste Anne Marine National Park**. Devote the next two days to the beaches and byways of Mahé, and walking in the stunning **Morne Seychellois National Park**, which has a little bit of everything: a colonial-era ruin, a tea factory and some fabulous hiking.

Next, cruise over to Praslin which closely resembles paradise. Ogle curvaceous *coco-de-mer* nuts in the Unesco World Heritage–listed **Vallée de Mai**, hike amid massive palm fronds and then flake out on the perfect, sugar-white sands at **Anse Lazio**, which is one of the prettiest beaches we know. Fill the next four days with snorkelling, diving and swimming off **Anse Volbert**, getting up close and personal with giant tortoises on **Curieuse Island**, home to a large breeding farm of giant Aldabra tortoises, and walking among cacophonous clouds of sea birds on **Cousin Island** with more than 300,000 birds and numerous endemic species – even amateur bird-watchers will want to spend more time here than most tours allow.

From Praslin, set sail for La Digue – if you thought Praslin was paradise, just wait until you lose yourself on La Digue. Three days is the perfect amount of time to lapse into La Digue's slow vibe. Visit **Anse Source d'Argent** – the archetypal idyllic beach, although it's by no means the only one on La Digue. Get there late afternoon for the best atmosphere and try to avoid high tide when the beach all but disappears. Take a snorkelling trip around nearby islands, then find solitude on the beaches of **Grand Anse** and **Petite Anse**. All too soon, it will be time to tear yourself away for the trip back to Victoria.

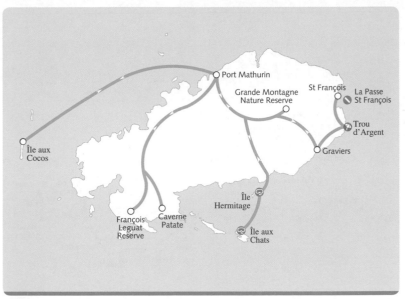

 Rodrigues – The Other Mauritius

Some call Rodrigues a mini-Mauritius, even though it's different in almost every way. What they really mean is that this is the closest you can get to what Mauritius was like before tourism took off, with a marked lack of development compared to the mainland. Few tourists make it out this far on the 1½-hour flight into the Indian Ocean. A week is ample time to discover the delights of this small, mountainous island. Depending on the weather you can divide the days between walking, diving and taking boat trips to nearby islands. It's a lot easier to fully experience the island's charms if you rent your own vehicle.

First, though, spend half a day strolling the streets of **Port Mathurin** and make sure it's a Saturday when the island's endearingly sleepy 'capital' springs into life, when it seems the entire population descends for the weekly market. Two of the not-to-be-missed sights on the island are the giant tortoises at **François Leguat Reserve** and the caves at **Caverne Patate**. Another day could be taken up by the classic coastal hike from **Graviers to St François**, passing en route a gem of a beach at **Trou d'Argent**. From St François either walk back the way you came or take a bus to Port Mathurin. Another day should be dedicated to the boat excursion to **Île aux Cocos** with its quiet beaches and lively seabird colonies, with a couple of hours set aside for a hike in search of endangered species in the **Grande Montagne Nature Reserve**.

You're spoilt for choice when it comes to diving. Top spots include the channel off St François, **La Passe St François**, on the edge of the lagoon, with more options beyond the reefs. There's good snorkelling around the little-visited **Île aux Chats** and **Île Hermitage** off the south coast.

And of course, you'll want to dedicate as much time as you can to simply kicking back on the beach for hours at a stretch and indulging in seafood feasts at one of the great family-run restaurants scattered around the island.

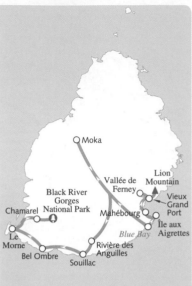

 ## Réunion's Sud Sauvage

 ## Southern Mauritius

Réunion's 'Wild South' offers volcanic landscapes, massive ravines, wave-lashed cliffs and sensational hiking trails. You can discover the best of the region in a reasonably leisurely week.

Start at **Ste-Rose** and head south to find the first tongues of lava tumbling down to the sea. Cross the threatening lava fields of **Le Grand Brûlé**, to spend a night or two near **St-Philippe** or **St-Joseph**; stay up in the hills for a real taste of rural life. From here you can hike the spectacular **Rivière des Remparts**.

Pass quickly through **St-Pierre** en route to the high plateau of **Plaine-des-Cafres** to visit the **Maison du Volcan**. Take the magnificent forest road up to **Piton de la Fournaise**, Réunion's restless volcano. Now drop back down to Plaine-des-Cafres, where you could spend a couple of days hiking to **Grand Bassin**, a village at the end of the world. Finally, head for **Plaine-des-Palmistes**, where the hikes through the **Forêt de Bébour-Bélouve** and to **Trou de Fer** provide unforgettable experiences.

The south of Mauritius offers the perfect combination of outstanding beaches and glorious natural scenery.

Blue Bay is everything its name suggests and its proximity to a host of postcard-pretty landscapes makes it the perfect base for the island's southeast. Don't miss the excursion to **Île aux Aigrettes** where you can spy pink pigeons and giant tortoises. **Vieux Grand Port** is where Mauritius' human story began centuries ago, and there's an untouched feel to the forests of **Vallée de Ferney**, home to the iconic Mauritius kestrel. **Lion Mountain** is a challenging but extremely rewarding hike. From your Blue Bay base, consider a day trip inland to Eureka in **Moka** high on the Central Plateau.

Now head west, pausing at La Vanille in **Rivière des Anguilles**, then in **Souillac** and **Bel Ombre** to enjoy the pretty coast. Continue on to Unesco World Heritage–listed **Le Morne** where dramatic hiking trails await. Climb up into the hills to **Chamarel**, with its terrific eating scene, the perfect base for scenic drives and hikes through **Black River Gorges National Park**.

Plan Your Trip
Diving

Though largely overshadowed by the iconic Maldives, scuba diving in Mauritius, Réunion and Seychelles is increasingly popular. Beneath the clear turquoise waters is a trove of unbelievable riches: rainbow-coloured fish and large pelagic species (and yes, sharks are part of the package), a dramatic seascape, a few wrecks and a host of drop-offs and reefs. It's not the cheapest place on earth to dive (Thailand or the Red Sea it ain't), but it's a great place to learn, and in turn love, scuba diving. Good news: bar a few areas, the dive sites are never crowded. For more on health and safety precautions, see p326.

Mauritius

So, you want variety? Abundant marine life, dramatic seascapes, atmospheric wrecks – Mauritius has it all, not to mention well-established, high-quality dive operators. Mauritius is almost entirely surrounded by a barrier reef, within which turquoise lagoons provide great possibilities for snorkellers, swimmers and novice divers. And there is the pièce de résistance: Rodrigues, which has virgin sites and outstanding fish life.

Where to Dive

The North

The north coast is a magnet for divers of all levels, and it's no wonder – there's a good balance of thrilling dives, wrecks, drop-offs and easy dives.

The islands off the coast (Île Plate, Coin de Mire) are the main highlights, with splendid sites and diverse fish life – not to mention a sense of wilderness. To the northwest, Trou aux Biches is the main jumping-off point to a variety of superb dives.

➡ **La Fosse aux Requins** This iconic site will make your spine tingle. On the northwestern side of Île Plate, a bowl-shaped basin carved into the cliff is home to an eerie concentration

Best Dives For...

Wrecks
Stella Maru (Mauriitus), Kei Sei 113 (Mauritius), Antonio Lorenzo (Réunion), Aldebaran (Seychelles)

Beginner Divers
Tug II (Mauritius), Le Pain de Sucre (Réunion), Le Jardin des Kiosques (Réunion), Anse Sévère (Seychelles)

Experienced Divers
Manioc (Mauritius), Shark Bank (Seychelles), Haï Siang (Réunion), Tombant de la Pointe aux Canonniers (Mauritius)

Shark Encounters
La Fosse aux Requins (Mauritius), Belmar Pass (Mauritius), Tombant de la Pointe au Sel (Réunion), Shark Point (Seychelles)

of blacktip sharks that keep swirling around. Why? Possibly because the waters here are rich in oxygen thanks to the swell. Good news for novice divers in search of excitement: this shallow dive (12m) is accessible with an open-water certificate, though the current can be a bit tricky. One proviso: the encounter with the sharks is probable but cannot be guaranteed!

➜ **The Wall** This dive is like looking down from the top floor of a skyscraper and wondering what it would be like to jump – only now, you can! You can soar right over an incredibly vertical face. Also impressive is the amount of healthy growth on the wall.

➜ **Djabeda** Near the Wall, this shipwreck is a former Japanese freighter that was scuttled in 1998 in 34m. It's more atmospheric than fishy.

➜ **Holt's Rock** Also known as Stenopus, this site features two rocky domes and clusters of big boulders in less than 25m. You're likely to see butterfly fish, parrot fish, massive moray eels, scorpion fish, angel fish and groupers.

➜ **Tombant de la Pointe aux Canonniers** Between Holt's Rock and Lobster Rock, this site is suitable for experienced divers, with an exhilarating drop-off that tumbles from 32m to about 60m. It has fairly good coral formations and tons of fish life.

➜ **Kingfish** Another splendid drop-off embellished with black coral and seafans. Small reef fish are plentiful, as are jacks and snappers.

➜ **Waterlily** & **Emily** These two photogenic barges were sunk in 1987 and are longstanding favourites for novice divers. They rest at a maximum depth of 26m.

➜ **Stella Maru** This Japanese freighter, scuttled in 1987 and resting upright in 25m, is a not-to-be-missed wreck. Over the years, it has become nicely encrusted and has attracted a host of colourful species, including moray eels, parrot fish and leaf fish.

The West

The Flic en Flac area ranks among the best in Mauritius when it comes to diving. Conditions are optimal year-round – it's protected from the prevailing winds – and visibility is usually excellent.

And the southwest coast? The area between Le Morne Peninsula and Black River (Rivière Noire) has a few diving hot spots, but they lack the 'wow' factor. The weak points are the average visibility and the fairly dull topography.

➜ **Rempart Serpent** (Snake Rampart) This is possibly the quirkiest dive in Mauritius. Located a 15-minute boat trip from Flic en Flac, it takes its name from the sinuous rock lying about 25m below the surface, which attracts perhaps the greatest concentration in the world of weird and wonderful scorpion fish, stonefish, moray eels and lionfish.

➜ **La Cathédrale** Be awed by a memorable seascape – think a warren of cavelets, stipples, passages and ledges. It's full of reef species, including fusiliers, surgeonfish, groupers, snappers, angelfish and lobsters. One downside: it's so popular that it's fairly congested.

➜ **Couline Bambou** Less crowded than La Cathédrale. This dive takes you through a kaleidoscope of changing scenery.

➜ **Manioc** A deep dive beloved by seasoned divers. It starts at -33m. Two massive rocky outcrops attract scores of reef species. Very atmospheric.

➜ **Kei Sei 113** Full of atmospheric wrecks, including the *Kei Sei 113*, scuttled in the 1980s. Resting at about 35m, it's accessible to seasoned divers only.

➜ **Tug II** Beginners rave about this 20m-long tugboat scuttled in 1981 that sits on the sand in about 20m. It's now home to thousands of colourful fish. Hint: lie without moving on the sandy bottom and you'll see swaying conger eels slip down into their burrows.

➜ **Passe St Jacques** The highlight of the site is the dazzling aggregation of barracudas, snappers and trevallies. The best opportunity to spot predators is during an outgoing current, when they patrol the pass in search of drifting lagoon fish.

The Southeast

Off the southeast coast it's the dramatic underwater terrain that impresses more than anything, making for unique profiles. You'll be rewarded with a profusion of caves, tunnels and giant arches – it's very scenic – as well as large numbers of pelagics thrown in for good measure. The hitch? From June to August most sites are exposed to the prevailing winds – expect choppy seas in rough weather.

➜ **Colorado** As befits its name, this site looks like an underwater version of the famous American valley. This 400m-long canyon is peppered with chasms, tunnels, crevices and boulders where masses of lobsters, jacks, groupers and barracuda seek shelter.

➔ **Roches Zozo** Another must-dive, close to Colorado. It features a huge rock that rises from the seabed to about 12m, pocked with crevices where lobsters hide.

➔ **Grotte Langouste** A cave brimming with lobsters.

➔ **Sirius** Great for wreck buffs. This 19th-century vessel rests in the 20m range off Mahébourg, but it's not in good shape.

➔ **Blue Bay** A safe, lovely spot to learn to dive, with a parade of reef fish to be observed on the sprawling reef. Blue Bay is the only place in Mauritius where you'll find patches of thriving coral.

The East

➔ **Belmar Pass** There is a fantastic parade of pelagic and reef fish to be observed in this pass. Strong tidal currents push the deep water back and forth through the passage, providing nutrients for a staggering array of species. The seascape is another draw; the passage is peppered with numerous chasms, gullies, coral canyons and sandy valleys. Sharks, especially bull sharks and grey sharks, regularly patrol the area. There are at least five different sites in the pass.

➔ **Passe de Trou d'Eau Douce** Another worthwhile site, though it's less spectacular than Belmar. It's usually done as a drift dive.

Rodrigues

This is the Indian Ocean at its best. A true gem, Rodrigues boasts numerous untouched sites for those willing to experience something different. There's a profusion of coral that you won't see anywhere else in Mauritius, and the density of fish life is astounding. The underwater scenery is another pull, with a smorgasbord of canyons, arches and caves.

➔ **La Passe St François** Rodrigues' signature dive, La Passe St François is a kilometre-long channel teeming with tuna, unicorn fish, groupers, turtles, rays and jacks (of the *Caranx ignobilis* variety) the size of a small car.

➔ **Le Canyon** This is a truly atmospheric dive site – you'll dive in a canyon that runs under the reef, with openings that allow beams of sunlight to pass through.

➔ **La Basilique** If surreal scenery is what makes you tick, don't miss this dive – it is like exploring an underwater medieval castle carved into the reef, full of galleries, faults and archways (but no coral).

DIVING WITH A CONSCIENCE

Please consider the following tips when diving, to help preserve the ecology and beauty of reefs:

➔ Encourage dive operators to establish permanent moorings at appropriate dive sites.

➔ Practise and maintain proper buoyancy control.

➔ Avoid touching living marine organisms with your body and equipment.

➔ Take great care in underwater caves, as your air bubbles can damage fragile organisms.

➔ Minimise your disturbance of marine animals.

➔ Take home all your rubbish, and any litter you may find as well.

➔ Never stand on corals, even if they look solid and robust.

➔ Do not buy or collect seashells, or buy any seashell or turtleshell products.

➔ Dive with a local dive operator that follows high safety, ethical and professional standards.

➔ **Karlanne** Another hot favourite, offering dense marine life and healthy coral formations, especially those of the *Acropora* and *Porites* genuses.

➔ **La Grande Passe** Many dive instructors consider La Grande Passe to be one of the very best medium-depth reefs in this area. To say it's fishy is an understatement, and you don't need to go below 20m to admire the full gamut of reef species.

Practicalities

Diving Conditions

Although Mauritius is diveable year-round, the most favourable periods are October to December, March and April (January and February are peak months for cyclone activity). During July and August, when the southeast trade winds are at their strongest, the seas are too rough and murky for diving all along the east coast and around Rodrigues. Visibility is heavily weather-dependent and thus varies a lot – from a low of 10m at certain sites at certain periods of the year to 40m at others.

Current conditions vary a lot, from imperceptible to powerful. Water temperatures range from a low of 22°C in August to a high of 28°C between December and February.

Dive Operators

There are at least 40 professional dive centres in Mauritius. Most belong to the **Mauritius Scuba Diving Association** (MSDA; ☑454 0011; www.msda.mu), which is affiliated with CMAS and makes regular and rigorous checks. Most dive centres are also affiliated with one or more of the internationally recognised certifying agencies, usually PADI or CMAS. Many dive centres in Mauritius are hotel-based, but they all welcome walk-in clients. In general, you can expect well-maintained equipment, good facilities and professional staff, but standards may vary from one centre to another, so it pays to shop around.

Réunion

Who said that diving in Réunion wasn't interesting? OK, the island is mostly famous for its trekking options, but it shouldn't be sneezed at. You'll be positively surprised: there's a wide choice of shallow dives inside the lagoon for novices and deeper dives (mostly 25m to 40m) just outside for more experienced divers, as well as a few

WHAT YOU'LL SEE

Let's be honest: the western Indian Ocean is not the richest marine realm in the world – some parts of the Caribbean, the South Pacific and the Red Sea boast more prolific fish life. But it's far from being poor – in fact, it has everything from tiny nudibranchs (sea slugs) to huge whale sharks. It's just a matter of quantities, not diversity.

Reef Fishes

Like technicolour critters? You'll encounter a dizzying array of reef species darting around the reef, including clownfish, parrotfish, angelfish, emperor-fish, butterflyfish and various types of grouper. Moray eels are also frequently encountered.

Pelagics

Pelagic fish – larger beasts that live in the open sea, such as tuna and barracuda – sometimes cruise quite close to the reef in search of prey. Of the shark species inhabiting these waters, the most common are the whitetip reef shark, the hammerhead shark and the reasonably docile nurse shark. Whale sharks are also regularly encountered.

Rays

The most common species of ray found around the Seychelles and Mauritius is the manta ray. One of the larger stingray species, often encountered at Shark Bank off Mahé, is the brissant (or round ribbon-tailed) ray. It can grow up to 2m across. The blue-spotted stingray is quite common in the sandy areas between the granite boulders of the Seychelles.

Turtles

The best place to see turtles in the wild is the Seychelles, where there are a number of important breeding grounds for hawksbill and green turtles.

Coral

Coral is not the strongest point. The Indian Ocean's shallow-water reefs were badly hit by 'coral bleaching' in 1997 and 1998. In parts of the Seychelles, up to 90% of hard corals (the reef-building corals) were wiped out. They are still struggling, but there are encouraging signs of new growth.

Above: Diver near a school of big-eye fish, Mauritius

Right: Turtle swimming in shallows

purpose-sunk wrecks thrown in for good measure.

Where to Dive

Most dive sites are located off the west coast between Boucan Canot and St-Pierre.

St-Gilles-les-Bains

If you want relaxed diving, St-Gilles will appeal to you. Diving here is focused on the reefs, which slope gently away in a series of valleys to a sandy bottom in about 25m – very reassuring. Pelagics are rare, but small reef species are prolific.

➡ **Tour de Boucan** A fantastic site suitable for all levels. Super underwater terrain, with a massive boulder that provides shelter to numerous species.

➡ **Le Pain de Sucre** The setting is the strong point, with a contoured terrain and lots of small critters in the recesses (damselfish, parrotfish, triggerfish, lobsters), as well as a few seafans. Great for beginners.

➡ **Petites Gorgones** (also known as Saliba) A relaxing site. Keep an eye out for leaf scorpion fishes and turtles.

➡ **La Passe de L'Hermitage** An exciting dive. The terrain is nicely sculpted, with little canyons and large boulders that act as magnets for a wealth of species. Sadly, visibility is often reduced.

➡ **Haï Siang** With a maximum depth of 55m, this wreck is accessible to very experienced divers only.

➡ **Navarra** Another great wreck, but the maximum depth is 55m.

➡ **La Barge** Off St-Paul, a relaxing wreck dive in less than 22m. Beginners will love it!

St-Leu

St-Leu features splendid wall diving and good coral fields. Here walls tumble steeply to several dozen metres.

➡ **Tombant de la Pointe au Sel** South of St-Leu, this is widely regarded as Réunion's best all-round dive site. In addition to great scenery, this stunning drop-off offers a fabulous array of fish life and seldom fails to produce good sightings of pelagics, especially tuna, barracudas and jacks, as well as hammerhead sharks between October and November.

➡ **Les Pyramides** Features two seamounts rising from 70m to 38m.

➡ **Le Jardin des Kiosques** With a depth ranging from 3m to 18m, it's very secure yet atmospheric for beginners. It's all about little canyons and grooves.

➡ **La Maison Verte** A relaxing site, blessed with good coral formations.

➡ **Antonio Lorenzo** Wreck enthusiasts will make a beeline for this well-preserved vessel that rests in about 35m on a sandy bottom off Pointe des Chateaux. Fish life is not dynamic – it's the ambience that's the pull.

St-Pierre & Étange-Salé-les-Bains

Savvy divers, this area is for you. This area is not hyped and that's why we enjoy it so much. There are a host of untouched sites between St-Pierre and Grand Bois. The main drawcard here is the topography, with numerous ridges, canyons and drop-offs.

➡ **Les Ancres & Le Tombant aux Ancres** A sloping reef festooned by healthy coral formations. You'll also see some old anchors dotted around the reef.

➡ **La Dérivante** 'The Drift' is self-explanatory – divers do a drift dive off Grand Bois along a huge rocky reef. Fish life is prolific.

Practicalities

Diving Conditions

While it is possible to dive all year, the best time is October to April, when the water is at its warmest (about 28°C). However, you might want to avoid February and March, which is cyclone season. Water temperatures can drop to about 21°C in August.

Dive Operators

The dive centres are concentrated around St-Gilles-les-Bains, St-Leu and St-Pierre. The standard of diving facilities is high. You'll find professional dive centres staffed with qualified instructors catering to divers of all levels. Staff members usually speak English. Most dive centres are affiliated with PADI, SSI or CMAS – all internationally recognised dive organisations.

Take note that a simple medical certificate stating you are fit enough to dive is compulsory for diving in France. You can get one from your doctor in your home country or have it faxed or emailed to the dive centre. Otherwise, you can get one from any doctor in Réunion.

Seychelles

Billed as one of the Indian Ocean's great diving destinations, the Seychelles almost rivals the Maldives, though it's much less hyped – all the better for you. You don't need to be a strong diver – there are sites for all levels.

There's excellent diving off Mahé, Praslin and La Digue, the three main islands, as well as off the other inner islands. The strong point is the underwater scenery, complete with big granite boulders and seamounts – it's as atmospheric as on land.

Where to Dive

Mahé

➡ **Shark Bank** Mahé's signature dive, for experienced divers only. The name is misleading, because there are very few sharks around this 30m-tall granite plateau 9km off Beau Vallon (Mahé). Instead, you'll encounter brissant rays the size of Mini Mokes, eagle rays, barracuda, batfish and teeming yellow snapper and big-eyes. There is nearly always a strong current at this site.

THE FIRST TIME

You've always fancied venturing underwater on scuba? Now's your chance. Mauritius, Réunion and the Seychelles are perfect starting points for new divers, as the warm waters and shallow reefs are a forgiving training environment. Most dive centres offer courses for beginners and employ experienced instructors.

Just about anyone in reasonably good health can sign up for an introductory dive (from €45), including children aged eight and over. It typically takes place in shallow (3m to 5m) water and lasts about 30 minutes, escorted by a divemaster.

If you choose to enrol in an open-water course, count on it taking about four days, including a few classroom lectures and open-water training. Once you're certified, your C-card is valid permanently and recognised all over the world.

➡ **Îlot** This granite outcrop just off north Mahé consists of several large boulders topped by a tuft of palm trees. The current in the channel can be quite strong, but the cluster of boulders yields one of the highest densities of fish life in the Seychelles. Golden cup coral festoons the canyons and gullies, and gorgonians and other soft corals abound. You're sure to see yellow-spotted burr fish, turtles, anemones and clownfish, peppered moray eels, Spanish dancer nudibranchs and thousands of hingeback shrimps. Îlot is about a 15-minute boat ride from Beau Vallon.

➡ **Brissare Rocks** About 5km north of Mahé, this granite pinnacle is accessed from Beau Vallon. The site features abundant fire coral and great concentrations of yellow snapper, wrasse, parrotfish and fusiliers, as well as groupers and eagle rays. It's covered with bright orange sponges and white gorgonians.

➡ **Twin Barges** If you need a break from offshore dives, these two adjoining shipwrecks will keep you happy. They sit upright on the seabed in about 20m in Beau Vallon bay.

➡ **Aldebaran** This boat was scuttled in 2010 off Anse Major, the maximum depth is 40m. It shelters moray eels, groupers and rays.

➡ **Alice in Wonderland** Famous for its healthy coral formations. Off Anse à la Mouche.

➡ **Jailhouse Rock** A high-voltage drift dive for experienced divers with prolific fish life. Off Pointe Lazare.

➡ **Shark Point** Whitetips, nurse sharks and grey reef sharks are commonly sighted here. Off Pointe Lazare.

Praslin & La Digue

➡ **Aride Bank** Off Aride Island, this pristine site can be accessed from Praslin if you don't mind the tedious 30-minute boat trip to get to the site. A hot fave among local divemasters, it features rays, snappers, nurse sharks, jacks, barracudas and Napoleon wrasses as well as magnificent seafans.

➡ **Booby Islet** Approximately halfway between Aride and Praslin, this exposed seamount consistently sizzles with fish action. In less than 20m of water, you'll come across parrotfish, Napoleon wrasses, moray eels, turtles, eagle rays and nurse sharks.

➡ **Anse Sévère** An easy site, close to the shore of La Digue.

➡ **Ave Maria Rocks** A seamount northwest of La Digue. Noted for its shark sightings.

SNORKELLING

If the idea of total immersion doesn't appeal to you, snorkelling is possible in the three countries. It's a great way to explore the underwater world with minimal equipment and without the costs associated with diving. Even the shallowest reefs are home to many colourful critters. In all three destinations, rental gear is widely available from dive centres.

Mauritius

Top spots include the marine park at Blue Bay and along the west coast off Flic en Flac and Trou aux Biches, not forgetting the lagoon around Rodrigues. Companies running trips on glass-bottomed boats will often include snorkelling in the deal.

Réunion

The lagoon along the west coast between St-Gilles-les-Bains and La Saline-les-Bains offers great snorkelling, with particularly good marine life off L'Hermitage-les-Bains. Take advice before leaping in as the currents can be dangerous.

Seychelles

The sheltered lagoons provide safe havens for swimming and snorkelling. The Ste Anne and Port Launay Marine National Parks are firm favourites in the waters around Mahé. In September and October, divers have a chance to snorkel alongside whale sharks. Around Praslin, try off Anse Lazio and Anse Volbert beaches, or take a boat trip from Anse Volbert to St Pierre islet. Close to La Digue, the submerged granite boulders around Coco, Grande Sœur and Marianne islands are teeming with fish life.

➡ **Cousin** An easy site.

➡ **Marianne Island** An islet east of La Digue, famous for its dense fish life (including grey sharks, stingrays, barracudas, eagle rays and nurse sharks) and contoured seascape.

➡ **South Cousine Island** A dive site similar to Cousin.

➡ **White Bank** About 200m west of Ave Maria Rocks. Stunning seascape (tunnels, arches) and prolific fish life, including shoals of jacks and the occasional guitar shark.

Other Inner Islands & Outer islands

For wealthy divers, the private islands of Desroches, Frégate, North, Silhouette and Denis offer fantastic diving options, with absolutely pristine sites and only one dive boat: yours. One step beyond, you'll find Aldabra, Cosmoledo and Astove, which are the stuff of legend. They feature the best sites in the eastern Indian Ocean, with electric fish action in a totally virgin territory and high-voltage drift dives. The

catch? They were not accessible at the time of writing due to the presence of Somali pirates in the area.

Practicalities

Diving Conditions

Diving in the Seychelles heavily hinges on the weather conditions, currents and direction of the wind, but it can be sampled over all of the seasons as there are always sheltered conditions. The calmest seas are from April to May and October to November. Due to currents and wind, visibility is temperamental and can drop to 5m. But in normal conditions you can expect 25m.

Dive Operators

The Seychelles' 15-odd diving centres have first-rate personnel and facilities. You'll find dive centres in Mahé, Praslin, La Digue, Ste Anne, Silhouette, Frégate, Denis, North and Desroches. Most centres are affiliated with PADI.

JEAN BERNARD CARILLET / GETTY IMAGES ©

Cirque de Mafate (p222)

Plan Your Trip

Hiking in Réunion

Hiking is the very best of what Réunion has to offer. Formed from one mighty dead volcano (Piton des Neiges) and one active volcano (Piton de la Fournaise), the island is a paradise for hikers, adventure-sports enthusiasts or indeed anyone who is receptive to the untamed beauty of a wilderness environment.

Hiking Tips

Safety is basically a matter of common sense and being prepared. Remember:

Before You Leave

Get a detailed and up-to-date map.

Double-check the state of the paths before setting out.

Check the weather report.

Tell people where you're going if you are hiking alone.

Leave early enough to reach your destination before dark.

Take Along

Comfortable hiking boots.

Wet-weather gear.

Plenty of water and energy-rich snacks.

A basic medical kit.

When to Hike

The best time to hike is during the dry season, from around late April to the end of October. May and June, as well as September and October, are probably the best months of all. July and August are a bit chilly, and during the rainy months a number of paths are not accessible. The weather is extremely changeable from one part of this small island to the other.

The weather in Réunion has a tendency to become worse as the day goes on. As the hours pass, the island's uplands seem to delight in 'trapping' any cloud that happens to come their way. An early start is therefore one of the best defences against the vagaries of the elements.

The next day's weather forecast is shown on the two main TV channels after the evening news. You can also get the forecast by telephoning the **Météo France voice service** (☎0892 68 02 00; per min €0.45). Cyclone bulletins are available on ☎0897 65 01 01 (€0.51 per call). Both these services are in French. Also check out the website www.meteo.re.

What to Bring

Good shoes are essential for hiking the trails of Réunion, which are made of gravel and stone and often very steep, muddy or slippery. Hiking shoes with good ankle support are better than sneakers.

Be sure to carry water (at least 2L for a day's hiking), wet-weather gear, a warm top, a hat, sunscreen, sunglasses, insect repellent, a whistle, a torch and a basic medical kit including plasters (Band-Aids), elastic bandages and muscle balm for blisters and minor muscle injuries. The *gîtes* provide sheets and blankets, but if you intend to sleep out at altitude, you'll need a decent sleeping bag, as temperatures in the Cirques can fall rapidly at night.

In most places to stay and places to eat, payment will be expected in cash, so bring a stash of euros with you. The only places to get euros in the Cirques are the ATMs at the post offices in Salazie and Cilaos, and these can't be depended on.

You will be able to buy most last-minute supplies at a sporting-goods store or one of the big supermarkets in Réunion as well as in Cilaos.

Hiking Trails

There are two major hiking trails, known as Grande Randonnée® Route 1 (GR® R1) and Grande Randonnée® Route 2 (GR® R2), with numerous offshoots. The GR® R1 does a tour of Piton des Neiges, passing through Cilaos, the Forêt de Bébour-Bélouve, Hell-Bourg and the Cirque de Mafate. The GR® R2 makes an epic traverse of the island all the way from St-Denis to St-Philippe via the three Cirques, the Plaine-des-Cafres and Piton de la Fournaise.

A third trail, the Grande Randonnée® Route 3 (GR® R3), does a tour of Cirque de Mafate and overlaps with some sections of the GR® R1 and GR® R2.

The trails are well maintained, but the tropical rainfall can eat through footpaths and wash away steps and handrails. Even experienced hikers should be prepared for tortuous ascents, slippery mud chutes and narrow paths beside sheer precipices. The routes are well signposted on the whole, but it's essential to carry a good map and you should check locally on the current situation; trails are occasionally closed for maintenance, especially following severe storms.

Information

Hiking information is provided by the **Centrale d'Information et de Réservation Régionale – Île de la Réunion Tourisme** (Map p180; ☎0810 160 000; www.reunion.fr), and by associated tourist offices, including those in Cilaos, Salazie, Hell-Bourg, Ste-Suzanne, St-Gilles-les-Bains, St-Pierre, St-Leu, Plaine-des-Palmistes, Ste-Anne, St-Joseph and Bourg-Murat. All these offices organise bookings for *gîtes d'étape et de randonnée* (walkers' lodges) and can give advice on which paths are currently closed. They can also arrange hiking tours.

By far the most useful website for hikers is that of the Centrale de Réservation – Île de la Réunion. It allows you to book your accommodation online.

The websites runrando.free.fr (in French) and www.gites-refuges.com are also useful.

For information on *état des sentiers* (closed trails), phone the voice service at ☎0262 37 38 39 (in French).

The **Fédération Française de la Randonnée Pédestre** (FFRandonnée; www.ffrandonnee.fr) is responsible for the development and upkeep of the GR® walking tracks.

The definitive guide to the GR® R1, GR® R2 and GR® R3 is the TopoGuides GR® Grande Rrandonnée *L'Île de la Réunion* (2012), published by the FFRandonnée. It uses 1:25,000 scale IGN maps and details the itineraries. The GR® R1 is described in six *étapes* (stages), the GR® R2 in 12 stages and the GR® R3 in five stages.

The FFRandonnée also publishes the Topo-guide PR® *Sentiers forestiers de L'Île de la Réunion* (2011), which covers 25 walks varying from one-hour jaunts to six-hour hikes.

Published locally by Orphie, *52 Balades et Randonnées Faciles* is designed with children in mind and describes outings that can be covered in less than four hours.

DANITA DELMONT / GETTY IMAGES ©

Cascade du Voile de la Mariée (p218), Cirque de Salazie

A broader range of walks is covered by *62 Randonnées Réunionnaises* (also by Orphie).

Maps

Réunion is covered by the six 1:25,000 scale maps published by the **Institut Géographique National** (IGN; www.ign.fr). These maps are reasonably up to date and show trails and *gîtes*. Map number 4402 RT is one of the most useful for hikers, since it covers Cirque de Mafate and Cirque de Salazie as well as the northern part of the Cirque de Cilaos.

EMERGENCIES

In a real emergency out on the trail, lifting both arms to form a 'V' is a signal to helicopter pilots who fly over the island that you need help. If you have a mobile phone, call the emergency services on ☎112.

JEAN BERNARD CARILLET

Hikers in the Cirque de Mafate (p222)

Tours & Guides

Réunion's hiking trails are well established and reasonably well signposted, but you may get more information about the environment you are walking through if you go with a local guide.

Fully qualified mountain guides can be contacted through the Centrale d'Information et de Réservation Régionale – Île de la Réunion Tourisme and local tourist offices. Rates are negotiable and vary according to the length and degree of difficulty of the hike; an undemanding one-day outing should start at around €50 per person (minimum four people).

➡ **Allons Bat Carré** (☑0692 43 06 79; recif.tigus@wanadoo.fr)

➡ Aparksa Montagne (p212)

➡ Austral Aventure (p219)

➡ **Kokapat Rando** (☑0692 69 94 14, 0262 33 30 14; www.kokapatrando-reunion.com)

➡ **Réunion Mer et Montagne** (☑0692 83 38 68; www.reunionmeretmontagne.com)

➡ **Réunion Randonnées** (☑0692 64 45 26; www.reunion-randonnees.com)

➡ Run Evasion (p213)

Sleeping & Eating

Most of the accommodation for hikers consists of *gîtes de montagne* (mostly found in isolated locations on the trails themselves) or of privately run *gîtes d'étape* along the walking trails. Both offer dorm beds and meals. There's often very little to separate the two types of *gîte* in terms of comfort or facilities. Almost all *gîtes* provide hot showers (they're solar heated). A third option consists of small, family-run *chambres d'hôtes* (mostly found in the villages at the ends of the hiking trails). Your choice of where to stay will most likely be based on where you can find a room. There are also a few hotels in Hell-Bourg and Cilaos for that last night of luxury (and central heating) before you set out on your hike.

One night's accommodation without food costs between €16 and €18. For half board, reckon on €40 per person.

You can also camp for free in some areas in the Cirques, but only for one night at a time. Setting up camp on Piton de la Fournaise (the volcano) is forbidden for obvious reasons.

The trail to Piton de la Fournaise (p227)

Most *gîtes* offer Creole meals, which are normally hearty, though a little rustic for some palates. The standard fare is *carri poulet* (chicken curry), *boucané* (smoked pork) or *rougail saucisses,* often with local wine or *rhum arrangé* (rum punch) thrown in. Breakfast usually consists of just a cup of coffee with *biscottes* (rusks) – or, if you're lucky, bread – and jam.

If you plan to self-cater, you will need to bring plenty of carbohydrate-rich food. Note that only a few *gîtes* are equipped with cooking facilities; you are best off bringing a camping stove. Bear in mind that you are not allowed to light fires anywhere in the forest areas. Some villages in the Cirques have shops where you can purchase a very limited variety of food.

Bookings

Book your accommodation before arriving in Réunion, especially during the busiest months (July, August and around Christmas). At other times it's best to book at least a couple of months in advance, particularly for popular places such as the *gîtes* at Caverne Dufour (for Piton des Neiges) and Piton de la Fournaise.

The *gîtes de montagne* are managed by the Centrale de Réservation – Île de la Réunion and must be booked and paid for in advance. This can be done through its website and at tourist offices. When you pay, you will receive a voucher to be given to the manager of the *gîte* where you will be staying. You must call the *gîte* to book your meals at least one day in advance; this can be done at the same time as the original booking if you'd rather, but meals still have to paid for on the spot.

For the privately owned *gîtes* things are less restrictive in terms of logistics; you can book directly through the *gîte*.

Best Multiday Hikes

The Haut Mafate

What's not to love in the Haut Mafate? Surrounded by ramparts, criss-crossed with gullies and studded with narrow ridges, Cirque de Mafate (p222) is the wildest and the most remote of Réunion's Cirques. The most scenic areas of the southern part of the Cirque can be completed in a four-day loop that takes in the hamlets of La Nouvelle, Roche-Plate and Marla, which all have *gîtes d'étape.* There are various access points into the Haut Mafate, but the most convenient option is the Col des Bœufs car park, in the Cirque de Salazie. This loop can easily be combined with the Bas Mafate and Tour des Cirques.

Highlights include the forested Plaine des Tamarins, the deep valley of the Rivière des Galets, the waterfall at Trois Roches and the ruins of Maison Laclos, which is said to be the oldest dwelling in the Cirque. Of course, you'll also enjoy phenomenal views.

IGN's 1:25,000 topographic map 4402 RT covers the area.

The Haut Mafate Hike at a Glance

➡ **Duration** 4 days
➡ **Distance** 20.4km
➡ **Difficulty** moderate
➡ **Start/Finish** Col des Bœufs car park
➡ **Nearest Town** Grand Îlet

RIEGER BERTRAND / GETTY IMAGES ©

JEAN-BERNARD CARILLET

Above: Forêt de Bébour-Bélouve (p230)

Left: Hikers enjoying a break in the Cirque de Mafate (p222)

ECOWALKING

To help preserve the ecology and beauty of Réunion, consider these tips when hiking.

Rubbish

➡ Carry out all your rubbish. Don't overlook easily forgotten items, such as silver paper, orange peel, cigarette butts and plastic wrappers. Empty packaging should be stored in a dedicated rubbish bag.

➡ Never bury your rubbish: digging disturbs soil and ground cover and encourages erosion. Buried rubbish will likely be dug up by animals, who may be injured or poisoned by it.

➡ Minimise waste by taking minimal packaging and no more food than you will need. Take reusable containers or stuff sacks.

➡ Sanitary products, condoms and toilet paper should be carried out despite the inconvenience. They burn and decompose poorly.

Human Waste Disposal

➡ Contamination of water sources by human faeces can lead to the transmission of all sorts of nasties. Where there is a toilet, use it. Where there is none, bury your waste.

Erosion

➡ Hillsides and mountain slopes, especially at high altitudes, are prone to erosion. Stick to existing tracks and avoid short cuts.

➡ If a well-used track passes through a mud patch, walk through the mud so as not to increase the size of the patch.

➡ Avoid removing any plant life – it keeps the topsoil in place.

The Bas Mafate

After (or before) a loop in the Haut Mafate, you might want to explore the Bas Mafate, which is even more secluded (and that is saying something) and less 'touristy' than Haut Mafate. The most popular circuit starts from the Rivière des Galets valley and takes in all the *îlets* (hamlets) of Bas Mafate, including Aurère, Îlet à Malheur, La Plaque, Îlet à Bourse, Grand Place Les Hauts, Grand Place, Cayenne, Les Lataniers and Îlet des Orangers – a great way to immerse yourself in local culture and sample authentic rural Réunionnais life. It's a four-day hike, but you can design a longer or shorter itinerary depending on how pressed and how full of beans you are.

If time allows, you can rejoin the Haut Mafate itinerary. A path connects Îlet des Orangers and Roche-Plate. From Les Lataniers, you can also get to Roche-Plate via the Sentier Dacerle.

Highlights include spectacular landscapes consisting of precipitous mountain slopes and steep-sided valleys.

IGN's 1:25,000 topographic map 4402 RT covers the area.

The Bas Mafate Hike at a Glance

➡ **Duration** 4 days

➡ **Distance** 30km

➡ **Difficulty** moderate

➡ **Start** Deux Bras

➡ **Finish** Sans Souci

➡ **Nearest Towns** Rivière des Galets and Sans Souci

Tour des Cirques

Simply magical. The Tour des Cirques (Round the Cirques) is a Réunion classic that is sure to leave you with indelible memories. Combining the best of the three Cirques, it will offer you three distinct atmospheres and various landscapes. As a bonus, you'll cross a few towns that are well equipped with cosy accommodation facilities.

OLIVIER CIRENDINI / GETTY IMAGES ©

Climbers at the top of Piton des Neiges (p214)

The walk roughly follows the path of GR® R1 and is best started in Cilaos, which has excellent facilities for walkers and the added advantage of a health spa where you can unwind after your hike. It can be completed in five days.

Tour des Cirques Hike at a Glance

➡ **Duration** 5 days

➡ **Distance** 51.5km

➡ **Difficulty** demanding

➡ **Start/Finish** Cilaos

Day Hikes & Short Walks

If you don't have time for a multiday trek, there are also plenty of great day hikes that will give you a taste of life in rural Réunion. A not-to-be-missed day hike is the climb up the Piton de la Fournaise (the volcano) from Pas de Bellecombe. Réunion's highest point, Piton des Neiges, can also be done in a day if you're super fit, but most people choose to stay overnight at Gîte de la Caverne Dufour.

Another popular activity related to hiking is exploring lava tubes on the southeast coast. You'll walk (make it scramble) over slippery wet rocks through tunnels and caves that were formed by the volcanic eruptions – see the boxed text on p245.

Tourist offices have plenty of recommendations for short, easy walks.

Islands at a Glance

Four unique island destinations cast adrift in the warm azure waters of the Indian Ocean; Mauritius, Rodrigues, Réunion and Seychelles can all stake a convincing claim to being a piece of paradise. But there are plenty of characteristics that set each island apart from the next – you can zero in on the islands that best suit you. Mauritius achieves perfect balance with its blend of culture and coast, while Réunion, with its surreal mountainous landscapes, is heaven on earth for activities enthusiasts. Beach bums will be better off in the Seychelles, which is blessed with some of the most alluring beaches in the world. Rodrigues is a rural gem that time forgot. It will delight those in search of something a little different.

Mauritius

Culture
Beaches
Watersports

Past & Present

Visitors are often overwhelmed by the sense of devotion that emanates from the incredibly colourful festivals – whether they are Hindu, Christian, Chinese or Muslim – held throughout the island. Architecture buffs will make a point of visiting the country's historic buildings, especially the colonial plantation houses.

Mind-Blowing Beaches

When it comes to beaches, you'll be spoilt for choice. Most resorts and guesthouses here have access to perfect white sand and amazing sapphire water. Good news: despite the crowds, it's easy to find your own slice of paradise.

Aquatic Delights

Mauritius is the place to be if you want to get your feet (and the rest) wet. Pretty much everything's on offer here, from kitesurfing and kayaking to windsurfing to excellent snorkelling and diving. Oh, and beachcombing counts too.

p46

Rodrigues

Diving
Village Life
Walking

Pristine Underwater World

The lack of resorts and a remarkably well preserved marine environment make Rodrigues one of the best places to dive in the Indian Ocean. Sharks, giant trevallies and barracudas galore!

Lost in Time

Slip into island time in Port Mathurin, the somniferous capital of Rodrigues, and savour the unhurried pace of life. Accessible homestays, small markets, stuck-in-time villages and welcoming smiles – you'll be hard-pressed to find a mellower destination to maroon yourself for a languid holiday

Coast Walks

The coastline between Graviers and St François in the island's east is extremely alluring: a string of hard-to-reach inlets and coves lapped by azure waters, with the mandatory idyllic beach fringing the shore, and vast expanses of rocks. Who knows, you may find a pirate's hidden booty!

p154

Réunion

Outdoors
Scenery
Food

Adrenaline Fix

With its extraordinarily varied terrain, Réunion is an incredible stage for the action seeker in search of anything from canyoning and paragliding to whitewater rafting and horseriding. And when it comes to hiking, Réunion is in a league of its own.

Scenic Mountains

Soaring peaks, lush valleys, majestic summits, sensational lookouts, waterfalls taller than skyscrapers, stunning forests and one of the world's most active volcanoes: Réunion's rugged topography will take your breath away.

Bon Appétit

Foodies of the world, rejoice. In Réunion, even the simplest meal has a flavour you're unlikely to forget. Imagine French gastronomy, prepared with the freshest ingredients, add a dash of Creole, a smidgen of Indian, and voilà!

p175

Seychelles

Beaches
Wildlife
Fabulous Resorts

Perfect White Sand

Many think the eye-catching brochure images of turquoise seas and shimmering white sands are digitally enhanced but, once here, they realise the pictures barely do them justice. The Seychelles is the tropical paradise you've always dreamed about.

Wildlife Spotting

The country is a nature-lover's dream. A variety of charismatic species can easily be approached and photographed. Scratch the neck of a giant tortoise, swim alongside a massive whale shark, observe thousands of nesting sooty terns or look for the smallest frog on earth. Don't forget your camera!

Lap of Luxury

Few islands have the concentration of world-class resorts that can be found in the Seychelles. Whether it's small and romantic, super-glamorous or back-to-nature luxury, you'll find the right resort here.

p270

On the Road

Seychelles
p270

Madagascar

Mauritius
p46

Rodrigues
p154

Réunion
p175

Mauritius

Why Go?

Mark Twain once wrote that 'Mauritius was made first and then heaven, heaven being copied after Mauritius'. For the most part, it's true: Mauritius is rightly famed for its sapphire waters, powder-white beaches and luxury resorts. But there's so much more to Mauritius than the beach when it comes to attractions. There's bird-watching and hiking in the forested and mountainous interior or world-class diving and snorkelling. Or there are boat trips to near-perfect islets and excursions to fabulous botanical gardens and colonial plantation houses. Either way, the possibilities can seem endless. And the *real* Mauritius – a hot curry of different cultures, traffic and quiet fishing villages – is never far away.

Ultimately, Mauritius is the kind of place that rewards even the smallest attempts at exploration. So, if your biggest discovery is the beach butler service at your hotel, then you'll need to plan a second visit!

Best Places to Eat

➡ Eureka Table d'Hôte (p59)

➡ Chez Tante Athalie (p84)

➡ Lambic (p54)

➡ Rasoi (p128)

➡ 1974 (p69)

Best Places to Stay

➡ Le Saint Géran (p126)

➡ Le Prince Maurice (p127)

➡ La Maison d'Été (p128)

➡ L'Oiseau du Paradis (p112)

➡ Le Preskîl (p113)

When to Go

➡ Mauritius enjoys a typically tropical climate with year-round heat. The summer months are from December to April, when it can be extremely humid, and the cooler winter, such as it is, runs from May to November.

➡ Peak cyclone months are January and February, with cyclones possible until April.

➡ Coastal temperatures range between 25°C and 33°C in summer and between 18°C and 24°C in winter. On the plateau it will be some 5°C cooler.

➡ High season roughly runs from November to April, with a Christmas–New Year peak, although other factors (French school holidays for example) can also cause spikes in prices and visitor numbers.

Driving in Mauritius

Driving a rental vehicle around Mauritius shouldn't pose too many problems or cause too much anxiety. Most roads are in reasonable condition, although be wary of unsigned potholes or poorly signed speed humps on minor or residential roads. The main concern for first-time drivers is that, apart from the motorway that links the airport with Grand Baie, many roads can be quite narrow – fine under normal conditions, but slightly trickier when buses, trucks and meandering cyclists are factored in. The only solution is to err on the side of caution and remain vigilant. Also watch out for other vehicles overtaking when it's not entirely safe to do so. See also p152.

ESSENTIAL FOOD & DRINK

Mauritius's complex mix of cultures has bequeathed to the island an equally complex culinary scene – Chinese, Indian, Creole and French influences are all evident. It's the Creole element that shines through most strongly at the *tables d'hôte*, the eating equivalent of a family-run guesthouse where diners often eat at a communal table and can enjoy a range of traditional dishes spread over a number of courses. If you don't eat at a *table d'hôte* at least once in Mauritius, you've missed an essential part of its gastronomic culture.

Seafood is the mainstay of all the different cuisines on the island. Prawns (*crevettes*) and octopus (*ourite*) are special highlights, and octopus in particular appears in all manner of varieties – salads, cooked in saffron, or in a curry (sometimes with green papaya). The fish of the day is nearly always a good order.

When it comes to meat, steaks can be terrific here, especially those from South Africa. Creole sausages are distinctive and are often cooked in a red Creole sauce.

When it comes to street food, *dhal puri* (lentil dhal served in a chapati pancake) and *boulettes* (tiny steamed Chinese dumplings) are fantastic.

Keeping Costs Down

➔ If your accommodation is based on a half-board regime, eat lunch outside the hotel

➔ Rent a car from a local (rather than international) company – their rates are invariably cheaper

➔ For most upmarket hotels, try to book through a travel agency – otherwise you'll pay the full rack rates

➔ For excursions, try to get a group together – quoted costs are usually for the vehicle or boat

AT A GLANCE

➔ **Currency** Mauritian rupee (Rs)

➔ **Language** French, English

➔ **Mobile phones** GSM network through Orange and Emtel; international roaming available

➔ **Money** ATMs widespread on main island, less common on Rodrigues

➔ **Visas** Not required for most nationalities for stays of up to three months

Fast Facts

➔ **Capital** Port Louis

➔ **Country code** 🖬 230

➔ **Population** 1.322 million

➔ **Time** GMT + four hours

Exchange Rates

For current exchange rates see www.xe.com.

A$1	Rs 26.9
C$1	Rs 28.5
€1	Rs 39.6
¥100	Rs 30.4
NZ$1	Rs 23.7
UK£1	Rs 46.4
US$1	Rs 29.6

Resources

➔ **Lonely Planet** (www.lonelyplanet.com/mauritius)

➔ **Mauritius Tourism Promotion Authority** (www.tourism-mauritius.mu)

➔ **Mauritian Wildlife Foundation** (www.mauritian-wildlife.org)

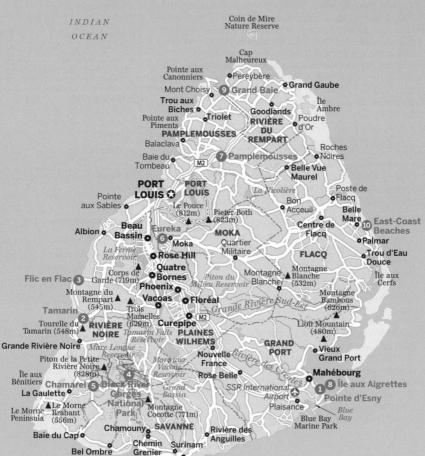

Mauritius Highlights

1 Enjoy *chambre d'hôte* charm along the beach in **Pointe d'Esny** (p110)

2 Spot breaching dolphins in **Tamarin** (p92)

3 Dive the cavernous drop-offs at **Flic en Flac** (p85)

4 Hike through the forests of **Black River Gorges National Park** (p95)

5 Pause for lunch in the mountain village of **Chamarel** (p96)

6 Uncover the island's plantation past at **Eureka** (p59)

7 Find weird-and-wonderful planet species at **Pamplemousses** (p82)

8 Discover how Mauritius once looked with a boat trip to **Île aux Aigrettes** (p110)

9 Snorkel on a boat trip from **Grand Baie** (p72)

10 Snap photos of azure lagoons along the rugged **east-coast beaches** (p120)

PORT LOUIS

POP 117.198

Port Louis (*por* loo-ee), the island's capital and largest city, can feel like a kaleidoscope of countries and cultures, with flashes of India, Africa, Europe, China and the Middle East. Unless you've essential business to transact here, or unless you're in the country for a prolonged visit, there aren't that many reasons to come – there are numerous other day excursions that we'd rank above Port Louis. But if you are here, it can be a good place to take the pulse of the country and to get an alternative slant on the island's rarefied world of resorts and private beaches. Most interest lies amid the bustle and chaos of the streets, the tangle of ethnic quarters and some wonderfully preserved colonial buildings. Apart from Le Caudan Waterfront, it all shuts down after dark when countless day commuters rumble out of town at sunset en route to their homes on the Central Plateau.

History

Port Louis was first settled in the 17th century by the Dutch, who called it Noordt Wester Haven. It was the French governor Bertrand François Mahé de Labourdonnais, however, who took the initiative and developed it into a busy capital and port after 1736. He was rewarded with a much-photographed statue in Place d'Armes.

Few cities have bounced back from as many natural disasters as Port Louis, or Port Napoleon as it was known briefly in the early 19th century before the British took the island. Between 1773 and 1892 a series of fires, plagues and tropical storms all tried, and failed, to level the town. In 1819 cholera arrived from Manila on the frigate *Topaz*, killing an estimated 700 Port Louis residents. Things quietened down until 1866, when malaria suddenly appeared on the scene, causing a further 3700 fatalities. Around this time people started heading for the cooler (and healthier) Central Plateau, so the town's population was mercifully small when the 1892 cyclone whipped through and destroyed 3000 homes.

The 20th century saw Port Louis become one of Africa's most important financial centres and ports – to which the ever-growing number of high-rise glass-fronted banks in the city centre attest.

⊙ Sights

Most of the following sights can be reached on foot, but consider a taxi or bus to reach the citadel and Père Laval's shrine (p58).

★ **Central Market**   MARKET
(⊙5.30am-5.30pm Mon-Sat, to 11.30pm Sun) Port Louis' rightly famous Central Market, the centre of the local economy since Victorian times, was cleaned up considerably in a 2004 renovation. Many comment that it's lost much of its dirty charm and atmosphere (you're far less likely to see rats, although it's possible), but it's still a good place to get a feel for the everyday life of many locals, watch the hawkers at work and buy some souvenirs. Most authentic are the fruit and vegetable sections (including Chinese herbal medicines and aphrodisiacs).

Place d'Armes   SQUARE
The city's most imposing boulevard, Place d'Armes is lined with royal palms and leads up to **Government House** (Place d'Armes), a beautiful French colonial structure dating from 1738. Outside there's a typically solemn **statue of Queen Victoria** in full 'we are not amused' mode. The **statue of Mahé de Labourdonnais** (Place d'Armes) at the quayside end of the avenue has become Port Louis' emblem throughout Mauritius.

Jardins de la Compagnie   GARDENS
(Company Gardens; ⊙6am-8pm Oct-Mar, 6am-7pm Apr-Sep) Jardins de la Compagnie is by far the most attractive garden in the city, with its vast banyan trees, huge number of statues, quiet benches and fountains. During the day it's perfectly safe, but you should avoid it at night when it becomes the city's favoured hangout for prostitutes and drug addicts. In early colonial times, the gardens were the vegetable patch of the French East India Company. Today, it's best known for its statues of local sculptor Prosper d'Épinay and the much-loved musician Ti-Frère.

**Natural History Museum
& Mauritius Institute**   MUSEUM
(⊘212 0639; La Chaussée St; ⊙9am-4pm Mon, Tue, Thu & Fri, to noon Sat) **FREE** The major attraction at this small but proud museum is the famous (though somewhat grubby) reconstruction of a dodo. Scottish scientists assembled the curious-looking bird in the late 19th century, using the only complete dodo skeleton in existence, although experts with whom we spoke suggest that the scale

Port Louis

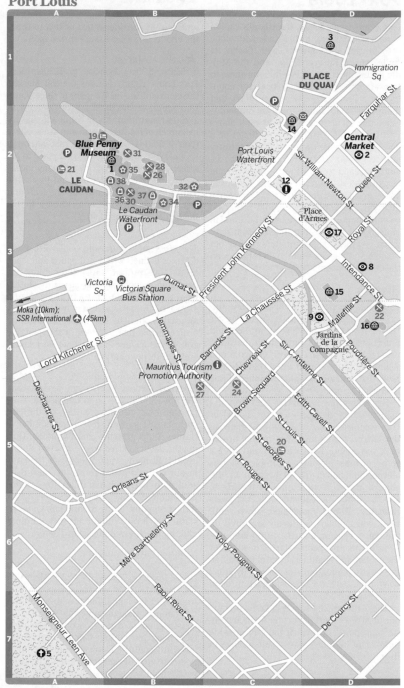

PLACE
DU QUAI

*Immigration
Sq*

Farquhar St

**Blue Penny
Museum**

19

31

21

**LE
CAUDAN**

35

38

28

26

32

36 30

37

34

*Le Caudan
Waterfront*

*Port Louis
Waterfront*

**Central
Market**

2

14

Sir-William-Newton St

Queen St

12

Place
d'Armes

17

Royal St

8

Intendance St

President John Kennedy St

*Victoria
Sq*

Victoria Square
Bus Station

Dumat St

La Chaussée St

15

Malefille St

22

16

Jardins
de la
Compagnie

9

*Moka (10km);
SSR International (45km)*

Lord Kitchener St

Jemmapes St

Barracks St

Chevreau St

Sir-C-Antelme St

Poudrière St

Edith Cavell St

Mauritius Tourism
Promotion Authority

27

24

Brown Sequard

Deschartres St

St Louis St

St Georges St

20

Dr Rouget St

Orleans St

Mère Barthelemy St

Volcy Pougnet St

De Courcy St

Raoul Rivet St

Monseigneur Leen Ave

5

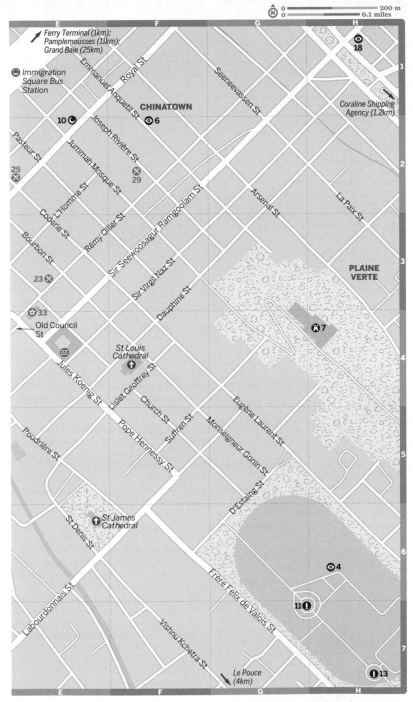

MAURITIUS PORT LOUIS

0 ——————— 200 m
0 ——————— 0.1 miles

Ferry Terminal (1km);
Pamplemousses (11km);
Grand Baie (25km)

Immigration
Square Bus
Station

CHINATOWN

10

6

18

Coraline Shipping
Agency (1.2km)

Royal St

Emmanuel Anquetil St

Seeneevassen St

Joseph Rivière St

Pasteur St

25

Jummah Mosque St

L'Homme St

Coderie St

Rémy Ollier St

Bourbon St

23

33

Old Council
St

Sir Seewoosagur Ramgoolam St

Sir Virgil Naz St

Dauphine St

Arsenal St

La Paix St

PLAINE
VERTE

7

29

St Louis
Cathedral

Jules Koenig St

Lislet Geoffrey St

Church St

Suffren St

Pope Hennessy St

Monseigneur Gonin St

Eugène Laurent St

Poudrière St

St Denis St

St James
Cathedral

D'Estaing St

4

11

Frère Felix de Valois St

Labourdonnais St

Vishnu Kchetra St

Le Pouce
(4km)

13

Port Louis

might be slightly larger than life. The rest of the museum's halls get marks for trying, with a good collection of stuffed endemic bird species, including the solitaire and red rail, both now extinct but nowhere near as famous as the dodo.

Chapel and Shrine of Marie
Reine De La Paix   CHURCH, RELIGIOUS SHRINE
(Monseigneur Leen Ave) The modern chapel and shrine of Marie Reine de la Paix is a popular spot for prayers, and the ornamental gardens offer views over the city. During Pope John Paul II's visit to the island he officiated his first Mass here.

Photography Museum   MUSEUM
(☑211 1705; www.voyaz.com/musee-photo; Old Council St; admission Rs 150; ⊙10am-3pm Mon-Fri) This small but engaging museum, down a cobbled lane opposite the Municipal Theatre, is the labour of love of local photographer Tristan Bréville. He's amassed a treasure trove of old cameras and prints, including several daguerreotypes (the forerunner of photographs) produced in Mauritius in 1840, just a few months after the technique

was discovered in France. The museum also contains a vast archive of historical photos of the island (however, only a fraction are on display).

Champ de Mars Racecourse   RACECOURSE
(Hippodrome; ☑211 2147; www.mauritiusturfclub. com) This racecourse was a military training ground until the Mauritius Turf Club was founded in 1812, making it the second-oldest racecourse in the world. Mauritian independence was proclaimed here in 1968. Within the racecourse stands a statue of King Edward VII by the sculptor Prosper d'Épinay, and the Malartic Tomb, an obelisk to a French governor.

The racing season lasts from around April to late November, with meetings usually held on a Saturday or Sunday. The biggest race of all is the Maiden Cup in September. If you're here on a race day, it's well worth joining the throng of betting-crazy locals. Tickets for the stands and loges range from Rs 50 to Rs 100, but admission to the rest of the ground is usually free. For race dates, contact the Mauritius Turf Club or check the local media.

Fort Adelaide
FORTRESS

(Citadel) Fort Adelaide resembles a Moorish fortress. Built by the British, the fort sits high on the crown of a hill, offering splendid views over the city and its harbour. The old barracks have been restored and transformed into a row of intriguing boutiques – good for a few minutes of window-shopping. The quickest route up is via Suffren St. Allow around 10 minutes for the climb.

SSR Memorial Centre
for Culture
CULTURAL CENTRE

(☑ 242 0053; Sir Seewoosagur Ramgoolam St, Plaine Verte; ☺ 9am-4pm Mon-Fri, to noon Sat) **FREE** This simple house museum near the Jardin Plaine Verte was home to Mauritius' father of independence, Sir Seewoosagur Ramgoolam, from 1935 until 1968. It's an interesting exhibit on his life, with some fascinating photographs, a collection of his personal belongings and even films about the great man, beloved by all Mauritians.

Chinatown
NEIGHBOURHOOD

The Chinese have traditionally occupied a quietly industrious position in the life of Port Louis. The region between the two 'friendship gates' on Royal St forms the centre of Port Louis' Chinatown. Here you'll see the rich mercantile life of the hard-working Chinese community, the busy Chinese restaurants and grocery stores, and the streets echoing with the unmistakable clatter of mah-jong tiles.

Jummah Mosque
MOSQUE

(Royal St; ☺ 8am-noon & 2-4pm Mon-Thu, Sat & Sun) The Jummah Mosque, the most important mosque in Mauritius, was built in the 1850s and is a delightful blend of Indian, Creole and Islamic architecture – it would look equally at home in Istanbul, Delhi or New Orleans! Visitors are welcome in the peaceful inner courtyard except on Fridays and during the month of Ramadan.

Aapravasi Ghat
HISTORIC BUILDING

(☑ 241 04 01; www.aapravasighat.org; 1 Quay St; ☺ 9am-5pm) Aapravasi Ghat, a small complex of buildings located on the seafront, served as the island's main immigration depot for indentured labourers from India. Britain pioneered their indentured servant scheme in Mauritius and from 1849 to 1923 over half a million immigrants were processed here before being shipped to various plantations or other colonial islands. Today, almost 70% of Mauritius' citizens can trace their roots back to Aapravasi Ghat. There isn't a whole lot to see besides having a wander around and taking in the surroundings. Some of the original stone buildings remain and there are strategically placed life-sized models of the immigrants. The ghat was listed as a World Heritage Site by Unesco in 2006 for its important role in the island's social history.

Mauritius Postal Museum
MUSEUM

(☑ 213 4812; www.mauritiuspost.mu; Place du Quai; adult/child Rs 150/90; ☺ 9.30am-4.30pm Mon-Fri, to 3.30pm Sat) This interesting museum beside the central post office houses a mishmash of commemorative stamps and other postal paraphernalia from around the world. A new exhibit details the history of the Mauritius post using a rich assortment of photographs and artefacts. Of particular interest is the display about mail delivery to the remote dependencies of Agaléga and St Bandon. The museum shop sells replica first-day covers of the famous 'Post Office' stamps of 1847.

★ Blue Penny Museum
MUSEUM

(☑ 210 8176; www.bluepennymuseum.com; Le Caudan Waterfront; adult/child Rs 245/120; ☺ 10am-5pm Mon-Sat) Whether or not you fully understand the philatelic obsession with the Mauritian one-penny and two-pence stamps of 1847, the Blue Penny Museum is far more wide-ranging than its name suggests, taking in the history of the island's exploration, settlement and colonial period and even detouring into the Paul and Virginia legend (see p82). It's Port Louis' best museum, with a fantastic selection of antique maps, engravings from different periods in history, and photographs that show a then-and-now look at Port Louis.

The pride of the museum's collection is two of the world's rarest stamps: the red one-penny and blue two-pence 'Post Office' stamps issued in 1847 (see p56). To preserve the colours, they are only lit up for 10 minutes at a time: every hour, at 25 minutes past the hour. The stamps are considered a national treasure and are probably the most valuable objects on the entire island.

On the ground floor you'll see the country's most famous work of art: a superbly lifelike statue by the Mauritian sculptor Prosper d'Épinay, carved in 1884. Based on Bernardin de St-Pierre's novel *Paul et Virginie*, the sculpture depicts the young hero carrying his sweetheart across a raging torrent.

🛏 Sleeping

We generally don't recommend staying in Port Louis – the selection of quality sleeps is minimal and the city is practically a ghost town after sunset.

Le St Georges Hotel HOTEL €€
(☑ 211 2581; www.saintgeorgeshotel-mu.com; 19 St Georges St; s/d from Rs 2250/3550; ✱ @ ⊚ ⊠) Towering above the surrounding residential neighbourhood in the AAA Tower, Le St Georges is excellent value for money. The rooms are fairly unexciting but they are clean and equipped with all the necessary comforts. The location is also good, just a five-minute walk from the centre of town.

★Labourdonnais Waterfront Hotel HOTEL €€€
(☑ 202 4000; www.labourdonnais.com; Le Caudan Waterfront; s/d from Rs 7500/8500; ✱ @ ⊚ ⊠) Definitely the best option in town, the Labourdonnais is an ultrasmart business hotel on the Caudan Waterfront. The rooms are excellent – even the standard rooms are huge. All are bathed in light, with cavernous bathrooms, and most have excellent views of the city and harbour, particularly the so-called 'turret rooms' at each top corner. Facilities include a gym, pool and business centre, and there are a number of eateries.

Le Suffren Hotel & Marina HOTEL €€€
(☑ 202 4900; www.lesuffrenhotel.com; Le Caudan Waterfront; r from €188; ✱ @ ⊚ ⊠) Le Suffren is the trendier sister hotel to the Labourdonnais Waterfront Hotel, just a short complimentary boat ride away. For better or for worse you feel like you're almost out of the city despite being just a couple of minutes from the waterfront. The rooms are smaller than at the Labourdonnais but the place has a very pleasant, convivial feel, with an excellent bar and restaurant.

✕ Eating

Port Louis has a great eating scene where the ethnic diversity of the city again comes up trumps. As the middle classes tend to reside outside the city, many places are only open for lunch – head to the Caudan Waterfront in the evenings and on weekends.

✕ City Centre

The Central Market, Chinatown and the bus stations provide happy hunting grounds for street-side nibbles, but you'll find stalls all over town peddling *samousas* (samosas), *gâteaux piments* (spicy cakes) and *dhal puri* (lentil pancakes). The general rule of thumb is to queue behind the longest line – gossip travels fast and everyone seems to simultaneously know who's serving up the best stall grub.

Bombay Sweets Mart SWEETS €
(7 Rémy Ollier St) Bombay Sweets Mart is famous for the Indian nibbles colourfully known as *caca pigeon* (literally, 'pigeon droppings').

Ru Yi CHINESE €
(☑ 217 9888; 32 Joseph Rivière St; mains from Rs 150; ⊘ 11am-2pm & 6-10pm) You can't go wrong with any of the restaurants in Chinatown, but this one is a favourite for its commitment to high-quality dishes. The atmosphere is a bit lacking, but then again when has an inner-city Chinese restaurant ever been featured in a design magazine? They do set menus for groups upon request.

First Restaurant CHINESE €
(☑ 212 0685; cnr Royal & Coderie Sts; mains from Rs 175; ⊘ noon-3pm & 6.30-9.30pm Tue-Sun) If the age-old rule that a good Chinese restaurant is full of Chinese diners applies, then First is a winner. Packed with large family groups enjoying vast feasts of delicious Cantonese cooking, this is one of Chinatown's finest and prices are extremely reasonable for the quality of the fare.

★Lambic MAURITIAN, INTERNATIONAL €€
(☑ 212 6011; 4 St Georges St; mains Rs 260-530; ⊘ 8am-10pm Mon-Thu, 8am-late Fri, 11am-10pm Sat) Set in a refurbished colonial home in the heart of the capital's chaos, Lambic is a beer buff's paradise with dozens upon dozens of local and imported beers, with a particularly rich selection from Belgium. If the dark-wood bar, antique timber beams and fanned napkins don't win you over, then you'll surely be impressed by the glass-faced pantries covering all the interior walls – they reveal hundreds upon hundreds of alcoholic imports. Waiters are well versed in the high art of matching platters to pints (yes, that's right – you match your meal *to* your beer here). The food includes all the usual fish and meat offerings, with some unusual local dishes such as Creole wild hare.

27 Brasserie
CAFE €€

(☑ 212 5823; www.27brasserie.com; 10 Intendance St; brasserie mains Rs 290-440, restaurant mains Rs 450-650; ⊘8am-4.30pm Mon-Fri) There's something rather Parisian about the bustle and brasserie-style ambience here, and its especially popular for a coffee or lunch for business meetings during the week. Dishes include Rodrigues-style pork curry or fish in ginger, but they won't look askance at you if you just order coffee and croissant.

Courtyard
EUROPEAN €€

(☑ 210 0810; cnr St Louis & Chevreau Sts; mains Rs 500-1200; ⊘noon-4pm Mon-Fri) Set around an attractive courtyard, this European-style restaurant also features a stylish indoor dining space built in a restored stone structure. The impressive menu focuses on a memorable assortment of fusion tastes and fresh cuisine, such as steaming seafood and finely sliced carpaccios.

✖ Le Caudan Waterfront

There's a wide variety of restaurants and cafes in the Caudan complex, from bustling food courts to upscale seaside dining.

Segafredo Zanetti Expresso
CAFE €

(☑ 211 7346; Le Caudan Waterfront; snacks & mains Rs 165-250; ⊘9am-5.30pm Mon-Sat) Finally a decent cup of coffee! Salads, paninis, wraps and pastries also refresh the curry-jaded palate.

Grand Ocean City
CHINESE €€

(☑ 211 8357; Le Caudan Waterfront; mains Rs 120-600, lunch/dinner buffet Rs 550/600; ⊘noon-2.30pm & 6.30-10pm) Excellent Shanghainese treats. Hands down the best place in Port Louis for dim sum lunches (on Monday, Thursday and Sunday), with lunch and dinner buffets on Fridays and Saturdays. Try the half Peking duck for a reasonable Rs 600.

Namaste
INDIAN €€

(☑ 211 6710; Le Caudan Waterfront; mains Rs 375-550, set menu Rs 1175-1800; ⊘11.30am-3pm & 6.30-10.30pm) Namaste is an atmospheric place that serves up excellent North Indian specialties such as tandooris, tikkas and butter chicken. The place gets lively on Saturday evenings when meals start at Rs 400 and are followed by Bollywood tunes to shake your body to.

> ### FIVE REASONS TO VISIT PORT LOUIS
>
> Need an excuse to visit the capital? These are the reasons we'd make the effort to get here.
>
> ⇒ See the dodo at the Natural History Museum & Mauritius Institute (p49)
>
> ⇒ See two of the world's rarest stamps at the Blue Penny Museum (p53)
>
> ⇒ Order your favourite Belgian beer at lovely Lambic (p54)
>
> ⇒ Wander Le Caudan Waterfront, Port Louis' statement of modernising intent
>
> ⇒ Buy a model ship at MAST (p56)

Le Capitaine
MAURITIAN, SEAFOOD €€

(☑ 213 0038; Le Caudan Waterfront; mains Rs 195-495; ⊘11.30am-4pm & 6-10pm) Small, stylish and reasonably priced, Le Capitaine serves up good if unexciting food on its pretty outdoor terrace with great views back to the city centre. Seafood and Mauritian classics are on offer, with the usual suspects such as chicken curry and grilled dorada in residence.

The Deck
SEAFOOD €€

(☑ 950 3134; Le Caudan Waterfront; mains Rs 550-750; ⊘noon-3pm & 6.30-10.30pm Mon-Sat) Inhabiting its own pontoon on the harbour, The Deck wins plaudits for its setting which is slightly removed from the clamour of the riverside bars and has good views. The food is good without getting really interesting – the calamari vindaloo caught our eye, but the grilled fish is also good.

La Rose des Vents
SEAFOOD €€

(☑ 202 4017; banquets@labourdonnais.com; Le Caudan Waterfront; mains Rs 400-1200; ⊘noon-3pm & 6.30-10.30pm Mon-Fri, 6.30-10.30pm Sat) The Labourdonnais Waterfront Hotel boasts this upmarket seafood restaurant, famed for its lobster dishes.

☕ Drinking & Nightlife

Port Louis is not exactly a happening place at night and come sunset the city is virtually silent as commuters retire to the Central Plateau towns. What evening life there is tends to be concentrated on Le Caudan Waterfront.

A MILLION-DOLLAR STAMP?

Philatelists (that's 'stamp collectors' to the rest of us) go weak at the knees at the mention of the Mauritian 'Post Office' one-penny and two-pence stamps. Issued in 1847, these stamps were incorrectly printed with the words 'Post Office' rather than 'Post Paid'. They were recalled upon discovery of the error, but not before the wife of the British governor had mailed out a few dozen on invitations to one of her famous balls.

These stamps now rank among the most valuable in the world. The 'Bordeaux cover', a letter bearing both stamps which was mailed to France, was last sold for a staggering US$3.8 million. In 1993 a consortium of Mauritian companies paid US$2.2 million for the pair of unused one-penny and two-pence stamps now on display in Port Louis' Blue Penny Museum (p53). This is the only place in the world where the two can be seen together on public view. Replicas can be bought at both the Blue Penny Museum and the Mauritius Postal Museum (p53).

☆ Entertainment

Port Louis Casino   CASINO
(☑210 4203; www.casinosofmauritius.mu; Le Caudan Waterfront; ☺9.30am-2am, gaming tables 8pm-4am Mon-Sat & 8pm-2am Sun) The mighty popular city casino is about the liveliest place in town after midnight – its salient (some would say tackiest) feature externally is its ship-shaped design, crowned at its prow by the campest lion imaginable. Miaow. There are slot machines downstairs and blackjack and American roulette on the 1st floor. Smart-casual dress is required.

Star Cinema   CINEMA
(☑211 5361; Le Caudan Waterfront; tickets from Rs 150) This is Port Louis' biggest and best cinema, with three screens offering mainstream international releases. Films are generally dubbed in French and there are usually four or five screenings a day.

Keg & Marlin   LIVE MUSIC
(☑211 6821; Le Caudan Waterfront; ☺noon-midnight Mon-Thu, to 3am Fri, to 1am Sat & Sun) At the weekends the Keg & Marlin transforms into Port Louis' only live-music venue. Standards vary enormously from rock outfits to *séga* (Mauritian folk dance).

Municipal Theatre   THEATRE
(Jules Koenig St; tickets from Rs 100) The appealing Municipal Theatre has changed little since it was built in 1822, making it the oldest theatre in the Indian Ocean region. Decorated in the style of the classic London theatres, it seats about 600 over three levels, and has an exquisitely painted dome ceiling with cherubs and chandeliers. Performances are in the evenings – usually at 8pm. Look for announcements in the local press or call the tourist office to find out what's on. Theatre tickets can be purchased at the box office in the theatre itself.

🛍 Shopping

Most of the city centre's main streets have clusters of merchants selling similar items. Bourbon St has swarms of flower sellers, Coderie St (also spelt Corderie St) has silk and fabric vendors, and La Chaussée St is where locals go to buy electronics.

The Caudan Waterfront is also the place to go for trendy knick-knacks and designer boutiques, including Floreal, Hugo Boss, Mango, Ralph Lauren and the like. There's even an iShop.

Central Market   MARKET
(☺5.30am-5.30pm Mon-Sat, 5.30am-11.30pm Sun) Port Louis' Central Market (p49) has a wide selection of T-shirts, basketry, spices and souvenirs; bargain to get a decent price.

Craft Market   MARKET
(☑210 0139; Le Caudan Waterfront; ☺9.30am-5.30pm) Based in the Caudan Waterfront, Craft Market is less fun but also less hassle than Central Market. You'll find more upmarket souvenirs, such as Mauritius glass, artworks and essential oils.

MAST   MODEL SHIPS
(☑211 7170, 674 6764; www.voiliersocean.intnet.mu; Le Caudan Waterfront; ☺9.30am-5pm Mon-Sat, 9.30am-noon Sun) The model ship manufacturer Voiliers de l'Ocean (p63) has an outlet just outside the Craft Market.

Power Music   MUSIC
(☑211 9143; Le Caudan Waterfront; ☺9.30am-5.30pm Mon-Sat) Power Music stocks a good selection of CDs by local and international artists.

Bookcourt BOOKS
(☑211 9146; Le Caudan Waterfront; ⊙10am-6pm Mon-Sat, to 12.30pm Sun) The country's best bookshop sells a broad range of English, French and Creole books, including guidebooks and an excellent range of books about Mauritius.

ⓘ Orientation

Port Louis is divided by Mauritius' only motorway, which runs by the harbour and Le Caudan Waterfront. The Caudan side is a sanitised city with smart shops and bars, while the vast majority of the city – dirty, colourful, chaotic – is on the other side of the road. The two are connected by at least two underground walkways, one next to the Mauritius Postal Museum that connects to the northwestern end of Sir William Newton St and the other in Le Caudan itself.

Port Louis' two main bus stations are located either side of the city centre, each a few minutes' walk from Place d'Armes. Arriving from the airport, you'll be dropped at the more southerly Victoria Sq bus station.

ⓘ Information

DANGERS & ANNOYANCES

Port Louis is a city with a big underclass and as such is not safe at night. After dark all travellers should stick to well-lit main streets and avoid the Jardins de la Compagnie (p49), a favoured hangout for all manner of unsavoury types. If you don't know your exact route, take a taxi.

During the daytime it's a very safe city but beware of pickpockets anywhere, particularly in the market and around the bus stations.

EMERGENCY

Ambulance (☑114)
Fire services (☑995)
Police (☑emergency 999, headquarters 203 1212; Line Barracks, Lord Kitchener St)

MEDICAL SERVICES

Dr Jeetoo Hospital (☑212 3201; Volcy Pougnet St) Provides 24-hour medical and dental

treatment and has a 24-hour pharmacy. Staff speak English and French.

TOURIST INFORMATION

Head to **Lonely Planet** (www.lonelyplanet.com/mauritius/port-louis) for planning advice, author recommendations, traveller reviews and insider tips.

Mauritius Tourism Promotion Authority (MTPA; ☑210 1545; www.tourism-mauritius.mu; St Louis St, 4-5th fl, Victoria House; ⊙9am-4pm Mon-Fri, 9am-noon Sat) Distributes maps of Port Louis and Mauritius, and can advise on car hire, excursions and hotels throughout the country.

ⓘ Getting There & Away

BUS

Port Louis' two bus stations are both located in the city centre. Buses for northern and eastern destinations, such as Trou aux Biches, Grand Baie and Pamplemousses, leave from **Immigration Sq**, northeast of the Central Market. Buses for southern and western destinations, such as Mahébourg, Curepipe and Flic en Flac, use the **Victoria Sq terminus** just southwest of the city centre.

The first departure on most routes is at about 6am; the last leaves at around 6pm.

FERRY

Ferries to Rodrigues and Réunion dock beside the passenger terminal on Quai D of Port Louis harbour, 1km northwest of town.

TAXI

Taxis from Port Louis to Grand Baie cost Rs 900. To Flic en Flac it's Rs 1000, to Mahébourg it's Rs 1300 and to Belle Mare it's Rs 1600. If you'd prefer a private vehicle, contact any of the island's rental agencies (p151) – they'll deliver the car to your hotel.

ⓘ Getting Around

TO/FROM THE AIRPORT

There are no special airport buses, but regular services between Port Louis and Mahébourg call

BUSES FROM PORT LOUIS

DESTINATION	FARE (RS)	DURATION (HR)	BUS STATION
Centre de Flacq	32	2	Immigration Sq
Curepipe	32	1	Victoria Sq
Grand Baie	32	1	Immigration Sq
Mahébourg	35	2	Victoria Sq
Pamplemousse	28	½	Immigration Sq

at Sir Seewoosagur Ramgoolam International Airport (p150); the stop is roughly 300m from the terminal buildings, near the large round-about. Heading to the airport from Port Louis, allow two hours to be on the safe side and make sure the conductor knows where you're going, as drivers occasionally skip the detour down to the airport.

Expect to pay Rs 1200 for a taxi from Port Louis to the airport – the ride takes at least one hour.

CAR

Given the number of traffic snarls, it's not worth trying to drive around Port Louis. Day-trippers are advised to leave their car in one of the car parks at Le Caudan Waterfront. These are open from 7am to 11pm and cost Rs 50 for the first four hours plus Rs 50 for each additional hour. The turn-off to Le Caudan is located at a marked roundabout south of the city centre. Thus, if you are coming from the north part of the island, you must drive all the way through the city, pass the waterfront complex, then make a U-turn back towards the city on a signposted side road.

Cars can be parked on the street for a maximum of two hours at a time; a marked parking coupon, available at any filling station and some smaller Chinese stores, must be displayed on the dashboard.

TAXI

As a general rule, do not take a taxi around the gridlocked city centre during daylight hours – you'll quickly notice that the pedestrians are moving faster than the cars. After dark, expect to pay Rs 100 for a short taxi ride across town. Always agree to a price beforehand.

CENTRAL PLATEAU

Home to a large majority of Mauritians, the cool and rainy centre of the island feels, for the most part, like a continuation of the urban chaos in Port Louis. There's very little to see in the corridor of towns that runs almost unbroken from the capital to Curepipe; in fact, it's pretty much the opposite of that postcard your friends sent you from their trip here last year.

For tourists interested in learning about life on the island beyond the sand and sun, there are a few worthwhile attractions hidden among the gridiron – the best is Eureka, a charming plantation home and museum. Visitors looking for retail therapy will also enjoy an afternoon of snooping around the local markets and factory outlets.

❶ Getting There & Around

The Central Plateau towns are serviced by frequent bus connections with Port Louis. Other useful routes include the direct services between Quatre Bornes and Flic en Flac, on the west coast, and between Curepipe and Mahébourg, to the southeast; the latter service passes via the airport.

Père Laval's Shrine

The **shrine** (☑242 2129; ⊘8.30am-noon & 1-4.45pm Mon-Sat, 10am-noon & 1-4pm Sun) of the French Catholic priest and missionary Père Jacques Désiré Laval is something of a Lourdes of the Indian Ocean, with many miracles attributed to visits to the priest's grave. The padre died in 1864 and was beatified in 1979 during a visit by Pope John Paul II. He is credited with converting 67,000 people to Christianity during his 23 years in Mauritius.

Today Père Laval is a popular figure for Mauritians of all religions. Pilgrims come here from as far afield as South Africa, Britain and France to commemorate the anniversary of his death on 9 September. Notice the coloured plaster effigy of the priest on top of the tomb – it's been rubbed smooth by miracle-wishing pilgrims.

At other times of year the shrine is fairly quiet, though the services held on Friday at 1pm and 5pm attract a reasonable crowd. In the same complex is a large modern church and a shop with a permanent exhibition of Père Laval's robe, mitre, letters and photographs.

To get here, take a bus signed 'Cité La Cure' or 'Père Laval' from the Immigration Sq bus station.

Pailles

POP 11,475

Just a few miles outside of the capital, the strange sugar-estate-turned-theme-park **Domaine Les Pailles** (☑286 4225; www.domainelespailles.net; ⊘10am-4.30pm) has been transformed into a cultural and heritage centre that makes for an enjoyable half-day excursion. The facilities include rides in horse-drawn carriages, a miniature railway, a working replica of a traditional ox-driven sugar mill, a rum distillery producing the estate's own brew, a spice garden, a quad-biking circuit and a children's playground. On weekdays it's also possible to horseback ride around the estate. Call the riding centre, **Les Écuries du Domaine** (☑286 4240; ⊘8am-5.30pm Mon-Fri, to noon Sat), to make a reservation. There are also a number of upmarket restaurants on the site.

To get to the Domaine, take any bus running between Port Louis' Victoria Sq terminus and Curepipe and ask to be let off at the turn-off for Domaine Les Pailles (it's clearly signposted). From the main road it takes less than half an hour on foot to the reception. Alternatively, it's a 10-minute taxi ride from Port Louis or Moka.

Moka

POP 8203

The most interesting of the Central Plateau towns, the country's academic centre and official home to the president of Mauritius, Moka is a great place to visit for a taste of Mauritian history. The scenery is dramatic here too, with waterfalls, valleys and the towering Le Pouce in the background. Moka's main attraction, though, is the captivating colonial mansion of Eureka. Almost perfectly preserved from the mid-19th century, it provides a window to the island's plantation past.

◉ Sights

Eureka   HISTORIC BUILDING

(☑433 8477; www.maisoneureka.com; admission house Rs 200, house & waterfall Rs 300; ⊘9am-5pm Mon-Sat, 9am-3pm Sun) If you're only going to visit one attraction related to Mauritius' rich colonial history, choose Eureka. This perfectly preserved Creole mansion was built in the 1830s and today it's a museum and veritable time machine providing incredible insight into the island's vibrant plantation past. The estate's unusual name is believed to have been the reaction of Eugène Le Clézio when he successfully won a bid to purchase the house at auction in 1856.

The main manor house is a masterpiece of tropical construction, which apparently kept the interior deliciously cool during the unbearably hot summers, and boasts 109 doors and more rooms than a Cluedo board. Rooms are adorned with an impeccably preserved collection of period furniture imported by the French East India Company – take special note of the antique maps, a strange shower contraption that was quite the luxury some 150 years ago and the mildewed piano with keys like rotting teeth.

OFF THE BEATEN TRACK

HIKING THE CENTRAL PLATEAU

The mountain ranges fringing the Central Plateau offer a variety of memorable rambles and hikes. Two of the best introductions to hiking in Mauritius are **Le Pouce** (812m), a thumb-shaped peak on the plateau's northern edge, and **Corps de Garde** (719m), a wedge-like ridge to the southwest that makes for a slightly more challenging endeavour.

Both hikes offer resplendent views down to the coastal plains, but are best appreciated when tackled with a local guide who can annotate the hike with detailed information about the local flora and history. If you decide to go at it alone, check out www.fitsy.com, a brilliant website that has mapped out the walks with extensive GPS and satellite detail. For planning purposes, allow about two hours for each hike if you're starting at the trailhead.

The courtyard behind the main mansion contains beautifully manicured grounds surrounded by a set of stone cottages – the former servants quarters and kitchen. Follow the trail out the back for 15 minutes and you'll reach the lovely **Ravin waterfall**.

🛏 Sleeping & Eating

Eureka Maison d'Hôte HISTORIC GUESTHOUSE €€

(☑433 8477; www.maisoneureka.com; r incl breakfast Rs 3500) If you wish to spend the night on a plantation, there are a handful of authentic cottages on the property that have been converted into lovely bedrooms with en suite facilities and kitchenettes. Both rooms at this so-called *maison d'hôte* have period furnishings from the French East India Company. The St George cabin, the smaller of the two units, was once the cell for the estate's priest.

★ Eureka Table d'Hôte MAURITIAN €€

(☑433 8477; www.maisoneureka.com; meals Rs 800; ⊘noon-3pm) Even if you don't stay the night, to deepen your Eureka experience, we recommend planning your visit around noon to enjoy a relaxing repast at the in-house *table d'hôte*. Sample an assortment of Mauritian classics like *marlin fumée* (smoked fish), lentils and curried fish while

Central Plateau

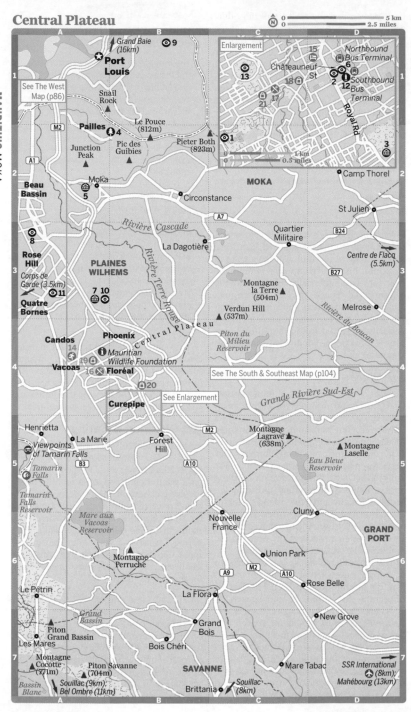

N

0 ——— 5 km
0 ——— 2.5 miles

Grand Baie
(16km)

9

**Port
Louis**

See The West
Map (p86)

Snail
Rock

Pailles **4**

Le Pouce
(812m)

Pieter Both
(823m)

Junction
Peak

Pic des
Guibies

Enlargement

15

Châteauneuf
St

6

13

18

2 **12**

Southbound
Bus
Terminal

Northbound
Bus Terminal

21 17

Royal Rd

1

0 ——— 1 km
0 ——— 0.5 miles

3

Moka **5**

MOKA

Circonstance

Camp Thorel

St Julien

**Beau
Bassin**

8

A7

La Dagotière

Rivière Cascade

Quartier
Militaire

B24

Centre de Flacq
(5.5km)

**Rose
Hill**

Corps de
Garde (3.5km)

11

**Quatre
Bornes**

**PLAINES
WILHEMS**

7 10

Rivière Terre Rouge

Montagne
la Terre
(504m)

Verdun Hill
(537m)

Piton du
Milieu
Reservoir

B27

Melrose

Rivière du Boucan

Candos

14

Phoenix

Central Plateau

Vacoas

19

16 **Floréal**

Mauritian
Wildlife Foundation

20

Curepipe

See Enlargement

See The South & Southeast Map (p104)

Grande Rivière Sud-Est

Henrietta

La Marie

Viewpoints
of Tamarin Falls

**Forest
Hill**

B3

A10

Montagne
Lagrave
(638m)

Montagne
Laselle

Tamarin
Falls

Eau Bleue
Reservoir

Tamarin
Falls
Reservoir

Mare aux
Vacoas
Reservoir

Nouvelle
France

Cluny

**GRAND
PORT**

Montagne
Perruche

Union Park

M2

A9 A10

Rose Belle

Le Pétrin

La Flora

New Grove

Grand
Bassin

Piton
Grand Bassin

Les Mares

Grand
Bois

Montagne
Cocotte
(771m)

Piton Savanne
(704m)

Bois Chéri

SAVANNE

Mare Tabac

SSR International
(8km)
Mahébourg (13km)

Bassin
Blanc

Souillac (9km);
Bel Ombre (11km)

Brittania

Souillac
(8km)

M2

A1

M2

Central Plateau

enjoying the delightful throwback atmosphere. Call ahead as sometimes the restaurant is closed for tour groups.

ⓘ Getting There & Away

To get to Eureka, take a bus from Curepipe or Victoria Sq in Port Louis and get off at Moka. Eureka is signed about 1km north of the bus stop. Otherwise, many hotels and most tour operatros can organise half-day excursions here from anywhere on the island.

Curepipe

POP 76,304

Effectively Mauritius' second city, Curepipe is a bustling highland commercial centre famous for its rainy weather, volcanic crater and retail shopping. Its strange name reputedly stems from the malaria epidemic of 1867 when people fleeing from lowland Port Louis would 'cure' their pipes of malarial bacteria by smoking them here (although it's more likely that the area was named after a fondly remembered town in France).

Curepipe is the highest of the plateau towns. At 550m above sea level, temperatures are refreshingly cool in summer, but according to lowlanders, Curepipe has two seasons: the little season of big rains and the big season of little rains. The damp climate gives the buildings an ageing, mildewed quality. Bring an umbrella.

◎ Sights

Hôtel de Ville　　　　　ARCHITECTURE
(Town Hall; Rue Chasteauneuf) Overlooking a small park in the centre of Curepipe, the Hô-

tel de Ville is one of Mauritius' best surviving structures from its colonial era. Notice the gable windows, verandah and decorative wooden friezes known as *dentelles* – all are signature traits of the island's early plantation architecture. The building was moved here from Moka in 1903.

Statue of Paul and Virginie　　STATUE
Near the town hall, you'll find a bronze copy of Prosper d'Épinay's famous statue of Paul and Virginie. The original is on display in Port Louis' Blue Penny Museum (p53).

Carnegie Library　　　LIBRARY, ARCHITECTURE
(☑674 2278; ◷9.30am-6pm Mon-Fri, to 3pm Sat) FREE Next to the town hall, the stone building with the distinctive neoclassical porch houses the municipal Carnegie Library. Its collection includes rare books on Mauritius dating back to the 18th century.

Domaine des Aubineaux　　HISTORIC BUILDING
(☑676 3089; Royal Rd; adult/child Rs 350/175; ◷8.30am-4pm Mon-Fri, to 1.30pm Sat) The manor house of the Domaine des Aubineaux was built in 1872 in a classic colonial style, and in 1889 it was the first residence on the island to be outfitted with electricity. The plantation was transformed into a museum in 2000, and today it marks the first stop on the historical La Route du Thé (p117). Keep an eye out for old photographs preserving the memory of the local colonial manses that have fallen victim to harsh weather and the relentless passage of time. Exotic plants fill the garden under the shade of camphor trees, and when you're ready for a break you can sip savoury teas in the converted billiard parlour.

Trou aux Cerfs
VOLCANO

About 1km west of central Curepipe, the Trou aux Cerfs is an extinct volcanic crater some 100m deep and 1km in circumference. The bowl is heavily wooded and from the road around the rim – a favourite spot for joggers and walkers – you get lovely views of the plateau. There are benches for rest and reflection, and a radar station for keeping an electronic eye on cyclone activity.

Botanical Gardens
GARDENS

(☺6am-6pm May-Sep, 7am-7pm Oct-Apr) FREE
The well-kept gardens of Curepipe were created in 1870 to foster foliage that thrived in cooler weather – the grounds in Pamplem-ousses proved far too sweltering for certain species.

🛏 Sleeping & Eating

Unless you're visiting family, it's hard to imagine why you'd want to stay in Curepipe – nowhere else in the island is more than an hour away by road.

Believe it or not, the cafeteria at the local hospital (Clinique de Lorette) serves a mean quiche at lunchtime – it's a local secret.

Auberge de la Madelon
GUESTHOUSE €

(☑670 1885; www.aubergemadelon.com; 10 Sir John Pope Hennessy St; r €20-40; ❋ @ 🛜 ⛼) Excellent value and centrally located, this well-run place is simple, small and surprisingly

---

A TOUR OF THE CENTRAL PLATEAU

The area southeast of, and inland from Port Louis can seem like one great connurbation, and in a sense it is. While most travellers pass right on by en route between the coasts, there are enough sights to warrant a day or half-day excursion by taxi – we suggest you don't drive yourself or you'll waste valuable time trying to find each place. In addition to the following, consider adding the highlights of Moka, Pailles and Curepipe to your tour.

The town of Rose Hill (pronounced row-zeel by locals), wedged between Beau Bassin and Quatre Bornes in the heart of the Central Plateau's urban sprawl, is virtually a suburb of Port Louis. Here, architecture buffs will appreciate the unusual Creole structure housing the Municipality of Beau Bassin-Rose Hill (St Jean Rd). The building was constructed in 1933 as a municipal theatre. The attractive Creole manse next door – Maison Le Carne (St Jean Rd) – houses the Mauritius Research Council.

Another satellite of Port Louis, Quatre Bornes has little to detain you, other than on Thursdays and Sundays when scores of locals flock to the city to rummage through stall upon stall at the bustling produce and textile market; there's also a popular vegie market on Saturdays.

In Phoenix, the Mauritius Glass Gallery (☑696 3360; mgg@pbg.mu; Pont Fer, Phoenix; admission Rs 50; ☺8am-5pm Mon-Sat) produces unusual souvenirs made from recycled glass. You can see them being made using traditional methods in the workshop, which also doubles as a small museum.

The neighbouring town of Vacoas is home to the oldest golf course in the Indian Ocean, Mauritius Gymkhana Club (☑696 1404; www.mgc.intnet.mu; Suffolk Close, Vacoas). It's the fourth-oldest fairway in the world (the three older courses are in Britain and India).

Another possibility is Floréal, the 'Beverly Hills' of Mauritius and a rather posh suburb northwest of Curepipe. The area has become synonymous with the high-quality knitwear produced by the Floreal Knitwear company. Fill your suitcase with clothes at Floréal Square (☑698 8011; Swami Sivananda Ave; ☺9.30am-5.30pm Mon-Fri, to 4pm Sat) on the main road from Curepipe.

If you're in the neighbourhood, we highly recommend seeking out La Clef des Champs (☑686 3458; www.laclefdeschamps.mu; Queen Mary Ave; set menu per person from Rs 1200; ☺noon-2pm & 7-11pm Mon-Fri), the table d'hôte – and pet project – of Jacqueline Dalais, chef to the stars. Known for her impressive library of self-created recipes, Jacqueline has earned quite the reputation on the island for her unparalleled cuisine – she is regularly called upon to cater government functions, especially when foreign dignitaries are in town. Dishes served in her quaint dining room lean towards Provençal flavours; the presentation is exquisite.

stylish, boasting comfy en suite rooms and very helpful management.

La Potinière
MAURITIAN €€

(☑670 2648; Bernardin de St-Pierre St; crêpes & mains from Rs 200; ⊙10am-3pm & 6.30-10pm Tue-Sat) Curepipe's most obviously upmarket restaurant hides in an unassuming concrete block, but inside all is starched linen and gleaming tableware. The menu features a selection of quintessential Mauritian eats – hearts of palm, wild boar and seafood.

🛍 Shopping

Curepipe is where the locals go to shop; you can find an incredible assortment of discounted items just by walking from the Royal College to the Galerie Currimjee.

Galerie des Îles
MALL

(☑670 7516; Arcade Currimjee; ⊙9.30am-5.30pm Mon-Sat) Try Galerie des Îles for a generous selection of local designs and artisans in more than a dozen shops.

Beauté de Chine
ANTIQUES

(Rue du Jardin, Les Arcades; ⊙9.30-5.30 Mon-Fri, to 1pm Sat) Beauté de Chine, one of the longest-running stores on the island, sells an assortment of old-world relics like copper, jade, silk and antique porcelain.

Voiliers de L'Océan
HANDICRAFTS

(☑676 6986, 674 6764; www.voiliersocean.intnet. mu; Bernardin de St-Pierre; ⊙9am-6pm) Travellers looking for model-ship showrooms and workshops should join the circuit and stop by Voiliers de L'Océan. Roughly 200 models are produced per month and visitors can watch the artisans at work.

ℹ Orientation

Curepipe is bisected by Royal Rd, which runs approximately north–south. Most of the city's banks, shops and restaurants gather around the junction of Royal Rd and Châteauneuf St. Head east along Châteauneuf St for the bus station. Most of the sights, such as the Trou aux Cerfs crater and the botanical gardens, are within walking distance of the town centre.

ℹ Getting There & Away

Curepipe is an important transport hub, with frequent bus services to Port Louis (Victoria Sq), Mahébourg, Centre de Flacq, Moka and just about anywhere else on the island. There are two terminals – the **northbound** and the **southbound**. Most services go from the north-bound (Port Louis, Rose Hill, Quatre Bornes); Mahébourg is served from the southbound. The terminals lie on either side of Châteauneuf St, at the junction with Victoria Ave.

From Curepipe, expect to pay Rs 1000 for a taxi ride to the airport, Rs 1600 to Grand Baie, Rs 1500 to Belle Mare, Rs 1000 to Port Louis, Rs 1000 to Flic en Flac and Rs 600 to Black River.

THE NORTH

Mauritius' tourism panache started in the north, and today there's plenty on offer for visitors. Although most of the area's spectacular beaches have been claimed by hotel construction, it's never hard to get away from it all and discover the little nooks that remain largely untouched by development.

Grand Baie is the eye of the tourist storm, boasting Mauritius' best nightlife and some of the island's best restaurants. The small beachside villages around Grand Baie – Trou aux Biches, Mont Choisy and Pereybère – are quickly developing in a similar fashion.

The inland plain of sugar-cane fields – pocked with piles of volcanic boulders stacked by indentured servants – is known as Pamplemousses and gently slopes towards the sea. Here you'll find the wonderful Sir Seewoosagur Ramgoolam Botanical Gardens and the rightly popular L'Aventure du Sucre – a museum dedicated to Mauritius' traditional colonial export.

ℹ Getting There & Around

The most useful bus routes in and around this area are those running from Port Louis' Immigration Sq bus station along the coast road to Trou aux Biches, Grand Baie, Pereybère and Cap Malheureux. There are also express services direct from Port Louis to Grand Baie. Port Louis is the starting point for buses via Pamplemousses to Grand Gaube.

To reach this area from the airport, change buses in Port Louis. Alternatively, a taxi costs Rs 800 from Port Louis to Balaclava, Rs 900 to Grand Baie and Rs 1000 to Grand Gaube. Add an additional Rs 1000 to reach the airport.

Most hotels and guesthouses have bikes for hire and can help organise car hire. Otherwise, you can approach the rental agencies directly. The largest concentration is in Grand Baie, and there are a smattering of outlets in and around Trou aux Biches and Pereybère.

Port Louis to Grand Baie

The northwest coast of Mauritius is quiet and quietly pretty with some good beaches, excellent hotels and a more tranquil air than Port Louis and Grand Baie at either end.

Balaclava, around 10km north of Port Louis, is named after the region's black-lava rocks. The narrow road passes through tiny **Pointe aux Piments** en route to relaxed **Trou aux Biches** and the neighbouring village of **Mont Choisy** (also spelt Mon Choisy). Trou aux Biches (Does' Watering Hole) in particular enjoys gorgeous stretches of casuarina-lined sand that continue almost unbroken all the way to sleepy Mont Choisy. Although things are changing, most of the beaches are pleasantly uncrowded during the week, but there's fierce competition for picnic spots on weekends.

Sights

Rivulet Terre Rouge Bird Sanctuary　　　　WILDLIFE RESERVE
(Map p66; ☺9am-2pm) **FREE** Just north of Port Louis, bird-watchers will want to take the signposted turn-off to the east that leads to the Rivulet Terre Rouge Bird Sanctuary. Sited on one of the largest estuary habitats in Mauritius, this Ramsar-recognised site draws countless migratory bird species, with large populations present from October to March in particular.

Baie de l'Arsenal Ruins　　　　RUINS
(Map p66) You can still see the ruins of the French arsenal – along with a flour mill and a lime kiln – within the grounds of the Maritim Hotel (p68) at Baie de l'Arsenal. Non-guests can obtain permission to visit the ruins from the security guard at the hotel entrance; the track begins about 30m inside the gate to the right.

Mauritius Aquarium　　　　AQUARIUM
(Map p66; ☏261 4561; www.mauritiusaquarium. com; Coastal Rd, Pointe aux Piments; adult/child/ family Rs 250/125/650; ☺9.30am-5pm Mon-Sat, 10am-4pm Sun) This small aquarium has a decent collection of tropical fish (including clown fish), but the real stars are the white-tip reef shark and the two hawksbill turtles. There's daily shark feeding at 11am and fish feeding three times daily.

🏃 Activities

Trou aux Biches and Mont Choisy are both important watersports centres. Activities on offer range from touring the lagoon in a glass-bottomed boat to parasailing, water-skiing, deep-sea fishing and diving.

Boat House　　　　WATERSPORTS
(Map p69; ☏728 4335; ☺9am-5pm) Snorkelling equipment (Rs 150 per day) can be rented at the boat house on Trou aux Biches' public beach. It also rents out pedalos and one-/two-person kayaks (Rs 300/500 per hour), and offers a variety of other activities, including glass-bottomed boat tours (Rs from 750 per hour per person), waterskiing (Rs 1500/1000 for beginners/non-beginners per 12 minutes) and parasailing (Rs 1500 per 10 minutes).

Diving

All of the following dive centres charge around Rs 1500/2000 per day/night dive and can arrange PADI accreditation courses.

Divers' Ocean　　　　DIVING
(Map p69; ☏265 5889; www.diversocean.com; Royal Rd, Mont Choisy; ☺9am-4.30pm) French-run centre offering diving and undersea walks.

Dive Dream Divers　　　　DIVING
(Map p69; ☏265 5552; www.dive-dream.org; off Trou aux Biches Rd, Mont Choisy; ☺8.30am-4.30pm Tue-Sun) A PADI-accredited centre.

Blue Water Diving　　　　DIVING
(Map p69; ☏265 6700; www.bluewaterdiving center.com; Royal Rd, Mont Choisy; ☺8am-4pm) A good dive option.

Horse Riding

In addition to the following place, horse riding is possible at the Maritim Hotel (p68) in Balaclava.

ℹ DIVING IN THE NORTH

Northern Mauritius is one of the best places on the island to dive, whatever your level. The following are our favourites, and are possible through the dive centres in Mont Choisy. To read more about these and other sites in the area, turn to p27.

➟ La Fosse aux Requins, Île Plate

➟ Carpenters & The Wall, Coin de Mire

➟ Holt's Rock, off Trou aux Biches

➟ Tombant de la Pointe aux Cannoniers

SHOPPING IN MAURITIUS

Mauritius is increasingly promoting itself as a shopping destination, not least because numerous prestigious international clothing brands are manufactured here.

Before we give you the rundown on shopping on the island, a couple of warnings. First, avoid any seashell, coral or turtleshell products – importing them into your country may be illegal. Secondly, taxi drivers in Mauritius usually earn up to 20% commission from certain shops and other businesses to which they take clients.

Clothing

Although the textile industry has been eclipsed by China, it is still one of Mauritius' biggest earners. Many of the brand-name clothes on sale in Europe, Australia and the USA are produced in the factories around Curepipe, Floréal and Vacoas. Shoppers can save by buying at the source, and many of the bigger suppliers have outlet stores where you can snap up items at a fraction of their usual retail price.

Floreal Knitwear in Floréal is renowned for its stylish sweaters and other knitted garments. The company supplies Gap, Next and other international outfitters, but you can buy the same items before the branded labels have been added for a fraction of the final cost at their Floréal emporium.

Handicrafts & Souvenirs

Locally produced basketry, essential oils, sugar, spices, rums, teas and T-shirts all make very portable souvenirs. The Craft Market (p56) in Port Louis' Caudan Waterfront complex offers perhaps the widest choice. Most of the crafts and souvenirs sold at Port Louis' Central Market and the Grand Baie Bazaar (p77) are of Malagasy origin, like leather belts and bags, masks, embroidery and semiprecious-stone solitaire sets. For Rodrigues' specialities, see p164.

Model Ships

It's difficult not to be impressed by the skill that goes into producing Mauritius' famous model ships. Small-scale shipbuilding has become a huge business and you'll see intricate replicas of famous vessels, such as the *Bounty*, *Victory*, *Endeavour*, *Golden Hind* and even the *Titanic*, for sale all over the island. Model shipbuilding dates back to only 1968, when an unknown Mauritian carved a model ship for fun and launched a whole new industry.

The models are made out of teak or mahogany (cheaper camphor wood is liable to crack), and larger ships take up to 400 hours to complete. Men usually work on the structure and the women do the rigging and sails, which are dipped in tea to give them a weathered look.

One of the best model-ship builders is Voiliers de L'Océan (p63), in Curepipe. The company also has an outlet, MAST (p56), in Port Louis' Caudan Waterfront complex.

To get your goods home safely, shops will pack the models for carry-on luggage or in sturdy boxes to go in the hold, and deliver them to your hotel or the airport at no extra charge.

Horse Riding Delights HORSE RIDING
(Map p69; ☑ 265 6159; www.horseridingdelights. com; Mont Choisy Sugar Estate, off Royal Rd; adult/ child Rs 2100/1900; ◷ 8am & 3pm Mon-Fri, 8am Sat) At this excellent riding school on the northern edge of Mont Choisy, you can take a 90-minute ride in over 200 hectares of land amid deer and giant tortoises.

Deep-Sea Fishing

Corsaire Club FISHING
(Map p69; ☑ 265 5209; off Royal Rd, Mont Choisy; half-/full-day Rs 24,000/28,000; ◷ 9am-5pm)

Deep-sea anglers should head for the Corsaire Club, which is run by Saïd Foorabally. It's located beside Le Pescatore (p70) restaurant in Mont Choisy; the restaurant is well signposted off Royal Rd.

Submarine Rides

Blue Safari Submarine SUBMARINE
(Map p69; ☑ 263 3333; www.blue-safari.com; Royal Rd, Mont Choisy; adult/child Rs 3900/2300; ◷ 9am-4pm) If you fancy diving but don't want to get wet, Blue Safari Submarine takes you down among the coral and fishes

The North

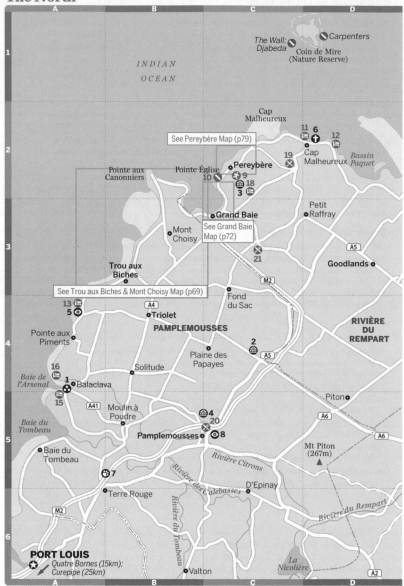

INDIAN OCEAN

The Wall; Djabeda
Carpenters
Coin de Mire (Nature Reserve)

Cap Malheureux

11 6 12
19 Cap Malheureux
Bassin Paquet

See Pereybère Map (p79)

Pointe aux Canonniers
Pointe Église
Pereybère
10 9
18
3

Petit Raffray

Grand Baie
See Grand Baie Map (p72)

A5

Mont Choisy

Goodlands

21

Trou aux Biches

M2

See Trou aux Biches & Mont Choisy Map (p69)

Fond du Sac

13
5

A4
Triolet
PAMPLEMOUSSES

RIVIÈRE DU REMPART

Pointe aux Piments

Plaine des Papayes

2
A5

16
Baie de l'Arsenal
1 Balaclava
15

Solitude

Piton

A41
Moulin à Poudre

4
20

A6

A6

Pamplemousses
8

Mt Piton (267m)

Baie du Tombeau

Rivière Citrons

Baie du Tombeau

7

D'Epinay

Terre Rouge

Rivière des Calebasses

M2

Rivière du Rempart

Rivière du Tombeau

PORT LOUIS
Quatre Bornes (15km); Curepipe (25km)

La Nicolière

A2

Valton

to a depth of 35m. The ride lasts roughly two hours, of which 40 minutes are spent underwater, with departures every hour according to demand. Reservations are recommended at least a day in advance and departures aren't possible when seas are rough.

🛏 Sleeping

It seems almost every building along this stretch of coast is available for rent in some form. Much of the accommodation is in the midrange bracket and consists of self-catering apartments, villas and bungalows,

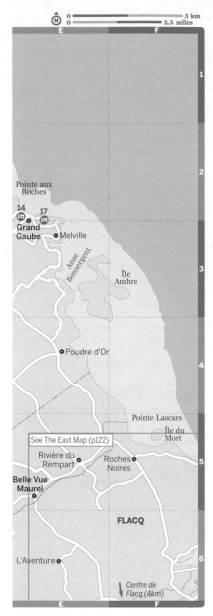

The North

◎ Sights

Above the restaurant of the same name and across the road from the beach, these two mini-apartments are outrageous value. Both have kitchens (microwave only).

★ **Le Récif Attitude** HOTEL €€
(Map p66; ☑ 261 0444; www.lerecif.com; Royal Rd, Pointe aux Piments; s/d garden view incl breakfast from €82/118, seaview €93/134; ❄ @ 🛜 ☲) Le Récif is a stylish three-star-superior beachfront resort with a surprisingly reasonable price tag. The rooms are attractively turned out. The soothing public areas are riddled with pillow-strewn nooks, and there's a spa centre, plunge pool and plenty of the island's trademark thatch umbrellas.

often with terraces or balconies for viewing the sunset.

Cafe International GUESTHOUSE €
(Map p69; ☑ 765 8735; anemariforever@gmail.com; Royal Rd, Trou aux Biches; apt €25-35; ❄ 🛜)

Casuarina Hotel HOTEL €€€
(Map p69; ☑ 204 5000; www.hotel-casuarina.com; Royal Rd, Trou aux Biches; s/d incl breakfast from €148/213; ❄ 🛜 ☲) Definitely one of the more interesting midrange places, Casuarina's Moorish style is matched by equally inventive

apartment layouts. It's also pleasantly small and feels very relaxed. You have to cross the road to the beach and the cheaper rooms are a little overpriced, but otherwise this place is great.

Le Sakoa
HOTEL €€€

(Map p69; ☎265 5244; www.lesakoa.com; Royal Rd, Trou aux Biches; d incl breakfast/half board from €175/225; ❊@☎≋) Easily the most stylish option in Trou aux Biches, Le Sakoa is instantly recognisable by its signature high-pitched roofs that match the neighbouring palms both in height and grandeur. Spacious accommodation is in wonderful two-storey thatched blocks radiating out from the fantastic beach. A charming dark-marble infinity pool anchors the hotel's centre, providing a luxurious setting for couples and families.

Maritim Hotel
HOTEL €€€

(Map p66; ☎204 1000; www.maritim.de; Royal Rd, Balaclava; s/d incl breakfast from €205/280; ❊@☎≋) This is a well-established German-owned hotel with an enviable position out of the wind on Turtle Bay. Its main plus points are a 25-hectare park, complete with a nine-hole golf course, tennis courts and riding stables. It has a great beach where guests can indulge in everything from snorkelling to waterskiing, and there's a choice of three restaurants, including a fantastic venue in a refurbished colonial manse. Don't miss the old arsenal (p64) that used to be a powder magazine.

Oberoi
LUXURY HOTEL €€€

(Map p66; ☎204 3600; www.oberoihotels.com; Pointe aux Piments; r incl breakfast from €370, with private pool from €685; ❊@☎≋) Set in expansive gardens, the Oberoi boasts a gorgeous beach and stunning grounds including a high-flowing waterfall that dominates the ensemble. The best villas here have their own pools and gardens, enjoying total privacy and making them perfect for honeymooners. Inside it's all understated luxury, an inventive mix of African and Asian design.

Trou aux Biches Hotel
HOTEL €€€

(Map p69; ☎204 6565; www.trouauxbiches-hotel.com; Royal Rd, Trou aux Biches; s incl half board €330-516, d €440-688; ❊@☎≋) Uber luxury is the name of the game at five-star Trou aux Biches Hotel with its clutch of traditionally inspired beachside suites and villas. The resort's design scheme incorporates rustic elements – like thatch, wicker, and hand-cut

boulders – into the unquestionably modern surrounds. Spas, pools and two kilometres of sand make this the most desirable address in Trou aux Biches.

Eating

Snack Kwan Peng
CHINESE €

(Map p69; Royal Rd, Trou aux Biches; meals Rs 70; ⏰9am-4pm) Queues form here at lunchtime for some of the simplest and best Chinese food on the island. You basically put your own meal together by pointing to the pots you wish to try – beef, *boulettes* (small steamed dumplings in a variety of flavours), noodles, soup – and it will be put together at breakneck speed; no matter how much you order it rarely jumps above Rs 70 for a filling meal, although drinks are extra. The small shopfront is just across the road from the beach, ideal for takeaway.

La Marmite Mauricienne
MAURITIAN €

(Map p69; ☎265 7604; Trou aux Biches Rd, Trou aux Biches; mains Rs 105-195; ⏰noon-2.30pm & 6-10pm) This basic but sweet place down Trou aux Biches Rd has a pleasant outdoor feel, with lots of tables on the terrace (although sadly it's on a rather busy road). The menu is Mauritian, featuring mostly seafood, noodles and curries.

Bollywood Curry
INDIAN €

(Map p69; ☎758 2404; A4, Triolet; mains Rs 140-250; ⏰10.30am-2.30pm & 5.30-10.30pm) Bollywood Curry serves out-of-this-world curries in uberbasic surrounds (think buzzing neon bulbs and cracked tiles) – it doesn't get more authentic than this! Kormas, biryanis and masalas are all there plus a few surprises. Coming from Grand Baie along the M2 and A4, it's around 500m on the left after the Mont Choisy turn-off.

★ Café International
INTERNATIONAL €€

(Map p69; ☎723 9214; Royal Rd, Trou aux Biches; mains Rs 140-600; ⏰10am-10pm Wed-Sat & Mon, noon-10pm Sun) This popular South African–run spot serves up an excellent assortment of dishes from around the world – burgers, curries and sandwiches are mainstays but the highlights are fresh fish and South African steaks that are so good we would (and, on at least one occasion, did) cross the island just to try one. It's all watched over by friendly Deon (a former bodyguard for Nelson Mandela), and there's a clothes shop and second-hand bookshop as well.

Trou aux Biches & Mont Choisy

Trou aux Biches & Mont Choisy

🎯 Activities, Courses & Tours
1 Blue Safari Submarine	C2
Blue Water Diving	(see 4)
2 Boat House	B3
Corsaire Club	(see 13)
3 Dive Dream Divers	B3
4 Divers' Ocean	C3
5 Horse Riding Delights	C2

🛏 Sleeping
6 Casuarina Hotel	B3
7 Le Sakoa	B4

8 Trou aux Biches Hotel	B3

🍴 Eating
1974	(see 14)
9 Bollywood Curry	D3
10 Cabanne du Peche	B4
11 Café International	B4
La Marmite Mauricienne	(see 12)
12 L'Assiette du Nord	B4
13 Le Pescatore	C3
14 Snack Kwan Peng	B4

★ **1974**   ITALIAN, SEAFOOD €€
(Map p69; ☎ 265 7400; Royal Rd, Trou aux Biches; mains Rs 300-500; ⊗ 6-11pm Tue-Thu, noon-2.30pm & 6-11pm Fri-Sun) This fabulous place in warm terracotta hues is the work of Italians Antonio and Giulia. The food includes pasta and seafood with an emphasis on fresh local produce – the menu changes daily.

L'Assiette du Nord   INTERNATIONAL €€
(Map p69; ☎ 265 7040; Trou aux Biches Rd, Trou aux Biches; mains Rs 150-450; ⊗ noon-2.30pm & 6-10pm) A popular option where you can opt

for the terrace or a slightly smarter dining area behind the fish-tank partition. Seafood features strongly, served in Chinese, Indian and Creole style. Try fish cooked in banana leaf with madras sauce or perhaps prawns in garlic butter.

Cabanne du Peche   MAURITIAN €€
(Map p69; ☑ 711 2729; Royal Rd, Trou aux Biches; mains from Rs 400; ⓢ noon-9pm) You just don't get experiences like this if you never leave your resort. This seaside kiosk is run by an all-female crew who serve fabulous local specialties, among them prawns or fish in red Creole sauce and fish curry with eggplant. Servings are large and the ramshackle tables right next to the beach could just be our favourites along this stretch of coast.

Le Pescatore   SEAFOOD €€€
(Map p69; ☑ 265 6337; off Royal Rd, Mont Choisy; set menus Rs 1500-4000, mains Rs 1000-3000; ⓢ noon-2pm & 7-9pm Mon-Sat) Wonderfully light decor and a great terrace overlooking the fishing boats in the sea below set the scene for a truly superior eating experience. Dishes such as lobster in ginger and sake sauce should give you an idea of what to expect, but the fine set menus are all worth considering.

ⓘ Information

Shibani Foreign Exchange (Royal Rd, Mont Choisy; ⓢ 8am-6pm Mon-Sat, to noon Sun)

ⓘ Getting There & Away

There are no bus services to Balaclava or Baie de l'Arsenal. A taxi from Port Louis will cost Rs 400 to 500.

Trou aux Biches and Mont Choisy are served by buses running between Port Louis' Immigration Sq bus station and Cap Malheureux via Grand Baie. There are bus stops about every

500m along the coastal highway. A taxi to Grand Baie costs around Rs 500.

Grand Baie

POP 9569

In the 17th century the Dutch used to call Grand Baie 'De Bogt Zonder Eynt', which meant the 'Bay Without End'. Today it appears as though it's the development – not the bay – that's without end. As such, Grand Baie has all the vices and virtues of beach resorts the world over. The virtues include good accommodation, bars and restaurants, while the vices can be found in water frontages consumed by concrete and touts, although the latter, in true Mauritian style, nudge rather than push. To escape the downtown scene, head for charming and quiet Pointe aux Canonniers.

ⓞ Sights

Grand Baie's prime attraction is the range of water-based activities on offer. Otherwise, the only specific sights are a couple of vividly colourful Tamil temples.

Surya Oudaya Sangam   HINDU TEMPLE
(Map p71; ⓢ 8am-5pm Mon-Sat) Surya Oudaya Sangam, located at the west end of town, is dedicated to Shiva. Visitors are welcome but shoes should be removed before entering.

Shiv Kalyan Vath Mandir   HINDU TEMPLE
(Map p72; Royal Rd; ⓢ 8am-5pm Mon-Sat) Shiv Kalyan Vath Mandir is a vividly coloured Tamil temple that's older than Grand Baie's other temple, Surya Oudaya Sangam. Remove your shoes before entering.

🏝 Beaches

The beach at Grand Baie is nothing special and the bay here is congested with boats.

BEST HORSE-RIDING OUTFITS

Mauritius has some lovely rambling countryside, which is perfect for riding excursions. There are heaps of equestrian outfits throughout the island – you'll find a couple of ranches in the west, an interesting farm in the south that rescues old race horses, and several outfits in the north. Our pick of the possibilities include:

➡ La Vieille Cheminée (p97), Chamarel

➡ Les Écuries du Domaine (p59), Pailles

➡ Horse Riding Delights (p65), Mont Choisy

➡ Domaine de l'Étoile (p119), southeastern Mauritius

➡ Haras du Morne (p103), Le Morne Peninsula

Pointe aux Cannoniers

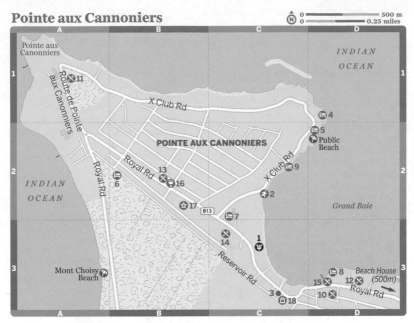

Instead, you're better off heading for **La Cuvette public beach** beside the Verandah Hotel (p74) towards Pereybère; it can get crowded on weekends. If you continue north, you'll find a series of sandy beaches accessible by small passages between the seemingly continuous string of private villas.

🏃 Activities

Skydive Austral ADVENTURE SPORTS
(📞 499 5551; www.skydiveaustral.com; sky dive Rs 11,500) 'Wanna get high?' asks Skydive Austral with a winked eye. This new adventure outfit offers travellers a whole new way to check out the island – from 3000m in the air as you zoom towards the earth after jumping from a plane. It's based at a clearing towards Roches Noires in the east, but touts and transfers make Grand Baie a good departure point.

Sportfisher FISHING
(Map p72; 📞 263 8358; www.sportfisher.com; Royal Rd; half/full day from Rs 23,000/26,450 per boat; ⏰ 7am-6pm) Based beside the Sunset Blvd jetty, Sportfisher has four boats, each taking up to six people (three anglers and three companions). Remember their policy: 'All fish belong to the boat. However, should

Grand Baie

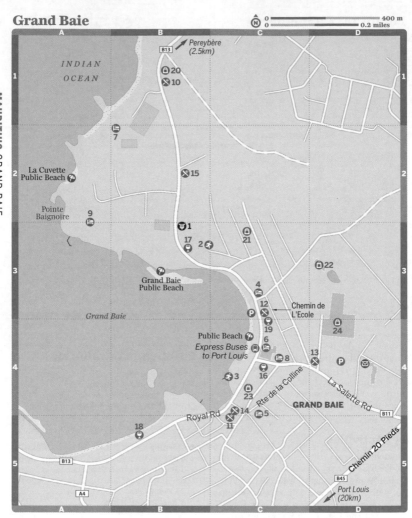

you wish to sample your fish we will gladly oblige'.

Grand Baie Gym & Hydro Spa   GYM, SPA
(Map p71; ☑263 4891; www.grandbaiegym.com; 3 X Club Rd; day membership Rs 690) The Grand Baie Gym & Hydro Spa has a fabulous pool and gym, and you can indulge in a huge range of spa treatments, steam yourself in the *hammam* (Turkish bath) or enjoy low-fat dishes at the cafe across the street.

Solar Sea Walk   ADVENTURE SPORTS
(Map p72; ☑263 7819; Royal Rd; per person Rs 1200; ☺8.30am-5pm) For nondivers, Captain

Nemo's Undersea Walk provides the unique experience of walking underwater wearing a diver's helmet and weight belt. Solar-powered pumps on the boat above feed oxygen to you during the 25-minute 'walk on the wet side'. Walks are available to everyone over the age of seven. There are trips every few hours from 9am to 3pm. In peak season it's advisable to book a day in advance.

Catamarans & Cruises

Catamaran day trips are the most popular activity in the north – most cruises depart from Grand Baie. In general, we advise

Grand Baie

booking with a company that is licensed to set foot on one of the northern islands. Prices range from €39 per person up to €65, and this should include a full lunch, drinks and snorkelling apparel. Check out www.mauritiuscatamaran.com for a rundown of catamaran possibilities and bookings.

Most operators also offer semisubmersible vessels for coral-viewing tours. Trips usually last just under two hours, with 30 minutes of snorkelling for those who wish to. Tickets are available from hotels and tour agents.

Croisières Australes   BOAT TOUR
(☑ 263 1669; www.croisieres-australes.mu; per person €40-65) Arguably the most professional outfit in town.

Yacht Charters   BOAT TOUR
(Map p71; ☑ 263 8395; www.isla-mauritia.com) The magnificent sailing ship, the *Isla Mauritia,* was built in 1852 and is claimed to be the world's oldest active schooner. Rates vary depending on the season, itinerary and number of people.

🛏 Sleeping

Grand Baie has two distinct classes of hotels: the grandiose resorts and the budget studios and apartments set back from the main drag; for the apartments there are some excellent deals around, especially if you arrive with friends in tow at a quiet time of the year. Despite Grand Baie's reputation as 'tourist central' there are fewer luxury resorts in the area than one might think, although a clutch of smart hotels occupies the east side of the bay. Those for whom Grand Baie is just a little too busy might want to consider Pereybère nearby.

★**Sous Le Badamiers**   GUESTHOUSE €
(Map p71; ☑ 263 4391; www.souslebadamier.com; Royal Rd, Pointe aux Canonniers; s €48-55, d €58-65; ❋@☎) Once known as Chez Vaco for the artist's enchanting paintings that adorn almost every wall, this wonderful li'l guesthouse now takes its name from the looming *badamier* trees that shade the charming cloister at the entrance. The delightful rooms are sponge painted in soothing neutral tones and furnishings are accented with patterns of woven rattan – there's a certain warm minimalism here that feels stylish yet homely. This place is a real find.

Résidence Peramal   APARTMENT €
(Map p71; ☑ 263 8109; www.residenceperamal.com; Royal Rd; studio €25, apt €30-40; ❋) This excellent-value self-catering accommodation is on a little promontory plum in the centre of Grand Baie.

Trendzone Apartments   APARTMENT €
(Map p72; ☑ 263 8277; www.trendzonemauritius.com; La Salette Rd; s/d apt €40/50; ❋☎) Modern apartment units above the Trendzone boutique in the heart of town between Super U and the sea.

Pépère Guest House   GUESTHOUSE, APARTMENT €
(Map p72; ☑ 696 3986; www.pepere-appartement.com; Royal Rd; s €20-30, d €30-40, 4-bed apt €50-60; ❋☎) Right in the heart of town, these

simple, no-frills rooms are well-priced and well-maintained by the friendly owners.

★ Esprit Libre
GUESTHOUSE €€

(Map p71; ☎ 269 1159; www.espritlibremaurice. com; rue Bourdet, Pointe aux Canonniers; r incl breakfast €60-100, ste €100-120; ❋ ≋ ≋) Easily one of the best value for money places on the island, this charming guesthouse is run by two friendly Québécois, Stéphane and André, who run their enclave of 'free spirits' with one mantra in mind: customer service. Rooms are simple and tastefully decorated and the on-site restaurant offers up an inventive menu that has lured in a faithful crowd of locals. To reach the guesthouse, turn left at the large elephant statue (you can't miss it) when coming from Grand Baie.

Ocean Villas
HOTEL €€

(Map p71; ☎ 263 6788; www.ocean-villas.com; Royal Rd, Pointe aux Canonniers; r incl breakfast from €55; ❋ @ ≋ ≋) Ocean Villas is recommended for its broad range of accommodation, from straightforward hotel rooms to self-catering units for up to eight people and sleek honeymoon suites with sunken baths. Facilities include an excellent pool plus a small strip of beach (with limited watersports on offer), a restaurant and the love nest – a private house on the beach.

Les Orchidées
HOTEL €€

(Map p72; ☎ 263 8780; www.lesorchideeshotel mauritius.com; Route de la Colline; d incl breakfast

---

GRAND BAIE VILLAS FOR RENT

As in most resort areas of Mauritius, Grand Baie has its share of agents offering seaside villas and apartments for rent. Some of the better options include the following.

CG Villas (☎262 5777; www.villas-maurice .com) Villas and apartments directly on the bay.

Grand Bay Travel & Tours (Map p72; ☎263 8771; www.gbtt.com; Royal Rd) Several multi-apartment properties from basic digs to luxury sleeps.

Idyllic Villas (www.idyllic-mauritius. com) Manages a gaggle of private seaside villas – good deals can be scouted in the charming Pointe aux Canonniers neighbourhood.

€44-54, half board from €68; ❋ ≋ ≋) Highly recommended and extremely popular (book ahead), this small hotel is set back from the coast in a quiet location just a short walk from the centre of town. Sweet, simple, brightly coloured rooms and a charming pool area make this a great option. There's wi-fi in the public areas.

Verandah Hotel
HOTEL €€

(Map p72; ☎ 209 8000; www.verandah-resorts. com; off Royal Rd; s/d incl breakfast from €111/158; ❋ @ ≋ ≋) The rather elegant public areas here give the Verandah a sense of exclusivity unusual for the price. The two pools, good facilities and a relatively recent refit of the rooms also help. The beach is fine, but no great shakes, although the location is handy for town and there's a full-service Seven Colours spa here to help with relaxation.

★ 20° Sud
LUXURY HOTEL €€€

(Map p71; ☎ 263 5000; www.20degressud.com; X Club Rd, Pointe aux Canonniers; d incl half board from €225; ❋ @ ≋ ≋) The boutiquiest boutique resort on the island, 20° Sud has a cache of chic, plantation-inspired rooms. Walls are lavished with generous coats of prim white paint; draped linen and elegant dark-wood mouldings perfectly accent the surrounds. Palatial oak doors initiate guests into the vine-draped public area, a lush palm grove with an inviting swimming pool and a cosy lodge-style library. 20° Sud also operates a popular catamaran day trip to Île Plate for snorkelling, sunbathing and an elegant barbecue feast in the stylishly half-renovated ruins of the old Governor's House (nonguests can join in as well, although you must book several days in advance as the trip is exceedingly popular).

Baystone Hotel & Spa
BOUTIQUE HOTEL €€€

(Map p71; ☎ 209 1900; www.baystone.mu; X Club Rd; r with seaview/direct beach access incl half board €350/390; P ❋ @ ≋ ≋) On a lovely quiet stretch of beach that looks across the bay at the town, this classy boutique hotel is one of our favourite upmarket places in town. Intimate where so many luxury hotels sprawl impersonally, this is luxury with a personal, discreet touch. The rooms are flooded with natural light and are supremely comfortable.

Royal Palm
LUXURY HOTEL €€€

(Map p72; ☎ 209 8300; www.royalpalm-hotel.com; off Royal Rd; r per person from €385 ; ❋ @ ≋ ≋) The world-famous flagship of the Beachcomber group is the pinnacle of luxury and a veritable playground for the rich and famous. Staff don safari-butler uniforms (stylish pith helmets!) and meticulously arranged flower bouquets are the centrepiece of every room.

✗ Eating

While the centre of town is packed with eateries, the very best tend to be slightly outside the heart of Grand Baie, particularly towards Pointe aux Canonniers and Pereybère. Street vendors and vegetable stands can be found all along Royal Rd. They tend to congregate near the public beaches.

★ Boulette Ti Kouloir   MAURITIAN €

(Map p72; Royal Rd; boulettes Rs 6.50; ⊙ 11.30am-4pm & 5.45-9pm Mon-Sat, 11.30am-4pm Sun) Follow the low-slung billboard for Paparazzi, pass the car park for the Sunset Boulevard shopping centre, then turn right – around 50m further along on the right, next to La Rougaille Créole, this is one of Grand Baie's best little snack joints. As the name suggests, this microscopic joint really is just a *ti couloir* (li'l hallway) where a couple of women cook up savoury *boulettes* (steamed balls, like mini Chinese dumplings) to unending lines of locals. Choose between chicken, pork, fish, calamari and lamb. Fabulous place.

★ Domaine   MAURITIAN €

(Map p66; ☑ 263 5286; Narainen St, Upper Vale, The Vale; mains Rs 75-150; ⊙ 4-11pm Mon, 11am-11pm Tue-Sun) 'Domaine' is the answer every local offers when travellers ask where to go to savour some Mauritian home cookin' while escaping the throngs of vacationers. So, naturally this inland haunt is starting to fill up with tourists. Go quick before someone else lets the cat out of the bag or tells the owner that his prices are remarkably low! The best dishes are those starred on the menu as local specialties – offerings such as *ourite safrané* (octopus cooked in ginger, garlic and turmeric) or chilli lamb.

It can be hard to find and you'll need a private vehicle or taxi. Take the M2 towards Port Louis, then turn left off the motorway at the first roundabout and follow the signs to The Vale. Once in the village, look for the 'Snack Mustapha' sign where the main road doglegs left – turn hard right and then take the second paved road on the left, around 250m down the hill.

Luigi's   ITALIAN €

(Map p72; ☑ 269 1125; luigis-restaurant.mu; Royal Rd; pizza Rs 170-300, pasta Rs 185-280; ⊙ 6-10.30pm Tue-Thu, 6-11pm Fri, noon-2.30pm & 6-11pm Sat) There are no frilly adornments at this place – just good wood-fired pizzas, excellent pasta dishes and a breezy dining area. No wonder it's full most of the time.

Coffee Garden   CAFE €€

(Map p71; ☑ 263 2270; www.coffeegarden.mu; Rte de Pointe aux Canonniers; specials Rs 375, snacks from Rs 120; ⊙ 8am-4pm; 🛜) A lovely little place out on Pointe aux Canonniers, Coffee Garden is classy and casual with free wi-fi, a menu of lunch specials that changes daily and paninis, omelettes and even smoked marlin sandwiches. Highly recommended.

Café Müller   CAFE €€

(Map p71; ☑ 263 5230; Royal Rd; brunch Rs 400; ⊙ 8am-5pm Mon-Sat, 10am-2pm Sun) This charming German-run option is a great place for cakes and coffee, while they also do an excellent Saturday brunch in their lovely grassy garden.

Coolen – Chez Ram   MAURITIAN, SEAFOOD €€

(Map p71; ☑ 263 8569; Royal Rd; mains Rs 175-425; ⊙ noon-2.30pm & 6.30-9.30pm Thu-Tue) The clear local favourite among Royal Rd's endless parade of restaurants, Coolen is usually filled to the brim with locals. Customers are welcomed with fish cakes and a splash of rum while they thumb through the menu of Creole and seafood staples. The octopus curry with papaya is as weird and wonderful as it sounds, and save room for the banana flambé.

La Rougaille Créole   MAURITIAN €€

(Map p72; ☑ 263 8449; off Royal Rd; mains Rs 225-500; ⊙ 12.30-3pm & 6.30-10.30pm) Tucked away behind the Sunset Boulevard shopping centre but well signposted, this friendly place does local dishes and does them extremely well without expecting to pay over the odds. The crab stir fry and red fish in Creole sauce both caught our eye.

Cocoloko   INTERNATIONAL €€

(Map p72; ☑ 263 1241; Royal Rd; mains Rs 220-575; ⊙ 11am-11pm; 🛜) Arranged around an inviting pebble-strewn courtyard across the street from the beach, Cocoloko brings a slice of cool and wannabe sophistication to downtown Grand Baie. Familiar international fare won't inspire devotion, but the atmosphere is very conducive to coffee sipping and cocktail clinking There's salads, steaks, tapas, sandwiches and pizza (or 'Pizzaloko' as it's known) and there's even sushi from 7pm to 11pm Monday to Saturday, plus free wi-fi for customers and live music four nights a week.

Happy Rajah   INDIAN €€
(Map p72; ☑263 2241; www.happyrajah.com; La Salette Rd; Rs 290-650; ☉11.30am-2pm & 6-10pm) Right next to the entrance of the Super U Hypermarket, on the 1st floor, this well-regarded Indian restaurant serves all the usual suspects. If you're going to splurge, do it with the lobster masala. Otherwise, curries, tikkas and tandooris dominate.

Hidden Reef   SEAFOOD €€
(Map p71; ☑263 0567; Royal Rd, Pointe aux Canonniers; mains Rs 360-790; ☉10am-3pm & 6pm-midnight Mon-Sat) Pronounced 'Eden Reef' by most locals, this popular spot features a dozen tables spread around a garden of lazy palms sprouting up from the crushed coral underfoot. The ambience is dimly lit and romantic – you'll need a torch to thumb through your menu (provided, of course), and when you can't decide what to order the waiter will let you try half-and-half appetiser samplers to go with your seafood main. The complimentary shot of homemade coffee rum is the perfect way to end the meal.

Le Capitaine   SEAFOOD €€
(Map p71; ☑263 6867; www.lecapitaine.mu; Royal Rd; mains Rs 470-695; ☉11.30am-3pm & 6.30-10.30pm) This is a popular place serving good standard seafood and fish dishes in a pleasant, convivial space that combines style with informality and great bay views. Fresh lobster is the pick of the menu, while other delicious mains include whole crab cooked in white wine, and lobster ravioli with fresh mushroom and cucumber quenelles. Reservations are essential in the evening.

Bistrot de Bacchus   INTERNATIONAL €€€
(Map p72; ☑263 3203; www.bistrot.mu; Royal Rd, Ventura Plaza; mains Rs 470-825; ☉noon-3pm & 7-11pm Mon-Sat) Styled like an old cellar with rounded brick arches and alcoves, this wine bar and restaurant features a small menu of brasserie-inspired dishes. But here's the real beauty: all by-the-glass wine is served at retail rather than restaurant prices.

La Langouste Grisée   MAURITIAN, SEAFOOD €€€
(Map p71; ☑263 1035; Royal Rd; mains Rs 1000; ☉lunch & dinner) This is a restaurant fre-quented by the great and the good of Grand Baie, offering very stylish dining overlooking an attractive garden and a swimming pool-like pond. As a winner of the Fourchette d'Or in 2005, 'The Tipsy Lobster' is generally recognised as one of the best restaurants on the island. Dishes from its imaginative Franco-Mauritian menu include dorado fillet with peanut sauce and banana slices. Lobster is obviously the speciality and vegetarians really shouldn't bother coming.

🍸 Drinking & Nightlife

If you're looking for a party in Mauritius, you'll find it in Grand Baie. Many of the area's restaurants, including Cocoloko (p75), have buzzing nightlife as well. Out near Luigi's (p75), located just north of the town centre, nightclubs come and go with the seasons, but it's always worth checking what's happening.

Banana Bar   BAR
(Map p72; ☑263 0326; Royal Rd; admission Rs 150; ☉10am-3am Mon-Sat, noon-3am Sun) In the Caltex parking lot, this is one of the best spots to grab a drink and catch up with friends. There's also live music at 8.30pm Wednesday to Saturday.

B52   COCKTAIL BAR
(Map p72; ☑263 0214; cnr La Salette & Royal Rds; ☉10am-midnight Mon-Sat) This large, popular spot serves up great cocktails all day long in its alfresco setting back from the main coastal road.

La Rhumerie   BAR, CAFE
(Map p72; ☑263 7664; Royal Rd; ☉7am-midnight) Friendly bar and cafe with a lethal selection of *rhum arrangés* (flavoured rums).

Beach House   BAR
(Map p72; ☑263 2599; Royal Rd; ☉11.30am-late Tue-Sun) Owned by a famous South African rugby player, this lively joint bustles with about as much energy as a sports match in overtime. The owner is sometimes seen roaming around shirtless signing autographs. A major draw is the unbeatable location, smack dab along the lapping waves of Grand Baie's emerald lagoon. Skip the uninspired pub grub and come early for sunset cocktails – you'll have front-row seats and get to carouse with the other patrons before everyone's soused. There's live music on Sunday afternoons.

Patch 'n Parrot
SPORTS BAR

(Map p71; ☑ 269 0374; Royal Rd; ⊘ noon-midnight Mon-Sat) Out on the road to Mon Choisy, this popular sports bar is one of the best places in town for those who love their sports – two massive screens broadcast pretty much nonstop. It's out of town so you'll need your own vehicle, but its proximity to Hidden Reef and Les Enfants Terribles mean that you could spend a whole night here without having to stray too far. Opening hours may vary with the seasons so it's worth ringing ahead to check they're open.

☆ Entertainment

★ Les Enfants Terribles
NIGHTCLUB

(Map p71; ☑ 263 8117; Royal Rd, Pointe aux Canonniers; ⊘ 7pm-3am Fri & Sat) The top pick for a night out on the town, the 'little terrors' has a roaring dance floor, a chilled-out lounge and a special VIP section that overflows with champagne. Walls bedecked with hundreds of crinkled photos of partiers confirm the sociable local vibe.

Kamikaze
NIGHTCLUB

(Map p72; ☑ 263 0521; Royal Rd; ⊘ 11.30pm-late) Next to Banana Bar and the Caltex Petrol Station, this relatively new offering styles itself as a 'lifestyle club'. Whatever that means, there's a packed dancefloor and music that's ideal for waving your hands in the air like you just don't care. A good in-town option.

🛍 Shopping

Sunset Boulevard
SHOPPING CENTRE

(Map p72; Royal Rd) Sunset Boulevard is home to chic boutiques, including knitwear specialists Floreal, Maille St and Shibani; Harris Wilson for menswear; and Hémisphère Sud for fabulous leather goods. Cheaper clothing stores are concentrated in and around the Super U Hypermarket.

Del Sol
ACCESSORIES

(Map p72; www.delsol.com; Royal Rd) Intriguing light-sensitive Del Sol products, from T-shirts to nail polish, are sold at a friendly boutique in Ventura Plaza.

Grand Baie Bazaar
HANDICRAFTS

(Map p72; ⊘ 9.30am-4.30pm Mon-Sat, 9am-noon Sun) A craft market hidden down an inland street away from Royal Rd. There's a broad range of touristy Mauritian and Malagasy crafts. Prices aren't fixed, but it's not expensive and there's minimal hassling from vendors.

Françoise Vrot
ART

(Map p71; ☑ 263 5118; Reservoir Rd; ⊘ 10am-1pm & 3-6.30pm) To purchase some original art, visit the studio of Françoise Vrot to see her expressive portraits of women fieldworkers.

Galerie Vaco
ART

(Map p72; ☑ 263 6862; off Royal Rd, Dodo Sq; ⊘ 10am-5pm Mon & Wed-Sat, to 1pm Tue) Head to Galerie Vaco to buy one of Vaco Baissac's instantly recognisable works.

Super U Hypermarket
SUPERMARKET, BOOKS

(Map p72; La Salette Rd; ⊘ 9am-8.30pm Mon-Fri, to 9.30pm Sat, to 1.30pm Sun) Located 200m inland from Grand Baie's main drag, the vast Super U Hypermarket is, by far, the best supermarket on the island and sells almost everything you can imagine, including the North's best range of books and magazines.

ℹ Information

Cyber cafes come and go in Grand Baie with very few lasting longer than a season or two. Wander along the main street in the town centre and you're bound to find one.

Mauritius Commercial Bank (MCB; Royal Rd; ⊘ bureau de change 8am-6pm Mon-Sat, 9am-noon Sun) Has an ATM.

State Bank (Royal Rd; ⊘ bureau de change 8am-6pm Mon-Sat, 9am-noon Sun) Has an ATM.

Thomas Cook (Royal Rd; ⊘ 8.30am-4.45pm Mon-Sat, to 12.30pm Sun) The best of the non-bank moneychangers.

ℹ Getting There & Away

There are no direct buses to Grand Baie from the airport, so it's necessary to change in Port Louis and transfer between two bus stations to do so. Almost all people will have a transfer provided by their hotel and for others arriving after a 12-hour flight, we definitely suggest taking a taxi – or better still, order one in advance via your hotel if your hotel is not one of the big players.

Express buses run directly between Immigration Sq (p57) in Port Louis and Grand Baie every half-hour. The terminus for express buses to/from Port Louis is on Royal Rd about 100m north of the intersection of Royal and La Salette Rds. Nonexpress buses en route to Cap Malheureux will also drop you in Grand Baie. Buses between Pamplemousses and Grand Baie leave roughly every hour. Nonexpress services via Trou aux Biches stop every few hundred metres along the coast road.

Expect to pay Rs 2000 to/from the airport. A return trip to Pamplemousses, including waiting time, should set you back Rs 600 or so.

⊙ Getting Around

BICYCLE

Many hotels and guesthouses can arrange bicycle hire and some even do so for free. Otherwise, rates vary, but expect to pay between Rs 150 and Rs 250 per day, less if you hire for several days. Most of the local tour operators have bikes for rent; just walk down Royal Rd and see what's on offer.

CAR

There are numerous car-hire companies in Grand Baie, so you should be able to bargain, especially if you're renting for several days. Prices generally start at around Rs 1050 per day for a small hatchback. Find out whether the management of your hotel or guesthouse has a special discount agreement with a local company. Motorbikes of 50cc and 100cc are widely available in Grand Baie; rental charges hover at around Rs 500 per day, less if you rent for several days.

ABC Car Rental (☑ 216 8889; www.abc-car rental.com; Super U Hypermarket, La Salette Rd) One of the more reliable operators with offices around the country.

Pereybère

As development continues to boom along the north coast, it's becoming rather difficult to tell where Grand Baie ends and Pereybère (peu-ray-bear) begins. This area is very much the second development on the north coast after Grand Baie and has found the sweet spot between being a bustling tourist hub and a quiet holiday hideaway.

⊙ Sights & Activities

Galerie du Moulin Cassé   ART GALLERY
(Map p79; ☑ 727 0672; Old Mill Rd; ⊙ 10am-6pm Fri) Housed in a charmingly restored sugar mill, the Galerie du Moulin Cassé features the vibrant floral scenes of painter Malcolm de Chazal (1902–82) and a collection of photographs by Diane Henry. The most impressive display, however, is the collection of over 20,000 terracotta pots lining the vaulted arcs of the ceiling.

Ocean Spirit Diving   DIVING
(Map p79; ☑ 263 4428; www.osdiving.org; Royal Rd; 1/3 dives Rs 1200/3360; ⊙ 8am-4.30pm) French-run with an office on the main road through town, this recommended outfit is the pick of the places in Pereybère itself.

Orca Dive Club   DIVING
(Map p66; ☑ 716 3167; www.orca-diveclub-merville. com) This professional German-run dive centre is based at the Merville Hotel between Pereybère and Grand Baie.

Surya Ayurvedic Spa   DAY SPA
(Map p79; ☑ 263 1637; www.spasurya.com; Royal Rd; ⊙ 9am-8pm) For some indulgent relaxation, head to the very smart Surya Ayurvedic Spa and treat yourself to an Indian massage or a steam in the *hammam*.

Chi   DAY SPA
(Map p66; The Spa; ☑ 263 9621; Old Mill Rd; ⊙ 9am-7pm) The 90-minute 'Chi Balance' (a footbath with five essential element oils) costs Rs 1325 – quite reasonable when compared to the in-house spas at the surrounding hotels.

🛏 Sleeping

While there are a few larger hotels on the beach side of the main road, the majority of accommodation here is made up of charming guesthouses and little hotels in the back streets, a short walk from the town centre and public beach.

Les Cases Fleuries   GUESTHOUSE €
(Map p79; ☑ 263 8868; casefle@intnet.mu; Beach Lane; studio/apt €40/45; ❄) Here you'll find a variety of studios and apartments for up to six people set in a flower-filled garden. Go for one of the prim white studios – the apartments are dour.

★ **Bleu de Toi**   GUESTHOUSE €€
(Map p79; ☑ 269 1761; www.bleudetoi.mu; Royal Rd; r €78-112; ❄@🛜🐟) Owned by friendly Belgians, this lovely B&B is the area's only worthy contender in the guesthouse category. Rooms are done up with simple yet tasteful furnishings and adorable arched doorways abound. Don't miss the charming *table d'hôte* (€12 to €18) in the evenings. Blue de Toi is quite pricey compared to the *chambres d'hôtes* in Pointe d'Esny, but it's highly recommended if you want to stay in the north. Things also get cheaper the longer you stay.

Pereybère Hotel & Apartments   HOTEL €€
(Map p79; ☑ 263 8320; www.pereyberehotel.com; Royal Rd; d/apt/ste €56/70/75; ❄@🛜🐟) Right in the thick of things and just across the road from the public beach, this old-timer may look rather dated from the front but the rooms are surprisingly neat. The promised sea views are more like peer-hopefully-through-the-trees-in-search-of-the-sea-views. And the Jacuzzis promised in some rooms are actually just showers with fancy nozzles and buttons.

Pereybère

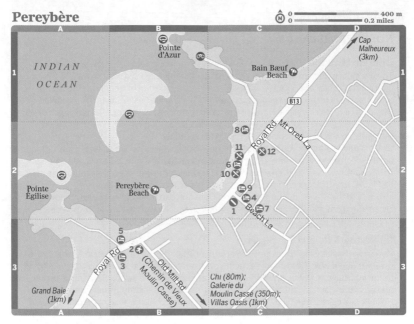

Ocean Beauty   HOTEL €€
(Map p79; 📞263 6039; www.ocean-beauty.com; Pointe d'Azur; r incl breakfast €55-220; ✴@🛜🏊) Ocean Beauty is a boutique hotel aimed squarely at honeymooners. This is boutique in the sense of an intimate feel, but it's also basic, all of which means the rooms are stylish and atmospheric, but there's very little else to the hotel. Despite this, it's a great spot for romance; breakfast is served on your balcony and there's direct access to the lovely town beach. Beware of the pool that plays Enya at you while you swim.

Le Beach Club   HOTEL €€
(Map p79; 📞263 5104; www.le-beachclub.com; Royal Rd; r with sea/garden view from €99/83, 4-bed apt from €134; ✴🛜) This complex of studios and two-bedroom apartments is one of the few places on the seafront and has a great little beach, perfect for swimming. Rooms have festive tropical colours and the location's brilliant. Complaints? We're nit-picking but the common areas are so tiny they feel like storage spaces for stacked furniture. Plan your check-in time before arriving – the reception has limited hours.

Flowers of Paradise Hotel   HOTEL €€
(Map p79; 📞934 5320; hotel-paradise-mauritius. mu; Beach Lane; s/d from €90/130; ✴🛜🏊) Set

Pereybère

🎯 Activities, Courses & Tours
1 Ocean Spirit Diving C2
2 Surya Ayurvedic Spa B3

🛏 Sleeping
3 Bleu de Toi B3
4 Flowers of Paradise Hotel C2
5 Hibiscus Hotel B3
6 Le Beach Club C2
7 Les Cases Fleuries C2
8 Ocean Beauty C2
9 Pereybère Hotel & Apartments C2

🍴 Eating
10 Caféteria Pereybère C2
11 Sea Lovers Restaurant C2
12 Wang Thai C2

back from the main road but a short walk from the beach, this gorgeous new hotel has a vaguely boutique hotel feel with beautifully appointed rooms and good service. Highly recommended.

Hibiscus Hotel   HOTEL €€
(Map p79; 📞263 8554; www.hibiscushotel.com; Royal Rd; s incl half-board €90-120, d €130-180; ✴🛜🏊) Hibiscus boasts a stone path that wends past thick jungle-like gardens, a super

MAURITIUS PEREYBÈRE

NORTHERN ISLANDS

Coin de Mire, Île Plate & Îlot Gabriel

The distinctive Coin de Mire (Gunner's Quoin), 4km off the coast, was so named because it resembles the quoin (wedge) used to steady the aim of a cannon. The island is now a nature reserve and home to a number of rare species, such as the red-tailed tropicbird and Bojer's skink. None of the major catamarans stop here as landing is often difficult. Despite the island's striking shape there's not much to see here anyway – it's the kind of place that looks far better from far away.

Most operators take you to the lagoon between Île Plate and Îlot Gabriel, 7km further north, which offers good snorkelling. Barbecue lunches are served on a sandy patch of Îlot Gabriel, while 20° Sud's (p74) luxury cruiser currently has the sole right to land on Île Plate – day-trippers eat in the charming ruins of the Governor's House.

Boats to the islands depart from Grand Baie. You can book online at www.mauritius catamaran.com, through any local tour agent or directly with the cruise companies. Prices are from Rs 1200 to 1500 per pers on, including lunch.

Île Ronde & Île aux Serpents

Île Ronde (Round Island) and Île aux Serpents (Snake Island) are two significant nature reserves about 20km and 24km respectively from Mauritius. It is not possible to land on them. Ironically, Île Ronde is not round and has snakes, while Île aux Serpents is round and has no snakes; the theory is that an early cartographer simply made a mistake.

Île Ronde covers roughly 170 hectares and scientists believe it has more endangered species per square kilometre than anywhere else in the world. Many of the plants, such as the hurricane palm (of which one lonely tree remains) and the bottle palm, are unique to the island. The endemic fauna includes the keel-scaled boa and the burrowing boa (possibly extinct), three types of skink and three types of gecko. Among the seabirds that breed on the island are the wedge-tailed shearwater, the red-tailed tropicbird and the gadfly (or Round Island) petrel. Naturalist Gerald Durrell gives a very graphic description of the island in his book *Golden Bats and Pink Pigeons*.

The smaller Île aux Serpents (42 hectares) is a renowned bird sanctuary. The birds residing on the island include the sooty tern, the lesser noddy, the common noddy and the masked (blue-footed) booby. Nactus geckos and Bojer's skinks are also found here.

pool and a private beach of sorts (although there's quite a bit of rock to negotiate). Accommodation is in clean, comfortable rooms in three-storey blocks.

Villas Oasis VILLAS €€€
(Map p66; ☑ 422 8435; www.oasis-villas-mauritius. com; Old Mill Rd; villas from €215; ❊ ❂ ❀) They take the use of the word 'oasis' seriously here and these luxurious villas are a steal if you're travelling with family or friends. Trendy Asian-inspired decor permeates the lavish open-air floorplans. Security is tight, privacy is held sacred and there's a real sense of being a VIP. The only downside is that you'll need a private vehicle to get to the beach.

✖ Eating & Drinking

Like in Grand Baie, most of Pereybère's restaurants also double as good places for a drink, though the neighbourhood is gener-

ally much quieter. There are still some top spots amid the frenzy of ever-growing eating options.

Caféteria Pereybère INTERNATIONAL, CAFE €
(Map p79; ☑ 263 8539; Royal Rd; mains Rs 135-275; ❂ 10.30am-10pm) This friendly all-day, no-frills cafe-restaurant behind the public beach offers grilled fish, curries, and steak and chips from an extensive menu. Portions are on the small side and it's cash only.

Wang Thai THAI €€
(Map p79; ☑ 263 4050; www.thai.mu; Royal Rd; mains Rs 250-330, set menus Rs 250-500; ❂ noon-2.30pm Mon-Wed, noon-2.30pm & 6-10pm Thu-Sun) Long the best restaurant in town and a pioneer of authentic Thai food in Mauritius, Wang Thai is a sophisticated, airy place with Buddha statues and raw silks setting the scene for surprisingly affordable cuisine. Treat your taste buds to such classics as

tom yum thalay (lemongrass-laced seafood soup), green curry, fish in tamarind sauce or *phad thai* (mixed fried noodles).

Sea Lovers Restaurant SEAFOOD €€
(Map p79; ☑ 263 6299; Royal Rd; mains Rs 395-825; ⏲ noon-2.30pm & 6-9pm) This is, without a doubt, the smartest restaurant setting in the area. There's a gorgeous terrace built right into the sand and the furniture is unquestionably stylish. The service, however, can be a bit lacking and the food doesn't live up to the locale, though the fish fillet wrapped in a banana leaf is reasonable. It's worth stopping by to take in the atmosphere – just stick to the drinks list.

❶ Getting There & Around

Buses between Port Louis and Cap Malheureux stop in Pereybère as well as Grand Baie. Services run roughly every 30 minutes.

You can rent cars, motorbikes and bicycles through the local tour agents. Cars start at Rs 1000 per day and motorbikes at Rs 500 for a 50cc or 100cc bike. Pedal bikes cost upwards of Rs 150 per day. Most of Grand Baie's car-hire companies will also drop off and pick up cars in Pereybère.

Cap Malheureux

The northern edge of Mauritius has stunning views out to the islands off the coast beyond, most obviously of the dramatic headland of Coin de Mire. Although it feels like rather a backwater today, 'Cape Misfortune' (thus named for the number of ships that foundered on the rocks here) is a place of great historical importance for Mauritius: it was here that the British invasion force finally defeated the French in 1810 and took over the island.

A little past the cape lies the minuscule fishing village also known as Cap Malheureux, with its much-photographed church, the red-roofed **Notre Dame Auxiliatrice**. It's worth a quick peek inside for its intricate woodwork and a holy-water basin fashioned out of a giant clamshell. A sign strictly prohibits newlyweds 'faking' a church wedding for the photographers here. You can attend Mass here at 6pm on Saturday and 9am on Sunday.

Heading around the coast the landscape becomes wilder and more rugged. A clutch of hotels occupies the few decent beaches in between the rocky coves and muddy tidal creeks. They offer a perfect hideaway for those who want to get away from it all.

🛏 Sleeping & Eating

Outside the hotel restaurants there are just a few eating options in the area, the best being Amigo.

Kuxville APARTMENTS €€
(Map p66; ☑ 262 8836; www.kuxville.com; studio/apt/villa from €70/105/190; ✳ 🛜) There's a huge choice of accommodation on offer at this perennially popular apartment complex about 1.5km west of Cap Malheureux village. Accommodation is in impeccably clean studios or apartments sleeping up to four people; 'gardenside' units are in a newer compound across the road. There's a fine little beach and a small kiteboarding and dive school headed up by the affable owner Nico Kux – check out www.sindbad.mu.

Le Paradise Cove RESORT €€€
(Map p66; ☑ 204 4000; www.paradisecovehotel.com; Anse la Raie; s/d/ste incl half-board from €375/525/825; ✳ @ 🛜 ✳) Paradise Cove is a five-star boutique resort aimed at honeymooners. Terribly understated but as utterly luxurious as its name suggests, it's built on an attractive small cove – the beach is at the end of an inlet from the sea, which gives it remarkable privacy. Other great touches include a golf course, tennis courts, free watersports, a dive centre, brightly painted and delightful rooms and 'love nests' on the promontory overlooking the northern islands. With three restaurants, a Cinq Mondes spa and award-winning gardens, this stylish place is a great destination for couples.

★ Amigo SEAFOOD €€
(Map p66; ☑ 262 8418; amigo.restaurant.mu; Royal Rd; mains Rs 220-825; ⏲ 11.30am-3.30pm & 6.30-11.30pm Mon-Sat) Everyone adores this friendly joint tucked behind the township near the cane farms. The writing's on the wall (literally) – contented customers have left myriad messages of love and affection on every flat surface in the restaurant. The tables, however, are graffiti-free – they're reserved for the excellent seafood specialities. Side note: the letters in the restaurant's name are the first initials of the owner (sadly now deceased) and his four sons. Ironically, the owner didn't speak a lick of Spanish. Delivery available.

ⓘ Getting There & Away

Buses run roughly every half-hour between Port Louis' Immigration Sq bus station and Cap Malheureux, via Grand Baie. A taxi to Port Louis will cost Rs 900, to Grand Baie Rs 400 and to the airport Rs 2000.

Grand Gaube

Grand Gaube, about 6km east of Cap Malheureux, is where the development of northern Mauritius currently ends, although expect that to change. Until it does, it remains a tiny fishing village with a good beach. Beyond the small rocky bays of Grande Gaube there are almost no beaches until a long way down the east coast, making any trip beyond here an illuminating glimpse into traditional Mauritian life without the tourists. In 1744 the *St Géran* foundered off Grand Gaube in a storm, inspiring the famous love story *Paul et Virginie* by Bernardin de St-Pierre.

It's possible to explore Île Ambre offshore on a sea kayaking trip with **Yemaya** (www.yemayaadventures.com; half-/full-day from Rs 1500/2000).

🛏 Sleeping & Eating

Verandah Paul & Virginie　　HOTEL €€€
(Map p66; ✆ 266 9700; www.paul-et-virginie-hotel.com; s/d incl breakfast from €115/164; ✴ @ 🛜 🌊) The longest-established hotel in Grande Gaube is a pleasant surprise. It's small enough not to be overwhelmed yet offers all the services and comforts required for luxury: two pools, a couple of restaurants, a

Seven Colours 'wellness' spa, plenty of entertainment and activities, and a kids' club. The style is colonial, although the atmosphere is very relaxed. The rooms are stylishly fitted out and spacious, all with sea views, and there's a small but attractive beach.

Lux* Grand Gaube　　LUXURY HOTEL €€€
(Map p66; ✆ 698 9800; www.luxresorts.com; r €183-2200; ✴ @ 🛜 🌊) This very large, stylish establishment enjoys an idyllic location miles from the mass tourism found further down the coast. Guests have the run of the pretty bay and the hotel's well-appointed surroundings. The hotel is feng shui themed.

ⓘ Getting There & Away

Buses run roughly every 15 minutes between Port Louis' Immigration Sq bus station and Grand Gaube. A taxi to Port Louis will cost Rs 900, to Grand Baie Rs 500 and to the airport Rs 2100.

Pamplemousses

One of the island's main attractions, the botanical gardens at Pamplemousses (roughly halfway between Grand Baie and Port Louis) are soothing, tranquil and brimful of endemic and foreign plant species. Also of interest is the decommissioned Beau Plan sugar factory nearby, which has been converted into a fascinating museum.

Pamplemousses itself was named for the grapefruit-like citrus trees that the Dutch introduced to Mauritius from Java. The town

---

PAUL & VIRGINIE

Mauritius' most popular folk tale tells the story of two lovers, Paul and Virginie, who encounter tragedy when the ship that is carrying Virginie founders on the reef. Although Paul swims out to the wreck to save her, Virginie modestly refuses to remove her clothes to swim ashore, and drowns; Paul dies of a broken heart shortly after.

The story was written by Bernardin de St-Pierre in the 18th century, but was inspired by a real-life tragedy that took place some years earlier. In 1744, the ship *St Géran* was wrecked during a storm off Île Ambre, to the southeast of Grand Gaube, with almost 200 lives lost. Among them were two female passengers who refused to undress to swim ashore and were dragged down by the weight of their clothes. The true story is more a tragedy of social mores than one of romance!

The *St Géran* was carrying a hoard of Spanish money and machinery from France for the island's first sugar refinery. A French dive expedition explored the wreck in 1966 and many of their finds are on display in Mahébourg's National History Museum (p107) and the Blue Penny Museum (p53) in Port Louis.

You'll run into Paul and Virginie everywhere in Mauritius. The statue by Prosper d'Épinay is perhaps the most famous memorial. The original is in the Blue Penny Museum and there's a copy near the town hall in Curepipe.

WORTH A TRIP

CHATEAU LABOURDONNAIS

If you've rented a taxi for the day to explore the botanical gardens and sugar museum at Pamplemousses, there's one more stop in the area that we highly recommend.

One of the loveliest examples of colonial architecture on the island, recently restored **Chateau Labourdonnais** (266 9533; www.unchateaudanslanature.com; Mapou; adult/child Rs 175/80, meals Rs 1100; 9am-5pm) was completed in 1859. Built in teak and sporting an Italian neoclassical style, the chateau is perfectly proportioned and filled with sober Victorian furnishings interspersed with some exceptionally lovely design flourishes. Compulsory guided tours last for 45 minutes. After the tour, wander through the lush gardens, taste the rum from the on-site distillery and stay for a meal at the restaurant where the menu changes daily.

To get here, head north along the M2 motorway for around 3km then take the exit for Mapou, then follow the signs.

is typically Mauritian and feels a million miles from Grand Baie or Trou aux Biches.

Sights

Sir Seewoosagur Ramgoolam Botanical Gardens
GARDENS
(Map p66; Jardins de Pamplemousses, Royal Botanical Gardens; admission Rs200; guide per person from Rs 40 ; 8.30am-5.30pm) Don't be put off if you've never been particularly interested in botany – after London's Kew Gardens the SSR Botanical Gardens is one of the world's best botanical gardens. It's also one of the most popular tourist attractions in Mauritius and is easily reached from almost anywhere on the island.

Labelling of the plants is a work in progress and they don't have maps, so we strongly recommend that you hire one of the knowledgeable guides who wait just inside the gardens' entrance; golf buggy tours are also available upon request for those with limited mobility. If you don't take a guide and go it alone you'll miss many of the most interesting species.

The gardens, named after Sir Seewoosagur Ramgoolam, the first prime minister of independent Mauritius, were started by Mahé de Labourdonnais in 1735 as a vegetable plot for his **Mon Plaisir Château** (which now contains a small exhibition of photographs). The landscape came into its own in 1768 under the auspices of the French horticulturalist Pierre Poivre. Like Kew Gardens, the gardens played a significant role in the horticultural espionage of the day. Poivre imported seeds from around the world in a bid to end France's dependence on Asian spices. The gardens were neglected between 1810 and 1849 until British

horticulturalist James Duncan transformed them into an arboretum for palms and other tropical trees.

Palms still constitute the most important part of the horticultural display, and they come in an astonishing variety of shapes and forms. Some of the more prominent are the stubby bottle palms, the tall royal palms and the talipot palms, which flower once after about 40 years and then die. Other varieties include the raffia, sugar, toddy, fever, fan and even sealing-wax palms. There are many other curious tree species on display, including the marmalade box tree, the fish poison tree and the sausage tree.

The centrepiece of the gardens is a pond filled with giant Victoria amazonica water lilies, native to South America. Young leaves emerge as wrinkled balls and unfold into the classic tea-tray shape up to 2m across in a matter of hours. The flowers in the centre of the huge leaves open white one day and close red the next. The lilies are at their biggest and best in the warm summer months, notably January.

Another highlight is the abundant birdlife – watch for the crimson hues of the Madagascar fody – while there are captive populations of deer and around a dozen giant aldabra tortoises near the park's northern exit, close to the chateau. Also nearby is the funerary platform where Sir Seewoosagur Ramgoolam was cremated (his ashes were scattered on the Ganges in India) while various international dignitaries have planted trees in the surrounding gardens, including Nelson Mandela, Indira Gandhi and a host of British royals.

L'Aventure du Sucre   MUSEUM
(Map p66; ☑ 243 0660; www.aventuredusucre.com; adult/child Rs 350/175; ☺9am-5pm) On the other side of the motorway's roundabout from the botanical gardens, the former Beau Plan sugar factory now houses one of the best museums in Mauritius. It not only tells the story of sugar in great detail, but also covers the history of Mauritius, slavery, the rum trade and much, much more. Allow a couple of hours to do it justice.

The original factory was founded in 1797 and only ceased working in 1999. Most of the machinery is still in place and former workers are on hand to answer questions about the factory and the complicated process of turning sugar cane into crystals. There are also videos and interactive displays as well as quizzes for children. At the end of the visit you can taste some of the 15 different varieties of unrefined sugar, two of which were invented in Mauritius.

✖ Eating

★Chez Tante Athalie   MAURITIAN €€
(Map p66; ☑ 243 9266; Centre de Flacq Rd, Mont Gout; menu Rs 450; ☺noon-2.30pm Mon-Sat) While you're in the neighbourhood of the Sir Seewoosagur Ramgoolam Botanical Gardens, it's worth grabbing a delicious Creole lunch at Chez Tante Athalie, the best-known *table d'hôte* in the area. The open-sided restaurant offers simple but fresh tastes overlooking a garden filled with vintage cars, and there's an oasis-like feel to the place. From the entrance to the botanical gardens follow the signs around 500m to the T-junction, turn left and then watch for a signposted driveway 2km further on on your left.

Le Fangourin   MAURITIAN €€
(Map p66; ☑ 243 0660; mains Rs 310-695; ☺11.30am-4pm) If all the sugar in L'Aventure du Sucre museum has set your taste buds working, you could sup a glass of sugar cane juice at Le Fangourin, a stylish cafe-restaurant in the museum grounds. It specialises in sophisticated Creole cuisine and all sorts of sugary delights.

🛍 Shopping

Le Village Boutik   FOOD & DRINK
(Map p66; ☺9am-5pm) Right next to the sugar museum, this impressive shop has sugar in all manner of gift packs, as well as rum made from local sugar cane. They encourage you to try before you buy.

ℹ Getting There & Away

Pamplemousses can be reached by bus from Grand Baie, Trou aux Biches, Grand Gaube and Port Louis. Services from Grand Baie and Trou aux Biches run approximately every hour and stop near the sugar museum on the way to the botanical gardens.

Buses from Port Louis' Immigration Sq bus station and Grand Gaube operate every 10 to 15 minutes. These buses only stop at the botanical gardens, from where it takes about 15 minutes to walk to the museum.

THE WEST

A world away from the shores of the north, Mauritius' western wonderland is the nation's most diverse coast. The bustling tourist hub of Flic en Flac may not be to everyone's taste, but the treasures that lie just beyond will satisfy even the pickiest holidaymaker. A veritable swatch book of lush greens and light browns, the area of Black River (Rivière Noire) has scalloping sandy bays that dimple the arable farmland. Then, further on, the tic-tac-toes of Tamarin's shimmering salt flats perfectly reflect the beaming sun and soaring hills of fauna-filled Black River Gorges National Park. Next is bucolic Chamarel nestled in the highlands, followed by the last iteration of sky-reaching stone, Le Morne Brabant; an awesomely photogenic crag that caps the coastline's southern tip. It all adds up to what could just be our favourite corner of the island.

ℹ Getting Around

The main bus routes in west Mauritius are those from Port Louis down to the southern end of Black River. There is also a regular service between Quatre Bornes on the Central Plateau, and Chamarel.

Your hotel or guesthouse should be able to arrange bike and car hire.

Note that there are only two petrol stations in the west – one at Flic en Flac and one in Black River near La Preneuse.

Albion
POP 5201

A small dent of coral-strewn tranquillity between Port Louis and Flic en Flac, the quiet waters of Albion are home to a lovely house reef offshore.

🏃 Activities

Vertical World ADVENTURE SPORTS
(Map p86; 📞 251 1107, 697 5430; www.verticalworld ltd.com) After a few too many days of beach-side lethargy, get the blood rushing again with an invigorating half-day rock-climbing session on the Belle Vue cliffs, about a 10-minute walk from the lighthouse. They also organise canyoning and hiking.

🛏 Sleeping

Club Med La Plantation d'Albion LUXURY HOTEL €€€
(Map p86; 📞 206 0700; www.clubmed.com; d per week incl full board €3500; ❄ @ 🛜 🏊) Forget what you know about the Club Med chain, this is one of the finest resorts on the island, with acres of groomed gardens and a savvy design scheme that fuses African and Zen motifs. The beach isn't tops here, but the luxurious swimming pools more than make up for it. Quirky side note: during particularly tumultuous rainstorms guests often find fragments of Ming dynasty china from a merchant vessel that ran aground in the reef many moons ago.

Flic en Flac

POP 2253

As wonderful and whimsical as the name sounds, Flic en Flac isn't quite the picture of paradise you saw on your travel agent's website. The area's moniker is thought to be a corruption of the old Dutch name Fried Landt Flaak (meaning 'Free and Flat Land'); the endless acreage of sandy shoreline was undoubtedly striking when explorers first arrived in the 18th century. Today, the public beach is peppered with weeping *filao* trees, and the area is exploding with apartment complexes, souvenir shops, moneychangers and pinchpenny holiday rentals. Although development in Flic en Flac has gone the way of Grand Baie, it's still about a dozen clubs and restaurants short of attracting a party crowd in earnest.

All is not lost, however; the beach is still one of the best in Mauritius and if you stay at any of the high-end resorts in the Wolmar area outside the town, you'll uncover some stellar stretches of sand, glorious diving and a handful of palate-pleasing restaurants.

ℹ DIVING IN THE WEST

Western Mauritius is the pick of the places to dive in Mauritius, with a couple of excellent dive centres in Flic en Flac and good year-round diving. The following, all accessible from Flic en Flac, are our favourites. To read more about these and other sites in the area, turn to p28.

➡ Rempart Serpent

➡ La Cathédrale

➡ Couline Bambou

➡ Tug II

◉ Sights

Casela Nature & Leisure Park ZOO
(Map p86; 📞 727 6076, 452 2828; www.casela yemen.mu; adult/child Rs 340/210; ⊙ 9am-5pm May-Sep, 9am-6pm Oct-Apr) This 14-hectare nature park is on the main road 1km south of the turn to Flic en Flac. When you arrive at the entrance gate you are greeted with a bewildering range of options – in addition to being a zoo, the beautifully landscaped reserve offers a variety of heart-pumping 'rando fun' like ziplines, suspension bridges, hiking, swimming spots hidden in canyons and quad-bike 'safaris' around the neighbouring 45-sq-km Yemen Reserve which is home to deer, wild pigs, fruit bats and monkeys. Children are well catered for with a petting zoo, a playground, giant tortoises, fishing and minigolf. Check out the website for a full list of prices or spend some time at the information desk before the main entrance to get a handle on how to spend your day.

If you simply pay the admission fee, you'll be free to wander the grounds, where you'll see tortoises, a huge range of exotic birds and a few primate species in cages. And make sure you pass by the Mirador restaurant (p91) which has fabulous sweeping views of the coastal plain. If you pay an extra Rs 100, you'll be taken in a safari vehicle where you get out and look at lions, tigers and cheetahs from viewpoints overlooking large, grassy enclosures. If you pay an extra Rs 250, you board another safari vehicle to drive through a much larger area roamed by lions, zebra etc.

The park is famous for offering 15-minute 'interactions' (Rs 500) with the big cats, which means you're actually in the enclosure with them armed with nothing more than a

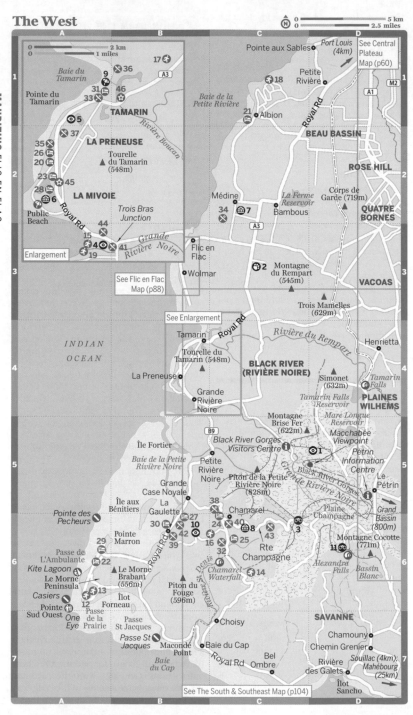

The West

MAURITIUS FLIC EN FLAC

large stick, and the hour-long 'walking with lions' experience (Rs 3000). We don't recommend either of these two options. These are wild animals, despite having been bred in captivity. Incidents in which visitors have been mauled by big cats in similar places in Africa aren't common but they do occur and participants are asked to sign an indemnity form before they draw near to the animals.

Médine Sugar Factory MUSEUM
(Map p86; ☑401 6000, 452 0400; www.medine. com/sugar) Rather unattractively spewing out smoke into the countryside around Flic en Flac is the Médine Sugar Factory, one of the country's biggest. During the cutting season (July to early November) it's possible to take a guided one-hour tour of the factory. You can also visit the distillery, where the 'waste' molasses is turned into rum. The visit ends with a tasting session. Call ahead for details. The factory is 6km northeast of Flic

en Flac. If you get stuck behind a sugar-cane truck overburdened by harvested crops, you can bet it's heading here.

🏃 Activities

In addition to the activities at Casela Nature & Leisure Park, the main activities in Flic en Flac are watersports.

Some of Mauritius' best dive sites can be found just beyond the emerald lagoon near Flic en Flac where the shallow waters suddenly give way to the deep. The most popular site in the area is La Cathédrale, with its signature stone arches and tucked-away cavern.

In addition to the places listed here, most of the upmarket hotels in Wolmar have their own diving operators, all of which are open to participants from outside the hotel. Check out www.msda.mu for a list of licensed and insured dive operators.

Flic en Flac

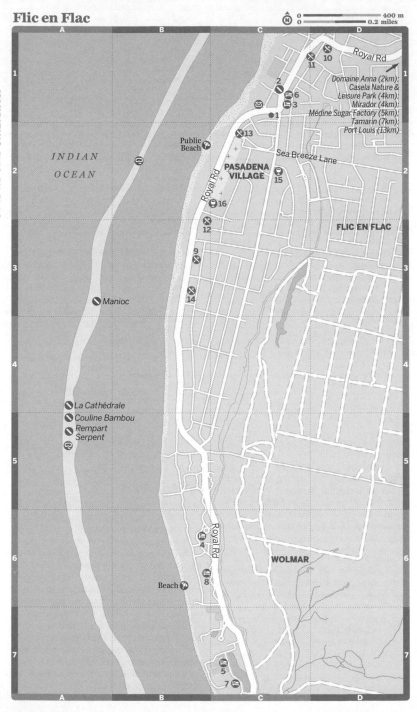

N
0 —————————— 400 m
0 —————————— 0.2 miles

INDIAN
OCEAN

Royal Rd

Domaine Anna (2km);
Casela Nature &
Leisure Park (4km);
Mirador (4km);
Médine Sugar Factory (5km);
Tamarin (7km);
Port Louis (13km)

Public
Beach

PASADENA
VILLAGE

Sea Breeze Lane

FLIC EN FLAC

Manioc

La Cathédrale
Couline Bambou
Rempart
Serpent

Royal Rd

WOLMAR

Beach

Royal Rd

Flic en Flac

☉ Activities, Courses & Tours
1 Blue Coral Tour C1
2 Sea Urchin Diving Centre C1
  Sun Divers .... (see 4)

⊜ Sleeping
  Aanari .... (see 1)
3 Easy World Hotel C1
4 La Pirogue B6
5 Maradiva C7
6 Résidence Art C1
7 Sands Resort C7
8 Sugar Beach Resort B6

⊗ Eating
9 Ah-Youn B3
10 Banane Créole D1
11 Canne à Sucre D1
12 Chez Pepe B3
13 Ocean Restaurant C2
14 Twin's Garden B3

⊜ Drinking & Nightlife
15 KenziBar C2
16 Shotz C2

Sun Divers   DIVING
(Map p88; ☑453 8441; www.sundiversmauritius.
com; 1/3 dives Rs 1675/4360; ◷8am-4pm Mon-Sat,
8pm-noon Sun) One of the top dive operators
in the area is Sun Divers, based at La Pirogue
hotel. It is one of the oldest outfits on the island. Three daily dives are scheduled at 9am,
noon and 2.30pm with a minimum of three
participants. There are discounts for those
who have their own equipment.

Sea Urchin Diving Centre   DIVING
(Map p88; ☑453 8825; www.sea-urchin-diving.
com; Royal Rd; dive for beginners/experienced Rs
2000/1200; ◷8am-6pm Mon-Sat, dives 9am,
11.30am & 1.30am Sat) This German-run centre
is professionally run and, conveniently, you'll
find them along the main road.

Blue Coral Tour   BOAT TOUR
(Map p88; ☑257 7202; www.bluecoraltour.com; Pa-
sadena Village) Boat trips to Île aux Cerfs and
Îlot Gabriel and fishing excursions.

🛏 Sleeping

Central Flic en Flac is decidedly *not* upmarket, with condos and apartment complexes
flanking every street. South of Flic en Flac, in
the Wolmar area, you'll find several charming luxury options directly on the sand.

As always, if you're considering one of the
pricier options, it is best to book through a
travel agent who should get significant discounts. Rack rates are quoted here.

Résidence Art   GUESTHOUSE €
(Map p88; Little Acorn; ☑453 5277; Royal Rd; s/d/
apt Rs 700/1100/1300, s/d with shared bathroom Rs
650/800; ⊛) Peeping out from behind a rusty
wrought-iron gate and overgrown foliage, this
ramshackle guesthouse is the first place you
should look if you're serious about pinch-
ing pennies. The rooms are basic – we'd say

bare if it weren't for the coy mosaics on the
wall – but everything's clean and most of the
bathroom fixtures are relatively new. If you
can, go for the apartment with a terrace on
the 2nd floor (Room 8). The elderly Chinese
owner is friendly and the eclectic wrought-
iron sculptures around the property were
done by her husband.

Easy World Hotel   HOTEL €
(Map p88; ☑453 8557; easyworld@intnet.mu;
Royal Rd; r/studio Rs 850/1100; ⊛) Basic, cheap,
though rather threadbare, the Easy World
Hotel is conveniently set along the main
road through town – ask for a room on one
of the upper floors – it's quite a climb but the
sea breezes should compensate.

Aanari   HOTEL €€
(Map p88; ☑453 9000; www.aanari.com; Royal Rd;
s/d from €80/112; ⊛@ 🛜 🏊) Perched atop the
Pasadena Village, Aanari is attempting boutique sophistication with a clutch of oriental
statues and special 'VIP perks' for guests
at eminently reasonable midrange prices.
Rooms feel distinctly Asian in theme with
lacquered furnishings, errant flower petals
and silk bed runners. The hotel's biggest
drawcard is the window-filled spa and fitness centre on the roof.

★La Pirogue   LUXURY HOTEL €€€
(Map p88; ☑403 3900; www.lapirogue.com; r incl
half board from €290; ⊛@ 🛜 🏊) Mauritius'
oldest resort shares the same management
as Sugar Beach next door, but there's a completely different feel here. Rather than a
colonial manse theme, La Pirogue opts for
a charming fishing village vibe with semi-
circular clusters of adorable hut-villas arranged along the 500m of spectacular sandy
beach. The resort was built around the same
time as the Sydney Opera House and if you

look carefully you'll notice that the thatch roofing is arranged in a similar fashion to the trademark cavalier helmet–like roofing on the iconic opera house. To some, it may feel like the resort is starting to show its age, but to most visitors, La Pirogue represents a classic paradigm of Mauritius' beachside hospitality.

Sands Resort
RESORT €€€

(Map p88; ☑ 403 1200; www.thesandsresort.mu; off Royal Rd, Wolmar; d incl half board from €278; ✴ @ 🛜 🌊) With gorgeous views from the beachside pool out onto Tamarin Bay and towards Le Morne, this sophisticated yet unpretentious option enjoys an airy, tropical elegance which permeates the open, timber-frame lobby. The bedrooms sport subtle earthy tones, generous bathrooms and sea-view balconies. There are two restaurants, a spa and plenty of sports activities, including a dive centre. Highly recommended.

Sugar Beach Resort
LUXURY HOTEL €€€

(Map p88; ☑ 453 9090; www.sugarbeachresort. com; Royal Rd, Wolmar; d incl half board from €310; ✴ @ 🛜 🌊) With its mock-plantation mansion look and wonderfully colonial lawns, Sugar Bay is a well-run resort catering to a huge number of people coming to enjoy the smart setting and great beach. It's a very family-friendly resort (think lots of kids in the pool and live entertainment at dinner) and shares facilities with La Pirogue next door.

Maradiva
LUXURY HOTEL €€€

(Map p88; ☑ 403 1500; www.maradiva.com; off Royal Rd, Wolmar; villas from €348; ✴ @ 🛜 🌊) Perfectly manicured grounds sprinkled with luxurious villas. This place oozes charm, serenity and impeccable service from the

---

HOLIDAY RENTALS

Flic en Flac trumps all of the island's other beach towns when it comes to cheap holiday rentals. None of the options are located directly on the beach as the coastal road cuts a line between development and the sandy shore, but there are still plenty of beach views to be had.

The most popular rental operator in the area, **Jet-7** (☑ 453 9600, 467 7735; www.jet-7.com), manages a handful of expansive multi-unit properties, including the Datier, Tamarinier, Latanier and Grenadier complexes.

---

entry gate to the sleek seaside resto-lounge. Rooms are large and beautifully presented.

 Eating

Flic en Flac has quite a paradoxical dining scene. Wealthier vacationers tend to stay on the grounds of their upmarket hotels to take advantage of their 'half-board' holiday packages, while budgetarians usually opt to self-cater or nibble on street fare. This leaves a strange void in the middle of the dining spectrum, and as a result there's a noticeable lack of out-of-this-world establishments in central Flic en Flac.

Foodies should consider booking a reservation at an in-house restaurant on the grounds of one of the top-end hotels, or drive down to Black River for a more memorable and eclectic assortment of eats.

For something a little more earthy, you'll find fast-food trucks parked under the weeping *filao* trees along the sand at the northern part of the public beach. They serve fruit, chips, drinks, kebabs and all manner of baguettes, all for no more than Rs 60. You can't see Le Morne from this part of the beach, but it's a scenic spot to enjoy a bite nonetheless.

Banane Créole
MAURITIAN €

(Map p88; Le Papayou; ☑ 453 9826; Royal Rd; mains Rs 100-250; ⊙ 9.30am-3pm & 6-10pm Mon-Sat) Service can come with a smile or a scowl at this tiny local joint, but that's all just part of the charm. It's lost a little since a change in management but you'll still find scores of locals flocking here on their lunch break for the cheap eclectic menu (paella, pizza etc) at pinchpenny prices. Try the signature dessert 'papayou' (cooked payapa sweetened with sugar and ice cream) with a cup of fresh coffee – Flic en Flac's finest.

Ah-Youn
CHINESE, MAURITIAN €

(Map p88; ☑ 453 9099; Royal Rd; mains Rs 200-350; ⊙ noon-3.30pm & 6-10pm) We're not sure how much of a compliment it is to say that Ah-Youn's best features are its swift service and generous portions, but alas it's true. Don't worry though, the food is perfectly palatable and, frankly, a much better choice than many of the other restaurants in town. The kitchen's focus is mainly Chinese fare, but Mauritian flavours have crept onto the menu as well.

★ Canne à Sucre
MAURITIAN €€

(Map p88; Chez May; ☑ 917 8282; Royal Rd; meals from Rs 600; ⊙ 8am-noon & 4pm-late) Now here's something special, an authentic slice of Mauritian life in the midst of Flic en Flac. May has converted her unpromising little roadside bar-restaurant into a cosy space that somehow captures the essence of coastal Mauritius. She offers good breakfasts, but likes nothing better than to serve up a multicourse dinner feast of Creole dishes – rice, chicken, octopus, Creole sausages and 'some vegetables you've never heard of before' – with dessert and rum thrown in for the price. You'll need to order the day before you plan to visit, and prices were expected to rise not long after we were there, but these are minor details. Don't miss it.

Mirador   MAURITIAN, INTERNATIONAL €€
(Map p86; ☑452 0845; Casela Nature & Leisure Park; mains Rs 300-425; ☺10.30am-4pm) It's well worth planning your visit to Casela around lunchtime to grab a bite at the on-site restaurant. This charming open-air cafe has photogenic views of the sea and western plains, and serves a variety of international and local dishes, including snacks, salads, paninis and pizzas.

Domaine Anna   CHINESE, SEAFOOD €€
(Map p86; ☑453 9650; www.domaineanna.net; Médine; mains from Rs 250; ☺11.30am-2.30pm & 6.30-10.30pm Tue-Sun) You'll need a taxi or rental car to get here, but you'll be really glad you made the trip. Flic en Flac's most refined dining experience sits in colonial-style pavilions with gauzy netting, wooden banisters and sky-scraping cane in the distance. The predominantly Chinese menu is the brainchild of chef Hang Leung Pah Hang and the food is excellent – locals come from all over the island to get their frequent fix of crab, calamari and succulent lobster.

Chez Pepe   ITALIAN €€
(Map p88; ☑453 9383; Royal Rd; mains Rs 250-650; ☺11.30am-late) Chez Pepe is a lively spot serving up Italian faves like pizza, pasta and rustic Tuscan meats. It won't be a particularly memorable meal, but it's one of the best place for a bite along Flic en Flac's beachside road.

Twin's Garden   MAURITIAN, INTERNATIONAL €€
(Map p88; ☑453 5250; Royal Rd; mains Rs 350-680, Fri buffet Rs 600; ☺noon-3pm & 7pm-late) A sprawling collection of agreeable outdoor tables just across the road from the beach, Twin's does dishes that range from the extremely well-priced (Rs 950) grilled lobster

flamed with local rum and garlic butter or the lamb shanks in Rodrigues honey to prime Australian steaks. Something, however, seems to have been lost in the translation in the 'cassoulette of the fisherman with seafood and lobster bisque'... On Friday nights it's a buffet dinner, a live *séga* floor show and then live bands playing music from the '60s through to the '80s. We prefer the other nights but each to their own.

Ocean Restaurant   SEAFOOD €€
(Map p88; ☑453 8549; Royal Rd; mains Rs 450-1200; ☺10am-3pm & 6.30-9pm) Set in slightly classier surrounds than we're accustomed to in Flic en Flac, this elegant place makes you pay a little over the odds but the seafood is excellent.

🍹 **Drinking & Nightlife**

You'll find plenty of bars around the Pasadena Village complex (you'll hear them before you see them) and across the road from the beach further south.

KenziBar   BAR
(Map p88; ☑453 5259; ☺6.30pm-midnight Tue-Sat) KenziBar, a block or two back from the waterfront, is your best bet for nightlife in Flic en Flac. There's tongue-tingling *rhum arrangés* (rum punch), fire-spurting torches, live music (on Fridays and Saturdays) and a mangy, pat-hungry dog that calls the bar home – welcome to Mauritius!

Shotz   BAR, NIGHTCLUB
(Map p88; ☑453 8644; Royal Rd; ☺11pm-4am Fri & Sat) Both lounge bar and nightclub, Shotz is about as jet-set as things get beyond the high walls of the upmarket resorts.

ℹ️ **Getting There & Around**

There is a bus from Port Louis to Flic en Flac and Wolmar every 15 to 20 minutes. Public buses constantly ply the coastal route in Flic en Flac and many tourists use it as a cheap and quick hop-on-hop-off service. A taxi from Port Louis to Flic en Flac will cost you Rs 1000. Figure on Rs 2000 for a taxi to the airport, Rs 1400 to Le Morne and Rs 1700 to Belle Mare. A ride to Black River costs Rs 500.

All accommodation and travel agencies in the area can help arrange bicycle and car hire. Count on Rs 250 for a bike. Cars start at Rs 900 for a manual; Rs1200 for an automatic. Numerous such agencies line the main road through town and most offer the exact same products and swipe identical commission.

Tamarin & Black River (Rivière Noire)

POP 11,287

The large swath of beach-fringed land between Flic en Flac and Le Morne is known to most Mauritians as Rivière Noire (Black River). One of the island's last coastal areas to witness development, this constellation of townships has grown by leaps and bounds over the last few years as unsightly salt flats morph into stylish housing projects for South African expats, and traditional hunting grounds get reimagined as scenic zoos and cycling paths. Despite the sudden appearance of modern structures, Black River is a great place to base yourself for a more active and authentic experience. Sensational hiking, scenic shorelines, top-notch fishing and interesting historical relics are all within arm's reach.

◎ Sights

Martello Tower   MUSEUM, FORT
(Map p86; ☑ 583 0178; ☉ 9.30am-5pm Tue-Sat, to 1.30pm Sun) FREE In the 1830s the British built five 'Martello' towers – copies of the tower at Mortella Point in Corsica (vowel order was apparently not a priority for the British) – to protect their young colony from predators (namely the French who were suspected of supporting a slave rebellion). Although the other towers have fallen into ruin, the one at La Preneuse has been converted into a small museum. Captions explain the tower's ingenious design – walls measure 3m in thickness and are crowned by a copper cannon that could apparently destroy a target 2km away.

La Route du Sel   HISTORIC SITE
(Map p86; ☑ 483 8764; Royal Rd; adult/child Rs 200/100; ☉ 8.30am-5pm Mon-Sat) Not quite a *route* like the Route du Thé, the 18th-century salt flats along the main road in Tamarin are a popular stopping point for camera-happy travellers. This is the last place in Mauritius where salt is still produced and the compulsory 15- to 20-minute guided tour takes you through the history of this fading industry with the chance for some good photos. There's also a small shop at the entrance.

La Balise Marina   YACHT HARBOUR
(Map p86; ☑ 483 7272; www.labalisemarina.com) The billboards are everywhere – La Balise Marina promises to revolutionise the tourism industry in Mauritius by creating the island's first port welcoming luxury yachts. Construction of the marina and its adjoining complex of shops and apartments is well underway (if behind schedule), but once complete, Black River is expected to overflow with some serious tourist traffic.

🏖 Beaches

Tamarin Beach   BEACH
(Map p86) Locals like to wax nostalgic about Tamarin Beach, and in many ways this sandy cove still feels like a throwback to earlier times – especially since the centrally located Tamarin Hotel looks like it hasn't been renovated since *Jaws* was in cinemas.

Once upon a time the area was known as Santosha Bay (you'll still find the word 'Santosha' scribbled on a few buildings in faded paint) and offered wave hunters some of the best surfing on the planet. In fact, before the bay earned the name Santosha, locals refused to give the beach a moniker because they didn't want outsiders to discover their cache of surfable seas!

Today the waves and currents have changed and surfing at Le Morne has really taken off, but Tamarin – unmarred by high-walled resort compounds – remains a popular place and during the evening live jazz tunes waft through the air.

The walk between Tamarin Beach and southern Wolmar is very scenic and not accessible by car (women are advised not to do it alone).

🏃 Activities

There are ample hiking opportunities at Black River Gorges National Park further inland and Le Morne Peninsula to the south.

Dolphin-Watching

Tamarin Beach's heyday as a surf hub may have subsided, but now tourists are flocking to the area to check out the friendly pods of bottlenose and spinner dolphins that swim by each morning. Speedboats departing from all over the island circle the western waters offering tourists a chance to jump in and swim with the gentle creatures.

The sudden increase in operators has called the sustainability of local dolphin-watching into question. Choose your tour boat carefully – companies who do not have the dolphins' wellbeing at heart should be avoided. Trips usually depart at 7am. Figure on around €40 for a two-hour excursion.

Check out www.mauritiuscatamaran. com for a short list of tour possibilities. La Pirogue Big Game Fishing also offers trips. Note that some dolphin-watching trips include a visit to Île aux Bénitiers.

JP Henry Charters Ltd BOAT TOUR
(☑729 0901; www.blackriver-mauritius.com) JP Henry Charters Ltd offers highly recommended dolphin trips on either a catamaran or speedboat.

Deep-Sea Fishing

The estuary at Black River suddenly plunges 700m down to the ocean floor making it one of the island's deep-sea fishing hubs. The peak fishing season is between November and March when you can catch just about anything from blue marlin to hammerheads. Black marlin and barracuda can be caught throughout the year, while the yellowfin season is from March to May and the wahoo season is around September to December.

There are a number of fishermen in the area that offer outings on fully equipped boats. Many of them congregate at **Le Morne Anglers' Club** (Map p86; ☑483 5801; www.morneanglers.com; ⊙6.30am-8.30pm), signposted beside the crumbling police station. In addition to fishing outings, it also offers boat charters and catamaran cruises along the coast for a spot of dolphin-watching, snorkelling and barbecue picnics.

La Pirogue Big Game Fishing FISHING, BOAT TOURS
(☑483 8054; www.lapiroguebiggame.com) Fishing outings and dolphin-watching can be arranged with La Pirogue Big Game Fishing

based at La Pirogue hotel (p89) in Flic en Flac.

Zazou Fishing FISHING
(Map p86; ☑788 3804, 729 9222; www.zazoufish ing.com; Ave des Rougets, Tamarin) Zazou Fishing is a reputable operator offering an excellent deal: Rs 16,000 for a half-day at sea (from 7am to 1pm) that can be extended to 4pm for an additional Rs 2000. There's a six-person maximum.

Golf

Tamarina Golf, Spa & Beach Club GOLF
(Map p86; ☑401 3006; www.tamarinagolf.mu; Tamarin Bay) The magnificent Tamarina Golf, Spa & Beach Club is an 18-hole course designed by Rodney Wright. It sprawls across 206 hectares along an old hunting estate situated between the coastal townships and the looming spine of the inland hills. The property also features two inviting restaurants – La Madrague (p95) and Le Dix-Neuf – and over a hundred rentable villas (p94).

🛏 Sleeping

Noticeably devoid of monstrous upmarket resorts, Black River prefers old-school inns, quiet villas and welcoming *chambres d'hôtes* tucked down narrow, tree-lined lanes.

The residential vibe in Black River means that there's a wide selection of private apartments and villas for rent.

EasyRent ACCOMMODATION SERVICES
(☑452 1010; www.easyrent.mu) The managers live in the area and have their finger on the pulse when it comes to local bargains.

DEEP-SEA FISHING

The fisheries around Mauritius support large maritime predators such as marlin, wahoo, tuna and sharks, luring big-game anglers from around the world. Annual fishing competitions are held in Black River in November and February.

Game fishing has far less environmental impact than commercial fishing, but the weight and the number of fish caught has shown a marked decline since its heyday in the 1970s. It's now rare to catch anything over 400kg. Using the practice of 'tag-and-release' is an option for those who want the thrill without depriving the ocean of these magnificent creatures.

Anglers get to take home a trophy such as the marlin's nose spike, or a couple of fillets, but the day's catch belongs to the operator, who sells it to be served up at local restaurants.

Most of the big hotels run boats, and there are several private operators based at Black River, Trou aux Biches and Grand Baie. Most outfits have a minimum hire time of around six hours, and each boat can normally take three anglers and three guests. Expect to pay upwards of Rs 22,000 per boat.

★ Les Lataniers Bleus
GUESTHOUSE €€

(Map p86; ✆483 6541; www.leslataniersbleus.com; d from €130; ❄@🔊☎) If you're hoping to partake in the Mauritian *chambre d'hôte* experience, look no further – Les Lataniers Bleus offers local hospitality at its finest. The formidable Josette Marchal-Vexlard is the head of the household, and she dotes upon her guests with effortless charm and an infectious smile. The darling rooms are spread across three houses situated on an ample, beachside orchard. Every comfort has been considered – there's even a powerpoint hidden in a tree trunk so you can update your blog while sitting in the sand! The evening *table d'hôte* on the verandah is a great way to meet other guests and learn about life on the island from the affable hostess.

Marlin Creek Residence
GUESTHOUSE €€

(Map p86; ✆483 7628; www.ilemauricelocation.fr; 10 Colonel Dean Ave; d/bungalow incl breakfast €100/160; ❄🔊☎) This new addition to Black River's sleeping scene sits along the cerulean bay just a stone's throw from the local jetty. The buzzing fisherfolk next door give the property a wonderfully local feel.

Bay Hotel
BOUTIQUE HOTEL €€

(Map p86; ✆483 6525; www.the-bay-hotel-mauritius.com; Ave des Cocotiers, La Preneuse; s/d from €74/140; ❄@🔊☎) What a find! The Bay comes pretty darn close to boutique chic while still keeping prices relatively low. The thoughtfully decorated rooms (think bright pillows and artsy wall hangings) are arranged on two floors around a white-walled courtyard. Don't miss the seaside restaurant and pool out the back. Half-board rates are available for an additional €20 per person.

La Mariposa
APARTMENT €€

(Map p86; ✆728 0506, 483 5048; www.lamariposa.mu; Allée des Pêcheurs, La Preneuse; apt incl breakfast €85-135; ❄🔊☎) Set directly along the sea and surrounded by a wild tropical garden, this quiet option features an L-shaped row of double-decker apartments. Rooms are breezy and simple, with cream-coloured walls, scarlet drapes and rounded balconies promising memorable sunset views. This is one of few hotels in Mauritius that openly advertises its gay-friendly credentials.

Tamarin Hotel
HOTEL €€

(Map p86; ✆483 6927; hoteltamarin.com; Tamarin Beach; s/d from €90/115; ❄@🔊☎) This welcoming address should be an entry in all film location scouts' Rolodexes, 'cause no

one does '70s retro quite like the Tamarin Hotel. Believe it or not the throwback colour scheme was a conscious choice during the renovation in 2002 – you'll either adore it or abhor it so it's best to click through a few pictures on the website before committing. Even if you don't decide to stay here it's well worth swinging by to take in the chilled-out atmosphere. There's a great pool, a sociable stretch of sand out front and a welcoming restaurant that usually hums with live beats. Watersports enthusiasts should ask at the front desk about surfing lessons.

Tamarina Golf, Spa & Beach Club
RESORT €€€

(Map p86; ✆404 0150, 404 8502; www.tamarina.mu; Tamarin; villa €350-700) Golf enthusiasts should consider leasing a luxurious villa here; rental packages include golfing privileges.

✗ Eating

The townships of the Black River area have a respectable selection of dining choices. In general, prices are quite high relative to the rest of the island as the target customers are usually expat South Africans and wealthy Franco-Mauritians.

Those in search of street eats will usually find *boulette* (meatball) vendors at Tamarin Beach (across from the eponymous hotel) on Saturday and Sunday between noon and 7.30pm. Locals say that these are among the best on the island.

Pavillon de Jade
CHINESE €

(Map p86; ✆483 6151; Royal Rd at Trois Bras Junction, Grande Rivière Noire; dishes Rs 100-350; ⊗noon-3pm & 6.30-9.30pm) You hardly ever see any diners at this no-frills Chinese joint above a faded supermarket, but the proud owner refuses to sell his land to the hungry developers of the Balise Marina project (smart guy!). If the owner caves, chances are high that you'll find this local haunt across the street from its original location.

Le Cabanon Créole
MAURITIAN €

(Map p86; ✆483 5783; Royal Rd, La Preneuse; mains Rs 200; ⊗11am-9.30pm) Friendly service and spicy spins on Creole home cooking make this family-run place a perennial favourite. There's a limited range of daily dishes, such as *rougaille saucisses* (spicy sausages) and chicken curry; specials, like lobster or whole fresh fish, can be ordered in advance. It's best to reserve in the evenings as there are only a handful of tables. Delivery available.

La Bonne Chute   MAURITIAN, SEAFOOD €
(Map p86; ☑483 6552; Royal Rd, La Preneuse; mains Rs 250-495; ⊘11am-2pm & 6.30-10.30pm Mon-Sat) Don't be dissuaded by the petrol-station-adjacent location, La Bonne Chute has built its reputation around its flavourful dishes and attractive garden setting. From venison and beef to steamed fish, crab and prawn cassoulette, the kitchen always seems to get it right. And don't forget to save room for one of the homemade desserts.

Cosa Nostra   ITALIAN €
(Map p86; ☑483 6169; cnr Anthurium Lane & Royal Rd, Tamarin; pizzas from Rs 250; ⊘lunch & dinner Tue-Sun) Two things make this popular pizza joint famous: the whisper-thin crust (you'll swear that you're just eating toppings) and the turtle-speed service (you'll think the servers went back to Italy to fetch your slice).

★**La Madrague**   INTERNATIONAL €€
(Map p86; The Beach Club; ☑483 0260; restaurants.tamarina.mu; Tamarina Golf, Spa & Beach Club, Tamarin Bay; mains Rs 350-750, Sun brunch Rs 800-1200; ⊘noon-10pm) Adorned with loads of stylish wicker and sleek wooden slatting, this feels like a poolside restaurant at a posh resort, yet there's no hotel in sight. Only the locals know about La Madrague – it's hidden at the end of the dirt track that splinters off from the entrance gate to the Tamarina golf grounds. The menu features an assortment of standard international dishes (think club sandwiches and lamb chops), but the real draw is the inviting infinity-edge swimming pool bedecked with shimmering dark marble. While away a sunny day under the shade of a coconut palm and when you're ready for some sand, simply scamper down the stairs to the semiprivate beach below.

Zucca   ITALIAN €€
(Map p86; ☑483 7005; Ruisseau Créole Shopping Complex, Grande Rivière Noire; lunch mains Rs 250-400, dinner mains Rs 350-700, pizza from Rs 225; ⊘noon-2pm & 7-10.30pm Tue-Sat, noon-2pm Mon, 7-10.30pm Sun) Owned by an Italian mama who saunters around her restaurant with a certain forceful alacrity. High-quality dishes like beef carpaccio, homemade pasta and osso bucco will have you wagging your hands like they do back in the mother country.

🍷 Drinking & Nightlife

Noticeably quieter than the scene in Grand Baie or even Flic en Flac, the communities of Black River prefer house parties to loud nights out at the club. Still, there are a couple places to go out for the evening, and many of the area's restaurants have a great after-hours vibe. Do keep in mind, though, that Flic en Flac is only a 15- to 25-minute drive up the coast (depending on where you're coming from).

If you're looking for a bit of live music, try the Tamarin Hotel. The owner is a jazz fanatic and plays the saxophone with his local band. It's best to call ahead – they only play twice a week and not always on weekends.

Big Willy's   BAR, NIGHTCLUB
(Map p86; ☑483 7400; www.bigwillys.mu; Royal Rd, Tamarin; ⊘3pm-2am Tue-Fri, 9am-2am Sat, 11am-2am Sun) Owned by a South African and perennially popular with the expat crowd, Big Willy's is the *it* spot for DJed dance beats and rugby on the tube.

Bali Copy   LOUNGE BAR
(Map p86; ☑483 8252; Tutti Frutti, La Preneuse; ⊘10am-midnight) Set within what looks like an office building, this lively joint is precisely what its name suggests: a Bali copy. There's a chilled-out tropical vibe, Buddha statues by the pool and the ambient beats rev up on weekends to attract the local surfing crowd.

ⓘ Getting There & Around

Buses headed for Tamarin leave Port Louis roughly every hour and Quatre Bornes every 20 minutes. These buses also stop in La Preneuse. A taxi from Port Louis costs Rs 1000. Expect to pay Rs 1700 for the airport, Rs 600 for Flic en Flac, Rs 700 for Le Morne and Rs 1700 to reach Belle Mare.

Black River Gorges National Park

Mauritius' biggest and best national park is a wild expanse of rolling hills and thick forest covering roughly 2% of the island's surface. It's difficult to overstate the importance of this park – it's the last stand for the island's forests and many of its native species. It's also the most spectacular corner of the island and if you make only one day trip from the coast make it here.

Once the island's prime hunting grounds, the area became a protected preserve in 1994 after scientists identified over 300 species of flowering plants, nine endemic species of bird and a population of giant fruit bats that numbered more than 4000. This is also an important habitat for three of the island's most endangered bird species – the Mauritius kestrel, the echo parakeet and the pink pigeon. Introduced wild boar, macaque monkeys and curious deer also wander through the vast swaths of old-growth ebony, and sightings are not uncommon.

🏃 Activities

There are numerous trails that criss-cross Black River Gorges National Park like unravelling shoestrings. While all of the trailheads are clearly marked along one of the two roads running through the park, many of the paths can quickly get obscured in the brush, leaving hikers confused. It's well worth stopping at one of the visitors centres to grab a crude map and check in about the current state of the trails. We recommend hiring a guide if you're serious about exploring the park and uncovering the majestic viewpoints. You can also contact the visitors centres ahead of time to enquire about hiring a ranger.

If you choose one of the one-way trails that ends at the Black River Gorges Visitor Centre, ring ahead to make sure that the road from Rivière Noire into the visitor centre is open – it's sometimes impassable by vehicle, which may prevent the taxi you aranged to meet you there from turning up!

The best time to visit the park is during the flowering season between September and January. Look for the rare *tambalacoque* (dodo tree), the black ebony trees and the wild guavas. Bird-watchers should keep an eye out for the Mauritius kestrel, pink pigeon, echo parakeet and Mauritius cuckoo-shrike.

ℹ️ Information

Staff at both of the visitors centres can offer advice on the different trails, brief you about the area's wildlife through captioned displays, and hand out fairly sketchy maps.

Black River Gorges Visitors Centre (☑258 0057; ⊙7am-5pm Mon-Fri, 9am-5pm Sat & Sun) At the park's western entrance, about 7.5km southeast of Black River's Trois Bras Junction.

Pétrin Information Centre (☑471 1128, 507 0128; ⊙8am-3.15pm Mon-Fri) At the eastern entrance to the park.

Chamarel

POP 786

Known throughout the island for its hushed bucolic vibe and cool breezes, Chamarel is a hidden hamlet tucked into the western hills. It's well-known for its excellent eating scene and we also love it as a stop en route to/from the Black River Gorges National Park.

⊙ Sights & Activities

Terres de 7 Couleurs   NATURAL LANDMARK
(Map p86; Chamarel Coloured Earths; ☑483 8298; adult/child Rs 125/75; ⊙7am-6pm) The Chamarel Coloured Earths, 4km southwest of Chamarel, has, for reasons that remain something of a mystery to us, become one

---

HIKING THE BLACK RIVER GORGES

The main trails are as follows. If you only have time to make one trek, choose between the Macchabée Trail, Macchabée Loop and the Parakeet Trail.

➡ Macchabée Trail (10km one-way, strenuous, four hours) Begin at the Pétrin Information Centre, hiking along the plateau to the stunning Macchabée Viewpoint, then down to the Black River Gorges Visitor Centre.

➡ Macchabée Forest Trail (14km return, moderate, three hours) Begin at the Pétrin Information Centre but remain on the plateau with a loop through some lovely tropical forest.

➡ Macchabée Loop (8km return, moderate, three hours) Hike along the plateau to the Macchabée Viewpoint then return along the same path to the Pétrin Information Centre.

➡ Parakeet Trail (8km one-way, strenuous, three hours) Begin at the Plaine Champagne Police Post (halfway between the Gorges Viewpoint and Alexandra Falls along the tarred road from Chamarel), following a ridge down into the gorge and then along the river to the Black River Gorges Visitor Centre.

➡ Mare Longue Reservoir (12km return, moderate, four hours) Begins and ends at the Pétrin Information Centre, taking in a dwarf native forest and a large reservoir at the little-visited northern tip of the park.

of the sights on the island's usual tourist circuit. Most travellers find it quite underwhelming after a long journey, but if you temper your expectations and approach an excursion here as a quirky side trip, then there's a greater chance of enjoying the variations of colourful sand – a result of the uneven cooling of molten rock. Tortoises are kept in an enclosure just below the coloured earths, which lie 3km inside the reserve.

The entire property was once the private estate of Charles de Chazal de Chamarel, who entertained Matthew Flinders during Flinders' captivity in Mauritius during the Napoleonic Wars.

Chamarel Waterfall   WATERFALL

About halfway (1.5km) between the Terres de 7 Couleur's entrance gate and the colourful sands is a scenic viewpoint over the Chamarel waterfall, which plunges more than 95m in a single drop. With a prior reservation, you can abseil with **Vertical World** (☑ 697 5430; www.verticalworldltd.com) from the top of the falls all the way into the pool at its base.

Rhumerie de Chamarel   MUSEUM

(Map p86; ☑ 483 7980; www.rhumeriedechamarel. com; Royal Rd; adult incl tasting Rs 350, child Rs 175; ⊙ 9.30am-4.30pm Mon-Sat) Set among the vast hillside plantations of Chamarel, the Rhumerie de Chamarel is a working distillery that doubles as a museum showcasing the rum-making process. The pet project of the Beachcomber hotel tycoon, the factory opened in 2008 and uses a special 'ecofriendly' production method ensuring that all materials are recycled. The rum is quite tasty and makes for a pleasant coda to a guided tour of the plant. It's best to time your visit with a lunchtime break at the onsite gourmet restaurant, L'Alchimiste (p99).

Yemaya   HIKING, MOUNTAIN-BIKING

(☑ 283 8187, 752 0046; www.yemayaadventures. com) Full- and half-day adventures can be arranged with professional 'cycle-path' Patrick Haberland at his outfit, Yemaya. They also arrange hikes through Black River Gorges National Park.

La Vieille Cheminée   HORSE RIDING

(Map p86; ☑ 483 5249; www.lavieillecheminee. com; 1-/2-hour trail ride Rs 1300/1600) La Vieille Cheminée, a farm and rustic lodge, offers guided trots on horseback through the hilly countryside and along its shady ravines.

ⓘ PREPARING TO HIKE

If you decide to attempt a trip under your own steam, you'll need a private vehicle as getting to the trailheads can be near impossible with public transport. The best option is to get a taxi to drop you off at a trailhead and then pick up a bus at the lower end of the park; the coast road is well covered by buses travelling between the main towns.

We suggest checking www.fitsy.com before you head out into the wild. This handy website features detailed trail information using GPS and satellite coordinates.

Note that there is nowhere to buy food or drinks in the park. Make sure you bring plenty of water and energy-boosting snacks. You'll also need insect repellent, wet-weather gear and shoes with good grip – no matter how hot and sunny the coast may be it is usually wet and humid within the park. Consider binoculars for wildlife-watching.

Parc Aventure Chamarel   ADVENTURE SPORTS

(Map p86; ☑ 234 4533, 234 5385; parcadventure@ intnet.mu; adult/child Rs 1100/550; ⊙ session 9.15am, 11.15am & 1.15pm) Tucked away in the forest within La Vallée des Couleurs, this adventure park offers tourists a few fun thrills like ziplines, mini suspension bridges and a ropes course. Reservations are required at least 24 hours in advance.

🛏 Sleeping

Le Coteau Fleurie   GUESTHOUSE €€

(Map p86; ☑ 733 3963; www.coteaufleurie.com; Royal Rd, Chamarel; d incl breakfast €80; ❋ @) Plucked from the sky-scraping ridges of Réunion, this lovely *chambre d'hôte* feels miles away from anything else in Mauritius. A quaint Creole-style option, it embraces its traditional roots and owners Geneviève and Gérard offer travellers a welcome retreat among fruit and coffee trees and thick jungle trunks.

Chalets en Champagne   CABINS €€

(Map p86; ☑ 483 6610; www.acoeurbois.com; 110 Rte Champagne, Chamarel; d incl half board €115-190; ❋) These beautiful log cabins are tucked into the mountainside amid gnarled tropical trees. The decor stays true to the wooded theme (think thatch roofs and stone-lined bath tubs) while gently incorporating modern touches (air-con, DVD players

SCENIC DRIVE: BLACK RIVER GORGES NATIONAL PARK

Although we strongly recommend that you explore the Black River Gorges National Park on foot, if that's not possible you can still get a taste for this beautiful region. Before we get started, a word of warning: if possible avoid making this trip on weekends as the otherwise quiet roads are flooded with locals driving slowly and stopping by the roadside while they hunt for wild berries.

Begin along the coast road on Mauritius' western coast at Case Noyale (around 1.5km north of La Gaulette and around 7km south of Black River), where a signpost points inland towards Chamarel; if you're looking for a landmark there's a cream church set back from the corner. After crossing the coastal plain, the road begins to climb steeply through increasingly dense forest. Around 4km after leaving the coast road, close to the top of the first ridgeline, a lookout on your right offers fine, sweeping views of the coastal plain and out to sea.

Passing through Chamarel, ignore the signs to Terres de 7 Couleurs (p96), which is not a patch on the scenery in the national park up ahead, and bear left through Chamarel. After passing the entrance to the Rhumerie de Chamarel, continue climbing through the forest for around 6km to the **Gorges Viewpoint**. On a clear day the views from here across the gorge rank among the best on the island. Look for the **Piton de la Petite Rivière Noire** (Black River Mountain peak; 828m) on your left, and keep an eye out for the Mauritius kestrel, tropic birds and fruit bats.

A further 2km along the paved road, you pass the **Plaine Champagne Police Post** (trailhead for the Parakeet Trail), with the turn-off for **Alexandra Falls** a further 2km on. Turn right off the main road, passing beneath a pretty honour-guard of trees, then follow the short path out to the falls' **viewpoint**. While there, you can admire the cloud forest of Mt Cocotte (771m) and the view down to the south coast.

Back on the main road, turn right towards Chamouny at the roundabout 2.5km beyond the Alexandra Falls turn-off and follow the road down the hill through the thinning forest. After around 3km, pull into the unpaved parking area on the right (west) side of the road – from the low ridge of dirt and rock there are good views down into a the crater lake called **Bassin Blanc**. If you wait here long enough, you might just see some of the region's rare birds passing through, although none breed here.

Return up the hill and continue straight ahead at the roundabout. After just over 2km, turn right and follow the signs to **Grand Bassin**, an important pilgrimage sight for the island's Hindus 2.5km from the turn-off. Long before you arrive, you'll see the massive, and curiously hypnotic Shiva statue that watches over this sacred spot.

Return the 2.5km to the main road and at the T-Junction you'll see the Pétrin Information Centre (p96). Even if you're not planning to hike, park your car and wander around the back to an enclosure where (at last count) six pairs of pink pigeons were being prepared for release into the wild.

etc). Hikers will appreciate the surrounding network of marked trails that weave across the tree-lined terrain.

Lakaz Chamarel LODGE €€€
(Map p86; ☑483 5240; www.lakazchamarel.com; Piton Canot; s/d incl half board from €118/185; ✳☏✳) This 'exclusive lodge' in the countryside around Chamarel is a wonderfully conceived collection of rustic (yet oh-so-elegant) cabins offering a blissful getaway amid gorgeous forests, gardens and streams. Rooms are tastefully decorated with chic safari-style trimmings. Not to be missed is the serene spa and the charming swimming pool adorned with stone goddess statues.

✘ Eating

Over the last few years, Chamarel has gained an island-wide reputation for its clutch of charming *tables d'hôtes* sprinkled around the hilltops. Lately, unscrupulous taxi drivers are capitalising on the area's newfound notoriety among foodies by overcharging tourists and demanding hefty commissions from the local restaurants. We recommend navigating the area with a private vehicle and choosing a dining option at your leisure. And remember: if a place is in this book and it's empty, its doesn't mean that it's no good, but rather the owner has most likely refused to pay the taxi drivers' commissions!

★ **Palais de Barbizon** MAURITIAN €
(Map p86; ☑ 495 1690; lebarbizon@yahoo.fr; Ste-Anne Rd; meals Rs 350; ☺ noon-4pm) It may not look like much from the outside but Barbizon has made quite the name for itself in the area, namely due to the lively and smiley owners. Marie-Ange helms the pots and pans whipping up traditional Mauritian flavours from her family's cookbook while Rico L'Intelligent (what a name!) entertains at the tables. He doesn't give you a menu. Instead he offers a feast of punch, rice, five vegetables, and fish or chicken, which could just be the best RS 350 you'll spend on the island.

★ **Domaine du Cachet** MAURITIAN, SEAFOOD €€
(Map p86; ☑ 483 5259; sdigumber@hotmail.com; La Montagne; mains from Rs 600, set menus Rs 1500-2300; ☺ 11.30am-4pm) Owned by the same people who run the ultrapopular Sirokan (p101) in La Gaulette, this classy restaurant oozes *table d'hôte* charm from behind the honey-tinged facade. If we could choose one place to eat in Chamarel and felt like a tranquil eating experience, this would win hands down. The restaurant is situated along the Baie du Cap–Chamarel Rd beyond the post office but before the Terres de 7 Couleurs.

**Le Chamarel
Restaurant** MAURITIAN, INTERNATIONAL €€
(Map p86; ☑ 483 6421; le-chamarel.restaurant.mu; La Crête; mains Rs 350-700; ☺ noon-3pm) Perched on the hillside 1km west of Chamarel along the descending road to Black River, this local mainstay is best known for its cantilevered verandah delivering a postcard-perfect panorama of the west coast. The food is also worth a mention – the finely tuned menu features an assortment of surf and turf mains that include octopus curry with green papaya, Australian beef, or grilled cockerel with tandoori spices. If you don't eat here, the view from the lookout 100m down the road is similar.

Chez Pierre Paul MAURITIAN €€
(Map p86; ☑ 483 5079; Rte Champagne; mains from Rs 450, set menu Rs 750; ☺ noon-4pm) No delusions of grandeur here, just simple Creole cuisine that hits the spot every time.

Don't be put off by the empty tables – this place is a match for most others in town.

Les Palmiers INDIAN, MAURITIAN €€
(Map p86; ☑ 483 8364; Royal Rd; mains from Rs 500; ☺ noon-4pm) This popular place does a roaring trade with curries and *faratas* (pan-fried flat breads) served in a pleasant dining area.

L'Alchimiste MAURITIAN €€
(Map p86; ☑ 483 7980; www.rhumeriedechamarel. com; Royal Rd, Rhumerie de Chamarel; mains Rs 500-700, set menus Rs 1000-1500; ☺ noon-3pm Mon-Sat) The Rhumerie de Chamarel's chic in-house restaurant boasts an impressive menu that promises to satisfy. The chef's philosophy is definitely gourmet; flavourful Mauritian favourites are whipped into eye-pleasing concoctions such as braised wild boar cooked in Chamarel rum.

Le Domaine de Saint-Denis MAURITIAN €€
(Map p86; ☑ 728 5562; www.domainedesaintdenis. com; Chamarel; mains from Rs 600; ☺ by reservation only) Features recipes from the kitchen of Jacqueline Dalais, the unofficial First Lady of Mauritian cuisine, who oversees this gem of a restaurant. Order the scallop carpaccio with olive oil and lime if it's on the menu. It's signposted off the road from Chamarel to Black River Gorges National Park.

OFF THE BEATEN TRACK

TAMARIN FALLS

Positioned on the outskirts of the Black River Gorges roughly 8km southwest of Curepipe in central Mauritius, this set of seven scenic cascades (some say 11) is a wonderful reward for those willing to take on a challenging hike.

Attempts to access the falls should not be done without a guide. Local guides (charging Rs 500 to 1000) usually wait around the bus station at Henrietta, a township near Curepipe, although we prefer linking up with Yanature at Trekking Île Maurice (p103).

For a truly unique and unforgettable experience, adventurers can abseil from chute to chute on a half- or full-day canyoning excursion with **Vertical World** (☑ 697 5430, 251 1107; www.verticalworldltd.com) or **Otélair** (☑ 251 6680; www.otelair.com). Both operators start their trips from Henrietta as well.

MAURITIUS CHAMAREL

GRAND BASSIN

According to legend, Shiva and his wife Parvati were circling the earth on a contraption made from flowers when they were dazzled by an island set in an emerald sea. Shiva, who was carrying the Ganges River on his head to protect the world from floods, decided to land. As he did so a few drops of water dripped from his head and landed in a crater to form a lake. The Ganges expressed unhappiness about its water being left on an uninhabited island, but Shiva replied that dwellers from the banks of the Ganges would one day settle there and perform an annual pilgrimage, during which water from the lake would be presented as an offering.

The dazzling island is, of course, Mauritius; the legendary craterlake is known as Grand Bassin (Ganga Talao). It is a renowned pilgrimage site, to which up to 500,000 of the island's Hindu community come each year to pay homage to Shiva during the Maha Shivaratri celebrations. This vast festival takes place over three days in February or March (depending on the lunar cycle) and is the largest Hindu celebration outside India.

The most devoted pilgrims walk from their village to the sacred lake carrying a *kanvar*, a light wooden frame or arch decorated with paper flowers. This is no easy feat – February is Mauritius' hottest month and it almost always rains during the festivities. Once the pilgrims arrive they perform a puja, burning incense and camphor at the lake shore and offering food and flowers.

Varangue sur Morne   MAURITIAN €€
(Map p86; ☑ 483 6610, 483 5910; acoeurbois.com; Plaine Champagne Rd; mains from Rs 650; ☼ noon-4.30pm) This former hunting lodge is an institution, and it's not too hard to see why. Its stunning location offers great views over the forested hillsides towards the ocean, and the superb menu reads like a veritable ode to your taste buds: tender braised wild boar, prawns flambéed in Île de France Rum, palm-heart salad with smoked marlin and a laundry list of clever cocktails. Reservations are advised.

❶ Getting There & Around

Although there's a bus service from Quatre Bornes to Chamarel, we highly recommend using private transport. Do not visit Chamarel by taxi – drivers are given exorbitant commissions for bringing tourists to the various attractions and *tables d'hôtes*. You can rent cars and bicycles from Ropsen in La Gaulette.

La Gaulette

POP 2343

South of Black River, the mountains draw ever closer to the coast. You'll find pinewoods and mangroves mingling with the lapping waves, but little in the way of habitation besides the pockets of impoverished shanty towns along the road. Then, a small township emerges under the shade of the nearby hills – it's a quiet place where the lazy fisherfolk lifestyle effortlessly mixes with the carefree surfer vibe. Welcome to La Gaulette.

◉ Sights & Activities

The area's most notable attraction is the lovely **Île aux Bénitiers**, which floats just above sea level in the technicolour reef offshore. The islet is considerably larger than many of the other outcrops in the lagoon (keep an eye out for the interesting rocky projection that looks like the top half of an hourglass) and sports a beautiful picnic-worthy beach, a small coconut farm and a colony of migratory birds. The island's keeper is quite the local character – he travels around with an ever-growing pack of chipper dogs.

Most of the fishermen docked at La Gaulette offer small excursions to the island. The number of boat operators that visit the island continues to grow each year and most of the products are identical: crowded catamarans and a picnic lunch on the sand. Check out www.mauritiuscatamaran.com to make heads or tails of the boat choices – try the Harris Wilson catamaran for a more luxurious (and less crowded) island experience. Note that many cruise operators combine a trip to Île aux Bénitiers with dolphin-watching.

☞ Tours

Ropsen TOURS
(Map p86; ☑255 5546, 451 5763; www.ropsen.net;
Royal Rd, La Gaulette) The village's top tour operator, Ropsen, also organises catamaran excursions, as well as dolphin-watching tours,
island tours, car rentals and accommodation.

🛏 Sleeping

Gaining popularity among the kitesurfing
crowd, La Gaulette represents an excellent
price-value ratio. There are currently two
notable options in the village and we suspect
that this number will quickly grow over the
next couple of years.

★ Ropsen APARTMENT, VILLA €
(Map p86; ☑451 5763; www.ropsen.net; Royal
Rd; studio & apt €30-60, 4-bed villa €100-125;
❋@🕏) From modern studios to large multi-
bedroom apartments, friendly Ropsen proffers such a vast array of high-quality options
that you'll start to think every building in
La Gaulette is a rentable villa in his name!
Insist on a sea view and you'll be treated to
some of the most spectacular vistas on the
island. Almost all of Ropsen's properties
have wi-fi, and guests without a laptop can
check their email at the computer terminal
in Ropsen's office.

Maison Papaye GUESTHOUSE €
(Map p86; ☑752 0918; www.maisonpapaye.com;
r €49-67; ❋@🕏🏊) Set among imposing
homes on a residential street away from the
sea, this stately *chambre d'hôte* is a real find.

Although the whitewashed facade, gabled
roofs and periwinkle shutters may hint at
a colonial past, the building is only a few
years old. The owners designed their retire-
ment getaway to invoke the island's plantation past and they keep tradition alive every
evening with their Creole-inspired *table
d'hôte* dinners (€15) served on the shaded
verandah. There's a minimum four-night-
stay policy.

Rusty Pelican GUESTHOUSE €
(Map p86; www.rusty-pelican.com; apt from €59;
❋@🕏🏊) This fabulous place at the northern end of town is a fine addition to La Gaulette's array of sleeping options. The rooms
are flooded with natural light and have excellent bathrooms. They also give you a mobile to use for the duration of your visit (you
just pay for calls) and they love helping you
plan your stay.

🍴 Eating

The small *superettes* (small self-service
grocery stores) that line the main street
through town cater for the legions of self-
caterers; there are only a few restaurants in
the area. For more options consider driving
up to Chamarel or Black River.

Sirokan SEAFOOD, MAURITIAN €
(Map p86; ☑451 5115; Royal Rd; mains Rs 250-400;
☉lunch & dinner) Bedecked with a pastoral
latticework of flowering twigs and bamboo
branches, Sirokan (a bastardisation of *sirop
de cane* or 'sugar cane') is our favourite La

SURFING, KITESURFING & WINDSURFING

A small scene led by Australian and South African surfers built up in the 1970s around
Tamarin on the west coast (the surf movie *The Forgotten Island of Santosha* was made
here), but the wave crashed during the 1980s.

These days, the scene around Tamarin comprises a small community of local and
Réunionnais surfers. You can plug into what's happening and rent surfboards from one
of the old-school establishments in Tamarin, like the Tamarin Hotel (p94). Le Morne is
the pick of the surf spots these days, with the season beginning in July.

The kitesurfing and windsurfing movements have grown in leaps and bounds over the
last decade – you'll find hundreds of wave hunters gathering along the west coast just
south of Tamarin. Otherwise, try:

➡ Kite Lagoon – on the west side of Le Morne, with a range of schools and good for
beginners

➡ One Eye – on the south side of Le Morne, and for experts only

➡ Cap Malheureux – a highly regarded kitesurfing school in the north

➡ Pointe d'Esny and Mahébourg – when the wind changes in the winter months, you'll
find great breaks in the southeast

MAURITIUS LA GAULETTE

Gaulette dining spot despite its unassuming position along the main road at the far north end of town. You'll have your choice of perfectly prepared steak or seafood. Try either one, or both – you really can't go wrong. The owners of Sirokan also run Domaine du Cachet (p99) in Chamarel.

Ocean Vagabond PIZZA €€

(Map p86; 451 5910; Royal Rd; pizza Rs 300-470; ⊘5-10pm Wed-Mon) Good pizzas and something of a surfer's vibe with DVDs and a Saturday evening happy hour. It all falls a bit flat when things are quiet but that changes when a crowd's in.

Enso MEDITERRANEAN €€

(Map p86; 451 5907; 1st fl, Village Walk Supermarket Centre, La Gaulette; mains Rs300-600; ⊘6pm-late Tue-Sat; 🛜) Styling itself as a lounge bar and restaurant, this place does cool very well, with its laid-back pool table and Saturday night DJs. The food itself is good without being spectacular – think pizzas, pasta and seafood.

🛈 Getting There & Around

Buses (every 20 minutes) between Quatre Bornes and Baie du Cap stop in La Gaulette. There are no direct buses from Port Louis. Instead you have to go via Quatre Bornes, or take the bus from Port Louis to Black River and change.

A taxi between Port Louis and La Gaulette will cost around Rs 1100; it's Rs 1700 to the airport. Do not take a taxi to Chamarel – rent a vehicle instead.

Le Morne Peninsula

Visible from much of southwestern Mauritius, the iconic Le Morne Brabant (556m) is a stunning rock crag from which this beautiful peninsula takes its name. Shaped like a hammerhead shark, the peninsula itself has some of the island's best beaches, now home to a number of upmarket hotels.

Beaches

Although the area's upmarket hotels have gobbled up most of the peninsula's sand-front property, the beaches themselves are still open to the public. Travellers not staying in one of the local resorts can find several access points along the public roads.

🏃 Activities

Hiking

Added to the Unesco World Heritage list in 2008, Le Morne is the star of many postcards as it slopes through the sky then

---

BEST HIKES

For those interested in more than the usual beach activities, Mauritius offers some attractive hikes. Most are in the areas where the Central Plateau meets the coastal plains. Many of the *domaines* in the southeastern part of the island offer beautiful trails through the island's oldest forests.

A fabulous resource for independent hikers, **Fitsy** (www.fitsy.com) is an outstanding website with detailed GPS and satellite imagery that maps out the course of each trail. We recommend, however, hiring a guide for any of the island's major hikes. Apart from making sure you stay on the right trail, a knowledgeable guide provides invaluable insight into the region's flora and fauna.

There are four main outdoor outfits on the island: Yemaya (p97), Trekking Île Maurice, Vertical World (p85) and Otélair (p99). Trekking Île Maurice is the only company that has permission to ascend Le Morne.

Although we haven't made the trek, locals assured us that it's possible to hike along the entire southern coast, beginning with the stretch from Blue Bay to Souillac. Otherwise, our favourite hikes in Mauritius include:

➡ Macchabée Trail, Black River Gorges National Park

➡ Parakeet Trail, Black River Gorges National Park

➡ Le Morne, Le Morne Peninsula

➡ Le Pouce and Corps de Garde, Central Plateau

➡ Vallée de Ferney, Southeast Mauritius

➡ East Coast of Rodrigues

LE MORNE: THE MOURNFUL ONE

Although almost totally uninhabited by locals, Le Morne has a deep resonance in Mauritian culture. According to legend, a group of escaped slaves fled to the peninsula in the early 19th century, hiding out on top of the mountain to remain free. The story goes that the slaves, ignorant of the fact that slavery had been abolished just before their escape, panicked when they saw a troop of soldiers making their way up the cliffs. Believing they were to be recaptured, the slaves flung themselves from the cliff tops to their deaths in huge numbers. And thus the crag earned its name – Le Morne means Mournful One. Although there are no historical records to substantiate the story, it's an important tale for Mauritians and was critical in Le Morne being granted Unesco World Heritage status in 2008.

plunges back down into the blue. Few tourists, however, realise that the view from the top is even more spectacular. As you ascend the crag you'll pass through an indigenous forest, which is the only place on the island where you'll find Mauritius' national flower, the *boucle d'oreille* ('earring'). And when you reach 500m, you'll be treated to unobstructed vistas of the colourful reefs to the west and south. The trail increases in difficulty the higher up you go – those with limited mobility can still take in the views from a midway point (around 260m).

Trekking Île Maurice   HIKING
(Yanature; ☑ 785 6177; www.trekkingilemaurice. com; half/full day per person €40/50) The best way to explore the heaping basalt mound is on a guided hike with this one-man operation headed up by friendly Yan. A nature enthusiast and eighth-generation Mauritian, Yan grew up at the base of Le Morne and wandered the snaking trails well into his teenage years; his father managed one of the five-star resorts nearby. Yan has exclusive permission from the Gambier family – the landowners of Le Morne – to bring tourists through. After Le Morne, consider tagging along on one of Yan's other hiking excursions through Black River Gorges National Park, or perhaps to

Tamarin Falls and the Corps de Garde. Discounts are offered to those who participate in multiple outings.

Windsurfing & Kitesurfing

The area is home to the ultimate surfing spot in all of Mauritius: **One Eye**, so named because surfers will see a small hole (or 'eye') appear in Le Morne's rockface when they are at the exact spot in the sea to catch the perfect wave. Beginners should start on the western side of the peninsula in the 'Kite Lagoon'; the southern winds are much more severe and unpredictable.

Son of Kite   KITESURFING
(☑ 972 9019; www.sonofkite.com; classes per person per hr €32.50-75, rental per hr €25) Kiteboarders of every ilk (from newbies to pros) can sign up for a class with the recommended professionals at Son of Kite.

Yoaneye Kite Centre   KITESURFING
(Map p86; ☑ 737 8296; www.yoaneye.com; 114 Villa Mona, Le Petit Morne) Yoaneye Kite Centre, an IKO-affiliated centre, offers courses.

Club Mistral   KITESURFING, WINDSURFING
(Map p86; ☑ 909 6010, 450 4112; www.club-mistral. com) The worldwide surfing organisation Club Mistral operates intensive kitesurfing and windsurfing courses from their school at the Indian Resort. Figure on around €75 for a one-hour private course.

Horse Riding

Haras du Morne   HORSE RIDING
(Map p86; ☑ 450 4142; harasdumorne.com; off Royal Rd, Le Morne; 60/90/120min ride Rs 3000/ 3500/4500) Expensive horse rides are on offer at this upmarket equestrian centre but the landscape through which they ride (the forest and beaches around Le Morne) are among the prettiest on the island.

❶ HIKING: THE WARNING SIGNS

As a general rule, when hiking you should pay attention to 'Entrée Interdit' (Entry Prohibited) signs – they may mean you're entering a hunting reserve. 'Chemin Privée' (Private Rd) signs are generally there for the benefit of motorists; most landowners won't object to the odd pedestrian. It's best to ask if you're unsure about where you should and shouldn't walk.

🛏 Sleeping & Eating

Largely the domain of five-star properties (rumours are sprouting that a 'six-star' resort is in the works), the fan-shaped swath of sand below the looming Le Morne Brabant is a wonderful place to spend your days on Mauritius if you're looking for a lazy beach holiday. You will need to rent a private vehicle (or pay taxis for day excursions) to get around.

Paradis LUXURY HOTEL €€€
(Map p86; ☑ 401 5050; www.paradis-hotel.com; d incl half board from €432; ❋ @ 🛜 ⛱) Stunning sea views, luxurious accommodation, a golf course and endless activities. What more could you ask for? Not to be missed is the fresh seafood at Blue Marlin, one of the in-house restaurants.

Dinarobin LUXURY HOTEL €€€
(Map p86; ☑ 401 4900; www.dinarobin-hotel.com; d incl half board from €526; ❋ @ 🛜 ⛱) Another ravishing Beachcomber beauty, with a sprawling campus of 172 suites. It was named for the first moniker given to the island by Arab merchants in the 10th century. Rated 'five-star plus' – and it lives up to the expectations.

The South & Southeast

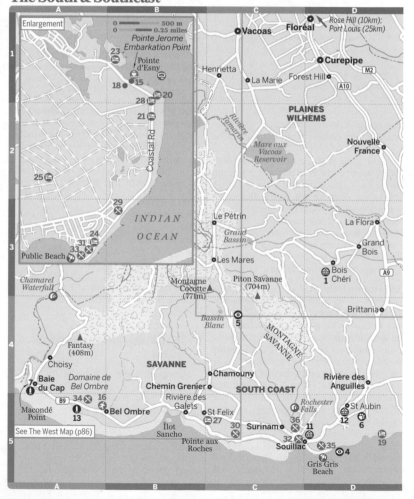

ℹ Getting There & Away

Buses en route between Quatre Bornes and Baie du Cap stop on the main road by the junction for Le Morne. These buses run roughly every hour. A taxi from Port Louis to the Le Morne hotels costs Rs 1700; figure on Rs 1900 to the airport, Rs 1500 to Flic en Flac and Rs 2400 to Belle Mare.

THE SOUTH & SOUTHEAST

With flashes of India, Ireland and the Caribbean, the wild unfolding south is an unde-niable favourite for many. Long considered too harsh to develop due to its steep, wind-battered cliffs, the south coast has managed to stave off the encroaching hands of developers until quite recently. A few luxury resorts have popped up over the last few years, but the area remains mostly rugged, with a plantation estate or two hidden among the towering cane.

The jagged southern cliffs taper off at the shimmering reefs in Blue Bay, and just beyond you'll uncover the gorgeous beach of Pointe d'Esny with its cluster of homely *chambres d'hôtes*. The gritty gridiron of Mahébourg anchors the southeast, providing

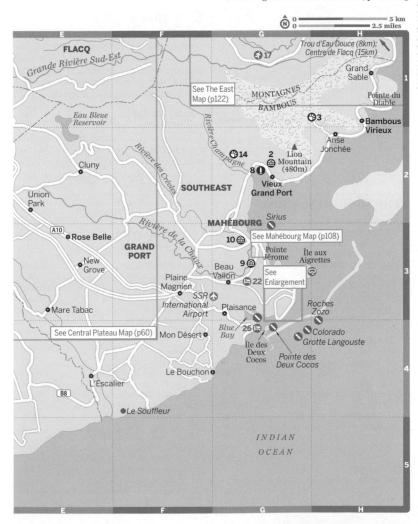

an interesting perspective on local life that starkly contrasts with the unfurling streamers of sand stretching beyond the sleepy commercial centre. Then, the coastal road cuts north, passing endless forests of green – the stomping ground of the island's first settlers some 400 years ago.

❶ Getting There & Around

Mahébourg is the main transport hub in this region, with buses departing from here for destinations along both the east and south coasts. The Mahébourg–Blue Bay area is also the best place to arrange car and bike hire.

Useful bus services include a route from Souillac to Curepipe and Port Louis, and from Baie du Cap up the west coast to Quatre Bornes.

If you're staying in the south or southeast of the island, we recommend one taxi driver in particular – Youssah (☑254 1731). Good for short hops to the airport or multiday excursions around the island, he's a friendly chap, an unusually careful driver and always cheaper than the drivers that wait all day outside the larger hotels.

Mahébourg

POP 15,153

There is something relentlessly charming about bite-size Mahébourg (my-boor), and it seems to have fooled most Mauritians into believing that it's the island's 'second city' (it's not). Although there are stalled plans for a mammoth Caudan-like waterfront complex, for now it's all about simple pleasures: an interesting museum, a buzzing market, spicy street food, good budget lodgings, a pretty backdrop and beautiful beaches to the north and south.

Founded in 1805, the town was named after the famous French governor Mahé de Labourdonnais. The town was once a busy port, but these days it's something of a backwater, with a small fleet of fishermen and a grid of dilapidated buildings.

❍ Sights

You can cover Mahébourg's smattering of sights in half a day, leaving plenty of time to wander the backstreets and take a stroll along the seafront. Everything can be tackled on foot, though you might want to hire a bike to get out to the biscuit factory.

Monday Market   MARKET
(Map p108; ☺8am-5pm) Don't miss the *foire de Mahébourg* in central Mahébourg near the waterfront. The initial focus was silks and other textiles, but these days you'll find a roaring produce section, rows of tacky

The South & Southeast

bric-a-brac and steaming food stalls. It's the perfect place to try some of the local snacks – *gâteaux piments, dhal puris, samousa* and chilli bites – usually dispensed from boxes on the backs of motorcycles. It doesn't take long to navigate the snaking rows of vendors, but it's well worth visiting if you found the market in Port Louis far too touristy. The market is open every day but it doubles in size on Mondays.

National History Museum   MUSEUM
(Map p104; ☑631 9329; Royal Rd; ◷9am-4pm Wed-Sat & Mon, 9am-noon Sun) **FREE** The colonial mansion housing this museum used to belong to the Robillard family and played an important part in the island's history. It was here in 1810 that the injured commanders of the French and English fleets were taken for treatment after the Battle of Vieux Grand Port (the only naval battle in which the French got the upper hand over their British foes). The story of the victory is retold in the museum, along with salvaged items – cannons, grapeshot and the all-important wine bottles – from the British frigate *Magicienne*, which sank in the battle.

The museum contains some fascinating artefacts, including early maps of the island and paintings of Mauritius' original fauna including, of course, the dodo; there are also a few bones of the dodo in a glass case, along with those of other disappeared species such as the red rail and Rodrigues solitaire. One real curio is an engraving of Dutch gentlemen riding in pairs on the back of a giant tortoise (a copy of this engraving is on sale in the Blue Penny Museum (p53) in Port Louis), a species that also went the way of the dodo.

The bell and a cache of Spanish coins from the wreck of the *St Géran* are also on display. The ship's demise in 1744, off the northeast coast of Mauritius, inspired the famous love story *Paul et Virginie* (see p82) by Bernardin de St-Pierre.

New additions to the museum include a retrofitted train carriage out back and a replica of Napoleon's boat used in the infamous battle defeating the English.

Notre Dame des Anges   CHURCH
(Map p108) The butter-coloured tower of Notre Dame des Anges church dominates the Mahébourg skyline. The original church was built in 1849, but it has been restored several times over the years, most recently in 1938. Take a quick peek inside at the baro-

nial roof timbers. Local people visit throughout the day to make offerings to Père Laval, whose statue stands to your right immediately inside the door. It's worth a visit just for the priceless 'beware of children' sign outside.

Rault Biscuit Factory   MUSEUM
(Map p104; ☑631 9559; adult/child with tasting Rs 175/125, without tasting Rs 140/100; ◷9am-3pm Mon-Fri) In 1870 the Rault family started producing manioc biscuits at their little biscuit factory on the northern outskirts of Mahébourg. It has changed hardly a jot since. The crispy, square cookies are made almost entirely by hand using a secret recipe passed down from generation to generation and baked on hotplates over stoves fuelled with dried sugar-cane leaves. The 15- to 20-minute guided tour ends with a chance to sample the end result – with a nice cup of tea, of course. The factory is on the far side of the Cavendish Bridge; when you cross the bridge turn left at the brown-and-white factory sign and then follow the further signs. Packets of the biscuits (we recommend butter flavour and reaching this decision involved pleasurable research...) are on sale for Rs 65.

🏃 Activities

The most popular activity in the area is an excursion by boat to the offshore islands nearby (Île aux Aigrettes, Île de la Passe, Île aux Vacoas and Île au Phare), or the uber-popular Île aux Cerfs further on. Most of the trips involve snorkelling and include lunch. Scores of boatswains park along the shores of Mahébourg and Blue Bay awaiting customers and offering relatively similar experiences.

Jean-Claude Farla   BOAT TRIPS
(☑423 1322, 631 7090) Our operator of choice is Jean-Claude Farla, a local fisherman and six-time national swimming champion who went on to compete in the Indian Ocean games. Not only is he somewhat of a local legend, he is the only person to offer sailing outings on a traditional 22ft pirogue (others have souped-up boats with motors). Figure on €20 for a half-day trip in the pirogue gliding through the blue and stopping periodically to snorkel and free dive. It's €50 for a full-day excursion to Île aux Cerfs with a stop at Île de Flamant and a BBQ lunch on Île aux Mangénie. It's best to call at least two days ahead to ensure that he's available (there's a six-person minimum).

Mahébourg

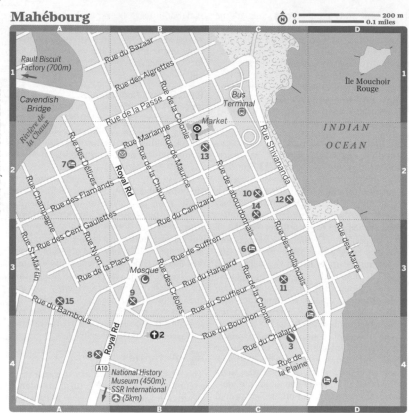

Mahébourg

Active Tours Mauritius   DIVING, KAYAKING
(Map p108; Case Nautiques; ☎631 5613; www.activetoursmauritius.com; 1 Shivananda Rd; boat excursion to île aux Cerfs from Rs 5000, kayak hire per hr Rs 350, boat & snorkelling trips from Rs 1700) Good for trips to Île aux Cerfs, island-hopping-and-snorkelling trips and kayak rental.

🛏 Sleeping

You won't come across any grand hotels in quaint Mahébourg, but you will find a proliferation of good, simple guesthouses, making the town an ideal base for budget travellers. Staying in Pointe d'Esny further down the coast is a good, quieter alternative.

Nice Place Guesthouse   GUESTHOUSE €
(Map p108; ✍631 9419; www.niceplace.orange.mu; Rue de Labourdonnais; r from Rs 700, with shared bathroom Rs 500; ❋❀) As the name suggests, this simple guesthouse has nice rooms – if simple and a bit faded – tended by a lovely Indian couple. For this price it's the best in town.

Hotel les Aigrettes   HOTEL €
(Map p108; ✍631 9094; www.hotellesaigrettes. com; cnr Rue du Chaland & Rue des Hollandais; small s/d Rs 800/1000, large incl breakfast Rs 1100/1400; ❋❀❊) Seemingly always under construction, Hotel les Aigrettes feels a bit like a Jenga tower with its stack of bedrooms and protruding balconies winding several storeys high. The rooms are clean (some even have sea views) with our pick Room 32 – the bathroom may be across the hall (although it's not shared) but the combination of views and comfort are splendid. The owner has a big smile.

Tyvabro   GUESTHOUSE €
(Map p108; ✍631 9674; www.tyvabro.com; Rue Marianne; r incl breakfast Rs 1000; ❋❀) This family-run operation earns high marks for friendly and eager service. Little perks like in-room DVD players and a welcoming roof deck with a hammock more than make up for the past-their-prime furnishings in the rooms.

Coco Villa   GUESTHOUSE €€
(Map p108; ✍631 2346; www.mahecocovilla.net; Rue Shivananda; s/d from Rs 1100/1600; ❋❀❊) Simple, light-filled spaces right by the water are what this place is all about but clean rooms are the order and most have unobstructed sea views.

✕ Eating

Like a microscopic Port Louis, Mahébourg has dozens of back alleys riddled with hidden eats known only to locals. If you're planning to swing by for a visit, make sure you come on a Monday when the local **market** is in full swing – you'll be treated to the colourful clanging of street stalls as vendors hawk savoury snacks to lines of shoppers. Mahébourg's the perfect place to get lost and stumble upon your own tucked-away treasures.

The face of Mahébourg's dining and drinking scene may change radically over the coming years as developers have their eye on the town's port with plans for a large waterfront complex to rival the Caudan in Port Louis.

An eclectic assortment of quality dining options also awaits the palate in Pointe d'Esny, just south of Mahébourg. For a supermarket, try **Kong** (Map p108; ✍631 9252; 47 Royal Rd; ⊙9am-7pm Mon-Sat, to noon Sun).

Tabagi Bambous   STREET FOOD €
(Map p108; ✍796 0070; Rue du Bambous; rotis Rs 10; ⊙7.30am-9.30pm) Dark, dimly lit and usually dingy, *tabagis* (convenience stores) line the streets of every town and township in Mauritius – they're an essential part of the local lifestyle. If you have yet to visit one, the unusually popular Bambous is the perfect place to lose your *tabagi* virginity. Customers come to visit Amrita, the proprietor, who is constantly dishing out her signature rotis while Bollywood heroines clink their bejewelled costumes on the TV screen. Amrita herself is quite the anomaly – it's very rare for a woman to run her own business in the less-developed parts of the country.

Shyam   MAURITIAN €
(✍764 2960; rotis & dhal puris Rs 10; ⊙11am-4pm) For the best *dhal puri* in town, look no further than Shyam (you can call him 'Sam'). He scoots around town scooping out flavourful snacks from an empty aquarium tank on the back of his motorbike. On Monday you'll find him at the market, and he always makes an appearance at the public schools when the students are set free from class in the afternoon. If you're desperate for *dhal puri*, just give him a ring and he'll come find you.

Pyramide   STREET FOOD €
(Map p108; ✍631 9731; Rue de Labourdonnais; kebabs Rs 50, small/large briani Rs 80/110; ⊙9.30am-4pm or 5pm Mon-Sat) This hero of the street-food scene is located beside the petrol station at the market grounds. Delicious *briani* (a rice dish cooked in a steel pot with various eastern spices and meat or fish) and 'kebabs' (salad, meat and sauce in a baguette) seem to emerge from the kitchen in factory proportions as fishermen and hawkers queue for a midday nibble. Whether eating in or having take away, order at the small counter on the right as you enter. Kebabs come with or without chilli and are spectacularly good whichever way you have them.

L'Ajoupa   MAURITIAN, INTERNATIONAL €
(Map p108; ✍290 1268; Rue du Souffleur; snacks & mains Rs 35-250; ⊙10.30am-3pm & 6.30-10pm Thu-Tue) L'Ajoupa is worth an honourable mention for its homely tree-lined garden

hidden behind a scratched picket fence – the perfect place to catch up with friends for a drink and some *poisson frit* (fried fish), rice or a burger.

Saveurs de Shin CHINESE, MAURITIAN €
(Map p108; ☑ 631 3668, 751 5932; Rue de Suffren; mains Rs 150-370; ☺10am-3pm & 6-10pm Wed-Mon) This place a block back from the water may not look like much but the quality is high, the prices are low and servings large – a winning combination in anyone's language. The half/full Peking duck is outrageously good value at Rs 450/800, but you could choose anything from this extensive menu and not be disappointed.

La Colombe MAURITIAN €
(Map p108; ☑631 8594; Rue des Hollandais; mains Rs 175-300; ☺11am-3pm & 6-9.30pm) Disco lights, kitsch decor and smiling staff await you at this lively venue located on a side street set back from the promenade. House specials include venison, wild boar and a smattering of seafood. Things liven up a bit on Saturday, which is occasionally *séga* night.

Chez Patrick MAURITIAN, CHINESE €
(Map p108; ☑631 9298; Royal Rd; mains Rs 225-275; ☺11.30am-3pm & 6-10pm) Patrick's is popular with locals and tourists for its unpretentious atmosphere and authentic Creole cooking. There's everything from octopus curry to Creole clams, and the seven-course seafood feast (Rs 625) is one of the south's best bargains, even if three of those courses are taken up by French fries, salad and vegetables.

Les Copains d'Abord MAURITIAN, SEAFOOD €€
(Map p108; ☑631 9728; Rue Shivananda; mains Rs 250-975; ☺9am-11pm) Hands down the best-located dining option in town (and the only one that has any real sense of nightlife), Les Copains d'Abord occupies an enviable position along the seafront promenade on the south side of town. Tasty Mauritian dishes (think fresh seafood curry, flavourful *rougaille saucisses* or wild boar ribs in Rodrigues honey), smart decor and frequent fits of live music will help you quickly forget that the menu is at times overpriced.

Getting There & Away

Mahébourg is an important transport hub. There are express buses every half-hour to/from Port Louis (Rs 35, two hours), from where there are connections to Grand Baie and other destinations. Most but not all of these buses stop at the airport en route; check before boarding. A shuttle to Blue Bay runs roughly every 30 minutes.

Buses running north from Mahébourg go to Centre de Flacq via Vieux Grand Port every 20 minutes or so. Heading south, there are less frequent services to Souillac via Rivière des Anguilles.

A taxi for the 15-minute hop from SSR international airport to Mahébourg costs Rs 500. You'll pay Rs 1500 to reach Port Louis, Rs 1500 to reach Flic en Flac and Rs 1300 for Belle Mare.

Getting Around

You'll find a variety of local car renters who also offer rides to the airport nearby. Your accommodation can hook you up with a vehicle.

Pointe d'Esny & Blue Bay

Mahébourg may be short on sand but Pointe d'Esny and Blue Bay more than make up for it. With one of the most beautiful stretches of beach on the entire island, this area has become one of the favoured spots for private villas and charming *chambres d'hôtes*. Pointe d'Esny is also the jumping-off point for those interested in visiting the nature reserve on Île aux Aigrettes.

Sights

Blue Bay Marine Park

In an effort to protect the area's rich underwater forest of rare corals from encroaching development, the government has given Blue Bay 'marine park' status. Besides a mandate barring high-speed watercrafts it seems that conservation plans are a bit laissez-faire and local environmentalists fear that irreversible coral bleaching is inevitable, which is a shame as this is the best snorkelling spot on the island.

There are no 'official' tours of the marine park like on Île aux Aigrettes – the protected patches of coral can be easily explored on a snorkelling outing or on an excursion aboard a glass-bottom boat (figure on around Rs 200 per person for one hour).

Île aux Aigrettes

This popular ecotourism destination is a 26-hectare nature reserve on an island roughly 800m off the coast. It preserves very rare remnants of the coastal forests of Mauritius and provides a sanctuary for a range of endemic and endangered wildlife species.

Visits are only possible as part of a guided tour.

As the guides to Île aux Aigrettes rightly point out, this is the last place in Mauritius where you can see it as the first explorers did almost five centuries before – everywhere else, the land has been tamed. Many of the animals and plants are unique to the area, like Aldabra giant tortoises, ebony trees, wild orchids and the endangered pink pigeon. The Mauritian Wildlife Foundation (p112) manages the reserve and conducts tours.

◉ Île des Deux Cocos

Île des Deux Cocos sits at the edge of the azure lagoon and was once used by Sir Hesketh Bell, the flamboyant British governor, to entertain guests. Today, the Lux hotel group has maintained the tradition of entertaining visitors by offering tourists a relaxing day of swimming, beach lazing and snorkelling. Welcome drinks, an immense buffet lunch and rum tasting are also included. Travellers with serious cash to burn can rent out the island's sole villa (constructed by Bell over a century ago) for an eye-popping €2000 per night, give or take a few hundred depending on the season. Transport to the island can be arranged by any of the Lux hotels. Visit www.iledesdeuxcocos.com for more information.

🏃 Activities

Boat Excursions

Just like Mahébourg to the north, Blue Bay is home to a variety of boat operators that offer journeys on glass-bottom boats and excursions to the nearby islands. Travellers should be careful, however, when choosing a boatswain here – the area has seen an increased number of drug dealers and addicts in recent years; always seek a recommendation from a local or your hotel before handing over any money. Also, the tides vary greatly in this part of the island; only a knowledgeable tour leader will know the optimal times for going to sea. In addition to the following, Jean-Claude Farla (p107) in Mahébourg is an excellent choice. Alternatively you can ask at

---

THE ÎLE AUX AIGRETTES STORY

In 1985, the Mauritian Wildlife Foundation (MWF; p112) took out a lease on Île aux Aigrettes, and began the difficult task of ridding it of introduced plants and animals, including rats and feral cats. They also began a massive planting program, removing introduced plant species and reintroducing native plants. Until the Foundation began their work, it was a popular place for day trips and most native plant species had been cut down for firewood. One exception was a small but significant stand of ebony forest. The forest survives, including some trees that may be 400 years old, and most guided tours pass through this forest.

With the habitat on its way to being restored, the foundation was able to bring some of the most endangered species in Mauritius to the island in the hope that they would find refuge and breed in a suitable natural habitat free from predators. Along with other sites, such as Round Island (off the north coast) and Black River Gorges National Park (in the southwest of Mauritius), the island became a bulwark against extinction, not to mention a stunning success story. The island is now home to, at last count, 43 pink pigeons (out of a total of just 400 left in the wild today), 34 olive white-eyes (out of 100 pairs) and 150 Mauritian fodies (out of 400). On most guided visits, there's a good chance of seeing the pink pigeon, but you'll need luck to see the other species.

Interestingly, not all endangered species made it here – the Mauritian kestrel was introduced here but didn't find the habitat to be suitable (the canopy was too low and there was not enough prey) and so they crossed the water and found more suitable habitats on the main island, including nearby Kestrel Valley (p119) and Vallée de Ferney (p118).

Other stars of the show include the 23 adult Aldabra or Seychelles tortoises (as well as a number of young), the last of the giant Indian Ocean tortoise species and one of very few places in Mauritius to see these soulful giants in the wild. Note also the five or so caged (and endangered) Mauritian fruit bats and around 450 Telfair's skinks (an important competitor for the Indian shrews, the only remaining mammal species on Île aux Aigrettes).

For more information on the endangered wildlife of Mauritius, see the box on p141.

your accommodation for additional recommendations – Le Preskîl, for example, runs outings on its private catamaran (available to nonguests as well).

Totof
BOAT TOUR

([image: phone] 751 1772, 790 3626; boatotof@yahoo.com; day trip per person incl lunch Rs 1800) In Blue Bay try Totof, an exuberant character who promises a memorable day of snorkelling, island-hopping and barbecues. He can also arrange evening cruises upon demand.

Diving

There are several dive sites of note lurking off the southeastern coast of Mauritius. These scuba hot spots – mostly wall dives and drop-offs – have interesting rock formations that plunge to 40m and attract a good amount of colourful fish. The most noteworthy sites are Colorado and Roches Zozo ('*zozo*' is Creole for bird; the site was named for the swarms of avians that orbit the area while swooping down to snag shallow fish).

Coral Diving
DIVING

(Map p104; [image: phone] 604 1084; www.coraldiving.com; lagoon/sea dive Rs 1800/2000; ⊙ 9am-5pm Mon-Sat, to 1pm Sun) Friendly Tony, one of the most knowledgeable divers in Mauritius, runs Coral Diving, the southeast's main scuba operator. It is primarily located on the sandy grounds of Le Preskîl hotel. The sea dive includes pool training for beginners.

Croisières Turquoise
SNORKELLING

(Map p104; [image: phone] 631 1640; www.croisieres-turquoise.com; Coast Rd; per person Rs 2100) Day-long boat trips to Île aux Cerfs departing from the Pointe Jerome embarkation point close to Le Preskil at 9.30am and returning at 4.30pm. The price includes snorkelling and a barbecue lunch.

🧭 Tours

Mauritian Wildlife Foundation
GUIDED TOURS

(Map p104; MWF; [image: phone] 631 2396; www.ile-aux-aigrettes.com; Coastal Rd, Pointe Jerome; short/long tour incl boat transfer Rs 800/1500; ⊙ booking office 9am-4pm Mon-Sat, to noon Sun; guided tours 9.30am, 10am, 10.30am, 1.30pm & 2pm Mon-Fri, 9.30am, 10am & 1.30pm Sat, 9.30am & 10am Sun) The Mauritian Wildlife Foundation manages the reserve and conducts tours of Île aux Aigrettes (revenues are ploughed back into its conservation efforts). The usual tours take between 1½ and two hours and start from Pointe Jérome, around 250m southeast of Le Preskîl hotel. Longer tours of two

to 2½ hours are also available which allow you more time on the island and let you meet some members of the scientific teams working on the island. Day tours that cross the line into volunteering are also possible. Bookings for either tour should be made a couple of days in advance by phoning the MWF, via email or in person at the booking office opposite the embarkation point. The tour of the island involves a good deal of walking; wear comfortable shoes and bring a hat, sunscreen and water. At the end of the tour there is a small museum and shop.

🛏 Sleeping

Pointe d'Esny and Blue Bay are among the epicentres of tourism in the south and there's a lot to be said for staying here. Close to the airport and to the charms of Mahébourg, the area also has a good mix of upmarket resorts, apartment complexes and charming *chambres d'hôtes*. And did we mention that the beaches are some of the best in the country? The area's one slight disadvantage is the rumble of departing planes from the nearby airport; there aren't many, but they can be awfully grumbly.

EasyRent
BOOKING SERVICE

([image: phone] 452 1010; www.easyrent.mu) Manages a variety of high-quality properties in the area, mostly at the upper end of the market.

Chez Henri
GUESTHOUSE €

(Map p104; [image: phone] 631 9806; www.henri-vacances.com; Coastal Rd; r incl breakfast Rs 1800; ✳@) Staying at Henri and Majo's welcoming *chambre d'hôte* feels like a trip to the countryside to visit your long-lost uncle and aunt. Rooms are lovingly filled with loads of wood and wicker, and each one sports a useful kitchenette. Don't miss the excellent three-course dinners (Rs 500 to Rs 600) served on the patio – it's a great opportunity to meet the other guests and listen to Henri recount his various adventures while rattling off an endless stream of double entendres (it helps if you speak French though).

★ L'Oiseau du Paradis
GUESTHOUSE €€

(Map p104; [image: phone] 729 3577, 631 5496; www.oiseauduparadis.com; Coastal Rd; standard/comfort r incl breakfast from €58/78, bungalow without breakfast €85; ✳@🖥✻) Our pick of Pointe d'Esny's coterie of guesthouses is undeniably stylish and remarkably homely. Rooms are coated in soothing colours and feature an eclectic mix of rustic wooden touches (stylish lamps and nightstands) and thoroughly modern fixtures (bucket sinks and rain showers). Although it's located on the far side of the coastal road, guests have access to the stunning beach via the owner's private villa across the street.

Pingouinvilla APARTMENTS €€
(Map p104; ☑637 3051; www.pingouinvillas.com; Rue Daurades, Blue Bay; studio €40-50, apt per week €45-60; ✹🔊) Charming complex of fully equipped apartments a few blocks back from the beach. Maid service twice per week.

Chantemer GUESTHOUSE €€
(Map p104; ☑631 9688; www.chantemer.mu; Coastal Rd; r incl breakfast €50-95) Attractive and well-run private guesthouse with a lovely garden leading down to the beach. All very tastefully decorated with family heirlooms and art, and Indra is an engaging hostess.

Noix de Coco GUESTHOUSE €€
(Map p104; ☑631 9987; www.noixdecocoguesthouse.com; Coastal Rd; r incl breakfast €63-81; ✹) Dorette has opened her charming home to travellers. Several rooms have sea views, though you'll spend most of your time lounging on the sand-swept terrace.

Villa Vakoa VILLA €€
(Map p104; ☑431 1099, 727 3216; villavakoa@gmail.com; villa €150-300; ✹🟰) Large two-storey property located 300m south of Le Preskîl, with travertine floors, an American-style kitchen and spacious bedrooms. Sleeps six.

Le Jardin de Beau Vallon HISTORIC HOTEL €€€
(Map p104; ☑631 2850; www.lejardindebeauvallon.com; Rue de Beau Vallon; s/d Rs 2500/3800, bungalows s/d 2300/3200; ✹🔊) Beau Vallon is primarily known for its charming restaurant (p114) set on the ground floor of an 18th-century colonial manor house. There are, however, several rooms on the property that make for a memorable vacation experience, as long as you don't mind being a 10-minute drive to the beach. Perched above the restaurant are two welcoming suites that draw their decorative inspiration from Madagascar and East Asia – vibrant tapestries tumble down the walls and four-poster beds are ensconced in a tornado of silky streamers. Several newer bungalows are arranged in a row just beyond the main building and are adorned with plantation-style incarnations of wood and wicker.

Le Preskîl RESORT €€€
(Map p104; ☑604 1000; www.lepreskil.com; Pointe Jérome; s/d incl half board from €165/207;

✹@🔊🟰) An unparalleled position on a secluded spit of sand? Check! A friendly staff that operates with Swiss efficiency? Check! Romantic views of the turquoise lagoon and rolling jungle mountains? Check! This four-star resort – with a subtle Creole design scheme – seems to have hit all the right notes and, after an extensive renovation, we can't find a reason not to stay at this slice of paradise. In addition to the usual bevy of watersports and activities, Le Preskîl boasts a popular kids club, expert scuba diving and a private catamaran shuttling vacationers to the nearby marine park and Île aux Cerfs.

Shandrani LUXURY HOTEL €€€
(Map p104; ☑603 4343; www.shandrani-hotel.com; s €324-600, d €432-592; ✹@🔊🟰) On the south side of Blue Bay, this relaxed and family-friendly resort rambles across a private peninsula garnished with luscious jungle foliage. It has no fewer than three beaches and boasts all the facilities you would expect from a heavy hitter in the top-end category: four restaurants, a golf course, tennis courts, a dive centre and more. It's the only five-star property on the island offering all-inclusive accommodation, which admittedly gives the hotel a slightly negative cruiseship-like stigma.

🍴 Eating

Despite the palpable residential vibe, Pointe d'Esny and Blue Bay have a few noteworthy options spread along the coastal road.

Jonquille Maryse MAURITIAN €
(Map p104; Chez Maryse; ☑978 8211; Coastal Rd; mains from Rs 250; ⊙11.30am-3pm & 6-9pm) After winning a 'women's empowerment' grant from the Mauritian government, friendly Maryse and her family opened a small restaurant in her backyard. Savoury Creole eats are stewed under her yellow tin roof and served to contented customers gathered around the haphazard collection of tables. The restaurant is across the street from L'Oiseau du Paradis.

Blue Bamboo ITALIAN, MAURITIAN €€
(Map p104; ☑631 5801; Coastal Rd; pizza Rs 240-390, mains Rs 380-480; ⊙11.30am-3pm & 6-11pm) Blue Bamboo has many charms: a cosy plant-filled cloister, delicious pan pizza, friendly owners and an inviting lounge on the 2nd floor. The upstairs bar is open every day, except Monday, from 6pm to midnight. In high season it's best to call ahead if you're eyeing a table in the bamboo-lined courtyard.

MAURITIUS POINTE D'ESNY & BLUE BAY

Le Bougainville
MAURITIAN €€

(Map p104; ✆ 631 8299; Coastal Rd; mains Rs 250-400; ⊙ 10am-10pm) Worth a mention for its breezy terrace, friendly atmosphere and convenient location across from Blue Bay beach, Le Bougainville is a popular hangout for locals and tourists alike. The menu is vast with salads, pizza, fish, curries etc.

Le Jardin de Beau Vallon
MAURITIAN €€

(Map p104; ✆ 631 2850; Rue de Beau Vallon; mains Rs 200-600; ⊙ noon-3pm & 7-10pm) Emerging from an inland thicket of trees and sky-scraping cane leaves, Beau Vallon is an enchanting colonial estate that has been carefully and lovingly refurbished over the last few decades. Romantic dark-wood panelling, flavourful island spices and the lazy spin of frond-shaped ceiling fans elicit fantasies found on the pages of a Ripling passage. Now if only the staff could be as charming and demure as the surrounds...

❶ Getting There & Around

Buses to and from Mahébourg run every 30 minutes. A taxi there will cost Rs 300, and it's Rs 600 to the airport.

All of the area's guesthouses can arrange car hire. Try Henri at **JH Arnulphy** (✆ 631 9806; www.henri-vacances.com) who offers cars from Rs 1450 per day. Arnulphy can also help with bicycle hire; rates start at Rs 150 per day.

South Coast

Mauritius' southern coast features some of the country's wildest and most attractive scenery. Here you'll find basalt cliffs, sheltered sandy coves, hidden falls and traditional fishing villages where fisherfolk sell their catch at roadside stalls. Beyond the shoreline lie endless sugar-cane fields and dense forests that clothe the hillsides in a patchwork of vibrant greens.

The region is known as Savanne and is noticeably devoid of any prominent towns save Rivière des Anguilles and Souillac. Both can be used as bases from which to explore the nearby parks and preserves, though we recommend staying elsewhere and visiting the far south during a day trip aboard a private vehicle.

Souillac

POP 4413

The largest settlement along the south coast is Souillac, 7km from Rivière des Anguilles.

The town itself has little to offer, but the clutch of (somewhat) interesting sights beyond just about make it worth a day trip. Souillac is named after the Vicomte de Souillac, the island's French governor from 1779 to 1787.

⊙ Sights

La Roche Qui Pleure
NATURAL LANDMARK

(Map p104; The Crying Rock) Right at the end of the headland after Gris Gris beach, 600m further on and well signposted, La Roche Qui Pleure resembles a crying man – you'll have to stand there puzzling it out for quite some time, and the waves really have to crash for the 'tears' to come out, but it's oddly satisfying when you finally get it.

Robert Edward Hart Museum
MUSEUM

(Map p104; ✆ 625 6101; ⊙ 9am-4pm Mon & Wed-Fri, to noon Sat) **FREE** Robert Edward Hart (1891–1954) was a renowned Mauritian poet, apparently appreciated by both the French and the English, although we've yet to meet anyone who's heard of him. His house, La Nef, is an attractive coral-stone cottage which was opened to the public as the Robert Edward Hart museum in 1967. On display are some originals and copies of Hart's letters, plays, speeches and poetry, as well as his fiddle, spectacles and trusty Britannic toilet. His award from the National Institute of Sciences for services to 'telepathy, hypnotism and personal magnetism' could do with some explanation. Sadly the captions are only in French. This is definitely rainy-day tourism.

Rochester Falls
WATERFALL

Rochester Falls are by no means the country's most spectacular falls, but they are worth a detour if you're in the area. Follow the makeshift signs from Souillac – the route is rather circuitous but reliable nonetheless, although it's a rough ride along the stone-strewn track. Prepare yourself for hawkers who want a tip for telling you where to park your car. The gushing cascade emerges from the cane fields after a five-minute walk from your vehicle.

🏖 Beaches

Gris Gris Beach
BEACH

Head east along the road past the Robert Edward Hart museum and you come to a grassy cliff top, which affords a view of the black rocky coastline and broken reef. A path leads down to the wild and empty

LE SOUFFLEUR

Le Souffleur, a hidden attraction known only to locals, requires a bit of gumption (and a 4WD) to tackle. But if you ask anyone in the know, they'll all say that it's well worth the adventure.

Situated on the coast about halfway between Souillac and Blue Bay, this geological anomaly is a half-formed grotto on the side of a cliff that spouts a geyser-like fountain of water (up to 20m in the air!) when the seas are rough. As the waves crash against the cliff the seawater pushes through a crack in the bluffs like a blowhole on a whale. If the seas aren't particularly rough during your visit, there's a natural land bridge nearby that's worth a camera click or two. It was formed when the roof collapsed on another naturally formed grotto.

To reach the super-secret souffleur, head for the Savannah sugar estate near the village of L'Escalier, cross the estate, then follow the snaking track once you reach the sea. Even if you don't seek permission to cross the sugar estate, which you probably should, we highly recommend bringing a local with you – otherwise you may never find the place.

Gris Gris beach; a wooden sign warns of the dangers of swimming here. The term *gris gris* traditionally refers to 'black magic', and looking at the tortuous coastline, you can see how the area got its name. Then again, another story suggests that the beach was named after the puppy (!) of a French cartographer who visited in 1753.

🛏 Sleeping & Eating

The best sleeping option in the area is the Andréa lodges bordering the Union Ducray Sugar Estate. The other choices are rather lacklustre and attached to popular eating establishments. If you're eating by the sea in Gris Gris, opt for something with seafood – it was probably caught offshore about 12m away.

Andréa & l'Exil   CABINS €€

(Map p104; Relais des Lodges; ☑471 0555; www.relaisdeslodges.com; s incl half board Rs 3000-4110, d incl half board Rs 4620-6340; ✳✭) The properties of Andréa and l'Exil each have a collection of 10 lovely cottages. The units at Andréa, along the sea, have gabled roofs and glass-panelled walls facing the rugged Ireland-esque coast. There's also an inviting swimming pool and reputable restaurant on-site.

Perched high in the hills, l'Exil's cache of serene bungalows has a distinctive adobe ranch–style architecture. Five rooms offer views of the distant sea while the other five face the rumbling waterfall nearby (a 20-minute walk) – all are surrounded by luscious fruit-bearing trees. Room rates include a guided hike through the interior forest beyond the sea of sugar cane. Guests can

also arrange 4WD excursions, quad biking and tours of the neighbouring sugar estate can be organised between December and June. At the time of research only the lodges at Andréa were open for visitors, although l'Exil should be back up and running fairly soon – check the website for updates.

Le Gris Gris   MAURITIAN, SEAFOOD €

(Map p104; Chez Rosy; ☑ 625 4179; Gris Gris Beach; mains Rs 150-290; ⊙11.30am-3pm) Rosy's place is a simple affair with a motley assortment of wicker and plastic furniture. The food, however, never misses the mark – locals and tourists rave about home-cooked Mauritian and Chinese dishes.

Le Rochester Restaurant   MAURITIAN €

(Map p104; ☑ 625 4180; mains Rs 275-400; ⊙noon-3pm & 6-9pm Wed-Mon, noon-3pm Tue) The charming Madame Appadu, who once ran the Cabane en Paille restaurant at the Vallée des Couleurs, now has her own family restaurant in an old colonial building by the bridge to Surinam. A delightful mix of Creole, Indian and Chinese staples are served on a shady terrace situated atop a gushing ravine. Upstairs you'll find three small guest rooms (singles/doubles including breakfast Rs 900/1600), but they're nothing to write home about.

Escale des Îles   MAURITIAN, SEAFOOD €€

(Map p104; ☑625 7014; mains Rs 250-450; ⊙11.30am-3pm & 6-9pm) Next door to Rosy's and slightly more serious (the staff wear uniforms), Escale des Îles is set within a brightly coloured building and has a popular sea-facing patio. There are a couple of rooms above the restaurant (doubles Rs 500), but we'd rather stay elsewhere.

Le Batelage MAURITIAN €€
(Map p104; ☑625 6084; Village des Touristes, Port Souillac; mains Rs 600-1250; ☉noon-3pm & 6-9pm) Drop down off the main road at the western end of Souillac for a lovely waterside eating experience. The food (the usual mix of Mauritian staples and seafood) is a touch overpriced, but it's still worth it for the setting.

❶ Getting There & Around

There are buses roughly every half-hour from Mahébourg to Souillac via the airport and Rivière des Anguilles. From Port Louis, buses run hourly, calling at Rivière des Anguilles en route. There are also frequent services to/from Curepipe, with three buses a day taking the coast road via Pointe aux Roches. Buses heading along the coast to Baie du Cap depart hourly.

Bel Ombre

Despite being miles from the bucket-and-spade atmosphere of Flic en Flac or Grand Baie, Bel Ombre has quickly developed into a cosy tourist bubble along the wild southern shores.

🏃 Activities

Domaine de Bel Ombre ADVENTURE
(Map p104; ☑ 623 5522; www.domainedebelombre.mu) The main attraction in Bel Ombre is the Domaine de Bel Ombre, an open nature reserve set on the old sugar plantation, which was developed by Charles Telfair between 1816 and 1833. Today it's a multifaceted venture with a brilliant golf course, Integrated Resort Scheme (IRS) properties, ruins from a colonial mill and the Valriche Nature Reserve – a haven for quad biking, hiking and touring on 4WDs.

🛏 Sleeping

The sumptuous Domaine de Bel Ombre also features two five-star hotels, Heritage Le Telfair and Heritage Awali, both run by Verandah Resorts.

Heritage Le Telfair LUXURY HOTEL €€€
(Map p104; ☑601 5500; www.heritageresorts.mu; s/d from €268/383; ❊@⊜⊜) The Heritage Le Telfair has perfectly captured the luxury and grandeur of the island's colonial yesteryears, with stately rooms, expansive grounds, exceptional service and an unrelenting attention to detail.

Heritage Awali LUXURY HOTEL €€€
(Map p104; ☑601 1500; www.heritageresorts.mu; s/d from €232/330; ❊@⊜⊜) The Heritage Awali celebrates an African heritage, with abounding masks, drums and tribal art. There's also an on-site golf course and spa complex for the ultimate indulgence.

 Eating

Le Château Restaurant FUSION, MAURITIAN €€€
(Map p104; ☑623 5522; mains from Rs 1200; ☉noon-3pm Mon-Thu, noon-3pm & 6.30-9pm Fri & Sat) The Domaine del Bel Ombre reserve has two lovely restaurants: an elegant dining venue at the golf club with views of the manicured greens, but we prefer Le Château Restaurant, set in a stunning conversion of the old Bel Ombre plantation house. This is the place for an exceptional meal of traditional Franco-Mauritian cuisine with contemporary flourish.

❶ Getting There & Away

There is regular bus service from Curepipe to Bel Ombre via Nouvelle France and Chemin Grenier.

Baie du Cap

POP 2400

The coastline between Baie du Cap and the stunning Le Morne Peninsula is some of the most beautiful in the country, and blissfully free of development. The only sights in the area besides the casuarina-lined beaches are a couple of low-key monuments. The first is the **Trevassa Monument**, about 1km beyond Bel Ombre village, which commemorates the sinking of the British steamer *Trevassa* in 1923. She went down 2600km off Mauritius. Sixteen survivors were eventually washed ashore at Bel Ombre after surviving 25 days in an open lifeboat.

The second is the **Matthew Flinders Monument**, which stands on the shore 500m west of Baie du Cap. It was erected in 2003 to honour the 200th anniversary of the arrival of Matthew Flinders, an English navigator and cartographer. He was less warmly received at the time; the poor bloke didn't know that England and France were at war and he was swiftly imprisoned for six years. For an interesting read on the subject, take a look at Huguette Ly-Tio-Fane Pineo's book *In the Grips of the Eagle: Matthew Flinders at the Île de France, 1803–1810*.

Bus services along here are limited. Baie du Cap is the terminus for buses from Souillac and Quatre Bornes (via Tamarin). Buses run approximately every 20 minutes.

Around the South Coast

The South Coast's hinterland has enough fascinating attractions to fill at least a day, with a wildlife park, some fine examples of colonial architecture and a take on the coloured-earth phenomenon, not to mention some fine hotels.

◉ Sights

La Vanille ZOO

(Map p104; ⚑ 626 2503; www.lavanille-reserve. com; adult/child Mon-Fri Rs 350/200, Sat & Sun Rs 200/90; ☺ 9.30am-5pm) This exciting zoo and reserve makes for a fantastic field trip with the kids. The park has the greatest number of giant tortoises in captivity in the world (over 1000), a result of a wildly successful breeding program for the Aldabra and radiata species. Chances are that you'll see the former breeding in front of your eyes. Almost as impressive as the tortoises is the unbelievably gigantic display of creepy-crawlies in the insectarium – it's worth coming to La Vanille just to check out this immense collection of mounted critters (over 23,000 species!). There's also a farm of Nile crocodiles (population 2000) which can grow up to 7m. Allow at least one hour for a complete visit.

The on-site **Hungry Crocodile Restaurant** (La Crocodile Affamé; mains Rs 250-650; ☺ 11am-5pm) specialises in all things crocodilian – croc curry, croc burger, croc fritters in a salad, croc cooked in a vanilla sauce... It also does more-conventional dishes like spaghetti bolognaise and beef burgers. Don't forget your mozzie repellent – you won't be the only one feasting at the lunch table.

La Vanille lies around 2km south of Rivière des Anguilles and is clearly signposted in the town.

St Aubin HISTORIC BUILDING

(Map p104; ⚑ 626 1513; www.saintaubin.mu; admission without/with restaurant set menu Rs 450/1100; ☺ 8am-4pm Mon-Sat) If you're following La Route du Thé, then the final stop after Bois Chéri is St Aubin, an elegant plantation house that dates back to 1819; it originally sat alongside the factory but was moved in the 1970s so that its owner could get a quieter night's sleep. The estate no longer produces sugar, but in the gardens of the house there is a traditional rum distillery and a nursery growing anthurium flowers and vanilla – you'll learn all about the fascinating history of vanilla production on the guided tour.

The height of the St Aubin experience is a meal at the wonderfully charming **table d'hôte** (mains Rs 375-1250; ☺ noon-3pm) in the main manor house. The dining room is one of best throwbacks to colonial times – dainty chandeliers cast ambient light over the white tablecloths and antique wooden furniture. The set menu showcases the fruits of the plantation: hearts of palm, pineapple, mango and chilli, to name a few. Reservations are recommended.

If you wish to stay the night, the on-site **Auberge de St Aubin** (per person incl half board Rs 2200-3200; ✱) has three rooms in the plantation manse across from the estate's main building. The bedroom at the front of the house perfectly captures the charming colonial ambience with creaky wooden floors and cotton gauzing over the four-poster bed – the two rooms in the back are noticeably more modern and have a bit less character.

LA ROUTE DU THÉ

La Route du Thé (www.larouteduthe.mu) offers tourists a window into the island's plantation past by linking together three of the island's remaining colonial estates. The first stop is the Creole manse-turned-museum at the Domaine des Aubineaux (p61) near Curepipe. Then the route veers south to the vast Bois Chéri Tea Plantation (p118). The final stop is the stately St Aubin, with its lush gardens and rum distillery. Despite the itinerary's name, the focus of the trip extends far beyond tea – each stop has a charming *table d'hôte*, a museum and the St Aubin even offers period-style accommodation.

True architecture buffs and historians should consider doing the route backwards and tacking on the resplendent Eureka (p59) estate at the end of the journey.

La Vallée des Couleurs NATURAL LANDMARK
(Map p104; ☑ 251 8666; www.lavalleedescouleurs.com; Mare Anguilles; adult/child Rs 250/125; ☉ 9am-5pm) Despite having 23 colours, as opposed to seven at Chamarel (p96), La Vallée des Couleurs is the less impressive of the island's two 'coloured earths'. The reserve does, however, have a scenic nature trail that passes some trickling waterfalls, memorable vistas, crawling tortoises and blossoming tropical flowers. It takes about an hour to complete the reserve's circuit.

Bois Chéri Tea Plantation MUSEUM
(Map p104; ☑ 507 0216; www.saintaubin.mu; admission without/with restaurant set menu Rs 400/700; ☉ 8.30am-4.30pm Mon-Fri, to 2.30pm Sat, restaurant 10.30am-3.30pm) This 250-hectare tea factory and museum is located about 12km north of Rivière des Anguilles amid an endless acreage of cane. Visitors can take an hour-long tour of the tea-processing facility, which ends with a stop at a small exhibition space annotating the island's tea history through machines and photos. The best part of the visit is undoubtedly the sampling session at the end. It's advisable to plan your trip during the morning as most of the action takes place before noon. After your tour, stick around for lunch – the in-house **restaurant** takes a formidable stab at gourmet cuisine and uses locally sourced ingredients. The commanding views over the riverine plains are also quite captivating.

🛏 Sleeping & Eating

Also consider the options at St Aubin and the restaurant at La Vanille.

Shanti Maurice LUXURY HOTEL €€€
(Map p104; ☑ 603 7200; shantimaurice.com; St Felix; r from €280; ❄@🛜🏊) One of the loveliest places to stay along the southern coast, the Shanti Maurice has large rooms, all of which face the sea.

Green Palm Restaurant INDIAN €€
(Map p104; ☑ 625 8100; Coastal Rd, Riambel; mains Rs 200-475; ☉ 11am-3.30pm & 6.30-10.30pm) Well-regarded Indian cuisine in a pleasant setting west of Souillac in the sleepy hamlet of Riambel. The beach is lovely so eating here means you can make a day of it. They're especially proud of their range of *naan* breads.

Southeast Mauritius

North of Mahébourg, the main road hugs the coast as it winds around the base of Lion Mountain (480m) and the Montagnes Bambous range. This area was the first settled by the Dutch early in the 17th century, and was one of the first parts of the country to lose its native ebony forest to the burgeoning sugarcane industry. Nevertheless, dense forest still cloaks the mountains. In recent years, several wealthy locals have purchased large tracts of land and turned them into forest reserves, tourist attractions and designated hunting grounds.

The best way to explore the region is by private vehicle; most tour operators can hook you up with a half- or full-day visit to any of the region's *domaines*. Opting for public transport is also possible, though significantly less convenient. Buses between Mahébourg and Centre de Flacq ply the coast road, passing through Vieux Grand Port, Anse Jonchée and Bambous Virieux. There are departures every 20 minutes or so.

Vallée de Ferney

Vallée de Ferney (Map p104; Ferney Valley; ☑ 729 1080, 634 0440; www.valleedeferney.com; admission without/with guided tour Rs 340/575, 4WD tour Rs 1093; ☉ 10am-3pm, guided tours 10am & 2pm) protects a 400-year-old forest. While that should be reason enough to visit, this is also an important habitat for the endangered Mauritius kestrel, one of the world's most at-risk raptors. A well-marked 3km trail winds through part of the forest, passing a number of viewpoints en route. We recommend taking the guided tour to make the most of your visit as your guide will point out fascinating flora and fauna that you may otherwise miss. But even if you don't pay for a guide you'll need to take the 4WD transfer from the park office to the trailhead – these leave every half hour. 4WD explorations of

---

A FAMOUS BATTLE

The sleepy Mauritian town of Vieux Grand Port may seem a long way from Paris, but this place has history. Not only is this where the story of human settlement on Mauritius began, the town is even more famous as the site of the only French naval victory to be inscribed on the Arc de Triomphe in Paris. Relics of the 1810 battle with the English are on display at the National History Museum (p107) in Mahébourg.

LION MOUNTAIN

Overlooking Vieux Grand Port and clearly visible from Mahébourg is Lion Mountain (480m), immediately recognisable from its sphinxlike profile. The mountain offers a splendid half-day hike with stunning views over the coast. It's a challenging but rewarding walk that climbs up the lion's 'back' to finish at an impressive viewpoint on the 'head'. We recommend hiring a local guide, though if you decide to go it alone you'll find the trailhead beside the police station at the north of Vieux Grand Port. Check out www.fitsy.com for detailed GPS information about the hike, though the main trail is fairly obvious and runs straight along the ridge and up over a rocky area to the peak. There are a few hairy scrambles over the rocks before you reach the flat area on the lion's head. From here you can see right across the interior of the island. Return the same way you came up. Allow three to four hours for the return trip.

the reserve are also possible. The walking trail begins and ends at the thatch-roofed **restaurant** (Vallée de Ferney Wildlife Reserve; mains from Rs 400; ⊘9am-4pm) where they serve up locally sourced venison vindaloo or roast venison.

As an important habitat for endemic species, Vallée de Ferney promises to be an important conservation and ecotourism area over the coming years. The Mauritian Wildlife Foundation (p139), which helps to train the guides here and provides important input into the reserve's policies, has ambitious plans to reintroduce a number of endangered species here, including the pink pigeon and echo parakeet.

The Ferney Valley is also well known as the site of a recent conservation demonstration that ignited when a Chinese paving company sought to construct a highway directly through the protected hinterland. Attempts at development were unsuccessful but scars remain – trees daubed with red paint alongside the walking trail signify those that were to be chopped down to make way for the road.

The turn-off to the 200-hectare reserve is clearly marked along the coastal road, around 2km south of Vieux Grand Port.

Domaine de l'Étoile

Teetering between the east and southeast realms of the island, the popular **Domaine de l'Étoile** (Map p104; TerrOcean; ☑448 4444, 7291050; www.terrocean.mu) forest reserve is set on over 2000 hectares of unspoilt terrain – the perfect hinterland to explore by horse, on foot or by quad bike. Mountain biking, guided hikes and archery are also on offer. Enjoy a bite at the on-site **restaurant** and, if you're lucky, you'll spot several Javanese

stags hiding in the forest – there are over 1000 living in the reserve.

Vieux Grand Port

POP 2962

'Old Grand Port' is the cradle of Mauritian history, the place where the first human inhabitants of the island landed on 9 September 1598 under the command of Wybrandt Van Warwyck. The Dutch later built a fort 3km further north in what is now the town of Vieux Grand Port, although a **monument** marks the actual landing point further south as well. It was the local headquarters of the Dutch East India Company until 1710, when the Dutch abandoned the island. The site was then taken over by the French.

The battered ruins of **Fort Frederik Hendrik** stand in a park near the church at the northern end of Vieux Grand Port and include the remains of an old Dutch church, a bakery, a prison, a forge, a powder magazine and a dispensary. A few clay pipes, wine bottles and other items left behind by both the Dutch and French occupants are now on display in the **Frederik Hendrik Museum** (Map p104; ☑634 4319; ⊘9am-4pm Mon-Sat) FREE. The museum also outlines the history of the Dutch in Mauritius.

Kestrel Valley

The scenic **Kestrel Valley** (Map p104; Domaine d'Anse Jonchée; ☑634 5011; www.kestrelvalley.com) is primarily a hunting reserve for Javanese deer. The 950 hectares of forested mountain terrain also act as a reserve for many endemic bird species, including the Mauritius kestrel – one of the world's rarest birds of prey. A portion of the reserve has been blocked off for hikers – there are four marked trails (from 2km to 6km long) that wind through the park.

The estate was closed for renovations when we visited, including its well-regarded restaurant and thatched bungalows. Call ahead to see if they've reopened.

Note that the reserve used to be known as the Domaine du Chasseur – the park now called Domaine du Chasseur is near the town of Nouvelle France.

THE EAST

Known by the rather romantic sobriquet of La Côte Sauvage (The Wild Coast), the island's east coast is a world away from the touts, nightclubs and souvenir shacks of Flic en Flac in the west and Grand Baie in the north. It does have its resorts, yes, but the east face of Mauritius feels blissfully untouched by mass tourism. Best of all, some of the island's very best beaches line this quiet coast. Not surprisingly, this is the most exclusive side of the island, and the congregation of luxury hotels attracts the kind of crowd likely to take a helicopter transfer from the airport when they arrive.

The closest the east comes to a resort is Trou d'Eau Douce, which has retained the feel of a sleepy fishing village despite rubbing shoulders with the grand hotels next door. It's the jumping-off point for the wildly popular Île aux Cerfs.

❶ Getting There & Around

The main transport hub for east Mauritius is the inland town of Centre de Flacq. You'll have to change here if you're arriving by bus from Port Louis, the Central Plateau towns or Mahébourg in the south. There are onward connections from Centre de Flacq to villages along the east coast, although some services are pretty infrequent. You can bank on bus transport from Centre de Flacq to Palmar and Poste Lafayette (with continuing service to Rivière du Rempart) but there are no buses to Belle Mare. Figure on at least Rs 500 for a taxi between the coastal towns and Centre de Flacq.

Most hotels and guesthouses have bikes for rent. Otherwise, you can rent bikes from any of the travel agencies in Trou d'Eau Douce. Car rentals can easily be arranged through your accommodation.

Trou d'Eau Douce

POP 5478

'Sweet water hole' sits at a set of major crossroads making it the unwitting tourism hub on this side of the island. It's a lovely little place, if a bit melancholic, where fishermen unravel their nets after a morning at sea and housewives walk around with baskets of vegies balanced on their heads. The sea is a stunning shade of blue here, but Trou d'Eau Douce's claim to fame is its easy access to the massively popular Île aux Cerfs, a favoured destination for day-tripping tourists. As a result, this seaside township makes a great base for exploring the east coast – especially for those on a tighter budget.

◎ Sights & Activities

Two of the island's best golf courses are here – the Touessrok's fairway masterpiece on Île aux Cerfs and the Ernie Els–designed dreamscape in the Anahita complex.

Natural Spring   SPRING
(Map p122) The actual *trou d'eau douce* for which the town is named can be found in a man-made stone hole next to the national coast guard's office. To find the natural spring, follow the fork in the main road away from the Gothic church as it slopes down the hill to the docks – the well is on the right side. Locals visit the stash of fresh water when the government supply gets corrupted after a strong storm.

Victoria 1840   ART GALLERY
(Map p122; ☑ 480 0220; www.maniglier.com; Victoria Rd; ☺ noon-3pm & 7-10pm Mon-Sat) Worth a look, Victoria 1840 is an old sugar mill that has been lovingly refurbished to house some of the works of Yvette Maniglier, a bewitching

❶ DIVING IN THE EAST & SOUTHEAST

There are very few dive centres in the island's east and south, but most major resorts can put you in touch with one. Otherwise, check online at www.msda.mu for a list of licensed and insured dive operators. The following are fabulous places to dive. To read more about these and other sites in the area, see p28.

➡ Colorado, off Pointe d'Esny & Blue Bay

➡ Roches Zozo, off Pointe d'Esny & Blue Bay

➡ Passe de Belle Mare, off Belle Mare

SCENIC DRIVE: THE HEART OF THE ISLAND

The divide between coastal Mauritius and the island's interior can be stark, but the small scale of everything here means that it's easy enough to experience both on a rather short drive.

Begin anywhere in the east and make your way to the regional centre of **Riviere de Rempart**. From there, head southwest, passing through small towns (some barely discernible) such as **Belle Vue Maurel** and **Barlow**; the signage can be a little confusing, but until you pass Barlow, follow the signs to Port Louis along the B21. After Barlow, the views open up with some decent views of the inland mountain where you're headed. At the crossroads around 11km after leaving Riviere de Rempart, turn left towards 'La Nicolière'. A lovely honour guard of trees arcs over you for around 2km, whereupon you take the right-turn, again following the signs for **La Nicolière**.

The traffic thins as you pass through more sugar-cane fields (no Ashok Leyland buses at last!), before crossing the dam wall. After the wall, the road climbs alternating between lovely thick forest and some fine views out over the coastal plains to the east. After around 4.5km of climbing, the road crosses a plateau haired with agriculture. At the T-junction (look for the 'Selazi Forest Service' sign). Around 2km further on, turn left at the T-junction, following signs for St-Pierre. You're largely back to civilisation with all the attendant construction, sugar cane and traffic, but it's worth it for the views away to the west from **Ripailles** and its approach – **Calebasses** (632m), **Pieter Both**, **Grand Peak** and **Le Pouce** are all stunning.

From Ripailles it's downhill all the way – literally. In St-Pierre, you could turn left (east) and return to the east of the island via Quartier Militaire. Another alternative is to pause in Moka to visit the tranquil tropical mansion of Eureka (p59).

French painter who spent a year under the wing of Matisse. The juxtaposition of industrial brick and splashy modern art works surprisingly well and is best appreciated while dining at the in-house restaurant, Le Café des Arts (p124). The mill-gallery is signposted from the stone Gothic church in the town centre.

🛏 Sleeping

There's more choice in and around Trou d'Eau Douce than anywhere else on the east coast, and you'll find a decent range of budget and midrange accommodation. The area's upmarket sleeps are, for the most part, a little way out of town and you'll need a taxi or private vehicle to reach them.

There is an endless parade of luxury hotels that march along the east coast all the way up to the northern part of the island.

Le Dodo APARTMENT €
(Map p122; ☑ 480 0034; christa0307@hotmail. com; Royal Rd; apt €20-30; ❄) Le Dodo is like an orphanage for outdated furniture, with decor that is horribly mismatched, but somehow it all seems to work. The owner is kind and the apartments come fully outfitted with retro fixtures. Ask for one of the apartments higher up – although there's no

elevator, the views over the cluttered village and azure sea are memorable.

Villa La Fourche APARTMENT €
(Map p122; ☑ 480 1194; www.villalafourcheltee. blogspot.com; 2-bedroom apt from €50; ❄❄) Tucked down a back street away from the coastal buzz, this quiet option is a good deal for large families, but the furnishings need updating.

★ Tropical Hotel Attitude HOTEL €€
(Map p122; ☑ 480 1300; tropical-hotel-mauritius. com; Royal Rd; s/d from €85/132; ❄@❄❄) Part of the Attitude chain, this place on Trou aux Douce's outskirts is a reshingly accessible slice of semi-luxury right on the waterfront. The rooms have a white-linen look and most face the sea. Highly recommended.

Les Toits Verts GUESTHOUSE €€
(Map p122; Chez Roseline Duvivier; ☑ 752 5552, 480 0503; rduvivier@intnet.mu; studio/apt per week €280/630; ❄❄) There are no signs directing travellers to this address – you'll have to keep your eyes peeled for the signature *toits verts* (green roofs). And boy will you be glad you made the effort! This is one of the best deals in Trou d'Eau Douce, and not just because of its seaside location (a rarity in the area). The charmingly decorated rooms have

The East

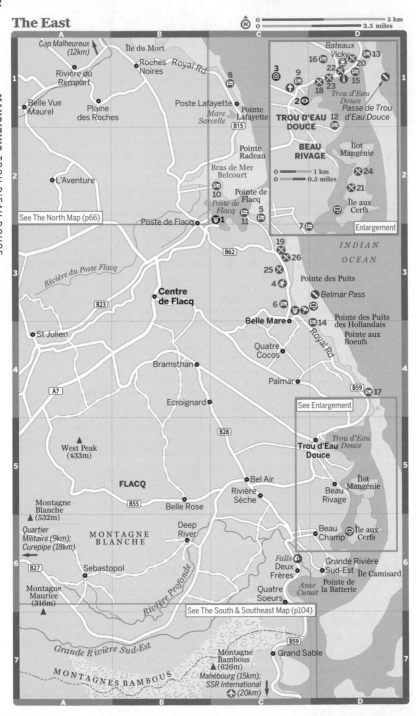

N
0 — 5 km
0 — 2.5 miles

Cap Malheureux (12km)

Île du Mort
Roches Noires
Royal Rd

Rivière du Rempart

8

Poste Lafayette
Pointe Lafayette

Belle Vue Maurel

Plaine des Roches

B15

Mare Sarcelle

Bateaux Vicky

16 22 20 13
3 9 23 15
   18 i

Trou d'Eau Douce
Passe de Trou d'Eau Douce

TROU D'EAU DOUCE

12

BEAU RIVAGE

Îlot Mangénie

0 — 1 km
0 — 0.5 miles

24

21

L'Aventure

Pointe Radeau

Bras de Mer Belcourt

10

Pointe de Flacq

5

11

Poste de Flacq

Poste de Flacq

1

Île aux Cerfs

7

Enlargement

19
26

25
4

INDIAN OCEAN

Rivière du Poste Flacq

B62

Pointe des Puits

Belmar Pass

B23

Centre de Flacq

6

Belle Mare

14

Pointe des Puits des Hollandais
Pointe aux Boeufs

St Julien

Quatre Cocos

Bramsthan

Palmar

Royal Rd

B59
17

Ecroignard

A7

See Enlargement

B28

Trou d'Eau Douce

Trou d'Eau Douce

West Peak (433m)

FLACQ

Bel Air

Rivière Sèche

Beau Rivage

Îlot Mangénie

Montagne Blanche (532m)

B55

Belle Rose

Quartier Militaire (9km); Curepipe (18km);

Deep River

MONTAGNE BLANCHE

Beau Champ

Île aux Cerfs

B27

Sebastopol

Rivière Profonde

Falls
Deux Frères

Grande Rivière Sud-Est
Île Camisard

Montagne Maurice (316m)

Quatre Soeurs

Anse Cunat

Pointe de la Batterie

See The South & Southeast Map (p104)

Grande Rivière Sud-Est

B59

Montagne Bambous (626m)

Grand Sable

MONTAGNES BAMBOUS

Mahébourg (15km); SSR International (20km)

See The North Map (p66)

Poste de Flacq

The East

all the mod cons and sit between the lapping waves and a lush, well-tended garden.

Villa Mahé
VILLA €€€

(Map p122; ☑452 1010; www.easyrent.mu; Royal Rd; villa €250-300; ❋🌐) For a spot of luxury at a very reasonable price, go for this endearing holiday home owned by the Montocchio family. There's a certain beachy charm about the place with its weathered white-wood exterior and slap-shut colonial shutters. The semidetached house sleeps 10 people and has stunning sea views from the wooden balconies.

Four Seasons Resort at Anahita
LUXURY HOTEL €€€

(Map p122; ☑402 3100; www.fourseasons.com/mauritius; Beau Champ; villas incl breakfast €750-5000; P❋@🌐🏊) Located in Beau Champ, slightly south of Trou d'Eau Douce, the Four Seasons Resort is part of a vast luxury complex known as Anahita. The draw at Anahita is the clutch of IRS bungalows, which offers foreigners the chance to purchase their very own piece of paradise – you'll see signs advertising these sales all across the island. For those who are looking for something a bit more temporary, the resort features a beautiful assortment of holiday villas. The design scheme plays with local materials, like tropical timber and volcanic rock, while seamlessly integrating every modern convenience. Four stone-cut pools, a spa and a stunning golf course are also big draws.

Le Touessrok
LUXURY HOTEL €€€

(Map p122; ☑402 7400; www.letouessrokresort.com; s €370-520, d €490-1430, ste €530-6280, villa don't even ask; P❋@🌐🏊) Where to begin? Le Touessrok has one of the best resort reputations on the island, and the accolades are well deserved. Rambling across a sandy peninsula, the hotel blends Moorish-inspired architecture to the thick patches of surrounding jungle. While amenities are undoubtedly aplenty, the resort distinguishes itself from the rest of the five-stars with its two offshore islands: the famous Île aux Cerfs and the totally exclusive, Robinson Crusoe–style hideaway, Îlot Mangénie. Don't forget to ask a staff member where the name 'Touessrok' comes from – we're pretty sure you'll be as surprised with the down-to-earth answer as we were.

🍴 Eating

Trou d'Eau Douce is the kind of place where you'll do perfectly fine just grabbing a chair and table at the first joint you stumble upon. It's a town of fishermen after all, so stick with the seafood. If you're looking for a more upmarket experience, you can't go wrong with any of the restaurants at Le Touessrok.

Palais de Chine
CHINESE €

(Map p122; Royal Rd; boulettes Rs 6; ⊙11am-9pm) Those lovely little piping-hot, steamed dumplings that are part-Chinese and now wholeheartedly Mauritian – *boulettes* – are pretty much all they serve at this place. A bowl of them, drowned in soup and served with chilli sauce makes for a fine, basic meal that has little to do with haute cuisine and has everything to do with satisfying hungry locals.

★ Chez Tino   MAURITIAN €€
(Map p122; ☑ 480 2769; Royal Rd; mains Rs 150-600; ☺10.30am-10pm Mon-Sat, lunch Sun) Pufferfish hanging in vast numbers from the ceiling greet you downstairs but head for the wonderful terrace on the first floor for the best views. They dish out superb meals of Mauritian cooking with a heavy focus on seafood (*langouste* in particular). Stand-out dishes include octopus curry with green pawpaw or seafood in Creole sauce. Tino also has a few rooms (without/with breakfast Rs 800/1000) on offer if you're looking for a place to spend the night.

Green Island Beach Restaurant   INTERNATIONAL €€
(Map p122; ☑251 7152; Royal Rd; mains Rs 200-525; ☺noon-2.30pm & 6-9pm Tue-Sun) The decor may be a little sparse, but the friendly staff and delicious assortment of international faves more than make up for it. Have some *rougaille saucisses* with a slice of pizza – the menu is extensive and everything's well priced.

Le Four à Chaud   SEAFOOD €€
(Map p122; ☑480 1036; www.lefourachaudresto. com; Royal Rd; mains Rs 525-1650; ☺noon-3pm & 7.30pm-midnight Sun-Fri, 7.30pm-midnight Sat) This is the smartest place in central Trou d'Eau Douce – head here for an evening of feasting on *fruits de mer* and a fantastic list of matched wines. Reserve ahead to get one of the few balcony tables with sea views, and note that the menu is exclusively seafood. The name is a play on words (it's opposite the old lime kiln, or *four à chaux*).

Le Café des Arts   MAURITIAN €€
(Map p122; ☑480 0220; www.maniglier.com; Victoria Rd; menu Rs 3400; ☺noon-3pm & 7-10pm Mon-Sat) This intriguing dining option is located within an old mill that has been transformed into Victoria 1840, an oddly charming gallery space. Crisp white cloths are draped over the tables and canvases of wicked brushstrokes adorn the cracked brick walls. The food, a modern nod to traditional island flavours, mirrors the old-meets-new surrounds.

ⓘ Information

Mauritius Tourism Promotion Authority
(MTPA; ☑480 0925; www.tourism-mauritius. mu; Royal Rd; ☺9am-4.30pm Mon-Fri, to 2.30pm Sat) Has a kiosk at the public beachfront near Le Four à Chaud restaurant but is of very little help as it only provides general

---

CATAMARANS & YACHT CRUISES

A catamaran day trip is one of the most popular activities in Mauritius. Hundreds of tourists each day board boats to zoom around the azure lagoon and wavy seas or stop at offshore islets and shallow reefs. Many such excursions include barbecue lunches and/or time for snorkelling.

The most romantic option is the sunset cruises offered by most operators. If you're looking for something a bit more traditional, you'll find myriad fishermen in Mahébourg and the surrounding beaches who have transformed their vessels into mini leisure crafts. Most operators include buffet lunches, alcohol and snorkelling. Make sure to shop around before choosing your cruise – some catamarans are not licensed to stop on any islands. Most cruises can be booked through tour agents and hotels. Check out www.mauritiuscatamaran.com for more information.

Some of the more popular excursions include:

➡ Île aux Cerfs – a stunning island off Trou d'Eau Douce on the east coast. Departures are also possible from Mahébourg. Île aux Cerfs is a good option for those who suffer from motion sickness as the boat never leaves the calm lagoon waters.

➡ Îlot Gabriel and Île Plate – Grand Baie is another major hub of cruise activity with dozens of vessels head for the wee islands in the north. These are probably our pick of the cruising options as the reefs are pristine, the beaches quieter and competition keeps the prices less inflated.

➡ Île aux Bénitiers – on the west side of the island, this popular cruising option is a half- or full-day trip with the possibility of dolphin-watching.

information about the island and a few brochures. It does not have details about getting to Île aux Cerfs and will simply refer you to the private operators.

Thomas Cook Foreign Exchange (Royal Rd; ⊘8.30am-4.30pm Mon-Sat)

❶ Getting There & Around

There are no direct buses between Port Louis and Trou d'Eau Douce – you'll need to change at Centre de Flacq, from where onward services to Trou d'Eau Douce run roughly every half-hour. Taxis cost around Rs 500 from Centre de Flacq, Rs 1800 to the airport and Rs 1600 to Port Louis.

SATURDAY NIGHTS ON ÎLE AUX CERFS

Taking a cue from Ibiza and Nikki Beach, the management of Le Touessrok turns the sands of Île aux Cerfs into a raging dance floor every Saturday night between October and March. The all-night romp fest starts at 11pm and DJed beats blare until 5am. Admission costs Rs 500 and includes boat service and one drink.

Île aux Cerfs

Like Marilyn Monroe and Cleopatra, Île aux Cerfs' killer looks have triggered its demise. Once sparsely populated by *cerfs* (stags; imported for hunting from Java), this picturesque island is now overrun with touts and tourists baking under the tropical sun or lazing in the perfect, gin-clear waters. The obtrusive crowds and general summer-camp vibe may be off-putting at first, but few people realise that the island boasts over 4km of sandy bliss. Hike a mere kilometre down the beach and you'll uncover an idyllic ocean vista all to yourself.

Much of the island's interior belongs to the stunningly manicured 18-hole golf course belonging to Le Touessrok (p123) – perhaps one of the most scenic spots to tee off in the world. Nonguests are welcome to play, although advance bookings are essential. Green fees are free for hotel guests, and €89 for everyone else for 18 holes. Island guests are politely asked to stay off the greens and fairways lest they be conked in the head by a soaring Titleist.

✖ Eating

All of the boat operators to Île aux Cerfs can arrange pricey barbecue lunches as part of their excursions. If you've just paid for the boat and no extras, either take food for a picnic or consider the island's two eating options.

La Chaumière Masala   INDIAN €
(Map p122; mains Rs 250-360; ⊘noon-3pm) This memorable dining experience offers Indian dishes refined to the European palate. Tables are perched in trees.

Paul & Virginie   SEAFOOD €€
(Map p122; mains Rs 400-500; ⊘noon-3.30pm) This is a sociable spot, located at the water-

sports centre and serving a scrumptious assortment of fresh fish and seafood. Popular with tour groups.

❶ Getting There & Away

Guests of Le Touessrok (p123), including those who have reserved a round of golf, get whisked over to the island for free on the hotel launch. Lesser mortals must choose from a variety of dizzying transport options and despite what the signs say, there is no public ferry to Île aux Cerfs – all services are run by private operators.

Dozens of boat operators run by former fishermen in Trou d'Eau Douce offer a water-taxi service to the island for Rs 350 round trip. Ask at your accommodation to be set up with a reliable option or try **Bateaux Vicky** (☎754 5597; bateauxvicky@yahoo.com; Royal Rd; ⊘9am-5pm). The taxi boats run roughly every 20 to 30 minutes between 9am and 4pm, with the last boat back at 5pm (the island 'closes' to visitors at 5pm sharp). The trip takes between 15 and 30 minutes depending on your point of departure. It's not necessary to book ahead. Many of these local operators also offer a side trip to the waterfalls at Grande Rivière Sud-Est (Rs 600) and/or a beachside barbecue on the island (Rs 1000 to Rs 1600 depending on your choice of food).

The other way to reach the island is on a popular catamaran day trip, which usually includes snorkelling, sunbathing and an expansive barbecue lunch. Check out www.mauritiuscatamaran.com for a list of day-trip options.

Belle Mare & Palmar

North of Trou d'Eau Douce as far as Pointe de Flacq, a 10km-long beach includes some of the best white sand and azure ocean in Mauritius. Unsurprisingly, the area is also home to an impregnable string of luxury resorts, although there are stretches of public beach, including around 4km and 8km north of Trou d'Eau Douce.

MAURITIUS BELLE MARE & PALMAR

◉ Sights & Activities

Hindu Temple
HINDU TEMPLE

(Map p122; ☺ dawn-dusk) Besides the endless vistas of azure, the area doesn't boast a whole lot when it comes to sights other than a white Hindu temple that sits on a teeny islet tenuously tethered to the mainland by a thin land-bridge. The views of the dazzling white bastion are best appreciated from Rasoi (p128), the Indian restaurant at Le Saint Géran.

Watersports

Mauritius' east coast has a few notable dive sites, including **Belmar Pass** nearby. The area's five-star hotels – including Le Saint Géran and Belle Mare Plage – all have reputable scuba outfits. Visit www.msda. mu for a complete list of insured operators here.

Le Waterpark & Leisure Village
AMUSEMENT PARK

(Map p122; ☑ 415 2626; Royal Rd; adult/child Rs 450/250; ☺ 10am-3.30pm) For a fun half-day away from the beach, swing by Le Waterpark & Leisure Village, which offers rides, slides and thrills aplenty spread across 10 hectares of an old sugar estate.

Golf

The endless proliferation of top-end sleeps means that there are plenty of places to tee off in the area. In addition to the golf courses further south at Anahita and Le Touessrok (p123), you'll find greens at Belle Mare Plage and Le Saint Géran.

Spas

Most of Mauritius' top-end resorts have an on-site spa, but if you're looking for a unique pampering experience try the Pedi:Mani:Cure Studio.

Pedi:Mani:Cure Studio
DAY SPA

(Map p122; ☑ 401 1688; Le Saint Géran, Pointe de Flacq; ☺ 9am-8pm) This spa at Le Saint Géran was developed by renowned French podiatrist Bastien Gonzalez. The not-to-be-missed treatment (Rs 5500) invigorates and revives tired hands and feet, giving them a radiant glow.

🛏 Sleeping

The sandy beaches of Belle Mare and Palmar provide sea frontage for a long string of up-market hotels, each one an opulent attempt to outdo the next. In addition to the endless row of top-end resorts, vacationers will be delighted to find a cache of stately seaside villas.

Most resorts should be booked well in advance through a travel agent – the public rates (listed here) can cause the eyes to water.

★ Emeraude
HOTEL €€

(Map p122; ☑ 415 1107; emeraudebeach-hotel -mauritius.com; Belle Mare; s/d incl breakfast from €84/117; ❋ @ 🛜 🏊) Set in a breezy garden facing the public beach in Belle Mare, Emeraude is a breath of fresh air from the sky-high walls of the neighbouring five-star compounds. Some 20 semidetached and extremely comfortable cottage units with gabled roofs frame a sociable pool area, an open-air restaurant and a bar.

★ Le Saint Géran
LUXURY HOTEL €€€

(Map p122; ☑ 401 1688; lesaintgeran.oneandonly resorts.com; Pointe de Flacq; ste incl half board from €420; ❋ @ 🛜 🏊) There's no other way to say

---

BEST GOLF COURSES

No leisure island would be complete without a handful of world-class golf courses and Mauritius has some fine examples of the genre, many of which are the preserve of five-star resorts. Our favourite fairways include:

➡ Mauritius Gymkhana Club (p62), Vacoas – the oldest course in the Indian Ocean

➡ Four Seasons Resort at Anahita (p123), Trou d'Eau Douce – course designed by Ernie Els

➡ Le Touessrok (p123), Trou d'Eau Douce – on idyllic Île aux Cerfs

➡ Le Saint Géran (p126), Belle Mare – on the east coast

➡ Tamarina (p93), Tamarin – magnificent complex on the west coast

➡ Domaine de Bel Ombre (p116), Bel Ombre – perfectly maintained course along the south coast

it, Le Saint Géran is classic Mauritian luxury at its finest. And the clientele seems to agree. The resort sees more repeat customers than any other top-end hotel on the island (and these aren't your average vacationers – the guest list is a veritable who's who of movie stars and politicos). Spacious rooms, under the signature bright-blue roofs, are arranged along the seemingly endless oceanfront – everyone has a to-die-for view. Watersports are aplenty, there's a charming kids club for the little ones, and the top-notch butler service caters to every request. Le Saint Géran has set the bar unobtainably high in the dining category as well. Of the numerous on-site restaurants, world-class Rasoi (p128), an Indian eatery set on a stunning pavilion, is the pick.

Belle Mare Plage LUXURY HOTEL €€€
(Map p122; ☑402 2600; bellemareplagehotel.con stancehotels.com; Pointe de Flacq; s/d/ste from €150/200/250; ❋@🛜🏊) One of Mauritius' most delightful and exclusive hotels, the Belle Mare Plage quite simply ticks every box. Pass through the inviting lobby – scented with vanilla and ylang-ylang, no less – before uncovering an enviable beach and cache of top-notch amenities. Golfers relish the two championship-level courses and well-respected academy, spa fanatics purr like kittens while being pummelled by expert massage therapists, and gourmet buffs are sated at the superb Blue Penny Café.

Residence LUXURY HOTEL €€€
(Map p122; ☑401 8888; www.theresidence.com; Belle Mare; r from €291; ❋@🛜🏊) Evoking the forgotten grandeur of colonial India, the Residence's vast complex of hotel rooms occupies an enviable stretch of sand. Rooms are simply decorated – white drapery everywhere and framed Darwin-esque animal sketches on the walls.

★Le Prince Maurice LUXURY HOTEL €€€
(Map p122; ☑413 9130; princemaurice.constance hotels.com; Pointe de Flacq; r incl half board €400-10,000; ❋@🛜🏊) The sense of grace and perfect tranquillity is immediately striking as you pass through the entryway – this is a world unto itself that knows no limit to luxury. The lobby's seamless melange of marble architecture and flowing infinity pools can only be described as sublime, and the opulent suites, hidden just beyond, continue the timeless elegance. The abundance of open-air pavilions and elegant thatch is meant to

---

BELLE MARE VILLAS

If private villas are more your style, tucked betwixt the five-star grandeur of rambling resorts is a noteworthy selection – the perfect choice for those seeking solitude. Like the hotels next door, the villas come equipped with daily maid and concierge services (you can even request an in-house chef for an additional fee).

EasyRent (☑452 1010; www.easy rent.mu) and Idyllic Villas (www.idyllic -mauritius.com) manage a wide selection of properties, and costs range from €150 to €1000.

---

elicit the ancient days of the spice trade – modern amenities are cleverly hidden and butlers are dressed in muted tones as they move across the grounds catering to every whim. Swimming pools, spas, access to Belle Mare Plage's golf courses and a floating restaurant (you'll see) round out the amenities list.

🍴 Eating

As the hotels here are so all-encompassing, there is little incentive for guests to leave their resorts and dine elsewhere. All of the hotels, however, welcome nonguests to dine at their à la carte restaurants, and the choice is superb. Prices are high, but the quality is almost always unimpeachable and it's well worth stopping by for a special occasion.

East Side MAURITIAN, CHINESE €€
(Map p122; ☑415 1254; Royal Rd, Belle Mare; mains Rs 350-450; ☉11am-10pm) This roadside restaurant does OK seafood dishes, local fare such as octopus in saffron and a range of Chinese dishes. Nothing to write home about, but easy on the wallet and handy if you're driving down the east coast.

**Seasons Restaurant
& Bar** SEAFOOD, MAURITIAN €€
(Map p122; www.orchidvillas.mu; Royal Rd, Belle Mare; mains Rs 300-500; ☉noon-2.30pm & 6-9pm Tue-Sat, noon-2.30pm Sun) Part of the Orchid Villas complex, this roadside restaurant doesn't have sea views, but the food and service are both surprisingly good. Try the grilled lobster in Creole sauce and lemongrass emulsion.

Symon's Restaurant   SEAFOOD, MAURITIAN €€
(Map p122; ☑415 1135; Belle Mare; mains Rs 350-800; ⊙11am-10pm) The best option in Belle Mare beyond the all-star line-up of in-house hotel restaurants, Symon's serves up a variety of Indian, Mauritian and Chinese dishes. The views are ho-hum, but at least you won't break the bank and some dishes – such as octopus curry with coconut milk, or the grilled catch of the day – are outstanding.

★**Rasoi**   INDIAN €€€
(Map p122; ☑401 1888; Le Saint Géran, Pointe de Flacq; mains Rs 950-2400; ⊙12.30-3.30pm & 7-10pm) Rasoi is the brainchild of Vineet Bhatia, a Michelin-star chef who made a name for himself in the London restaurant scene. The dining area is situated on an open-air verandah made of slatted jungle trunks tucked under an awning of thatch. While appreciating the views of the lagoon, cane-draped hills and a Taj Mahal–like temple, guests savour a dynamic assortment of Indian-inspired dishes. The lunch menu features a more casual selection of *naan* wraps and seafood samplers (the salmon is breathtaking); dinner is decidedly more sophisticated; the highlight is the curry leaf and ginger-infused lobster tail. Reservations required.

Poste de Flacq & Poste Lafayette

POP 8522

Even quieter and more rugged than the sandy streamers of Belle Mare, this calm area bordering the island's north still has a distinctive Creole vibe and is generally unmarred by upmarket developers. Holidaymakers seeking tranquillity should look no further than the lovely selection of private villas dotting the stone-strewn coast.

🛏 Sleeping & Eating

With a noticeable lack of resorts, Poste de Flacq is a haven for upscale villa rentals that work out to be a much better deal than many of the luxury hotel packages (especially if you're travelling with friends and/or family). Contact **CG Villas** (☑262 5777; www.villas-maurice.com) to organise your stay – they manage a sizeable collection of beach houses in the area.

Besides the case-like superettes dotting the coastal road, there's only one restaurant of note in this area of the east coast. If you're staying at a villa and are interested in freshly caught seafood, ask your villa operator to contact one of the local fishermen – they'll deliver whole fish and *langoustes* directly to your door.

★**La Maison d'Été**   BOUTIQUE HOTEL €€
(Map p122; ☑410 5039; www.lamaisondete.com; Poste Lafayette; r incl breakfast €135; ❋@令❀) La Maison d'Été is ranked as one of Mauritius' top B&Bs on a certain trip-advising website, and we can definitely understand why. The Franco-Mauritian owners have hit the nail on the head; an effortless tropical charm pervades the collection of poolside rooms, each one decorated with tasteful tributes to island life. The property also has an inviting restaurant, Auberg'inn, two pools and its own private beach. They had plans to renovate not long after we were there so it may be about to get even better.

Auberg'inn   MAURITIAN €€
(Map p122; ☑410 5039; Poste Lafayette; pizzas Rs 250, mains Rs 290-1600; ⊙noon-3pm & 7-9.30pm Mon-Sat, 7-9.30pm Sun) La Maison d'Été's in-house restaurant is run like a stand-alone establishment serving up an enticing assortment of pasta, fish and 'fusion food' of the highest quality. The inn's owner often moonlights as the chef and takes special care when preparing locally sourced dishes matched with international wines. The menu is limited to pizza on Sunday evenings. Ring ahead for a reservation if you're not staying here. Highly recommended.

UNDERSTAND MAURITIUS

Mauritius Today

A symbol of just how Mauritius is travelling can be answered by a simple question: when was the last time Mauritius made international headlines? The answer, with one notable exception, is almost never. Despite a robust political culture, the country remains stable, democratic and relatively properous for the region.

The island's brief foray into the international media occurred in late March 2013, when intense rains swept across the island. While often in the path of cyclones and other vagaries of Indian Ocean weather, the rains left a trail of devastation in Port Louis – flooding, largely the result of blocked drains, left 11 people dead. The tragedy was a wake-up call for the authorities who, critics said, had failed to heed earlier warning signs that the island's infrastructure was at best poorly maintained and at worst inadequate.

On the economic front, the diversification of the Mauritian economy continues to pay dividends – although sugar is grown on 90% of the island's agricultural lands, it now accounts for just 15% of the country's exports. The sugar industry is being downsized and vast work forces have been laid off because of increased mechanisation or factory closures.

Former prime minister Paul Bérenger envisaged Mauritius enjoying a 'quantum leap' to a 'knowledge island' during his brief premiership, making Mauritius the Indian Ocean's internet hub, and while progress continues to be made along these lines, traditional agricultural activities, tourism and textiles continue to provide most of the jobs in the country. You can expect to see lots more call centres here (with much of the population speaking fluent Hindi or Mandarin there's plenty of scope for service industries for both China and India being based here) as well as IT free-trade zones. The banking industry – Mauritius' secret world of international money transfers and tax loopholes – also continues to see huge benefits for the economy despite the global downturn.

In difficult international economic conditions, the 3.4% growth of the country's economy in 2012 is a pretty respectable figure, while GDP per capita for Mauritians stood at an impressive US$15,600 in the same year. Unemployment was 8%, a figure that was the envy of many a European country during the same period.

History

Mauritius had no native population predating the European colonisers (unless you count the ill-fated dodo), and so unlike many other small islands for which colonisation resulted in the savage destruction of the native inhabitants a short period later, Mauritius' initial history is pleasantly guilt-free (again, unless you count the dodo), at least until the advent of slavery. This historical point is important to understanding the country's inclusive culture of tolerance and easy acceptance of all people: there's nobody in the ethnic melting pot able to claim precedence over the others. Broadly speaking, Mauritius experienced four distinct historical periods in its colonisation leading up to full independence from the UK in 1968.

The First Colonisers

Although Arab traders knew of Mauritius – which they rather unfairly called Dina Arobi (Isle of Desolation) – perhaps as early as the 10th century, the first Europeans to discover these uninhabited islands were the Portuguese, around 1507. They, too, were more interested in trade and never attempted to settle.

In 1598, a group of Dutch sailors landed on the southeast coast of the island at what is now called Vieux Grand Port, and claimed the island for the Netherlands. For the next 40 years the Dutch used Mauritius as a supply base for Batavia (Java), before deciding to settle near their original landing spot. Settlement ruins and a museum (p119) can still be seen at Vieux Grand Port, near Mahébourg.

The colony never really flourished, however, and the Dutch abandoned it in 1710. Nevertheless, they left their mark: the Dutch were responsible for the extinction of the dodo and for introducing slaves from Africa, deer from Java, wild boar, tobacco and, above all, sugar cane.

Île De France

Five years later it was the turn of the French, when Captain Guillaume Dufresne d'Arsel sailed across from what is now Réunion and claimed Mauritius for France. The island was rechristened Île de France, but nothing much happened until the arrival in 1735 of the dynamic governor Bertrand François Mahé de Labourdonnais, Mauritius' first hero. He not only transformed Port Louis into a thriving seaport, but also built the first sugar mill and established a road network.

It was around this time that Mauritius' best-known historic event occurred when the *St Géran* went down during a storm off the northeast coast in 1744. The shipwreck inspired Bernardin de St-Pierre's romantic novel *Paul et Virginie,* an early bestseller. For more on this legend, see the boxed text on p82.

As the English gained the upper hand in the Indian Ocean in the late 18th century,

DIEGO GARCIA & THE CHAGOSSIAN BETRAYAL

One of the most prolonged betrayals in British colonial history is that surrounding the secret exile of the Chagos Islanders from their homeland in the 1960s and 1970s, in order to lease the main island, Diego Garcia, to the USA for use as a military base.

The Chagos Islands were excised from Mauritian territory by the British prior to independence in 1965 and Mauritius and the UK continue to dispute sovereignty. The islanders were 'resettled' in Mauritius and the Seychelles between 1965 and 1973. Some 5000 now live in abject poverty in the slums of Port Louis, where they continue to fight for their right to return home. The islanders won derisory compensation of £4 million from the British in 1982, which was paid out to the poverty-stricken islanders in return for them signing away their rights – many of them not realising at the time what the legal documents they were signing meant.

In 2000 the High Court in London ruled that the Chagossians had been evicted illegally and upheld their right to be repatriated. Nothing happened, so the Chagossians went back to court. In October 2003 the judge rejected their claim for further compensation, though he acknowledged that the British government had treated the islanders 'shamefully' and that the compensation had been inadequate. In May 2007 the Chagossians won a further case at the Court of Appeal in London, in which the government's behaviour was condemned as unlawful and an abuse of power. The judges in the case also refused to place a stay on the ruling, meaning the Chagossians were free to return to all islands (with the exception of Diego Garcia itself) with immediate effect. In 2008 the case was overturned. The Chagos Archipelago has now been ceded to the US military until 2016, while the islanders continue to pursue their rights through the European Court of Human Rights.

John Pilger gives his angle on the story in his documentary *Stealing a Nation* (2004). You can watch it online at www.jonhs.net/freemovies/stealing_a_nation.htm. Further information and ways to help the Chagossians can be found here: www.chagossupport. org.uk. For additional information on the Chagos Islanders, check out David Vine's book *Island of Shame*.

Port Louis became a haven for pirates and slightly more respectable corsairs – mercenary marines paid by a country to prey on enemy ships. The most famous Franco-Mauritian corsair was Robert Surcouf, who wrought havoc on British shipping.

In 1789, French settlers in Mauritius recognised the revolution in France and got rid of their governor. But they refused to free their slaves when the abolition of slavery was decreed in Paris in 1794.

British Rule

In 1810, during the Napoleonic Wars, the British moved in on Mauritius as part of their grand plan to control the Indian Ocean. Things started badly when they were defeated at the Battle of Vieux Grand Port. Just a few months later, however, British forces landed at Cap Malheureux on the north coast and took over the island.

The new British rulers renamed the island Mauritius, but allowed the Franco-Mauritians to retain their language, religion and legal system, and the all-important sugarcane plantations on which the economy depended. The slaves were finally freed in 1835, by which time there were over 70,000 on the island. They were replaced or supplemented by labour imported from India and China. As many as 500,000 Indians took up the promise of a better life in Mauritius, often to find themselves living and working in appalling conditions on minimum pay.

By sheer weight of numbers, the Indian workforce gradually achieved a greater say in the running of the country. Their struggle was given extra impetus when Indian political and spiritual leader Mahatma Gandhi visited Mauritius in 1901 to push for civil rights. However, the key event was the introduction of universal suffrage in 1959, and the key personality Dr (later Sir) Seewoosagur Ramgoolam. Founder of the Labour Party in 1936, Seewoosagur Ramgoolam led the fight for independence, which was finally granted in 1968.

Independence

The prime minister of newly independent Mauritius was, not surprisingly, Sir Seewoosagur Ramgoolam. He remained in office for the next 13 years and continued to command great reverence until his death in 1986, since then a host of public buildings have been named in his honour.

The political landscape has largely been dominated by the trio of Anerood Jugnauth, the Indian leader of the Mouvement Socialiste Mauricien (MSM), the Franco-Mauritian Paul Bérenger, with his leftist Mouvement Militant Mauricien (MMM), and Navin Ramgoolam, son of Sir Seewoosagur and leader of the Mauritian Labour Party. The former two parties formed their first coalition government in 1982, with Jugnauth as prime minister and Bérenger as finance minister. In the years that followed, the two men were in and out of government, sometimes powersharing, at other times in opposition to each other, according to the complex and shifting web of allegiances that enlivens Mauritian politics. In 1995 and again in 2005, Navin Ramgoolam beat the MSM-MMM coalition with his Alliance Sociale coalition.

On the economic front meanwhile, Mauritius was undergoing a minor miracle. Up until the 1970s the Mauritian economy could be summed up in one word – sugar. Sugar represented more than 90% of the country's exports, covered most of its fertile land and was its largest employer by far. Every so often, a cyclone would devastate the cane crop, or a world drop in sugar prices would have bitter consequences.

From the 1970s the government went all out to promote textiles, tourism and financial services, much of it based on foreign investment. Soon Mauritius was one of the world's largest exporters of textiles, with Ralph Lauren, Pierre Cardin, Lacoste and other famous brands all manufactured on the island. Income from tourism also grew in leaps and bounds as the government targeted the luxury end of the market.

The strategy paid off. The 1980s and 1990s saw the Mauritian economy grow by a remarkable 5% a year. Unemployment fell from a whopping 42% in 1980 to less than 6% by 2000 and overall standards of living improved. Even so, rates of unemployment and poverty remained high among the Creole population (people of mixed Afro-European origin), many of whom also felt frustrated at their lack of political power in the face of the Indian majority. These tensions spilled out onto the streets of Port Louis in 1999, triggered by the death in police custody of the singer Kaya, an ardent campaigner for the rights of the disadvantaged Creole population. The riots brought the country to a standstill for four days and forced the government to make political concessions.

The Culture

Mauritius is often cited as an example of racial and religious harmony, and compared with most other countries it is. On the surface, there are few signs of conflict. However, racial divisions are still apparent, more so than in Réunion or the Seychelles. Tensions between the Hindu majority and Muslim and Creole minorities persist despite the general respect for constitutional prohibitions

MAURITIUS THE CULTURE

ETIQUETTE IN MAURITIUS

The people of Mauritius have a well-deserved reputation for being exceptionally tolerant – if you breach some unknown code of etiquette you're likely to be quickly forgiven. That said, there are a few 'rules' of behaviour that you should try and abide by.

Although beachwear is fine for the beaches, you will cause offence and may invite pestering if you dress skimpily elsewhere. Nude bathing is forbidden, while women going topless is tolerated around some hotel pools, but rarely on the beaches.

Mauritius has many temples and mosques. You are welcome to visit, but should dress and behave with respect: miniskirts and singlet tops are no-nos, and it is normal to remove your shoes – there's usually a sign indicating where to leave them. Many temples and mosques also ask you not to take photos, while some Hindu temples request that you remove all leather items, such as belts. At mosques, you may be required to cover your head in certain areas, so remember to take along a scarf. Never touch a carving or statue of a deity. If at any time you're unsure about protocol, the best thing to do is ask.

WOMEN IN MAURITIUS

➡ Maternal mortality rate per 100,000 live births: 60 (UK:12)

➡ Life expectancy at birth for men/women (years): 71.25/78.35

➡ Adult literacy for men/women (%): 90.9/86.2

➡ Youth unemployment for males/females (%): 19.4/29

➡ Average age of school completion for boys/girls (years): 13/14

➡ Female MPs as proportion of total: 18.4%

➡ Women over 25 years old with a secondary education: 45%

identity for many Mauritians, a strong sense of national identity in Mauritius transcends racial and cultural ties.

Of the various forces binding Mauritians together, the most important is language – not the official language of English, but Creole, which is the first language of 70% to 80% of the population and understood by virtually all Mauritians. Another common bond is that everyone is an immigrant or descended from immigrants with no community being able to lay claim to being the island's indigenous inhabitants. Food and music are also unifiers, as is the importance placed on family life. Mauritius is a small, close-knit community. Living in such close proximity breaks down barriers and increases understanding between the different groups. Respect for others and tolerance are deeply ingrained in all sectors of society, despite the occasional flare up of racial tension.

against discrimination and constitute one of the country's few potential political flash points, although these rarely simmer to the surface except during elections when political parties aren't averse to playing the race card.

Living Standards

As a result of the ongoing economic boom and political stability, overall living standards have improved in recent years and the majority of houses now have piped water and electricity. However, the gap between rich and poor is widening. It is estimated that the top 20% of the population earns 45% of the total income and that 10% lives below the poverty mark. A labourer's wage is just Rs 6000 per month, while a teacher might earn Rs 12,000. You'll find a few beggars around the markets and mosques, but the visible presence of poverty on the streets is relatively discreet.

Mauritians place great importance on education – not just to get a better job, but as a goal in its own right. Lawyers, doctors and teachers are regarded with tremendous respect. The pinnacle of success for many is to work in the civil service, though this is beginning to change as salaries rise among artisans and businesspeople.

A National Identity?

Despite being a relatively young country with a diverse population, and although ethnic identity is often a primary source of

Family Life & the Role of Women

In general, each ethnic group maintains a way of life similar to that found in their countries of origin, even if they are second- or third-generation Mauritian.

Often, several generations live together under one roof and the main social unit is the extended family – as witnessed by the size of family parties on a Sunday picnic. There is minimal social-security provision in Mauritius; people rely on their family in times of need. Mauritians are usually married by the age of 25. The majority of wives stay home to raise the family, while the husband earns the daily bread. Arranged marriages are still the norm among Indian families, while the Hindu caste system has also been replicated to some degree. Among all groups, religion and religious institutions continue to play a central role in community life.

As with elsewhere, this very traditional pattern is starting to break down as the younger generation grows more individualistic and more Westernised. They are far more likely to socialise with people from other communities, and intermarriage is on the rise. Other forces for change are the rise in consumerism and the emergence of a largely Indian and Chinese middle class. Middle-class couples are more likely to set up their own home and to have fewer children, while the wife may even go out to work. Statistics also show a slight decline in the number of marriages, while the divorce rate has doubled over the last 20 years.

Women's equality still has a long way to go in Mauritius. Many women have to accept low-paid, unskilled jobs, typically in a textile factory or as a cleaner. Even highly qualified women can find it hard to get promotions in the private sector, though they do better in the public service. In 2003 the government passed a Sex Discrimination Act and set up an independent unit to investigate sex discrimination cases, including sexual harassment at work. The unit's also charged with raising awareness levels and educating employers about equal opportunities.

People of Mauritius

Mauritius is made up of five ethnic groups: Indo-Mauritian (68%), Creole (27%), Sino-Mauritian (3%), Franco-Mauritian (1%) and the new kids on the block – South African expats (1%). Another small group you might come across are the Chagos Islanders.

INDO-MAURITIANS

The Indian population (the majority of which is Hindu) is descended from the labourers who were brought to the island to work the cane fields. Nowadays, Indians form the backbone of the labouring and agricultural community and own many of the island's small- and medium-sized businesses, typically in manufacturing and the retail trade. Central Plateau towns such as Rose Hill have a strong Indian flavour.

Indians also tend to be prominent in civic life. Local elections are always racially aligned, and since the Indians are in the majority, Hindus always win at the polls. The prime minister between 2003 and 2005, Franco-Mauritian Paul Bérenger, was the first non-Indian at the helm in the country's history, and he only managed that through a deal struck with his predecessor, Indian Anerood Jugnauth.

CREOLES

After the Indo-Mauritians, the next largest group is the Creoles, descendants of African slaves, with varying amounts of European ancestry. Creoles as a whole form the most disadvantaged sector of society. Despite the fact that all forms of discrimination are illegal under the Mauritian constitution, it is widely recognised that the Creole minority has been socially, economically and politically marginalised.

The majority work in low-paid jobs or eke out a living from fishing or subsistence farming. and it's a vicious circle. Creoles find it harder to get work, partly because of low levels of literacy, but few Creole children complete secondary school because they're needed to help support the family. Expectations are also lower – and so it goes on.

Rodrigues is the epicentre of Mauritian Creole culture, with Creoles making up 98% of the population.

SINO-MAURITIANS

Mauritius' 30,000 Sino-Mauritians are involved mostly in commerce. Despite their small numbers, the Chinese community plays a disproportionate role in the country's economy, though they tend to avoid politics. Most came to the country as self-employed entrepreneurs and settled in the towns (particularly Port Louis), though most villages have at least one Chinese store.

FRANCO-MAURITIANS & SOUTH AFRICAN EXPATS

Franco-Mauritians, the descendants of the *grands blancs* (rich whites), have their hands on Mauritius' purse strings. Most of the sugar mills, banks and other big businesses are still owned by Franco-Mauritians, who tend to screen themselves off from their former labourers in palatial private residences in the hills around Curepipe, and own almost all the luxurious holiday homes along the coast. Many others have decamped completely to live in South Africa and France. In fact, there are now more South African expats living on the island

KAYA

It was a black day for Mauritius, and a blacker one still for the Creole community. On 21 February 1999, the singer Joseph Topize (aka Kaya) was found dead in his police cell, seemingly a victim of police brutality, after being arrested for smoking cannabis at a pro-legalisation rally.

As the pioneer of *seggae*, a unique combination of reggae and traditional *séga* beats, Kaya provided a voice for disadvantaged Creoles across the country. His death in the custody of Indian police split Mauritian society along racial lines, triggering four days of violent riots that left several people dead and brought the country to a standstill.

An autopsy cleared the police of wrongdoing, but the events forced the Indian-dominated government to acknowledge *le malaise Créole*, Creoles' anger at their impoverished status in a country that has been dominated by Indians since independence. It is an anger that still simmers almost 15 years after the singer's death.

In contrast to these violent scenes, Kaya's music is full of positive energy. The classic album *Seggae Experience* is a tribute to the singer's unique vision.

(congregated on the west coast) than there are Franco-Mauritians.

Religion

There is a close link between religion and race in Mauritius and a remarkable degree of religious tolerance. Mosques, churches and Hindu temples can be found within a stone's throw of each other in many parts of the country and we know of one case in Floréal where they are separated only by a shared wall.

Official figures put the number of Hindus at 48% of the population, and all of these are Indian in origin or ethnicity. Festivals play a central role in the Hindu faith and the calendar's packed with colourful celebrations.

There's a certain amount of resentment against the Hindus in Mauritius, not for religious reasons but because the Hindu majority dominates the country's political life and its administration. Up until now, with the economy in full swing, this has merely resulted in grumbling about discrimination and 'jobs for the boys', but there's a fear this might change if the economy really begins to falter.

Around one-quarter of the population is Roman Catholic. Catholicism is practised by most Creoles, and it has picked up a few voodoo overtones over the years. Most Franco-Mauritians are also Catholic and a few Chinese and Indians have converted, largely through intermarriage.

Muslims make up roughly one-fifth of the population. Like the Hindus, Mauritian Muslims originally came from India. In Mauritius, where Islam coexists in close proximity to other religions, it tends to be fairly liberal, though attendance at mosque is high and many Muslim women wear the hijab.

Sino-Mauritians are the least conspicuous in their worship. The one big exception is Chinese New Year, which is celebrated in Port Louis with great gusto. There are a few Chinese temples scattered around Port Louis.

Arts

Mauritian architecture, literature and fine arts are all firmly based in the French tradition. The country's music, however, is African in origin and is very much alive and kicking.

LITERATURE

Mauritius' most famous contribution to world literature – one that has become entangled in the island's history – is the romantic novel *Paul et Virginie* by Bernardin de St-Pierre, which was first published in 1788 (see p82). An English translation of the novel is widely available in Mauritius. The author captures the landscapes beautifully, though his ultra-moralistic tearjerker is less likely to appeal to modern tastes.

Joseph Conrad's oblique love story *A Smile of Fortune,* collected in *'Twixt Land and Sea* (1912), is set in Mauritius, although it's hardly very flattering about the place. Set in the late 19th century it does, however, give a taste of the mercantile activity of the time and the curious mix of 'negroes', Creoles, 'coolies' and marooned Frenchmen who populated the island then. Visitors to the island will certainly identify with Conrad's description of Mauritius as the 'Pearl of the Ocean...a pearl distilling sweetness on the world', but will undoubtedly find the current inhabitants far more pleasant to deal with than the characters described in the story.

Those who want to read a 20th-century Mauritian novel should try something by Malcolm de Chazal, whose most famous works are *Sens Plastique,* available in translation, and *Petrusmok.* Chazal was an eccentric recluse, but he inspired a whole generation of local writers. His works are a highly original blend of poetry and philosophy, and are peppered with pithy statements, such as 'Avoid clean people who have a dirty stare'.

Of living writers, perhaps the best-known internationally is Carl de Souza. In his novel *Le Sang de l'Anglais* he looks at the often ambivalent relationship between Mauritians and their countries of origin, while *La Maison qui Marchait Vers le Large,* set in Port Louis, takes inter-community conflict as its theme. *Les Jours Kaya* is a coming-of-age book set against the violence following Kaya's death.

Other contemporary novelists to look out for include Ananda Devi, Shenaz Patel and Natacha Appanah-Mouriquand. Unfortunately, their works as yet are only available in French, which is regarded as the language of culture.

In more recent times, the French author JMG Clézio, whose father was Mauritian, has also set a number of novels in Mauritius, of which *Le Chercheur d'Or* (The Prospector) has been translated into English.

MUSIC & DANCE

You'll hear *séga* everywhere nowadays, but in the early 20th century it fell seriously out of fashion. Its revival in the early 1950s is credited to the Creole singer Ti-Frère, whose song 'Anita' has become a classic. Though he died in 1992, Ti-Frère is still the country's most popular *séga* star. More recent Creole groups and singers with a wide following include Cassiya, Fanfan and the prolific Jean-Claude Gaspard.

Séga evolved slightly differently in Rodrigues. Here the drum plays a more prominent role in what's known as *séga tambour.* The island's accordion bands are also famous for their surprising repertoire, which includes waltzes, polkas, quadrilles and Scottish reels. Over the years these were learned from passing European sailors and gradually absorbed into the local folk music. They're now an essential part of any Rodriguan knees-up.

A newer Mauritian musical form was invented by Creole musician Kaya in *seggae,* which blends elements of *séga* and reggae. With his band Racine Tatane, Kaya gave a voice to dissatisfied Creoles around the island. Tragically, the singer died in police custody in February 1999. Following in Kaya's footsteps, Ras Natty Baby and his Natty Rebels are one of most popular *seggae* groups; sales gained an extra boost when Ras Natty Baby was imprisoned for heroin trafficking in 2003.

SÉGA!

Séga is the powerful combination of music and dance originally conceived by African slaves as a diversion from the injustice of their daily existence. At the end of a hard day in the cane fields, couples danced the *séga* around campfires on the beach to the accompaniment of drums.

Because of the sand (some say because of the shackles), there could be no fancy footwork. So today, when dancing the *séga,* the feet never leave the ground. The rest of the body makes up for it and the result, when the fire is hot, can be extremely erotic. In the rhythm and beat of *séga,* you can see or hear connections with the Latin American salsa, the Caribbean calypso and the African origins of the people. It's a personal, visceral dance where the dancers let the music take over and abandon themselves to the beat.

The dance is traditionally accompanied by the beat of the *ravanne,* a primitive goatskin drum. The beat starts slowly and builds into a pulsating rhythm, which normally carries away performers and onlookers alike. You may be lucky enough to see the dance being performed spontaneously at beach parties or family barbecues. Otherwise, you'll have to make do with the less authentic *séga* soirees offered by some bars and restaurants and most of the big hotels, often in combination with a Mauritian buffet.

BEST COLONIAL ARCHITECTURE

The following colonial-era mansions are all open to the public and well worth visiting. Apart from the buildings' innate historical and aesthetic values, visiting them makes a statement that these are places of beauty *and* value, which may just lead to more of them being preserved.

➡ Eureka (p59), Moka

➡ Government House (p49), Port Louis

➡ Chateau Labourdonnais (p83), Mapou

➡ National History Museum (p107), Mahébourg

➡ Hôtel de Ville (p61), Curepipe

➡ Le Jardin de Beau Vallon (p114), Near Mahébourg

➡ Domaine des Aubineaux (p61), Curepipe

➡ St Aubin (p117), Rivière des Anguilles

➡ Le Chateau Restaurant (p116), Bel Ombre

Recently, *ragga*, a blend of house music, traditional Indian music and reggae, has been gaining a following. Mauritian *ragga* groups include Black Ayou and the Authentic Steel Brothers.

ARCHITECTURE

Caught up in the need to develop its economy, Mauritius paid little attention to its architectural heritage until recently. As a result many (bit not all) splendid colonial mansions and more humble dwellings have been lost under the sea of concrete. The reasons, for the most part, are simple: rescuing these houses is extremely expensive and even more time-consuming. Many of the raw materials, such as tamarind wood, are in short supply. It's easier and cheaper to rip down the old timber frames and throw up brand-new concrete blocks on the sturdy foundations beneath.

The majority of Mauritians now live in nondescript concrete apartment blocks in the towns and cities. Middle-class families might possibly afford a seaside apartment or villa. The coast around Trou aux Biches and Flic en Flac is lined with these unin-spiring boxes, all cheek by jowl. A few more enlightened developers are beginning to add traditional flourishes, such as *lambrequins* (decorative wooden borders) and bright paintwork. Hotels and restaurants are also getting better at incorporating a bit of local colour.

COLONIAL ARCHITECTURE

In 2003 the government set up a National Heritage Fund charged with preserving the country's historic buildings. The plantation houses dating from the 18th and 19th centuries have fared best, you'll still see them standing in glorious isolation amid the cane fields. Many are privately owned and closed to the public, such as Le Réduit, near Moka, which is now the president's official residence. Others have been converted into museums and restaurants.

The first French settlers naturally brought with them building styles from home. Over the years the architecture gradually evolved until it became supremely well suited to the hot, humid tropics. It's for this reason that so many of the grand plantation houses have survived the ravages of time.

In many of these buildings, flourishes that appear to be ornamental – vaulted roofs and decorative pierced screens, for example – all serve to keep the occupants cool and dry. The most distinctive feature is the shingled roof with ornamental turrets and rows of attic windows. These wedding-cake touches conceal a vaulted roof, which allows the air to circulate. Another characteristic element is the wide, airy *varangue* (verandah), where raffia blinds, fans and pot plants create a cooling humidity.

The roofs, windows and overhangs are usually lined with delicate, lace-like *lambrequins* (decorative wooden borders), which are purely ornamental. They vary from simple, repetitive floral patterns to elaborate pierced friezes; in all cases a botanical theme predominates.

Lambrequins, shingle roofs and verandahs or wrought-iron balconies are also found in colonial-era town houses. The more prestigious buildings were constructed of brick, or even stone, and so are better able to withstand cyclones and termites. In Port Louis, Government House and other buildings lining Place d'Armes are all fine examples.

At the other end of the scale, traditional labourers' houses typically consist of two rooms (one for sleeping, one for eating) and a verandah; because of the fire risk the kitchen is usually separate. Nowadays they are built of corrugated iron rather than termite-resistant hardwood, but are still painted in eye-catching colours that offset the white *lambrequins*. The garden overflowing with edible and ornamental plants is almost as important as the house itself.

CONTEMPORARY ARCHITECTURE

A few attempts at daring contemporary structures have been made but the most prestigious in recent times has been Port Louis' Caudan Waterfront development. Given its location at the very heart of the capital, the architects decided to incorporate elements of the traditional architecture found around nearby Place d'Armes. Further inspiration came from the nearby stone-and-steel dockyard buildings to provide another link with the past. Plans are now underway, although they have stalled in recent years, to build a Caudan-like complex in sleepy Mahébourg, and the country's first luxury yacht port, La Balise Marina, is planned in Black River.

VISUAL ARTS

Historically, Mauritian artists took their lead from what was happening in Europe and, in particular, France. Some of the 18th- and 19th-century engravings and oils of Mauritian landscapes you see could almost be mistaken for Europe. The classical statue of Paul and Virginie in Port Louis' Blue Penny Museum (p53) and the one of King Edward VII at the city's Champ de Mars Racecourse (p52) were both created by Mauritius' best-known sculptor, Prosper d'Épinay.

In the 20th century, the surrealist writer and painter Malcolm de Chazal injected a bit of local colour into the scene. Inspired by the island's prolific nature, his paintings are full of light and energy. You'll see numerous copies of the *Blue Dodo* and other Chazal works around, but originals are extremely rare. The Galerie du Moulin Cassé (p78) in Pereybère features some of his work.

Contemporary Mauritian art tends to be driven by the tourist market. One artist you'll find reproduced everywhere is Vaco Baissac, instantly recognisable from the blocks of colour outlined in black, like a stained-glass window. His Galerie Vaco (p77) is in Grand Baie.

Other commercially successful artists include Danielle Hitié, who produces minutely detailed renderings of markets as well as rural scenes, and Françoise Vrot, known for her very expressive portraits of women field-workers. Both artists are exhibited in galleries in Grand Baie, where Vrot also has her studio (p77).

Keep an eye out for exhibitions by more innovative contemporary artists, such as Hervé Masson, Serge Constantin, Henri Koombes and Khalid Nazroo. All have had some success on the international scene, though are less visible locally.

Food & Drink

Mauritian cuisine is very similar across the island – a rich and delicious mix of Indian spices and fresh local seafood and fish prepared with strong influences from Chinese, French and African cuisine. The cuisine of Rodrigues is quite different – less spicy but with more fresh fruit and beans used as ingredients.

Staples & Specialities

In Mauritius, rice, noodles, fish and seafood are the staples of everyday life, although to a great extent what people eat depends on their ethnic background. A Sino-Mauritian may well start the day with tea and noodles, a Franco-Mauritian with a *café au lait* and croissant, and an Indo-Mauritian with a chapati. However, come lunchtime nearly everyone enjoys a hot meal – whether it be a spicy seafood *carri* (curry) or *mines* (noodles) and a cooling beer. Dinner is the main meal of the day and is usually eaten *en famille* (with family). The Mauritians love their cocktail hour, and so you'll nearly always have an *apéro* (aperitif) or a *ti punch* (small punch) – usually a rum-based fruit cocktail. While meat is widely eaten (especially in Chinese and French cuisine) – venison and wild boar are mainstays around Mahébourg – the most common elements are fish and seafood. Marlin is a big favourite, as are mussels, octopus, prawns, lobster and calamari.

Drinks

Unsurprisingly the national drink is rum. Although most experts agree that Mauritian rum isn't up to the standard of the Caribbean equivalent, there are still some excellent brands produced, particularly Green Island – the dark variety of which is superb. Despite a long history of rum production in

Mauritius, the socially preferred spirit tends to be whisky – a hangover from the 150-year British rule.

The national beer is Phoenix, an excellent pilsner produced at the **Phoenix Brewery** since the 1960s and a regular prizewinner at festivals around the world. The other premium brand of the brewery, Blue Marlin, is also very good.

The Mauritians are also great tea drinkers and you shouldn't miss trying the range of Bois Chéri teas on sale throughout the country. The vanilla tea is the most famous and is quite delicious and refreshing even in the heat of the day. You'll have a chance to see it being made and can taste it at the Bois Chéri tea plantation (p118) in southern Mauritius.

During Hindu and Muslim festivals, deliciously flavoured drinks such as *lassi* (Indian yoghurt drink) and almond milk (almond- and cardamom-flavoured milk) are prepared.

Where to Eat & Drink

There tends to be quite a bit of segregation between 'tourist' restaurants and 'local' ones, particularly around bigger resort areas. In places such as Port Louis and the central highlands this is a lot less pronounced, and most places have a mixed clientele.

Nearly all restaurants have menus in English, or at least staff who speak English, so communication difficulties are at a minimum.

Most restaurants have several cuisines served up cheek by jowl, although they're nearly always separated from each other on the menu. While in better restaurants this will mean each cuisine is prepared by a different expert chef, on the whole most chefs are decent at cooking one cuisine and prepare the remaining dishes with something approaching indifference. The rule is a fairly obvious one – don't go to a Chinese restaurant for a good curry.

The best places to eat throughout the country tend to be *tables d'hôtes*, privately hosted meals often given by people who run guesthouses as well, but just as often offered alone. These give you a unique insight into local life, as you'll usually dine with the host couple and often their children, plus any other travellers who've arranged to come by (or people staying in the guesthouse). It's nearly always necessary to book a *table d'hôte*, preferably a day in advance, although it's always worth asking – bigger operations will sometimes be able to accommodate last-minute additions.

Opening hours tend to be quite flexible (and unpredictable in smaller places!), although as a rule it's good not to leave eating too late – even though many places are officially open until 11pm, if they're empty by 10pm there's a chance they'll shut early. Port Louis is a ghost town for everything, including eating, in the evening as the middle classes tend to live out of town, so it's usually the Caudan Waterfront or nothing after dark.

QUICK EATS

Places to enjoy eats on the run are in plentiful supply in Mauritius. Street vendors are at every bus station and town square, and takeaway shops can be found in numerous shopping centres and markets; both offer inexpensive local treats, including Indian, French and Chinese delicacies. Almost all restaurants, except the most upmarket, will do takeaway. Roadside food stalls serving dinner dishes such as *biryani* (curried rice), Indian rotis and *farattas* (unleavened flaky flour pancakes) are popular. Street eats cost around Rs 5 to Rs 10 for snacks like rotis, *dhal puris* (Indian snacks) and *boulettes* (meatballs) served at markets, along public beaches and in the capital.

The atmospheric markets are worth visiting for the popular *gâteaux piments* (deep-fried balls of lentils and chilli), which are cooked on the spot. You should also try the delicious *dhal puris*, rotis, samosas and *bhajas* (fried balls of besan dough with herbs or onion).

Indian and Chinese restaurants offer quick and inexpensive meals and snacks. Remember to buy some Indian savouries such as *caca pigeon* (an Indian nibble) or the famous Chinese *char siu* (barbecue pork).

Vegetarians & Vegans

Vegetarians will fare well in Mauritius, although they may be disappointed by the lack of variety. Indian restaurants tend to offer the best choice, but often this is limited to a variation on the theme of *carri de légumes* (vegetable curry). Chinese restaurants are also good for vegetarians, while Creole and French places are much more limiting. That said, almost everywhere has a vegetable curry on the menu. Pescatarians will be spoiled for choice as almost every eatery in the country offers fresh seafood and freshly caught fish cooked to perfection.

Vegans will find things harder, but not unassailably so – most resorts will be able to offer vegan options with advance warning, and again Indian restaurants will offer the most choice.

Habits & Customs

Eating habits vary across ethnic groups. Some groups eat with their fingers, others don't eat meat on Fridays and some abstain from eating pork – it's hard to generalise across the community.

Other than in hotels and *chambres d'hôtes* where buffets are the norm, breakfasts are normally very quick and informal. Lunch is also a fairly casual affair, although at the weekend it tends to be more formal, when family and friends gather to share the pleasures of the table. In restaurants, special menus are offered for weekend lunches. Before dinner, which is a very formal occasion, *gajacks* (predinner snacks) and *un apéro* or *un ti punch* (pre-dinner drinks) are commonly served; during the meal, wine or beer is usually served.

As eating and drinking are important social activities, behaviour at the table should be respectful. Locals can be strict about table manners, and it's considered rude to pick at your food or mix it together. You are also expected to be reasonably well dressed. Unless you are in a beach environment, wearing beachwear or other skimpy clothing won't be well received – casual but neat clothing is the norm. When invited to dine with locals, bring a small gift (perhaps some flowers or a bottle of wine).

If you are attending a traditional Indian or Chinese meal or a dinner associated with a religious celebration, follow what the locals do. Generally, your hosts will make you feel comfortable, but if you are unsure, ask about the serving customs and the order of dishes. Definitely attend an Indian or a Chinese wedding if you get the opportunity – these celebrations are true culinary feasts.

Environment

The Land

Mauritius is the peak of an enormous volcanic chain that also includes Réunion, though it is much older and therefore less rugged than its neighbour.

The island's highest mountains are found in the southwest, from where the land drops slightly to a central plateau before climbing again to the chain of oddly shaped mountains behind Port Louis and the Montagne Bambous to the east. Beyond these mountains a plain slopes gently down to the north coast.

Unlike Réunion, Mauritius has no active volcanoes, although remnants of volcanic activity abound. Extinct craters and volcanic lakes, such as the Trou aux Cerfs crater (p62) in Curepipe and the Grand Bassin holy lake (p100), are good examples. Over the aeons, the volcanoes generated millions of lava boulders, much to the chagrin of the indentured farm labourers who had to clear the land for sugar cane. Heaps of boulders dot the landscape. Some that have been piled into tidy pyramids are listed monuments!

Mauritius also includes a number of widely scattered inhabited islands, of which the most important is Rodrigues, 600km to the northeast. Rodrigues is another ancient volcanic peak and is surrounded by a lagoon twice the size of the island itself. Mauritius also owns the sparsely inhabited islands of Cargados Carajos, northeast of the mainland, and the Agalega Islands, two islands adjacent to the Seychelles.

Mauritius also stakes territorial claim to the Chagos Archipelago, officially part of the British Indian Ocean Territory and controversially ceded to the US military until 2016.

Wildlife

The story of Mauritian wildlife certainly didn't end with the dodo. In fact, the island's reputation for extinction has been transformed by a program of saving endangered species with a dramatic success rate.

The best source of information is the **Mauritian Wildlife Foundation** (MWF; ☏ 697 6117; www.mauritian-wildlife.org; Grannum Rd, Vacoas; ⊙ 9am-5pm Mon-Fri) which was founded in 1984 to protect and manage the country's many rare species. The MWF vigorously supports the creation of national parks and reserves, and the monitoring of whales, dolphins and turtles. It has had significant success in restoring the populations of several endangered bird species and in conserving endemic vegetation. While you're welcome to visit their office to get information it can be difficult to find. In any event, their website is a useful resource, and they have staff who work in the vicinity of the Petrin Information Centre and Black River Gorges Visitors Centre at the Black River Gorges National Park; ask the national park staff at the centres to speak with one if you have a specific question. And, of course, a visit to MWF-run Île aux Aigrettes is a highlight of any visit to the island.

MAMMALS

Mauritius has only one native mammal, the wonderful fruit bat – they're a common sight at twilight each evening as they come to life and begin their night's foraging.

All other mammals present on the island were introduced with varying degrees of success by colonists. Mongooses are typical of the slapdash ecological management of the past – they were introduced from India in the late 19th century to control plague-carrying rats. The intention was to import only males, but some females slipped through and they bred like, well, mongooses. Soon there were mongooses everywhere. They remain fairly common, as are the bands of macaque monkeys that hang out around Grand Bassin and the Black River Gorges. Java deer, imported by the Dutch for fresh meat, and wild pigs, also introduced, roam the more remote forests.

REPTILES

Native reptiles include the beautiful turquoise-and-red ornate day gecko and Telfair's skink (a clawed lizard), both of which can be seen on Île aux Aigrettes. You can rest easy if you see a slithering critter – there are no dangerous reptiles in Mauritius.

TORTOISES

Mauritius, along with Réunion and Seychelles, once had the highest density of giant tortoises on the planet, a veritable Galapagos of distinct species, of which Mauritius and Rodrigues had one each. In 1691, the French settler François Leguat wrote of Rodrigues: 'There are so many tortoises on this island, sometimes there are groups of two or three thousand, so that one can take more than a hundred steps on their shell without touching the ground'. Such abundance didn't last long, and both were driven to extinction during the colonial period when sailors and settlers favoured tortoises as an easy-to-catch and long-lasting source of meat; tortoises could be kept alive on very little food, ideal for long-distance ocean journeys.

The only surviving species in the region, the Aldabra Giant Tortoise from the Seychelles, was introduced onto Île aux Aigrettes (20) in 2000 and onto Round Island (12) in 2007. The number of wild tortoises has since grown to an estimated 125 individuals.

Captive populations are also present at:

➡ François Leguat Reserve (p155), Rodrigues

➡ La Vanille (p117), Rivière des Anguilles

➡ Sir Seewoosagur Ramgoolam Botanical Gardens (p83), Pamplemousses

➡ Casela Nature & Leisure Park (p85), Flic en Flac

➡ Terres de 7 Couleurs (p96), Chamarel

BIRDS

The dodo may be Mauritius' most famous former inhabitant (other species that were driven to extinction during the early colonial period include the red rail and the solitaire), but Mauritius should be just as famous for the birds it has saved. In fact, an academic study in 2007 found that Mauritius had pulled more bird species (five) back from the brink of extinction than any other country on earth.

The birds you're most likely to see, however, are the introduced songbirds, such as the little red Madagascar fody, the Indian mynah (its yellow beak and feet giving it a cartoon-character appearance) and the red-whiskered bulbul. Between October and May the Rivulet Terre Rouge Bird Sanctuary (p64) estuary north of Port Louis provides an important wintering ground for migratory water birds such as the whimbrel, the grey plover, and the common and curlew sandpipers.

MAURITIUS KESTREL

In 1974, the rather lovely Mauritius kestrel (which once inhabited all corners of the island) was officially the most endangered bird species on the planet, with just four known to survive in the wild, including, crucially, one breeding female. There were a further two of the raptors in captivity. The reason for its dire position was all too familiar: pesticide poisoning, habitat destruction and hunting. A captive-breeding program and an intensive project of building predator-proof nesting boxes in the wild has led to an amazing recovery, with numbers around 400.

LOCAL KNOWLEDGE

BEST PLACES TO SEE...

While in Mauritius we spoke with Dr Vikash Tatayah, director of the Mauritian Wildlife Foundation (p139).

Where is the best place to see the Mauritian kestrel? There are two main populations, with around 250 in southeastern Mauritius and approximately 150 in the southwest. They are easiest to see during the breeding season, which in the southeast runs from August to February, and in the southwest from September to February. Sightings are possible although difficult in Black River Gorges National Park. The places where you are most likely to see them are all in the southeast: Vallée de Ferney (p118), Lion Mountain (p119) and, if it has reopened, Kestrel Valley (p119).

And the pink pigeon? The pigeon is present throughout Black River Gorges National Park (p95) and can be seen close to the two visitors centres and elsewhere. But the best place is Île aux Aigrettes (p110).

The echo parakeet? Although the parakeets are present throughout the park, the easiest place to see them is along Parakeet Trail in Black River Gorges National Park. They're also present in the hinterland of Bel Ombre in the far south.

What about other important bird species? Île aux Aigrettes is good for other endangered species such as the elusive olive white eye and the Mauritian fody. All of the offshore islands are good for seabirds.

And giant tortoises? The only free-ranging giant tortoises (apart from a population we've established on Round Island which isn't open to the public) are on Île aux Aigrettes. Otherwise, the best places to see them are La Vanille (p117), close to Souillac in the south, and the outstanding François Leguat Reserve (p155) on Rodrigues.

What's next for Mauritian conservation? Apart from building on our success in saving a number of endangered species by ensuring their long-term survival, we have big plans for Vallée de Ferney – we're hoping to reintroduce the pink pigeon and echo parakeet there. We also have a number of ecotourism projects that we're hoping to develop on Mauritius and Rodrigues. People can check our website to see how these are progressing.

Apart from going to see the wildlife, how can individuals help? We do accept volunteers but only for longer periods of around six months. We also have a program of longer visits to Île aux Aigrettes, whereby people can spend a whole day on the island and help out with weeding invasive species or helping out in the plant nursery. They also get to spend time talking with some of our scientists and researchers working on the island. It is also possible to adopt one of four endangered species (the Mauritian fody, olive white eye, pink pigeon, ornate day gecko and giant tortoise) – for an annual fee of Rs 1000 you get a free visit to Île aux Aigrettes, information on your chosen species and three MWF newsletters. Otherwise, people can always make a donation.

PINK PIGEON

The pretty pink pigeon has also been pulled back from the brink. In 1986, this once-widespread bird was down to just 12 individuals in the wild, close to Bassin Blanc in the southern reaches of Black River Gorges National Park. In that year all five nesting attempts were unsuccessful due to rats. The species appeared doomed. Again, an intensive program of captive breeding and reintroduction into the wild has seen numbers soar, with around 470 thought to be present throughout Black River Gorges National Park and on Île aux Aigrettes (where there were 43 at last count). The MWF hopes that captive species in European zoos may one day form part of the program as a means of ensuring the species' genetic diversity.

ECHO PARAKEET

The vivid colours of the echo parakeet, too, were almost lost to Mauritius. In 1986, between eight and 12 survived. And to make matters worse, it was the last of six endemic parrot species that once inhabited the island. You know the story: captive breeding, reintroduction and intensive conservation

DEAD AS A DODO

Illustrations from the logbooks of the first ships to reach Mauritius show hundreds of plump flightless birds running down to the beach to investigate the newcomers. Lacking natural predators, these giant relatives of the pigeon were easy prey for hungry sailors, who named the bird *dodo*, meaning 'stupid'. It took just 30 years for passing sailors and their pets and pests (dogs, monkeys, pigs and rats) to drive the dodo to extinction; the last confirmed sighting was in the 1660s.

Just as surprising as the speed of the dodo's demise is how little evidence remains that the bird ever existed. A few relics made it back to Europe during the 18th century – a dried beak ended up at the University of Copenhagen in Denmark, while the University of Oxford in England managed to get hold of a whole head and a foot – but until recently our knowledge of the dodo was mainly based on sketches by 17th-century seamen.

However, in 1865 local schoolteacher George Clark discovered a dodo skeleton in a marshy area on the site of what is now the international airport. The skeleton was re-assembled by scientists in Edinburgh, and has formed the basis of all subsequent dodo reconstructions, one of which is on display in the Natural History Museum (p49) in Port Louis. There is also an accurate reconstruction of a dodo in bronze in the ebony forest on Île aux Aigrettes.

For the full story of the dodo's demise, read Errol Fuller's fascinating book *Dodo: From Extinction to Icon*. For a more wide-ranging look at species evolution and extinction on islands, try David Quammen's excellent *Song of the Dodo*, which includes some lengthy passages on Mauritius.

management has seen the species recover to around 540, all within Black River Gorges National Park. A word of warning: the echo parakeet closely resembles the introduced ringed parakeet which is far more common and widespread throughout the island.

OTHER SPECIES

The numbers of olive white eye, a small Mauritian songbird, is down to no more than 150 pairs in the wild, with 35 birds on Île aux Aigrettes. The Mauritian fody has also found a refuge on Île aux Aigrettes which will serve as a base for future reintroduction programs.

Over on Rodrigues, the saving of the Rodrigues warbler (from 30 in the 1970s to over 4000 today) and Rodrigues fody (six pairs in 1968, 8000 individuals today) are almost unparelled in the annals of wildlife conservation.

PLANTS

Almost one-third of the 900 plant species found in Mauritius are unique to these islands. Many of these endemic plants have fared poorly in competition with introduced plants such as guava and privet, and have been depleted by introduced deer, pigs and monkeys. General forest clearance and the establishment of crop monocultures have exacerbated the problem, so that less than 1% of Mauritius' original forest is intact.

Mauritius' forests originally included the *tambalacoque* tree, which is also known as the dodo tree and is not far from extinction itself. It's a tall tree with a silver trunk and a large, tough seed that supposedly only germinates after being eaten by, and passing through the stomach of, a dodo. Scientists are sceptical about this rumour, but there's no denying the tree is extremely difficult to propagate. The easiest place to find this and other rare plant species is in the botanical gardens at Pamplemousses.

For a tropical island, Mauritius is not big on coconut palms. Instead, casuarinas (also known as *filaos*) fringe most of the beaches. These tall, wispy trees act as useful windbreaks and grow well in sandy soil. The government planted them along the shores to help stop erosion; eucalyptus trees have been widely planted for the same reason.

Other impressive and highly visible trees are the giant Indian banyan and the brilliant red flowering flamboyant (royal poinciana).

Staying with shades of red, one flower you will see in abundance is anthurium, with its single, glossy petal and protruding yellow spadix. The plant originated in South America and was introduced to Mauritius in the late 19th century. The flower, which at first sight you'd swear was plastic, can last up to three weeks after being cut and is therefore a popular display plant. Now grown in commercial quantities for export, it is used to spruce up hotels and public meeting places.

Mangroves are enjoying a renaissance in Mauritius today. Originally cut down to reduce swamp areas where malarial mosquitos could breed, they've been discovered to be an important part of the food chain for tropical fish, and thus large projects to develop mangrove areas have been undertaken, particularly on the east coast.

National Parks

Since 1988, several international organisations have been working with the government to set up conservation areas in Mauritius. About 3.5% of the land area is now protected either as national parks, managed mainly for ecosystem preservation and for recreation, or as nature reserves.

The largest park is the Black River Gorges National Park, established in 1994 in the southwest of the island. It covers some 68 sq km and preserves a wide variety of forest environments, from pine forest to tropical scrub, and includes the country's largest area of native forest. Two of the most important nature reserves are Île aux Aigrettes (p110)

and Île Ronde (the latter is closed to the public), both of which are being restored to their natural state by replacing introduced plants and animals with native species.

In 1997 marine parks were proclaimed at Blue Bay (near Mahébourg on the southeast coast) and Balaclava (on the west coast), but the number of visitors to the area makes it difficult to establish rigorous controls and there is a need to encourage local fishermen to use less destructive techniques.

There is also the new and tiny national park of Bras d'Eau, closed to Poste Lafayette on Mauritius' east coast.

Environmental Issues

The natural environment of Mauritius has paid a heavy price for the country's rapid economic development. And despite recent economic setbacks, the government seems more keen than ever to encourage more tourists – at least, the rich ones – to continue plugging the gap left by a declining sugar industry and waning textile industry. However, the expansion of tourist facilities is straining the island's infrastructure and causing problems such as environmental

MAURITIUS ENVIRONMENT

IMPORTANT NATIONAL PARKS & RESERVES

PARK	FEATURES	ACTIVITIES	BEST TIME TO VISIT
Balaclava Marine Park	lagoon, coral reef, turtle breeding grounds	snorkelling, diving, glass-bottomed boat tours	all year
Black River Gorges National Park	forested mountains, Mauritius kestrel, echo parakeet, pink pigeons, black ebony trees	hiking, bird-watching	Sep-Jan for flowers
Blue Bay Marine Park	lagoon, corals, fish life	snorkelling, diving, glass-bottomed boat tours	all year
Bras d'Eau National Park	Mauritius paradise flycatchers	bird-watching	all year
Grande Montagne Nature Reserve	Rodrigues fody and warbler, native reforestation, rare plants	hiking	all year
Île aux Aigrettes Nature Reserve	coral island, ebony forests, pink pigeons, olive white eye, Aldabra giant tortoise, Telfaïrs skink	ecotours	all year
Île aux Cocos	nesting seabirds, lagoon scenery	bird-watching, snorkelling, swimming	all year
Vallée de Ferney	Mauritius kestrel, white-tailed tropicbirds, native forest	hiking, bird-watching	Sep-Jan

degradation and excessive demand on services such as electricity, water and transport.

One area of particular concern is the amount of construction along the coast – almost every beach has been developed, most of it tourist related. However, Mauritians are very keen to put environmental concerns first: a proposal for a hotel on Île des Deux Cocos in Blue Bay, for example, met with such fierce resistance that it has been abandoned. Conservationists also fervently (and successfully) combated plans to construct a highway through the old forests in the southeast.

The government now requires an environmental impact assessment for all new building projects, including coastal hotels, marinas and golf courses, and even for activities such as undersea walks. Planning regulations for hotel developments on Rodrigues are particularly strict: they must be small, single-storey, built in traditional style and stand at least 30m back from the high-tide mark. Since water shortages are a problem on Rodrigues, new hotels must also recycle their water.

To combat littering and other forms of environmental degradation, the government has established a special environmental police force charged with enforcing legislation and educating the local population. To report wrongdoers, there is even a **hotline** ( 210 5151).

If anything, the marine environment is suffering even more from overexploitation. The coast off Grand Baie is particularly affected by too many divers and boats concentrated in a few specific locations. In addition, silting and chemical pollution are resulting in extensive coral damage and falling fish populations. In the west, dolphin-watching is an extremely popular activity for tourists; however, the sudden increase in operators has called into question its sustainability. Choose your tour boat carefully – companies who do not have the dolphins' wellbeing at heart should be avoided.

SURVIVAL GUIDE

ℹ Directory A–Z

ACCOMMODATION

By sheer volume alone, Mauritius offers the greatest range of sleeping options among the islands in the area. There are three main types of accommodation: fully equipped vacation rentals, locally run guesthouses, and larger hotels and resorts.

Seasons

In general, high season runs from around October to March, with a focus on the European winter months. Prices soar at the end of December and beginning of January. From May to September travellers can expect prices to dip during the low-season months, often called 'green season'.

Apartments & Villas

Renting a holiday apartment or villa is by far the most economical option in Mauritius, especially if there are a number of people travelling with you. There are hundreds of rental options available for tourists ranging from small studios in factory-sized complexes to lavish seaside mansions fit for a movie star. If you're travelling with your family or friends, a large high-end property can cost as little as €25 per person, which more than rivals the hostel-esque relics from an earlier era of travel on the island. But remember, even though rentals represent a better price-value ratio on the whole, you always get what you pay for.

Most of the accommodation in this category is privately owned and managed by an umbrella agency that markets a large pool of crash pads. While choices can vary greatly you should expect, in all but the cheapest places, that your home-away-from-home comes with daily maid service, a fully equipped kitchen, air-con and concierge service provided by the property manager (make sure to double-check).

Guesthouses & Chambres d'Hôtes

If you're looking for an island experience that doesn't involve the term 'all-inclusive', Mauritius' guesthouses and *chambres d'hôtes* (B&Bs) are well worth considering. This category of accommodation is managed by locals – often families –

SLEEPING PRICE RANGES

Throughout this chapter, the order of accommodation listings is by price, from the least to the most expensive. Each place to stay is accompanied by one of the following symbols (the price relates to a double room with private bathroom). Hotels list their rates in both euros and Mauritian rupees – it's usually fine to pay in either other than in top-end hotels.

€ less than €60 (around Rs 2350)

€€ €60–150 (Rs 2350–5800)

€€€ more than €150 (Rs 5800)

who often dote on their guests with genuine hospitality. It's a fantastic way to learn about the *real* Mauritius hidden from package-deal tourists. In fact, you'll sometimes have the chance to dine with your accommodation's proprietors at their *tables d'hôtes*.

Over the last few years the government has begun issuing security mandates for all tourism-related properties. Panic buttons and 24-hour security have become a compulsory expense for owners, forcing guesthouses to jack up their prices beyond the budget range to pay the bills. As a result, the island's *chambres d'hôtes* are starting to be under threat, especially since all-inclusive resorts have been known to offer bargain-basement prices to stay competitive during the economic downturn. Nonetheless, there's still a scatter of charming spots sprinkled around the island that are, now more than ever, promoting a 'local experience'. You'll find a cluster in Pointe d'Esny, and *chambres d'hôtes* are particularly popular in Rodrigues.

Hotels & Resorts
Rounding out the sleeping circuit is Mauritius' best-known brand of accommodation – the dreamy resorts found on the pages of magazines and in TV commercials for credit cards. And, despite the global economic recession, dozens of these opulent properties continue to spring up each year. There are, however, two distinct categories of hotels in Mauritius – the luxury over-the-top resorts that stretch along the sea, and the old-school midrangers that need some serious TLC. It's best to avoid the latter as many of the posh properties offer vacation incentives that rival the has-beens, and the guesthouses (which are often cheaper) are generally in better shape. Upscale properties come in various tiers of luxury – there are three-, four- and five-star resorts. You'll do perfectly well with a three-star charmer, and while the five-star price tags may be out of reach for many travellers, it is well worth checking with travel agents about hotel-and-flight vacation packages. In fact, no up-market sleeps should be booked with the public rates – agency rates are always cheaper. If you have your sights set on a luxury vacation, expect to pay €100 per person per night (including half board) at the very minimum. Prices quickly climb all the way up to €1000.

ACTIVITIES
There's much more to Mauritius than sun worship – listed throughout this chapter you'll find plenty of ways to get the blood pumping after one too many days of baking on the beach. For details on diving opportunities see p27. And one thing to remember about those beaches: all beaches below the high-tide line are public property, so you are entitled to plop your towel down on the sand, whatever some over-officious security guard from an upmarket resort might tell you.

CHILDREN
Travelling with children in Mauritius presents no particular problems. In fact, kids generally have a ball.

To put their holiday in context, there's a wonderful series of cartoon books by Henry Koobes (published locally by Editions Vizavi Ltd). The English-language titles include *In Dodoland, SOS Shark* and *Meli-Melo in the Molasses*.

For more information, see Lonely Planet's *Travel with Children*.

Accommodation
Most of the high-end hotels have dedicated facilities (like 'kids clubs') for children and those that don't often have a small children's playground somewhere in the grounds. Most top-end hotels also include babysitting services. The

TOP ATTRACTIONS FOR CHILDREN

Besides the seaside, Mauritius has numerous attractions that make for excellent day excursions for families. Remember, however, that some activities may be subject to minimum-age requirements – phone ahead or check the relevant website before getting the kids all excited. Our favourite attractions for children include:

➡ La Vanille (p117), Rivière des Anguilles

➡ Île aux Aigrettes (p110), Pointe d'Esny

➡ Dolphin-watching (p92), Tamarin

➡ Snorkelling, anywhere...

➡ Casela Nature & Leisure Park (p85), Flic en Flac

➡ Le Waterpark & Leisure Village (p126), Belle Mar

➡ Mauritius Aquarium (p64), Pointe aux Piments

proliferation of villa leases has made it easy to bring the entire family on vacation, while many hotels and even some *chambres d'hôtes* offer family rooms.

CUSTOMS REGULATIONS

In Mauritius, visitors aged 16 years and over may import 200 cigarettes or 250g of tobacco; 1L of spirits; 2L of wine, ale or beer; 250mL of *eau de toilette;* and up to 100mL of perfume.

There are restrictions on importing food, plants and animals, for which import permits are required. Other prohibited and restricted articles include spear guns and items made from ivory, shell, turtleshell or other materials banned under the Convention on International Trade in Endangered Species (CITES); it is also illegal to take such items out when you leave.

EMBASSIES & CONSULATES

Many countries do not have representatives in Mauritius, and usually refer their citizens to the embassy in Pretoria, South Africa. Countries with diplomatic representation in Mauritius include the following:

Australian High Commission (☑202 0160; www.mauritius.embassy.gov.au; 5 President John Kennedy St, 2nd fl, Rogers House, Port Louis; ☺8.30am-3.30pm Mon-Fri)

Canadian Consulate (☑212 5500; canada@intnet.mu; 18 Jules Koenig St, Port Louis; ☺9am-noon Mon-Fri)

French Embassy (☑202 0100; www.ambafrance-mu.org; 14 St Georges St, Port Louis; ☺8am-noon Mon-Fri)

UK High Commission (☑202 9400; bhc@intnet.mu; Edith Cavell St, 7th fl, Les Cascades Bldg, Port Louis; ☺7.45am-3.45pm Mon-Thu, 7.45am-1.30pm Fri)

US Embassy (☑202 4400; mauritius.usembassy.gov; President John Kennedy St, 4th fl, Rogers House, Port Louis; ☺7.30am-4.45pm Mon-Thu, 7.30am-12.30pm Fri)

GAY & LESBIAN TRAVELLERS

Mauritius has a paradoxical relationship to homosexuality. While gay and lesbian rights are legally guaranteed and much of the population is young and progressive, there remains a rigidly conservative streak to the Mauritian character. As a result gay life remains fairly secretive – mainly existing on the internet, in private and at the occasional party. While there were no gay or lesbian bars or clubs on the island at the time of writing, there are monthly underground club nights organised by text message.

For gay and lesbian travellers there's little to worry about. We've never heard of any problems arising from same-sex couples sharing rooms during their holidays. You're still best to avoid public displays of affection outside your hotel and generally to be aware that what might be entirely normal at home may not be viewed in the same light here.

INSURANCE

A travel-insurance policy to cover theft, loss and medical problems is a good idea. Some policies specifically exclude dangerous activities, which can include scuba diving, motorcycling and even hiking. Always check the small print and make sure that the policy covers ambulances or an emergency flight home. If you plan on diving, we strongly recommend purchasing dive-specific insurance with **DAN** (www.diversalertnetwork.org).

Worldwide travel insurance is available at www.lonelyplanet.com/travel_services. You can buy, extend and claim online anytime – even if you're already on the road.

INTERNET ACCESS

Most towns have at least one internet cafe and access can be found at most resorts, hotels and guesthouses and wi-fi connections are increasingly the norm – most often wi-fi access is restricted to public areas, although it may extend to some rooms.

PRACTICALITIES

→ **Electricity** 220V, 50Hz; both British-style three-pin sockets and continental two-pin variety are commonly used.

→ **Newspapers** French-language *L'Express* (www.lexpress.mu) and *Le Mauricien* (www.lemauricien.com); *News on Sunday* and the *Mauritius Times* are English-language weeklies.

→ **Radio** Huge number of local commercial stations broadcasting in Creole and Hindi, and the BBC World Service and Voice of America readily available. Most popular include Kool FM 89.3 Mhz and Taal FM 94.0 Mhz.

→ **Television** Three free television channels run by the state Mauritius Broadcasting Corporation (MBC) – MBC1, MBC2 and MBC3 – and numerous pay channels. Programming is mainly in Creole but with foreign imports in French, English and Indian languages.

→ **Weights and measures** Mauritius uses the metric system.

LEGAL MATTERS

Foreigners are subject to the laws of the country in which they are travelling and will receive no special consideration because they are tourists. If you find yourself in a sticky legal predicament, contact your embassy.

In general, travellers have nothing to fear from the police, who rarely harass foreigners and are very polite if you do need to stop them. Talking on your mobile phone while driving will definitely get you pulled over, but if you're in any sort of minor trouble it's best to play up your tourist naiveté and you'll most likely be let off the hook (speaking in English helps even more).

MAPS

Although Mauritius markets itself heavily as a major tourism destination, the island has a frustrating lack of decent maps (a ploy to keep you within the walls of your resort perhaps?). The best map of the island is the satellite imagery on Google Earth. If you don't have printing facilities on hand, try the map produced by the **Institut Géographique Nationale** (IGN; www.ign.fr). The Globetrotter travel map is also a good choice. Both should be available from local bookstores and supermarkets. Otherwise, see if you can pick up the reasonable *Tourist Map of Mauritius & Rodrigues* by ELP Publiations – we found it at Le Village Boutik (p84) in Pamplemousses (Rs 230).

MONEY

The Mauritian unit of currency is the rupee (Rs), which is divided into 100 cents (¢). There are coins of 5¢, 20¢ and 50¢, and Rs 1, Rs 5 and Rs 10. The banknote denominations are Rs 25, Rs 50, Rs 100, Rs 200, Rs 500, Rs 1000 and Rs 2000. While the Mauritian rupee is the island's currency, almost all villas, guesthouses and hotels (and several high-end restaurants usually affiliated with hotels) tether their prices to the euro to counterbalance the rupee's unstable fluctuations and it is possible (and sometimes required) to pay in euros at such places.

ATMs

Armed with your PIN, it's perfectly possible to travel on plastic in Mauritius since ATMs are widespread. Even Rodrigues has a smattering of them. They're mostly located outside banks, though you'll also find them at the airports, at larger supermarkets and in some shopping malls. The majority of machines accept Visa and MasterCard, or any similar cards in the Cirrus and Plus networks, while Amex now has a tie-in with Mauritius Commercial Bank (MCB). Remember, however, that bank fees, sometimes significant ones, can apply – check with your home bank before setting out for Mauritius.

EATING PRICE RANGES

The following price ranges refer to a standard main course. Unless otherwise stated, service charges and taxes are included in the price. For more information on Mauritian cuisine, see p137.

€ under Rs 300

€€ Rs 300 to Rs 750

€€€ over Rs 750

Credit Cards

Visa and MasterCard are the most commonly accepted cards, though Amex is catching up quickly. Nearly all tourist shops, restaurants and accommodation accept payment by credit card, as do car-hire companies, tour agents and so forth. Any establishment well outside the tourist bubble will still expect payment in cash.

A few places add on an extra fee, typically 3%, to the bill to cover 'bank charges'. The cheaper car-hire companies are the worst offenders. To be on the safe side, always ask. Cash advances on credit cards are available from most major banks, including MCB, Barclays, the State Bank and HSBC. Just remember to take your passport.

Moneychangers

Major currencies and travellers cheques can be changed at the main banks, exchange bureaus and the larger hotels. Bureaux de change sometimes offer slightly better rates than banks, but there's usually little difference. Hotels tend to have the worst rates and may add an additional service commission. As a general rule, travellers cheques bring a better rate than cash. There is no blackmarket in Mauritius.

Banks don't charge commission on changing cash. As for travellers cheques, the system varies. Some banks, such as HSBC, charge 1% of the total, with a minimum of Rs 200, while MCB and the State Bank levy Rs 50 for up to 10 cheques. Don't forget to take along your passport when changing money. And make sure you hang on to the encashment form, which will have to be presented if you want to change Mauritian rupees back into foreign currency at the end of your stay.

Taxes

Most items apart from unprepared food are subject to 15% VAT. There's no clear rule about whether this tax is included in prices quoted for meals, rooms and activities. If it's not clear, be sure to ask or you may be in for a shock.

Tipping

Tipping is not generally practiced in Mauritius and is never an obligation. Top-end hotels and restaurants sometimes add a service charge of about 10% to 15% to the bill.

OPENING HOURS

Banks 9am to 3.15pm Monday to Friday (extended hours in tourist hubs like Grand Baie and Flic en Flac)

Government offices 9am to 4pm Monday to Friday, 9am to noon Saturday (closed during religious and public holidays)

Post offices 8.15am to 4pm Monday to Friday, 8.15am to 11.45am Saturday (the last 45 minutes are available for stamp sales only)

Restaurants noon to 3pm and 7pm to 10pm; many restaurants close on Sunday

Shops 9am to 5pm Monday to Friday, 8am to noon Saturday; opening hours are usually longer in larger seaside resort towns; most stores – especially the ones located on the Central Plateau – will also close early (around 1pm) on Thursdays; on Rodrigues shops and offices generally close earlier

PUBLIC HOLIDAYS

New Year 1 and 2 January

Thaipoosam Cavadee January/February

Chinese Spring Festival January/February

Abolition of Slavery 1 February

Maha Shivaratri February/March

Ougadi March/April

National Day 12 March

Labour Day 1 May

Assumption of the Blessed Virgin Mary 15 August

Ganesh Chaturti August/September

Divali (Dipavali) October/November

Arrival of Indentured Labourers 2 November

Eid al-Fitr November/December

Christmas Day 25 December

SAFE TRAVEL

In most destinations, dangerous actions beget dangerous consequences, and Mauritius is no different. Your biggest annoyance is likely to be environmental (mosquitoes, sunburn and the occasional upset stomach).

The Indian Ocean is a warm tropical ocean, so there are several aquatic nasties to watch out for. Fortunately, few travellers encounter anything more serious than the odd (and often quite painful) coral cut.

Coconuts

Lying under a coconut palm may seem like a tropical idyll, but, as silly as it may sound, there have been some tragic accidents. Take care when walking under coconut trees and don't lie (or park your car) beneath them.

Cyclones

Mauritius lies within the cyclone belt. Most cyclones occur between December and March, although they are not unheard-of as late as April. While direct hits are relatively uncommon, storms miles away can bring very strong winds.

As soon as a cyclone is detected, a system of alerts is used to inform the public of the level of danger. In Mauritius there are four levels of alert. The alerts and then regular bulletins are broadcast on radio and TV. For current warnings check out metservice.intnet.mu.

Theft

Petty theft and break-ins can be somewhat of a common occurrence beyond the walls of your resort. Favourite haunts for thieves are the beaches and Île aux Cerfs is a particular hot spot. The best strategy is not to take any valuables to the beach – and never tempt a passing thief by leaving your belongings unattended.

Be extra careful in crowded places such as markets and avoid walking around with your valuables casually slung over your shoulder. When travelling on public transport, keep your gear near you.

If you hire a car, it's best not to leave anything valuable in it at all. If you must do so, hide everything well out of sight. Wherever possible, park in a secure car park or at least somewhere busy – never park in an isolated spot, especially at night.

Don't leave vital documents, money or valuables lying about in your room. Many hotels provide room safes, which are well worth using. Otherwise, leave your valuables in the safe at reception and get a receipt. While most hotels are reliable, to be extra sure, pack everything in a small, double-zippered bag that can be padlocked, or use a large envelope with a signed seal that will reveal any tampering. Count money and travellers cheques before and after retrieving them from the safe.

If you do have something stolen, report it to the police. The chances of them recovering anything are remote, but you'll need a statement proving you have reported the crime if you want to claim insurance.

TELEPHONE

Although Mauritius may feel lost in the Indian Ocean, the island's telephone services are generally reliable. In fact, Mauritius offers some of the cheapest mobile-phone services in the world.

The state-controlled **Mauritius Telecom** (www.mauritiustelecom.com) has a virtual monopoly on landlines, although there's an open market for mobile services.

The rate for a call to Australia, Europe or the USA is about Rs 25 per minute. These rates fall by around 25% during off-peak hours (10pm to 6am from Monday to Friday and noon on Saturday to 6am the following Monday).

When phoning Mauritius from abroad, you'll need to dial the international code for Mauritius (☎230), followed by the seven-digit local number. There are no area codes in Mauritius.

Mobile Phones

Coverage on Mauritius and Rodrigues is generally excellent and mobile phones are a cheap way to communicate with others. In fact, many Mauritians have more than one mobile phone. If you have a GSM phone and it has been 'unlocked', you can keep costs down by buying a local SIM card from either **Orange** (☎203 7649; www. orange.mu; Edith Cavell St, Mauritius Telecom Tower, Port Louis) or **Emtel** (☎212 5400; www. emtel-ltd.com; President John Kennedy St, Air Mauritius Bldg, Port Louis). A starter pack costs around Rs 100 including Rs 86 worth of calls. To top-up your credit you can buy prepaid cards almost anywhere. When buying a SIM card you'll usually need to bring along your passport and a sponsor's signature.

Local calls are charged at between Rs 1.20 and Rs 3.60 per minute depending on whether you're calling someone on the same network or not. International calls cost a couple of rupees per minute on top of the standard Mauritius Telecom rates.

Purchasing a SIM card package – even for one call home – is much less costly than buying a local phonecard.

TIME

Mauritius is GMT plus four hours, both on the mainland and on Rodrigues. When it's noon in Port Louis, it's 8am in London, 9am in Paris, 3am in New York and 6pm in Sydney. Mauritius does not operate a system of daylight savings; being equatorial its sunset and sunrise times vary only slightly throughout the year.

TOURIST INFORMATION

Although independent travellers are definitely in the minority, there are two corporate entities dedicated to those who don't fall into the package-getaway category. Both have desks in the arrivals hall at the airport. They can assist with hotel bookings and general island information.

Also useful is Mauritius Telecom's 24-hour phone service, **Tourist Info** (☎152). At any time of day or night you can speak to someone (in English) who will at least try to answer your questions.

Mauritius Tourism Promotion Authority (MTPA; ☎208 6397; www.tourism-mauritius. mu) The Mauritius Tourism Promotion Authority is a government-run body essentially responsible for promoting the island and its

virtues to foreign markets. MTPA has a constellation of kiosks peppered across the island, although, to be perfectly frank, we found these stations disappointing – many were empty during prime business hours, and when we did find someone staffing a booth they tossed us an outdated island map and offered very limited information. You're better off asking tour operators, hotel staff or anyone else accustomed to dealing with the usual onslaught of traveller's queries.

Association des Hôteliers et Restaurateurs de l'Île Maurice (AHRIM; ☎637 3782; www. mauritiustourism.org) The recommended Association des Hôteliers et Restaurateurs de l'île Maurice is an association of high-quality hotels, guesthouses and restaurants. AHRIM is starting to offer guesthouse-plus-airfare packages – an attempt to empower tourists to have a local experience while also benefiting from discounted airfares. Check out its website for details.

TRAVELLERS WITH DISABILITIES

Mauritius makes a relatively decent provision for those with mobility problems. Modern buildings conform to international standards for disabled access, although public toilets, pavements and lifts tend not to be as good. Most top-end hotels have wheelchair access, lifts and specially equipped bathrooms. In big hotels, there are always plenty of staff around to help and it is often possible to hire an assistant if you want to go on an excursion or a boat trip. With a bit of extra warning, some riding stables, dive centres and other sports operators can cater for people with disabilities.

None of the public transport systems offer wheelchair access. Anyone using a wheelchair will be reliant on private vehicles.

VISAS

You don't need a visa to enter Mauritius if you are a citizen of the EU, the USA, Australia, Canada, Japan, New Zealand or a number of other countries. You can find more information on the government website (www.passport.gov. mu). Initial entry is granted for a maximum of three months and proof of a planned and paid-for departure is required, although not always asked for.

Extensions for a further three months as a tourist are available from the **Passport & Immigration Office** (☎210 9312; fax 210 9322; Lislet Geoffroy St, Sterling House, Port Louis). Applications must be submitted with one form, two passport-size photos, your passport, an onward ticket and proof of finances. Two letters may also be necessary – one from you explaining why you want to stay longer, and one by a local 'sponsor' (it can be someone providing accommodation). Providing you can satisfy these demands there should be no further problems, but since quite a few visitors overstay their entry permits, there are 'get tough' periods.

WOMEN TRAVELLERS

There are no particular dangers for women in Mauritius, and you won't feel out of place travelling solo either. It's still sensible to avoid walking alone along heavily forested trails and roaming around late at night outside of resorts, particularly as most places have very poor or nonexistent street lighting. Port Louis is one extreme example where it really would be foolish to walk about alone after dark, especially near the Jardins de Compagnie (a favoured hangout of pimps, drug addicts and prostitutes).

ⓘ Getting There & Away

AIR

Mainland Mauritius' only airport is **Sir Seewoosagur Ramgoolam International Airport** (SSR; ☎603 6000; aml.mru.aero). If you're going to be island-hopping around the region, you can cut the cost of individual fares by buying an Indian Ocean Pass. The pass covers Air Mauritius, Air Austral and Air Seychelles flights between Mauritius, Réunion and the Seychelles and their services to Madagascar, Comoros, Mayotte and the Maldives. The pass, which is valid for two months, must be purchased outside the region from any of the three participating airlines. You must make a minimum of three different flights. Fares are discounted by about 30%. For details of prices contact the participating airlines.

Air Austral (☎202 6677; www.air-austral.com; 5 President John Kennedy St, Rogers House, Port Louis)

Air France (☎202 6747; www.airfrance.com; 5 President John Kennedy St, Rogers House, Port Louis)

Air Madagascar (☎203 2150; www.airmadagascar.com; IBL House, Le Caudan Waterfront, Port Louis)

Air Mauritius (☎207 7212; www.airmauritius.com; President John Kennedy St, Air Mauritius Centre, Port Louis)

Air Seychelles (☎202 6671; www.air-seychelles.com; 5 President John Kennedy St, Rogers House, Port Louis)

British Airways (☎202 8000; www.britishairways.com; IBL House, Le Caudan Waterfront, Port Louis)

Emirates (☎204 7700; www.emirates.com; 5th fl, Newton Tower, cnr Sir William Newton & Remy Ollier Sts, Port Louis)

SEA

The Mauritius Shipping Corporation (p151) operates the *Mauritius Trochetia* and the *Mauritius Pride* between Réunion and Mauritius at least once a week in low season. The journey takes about 11 hours. The return fare from Mauritius is €160/175 in low/high season.

ⓘ Getting Around

BICYCLE

Cycling isn't really a practical means of long-distance transport in Mauritius – there is simply too much traffic and drivers rarely take cyclists into consideration – but bikes are fine for short hops along the coast. Given that the coast is pleasantly flat, it's amazing how much ground you can cover in a day. The coast roads are also quieter than those in the interior.

In general, the roads are well maintained, but look out for potholes along country lanes, especially in the western part of the island. Avoid cycling anywhere at night, as most roads are poorly lit.

Most hotels and guesthouses can help you arrange bike rentals (usually mountain bikes). Although many offer this as a complimentary service for guests, expect to pay around Rs 250 per day for a quality bike at those places that don't. You'll usually be asked for a deposit of Rs 5000, either in cash or by taking an imprint of your credit card. Most bikes are in pretty reasonable condition, but be sure to check the brakes, gears and saddle (some are mighty uncomfortable) before riding off into the blue beyond. The bike should have a lock; use it, especially if you leave your bike at the beach and outside shops.

CLIMATE CHANGE & TRAVEL

Every form of transport that relies on carbon-based fuel generates CO_2, the main cause of human-induced climate change. Modern travel is dependent on aeroplanes, which might use less fuel per kilometre per person than most cars but travel much greater distances. The altitude at which aircraft emit gases (including CO_2) and particles also contributes to their climate-change impact. Many websites offer 'carbon calculators' that allow people to estimate the carbon emissions generated by their journey and, for those who wish to do so, to offset the impact of the greenhouse gases emitted with contributions to portfolios of climate-friendly initiatives throughout the world. Lonely Planet offsets the carbon footprint of all staff and author travel.

BOAT

Various private operators offer cruises to offshore islands, or snorkelling and fishing excursions.

Otherwise, two boats, the *Mauritius Pride* and *Mauritius Trochetia*, have three to four monthly passenger services in both directions between Port Louis (Mauritius) and Port Mathurin (Rodrigues). The journey can take anywhere between 25 and 36 hours.

The *Mauritius Pride* has only first-class cabins which cost US$135/81 per adult/child.

The *Mauritius Trochetia* has four different classes, ranging from second class (adult/child US$110/66) up to deluxe cabins (US$185/111).

Tickets and information are available through travel agents or direct from the two shipping company offices listed here. These are popular services – book ahead.

Coraline Shipping Agency (☏ 217 2285; www. mauritiusshipping.intnet.mu; 1 Military Rd, Nova Bldg, Port Louis) In Port Louis.

Mauritius Shipping Corporation (Map p161; ☏ 831 0640; www.mauritiusshipping.intnet. mu; Rue François Leguat, Port Mathurin; ☺ 8.15am-3pm Mon-Fri, 8.15-11am Sat) On Rodrigues.

BUS

Anyone on a budget will fare well using the network of bus routes that criss-cross the island. Bus travel is cheap and fun – you'll usually find yourself chatting to gregarious locals – and although you won't set any land-speed records, it's generally a fairly easy and reliable way to get around.

The buses are almost always packed, especially on the main routes, but turnover is quick at all the stops. If you start the trip standing, you're likely to end up sitting.

Be warned that you could have problems taking large bags or backpacks on a bus. If it takes up a seat, you will probably have to pay for that extra seat. A few travellers have even been refused entry to a full bus if they have a large bag.

Bus Types

There is no countrywide bus service for Mauritius. Instead there are several large regional bus companies and scores of individual operators.

It's best to stick to express buses whenever possible, as standard buses seem to stop every few metres and can take up to twice as long to reach the same destination. To give an idea of journey times, it takes approximately an hour by standard services from Mahébourg to Curepipe, an hour from Curepipe to Port Louis, and an hour from Port Louis to Grand Baie.

The buses are single-deck vehicles bearing dynamic names such as 'Road Warrior', 'Bad Boys' and 'The Street Ruler'. Thus encouraged,

it's perhaps not surprising that some drivers harbour Formula One racing fantasies; fortunately, the frequent stops slow things down a touch. Though the buses are in varying states of disrepair, the fleet is gradually being upgraded.

Bus Schedules

Unfortunately, there are no published timetables available. Your best source of information is to phone the umbrella body, the **National Transport Authority** (☏ 202 2800). Locals also usually know the best way to get from A to B.

Long-distance buses run from around 6am to 6.30pm, though there is a late service between Port Louis and Curepipe until 11pm. Generally there are buses every 15 minutes or so on the major routes, with less frequent buses on the express services. Buses in country areas can be few and far between.

Fares & Tickets

Fares range from Rs 15 for a short trip to a maximum of Rs 35 for the run from Port Louis to Mahébourg. Air-conditioned express buses may be a couple of rupees extra. Tickets are available from the conductor or porter (the conductor's 'assistant'); keep some small change handy. Retain your tickets, as inspectors often board to check them, and press the buzzer when you want to get off.

Advance reservations are not possible.

CAR & MOTORCYCLE

By far the easiest and quickest way to get around Mauritius and Rodrigues is to hire a car. Prices aren't as low as they could be, considering the numbers of visitors who rent vehicles, but you should be able to negotiate a discount if you're renting for a week or more.

Mauritian roads range from the one stretch of motorway – running from SSR international airport to Grand Baie via Port Louis – to pot-holed minor roads. Even on the motorway you'll find people wandering across the road and a generally relaxed attitude. As in most places, the greatest danger comes from other drivers, not the roads. Mauritian drivers tend to have little consideration for each other, let alone for motorbikes. Buses are notorious for overtaking and then pulling in immediately ahead of other vehicles to pick up or drop off passengers; always use extra caution when a bus comes in sight. At night be aware that you'll face an assault course of ill-lit oncoming vehicles, totally unlit bikes and weaving pedestrians. If you sense that you've hit something while driving at night, proceed to the nearest police station. Motorcyclists should also be prepared for the elements, as sudden rain showers can come out of clear skies.

Car Hire

Generally, drivers must be more than 23 years of age (some companies only require a minimum age of 21) and have held a driving licence for at least one year, and payment must usually be made in advance. You can pay by credit card (Visa and MasterCard are the most widely accepted), though small companies might add a 3% 'processing fee' for this service. All foreigners are technically required to have an International Driving Licence. Few rental agencies enforce this, but it's safest to carry one as the police can demand to see it.

Rates for the smallest hatchback start at around Rs 1000 a day (including insurance and unlimited mileage) with one of the local operators. Expect rates to start at Rs 1200 when using an international chain, although daily prices can even start as high as Rs 1600. On top of that you will be required to pay a refundable deposit, usually Rs 15,000; most companies will take an imprint of your credit card to cover this. Policies usually specify that drivers are liable for the first Rs 15,000 of damage in the event of an accident.

Although there are dozens of operators on the island, it is best to book ahead during the high-season months (the European winter holidays). The following car-hire companies have airport desks or can deliver to the airport.

ABC (☑ 216 8889; www.abc-carrental.com; 3B, Sir Seewosagur Ramgoolan International Airport)

Avis (☑ 405 5200; www.avismauritius.com; 4B, Sir Seewosagur Ramgoolan International Airport)

Budget (☑ 467 9700; www.budget.com.mu; 1A, Sir Seewosagur Ramgoolan International Airport)

Claire & Sailesh Ltd (☑ 754 6451, 798 5913; www.clairesaileshltd.com)

Europcar (☑ 637 3240; www.europcar.com; 3A, Sir Seewosagur Ramgoolan International Airport)

Hertz (☑ 670 4301, 604 3021; www.hertz.com; 17A, Sir Seewosagur Ramgoolan International Airport)

Kevtrav Ltd (☑ 465 4458; www.kevtrav.com; St Jean Rd, Quatre Bornes)

Ropsen (☑ 451 5763; www.ropsen.net; Royal Rd, La Gaulette)

Sixt (☑ 427 1111; www.sixt.com; 7B, Sir Seewosagur Ramgoolan International Airport)

Motorcycle Hire

There are only a few places where you can hire motorbikes, which is a shame as this is a great way to explore the quiet coastal roads – especially in traffic-free Rodrigues. While you'll occasionally find a 125cc bike, most are 100cc or under; the smaller models are referred to as scooters.

Expect to pay upwards of Rs 500 per day (Rs 600 in Rodrigues). As with car hire, payment is requested in advance along with a deposit of Rs 5000 or so.

Towns offering motorcycle hire include Grand Baie, Flic en Flac, Mahébourg and Port Mathurin. Your best bet is to ask around your hotel. You should be aware that most motorcycle hire is 'unofficial' so you may not be covered in case of a collision.

Parking

Parking is free and not a problem in most of Mauritius, although it's best not to leave your car in an isolated spot. City parking requires payment. There are supervised car parks in Port Louis, but elsewhere you'll have to park on the street, which in a handful of towns involves buying parking coupons – ask a local if you're not sure. These are available from petrol stations and cost from Rs 50 for 10 coupons, with each coupon valid for 30 minutes. The same coupons can be used all over the island. Street parking is generally free at night and on weekends; the exact hours, which vary from one town to another, are indicated on signposts.

Road Rules

Local motorists seem to think they'll save electricity by not switching on their headlights, and the police are better at people control than traffic control. Traffic congestion is heavy in Port Louis. There are many pedestrian zebra crossings, but cross with care. Don't expect courtesy and don't expect drivers to be worried about insurance – you'll get knocked over.

Driving is on the left and the speed limit varies from 30km/h in town centres to 110km/h on the motorway – speed limits are usually marked. Even so, not many people stick to these limits and the island has its fair share of accidents. Remember also that the motorway has a series of roundabouts – bearing down on them at 110km/h is a dangerous pastime best avoided.

Drivers and passengers are required to wear seat belts. For lack of sufficient breathalysers, the alcohol limit (legally 0.5g/L) is defined by the police as one glass of beer.

HELICOPTER

Air Mauritius also offers helicopter tours and charters from SSR international airport to a number of major hotels. A hotel transfer anywhere on the island costs Rs 22,000, while a full one-hour island tour costs Rs 34,000 for up to two passengers; a quick 15-minute jaunt will set you back Rs 13,000. For information and reservations, contact **Air Mauritius Helicopter Services** (☑ 603 3754; www.airmauritius.com/helicopter) or ask your hotel to organise a transfer or trip.

HITCHING

Hitching is never entirely safe in any country in the world, and we don't recommend it. Travellers who decide to hitch should understand that they are taking a small but potentially serious risk. People who choose to hitch will be safer if they travel in pairs and let someone know where they are planning to go.

Getting a lift in Mauritius is subject to pretty much the same quirks of luck and fate that you experience hitching anywhere. The only place where it really does come in handy is Rodrigues. Since few people there own cars, hitching is a popular way to get around, especially on Sundays, when buses are few and far between. Those driving in Rodrigues will make friends by offering lifts to locals who'll try and flag you down almost anywhere. Obviously, proceed with caution and don't offer lifts to groups if you're alone.

TAXI

It's sometimes possible to imagine that every adult male in Mauritius is a taxi driver. Taxi drivers will often shout out at travellers they see wandering around Port Louis or Grand Baie, while ranks outside hotels usually overflow with drivers. Negotiation is key – meters are rarely used and you'll usually be ripped off if you get in a taxi without agreeing on a price first. During the journey most drivers will also tout for future business; if you aren't careful, you may find that you've agreed to an all-day island tour. If you aren't interested, make this very clear, as many drivers won't take no for an answer.

Many guesthouse managers/owners have attempted to mitigate their guests' constant frustration with rip-offs by arranging prices with local taxi drivers. The quotes given under such arrangements, particularly those from small guesthouses, are often acceptable; they can usually arrange competitively priced airport pick-ups as well. Once you've got a feel for the rates, you can venture into independent bargaining. You'll find that these prices are fairly standard throughout – you may be able to knock off Rs 100 or Rs 200 here and there, though don't be crestfallen if you can't whittle the driver

down to the exact price you're expecting (after all, they have had more practise at the taxi game than you!).

Taxis charge slightly more at night and may ask for an extra fee if you want the comfort of air-con. It's also worth remembering that some taxis charge around Rs 1 per minute waiting time. It seems minimal, but it adds up if you stop for lunch or do some sightseeing on foot. Your best bet is to negotiate a set fare with the driver that includes waiting time.

Upon arrival at the airport, there is a taxi desk with set prices for just about anywhere on the island.

Taxi Hire

For around Rs 2000 you can hire a taxi for a full-day tour of sights along one or two coasts of the island. You can cut costs by forming a group – the price should *not* be calculated per person. Once you've agreed to a price and itinerary, it helps to get the details down in writing. Although most drivers can speak both French and English, double-check before setting off to ensure you won't face a day-long communication barrier. If you're lucky, you'll get an excellent and informative guide, but note that most drivers work on a commission basis with particular restaurants, shops and sights. If you want to go to a restaurant of your choice, you may have to insist on it. Again, small guesthouses can usually recommend a reliable driver.

Share Taxi

When individual fares are hard to come by, some taxis will cruise around their area supplementing the bus service. For quick, short-haul trips they pick up passengers waiting at the bus stops and charge just a little more than the bus. Their services are called 'share taxis' or 'taxi trains'. Mind you, if you flag down a share taxi, you'll only be swapping a big sardine can for a small one, and if you flag down an empty taxi, you may have to pay the full fare.

Rodrigues

Best Places to Eat

➜ Nyeusi (p163)

➜ Le Marlin Bleu (p163)

➜ Mazavaroo (p164)

➜ Aux Deux Frères (p163)

➜ Cases à Gardenias (p164)

Best Places to Stay

➜ Tekoma (p162)

➜ Bakwa Lodge (p162)

➜ Cases à Gardenias (p161)

➜ La Belle Rodriguaise (p162)

➜ Chez Bernard & Claudine (p162)

Why Go?

Blissfully isolated over 600km northeast of the mainland, this tiny volcanic outcrop surrounded by a massive turquoise lagoon is a stunning mountainous gem that barely feels connected to its big sister, Mauritius, let alone the wider world.

Often billed as the 'Mauritius of 25 years ago', Rodrigues actually bears little resemblance to its neighbour beyond the scenic strips of peach-tinged sand. The island's population of around 40,000 is predominantly African and Creole – a far cry from the ethnic melting pot next door. You won't find a stalk of sugar cane here either – Rodrigues' hilly interior is clothed with fruit-bearing trees and vast acreages of vegetable patches. The pace of life is undeniably slow – which gives the island its time-warped vibe. Great food, some fine natural sites and a host of activities round out an experience that lives long in the memory.

When to Go

➜ November to February is high season with high prices, although cyclones are possible from January. Accommodation and air tickets can be hard to come by so book well in advance if travelling at this time.

➜ October, March and April are still considered high season in places, but there are generally fewer crowds. Underwater visibility is especially good for diving and snorkelling at this time and it's generally a nice time to be on the island.

➜ Generally you'll find lower prices and milder temperatures from May to September, and no chance of cyclones.

⊙ Sights

Besides Rodrigues' golden beaches – the best of which flank the island's eastern ridges – there are several interesting sights to take in, including a couple of caves and several noteworthy architectural contributions. It's also worth noting that Rodrigues has few structured towns so we've included the island's main sights below.

⊙ Port Mathurin

This tiny port is the island's hub, largest town and, for want of a better word, its capital. The word 'soporific' may come to mind, but during the day the town has a friendly vibe, especially around the buzzing market stalls.

Saturday Market   MARKET
(Map p161; ⊙ 4.30-10am) The Saturday market is as busy as Rodrigues gets and a good place to shop for fresh produce and souvenirs. It's

open the rest of the week but really gears up on Saturdays when much of the island turns out. It's next to the bridge near the post office. Turn up later than 10am and you'll wonder what all of the fuss is about.

La Résidence   ARCHITECTURE
(Map p161; Rue de la Solidarité) One of the oldest buildings still standing in Port Mathurin, La Résidence dates from 1897, when it provided a fairly modest home for the British chief commissioner. Its facilities are now used as function rooms for the new Regional Assembly. As such, it is closed to the public although it is possible to get an idea of the structure from the verandah of the tourist office (p164) across the road.

⊙ Around Rodrigues

★ **François Leguat Reserve**   WILDLIFE RESERVE
(Map p156; ☑ 832 8141; www.tortoisescavereserve
-rodrigues.com; adult/child incl tortoises & cave

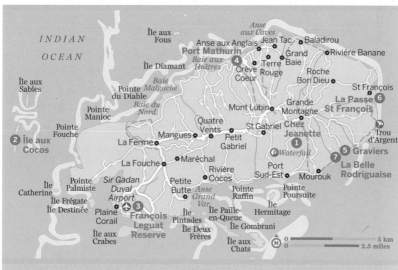

Rodrigues Highlights

❶ Savour traditional Rodriguan cuisine at a local *table d'hôte* like **Chez Jeanette** (p163)

❷ Take a boat ride out to the seabird colonies of pretty **Île aux Cocos** (p158)

❸ Cavort with hundreds of curious tortoises at the **François Leguat Reserve** (p160)

❹ Get up early and immerse yourself in the busy **Saturday Market** in Port Mathurin

❺ Hike past Rodrigues best beaches from **Graviers to St François** (p158)

❻ Dive the pristine waters off the east coast at **La Passe St François** (p159)

❼ Sleep by the sea at **La Belle Rodriguaise** (p162)

Rodrigues

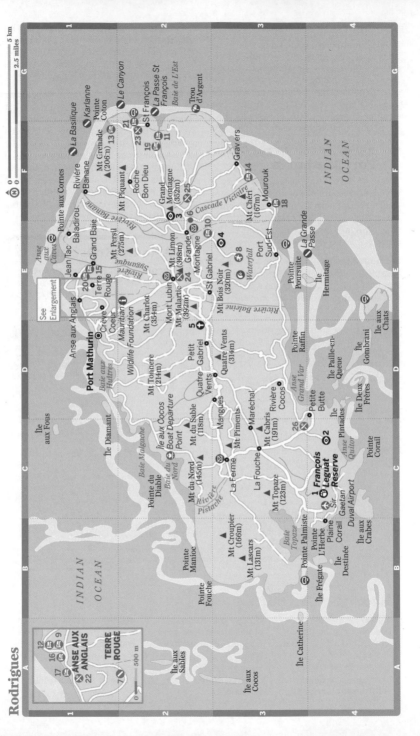

INDIAN OCEAN

INDIAN OCEAN

Baie de L'Est

Trou d'Argent

La Passe St François

St François

Le Canyon

Pointe Coton

Karlanne

La Basilique

Gravers

Mt Chéri (167m)

Mourouk

Cascade Victoire

Grand Montagne (352m)

Mt Grenade (206m)

Mt Piquant

Roche Bon Dieu

Banane

Rivière

Pointe aux Cornes

Pointe aux Cornes

Anse aux Cleves

Jean Tac

Baladirou

Grand Baie

Terre Rouge

Mt Persil (275m)

Rivière Banane

Rivière Susangue

Mt Limon (398m)

Grande Montagne

St Gabriel

Port Sud-Est

Pointe Poursuite

La Grande Passe

Île Hermitage

Île aux Chats

Île Gombrani

Pointe Raffin

Rivière Baleine

Mt Bois Noir (320m)

Waterfall

Quatre Vents (314m)

Mt Malartic (392m)

Mt Lubin

Mt Charlot (35+m)

Mauritian Wildlife Foundation

Crève Coeur

Anse aux Anglais

Port Mathurin

Baie aux Huîtres

Île aux Cocos

Boat Departure Point

Île Diamant

Île aux Fous

Baie Malgache

Baie du Nord

Pointe du Diable

INDIAN OCEAN

Pointe Fouche

Pointe Manioc

Mt Lascars (131m)

Mt Croupier (166m)

Mt du Nord (145m)

La Ferme

Rivière Pistache

La Fouche

Mt Topaze (123m)

Mt du Sable (118m)

Mangues

Maréchal

Mt Piments

Rivière Cocos

Mt Cabris (191m)

Petite Butte

Anse Grand Var

Île Paille-en-Queue

Île Deux Frères

Pointe Corail

Anse Quitor

Anse Pintades

Petit Gabriel

Quatre Vents

Mt Tonnerre (214m)

François Leguat Reserve

Plaine Corail

St. Gaetan Duval Airport

Île aux Crabes

Île Destinée

Baie Topaze

Pointe L'Herbe

Pointe Palmiste

Pointe Frégate

Île Catherine

Île aux Cocos

Île aux Sables

Pointe Corail

Enlargement

See Enlargement

ANSE AUX ANGLAIS

TERRE ROUGE

Rodrigues

Rs 285/135, tortoises only Rs 155/90; ⊙9am-5pm, tours at 9.30am, 10.30am, 12.30pm & 2.30pm) In 1691, François Leguat wrote that there were so many tortoises on Rodrigues that 'one can take more than a hundred steps on their shell without touching the ground'. Sadly the Rodrigues version of the giant tortoise went the way of the dodo, but this giant tortoise and cave reserve has grand plans to re-create the Eden described in the logbooks of the island's early explorers. The project is well underway – hundreds of tortoises roam the grounds (the outcome of a successful breeding program); there's a small enclosure with several giant fruit bats (the island's only endemic mammal); and over 100,000 indigenous trees have been planted over the last four years. The on-site museum recounts the history and settlement of the island, and offers detailed information about the extinct solitaire, cousin of the like-fated dodo. Don't miss the guided tours of the on-site caves. Spirited tour leaders point out quirky rock shapes and discuss the island's interesting geological history. Keep an eye out for the tibia bone of a solitaire that juts out from the cavern's stone ceiling. The reserve is in the island's southwest, and is signposted off the main road around 1.5km northeast of the airport.

Caverne Patate   CAVE
(Map p156; guided tours Rs 100; ⊙guided tours 9am, 11am, 1pm & 3pm) Caverne Patate, in the southwest corner of the island, is an impres-

sive cave system with a few stalagmite and stalactite formations. Visit is by guided tour during which a guide points out formations with uncanny resemblances to a dodo, Buckingham Palace and even Winston Churchill! The 700m tunnel is an easy walk, but gets slippery in wet weather; wear shoes with a good grip and take a light jacket or pullover.

The track to the caves is signposted off the road from La Ferme to Petite Butte. Buses en route to La Fourche can drop you off at the turn-off.

Grande Montagne
Nature Reserve   NATURE RESERVE
(Map p156; ☎832 5737; www.mauritian-wildlife. org; Grande Montagne; ⊙8am-3pm Mon-Fri) One of the last remaining stands of forest on Rodrigues, this nature reserve crowns the highest part of the island. The Mauritian Wildlife Foundation (MWF; p164) has overseen the planting of over 150,000 native plant species, and the restoration of this ecosystem has ensured the survival of the Rodrigues fody and Rodrigues warbler; for more information see p139. A series of trails pass through the forest – although they're not especially well marked, it's difficult to get too lost. Pick up the useful (and free) *Grande Montagne Nature Reserve Field Guide* at the entrance to help with plant and bird identification. The MWF has plans to run guided walks through the reserve – contact them for details.

Saint Gabriel Church CHURCH

(Map p156) This surprisingly grand church in the middle of the island has one of the largest congregations in the Port Louis diocese. Constructed between 1936 and 1939, it was built by local volunteers who arduously lugged stone, sand and coral from all corners of the island. Christianity is an integral part of life on the island – hundreds upon hundreds of Rodriguans gather here every Sunday.

Jardin des 5 Sens GARDENS

(Map p156; ☑ 831 5860; Montagne Bois Noir; admission incl guided tour Rs 250; ⊙ guided tours 10am, 11am, 1pm, 2pm & 3pm) This pretty little botanical garden of indigenous Rodriguan plants is an interesting way to spend an hour, not to mention a good initiative. Time your visit to coincide with lunch at the attached Chez Jeanette (p163).

🏃 Activities

Hiking

Hiking is the best way to uncover the island's natural treasures – most notably, its wild, undeveloped beaches. The *Carte Verte de Rodrigues*, published by the Association Rodrigues Entreprendre Au Féminin, charts the island's eight most popular hikes and provides detailed information on how to access each trailhead using public transportation.

The island's most famous walk (No 4 on the Carte Verte) is the classic coastal trail from **Graviers to St François** in the island's east. On the way you'll pass the island's most stunning stretches of sand, including **Trou d'Argent**, the supposed location of a pirate's hidden booty. If you're relying on public transport, we recommend beginning in Graviers – buses run to Graviers in the morning but are extremely

---

WORTH A TRIP

ÎLE AUX COCOS

There are 17 small islands sprinkled around Rodrigues' lagoon and the most interesting of these to visit is Île aux Cocos. Around 1.5km long and 150m wide at its broadest point, Île aux Cocos is a nature reserve and the only island on the Indian Ocean where four seabirds – the lesser noddy, brown noddy, fairy tern and sooty tern – all breed on the same island. The southern quarter of the island is fenced off as a restricted zone. Elsewhere, there is a virgin quality to the island here – the lesser noddies and fairy terns are remarkably tame, just as all wildlife (including the ill-fated dodo) was when the first sailors arrived on Mauritius and Rodrigues.

The reserve is overseen by Discovery Rodrigues (p164) – they meet all boat arrivals and give a brief (and mostly French) overview of the island's more interesting features. They do not, however, organise the boat trips themselves. To do that you will need to make the arrangements through your hotel, a tour operator or directly through the boat owners.

Most boat trips depart from Pointe du Diable, although check with the boat owner when making the booking. If you don't have your own wheels, the owners may be able to arrange a pick-up from your hotel. Departure time could be anywhere from 7am to 10am depending on the tides, and the boat trip takes an hour each way. You'll probably end up spending around three hours on the island – bring your swimmers.

A trip to Île aux Cocos will cost around Rs 1500 if you organise it through your hotel, but will cost significantly less (Rs 900 to Rs 1000) if you go directly to the boat owner. This price includes boat trip, park admission and a picnic lunch.

Boat owners we recommend include:

Rico François (☑ 875 5270) Departure from Pointe du Diable.

Tonio Jolicouer (☑ 875 5720) Departure from Pointe du Diable.

Berraca Tours (☑ 875 3726) Departure from Pointe du Diable.

Joe 'Cool' (☑ 876 2826) Departure from Pointe La Guele.

Christophe Meunier (☑ 875 4442, 429 5045) Departure from Anse aux Anglais. Christophe also uses a sailing boat (rather than one with an outboard motor) and sometimes factors in extra time for snorkelling.

scarce in the afternoon when you're likely to have far better luck in St François.

The Carte Verte is available for purchase (Rs 100) at a kiosk in central Port Mathurin outside the Alfred Northcoombes Building. If you find them closed (which is often) or they've run out of stock (ditto), call ☎ 876 9170 and they should be able to locate you a copy. La Belle Rodriguaise (p162) also had them for sale at the time of research.

Diving

In general, Rodrigues' marine environment is remarkably well preserved and the best sites for divers lie off the east and south coasts. For more information see p29.

The three main dive centres are all based in hotels but nonguests are always welcome – just ring ahead. Figure on around Rs 1800 for a dive and equipment.

Good snorkelling detsinations include Île Hermitage, a tiny island renowned for its beauty (and possible hidden treasure), and Île aux Chats. Both are accessible by boat from Port Sud-Est.

Cotton Dive DIVING, KITESURFING
(Map p156; ☎ 831 8001/8208; www.cottonbayhotel. biz/diving) At the Cotton Bay Hotel.

Bouba Diving DIVING
(Map p156; ☎ 832 3063; www.boubadiving.com; 1/3 dives incl equipment Rs 1850/5270) At the Mourouk Ebony Hotel.

Rodriguez Diving DIVING
(Map p156; ☎ 831 0957; rodriguez-diving.tripod. com; dives from €25) At Pointe Vénus Hotel & Spa and Les Cocotiers.

Kitesurfing & Windsurfing

All the pros agree – Rodrigues is one of the best places in the world to kitesurf. Cotton Dive or Osmowings can set you up.

Osmowings KITESURFING
(Map p156; ☎ 832 3051; www.kitesurf-rodrigues. com) The top outfitter is Osmowings based at the Mourouk Ebony Hotel. A two-hour 'initiation' course costs €65 per person. Experienced kitesurfers can rent equipment for €19 an hour.

Fishing

Rod Fishing Club FISHING
(Map p161; ☎ 875 0616; www.rodfishingclub.com; Terre Rouge) The island's leading deep-sea fishing experts are the Rod Fishing Club run by Yann Colas, skipper of the Black Marlin, which makes frequent jigging sorties from

ⓘ WATER

The water that comes out of the tap on Rodrigues is not safe for drinking – stick to bottled water.

Port Mathurin. Book via the website and meet at the pier.

Ziplining

Tyrodrig ADVENTURE SPORTS
(Map p156; ☎ 499 6970; www.tyrodrig.com; Montagne Bois Noir; per person Rs 1000; ⊙9am-noon & 1-5pm) If your idea of fun is zipping down a rope suspended over a canyon, then this adrenaline rush is all yours. Five cables hang out over the void, ranging from 420m long to 110m, with a drop beneath you of between 50m and 100m. It's signposted off the main road between Mont Lubin and Grande Montagne.

Tours

Guided tours led by locals are the best way to explore Rodrigues. There are several excellent travel agencies in town offering a range of activities, accommodation, tours and vehicle rentals. The tourist office has a small photocopied sheet with the phone numbers of a dozen boatswains willing to take tourists out to the various islets in the turquoise lagoon.

2000 Tours TOURS
(Map p156; ☎ 831 4703; www.rodrigues-2000tours. com; Rue Max Lucchesi)

Beraca TOURS
(☎ 831 2198; tropicalguy17@caramail.com; Baie aux Huitres)

JP Excursions TOURS
(Map p161; ☎ 831 1162; www.jpexcursion-rodrigues. com; Rue Barclay)

Gariko Tours TOURS
(Patriko Tours; Map p161; ☎ 831 2044; garikotours. wordpress.com; Rue François Leguat)

Rotourco TOURS
(Map p161; ☎ 831 0747; www.rotourco.com; Rue François Leguat)

🛏 Sleeping

The main concentration of hotels and guesthouses is found 2km east of Port Mathurin at Anse aux Anglais, at St François on the east coast and along the south coast. Elsewhere, the guesthouses in the quieter parts of the island offer the getaway-from-it-all experience par excellence.

Port Mathurin & Around

Port Mathurin makes a convenient base if you are travelling by bus, but frankly it lacks the quality you'll find elsewhere on the island.

Residence Foulsafat   GUESTHOUSE €
(Map p156; ☎831 1760; www.residencefoulsafat.com; Jean Tac; d incl half board €60) High up in the hills with memorable views of the infinite blue, this friendly option has three charming houses each with a unique design and theme. Our favourite was the adorable honeymooners' cottage with stone walls and attached gazebo covered with gingerbread trim.

Rotourco   APARTMENTS €
(Map p161; www.lacabanedete.com; Rue François Leguat; 4-/8-bed apt Rs 1500/3000) Offers adorable studio accommodation in Baie Malagache. Highly recommended.

Auberge Lagon Bleu   GUESTHOUSE €
(Map p156; ☎831 0075; www.aubergelagonbleu.com; Caverne Provert; s/d/tr Rs 600/800/1000; ❄) Wicker baskets and colourful paintings abound at this very casual guesthouse on the road towards Jean Tac. Guests congregate in the sociable eating area tucked under tin roofing and drooping laundry lines. Colourful paintings on the walls spruce up the otherwise Spartan bedrooms. It's an additional Rs 600 per person for half board.

Lataniers Jeune   GUESTHOUSE €€
(Map p161; ☎875 0591; Rue de la Solidarité, Port Mathurin; per person incl half board Rs 1400) The newest venture by Françoise Baptiste who runs La Belle Rodriguaise, this four-room guesthouse was due to open not long after we were there and, if her other ventures are anything to go by, it should become the place to stay in Port Mathurin.

Coco Villas   GUESTHOUSE €€
(Map p156; ☎831 0449; www.rodrigues-cocovilla.com; Caverne Provert; per person incl half board Rs 1200; ❄☎) Simple rooms at this family-run place make a quieter alternative to Anse aux Anglais just down the road. Rooms are nothing special but the price is about right.

Le Récif   GUESTHOUSE €€
(Map p156; ☎831 1804; www.lerecifhotel.com; Caverne Provert; s/d incl half board Rs 2600/3800; ❄) Perched on the cliff just east of Anse aux Anglais, Le Récif has fabulous views from its balcony out over the emerald lagoon. We reckon it's a touch overpriced and it can have a vaguely abandoned air when things are quiet, but the rooms are large and the views are hard to beat anywhere on the island.

L'Amphore   GUESTHOUSE €€
(Map p156; ☎832 1287; www.lamphore.vpweb.fr; Grand Baie; per person incl half board Rs 1400; ☎) This eccentric little place at the entrance to Grand Baie has just two rooms but they're kitted out in an eclectic mix of homey furnishings fashioned by the owner (who can organise diving excursions) himself. There's even a fish pond where they bite your legs

---

THE RAREST PLANT ON EARTH?

In 1980, a school teacher asked his students to bring in a local plant as part of a school project. One brought in a plant that baffled everyone. Finally the experts at the UK's Kew Gardens identified the plant as café marron (*Ramosmania rodriguesii*), which was long thought extinct. Locals had for centuries used the plant as an aphrodisiac and as a treatment for sexually transmitted diseases, and news of the plant's discovery leaked out. The plant was fenced off but locals continued to find a way through. In 1986 an international operation was mounted – a cutting of the plant was flown from Rodrigues to London where, within 24 hours, it was in Kew Gardens.

Cuttings were taken and it is from these that the Mauritian Wildlife Foundation has been able to grow more in its plant nursery. The plant is not yet out of danger – one of the plants in the Grande Montagne Nature Reserve (p157) was stolen (a younger, yet-to-flower replacement is labelled and can be seen alongside the main trail), as was another from their plant nursery. Even so, more than 50 have been successfully planted in the reserve. No other wild plants have ever been found but, for the first time in living memory, the original plant recently began to grow fruit.

Port Mathurin

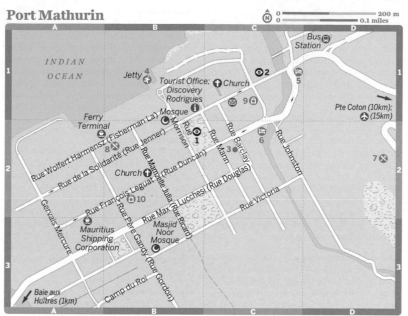

in some weird therapy ritual that the owner swears by.

Les Cocotiers HOTEL €€€
(Map p156; ☏ 831 1058; www.blue-season-hotels.com; Anse Aux Anglais; s/d with half board from €126/180; ❉ ◼) A great choice at the end of the coastal road, this friendly resort comes with an airy restaurant, an inviting swimming pool and a popular on-site dive centre. Vaco paintings adorn the walls in the rooms, and the beds have colourful duvets to match.

Around Rodrigues

Chez Jeanette GUESTHOUSE €€
(Le Tropical; Map p156; ☏ 831 5860; www.gite-letropical.com; Montagne Bois Noir; per person incl half board Rs 1200; ☏) Set high on a hill, this fine house, built partly of stone, has eight large, simple rooms that are blissfully quiet. The kitchen here serves up fine food and there's even an on-site botanical garden (p158). The perfect mountain retreat.

★ **Cases à Gardenias** GUESTHOUSE €€
(Map p156; ☏ 832 5751; www.casesagardenias-rodrigues.com; Montagne Bois Noir; per person incl half board €60; @ ☏) Cases à Gardenias is the most stylish guesthouse on the island.

Port Mathurin

It's the pride and joy of the lovely owners, a Belgian-Mauritian couple, who have built up their property from scratch. The beautiful plantation-inspired bedrooms have lovely stonewashed furniture (made by hand), and in the morning guests can wander the orchards in search of fresh fruit or help the beekeeper tease out the sticky honey from the colourful apiary. The owner also has plans to run cooking classes, including a trip with her to the market. It's not signposted – take the turn-off towards Chez Janette off the main road between Mont Lubin and Grande Montagne and it's the peach-coloured complex around 1km from the turn-off.

Chez Bernard & Claudine GUESTHOUSE €€
(Map p156; ☑ 831 8242; cbmoneret@intnet.mu; St François; per person incl half board Rs 1300) When St François was known for its end-of-the-world seclusion, this charming Tudor-style lodge was the only place to hang your hat. The well-maintained rooms have moved into a newer building out the back and are large, light and airy. Meals here are delicious, the owners are friendly and you're well placed for walks along the east coast.

La Belle Rodriguaise GUESTHOUSE €€
(Map p156; ☑ 832 4040; www.labellerodriguaise. com; Graviers; per person incl half board Rs 2000; ✦✦) Françoise Baptiste's inviting seaside retreat, near the quaint township of Graviers, has sun-drenched rooms in charming *case*-style abodes, all with wonderfully unobstructed sea views. Up the hill guests will find an inviting amoeba-shaped pool and a breezy dining room set on a sweeping verandah.

★ **Bakwa Lodge** HOTEL €€€
(Map p156; ☑ 686 7662; www.bakwalodge.com; Var Brulé, Mourouk; s Rs 2075-4280, d Rs 3990-7720; ✦✦) One of the most beautiful places to stay on the island, this all-white oasis where the road ends in Mourouk is luxury in a classy, understated style. The rooms are large and decorated with cuts from old wooden pirogues and each room is flooded with natural light; most have both indoor and outdoor showers. The beach here is good, which for most makes up for the lack of a swimming pool.

★ **Tekoma** LUXURY HOTEL €€€
(Map p156; ☑ 265 5244; www.tekoma-hotel.com; St François; d incl half-board €243 -417; ✦✦✦✦) ⌀ Arguably the finest address on Rodrigues, this stunning new place opened in late 2012. Supremely comfortable, freestanding cabins are arrayed around a rocky headland that slopes down to a good beach, and there's a blissful sense of isolation. They also have the aim of being powered entirely by renewable energy, and the food is superb.

Pirate Lodge HOTEL €€€
(Map p156; ☑ 831 8775; www.piratelodge.com; St François; ste incl breakfast €160; ✦) These attractive four- to six-bed apartments are set in a scenic palm grove visited by chirping birds. The outside design incorporates colourful Creole-inspired details while the interiors are much more modern – IKEA-esque knick-knacks dot the living rooms and fully equipped kitchens.

Cotton Bay Hotel HOTEL €€€
(Map p156; ☑ 831 8001; www.cottonbayhotel.biz; Pointe Coton; s incl half board €200-278, d €244-334, ste €298-404; ✦✦✦) Still going strong after 18 years in the biz, charming Cotton Bay is the island's oldest hotel. The design scheme has a lovely Creole motif – floral trim and tropically inspired prints adorn the rooms. Perks include a lovely pirogue-themed restaurant, outings on a private catamaran and endless streamers of honey-tinged sand.

Mourouk Ebony Hotel HOTEL €€€
(Map p156; ☑ 832 3351; www.mouroukebonyhotel. com; Mourouk; s/d incl half board from €140/200; ✦✦) The Mourouk Ebony waits at the end of a wiggling mountain road, and is easily recognised from afar by its bright-orange roofing. The grounds feature gorgeous gardens full of orchids and wildflowers that abut the out-of-this-world beach. Gentle Creole beats waft over the lobby's hand-dyed wicker lounge chairs. The rooms, however, could use a little sprucing up.

✖ Eating

The highlight of any visit to Rodrigues is sampling the unique local cuisine at one of the island's many *tables d'hôtes*. Rodriguans cook a variety of recipes that are quite different from their Mauritian neighbours – less emphasis is placed on spiciness and most meals are cooked with minimal amounts of oil.

Meals at the best and most well-known 'hosts' tables' on the island range from Rs 350 to Rs 700, and you should always call at least one day ahead to make a reservation.

✖ Port Mathurin & Around

Restaurant du Quai MAURITIAN, SEAFOOD €
(Map p161; ☑ 831 2840; Rue Wolfert Harmensz, Fisherman Lane; mains Rs 145-285; ⊙ 11am-2pm

LOCAL KNOWLEDGE

THE GOURMAND'S CHECKLIST

A list of Rodrigues' must-eats according to Françoise Baptiste; author, hostess and chef extraordinaire.

➡ *Ourite* – octopus salad with lemon juice, olive oil, pepper, onions and salt. The dried variety has a rather pungent taste and admittedly isn't for everyone.

➡ *Vindaye d'ourite* – boiled tender octopus flavoured with grated curcuma (such as ginger or turmeric), garlic, vinegar, lemon juice and a sprinkle of local spices.

➡ *Saucisses Créole* – a variety of meats that are dried and cured locally.

➡ *La torte Rodriguaise* – a small cake of papaya, pineapple or coconut mixed with a cream made from a local root called *corn-floeur*.

& 6-9pm Tue-Sun) This friendly place by the harbour is always full in the evenings with local families and visitors enjoying its fine seafood and lobster dishes. Staff are very keen to please and make a damn fine punch cocktail as an aperitif.

Chez Ram MAURITIAN, SEAFOOD €
(Map p161; ☑ 787 0375; Baie Lascars; mains Rs 145-285; ⊙ 11.30am-2pm & 6-9pm Thu-Tue) Roadside Chez Ram offers up excellent local cuisine – it has the *exact* same menu as Restaurant du Quai (owned by the same family).

Aux Deux Frères MAURITIAN, INTERNATIONAL €
(Map p161; ☑ 831 0541; 1st fl, Patriko Bldg, Rue François Leguat; mains Rs 240-365; ⊙ 8.30am-2.30pm Mon-Sat & 6.30-10pm Fri & Sat) Perched above a plaza of tour operators, Port Mathurin's slickest haunt serves local and international dishes in swish surrounds. The *marlin fumé avec gingembre* (smoked marlin with ginger) as a starter is small and simple but filled with taste. Aux Deux Frères also does pizza, pork brochettes and Creole sausages (the latter when they're available).

Le Marlin Bleu SEAFOOD, INTERNATIONAL €€
(Map p156; ☑ 832 0701; Anse aux Anglais; mains Rs 225-350; ⊙ 11am-2.30pm & 6-9.30pm Wed-Mon) The most sociable spot in Anse aux Anglais, this restaurant gets the thumbs-up from expats and is dominated by larger-than-life Mega, the friendly owner who makes sure that everyone's having a good time. The food is excellent (we especially loved the seafood salad), with a good mix of seafood, pizza and local dishes. Live football on the miraculously appearing big screen (or any excuse really) means the bar often stays open long after the kitchen closes.

Around Rodrigues

★**Nyeusi** MAURITIAN, FUSION €
(Map p156; ☑ 832 4533; www.rodriguesrestaurants.com; Coromandel; mains Rs 300-400; ⊙ 11.30am-2pm Sun-Thu, 11.30am-2pm & 6.30-9pm Fri & Sat) What a fabulous little place this is. Overseen by Veronique and Guillaume, Nyeusi is effortlessly classy and casual with a lovely semi-outdoors eating area surrounded by forest and a menu that fills a gap in Rodrigues restaurants with local dishes fused to an often Asian theme. All ingredients are local and fresh and the punch to get you started is the best we tasted on the island. They've plans for a guesthouse nearby.

Chez Jeanette RODRIGUAN €
(Le Tropical; Map p156; ☑ 831 5860; www.gite-tropical.com; Montagne Bois Noir; meals Rs 400-500; ⊙ 11am-2pm & 7-9pm) Traditional Rodriguan flavours is what you'll get at this friendly spot hidden in the hills. Dishes always feature an assortment of vegetables grown in the property's gardens.

Resto La Caverne MAURITIAN €
(Map p156; Petit Butte; mains from Rs 160; ⊙ 11am-2pm & 6-9pm) If you're visiting Caverne Patate (p157) or the François Leguat Reserve (p155), you could do worse than stop by this quiet little local place above a small grocery store. The octopus dishes are particularly memorable. It's opposite the turn-off to Caverne Patate.

Mengoz Snack STREET FOOD €
(Map p156; Route de l'Autonomie, Mont Lubin; mains Rs 45-120; ⊙ 8am-4pm Mon-Sat) It doesn't get much simpler than this but that's why we like it. Next to where the main road through the island branches to Grande Montagne,

Port Mathurin and the southwest, this fine little snack bar serves up fried rice or noodles, often with a main dish such as chop suey, and packs them in at lunchtime. A real slice of local life.

Mazavaroo
MAURITIAN €

(Map p156; ☎716 2282; St François; mains around Rs 300; ⊗10am-3pm & 6-9pm Sun-Fri) Hikers tackling a scenic east-coast jaunt can take a lunch break at this very casual affair. Savour the home-cooked seafood (smoked marlin, grilled fish, prawns and lobster), while the house specialty is *ceviché de thon jaune*, which is kind of like a yellow-fin tuna tartar, all served on painted pastel tables. Expats swear by this place.

★La Belle Rodriguaise
RODRIGUAN €€

(Map p156; ☎832 4040; Graviers; meals Rs 500-600) Perfected recipes by Françoise, author of a respected cookbook of Rodriguan recipes, are served on a breezy verandah with never-ending ocean views. Meals are mostly for guests of the hotel (p162), but ring ahead if you'd like to crash the party.

Chez Bernard & Claudine
RODRIGUAN €€

(Map p156; ☎831 8242; St François; meals Rs 500) This dinner-only option is the pick of the little *tables d'hôtes* scattered around St François. Ring ahead because they only take nonguests if they've room.

Cases à Gardenias
RODRIGUAN €€

(Map p156; ☎832 5751; Montagne Bois Noir; meals from Rs 500) The friendly hosts at Cases à Gardenias serve a smorgasbord of homemade goodies: wine, honey, fresh fruit, preserves and cured meats.

🛍 Shopping

Care-Co
HANDICRAFTS

(Map p161; Rue de la Solidarité; ⊗8am-4pm Mon-Fri, to noon Sat) Care-Co sells coconut-shell items, honey and model boats made by people (mostly beekeepers) with disabilities.

SHOPPING IN RODRIGUES

Rodrigues is famous for its honey and lemon and chilli preserves; you can also take home a very natty *vacoas*-leaf hat or basket. Jewellery and other items made from coconut shell by people with disabilities are available from Care-Co in Port Mathurin.

Island Books & Clothing Spot
BOOKS

(Map p161; ☎440 0040, 832 1564; Rue Francois Leguat; ⊗8.30am-4pm Mon-Fri, to 2pm Sat) This small bookshop has a handful of books about Rodrigues and Mauritius, including (while stocks last) the French-language flora and fauna guide to Île aux Cocos. They've another shop at the airport that opens just before and after flights arrive and depart.

❶ Information

INTERNET ACCESS

A growing number of hotels and guesthouses have wireless internet connections, but usually only in public areas, not rooms. Remember also that this is not an island of high-speed connections.

One public place with free (if slow) wireless access is outside the Alfred Northcoombs Building in central Port Mathurin. Among other tenants, it's home to the **Rodrigues Regional Library** which offers free wi-fi – hence the laptop-toting locals camped outside.

For an internet cafe with the usual slow connections, try Rotourco (p159).

MONEY

Most of the island's banks are in Port Mathurin and flank Rue Max Lucchesi. Mont Lubin and La Ferme also have banks, and there's an ATM at the airport. For exchange rates, see p47.

TOURIST INFORMATION

Tourist Office (Map p161; ☎832 0867; www.tourism-rodrigues.com; Rue de la Solidarité, Port Mathurin; ⊗8am-4pm Mon-Fri, to noon Sat) Small but helpful tourist office opposite La Résidence (p155).

Discovery Rodrigues (Map p161; ☎832 0867; Rue de la Solidarité; ⊗8am-4pm Mon-Fri, to noon Sat, to 10am Sun) Sharing an office and staff with the tourist office, this body oversees visits to Île aux Cocos. Although they organise tours they do not organise boat trips over (see p158).

Mauritian Wildlife Foundation (MWF; Map p156; ☎831 4558; www.mauritian-wildlife.org; Forestry Quarters, Solitude) Climbing the main road from Port Mathurin to Mont Lubin, take the second road on your left after passing the colourful painted sign for the Corail Restaurant. The MWF is in the second building you come to on your right at the bottom of the hill.

❶ Getting There & Away

AIR

The island's main **Air Mauritius office** (☎831 1632; fax 831 1959; Rue Max Lucchesi, ADS Bldg) is in Port Mathurin. There is also an office at the **airport** (☑ 832 7700), which is open for all arrivals and departures. It's a good idea to phone the airline the day before you leave anyway, just to make sure there's been no change to the schedule. There are six flights a day in high season, with just two at other times. Whenever you travel book early as seats can be hard to come by if you leave it late.

There is a luggage limit of 15kg per person, with excess charged at Rs 50 per kg.

SEA

The *Mauritius Pride* and *Mauritius Trochetia* make the voyage from Port Louis to Rodrigues three to four times a month, docking at the **passenger terminal** (Map p161; Rue Wolfert Harmensz) in Port Mathurin; see p151 for details.

ⓘ Getting Around

TO/FROM THE AIRPORT

Flights arrive at **Sir Gaetan Duval airport** (Plaine Corail Airport; Map p156; ☑ 831 6301) at the southwest tip of the island. A public bus runs between the airport and Port Mathurin roughly every 30 to 40 minutes from 6am to 4pm. The most hassle-free way to get to and from the airport is to pre-organise a ride with your accommodation of choice. Some hotels and guesthouses will include the price of a pick-up in their room rate. Figure on Rs 600 for a taxi to Port Mathurin.

BICYCLE & MOTORCYCLE

If your hotel or guesthouse doesn't offer bike or motorcycle rental, contact **Rotourco** (☑ 831 0747; www.rotourco.com; Rue François Leguat) or one of the other travel agencies in Port Mathurin. The going rate is around Rs 200 per day for a bike and Rs 600 to Rs 650 for a scooter. It costs Rs 350 to fill a scooter's petrol tank. Note that we recommend a scooter over a bicycle, as many of the interior roads can be discouragingly hilly.

BUS

The main bus station is in Port Mathurin. In addition to the airport bus, the most useful bus routes are those to Grand Baie and Pointe Coton in the east of the island, and to Graviers, Port Sud-Est and Rivière Cocos on the south coast. All apart from the Grand Baie buses pass through Mont Lubin in the centre of the island. Most buses operate every 30 to 60 minutes from about 7am to 4pm Monday to Saturday on most routes. The Sunday service is fairly sporadic. Expect to pay Rs 12 to Rs 35 depending on your destination.

CAR

The road system in Rodrigues has improved enormously and sealed roads now lead to most parts of the island. Though 4WD vehicles are no longer strictly necessary, most hire cars are still sturdy pick-ups.

Car rental can be arranged through most hotels and guesthouses and local tour operators, who will deliver all over the island. Expect to pay at least Rs 1200 per day and the price is usually the same whether you have a sedan or a pick-up. Most importantly, make sure you have sufficient petrol before setting off for the day – the island's only **petrol station** (Rue Max Lucchesi; ⊙ 6am-6.30pm Mon-Sat, to 3pm Sun) is in Port Mathurin.

TAXI

Most taxis on Rodrigues are 4WD pick-ups. Expect to pay between Rs 500 and Rs 1000 depending on your location. You can also hire taxis by the day for an island tour; expect to pay in the region of Rs 2000 to Rs 3000.

UNDERSTAND RODRIGUES

Rodrigues Today

Rodrigues has long felt itself ignored by policymakers on the main island of Mauritius, and even with greater autonomy formally granted in 2002, some are looking to take the next step. As such, complete independence remains a fervent desire for some and in April 2010, the Muvman Indepedantis Rodriguais (MIR) was launched when two candidates ran for government positions as 'Rodriguans' rather than 'Mauritians'. Although they were rebuffed, the issue won't go away any time soon.

In the meantime, Rodrigues' regional assembly is trying to tackle the overriding problems of population growth, poverty and critical water shortages. This latter problem is a grave one with year-round rationing. New hotels and many exisiting ones are being forced to look towards sustainable water options (including desalinisation), so conserve water whenever you can.

History

Rodrigues is named after the Portuguese navigator Don Diégo Rodriguez, who was the first European to discover the uninhabited island in 1528. Dutch sailors were the next to pay a call, albeit very briefly, in 1601, followed a few years later by the French.

At first Rodrigues was simply a place where ships could take refuge from storms and replenish their supplies of fresh water and meat. Giant tortoises were especially prized since they could be kept alive on board for months. Over the years thousands were taken or killed until they completely died out. Rodrigues also had a big flightless bird, the solitaire, which went the same sorry way as its distant cousin, the dodo.

The first serious attempt at colonisation occurred in 1691 when Frenchman François Leguat and a band of seven Huguenot companions fled religious persecution at home in search of a 'promised land'. Crops grew well and the island's fauna and flora were a source of wonder. Even so, after two years, life on a paradise island began to pall, not least due to the lack of female company. With no boat of their own (the ship they arrived on failed to return as promised), Leguat and his friends built a craft out of driftwood and eventually made it to Mauritius.

In 1735, the French founded a permanent colony on Rodrigues with a small settlement at Port Mathurin, but the colony never really prospered. When the British – who wanted a base from which to attack French-ruled Mauritius – invaded in 1809, they were met with little resistance.

In 1967, Rodriguans distinguished themselves by voting against independence from Britain by a whopping 90% (the rest of Mauritius voted strongly in favour). It was a dramatic illustration of the difference in outlook between the two islands. Following independence, Rodriguans continued to argue that their needs were significantly different from the rest of the country and that, in any case, they were being neglected by the central government.

The campaign was led by Serge Clair and his Organisation du Peuple de Rodrigues (OPR), founded in 1976. His patience and political skill eventually paid off. In 2001 it was announced that Rodrigues would be allowed a degree of autonomy, notably in socioeconomic affairs and in the management of their natural resources. The following year 18 councillors were elected; the Regional Assembly was formally inaugurated in 2002 with Serge Clair as chief commissioner.

NEIL FARRIN / GETTY IMAGES ©

A Glimpse of Paradise

Beaches that defy all superlatives, wild landscapes that will forever be etched into your memory, loads of adventure options, captivating festivals and a glimpse of history – it's impossible to be bored in Mauritius, Réunion and Seychelles. Paradise found? You be the judge.

Contents
➡ **Outdoor Adventures**
➡ **History & Culture**
➡ **Idyllic Beaches**
➡ **The Ultimate Honeymoon**

Above Aerial view over Mauritius (p46)

168

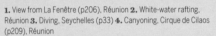

1. View from La Fenêtre (p206), Réunion 2. White-water rafting, Réunion 3. Diving, Seychelles (p33) 4. Canyoning, Cirque de Cilaos (p209), Réunion

DANITA DELIMONT / GETTY IMAGES ©

RAINER VON BRANDIS / GETTY IMAGES ©

JEAN-BERNARD CARILLET

Outdoor Adventures

Sure, these divine islands strewn across the peacock-blue Indian Ocean were designed for lounging on a beach or luxuriating in sensuous nature. But when you've finished sipping your cocktail, you may want to get the blood flowing a little more. Plenty of adventure options are readily available.

Underwater Activities

Mauritius, Réunion and the Seychelles are a divers' mecca thanks to a combination of unique features. Healthy reefs, canyon-like terrain, shallow shelves, exciting shipwrecks, seamounts and quick shoreline drop-offs give snorkellers and divers almost instant access to a variety of environments. The water is warm and clear, and teeming with life from the tiniest juvenile tropical fish to the largest pelagic creature.

Canyoning

There's no better way to immerse yourself in grandiose scenery than by exploring the atmospheric canyons in the Cirque de Cilaos or Cirque de Salazie in Réunion; expect various jumps, leaps in crystal-clear natural pools and rappelling. In Mauritius, adventurers abseil down the seven chutes at Tamarin.

Hiking

Crisscrossed with a network of paths ranging from simple nature trails to more challenging itineraries, Réunion has all the flavours of superlative hiking. Mauritius and Rodrigues also boast excellent walking options. The biggest surprise? The Seychelles. On top of world-renowned beaches, this archipelago offers divine coastal ambles and lovely jungle walks.

White-Water Rafting

The wealth of scenic rivers that decorate eastern Réunion make it a water-lover's dream destination. Rivière des Marsouins, Rivière des Roches and Rivière Langevin offer top-class runs to get the blood racing.

JEAN-BERNARD CARILLET / GETTY IMAGES ©

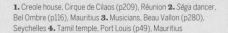

1. Creole house, Cirque de Cilaos (p209), Réunion **2.** *Séga* dancer, Bel Ombre (p116), Mauritius **3.** Musicians, Beau Vallon (p280), Seychelles **4.** Tamil temple, Port Louis (p49), Mauritius

HOLGER LEUE / GETTY IMAGES ©

2

History & Culture

Although many come to Réunion, Mauritius and Seychelles for the incredible beaches and nature, these islands have rich and diverse cultures, influenced by the waves of migrants who gradually populated the islands. Culture buffs with a penchant for architecture and festivals will be in seventh heaven.

Multiculturalism

You'll see almost every shade of skin and hair imaginable, arising from a mixture of African, Indian, Chinese, Arab and French genes. So don't be surprised to see a cathedral, a Tamil temple, a mosque and a pagoda lying almost side by side in larger cities.

Creole Architecture

Some wonderfully preserved colonial buildings can be found in Réunion, Mauritius and Seychelles. From splendid plantation houses and captivating mansions to humble *cases créoles* and grand colonial buildings harking back to the French East India Company, you're sure to be awed.

Cultural & Religious Festivals

Fabulous festivals provide visitors with a peek into local culture. Diwali, the Festival of Lights, is celebrated in the three countries in October or November. In Mauritius and Réunion, impressive fire-walking ceremonies take place in December or January. The Seychelles prides itself on its exuberant carnival.

Music & Dance

In this part of the Indian Ocean, music and dance are part of daily life, from the smallest village to the largest cities. In June, top-name *maloya*, *séga*, salsa, reggae and electro performers from throughout the Indian Ocean and beyond gather in St-Pierre during the three-day Sakifo festival.

HOLGER LEUE / GETTY IMAGES ©

4

1

1. Anse Source d'Argent (p305), Seychelles **2.** Anse Georgette (p297), Seychelles **3.** Anse Cocos (p306), Seychelles **4.** Pointe d'Esny (p110), Mauritius

3

2

RUTH EASTHAM & MAX PAOLI / GETTY IMAGES ©

Idyllic Beaches

Believe the hype: the Seychelles and Mauritius have some of the most dreamy and dramatic beaches you'll find this side of Bora Bora. Take your pick!

Anse Cocos (La Digue)

Anse Cocos is a died-and-gone-to-heaven vision of a beach – a frost-white strip of sand fringed by electric-blue waters. It can be reached by foot only, meaning that it always feels secluded.

Anse Georgette (Praslin)

It's like an apparition: the water is so scintillating and the sand so dazzling white that you'll rub your eyes. Despite having been engulfed by a resort, Anse Georgette is public property, so you are entitled to plop your towel down on the sand.

Anse Source d'Argent (La Digue)

OK, we thought the brochure spiel about 'the most photogenic beach in the world' was hype until we clapped eyes on the crystalline emerald waters and powder-soft sands of Anse Source d'Argent. It's even more astounding when seen from the summit of the granite hills that loom above the coast.

Pointe d'Esny (Mauritius)

This is it – that celebrity of all of the beaches of southern Mauritius is Pointe d'Esny. Immense, crystalline and glossy, it doesn't disappoint the bevy of swimmers and snorkellers who dabble in its gorgeous, lucent depths.

Rodrigues' East Coast

Between Graviers and St François in the island's east, the jagged coastline is regularly punctuated by appealing coves and stretches of gorgeous beach. The beauty of these stunning swaths of sand lies in the fact that they're totally secluded and there's no road here.

4

OLIVIER CIRENDINI / GETTY IMAGES ©

Fregate Island Private (p312), Frégate, Seychelles

The Ultimate Honeymoon

White-sand beaches. Secluded coves. Coral-coloured sunsets. Swish hotels. Hushed spas. It's not surprising that honeymooners and those seeking a glamorous tropical getaway have long had the Seychelles and Mauritius at the top of their wish lists.

Le Saint Géran (Mauritius)

Le Saint Géran is a sumptuous, impressive place that manages to get it right on so many levels – it's classy and stylish without being too formal, it's romantic without being too quiet and it's welcoming to families without allowing kids to run riot.

Desroches Island (Seychelles)

Many VIPs, including Prince William and Kate Middleton, choose to play Robinson Crusoe in style on Desroches. It's no wonder – the resort is romantic and extremely quiet. With its canopy of palm trees and surrounding splendid white beaches, Desroches conforms exactly to the tropical-island stereotype.

Silhouette (Seychelles)

If you want to combine romance, outdoors and affordable luxury, Silhouette is your answer. Here, stylish bungalows complement an already stunning island. Diving, snorkelling, fishing and walking are available.

Frégate (Seychelles)

If you want to live out that stranded-on-a-deserted-island fantasy, you've come to the right place. The 16 opulent villas are so delicious you might not want to leave, except for a beauty treatment in the serene spa, which uses only local, edible products (will it be a chocolate massage or a mango facial today, darling?).

Réunion

Best Places to Eat

➡ Les Letchis (p252)

➡ L'Eveil des Sens – Le Blue Margouillat (p203)

➡ Table Paysanne Chez Fiarda (p243)

➡ Le P'tit Zinc (p194)

Best Places to Stay

➡ Senteur Vanille (p193)

➡ Le Platane (p214)

➡ Rougail Mangue (p242)

➡ Villa Belle (p232)

Why Go?

Réunion is one of the Indian Ocean's last great island adventures. The diversity of landscapes is truly astonishing for such a small pocket. Jutting out of the ocean like a basaltic shield cloaked in green, this scenically magical island is a mini-Hawaii. What to expect? Emerald forests, tumbling waterfalls, awesome mountainscapes, twisting roads, soul-stirring panoramas, energetic coastal cities and a sprinkling of white- or black-sand beaches. The formidable Piton de la Fournaise, one of the world's most accessible active volcanoes, adds to the thrill. Small wonder that Réunion is a dream destination for nature and outdoor lovers. Hiking is the number-one activity, but canyoning, paragliding, rafting, horseback riding, diving, whale watching and climbing are also available.

There's also plenty to compel culture aficionados. Réunion has a fascinating Creole, African, Indian, Chinese and French heritage, with a wealth of architectural treasures and vibrant festivals that are a great occasion to immerse yourself in local culture.

When to Go

➡ Réunion's climate experiences only two distinct seasons: the hot, rainy summer from December to April and the cool, dry winter from late April to November.

➡ The peak tourist season is during the French school holidays from July to early September. From October through to the New Year holidays is also busy, but after this everything eases down during cyclone-prone February and March.

➡ Temperatures on the coast average 22°C in winter and 27°C in summer. In the mountains, they drop to 11°C and 18°C respectively.

➡ The drier winter months are the most favourable for hiking, as some of the trails are simply impassable when it's wet. The east coast is considerably wetter than the west.

➡ The whale watching season runs from June to October.

AT A GLANCE

⇒ **Currency** Euro (€)

⇒ **Languages** French, Creole

⇒ **Mobile phones** GSM network through Orange and SFR; international roaming and local SIM cards available

⇒ **Money** ATMs in major towns; credit cards widely accepted

⇒ **Visas** Not required for most Western nationals for three-month stays

Fast Facts

⇒ **Capital** St-Denis

⇒ **Country code** ☎262

⇒ **Population** 840,000

⇒ **Time** GMT + four hours

Exchange Rates

For current exchange rates see www.xe.com

A$1	€0.67
C$1	€0.72
¥100	€0.77
NZ$1	€0.60
UK£1	€1.17
US$1	€0.75

Resources

⇒ **Lonely Planet** (www.lonelyplanet.com)

⇒ **Île de la Réunion Tourisme** (www.reunion.fr)

⇒ **Allons La Réunion** (www.allonslareunion.com)

Arriving in Réunion

All long-distance flights to Réunion arrive at St-Denis, landing at Roland Garros international airport, which is located about 10km east of St-Denis. Taxis from just outside the airport cost from €20 to central St-Denis. Between 6.30am and 6pm, there's also a regular shuttle bus service from the airport to central St-Denis (€4, 12 daily). The ride takes about 20 minutes.

ESSENTIAL FOOD & DRINK

Réunion is a culinary delight: thanks to a mix of cuisines and prime fresh ingredients (plentiful seafood, succulent meat, spices, aromatic plants, and fruit and vegetables bursting with flavours), you're certain to eat well wherever you go. National favourites include *rougail saucisse* (sausages cooked in tomato sauce) and *carri* (curry), served with rice and vegetables.

Given that Réunion is an island, it's hardly surprising that seafood features prominently on the menu. Gorge yourself on fish and freshwater crayfish.

Desserts are equally exciting, with tropical fruit pies and jams, delicious cakes, exotic sorbets and ice creams. ·

In towns and cities, you'll also find plenty of patisseries selling croissants and pastries. Baguettes can be bought from every street corner.

What about drinks? Flavoured rum is Réunion's signature drink: there are dozens to try, from vanilla to lychee. Local wine is also great, if not exceptional.

Restaurants range from modest to top-end establishments. You'll also find *snacks* (fast food outlets) and food trucks; they are cheap and serve no-frills, typical Creole fare and sandwiches. The tastier Creole food is often served at B&Bs, which are famous for their *tables d'hôtes* meals (home cooked meals).

Keeping Costs Down

⇒ Buy simple Creole dishes at takeaway outlets

⇒ If you'd like to try an upmarket restaurant, go for lunch – lunch menus are much easier on the wallet than à la carte evening dining

⇒ Get around the island by bus

⇒ It's always better to arrange car hire before you arrive

⇒ Opt for B&Bs or *gîtes*, preferably in the Hauts (hills)

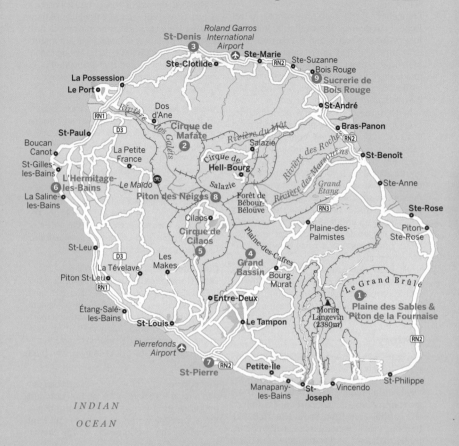

Réunion Highlights

1 Gorge your senses on the Martian landscapes of the **Plaine des Sables** (p228) and **Piton de la Fournaise** (p227)

2 Explore the mystical, rugged topography of **Cirque de Mafate** (p222)

3 Go heritage-hunting among the Creole buildings of **St-Denis** (p178)

4 Swap stress for bliss in the valley-village seclusion of **Grand Bassin** (p224)

5 Try canyoning in **Cirque de Cilaos** (p209)

6 Immerse yourself in **L'Hermitage-les-Bains'** (p198) steamy nightlife

7 Discover the colonial heritage and great nightlife of **St-Pierre** (p230)

8 Huff to the top of **Piton des Neiges** (p214) for sensational views

9 Learn how rum is prepared at **Sucrerie de Bois-Rouge** (p249)

ST-DENIS

POP 140,000

Francophiles will feel comfortable in St-Denis (san-de-*nee*), the capital of Réunion. Except for the palms and flamboyant trees to remind you that you're somewhere sunnier (and hotter), St-Denis could be easily mistaken for a French provincial enclave, with a flurry of trendy shops, brasseries, bistros and *boulangeries* (bakeries).

With most of Réunion's tourist attractions located elsewhere on the island, most visitors only stay long enough to book *gîtes de montagne* (mountain lodges), pick up a few tourist brochures and rent a car before dashing off to more magnetic locations. But St-Denis warrants more than a fleeting glance. Scratch beneath the French polish and you'll soon realise that the city also boasts an undeniably Creole soul, with a portfolio of delightful colonial and religious buildings and a casual multi-ethnic atmosphere.

If that's not enough, there are always epicurean indulgences. Sip a black coffee at a chic pavement cafe listening to a *séga* or *maloya* soundtrack or indulge in fine dining at a gourmet restaurant.

History

St-Denis was founded in 1668 by the governor Regnault, who named the settlement after a ship that ran aground here. But St-Denis didn't really start to develop until the governor Mahé de Labourdonnais moved the capital here from St-Paul in 1738; the harbour was in general more sheltered and easier to defend, and water more abundant.

The 19th century ushered in St-Denis' golden age. As money poured in from the sugar plantations, the town's worthies built themselves fine mansions, some of which can still be seen along Rue de Paris and in the surrounding streets. But in the late 1800s the bottom dropped out of the sugar market and the good times came to a stuttering end. St-Denis' fortunes only began to revive when it became the new departmental capital in 1946. To cope with the influx of civil servants, financiers and office workers, the city expanded rapidly eastwards along the coast and up the mountains behind. Even today the cranes are much in evidence as St-Denis struggles to house its ever-growing population.

◉ Sights

St-Denis is devoid of beach, but it boasts a gaggle of well-preserved colonial buildings harking back to the city's heyday in the 19th century. The larger colonial piles are mainly strung out along Rue de Paris, Ave de la Victoire, Rue Pasteur and Rue Jean Chatel. It's also home to a smattering of impressive religious buildings.

Anciens Magasins Aubinais HISTORIC BUILDING
(37 Rue Jean Chatel) This massive colonial building made of stone was constructed in the 1830s as a theatre but was used as a warehouse. It's neo-classical in style. Today it houses various shops.

Maison Kichenin HISTORIC BUILDING
(42 Rue Labourdonnais) This perfectly preserved Creole mansion was built in the 1790s and is considered one of the oldest of its kind in St-Denis. The well-proportioned fountain in the garden is a highlight.

Conseil Général de la Réunion – Direction de la Culture HISTORIC BUILDING
(Villa du Département; 18 Rue de Paris) You can't miss this villa – it's one of the most elegant of St-Denis' Creole buildings, with a superb *varangue* (veranda), finely crafted *lambrequins* (filigree-style decoration), and a manicured garden with a fountain. It was built in 1804.

Préfecture HISTORIC BUILDING
(Place de la Préfecture) One of the grandest buildings in St-Denis, the Préfecture began life as a coffee warehouse in 1734 and later served as the headquarters of the French East India Company.

Former Hôtel de Ville HISTORIC BUILDING
(Town Hall; Rue de Paris) Many consider the neoclassical Former Hôtel de Ville, at the north end of Rue de Paris, to be the city's most beautiful building; it's certainly very imposing, with its regimented columns, balustrades and jaunty clock tower.

Palais Rontaunay HISTORIC BUILDING
(Rue Rontaunay) Built in 1854, the much-photographed Palais Rontaunay is a bourgeois villa which has preserved the elegant style of the 19th century.

Maison Deramond-Barre HISTORIC BUILDING
(15 Rue de Paris) This colonial structure dating from the 1830s was the family home of former French prime minister Raymond Barre and the birthplace of the poet and

painter Léon Dierx. It's well worth a peek for its well-preserved architecture and harmonious proportions.

Mosquée Noor E Islam   MOSQUE
(121 Rue Maréchal Leclerc; ⊙9am-noon & 2-4pm except prayer times) One of St-Denis' most iconic buildings, the Grande Mosquée dominates the centre with its tall minaret. Its cool white-and-green interior is a haven of peace. The Islamic community in St-Denis is very traditional, so if you wish to visit, dress and behave with respect.

Cathédrale de St-Denis   CHURCH
(Place de la Cathédrale) Ambling down Ave de la Victoire, you'll come across the fairly unassuming, Tuscan-style Cathédrale de St-Denis.

Pagode Guan Di   BUDDHIST
(Rue Sainte-Anne; ⊙8.30-11am Mon, Wed & Sun) Blink and you'll miss this discreet pagoda, which is used by the Chinese community.

Tamil Temple   HINDU
(Kovil Kalikambal Temple; 259 Rue Maréchal Leclerc) St-Denis' small but wildly colourful Hindu temple stands out among a row of shops on a busy road. Visitors are not allowed inside the temple.

Musée Léon Dierx   MUSEUM
(☑0262 20 24 82; 28 Rue de Paris; admission €2; ⊙9.30am-5pm Tue-Sun) Housed in the former bishop's palace, built in 1845, this museum hosts Réunion's most important collection of modern art. The more high-profile works may include paintings, sculptures and ceramics by Picasso, Renoir, Gauguin and Matisse (the works exhibited change every three months). You can also see a few paintings by the Réunionnais poet and painter Léon Dierx (1838–1912).

L'Artothèque   GALLERY
(☑0262 41 75 50; 26 Rue de Paris; ⊙9.30am-5.30pm Tue-Sun) **FREE** This contemporary art gallery hosts changing exhibitions of works by local artists and those from neighbouring countries. It's housed in a handsome pale-yellow villa.

Maison Carrère   MUSEUM
(☑0262 41 83 00; 14 Rue de Paris; admission €3; ⊙9am-6pm Mon-Sat) This meticulously restored mansion dating from the 1820s is a beautiful example of Creole architecture, with its elaborate verandah and intricate *lambrequins* on the front of the eaves.

It does an excellent job of explaining the city's colonial past. It also houses the tourist office.

Musée d'Histoire Naturelle   MUSEUM
(☑0262 20 02 19; Jardin de l'État; admission €2; ⊙9.30am-5.30pm Tue-Sun) Go eye to eye with lemurs and other stuffed specimens in this museum located in the Jardin de l'État. Besides impressive lemurs, you'll see a good insect and bird collection on the 1st floor.

Jardin de l'État   GARDENS
(Botanical Gardens; ⊙7am-6pm) **FREE** Created in 1763, the attractive Jardin de l'État, at the southern end of Rue de Paris, is a good place to recharge the batteries and be introduced to a variety of tropical plants and trees. The Musée d'Histoire Naturelle stands at the far end of the gardens.

Le Barachois   WATERFRONT
This seafront park, lined by cannons facing out to sea, is a good place to catch the sea breeze in St-Denis. It has an area set aside for *pétanque* (a game similar to bowls), cafes and a **monument** to the Réunion-born aviator Roland Garros, leaning nonchalantly on a propeller.

🛏 Sleeping

Most hotels tend to be dull multistorey blocks that are designed with business travellers in mind. Budget beds are an endangered species and the choice of upmarket accommodation is limited.

Pension Zoulékan Limbada   GUESTHOUSE €
(☑0262 41 05 00; 35 Rue Issop Ravate; s/d without bathroom €25/30) This Indian-run guesthouse occupying a virginal-white building has a quiet location near the Petit Marché. The four fan-cooled rooms are monastic and a bit sombre but well-kept and clean-smelling, which is all that really matters. Towels are not provided.

Hôtel Phoenix   GUESTHOUSE €€
(☑0262 41 51 81; phoenix.dupont@wanadoo.fr; 1 Rue du Moulin à Vent; s €48, d €50-55, incl breakfast; ❄🛜) A reliable option for budgeteers, this little number is in a tranquil street within stumbling distance of the centre. The rooms do need updating – the bathrooms in particular – but on the whole, the place is clean and not bad value, especially if you consider that rates include breakfast, there's air-con (from 7pm to 7am only), free wi-fi and credit cards are accepted. Some rooms

RÉUNION ST-DENIS

St-Denis

Map Labels

INDIAN OCEAN

LE BARACHOIS

Blvd Gabriel Macé

Place Sarda Garriga

Place Général de Gaulle

Place Mât du Pavillon

Rue Doret

Rue de Nice

Rue Four à Chaux

Rue de la Victoire

Ave de la Victoire

Rue L'Amiral Lacaze

Rue Pontaunay

Place de la Préfecture

Rue du Moulin à vent

Rue Juliette Dodu

Rue des Sables

Rue Labourdonnais

Place Joffre

Blvd Joffre

Place Étienne Regnault

Rue Charles Gounod

Rue Alexis de Villeneuve

Rue Victor Mac Auliffe

Rue Pasteur

Rue Maréchal Leclerc

Rue Laferrière

Rue Issop Ravate

Blvd Lancastel

Blvd de l'Océan

Car Jaune

St-Denis Pôle d'Échanges Océan (50m); Roland Garros International (7.5km)

University

Place de la Cathédrale

Rue de la Compagnie

Mairie (Town Hall)

Rue de la Boulangerie

Rivière St-Denis

Rue du Pont

PETITE ÎLE

Le Port (20km); St-Gilles-les-Bains (35km)

RN1

Centrale d'Information et de Réservation Régionale – Île de la Réunion Tourisme

0   200 m
0   0.1 miles

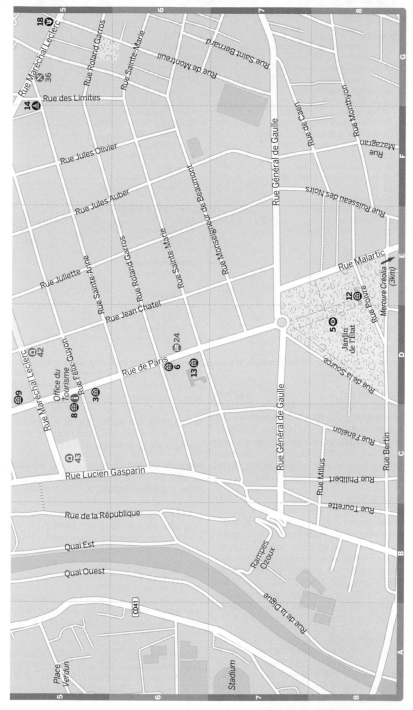

Rue Maréchal Leclerc
18
36
Rue Roland Garros
Rue Sainte-Marie
Rue de Montreuil
Rue Saint Bernard
Rue des Limites
14
Rue Monthyon
Rue de Caen
Rue Mazagran
Rue Jules Olivier
Rue Général de Gaulle
Rue Jules Auber
Rue Ruisseau des Noirs
Rue Juliette
Rue Sainte-Anne
Rue Roland Garros
Rue Monseigneur de Beaumont
Rue Sainte-Marie
Rue Malartic
Rue Poivre
12
Mercure Créolia (3km)
Rue Jean Chatel
5
Jardin de l'Etat
24
Rue de Paris
6
13
Rue de la Source
42
Office du Tourisme
Rue Félix-Guyon
Rue Maréchal Leclerc
9
8
3
Rue Fénelon
Rue Général de Gaulle
Rue Bertin
43
Rue Milius
Rue Philibert
Rue Tourette
Rue Lucien Gasparin
Rue de la République
Quai Est
Rampes Ozoux
Quai Ouest
CD41
Rue de la Digue
Place Verdun
Stadium

St-Denis

face a concrete wall; try for rooms 5, 6 or 7, which have a balcony.

Central Hôtel　　　　　　　　　HOTEL €€
(☏0262 94 18 08; www.centralhotel.re; 37 Rue de la Compagnie; s €56-96, d €76-108, incl breakfast; P❄🛜) The Central gets by on its handy location, a waddle away from restaurants, bars and shops. It offers bland, fairly identical-looking hotel rooms without much island flavour. Warning: there are no elevators.

Austral Hôtel　　　　　　　　　HOTEL €€
(☏0262 94 45 67; www.hotel-austral.fr; 20 Rue Charles Gounod; s €79-87, d €92-100; P❄@🛜♨) Distinctly unimpressive for the price, the Austral is not quite the three-star heavyweight it thinks it is, but the rooms have the requisite comforts, location is tip-top, facilities are good and there's a small pool. If you plan to stay here, aim high – the rooms and views get better the higher you go. Angle for rooms 302 or 308, which have sea views.

Le Juliette Dodu　　　　　　　　HOTEL €€€
(☏0262 20 91 20; www.hotel-jdodu.com; 31 Rue Juliette Dodu; s €110-165, d €160-190, ste €215-250, incl breakfast; P❄@🛜♨) Live like a colonial administrator in this stylish Creole building dating from the early 19th century. Al-

though the cheaper rooms feel claustrophobic and are unextraordinary, there are still enough vintage touches in the reception area – period furnishings, plump armchairs and old-fashioned tiles – to satisfy the snob within, with the added lure of a pool and a cosy restaurant. It's a two-minute strut south of the Barachois.

Mercure Créolia　　　　　　　　HOTEL €€€
(☏0262 94 26 26; www.accor.com; 14 Rue du Stade, Montgaillard; d €120-215; P❄@🛜♨) Located some 4km south of the city centre in a tranquil neighbourhood, your efforts in getting here are rewarded with splendid views over the coast. Rooms are functional and unflashy, and the decor is nothing special, but the setting and the relaxed feel more than make up for the slightly dated sense of style. Note that the cheaper rooms don't have sea views. Amenities include a bar, a restaurant and a gym. Best asset is the pool, one of the biggest in Réunion. Booking online gets you the best deals.

Villa Angélique　　　　　　BOUTIQUE HOTEL €€€
(www.villa-angelique.fr; 39 Rue de Paris; s €145-175, d €185-205, ste €220-250, incl breakfast; ❄🛜) The closest thing St-Denis has to a boutique

hotel, the Villa Angélique occupies a nicely renovated historic building and is just oozing with atmosphere. It's a modern twist on colonial decor: there are polished wood floors, beautiful wooden furniture, rich fabrics, sparkling bathrooms and beds that seem custom designed to give sweet dreams. On the downside, the on-site restaurant is overpriced and there's no private parking.

✖ Eating

Thanks to the French passion for gastronomy, St-Denis is a nirvana for food-lovers, with a smorgasbord of eateries to suit all palates and budgets.

Note that many bars also serve food.

★ L'Igloo
ICE CREAM €

(📋 0262 21 34 69; 67 Rue Jean Chatel; ice creams from €2, mains €9-21; ⊙ 11am-midnight Mon-Thu, 11am-1am Fri-Sat, 3-11pm Sun) You say you're itching for an ice-cream fix? Good, because it's hard to resist the fresh fruit sorbets and creamy delights at this iconic ice-cream parlour. Try the outstanding *glace au yaourt aux fruits des bois* (yoghurt with fruits of the forest berries) and you'll imagine you're eating the pulped fruits on a cold day. Also serves up snack options and light meals, including salads and omelettes, at lunchtime.

Petit Marché
SELF-CATERING €

(Rue Maréchal Leclerc; ⊙ 6am-6pm Mon-Sat, to noon Sun) For fresh fruit and vegetables, there is a wide range of cheap produce at the Petit Marché.

Le Massalé
DESSERTS €

(📋 0262 21 75 06; 30 Rue Alexis de Villeneuve; sweets from €0.50; ⊙ 10am-8pm Mon-Thu & Sat, 2-8pm Fri, 11am-8pm Sun) This teeny outlet tempts you with its colourful array of Indian snacks and sweets to eat in or take away. Perennial favourites include samosas as well as candy-pink or apple-green *balfi*. Wash it down with a glass of cardamom tea.

Le Caudan
INDIAN €

(📋 0262 94 39 99; 38 Rue Charles Gounod; mains €8-12; ⊙ lunch Tue-Sun, dinner Tue-Sat) Tasty Indo-Mauritian snacks and ready-made meals are the order of the day at this under-the-radar neighbourhood venture set in a small Creole house. The homemade biryani is the speciality here. A glass of *alouda* (sweet, milky drink) and a devilish *goolab* (fritters flavoured with cardamom) will round things off nicely. Takeaways available.

★ 12
FRENCH, FUSION €€

(📋 0262 40 12 12; 12 Rue de Nice; mains €14-29; ⊙ lunch & dinner Tue-Sat) A surprisingly hip restaurant inside a Creole house complete with dark-wood interior, this cool culinary outpost specialises in French-inspired cuisine with a twist. If you want a recommendation, go for the 12 Burger, with homemade bread. It's also a good place to hang out and just enjoy the tropical atmosphere while noshing on tapas on the shady terrace – the bar section is open from 3pm.

Café Edouard
FRENCH, PIZZERIA €€

(📋 0262 28 45 02; 13 Ruelle Edouard; mains €10-13, lunch menu €13; ⊙ lunch & dinner Mon-Sat; 🛜) The place to hang out, this buzzy eatery with outdoor tables has free wi-fi, good pizzas, crunchy salads and tasty daily specials. The lunchtime menu is excellent value.

Le Roland Garros
BRASSERIE €€

(📋 0262 41 44 37; 2 Place Sarda Garriga; mains €11-22, lunch menu €15; ⊙ lunch & dinner; 🛜) *Oh la la,* this St-Denis institution has the feel of a true Parisian bistro – packed, buzzing and full of attitude. The food is nothing spectacular but there's a good choice, ranging from Creole staples and tartares to grilled dishes and pastas. It's also a good place to enjoy a drink any time of the day. Free wi-fi.

Planète Nature
FRENCH €€

(📋 0262 46 53 97; 26 Rue Jean Chatel; mains €12-20; ⊙ lunch Mon-Sat, dinner Thu-Sat) Kudos to the chef for transforming the main-course salads – so often the dullest dish on the menu – into something fresh, tasty and filling. Everything is freshly made and most accompaniments are organic and locally sourced. Vegetarians will find options, too, such as the signature *tarte aubergine feta* (pie with eggplant and feta cheese). Service is zippy and friendly.

K*Rem
VEGETARIAN €€

(📋 0692 80 85 95; 11 Rue Laferrière; mains €14-19; ⊙ lunch daily, dinner Mon-Sat) A vegetarian restaurant in Réunion? Yes it's possible. This discreet eatery occupying a tastefully restored Creole building serves well-executed vegetarian dishes. Wash it all down with a glass of carrot and apple juice. Despite the fact that the menu is limited and there are only a few tables, service is a bit slow.

L'Arto Carpe
FRENCH, INTERNATIONAL €€

(📋 0262 21 55 48; 9 Ruelle Edouard; mains €14-25; ⊙ lunch & dinner Tue-Sat) On a pedestrianised

RÉUNION ST-DENIS

alley behind the cathedral, this European-style restaurant features a stylish indoor dining space built in a restored stone structure. The tempting menu focuses on a memorable assortment of fusion tastes and fresh cuisine, such as tuna steak served in a teriyaki sauce. Tapas (€5 to €9) are served from 6pm.

★ **Le Reflet des Îles** CREOLE €€€
(☑ 0262 21 73 82; 114 Rue Pasteur; mains €15-36; ☺ lunch & dinner Mon-Sat) This much-lauded eatery is the best place in St-Denis to try out authentic Creole food, with an assortment of tempting *carris* (curries) and *civets* (stews), but there are also Western-style options on offer if your tummy and palate are timid. Most dishes cost less than €20. The menu is translated into English – a rarity in Réunion.

Helios FRENCH €€€
(☑ 0262 20 21 50; 88 Rue Pasteur; mains €13-30; ☺ lunch & dinner Tue-Sat) This St-Denis icon has a good repertoire of flavoursome *métro* (French) dishes, best enjoyed on the flowery terrace. Skip the menu and stick to the daily specials.

Le DCP SEAFOOD €€€
(☑ 0262 20 10 14; 46 Rue Jules Auber; mains €18-26; ☺ lunch & dinner) If you have a weakness for ultrafresh fish, Le DCP is the place to indulge. The decor is another clincher: it occupies a restored Creole building with an agreeable terrace. Inside, aquatic murals and shades of blue and white create a *20,000 Leagues Under the Sea*–like ambience.

L'Atelier de Ben FUSION €€€
(☑ 0262 41 85 73; www.atelier-de-ben.com; 12 Rue de la Compagnie; mains €26-30, lunch menus €21-26; ☺ lunch & dinner Tue-Sat) A true alchemist, the French chef Benoît Vantaux has got the magic formula right, fusing French with Asian to create stunning cuisine. How does beef fillet with wasabi ice cream sound? Shame it doesn't have outdoor seating.

🍷 Drinking & Entertainment

Most of Réunion's action is down the coast at L'Hermitage-les-Bains and St-Pierre, but there's a handful of OK nightspots to keep you entertained in St-Denis.

Le Zanzibar BAR
(☑ 0262 20 01 18; 41 Rue Pasteur; ☺ 5pm-midnight) Le Zanzibar is the hang-out of well-connected locals and serves devilishly good tropical potions.

O'Bar BAR
(☑ 0262 52 57 88; 32 Rue de la Compagnie; ☺ 8am-midnight Mon-Sat) A funky drinking spot right in the centre. The streetside terrace allows for a dash of people-watching. Food is only so-so.

Le K-T Dral BAR
(☑ 0692 95 92 00; 5 Ruelle Saint-Paul; ☺ 10am-midnight Mon-Sat) Tucked in an alley behind the cathedral, this congenial bar is packed to the rafters on weekends and you come here as much for a cocktail as for the trendy atmosphere. Don't miss the *concert* (live band) on Friday evening.

Le Prince Club GAY
(☑ 0692 38 28 28; 108 Rue Pasteur; ☺ 10.30pm-4am Fri-Sat) Gay-friendly.

🛍 Shopping

The main shopping streets are the semi-pedestrianised Rue Maréchal Leclerc and Rue Juliette Dodu.

Boutique Pardon CLOTHING
(☑ 0262 41 15 62; www.pardon.net; cnr Rue Maréchal Leclerc & Rue Jean Chatel; ☺ 9am-6.30pm Mon-Sat) Get glammed up at this trendsetting boutique stocking island-made shirts, T-shirts, dresses and accessories.

Grand Marché MARKET
(2 Rue Maréchal Leclerc; ☺ 8am-6pm Mon-Sat) This place has a mishmash of items for sale, including Malagasy wooden handicrafts, fragrant spices, woven baskets, embroidery, T-shirts, furniture and a jumble of knick-knacks.

Petit Marché MARKET
(Rue Maréchal Leclerc; ☺ 6am-6pm Mon-Sat, to noon Sun) On the east side of town, this is mainly a fresh-produce market, but you can buy herbs and spices here at competitive prices.

ℹ Information

BC Games (☑ 0262 21 50 10; 174 Rue Jean Chatel; per hr €3; ☺ 8.30am-6.30pm Mon-Sat) Internet access and printing services.
Cabinet Médical de Garde Saint-Vincent (☑ 0262 47 72 10; cnr Rue de Paris & Rue Maréchal Leclerc; ☺ 7pm-midnight Mon-Fri, 2pm-midnight Sat, 8am-midnight Sun) A small clinic (two doctors) that's open outside regular business hours.
Centre Hospitalier Félix Guyon (☑ 0262 90 50 50; Allées des Topazes, Bellepierre) Réunion's

main hospital has 24-hour medical and dental treatment and English-speaking staff.

Office du Tourisme (0262 41 83 00; www.lebeaupays.com; 14 Rue de Paris, Maison Carrère; ⊙9am-6pm Mon-Sat; 🖲) Housed in a historic building, the St-Denis tourist office has English-speaking staff and can provide plenty of information, maps and brochures. It also runs excellent cultural tours focusing on St-Denis' rich architectural heritage (minimum two people, €8) and biking tours (€25). Bookings for *gîtes de montagne* can also be made here. There's internet and wi-fi access (one hour free).

ⓘ Getting There & Away

AIR

For details of flights from Roland Garros international airport, see p268.

The following airlines have offices in St-Denis. All airlines also have an office at the airport, which is usually open every day.

Air Austral (☑0825 01 30 12; www.airaustral.com; 4 Rue de Nice; ⊙8.30am-5.30pm Mon-Fri)

Air France (☑0820 82 08 20; www.airfrance.re; 7 Ave de la Victoire; ⊙9am-5pm Mon-Fri)

Air Madagascar (☑0892 68 00 14; www.airmadagascar.com; 31 Rue Jules Auber; ⊙8.15am-noon & 1.30-5.45pm Mon-Fri, to 4.45pm Fri)

Air Mauritius (☑0262 94 83 83; www.airmauritius.com; 13 Rue Charles Gounod; ⊙8.30am-5.30pm Mon-Fri)

Corsair (☑0820 04 20 42; www.corsair.fr; 2 Rue Maréchal Leclerc; ⊙9am-1pm & 2-5.30pm Mon-Fri)

BUS

St-Denis Pôle d'Échanges Océan (Gare Routière; ☑ 0262 41 09 59, 0810 123 974; Blvd Joffre), the main long-distance bus station, is on the seafront. From here Car Jaune (p268) operates various services. Information for Car Jaune, including all its routes and *horaires* (timetables) around the island and the airport bus service, is available from the information counter at the bus terminal. Some of the more useful routes include the following:

Line A West to St-Pierre via Le Port, St-Paul, St-Gilles-les-Bains, St-Leu, Étang-Salé-les-Bains and St-Louis (€4.20, two hours, about 10 daily, less on Sunday).

Lines F or G East to St-Benoît via Ste-Suzanne, St-André and Bras-Panon (€2.80, one hour, about 15 daily, less on Sunday).

Z'éclair 1 (express) West to St-Pierre, direct (€7, one hour, about 18 daily, five on Sunday).

Z'éclair 2 (express) East to St-Benoît via St-André (€3.50, one hour, about 15 daily, three on Sunday).

CAR & MOTORCYCLE

There's not much point in having a car in St-Denis unless you're using it as a base to explore the rest of the island. If that's the case, you can either pick a car up at the airport or avoid paying the airport surcharge (around €26) by having it delivered to your hotel. For car rental, see p269.

FERRY

St-Denis' ferry terminal is at Le Port, located 20km west of St-Denis.

ⓘ Getting Around

St-Denis is relatively small and getting around the centre on foot is a breeze.

TO/FROM THE AIRPORT

Taxis between St-Denis and Roland Garros International Airport cost around €20 during the day and €30 at night. Cheaper and almost as convenient is the regular Navette Aéroport service, which runs from L'Océan bus terminal to the airport about once an hour between 6.30am and 6pm (between 6am and 6.15pm coming from the airport). The fare is €4 and the journey takes a minimum of 20 minutes.

TO/FROM LE PORT

The terminal for passenger ferries to Mauritius is in Le Port, 20km west of St-Denis. There are no bus services direct to the terminal. All nonexpress buses between St-Denis and St-Pierre stop at the bus station in Le Port, from where locally operated buses depart roughly every 30 minutes for the Gare Maritime, Port Est. You're better off splashing out on a taxi (€45 from St-Denis).

WORTH A TRIP

DOS D'ANE

After braving St-Denis' busy streets and before tackling the seaside resorts further south, a drive up to the isolated village of Dos d'Ane, in the hills above Le Port (take the D1), will give you a breath of fresh air. It's an excellent base for **hikes** in the interior; from here you can walk to the Plaine d'Affouches and La Roche Écrite, as well as into the Cirque de Mafate via the Rivière des Galets route. For a shorter ramble, there are superb views to be had from the **Cap Noir** kiosk, about 20 minutes from the Cap Noir car park above Dos d'Ane (it's signposted), or from the **Roche Verre Bouteille** lookout, less than an hour's walk from the car park. It's possible to do a loop combining the two lookouts (about 1½ hours).

If you like peace, quiet and sigh-inducing views, you'll have few quibbles with **Les Acacias – Chez Axel et Patricia Nativel** (☑0262 32 01 47; Rue Germain Elisabeth, Dos d'Ane; dm €17, d incl breakfast €45), which offers two *chambres d'hôtes* and three spick-and-span six-bed dorms. The hearty evening meals (dinner €20) go down well after a day's tramping and the views from the terrace are stupendous.

There is a small information desk at the ferry terminal, open for arrivals, but no other facilities for tourists. Taxis wait on arrival.

TAXI

Taxis around town are generally expensive. A trip across town will set you back at least €8.

During the day you should have no problem finding a taxi. It gets more difficult at night, when you might have to phone for one. A reliable company offering a 24-hour service is **Taxis Paille-en-Queue** (☑ 0262 29 20 29).

THE WEST

Welcome to Réunion's Sunshine Coast, or Réunion's Riviera, or the leeward coast. However you label it, say hello to this 45km-long string of seaside resorts and suburbs running from St-Paul to St-Louis. It has a wealth of developed tourist facilities and attractions, including the best of the island's beaches (which is not saying a lot).

Sea, sand and sun are not the only *raison d'être* on the west coast. There's also a superfluity of activities on land and sea. Steep drop-offs tempt divers, spectacular slopes beckon mountain bikers, while paragliders soar over the lagoon.

Despite the fact that tourist development has got a little out of hand to the south of St-Paul, there remain hidden corners of untouched wonder in this most populous, most visited region. It's easy to leave the Route des Tamarins that zips along the flanks of the mountains and explore the glorious hinterland and its bucolic offerings – think sugar-cane fields, lush orchards, geranium

plantations and cryptomeria forests swathing the slopes of the mountains, studded with character-filled villages that retain a palpable rural air.

With the exception of St-Louis and the Hauts (Hills), this region is predominantly Zoreilles (mainland French) territory and feels closer to France than South Africa. Brush up on your French!

St-Paul

POP 20,000

Lively if not jaw-dropping in beauty, Réunion's second-largest *commune* (administrative district) after St-Denis deserves a quick stop if you're into history. It's also an obvious transit point if you plan to reach Le Maïdo by public transport.

◉ Sights

Most tourists who do come here visit the bright and well-kept **Cimetière Marin**, the cemetery at the southern end of town. It contains the remains of various famous Réunionnais, including the poet Leconte de Lisle (1818–94) and the pirate Olivier 'La Buse' Levasseur (The Buzzard), who was the scourge of the Indian Ocean from about 1720 to 1730.

You'll also find a few well-preserved **colonial buildings** along the seafront. On a street running parallel to the seafront lies the colourful **Hindu temple**, built in 1871.

Make sure you save energy for the animated **market** on the seafront promenade. It's held all day on Friday and on Saturday morning. With heaps of local vegetables,

Western Réunion

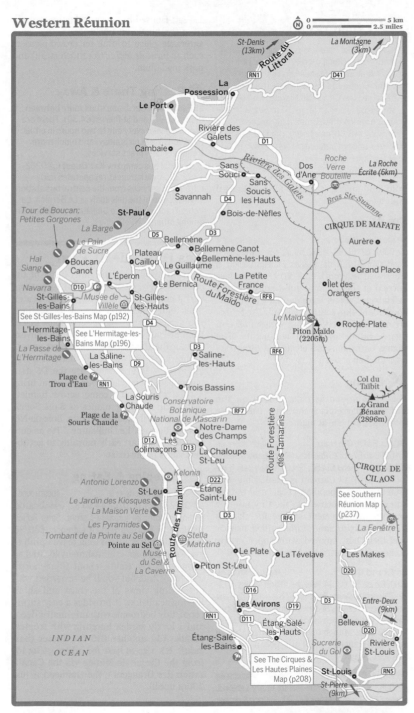

St-Denis
(13km)

Route du Littoral

La Montagne
(3km)

RN1

D41

La Possession

Le Port

Rivière des Galets

D1

Cambaie

Rivière des Galets

Sans Souci

Sans Soucis les Hauts

Dos d'Ane

Roche Verre Bouteille

La Roche Écrite (6km)

Savannah

D4

Bras Ste-Suzanne

St-Paul

Bois-de-Nèfles

CIRQUE DE MAFATE

Tour de Boucan; Petites Gorgones

La Barge

D5

Bellemène

D3

Aurère

Le Pain de Sucre

Plateau Caillou

Bellemène Canot
Bellemène-les-Hauts

Grand Place

Haï Siang

Boucan Canot

Le Guillaume

Le Bernica

La Petite France

Route Forestière du Maïdo

Îlet des Orangers

Navarra

D10

L'Éperon

St-Gilles-les-Bains

Musée de Villèle

St-Gilles-les-Hauts

RF8

Le Maïdo

Roche-Plate

See St-Gilles-les-Bains Map (p192)

D4

Piton Maïdo (2205m)

L'Hermitage-les-Bains

See L'Hermitage-les-Bains Map (p196)

D3

Col du Taïbit

La Passe de L'Hermitage

La Saline-les-Bains

Saline-les-Hauts

RF6

Le Grand Bénare (2896m)

D9

Plage de Trou d'Eau

RN1

Trois Bassins

La Souris Chaude

Conservatoire Botanique National de Mascarin

RF7

Route Forestière des Tamarins

CIRQUE DE CILAOS

Plage de la Souris Chaude

Notre-Dame des Champs

D12

Les Colimaçons

D13

La Chaloupe St-Leu

See Southern Réunion Map (p237)

Antonio Lorenzo

Kelonia

D22

St-Leu

Étang Saint-Leu

La Fenêtre

Le Jardin des Kiosques

La Maison Verte

D3

RF6

Les Makes

Les Pyramides

Tombant de la Pointe au Sel

Stella Matutina

Le Plate

La Tévelave

Pointe au Sel

Route des Tamarins

D20

Musée du Sel & La Caverne

Piton St-Leu

Entre-Deux (9km)

D16

Les Avirons

D19

D3

Bellevue

RN1

D11

Étang-Salé-les-Hauts

D20

Rivière St-Louis

INDIAN OCEAN

Étang-Salé-les-Bains

Sucrerie du Gol

See The Cirques & Les Hautes Plaines Map (p208)

St-Louis

RN5

St-Pierre (9km)

ⓘ LE MAÏDO BY BUS

Walkers, take note: from the central bus station in St-Paul, there's a special bus to Le Maïdo (that takes you to the start of the Sentier de Roche-Plate, the footpath into the Cirque de Mafate, which strikes off the road about 4km below the summit) three times daily except Sunday (€1.50, one hour); the first bus leaves at 6am and the last one down is at 5.20pm.

---

fruits and spices, it makes for a colourful experience.

🛏 Sleeping

Le Caillou Blanc GUESTHOUSE €
(☑ 0692 87 51 92, 0262 55 71 55; www.caillou blanc.com; 20 Rue des Merles, Plateau Caillou; d with shared bathroom €35; 🅿 ⧉) Life feels less hurried at this tranquil guesthouse located in Plateau Caillou, a residential neighbourhood about 4km south of St-Paul. The rooms are neat and functional, but without air-con they're rather airless on hot nights. The shared bathrooms are clean and all guests have kitchen access.

🍴 Eating

The *camions-snacks* (snack vans) on the seafront marketplace operate from late morning until late at night.

★ **Au Petit Carreau** FRENCH, CREOLE €€
(☑ 0262 45 67 46; 25 Rue de la Congrégation; mains €13-17, lunch menu €14.50; ⊘ lunch Mon-Sat) The food at Au Petit Carreau is wholesome, unpretentious and popular. Locals and in-the-know visitors squeeze into the tiny interior or onto the pavement terrace for classics such as *rougail zandouille*, grilled fish or beefsteak, best enjoyed with super crispy homemade French fries. Near the church.

Le Grand Baie FRENCH, CREOLE €€
(☑ 0262 22 50 03; 14 Rue des Filaos; mains €13-22; ⊘ lunch & dinner Tue-Sun) This local haunt rarely registers on St-Paul's tourism radar because it's tucked behind the Cimetière Marin. Big mistake. Munch on well-prepared Creole and *métro* dishes while the ocean crashes just feet away.

Le Bout' Chandelle FRENCH €€
(☑ 0262 27 47 18; 192 Rue Marius et Ary Leblond; mains €17-22, lunch menus €17-20; ⊘ lunch & dinner Tue-Sat) Housed in a welcoming house back from the bustle on the seafront, this is an agreeable place to dine on crowd-pleasers such as *pavé de légine* (toothfish steak) and pork medallion.

ⓘ Getting There & Away

St-Paul lies on Car Jaune's bus route between St-Denis (€2.70) and St-Pierre (€4.30). There are express buses every one to two hours in either direction (fewer on Sunday) and much more frequent nonexpress services.

The local bus company **Kar'Ouest** (☑ 0262 45 72 30; www.karouest.re) operates fairly infrequent services from the central bus station to villages up in the hills such as Le Bernica, La Petite France, Villèle, Le Guillaume and L'Éperon, among others.

Les Hauts de St-Paul

A world away from the hurly-burly of the coast, the verdant Hauts de St-Paul is wonderful country for exploring off the beaten track but, unless you have a lot of time, you need a vehicle. Buses serve most places from St-Paul, but they aren't really convenient for the Hauts. We won't suggest any set itinerary, for this area lends itself to a DIY approach – from St-Paul, use the D5 as a launchpad, then follow your nose (but bring a good map). You'll come across hamlets with such charming names as Sans Soucis les Hauts, Bellemène-les-Hauts, Bois-de-Nèfles, Le Bernica, Le Guillaume... It's as cute as it sounds! Start early morning to get the best views of the coast.

🛏 Sleeping & Eating

La Caz des Orangers GUESTHOUSE €
(☑ 0692 08 23 12, 0262 44 50 32; www.lacazde sorangers.com; 24 Impasse Cernot, Sans Soucis les Hauts; d €49, s/d without bathroom €30/36, incl breakfast; 🅿 ⧉) It's a long drive uphill to get to this sweet establishment located in Sans Souci Les Hauts, about 10km northeast of St-Paul, but you'll be rewarded with enchanting views of the coast and shimmering sea below. It provides a cosy sitting room, tidy bedrooms with minimalist decor and a lovely garden bursting with tropical plants. Add another €10 for dinner (bargain!). It's a great base for hikers going to/from the Cirque de Mafate via the Canalisation des Orangers – the trailhead is just 200m uphill.

Chez Suzy et Gaia   B&B €€

(☑ 0692 52 82 59, 0262 32 45 14; www.chez-gaya-etsuzie.sitew.com; 197 Route Hubert-Delisle, Belle-mène Canot; d incl breakfast €46; ℗) This simple *chambre d'hôte* run by a hospitable Indian couple has two modest but tidy rooms – be sure to ask for the *'vue mer'* (room with a sea view). The dinner menu (€25) is based on good-quality local produce, including home-grown vegetables.

Le Maïdo & Around

Be prepared to fall on your knees in awe: far above St-Paul and St-Gilles-les-Bains on the rim of the Cirque de Mafate, Le Maïdo is one of the most impressive viewpoints in Réunion. The lookout is perched atop the mountain peak at 2205m and offers stunning views down into the Cirque and back to the coast. As with other viewpoints, you should arrive early in the day – by 7am if possible – if you want to see anything other than cloud.

Getting there is half the fun. The sealed Route Forestière du Maïdo winds all the way up to the viewpoint from Le Guillaume (14km) in the hills above St-Gilles-les-Bains, offering a scenic drive through majestic cryptomeria forests. On the way, the hamlet of La Petite France (1000m) is famous for its traditional distilleries producing essential oils from geranium, cryptomeria and vetiver leaves (nice smell!). You'll also find a smattering of attractions along the way to keep you entertained.

A word of warning: expect traffic snarls on Sunday when hundreds of picnicking families set up base in the shade of trees along the road.

🏃 Activities

La Forêt de L'Aventure   OUTDOORS

(☑ 0692 30 01 54; Route Forestière des Cryp-tomérias, La Petite France; adult/child €20/15; ☺ Wed, Fri, Sat & Sun by reservation) For Tarzan types, La Forêt de L'Aventure has set up two wonderful adventure circuits in a 3-hectare perimeter, with a variety of fixtures, including Tyrolean slides. There's a 'Mini Forêt' for the kiddies (over five). It's signposted, about 500m to the north of La Petite France, after L'Alambic Bègue.

Le Relais du Maïdo   OUTDOORS

(☑ 0262 32 40 32; Route du Maïdo; ☺ Tue-Sun) At an altitude of 1500m, the Relais du Maïdo is a kind of theme park, with a smattering of attractions, mostly geared to children, including pony rides (€5), quad bikes (€5 to €10) and archery (€6).

Hiking

Hiking options abound near Le Maïdo. The peak is the starting point for the tough walk along the Cirque rim to the summit of Le Grand Bénare (2896m), another impressive lookout. Hikers can also descend from Le Maïdo into the Cirque de Mafate via the Sentier de Roche-Plate, which meets the GR® R2 variant. For more information see p35.

Mountain Biking

The Maïdo area, with its thrillingly steep descents and spectacular mountain scenery, is a top two-wheel destination.

RÉUNION LE MAÏDO & AROUND

DON'T MISS

THRILLING DOWNHILLS

The spectacular flanks of Le Maïdo will prove a sort of nirvana for mountain bikers who prefer sitting back and letting gravity do the work. The 35km, 2205m descent follows trails that wind through tamarind and cryptomeria forests and sugar-cane fields. Throughout the ride you're presented with astounding views of the lagoon and the coast.

Rando Réunion Passion (p193) is a professional set-up that offers a range of mountain-bike trips for riders of all levels. The most popular ride is the 'Classique du Maïdo' descent, from the lookout to the coast. If you're a beginner, fear not! You won't ride at breakneck speed, and various stops are organised along the way, where the guide will give you the lowdown on flora and fauna. Half-day packages including bike hire, transport to the start (by minivan) and a guide cost around €55 per person (minimum four). Children over 12 are welcome.

If you want to open up the throttle a little more, opt for the 'Maïdo Sportif' (€55) or the 'Méga, Tête Dure' (€90) descents.

✲ Festivals & Events

The **Megavalanche Mountain Race** – the biggest downhill race in the Indian Ocean region – takes place here each year in late November or early December. It is a 2205m descent using a mass start and draws riders from across Réunion and the world.

⊨ Sleeping & Eating

Chez Dominique et Rose Magdeleine B&B €
(✐0262 32 53 50; Chemin de l'École, La Petite France; d incl breakfast €40) Run by an elderly Creole lady, this good-value B&B is a real home away from home. It has few frills but the four rooms are clean as a pin, and the location, just off the main road in La Petite France, makes a convenient base for an early-morning start up to Le Maïdo.

Chez Doudou et Alexandra CREOLE €€
(✐0262 32 55 87; Route de Maïdo, PK 3; menu €20; ⊙lunch Thu-Sun) With its barnlike surrounds, Chez Doudou boasts a kind of ramshackle charm but has no views to speak of. The onus is on earthy regional food, so roll up for comforting Creole *carris* served with all the traditional accompaniments. It's full to bursting at weekends – reservations are advised.

Le Relais du Maïdo CREOLE, BUFFET €€
(Route du Maïdo; mains €10-15, Sunday buffet €17; ⊙lunch Tue-Sun) Adjacent to the eponymous theme park, this eatery with a rustic charm specialises in Creole classics. The menu is down-to-earth, inexpensive and perfectly acceptable as long as you are not expecting cordon bleu. The homemade pastries, especially the coconut and banana pie, are to die for. The Sunday buffet is very popular.

🛍 Shopping

Distillerie du Maïdo – Chez Nanou Le Savoyard DISTILLERY
(✐0692 61 75 43; www.ladistilleriedumaido.com; La Petite France; ⊙8.30am-6pm) Here you can stock up on essential oils, perfumes, soaps and other natural health products. Also sells *rhum arrangé* (flavoured rum), honey and jam.

L'Alambic Bègue DISTILLERY
(✐0692 64 58 25; La Petite France; ⊙8.30am-6pm) A longstanding distillery with an excellent reputation. It features a range of essential oils and health products.

❶ Getting There & Around

Kar'Ouest (p188; line 2) runs three buses a day (Monday to Saturday) taking walkers from St-Paul to the start of the Sentier de Roche-Plate, the footpath into the Cirque de Mafate, which strikes off the road about 4km below the summit. The first bus up the hill leaves at 6am and the last one down is at 5.20pm (€1.50, one hour).

Boucan Canot

POP 2000

The 'Boucan' checklist: skimpy bikini, designer glasses (imitations may be sniggered at), sunscreen. This attitude-fuelled little resort town isn't dubbed the Réunionnais St-Tropez for nothing.

🏖 Beaches

The **main beach** has been listed as one of Réunion's best, and once you get a glimpse of the gentle curve of the bright white sand, lined with palms and casuarina trees and framed with basalt rocks and cliffs, you'll see why. It gets packed on weekends. Caveat: currents can be strong.

There's also the smaller, much quieter **Plage de Petit Boucan**, further south.

⊨ Sleeping

La Villa Du Soleil HOTEL €€
(✐0262 24 38 69; www.lavilladusoleil.com; 54 Route de Boucan Canot; d €56-96; ❄❀🅟🌐) Near the highway (noise!), this low-key hotel with 13 rooms was being upgraded at the time of research. Ask for a room upstairs to make the best of the light; downstairs, rooms 12 and 14, which overlook the (tiny) pool, are also good. The property feels a tad compact and there's no beach frontage, but Plage de Boucan Canot and Plage de Petit Boucan are a short amble away. Note that prices vary depending on season, and they're an extra €10 on Saturday.

Résidence Les Boucaniers APARTMENTS €€
(✐0262 24 23 89; www.les-boucaniers.com; 29 Route de Boucan Canot; d €78; 🅟❀🌐) These self-catering studios and apartments are a tad long in the tooth but have lovely views of the beach, and the location is just right. Prices drop after two nights.

Le Saint-Alexis Hotel & Spa LUXURY HOTEL €€€
(✐0262 24 42 04; www.hotelsaintalexis.com; 44 Route de Boucan Canot; d from €170, ste from €300; 🅟❀@🌐) Le Saint-Alexis is a beautifully designed resort at the southern tip of the

main beach. The rooms are attractively decorated, although some of the standard ones are looking a little threadbare these days. Facilities include a gym, a small spa and a large pool. Frequent online promotional deals provide real value.

Le Boucan Canot LUXURY HOTEL €€€
(📞0262 33 44 44; www.boucancanot.com; 32 Route de Boucan Canot; d/ste incl breakfast from €220/280; P❄🛜🏊) Though ageing a bit, this four-star bigwig at the northern end of the beach is still a commendable option provided you score a room with a sea view. There's a reputable on-site restaurant if you're feeling too lazy to travel elsewhere.

🍴 Eating

There's a clutch of snack stands and laid-back cafe-restaurants along the seafront promenade.

La Boucantine FRENCH, CREOLE €€
(Route de Boucan Canot; mains €10-23; ⊙lunch & dinner Thu-Tue) One of the better (and quieter) restaurants on this seaside strip, with an inviting terrace that affords lovely sea views. High marks go to the *souris d'agneau aux épices* (morsel of lamb with spices) and the catch of the day. There are mouthwatering desserts, too.

Bambou Bar BRASSERIE €€
(📞0262 24 59 29; Route de Boucan Canot; mains €10-24; ⊙lunch Tue-Sun, dinner daily) A longstanding favourite, the Bambou Bar distinguishes itself with its atmospheric decor – think a thatched roof and plenty of wood and greenery. Order anything from coffee and cocktails to pizzas, Creole staples, seafood, burgers, salads and meat dishes.

Ti Boucan BRASSERIE €€
(📞0262 24 85 08; Route de Boucan Canot; mains €12-21, lunch menu €14; ⊙lunch & dinner) On the main strip, this cheerful place is no place to escape the crowds, but the food is tasty and great value. Fish lovers can opt for the *tartare à la mangue* (tuna tartare with mango), while meat-eaters will plump for the kangaroo fillet or the sirloin steak. Copious salads provide a tempting alternative. The service is friendly and the outside terrace is a delight.

❶ Getting There & Away

Car Jaune's lines B and C between St-Denis and St-Pierre run through the centre of Boucan-Canot.

St-Gilles-les-Bains
POP 6000

The tourism machine shifts into overdrive in the large resort complex of St-Gilles-les-Bains, with white sands, restaurants, nightclubs and a boisterous atmosphere on weekends. During the week, however, the atmosphere is much more relaxed and you shouldn't have to fight for a space to lay your towel. There are numerous water activities on offer, from diving to deep-sea fishing.

But let's be frank: it's got that generic resort feel and there's no discernible Creole character. If you're after more authenticity, clunk in your seat belt, jump on a serpentine country road and drive up to some rustic and authentic villages in the Hauts.

⊙ Sights

Aquarium de la Réunion AQUARIUM
(📞0262 33 44 00; www.aquariumdelareunion.com; Port de Plaisance; adult/child €9/6; ⊙10am-5.30pm Tue-Sun) In the modern Port de Plaisance complex, the quite engaging Aquarium de la Réunion houses a series of excellent underwater displays, including tanks with lobsters, barracudas, groupers and small sharks.

🐠 Beaches

Plage des Roches Noires, in the heart of town, is crowded and neatly striped with sunbeds and parasols, but, beneath all this, it remains an attractive stretch of beach excellent for families, with shallow waters and plenty of restaurants. One section is dedicated to surfers. On the southern side of the Port de Plaisance, **Plage des Brisants** is less ideal for swimming but is surprisingly more quiet.

🏃 Activities

Boat Excursions & Whale-Watching

The best way to discover St-Gilles' iridescent lagoon is by joining a boat excursion. Various operators offer *promenades en mer* (boat excursions) and *observation sous-marine* (glass-bottomed tours) along the coast towards St-Leu or St-Paul. 'Safaris dauphin' (dolphin encounters), whale-watching trips (from June to September or October), sunset cruises and day-long catamaran cruises are also available. Tours go every day but are weather-dependent.

St-Gilles-les-Bains

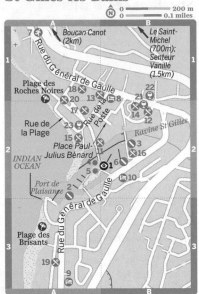

Le Grand Bleu   BOAT TOUR
(☎0262 33 28 32; www.grandbleu.re; Port de Plaisance, St-Gilles-les-Bains; ☉daily) This reputable operator has the largest range of tours, from sunset cruises to whale- and dolphin-watching trips. Depending on the duration of the cruise (the shortest tours last 45 minutes) and the type of boat, rates range from €10 to €90 per adult and from €5 to €50 per child.

Visiobul   BOAT TOUR
(☎0262 24 37 04; www.runevasion.com/visiobul; Port de Plaisance, St-Gilles-les-Bains; adult/child €12.50/7.50; ☉daily) This company specialises in glass-bottomed tours.

Lady La Fée   BOAT TOUR
(☎0692 69 12 99; www.ladylafee.com; Port de Plaisance, St-Gilles-les-Bains; half-/full-day trip €50/90; ☉daily) This small outfit offers half- and full-day trips aboard a catamaran along the west coast. The itinerary is flexible. Sunset cocktail cruises cost €30.

Diving & Snorkelling
The waters off St-Gilles offer plenty of scope for diving (including the chance to explore a few wrecks), whatever your level. See p32 for more information on dive sites.

Bleu Marine Réunion   DIVING
(☎0262 24 22 00; www.bleu-marine-reunion.com; Port de Plaisance; ☉daily) A fully fledged, well-organised dive shop offering a full menu of underwater adventures, including introductory dives (€60), single dive trips (€41 to €50), snorkelling trips (€25) and certification courses.

Corail Plongée   DIVING
(☎0262 24 46 38; www.corail-plongee.com; Port de Plaisance; ☉daily) A reputable dive operator. Has introductory dives (€60), single dives (€35 to €48), snorkelling trips (€25), certification courses and various packages.

Ô Sea Bleu   DIVING
(☎0262 33 16 15; www.reunion-plongee.com; Port de Plaisance; ☉daily) Professional dive shop that offers the full range of scuba activities. Introductory dives go for €60 while single

dives cost €50 (€35 if you have your own gear). Snorkelling trips (€35), certification courses and dive packages are also available.

Mountain Biking

Rando Réunion Passion   MOUNTAIN BIKING
(☑ 0692 21 11 11, 0262 45 18 67; www.descente-vtt. com; 3 Rue du Général de Gaulle) Downhill rides from Le Maïdo can be arranged with Rando Réunion Passion.

Sportfishing

St-Gilles is a good base for fans of Ernest Hemingway. The waters off the west coast are a pelagic playpen for schools of marlin, swordfish, sailfish, shark and tuna. A fishing trip (four to six people) costs from €400/800 per half/full day. Three recommended outfits:

Blue Marlin   FISHING
(☑ 0692 65 22 35; www.bluemarlin.fr; Port de Plaisance) A well-established operator.

Maevasion   FISHING
(☑ 0262 33 38 04; www.maevasion.com; Port de Plaisance) Good credentials.

Réunion Fishing Club   FISHING
(☑ 0262 24 36 10; www.reunionfishingclub.com; Port de Plaisance)

🛏 Sleeping

There's plenty of accommodation in the area, but almost everything is booked out during holiday periods and on weekends. The more appealing hotels and *chambres d'hôtes* are in the countryside just north of town or to the south in L'Hermitage-les-Bains.

Thimloc   APARTMENT €€
(☑ 0262 24 23 24; www.thimloc.fr; 165 Rue du Général de Gaulle; d €60; ✳🛜) Six adjoining rooms in a shady garden. They're fairly unexciting but they're clean and equipped with all the necessary comforts. Prices drop to €54 for stays of more than two nights. The managers rent cars at unbeatable rates.

Hôtel de la Plage   HOTEL €€
(☑ 0692 80 07 57, 0262 24 06 37; www.hoteldelaplage.re; 20 Rue de la Poste; d €65, without bathroom €42-55; ✳🛜) The highlights of this long-established and well-run, hostel-like venture are its ultra-central location and colourful communal areas. The eight rooms are nothing special but get the job done and have good mattresses and flat-screen TVs. Some have bathrooms, some don't, some are spacious, some are boxy, some open onto a terrace, some don't. Rooms 114, 115 and 116

are the best. Breakfast costs €6. Prices drop after two nights. Book ahead.

Le Saint-Michel   HOTEL €€
(☑ 0262 33 13 33; st-michel.hotel@wanadoo.fr; 196 Chemin Summer; s/d incl breakfast €76/98; P✳🛜🏊) Under new management, this great little number amid a tropical garden on the outskirts of town was being renovated at the time of writing and should feature 28 modernised rooms (some with sea views) by the time you read this. The on-site restaurant offers really superb French cuisine with a Creole twist (menus from €15). It's a two-minute drive to the centre and the beach.

Hôtel des Palmes   HOTEL €€
(☑ 0262 24 47 12; fax 0262 24 30 62; 205 Rue du Général de Gaulle; d €90; P✳🏊) This two-star offers good-sized villas, but its location ain't so great – it's sandwiched between the highway and the main road to L'Hermitage. The pool is a joke. An acceptable plan B.

★Senteur Vanille   LODGE, VILLA €€€
(☑ 0692 78 13 05, 0262 24 04 88; www.senteurvanille.com; Route du Théâtre; studio d €85-100, villa q €160-190, lodge d €145, lodge q €160-185; P✳🛜) A true find for peace seekers, Senteur Vanille makes you feel like you've stepped into a Garden of Eden, with mango, lychee and papaya trees all over the grounds (the owner is a major fruit producer in Réunion). Curl up in a well-equipped lodge or in a cute-as-can-be Creole house. The wonderful setting makes it easy to meet the three-night minimum stay. No swimming-pool, but the nearest beach is a 20-minute walk down a path. It's a few kilometres east of the centre, in the direction of St-Gilles-les-Hauts, signed down a lane beside the Total petrol station. No credit cards.

🍴 Eating

St-Gilles is well endowed with eating places. Standards tend to be more variable than elsewhere on the island.

As well as restaurants, you'll find several *camions-pizzas* (mobile pizza vans) on the main street; they're a good bargain. They operate in the evening.

★Chez Loulou   BAKERY, FAST FOOD €
(☑ 0262 24 40 41; 86 Rue du Général de Gaulle; mains €6-8; ⏰7am-1pm & 3-7pm Mon-Sat, 7am-1pm Sun) The most iconic Creole *case* (house) for miles around, with a distinctive turquoise facade on the main drag. The belt-bustingly good samosas, *macatias* (a variety

MUSÉE DE VILLÈLE

If all these beaches start to overwhelm, head to the **Musée de Villèle** (☑0262 55 64 10; St-Gilles-les-Hauts; admission €2; ⊙9.30am-12.30pm & 1.30-5pm Tue-Sun), a 20-minute drive from St-Gilles-les-Bains, on the D6. It's set in the former home of a wealthy coffee and sugar baroness who, among other things, owned 300 slaves. Legend has it that she was a cruel woman and that her ghost inhabits the Piton de la Fournaise; supposedly her tormented screams can be heard from the hellish fires whenever the volcano is erupting. She died in 1846 and her body lies in the **Chapelle Pointue**, on the D6 by the entrance to the museum. The house itself, which is only accessible on a guided tour (in French only), was built in 1787 and is full of elegant period furniture. After the tour, you're free to wander the outbuildings and the 10-hectare park, which contains the ruins of the sugar mill.

of bun), croissants and tarts continue to torment us! Good sandwiches and takeaway meals at lunchtime, too.

Le Glacier de Marie B ICE CREAM €
(☑0262 24 53 06; 13 Rue de la Poste; ice creams from €1.80; ⊙11am-7pm Tue-Sun, to 11pm Sat) You'll lose all self-control at this drool-inducing ice-cream parlour. Amid a mind-boggling array of flavours, the electric purple pitaya screams 'try me'. Good pancakes and waffles, too.

La Case à Pain BAKERY, SANDWICHES €
(☑0262 33 27 89; Port de Plaisance; sandwiches €4.50; ⊙6.30am-7pm) Hmm! We can still smell the scent of freshly baked bread and cakes wafting from the door. It also churns out excellent sandwiches.

★**Le P'tit Zinc** CREOLE €€
(☑0262 24 07 50; 58 Rue du Général de Gaulle; mains €14-20, menu €19; ⊙dinner Mon-Sat) This venue has a tantalising menu showcasing all the classics of Creole cuisine, served in snug surrounds complete with wood beams, elegant furnishings and tropical plants. Feeling adventurous? Go for the *carri pat' cochon* (pig's trotter curry). The spiffing balcony on the 1st floor (two tables only) is a good place to linger over a meal.

Ice Spot BRASSERIE €€
(☑0262 33 26 77; www.restaurant-ice-spot.fr; 2 Rue du Port; mains €10-22; ⊙breakfast & lunch daily, dinner Thu-Sat) This bustling eatery enjoys an ace position with a sprawling terrace overlooking the beach. The menu is surprisingly down-to-earth and perfectly acceptable as long as you are not expecting cordon bleu. Expect salads, seafood, meat dishes and

tartines (a slice of bread with toppings). The brunch formula (€15) is served until 10.30am.

O'Casier FRENCH €€
(☑0262 33 17 38; 190 Rue du Général de Gaulle; mains €11-25; ⊙lunch & dinner Tue-Fri & Sun, dinner Sat) This sassy *bistrot chic* (gastropub) churns out excellent charcuterie and cheese platters (€12), as well as tempting *métro* dishes. Since wine also features here, get stuck into the list of well-chosen French tipples, available by the glass.

Au Bord de L'Eau CHINESE, CREOLE €€
(☑0262 33 47 63; www.auborddeleau.re; 59 Blvd Roland Garros; mains €14-22; ⊙lunch Tue-Sun, dinner Tue-Sat) It was the braised chicken that clinched it for us. The onus is on well-executed Chinese and Creole classics. The inconspicuous entrance brings you to a cheery terrace that enjoys prime position overlooking the marina. Fair value.

★**Chez Bobonne** FUSION €€€
(☑0262 39 27 96; 3 Rue St-Alexis; mains €23-30; ⊙dinner) Indulge in delicious, flawlessly prepared dishes at this fine-dining restaurant with a contemporary decor. The small menu is chalked on the board and changes weekly. There's also a thoughtful wine list. It's tucked away from the main drag.

Chez Nous FUSION €€€
(☑0262 24 08 08; 122 Rue du Général de Gaulle; mains €16-23; ⊙lunch & dinner) This bold bistro is beloved by all who come here. The blackboard menu features flavourful meat and fish dishes, some with an exotic twist. The service may see you twiddling your thumbs when it's crowded. It doubles as a bar.

Sel et Poivre FRENCH €€€

(☎0262 43 18 08; 29 Blvd Roland Garros; mains €16-32; ☺lunch & dinner Thu-Tue) The modern menu at this sophisticated restaurant offers a creative take on otherwise typical French fare. One of the more upmarket places in the centre, it's the sort of place you should eat at as a treat to yourself, but it's also popular with a more informal lunchtime crowd.

Drinking

St-Gilles is one of the top places in Réunion (on an equal footing with St-Pierre) for bar-hopping. The atmosphere is very Zoreilles – you could be mistaken for thinking you're in the French Côte d'Azur. Most places are scattered along Rue du Général de Gaulle and the chichi seafront. As the bars fade from about midnight on, the centre of pleasurable gravity shifts to L'Hermitage. Most bars also serve food.

Cubana Café BAR

(☎0262 33 24 91; 122 Rue du Général de Gaulle; ☺7pm-5am Tue-Sat) Kick off the night with a few shots at this salsa-inspired venue featuring bordello-red curtains.

Esko Bar BAR

(☎0262 33 19 33; Rue du Général de Gaulle; ☺7pm-2am Mon-Sat) Opened in 2012, this chic venue has excellent cocktails and themed nights – check the Facebook page.

L'Acacia BAR

(☎0262 27 36 43; 1 Rue de la Poste; ☺11am-midnight) A fashionable open-air bar and restaurant on the seafront. Its 'pool parties' are legendary.

Chez Nous BAR

(☎0262 24 08 08; 122 Rue du Général de Gaulle; ☺7pm-2am) A hip bar with a loungey feel.

ⓘ Information

ATM-clad commercial banks can be found along the main drag in St-Gilles.

Hotwave (☎0262 24 04 04; 37 Rue du Général de Gaulle, St-Gilles-les-Bains; per hr €9.80; ☺10am-7pm Mon-Sat; ☎) Internet cafe. Also has wi-fi and printing services.

Office du Tourisme (☎0810 79 77 97; www. saintpaul-lareunion.com; 1 Place Paul-Julius Bénard, St-Gilles-les-Bains; ☺10am-1pm & 2-6pm; ☎) Has helpful English-speaking staff. Free wi-fi. Does bookings for *gîtes de montagne*.

ⓘ Getting There & Away

Car Jaune's nonexpress buses between St-Denis and St-Pierre (lines B and C) run through the centre of St-Gilles down Rue du Général de Gaulle. The trip to St-Denis takes at least one hour and costs €2.80.

ⓘ Getting Around

CAR & MOTORCYCLE

There are numerous local operators and a few international outlets in St-Gilles. Find them along Rue du Général de Gaulle.

BICYCLE

Rando Réunion Passion (p193) rents out mountain bikes (from €15 per day).

L'Hermitage-les-Bains

POP 6000

L'Hermitage has the bulk of the island's major resorts, a good selection of restaurant and entertainment options, and what is possibly Réunion's most scenic beach. Here, the island has the feel of a vacation destination.

◉ Sights

Le Jardin d'Eden GARDENS

(☎0262 33 83 16; www.jardindeden.re; 155 RN1; adult/child €7/3.50; ☺10am-6pm Sat-Thu) Appealing to a wider audience than just plant lovers and gardeners, Le Jardin d'Eden, across the main road from L'Hermitage, is definitely worth an hour or so for anyone interested in tropical flora. Sections of the gardens are dedicated to interesting concepts such as the sacred plants of the Hindus, medicinal plants, edible tropical plants, spices and aphrodisiac plants.

Beaches

Further south of St-Gilles' Plage des Roches Noires, lined with casuarina trees, is **Plage de L'Hermitage**, which is another alluring place to fry in the sun. It is safe for swimming and extremely popular on weekends. Snorkelling is better at Plage de L'Hermitage than at Plage des Roches Noires.

🛏 Sleeping

Camping Ermitage Lagon CAMPGROUND €

(☎0262 96 36 70; camping@tamarun.fr; 60 Ave de Bourbon; camp site 1-6 people €15-30) This relatively new camping ground has modern, functional facilities, but is located near

RÉUNION L'HERMITAGE-LES-BAINS

L'Hermitage-les-Bains

0 — 200 m
0 — 0.1 miles

Le Jardin d'Eden

Ave des Mascareignes

RN1

Plage de L'Hermitage

St-Leu (13.5km)

L'HERMITAGE-LES-BAINS

Ave de la Mer

Ave des Badamiers

Ave des Letchis

Ruelle des Bougainvilliers

INDIAN OCEAN

Blvd Leconte de Lisle

Ave de Bourbon

Lux (400m)

L'Hermitage's clubs, so it may not be quiet on weekends. Shade is in short supply (until the recently planted trees mature) but you're within spitting distance of the beach. You can rent out a whole 'safari tent' for €30 – quite a good deal by L'Hermitage standards.

Résidence Coco Island   GUESTHOUSE €
(☑0692 37 71 12, 0262 33 82 41; www.cocoisland -reunion.com; 21 Ave de la Mer; d €41-71; ❄🐕📶⛱) This is a popular budget option, with 20 unimaginative rooms of varying size and shape – have a look before committing. Cheaper rooms share toilets but have cubicle showers plonked in the corner. Guests can use the communal kitchen and the small pool in the garden beside the reception. Prices drop for stays longer than five nights.

★**Les Créoles**   HOTEL €€
(☑0262 26 52 65; www.hotel-les-creoles.com; 43 Ave de Bourbon; d from €110; P❄🐕📶⛱) On an island where affordable-but-beautiful hotels are a rarity, this small-scale venture opened in 2011 is a no-brainer. It attracts holiday-makers looking for comfortable, modern rooms. Facilities include a bar, a pool and a small restaurant. One quibble: it's not on the beach. Check out the website for off-season discounts.

Villa des Tisserins   APARTMENTS €€
(☑0262 33 15 23; villa.des.tisserins@wanadoo.fr; 25 Ave de la Mer; d €45-65; P❄🐕📶⛱) If you're looking to save and be close to the beach, this laid-back villa with five studios and one bungalow is a bonanza. The decor is a tad faded but at this price nobody's complaining. Mellow out in the garden or take a dip in the kidney-shaped pool.

Les Bougainvilliers   GUESTHOUSE €€
(☑0262 33 82 48; www.bougainvillier.com; 27 Ru-elle des Bougainvilliers; d €56-66; P❄🐕📶⛱) For something personal, try this jolly, hospitably run little bolt-hole with 14 rooms. Firm mattresses, colourful walls, flat-screen TVs, a pool, plus a communal kitchen and a flower-filled garden, all just a stroll from the beach. The catch? It's a wee compact – the pool almost licks the terrace of the downstairs

room. Bikes are available for free. Discounts are offered for longer stays.

Lux
RESORT €€€

(✆0262 70 05 00; www.luxresorts.com; 28 Rue du Lagon; d incl breakfast from €375; P ✳ @ ⓢ ☒) Lux pays elegant homage to luxurious colonial architecture, with a gaggle of Creole-style villas scattered amid a verdant property at the very south end of the beach at L'Hermitage. Facilities include two restaurants, a huge pool and a bar. For the price, we'd expect a spa. Frequent special offers can mean you often only pay €180 for a room.

Le Récif
RESORT €€€

(✆0262 70 05 00; www.hotellerecif.com; 50 Ave du Bourbon; d incl breakfast from €250; P ✳ ⓢ ☒) While not as luxurious as Lux (its sister property), this sprawling resort is still a reliable base, especially if you can score promotional rates (around €135 in low season). Rooms and communal areas are pretty tired, so don't come expecting cutting-edge design. Its main selling point is its location, a coconut's throw from the beach.

✗ Eating & Drinking

Snack Chez Herbert
CREOLE, SANDWICHES €

(✆0262 32 42 96; 40 Blvd Leconte de Lisle; mains €2.50-8; ⊙lunch & dinner Tue-Sun) This popular joint is worth visiting for its cheap and wholesome Creole staples. Snacks, salads, sandwiches and other nibbles are also available. Take your plunder to the beach or grab a (plastic) table on the shaded pavement.

Snack Chez Racine
CREOLE, SANDWICHES €

(42 Blvd Leconte de Lisle; mains €3-10; ⊙lunch & dinner Wed-Mon) If you're looking for a quick food fix, check out the options at this casual hang-out near the beach.

★ La Bobine
SEAFOOD, FRENCH €€

(✆0262 33 94 36; Blvd Leconte de Lisle; mains €17-25; ⊙lunch & dinner) This sprightly restaurant with an exotic feel – the wood and thatch are imported from Madagascar – enjoys a perfect location, slap bang on the beach. The wide-ranging menu features delicious fish or meat dishes. There's also a snack section (until 5pm), with a choice of sandwiches, salads and light meals. It's also a fantastic place to sip a cocktail (€7).

Coco Beach
FRENCH, CREOLE €€

(✆0262 33 81 43; Blvd Leconte de Lisle; mains €15-23, menus €20-47; ⊙lunch & dinner) This peren-

nial fave overlooking the beach serves grills and ultra-fresh fish, salads and tapas (from 5.30pm). It's also a good place to hang out and just enjoy the tropical atmosphere and fashionable buzz with a fresh Dodo beer in hand. There's live music on Friday and Saturday evening.

Au K'Banon
FRENCH, SEAFOOD €€

(✆0262 33 84 94; Blvd Leconte de Lisle; mains €16-23; ⊙breakfast & lunch daily, dinner Mon-Sat) This friendly restaurant with a casual atmosphere occupies a privileged spot on the beach. The menu runs the gamut from fish dishes and grilled meats to salads and ice creams. What sets it apart, though, is the *formule petit déjeuner au bord du lagon* (lagoonside breakfast, served from 9am; €7.50). Hmm, croissants and baguettes metres from the turquoise waters...

La Marmite
CREOLE, BUFFET €€

(✆0262 33 31 37; Blvd Leconte de Lisle; buffet €20, menus €37-47; ⊙lunch & dinner) You'll need to fast the day before – lunch and dinner at La Marmite are buffet-style, with 14 wood-fired *carris* on offer.

Le Manta
SEAFOOD, INTERNATIONAL €€

(✆0262 33 82 44; Blvd Leconte de Lisle; mains €12-24; ⊙lunch & dinner) Concealed in a wonderfully overgrown garden, this well-respected restaurant has a great selection of fish and meat dishes, as well as a few Creole classics and salads. Toothsome specialities include *salade manta,* comprising smoked marlin and tuna, and *espadon grillé* (grilled swordfish). No, it's not right on the beach – it's just across the road.

La Gueule de Bois
BAR, RESTAURANT

(✆0262 22 90 06; 5 Rue des Îles Éparses; ⊙6.30pm-midnight Tue-Sun) The name of this

RÉUNION L'HERMITAGE-LES-BAINS

DON'T MISS

BEST PICNIC SPOTS

➡ The beach at L'Hermitage-les-Bains (p195) – fun and casual

➡ Belvédère de l'Eden (p250) – our favourite (shh...)

➡ Anse des Cascades (p254) – in a lovely coconut grove

➡ Le Maïdo (p189) – fresh air galore

➡ Rivière Langevin (p241) – wildly popular at weekends

cheerful den is a French expression meaning 'hangover', which is pretty appropriate given the incendiary rums on offer. It hosts live bands on Saturday and Sunday evening. Food is also served.

☆ Entertainment

Party, party, party! L'Hermitage rocks on weekends. The unchalleged capital of Réunion's club scene, it has the greatest density of discos on the island. The fun starts late – after midnight – and places typically close around 5am. Cover charges vary between €10 and €15 at most venues (but some are free). You don't need to be completely dolled up but if you're wearing shorts or flip-flops you'll be turned away.

La Villa Club   CLUB
(🖉 0692 60 19 00; www.lavilla-club.com; 71 Ave de Bourbon; ⊗ Fri & Sat) L'Hermitage's top nightspot positively sizzles on a Friday and Saturday night when the dance floors are packed. Tropical, electro and dance music dominate the play list.

Le Klub   CLUB
(🖉 0692 85 86 72; www.leklub.re; 2 Mail Rodrigue; ⊗ Fri & Sat) House, dance and electro grooves thump 'n' bump under ultraviolet and stroboscopic lights.

Moulin du Tango   CLUB
(🖉 0262 24 53 90; www.moulin-du-tango.re; Ave de Bourbon; ⊗ Fri & Sat) Bump your hips with a mature crowd in this dance club famous for its themed nights.

Le Loft   CLUB
(🖉 0262 24 81 06; 1 Rue des Îles Éparses; ⊗ Fri & Sat) A pulsating club playing a little bit of this and a little bit of that.

❶ Getting There & Away

Car Jaune's nonexpress buses between St-Denis and St-Pierre (lines B and C) run through L'Hermitage. The trip to St-Denis costs €2.80.

La Saline-les-Bains & Around

POP 2750

If you find the scene in St-Gilles and L'Hermitage a little too much, head to La Saline-les-Bains. Though immediately to the south of L'Hermitage along the coast, it has a distinct atmosphere. Here it's more mellow, more alternative, more nonconformist.

That said, there are plans to build a couple of hotels near the beach, which may change the allure of La Saline-les-Bains.

🏊 Beaches

The main beach is a stellar stretch of white sand and is usually less crowded than its northern counterparts at St-Gilles or L'Hermitage. It has shallow, calm waters, making it an ideal location for families. Its southern section is known as **Plage de Trou d'Eau** and is a nice place to relax and have a swim.

Not a fan of tan lines? Head further south and lay your towel on **Plage de la Souris Chaude**, which is a favourite among nudists (only just tolerated) and gay men (head to the northern tip of the beach). It remains largely off the tourist radar, not least because it's a bit hard to find.

🏃 Activities

Kayaking is a great way to explore the lagoon at a gentle pace. The beachfront restaurant Planch'Alizé (p199) rents canoes, kayaks and paddleboats (from €5 per hour).

The area is also popular for **surfing**, especially for beginners. To the south of La Saline, surfers gather at the Pointe des Trois Bassins, where the waves are generally easier and more consistent than around St-Leu.

Ecole de SUP du Lagon   STAND-UP PADDLE BOARDING
(🖉 0262 24 63 28, 0692 86 00 59; La-Saline-les-Bains) Fancy trying stand-up paddle boarding? Contact Ecole de SUP du Lagon, which offers one- or two-hour courses run by a qualified instructor.

Aileron   WINDSURFING
(🖉 0693 03 36 12; http://dtmi.free.fr; La-Saline-les-Bains) If you want to learn to windsurf, Aileron can arrange windsurfing courses (from €30 per person) for all levels.

🛏 Sleeping

L'Amarina   GUESTHOUSE €
(🖉 0693 97 02 81; www.amarinareunion.fr; 30 Rue des Ormeaux; d without bathroom €30-43, studio €45-55; 🕲🐾) A 10-minute stroll from the beach, this friendly, well-run guesthouse is nicely small scale, with just five fan-cooled rooms and one studio, and is surprisingly decent at a bargain price. Rooms are neat, fuss-free and airy. Common areas include a sitting room/library, kitchen and swimming

pool. A minimum two-day stay is required. L'Amarina is a bit tricky to find – check the website for directions. Pricing varies according to the season.

Le Vacoa
HOTEL €€

(☑ 0262 24 12 48; www.levacoa.com; 54 Rue Antoine de Bertin; d €54-60; ❄ 🎤 🗄) A five-minute stroll from the beach, this little two-storey *résidence hôtelière* (mini-resort) won't knock your socks off but it contains 15 modern, well-appointed (albeit hanky-sized) rooms arranged around a central courtyard. There's a kitchen for guests' use and a pocket-sized pool. Prices drop after three nights. Bonus: four bikes are available (free).

La Maison du Lagon
HOTEL €€

(☑ 0262 24 30 14; www.lamaisondulagon.com; 72 Rue Auguste Lacaussade; s €68-102, d €88-123, ste €190, incl breakfast; ❄ 🎤 🗄) This villa has a compact but respectable collection of various-sized rooms, but only two rooms have direct sea views. Tip for couples: book the stand-alone Zen chalet (€99), which is a sweet spot. The real plus here is the location – it's *les pieds dans l'eau* (right by the beach). The pool at the entrance of the property is a bit of a joke, though. Kids under 12 are not accepted.

La Villa Elixène
B&B €€

(☑ 0692 00 40 91; www.villaelixene.com; La Souris Chaude; s/d incl breakfast €89/99; P ❄ 🎤 🗄) Florian gives his guests a genuinely warm welcome at this smart B&B a thong's throw from Plage de la Souris Chaude. It's a lovely spot to while away a few peaceful days. The large bright rooms have a luxurious feel with their minimalist lines, soothing colour accents and sparkling bathrooms. Laze on the shady terrace, lounge by the pool, enjoy the sea views or step down to the beach just below. Gay-friendly.

Le Dalon Plage
BUNGALOW €€

(☑ 0692 04 94 26, 0262 34 29 77; www.ledalon. jimdo.com; 6 Allée des Tuits Tuits, La Souris Chaude; d €55-65; P ❄ 🎤 🗄) It's just a short amble from the Plage de la Souris Chaude to this hedonistic, gay-friendly place. Guests are allowed (if not incited) to swim naked in the gleaming pool. Too prudish? Slumber in the fully equipped, solar-heated bungalow or in the well-appointed studio. The flowery garden is a feast for the eyes – it helps that François, one of the two owners, is a gardener. Breakfast/dinner cost €10/20. A good deal.

★ La Closerie du Lagon
APARTMENT €€€

(☑ 0692 86 32 47, 0262 24 12 56; www.closerie-du-lagnon.fr; 78ter Rue Lacaussade; d €110; P ❄ @ 🎤) Alain and Charles are your kindly hosts at this ravishing abode, which consists of a splendid villa with all mod cons in a peaceful property by the beach. It's fully equipped. Intimate, chic and gay-friendly. There's a two-night minimum stay.

Hôtel Swalibo
HOTEL €€€

(☑ 0262 24 10 97; www.swalibo.com; 9 Rue des Salines; s €110-150, d €140-190, incl breakfast; P ❄ 🎤 🗄) This small (some would say 'cramped') two-storey hotel is a good deal if you can get online specials. The rooms sport colourful frescoes and are arranged around a gleaming pool. They're well appointed but the bathrooms are itty-bitty. There's an on-site restaurant. It's 200m away from the beach.

✖️ Eating & Drinking

★ La Petite Vague
SEAFOOD, BURGERS €€

(☑ 0692 08 16 76; Route du Trou d'Eau; mains €10-19; ☉ lunch daily, dinner Wed-Sun) Sweet! La Petite Vague is right on the beach, and it serves good, fresh food at competitive prices given the five-star location. The menu has something for all: burgers, tuna tartare, salads, meat dishes and seafood. Come for lunch rather than dinner, and enjoy the setting.

★ Planch'Alizé
SEAFOOD, SANDWICHES €€

(☑ 0262 24 62 61; www.planchalize.net; Rue des Mouettes; mains €8-18; ☉ lunch daily, dinner Wed-Sun, bar 9am-late) Visitors and locals flock to this bustling little *paillotte* (beach restaurant) for reliable seafood – the swordfish tartare is excellent – as well as meat dishes and lavish salads. All at very honest prices. For a snack, call by the adjacent takeaway outlet, which turns out tasty sandwiches, salads and homemade desserts. It's also a fantastic spot for a drink any time of the day. Live bands play here on Friday from 6.30pm.

La Bonne Marmite
CREOLE €€

(☑ 0262 39 82 49; Route du Trou d'Eau; mains €10-16, dinner buffet €17; ☉ dinner Mon-Sat) Pounce on La Bonne Marmite's excellent-value dinner buffet, which features 10 wholesome *carris*, and you'll leave perfectly sated. It's a coconut's throw from the beach (with the sea just out of sight, alas).

RÉUNION LA SALINE-LES-BAINS & AROUND

La Bodega
FRENCH €€

(Plage de Trou d'Eau; mains €14-18; ⊘ breakfast, lunch & dinner) Visitors and locals flock to this casual little *paillotte* that serves a wide range of dishes, including tapas and seafood. More than the food, though, it's the beachside location that's the real draw.

Le Copacabana
FRENCH €€€

(🖉 0262 24 16 31; www.copacabana-plage.com; 20 Rue des Mouettes; mains €16-28; ⊘ lunch daily, dinner Fri & Sat, bar 9am-late daily; 🛜) This trendy bar-restaurant has a peerless position right on the beach. Enjoy well-prepared fish and meat dishes as well as excellent homemade desserts. Le Copa is also the most fashionable spot for a night-time tipple or a refreshing fruit juice any time of the day. The catch? It's pretty expensive.

St-Leu

POP 25,000

Since the good old days of the sugar industry ended, forward-looking St-Leu has transformed itself into a mecca for outdoor enthusiasts. This is the place to get high – legally: no doubt you'll be tempted to join the paragliders who wheel down from the Hauts to the lagoon. Scuba divers also swear that the drop-offs here are the best on the island.

And culture? St-Leu has a smattering of handsome stone buildings dating from the French colonial era, such as the *mairie* (town hall) and the church opposite. Other attractions are the shady park along the seafront and a protected beach that is popular with families.

St-Leu is also optimally placed for explorations of the coast and forays into the Hauts.

◎ Sights

Kelonia
MUSEUM

(🖉 0262 34 81 10; www.kelonia.org; Pointe des Châteaux; adult/child €7/5; ⊘ 9am-5pm) Don't miss this ecologically conscious marine and research centre dedicated to sea turtles, about 2km north of St-Leu. It features exhibits, interactive displays and big tanks where you can get a close-up look at the five different varieties of turtle found in the waters around Réunion, especially the green turtle *(Chelonia mydas)*. Kids love the place but adults will also be blown away by this well-organised venture. Guided tours are available.

Notre-Dame de la Salette
CHURCH

(St Leu) The little white chapel of Notre-Dame de la Salette, perched on the side of the hill to the east of town, was built in 1859 as a plea for protection against the cholera epidemic sweeping the entire island. Whether by luck or divine intervention, St-Leu was spared from the epidemic, and thousands of pilgrims come here each year on 19 September to offer their thanks.

Musée du Sel & La Caverne
MUSEUM

(🖉 0262 34 67 00; Pointe au Sel; ⊘ 9am-noon & 1.30-5pm Tue-Fri) FREE On the cliffs at Pointe au Sel, between St-Leu and Étang-Salé-les-Bains, this museum, housed in an old salt warehouse, traces the local salt-harvesting history. It's flanked by salt evaporation ponds. After visiting the museum, follow the path that leads to La Caverne (no sign), a large, wonderful rock pool with turquoise waters only known to locals. It's ideal for splashing about, sunbathing or picnicking.

🐠 Beaches

St-Leu's beach is a very good stretch of sand that's particularly popular with locals; it comes to life on weekends with loud music and smells of *carri* cooking.

🏃 Activities

Diving

The dive spots off Pointe au Sel to the south of St-Leu offer some of the best underwater landscapes in Réunion, while the lagoon closer to St-Leu is good for coral. See p32 for more details on dive sites.

Abyss Plongée
DIVING

(🖉 0262 34 79 79; www.abyss-plongee.com; 17 Blvd Bonnier; ⊘ daily) This reputable outfit has a full menu of reef and wreck dives (from €35) and runs certification courses. An introductory dive costs €62.

Bleu Océan
DIVING

(🖉 0262 34 97 49; www.bleuocean.fr; 25 Rue du Général Lambert; ⊘ daily) A professional centre that caters just as well to beginners as it does to advanced divers. Single/introductory dives cost from €36/65. There are special rates for multiday diving.

Excelsus
DIVING

(🖉 0262 34 73 65; www.excelsus-plongee.com; Pointe des Châteaux; ⊘ daily) This efficient operation offers a full range of dives and various dive packages. It charges €60 for an introductory dive and from €38 for a single dive.

Réunion Plongée
DIVING

(☑ 0692 85 66 37, 0262 34 77 77; www.reunion-plongee.com; 13 Ave des Artisans; ⊘ Tue-Sun) A small outfit with good credentials. Offers introductory dives (€65), singles dives (from €38), Nitrox dives and dive packages.

Paragliding

St-Leu is one of the world's top spots for paragliding, with excellent uplifting thermals year-round. If you're new to dangling yourself in the air, you can tandem paraglide with one of the many operators offering flights (from €75 to €110 for a 15-minute to a one-hour aerial buzz). They also run introductory courses from €270. The most popular launch pad is at an altitude of 800m, high above the town. There's another launch pad at 1500m. The descent from the mountain is amazing, with heart-stopping views over the lagoon and the coast. Children over six are welcome.

Airanx
PARAGLIDING

(☑ 0692 68 81 81; www.airanx-parapente.com; 38 Rue du Général Lambert; ⊘ daily) Offers paragliding and paramotoring.

Azurtech
PARAGLIDING

(☑ 0692 85 04 00; www.azurtech.com; Pointe des Châteaux; ⊘ daily) A longstanding favourite.

Bourbon Parapente
PARAGILDING

(☑ 0692 87 58 74; www.bourbonparapente.com; Rue du Général Lambert; ⊘ daily) An experienced outfit.

Parapente Réunion
PARAGLIDING

(☑ 0692 82 92 92, 0262 24 87 84; www.parapente-reunion.fr; 1 Route des Colimaçons; ⊘ daily) This is a well-established operator.

Surfing

The surf break known as **La Gauche de St-Leu** ('the Left of St-Leu') has achieved cult status among surfers from all over the Indian Ocean. Certainly not for the faint-hearted, it instils profound respect (if not fear) even in the most seasoned surfers. The best season runs from May to October.

Beginners should make for a spot called **La Cafrine**, which is a bit more innocuous, or head to Pointe des Trois Bassins or St-Gilles-les-Bains.

That said, the surfing scene is no longer what it used to be, following several shark attacks that occurred quite recently off Bou-

TOP FIVE PLACES TO GET OUTDOORS

➡ Piton de la Fournaise (p228) – scale Réunion's number-one attraction

➡ Le Maïdo (p189) – quicken your pulse with a rip-roaring mountain-bike descent

➡ St-Leu – try paragliding and see the lagoon from above

➡ St-Benoît (p251) – test your mettle on a white-water run on Rivière des Marsouins

➡ Cilaos (p212) – learn the ropes (literally) of canyoning in the gentle Canyon de Gobert

can Canot, Pointe des Trois Bassins and St-Gilles-les-Bains. It's wise to seek local advice before hitting the waves.

Festivals & Events

Leu Tempo
THEATRE

(www.lesechoir.com; ⊘ May) A very popular theatre festival at Le K - Le Séchoir venue. Also features dance, circus and music.

Fête de Notre-Dame de la Salette
RELIGIOUS

(Festival of Notre Dame de la Salette; ⊘ Sep) Pilgrimage to the miracle-working Madonna at the chapel of Notre-Dame de la Salette (p200). Fair and street events over 10 days.

Sleeping

Ti Som
HOSTEL €

(☑ 0692 24 18 12; 228bis Rue du Général Lambert; dm €17, d with shared bathroom €35; ❀) The cheapest place to stay for miles, with a brightly painted 12-bed dorm. If privacy is a priority, opt for the no-frills but OK doubles. The shared kitchen is a plus.

Dodo Spot
GUESTHOUSE €

(☑ 0262 34 76 98; www.dodospot.com; 67 Rue du Général Lambert; d without bathroom €29, studios €44-54; ❀) On the northern edge of town, this is an acceptable standby, if you can forgive some flagrant omissions in the brochure and on the website. Sure, it's almost 'two steps away from the lagoon', but there's no mention of the noisy highway in between! The whole place feels a bit cramped, especially the coffin-sized rooms; it's worth dropping the extra €15 to grab a more spacious studio.

Palais d'Asie
APARTMENTS €

(☑0692 86 48 80, 0262 34 80 41; lepalaisdasie974@wanadoo.fr; 5 Rue de l'Étang; d €40-45; ❋🛜🏊) One of St-Leu's best bargains, though the 'Palais' bit is a gross misnomer. It's comfortably central, with minimally furnished but functional rooms. And no, that icon's not a misprint – it really does have its own (tiny) swimming pool. Prices drop to €35 to €40 for stays longer than two nights.

Résidence Les Pêcheurs
BUNGALOWS €€

(☑0692 85 39 84, 0262 34 91 25; les.pecheurs.pagesperso-orange.fr; 27 Rue des Alizés; d/q €52/82; 🅿🏊) On the southern edge of town there's great value to be found at this clean, friendly and well-run venture. It consists of six bungalows with partial sea views. They're spacious, practical and well kitted out. There's no beach nearby, but guests can chill by the lovely pool. Three nights minimum.

Repos Laleu
APARTMENTS €€

(☑0262 34 93 84; 249 Rue du Général Lambert; d/q €60/75; 🅿❋🛜) Offers eight fully equipped studios, smack dab in the centre. Note that one-week stays are preferred.

★ Le Blue Margouillat
BOUTIQUE HOTEL €€€

(☑0262 34 64 00; www.blue-margouillat.com; Impasse Jean Albany; d from €165; 🅿❋🛜🏊) This delightful hotel on the southern outskirts of St-Leu adds a welcoming touch of glam to the local hotel scene, with just 14 artfully designed and sensitively furnished rooms, an award-winning restaurant, an inviting pool and smashing views. Overall this is a real treat for couples looking for a perfect high-style escape.

Iloha
HOTEL €€€

(☑0262 34 89 89; www.iloha.fr; Pointe des Châteaux; s €75-85, d €90-155, bungalows €125-185; 🅿❋🛜🏊) This recently upgraded place is a very good all-round hotel-cum-resort. Its rooms and bungalows offer a great choice for everyone from couples to families. While the standard rooms feel a bit claustrophobic, the bungalows offer ample space. Visitors after more privacy can choose a room in the newish Guetali building, which shelters enticing rooms with contemporary lines. Precious perks include two pools, two restaurants, a spa and sprawling gardens. Views take in the lagoon. Check the website for special offers. It's on Route des Colimaçons, north of town.

Eating

★ L'Orange Givrée
CAFETERIA €

(☑0262 54 74 63; Rue Le Barrelier; mains €5-10; ⏲8am-4pm Mon-Sat) Blink and you'll miss the tiny entrance of this funky little den next to the tourist office. It whips up appetising salads, *plats du jour* (daily specials), sandwiches and other treats at wallet-friendly prices. Everything is fresh and homemade – unfussy *cuisine de marché* (market cuisine) at its best. Make sure you save a corner for the criminally addictive chocolate mousse. Good breakfast too (€6).

★ Au Bout La Bas
EUROPEAN €€

(☑0262 55 98 72; 37 Rue du Lagon; mains €9-19; ⏲lunch & dinner Tue-Sat) Brimming with good cheer, this tropical cocoon in a street running parallel to the seafront serves excellent value-for-the-money food. A sampling of choices might include Leu French cheeseburger (yes!) and fresh fish or a toothsome *tartine* (a slice of bread with toppings). Special mention should also go to the giant-sized salads. The homemade desserts are every bit as devastatingly delicious as they sound. Hmm, the chocolate mousse.

Le Zat
CREOLE, SEAFOOD €€

(☑0262 42 20 92; 14 Rue de la Compagnie des Indes; mains €13-17; ⏲lunch) Near the harbour, this unpretentious venture majors in fish and meat dishes. The menu changes daily, as displayed on a handwritten blackboard.

Villa Vanille
EUROPEAN €€

(☑0262 34 03 15; 69 Rue du Lagon; mains €13-23; ⏲lunch & dinner Wed-Mon) No plastic chairs (sweet mercy!) at this popular eatery, but teak furnishings and an agreeable terrace. The food is nothing special but the menu is extensive – choose from frondy salads, meat and fish dishes and ice creams. Lounge on the beach across the road once you've finished your meal – this is the life!

Le Lagon – Tilbury
BRASSERIE, PIZZERIA €€

(☑0262 34 79 13; 2 Rue du Lagon; mains €10-25; ⏲lunch & dinner Tue-Sun) This beachfront place won't start a revolution but the menu covers enough territory to please most palates.

Il Etait Une Fois
FRENCH €€€

(☑0692 68 96 19; 1 Ruelle Rivière; mains €24-29; ⏲dinner Tue-Sat) Tucked away on a side street running perpendicular to the main road, 'Once Upon a Time' is that easy-to-miss 'secret spot' that local gourmands like to recommend. There's no menu, just a selection of the day's dishes depending on seasonal produce and the chef's mood. Its rustic, plant-filled terrace is also a welcoming place to eat.

L'Eveil des Sens – Le Blue Margouillat
EUROPEAN €€€

(☑0262 34 64 00; www.blue-margouillat.com; Impasse Jean Albany; mains €24-37, menu €80; ☺lunch Sun, dinner daily) This elegant restaurant inside Le Blue Margouillat scores a perfect 10 on the 'romance meter'. But even if your date doesn't make you swoon, Marc Chappot's culinary magic ensures a memorable meal. The menu may feature *canard rôti laqué au miel* (roasted duck lacquered with honey) and *langouste rôtie au chorizo* (roasted lobster with chorizo). Another draw is the setting – tables are set around the pool or on the colonial-style terrace. Pricey, but well worth it for the experience.

Drinking & Entertainment

6Bar
BAR

(☑0262 27 65 51; www.sixbar.re; Rue Barrelier; ☺10am-midnight Tue-Sun; 🛜) This tiny venue run by two young Zoreilles is St-Leu's trendiest spot (an easy distinction, given the lack of competitors). Come for the good fun, great mix of people, wicked cocktails and flavoursome tapas – not to mention free wi-fi. Tables get pushed aside after 9pm on Thursday, Friday and Saturday for DJs.

Rondavelle Les Filaos – Chez Jean-Paul
LIVE MUSIC

(Beach; ☺7.30am-9pm) Like bees to Bacardi, St-Leusiens swarm on this modest, open-air bar close to the beach when live bands perform on Friday and Sunday evenings. Good blend of electro, *maloya* (traditional dance music), rock and jazz. During the day the place is esteemed for its cheap sandwiches, freshly squeezed fruit juices and cold beers.

Le K – Le Séchoir
CONCERT VENUE

(☑0262 34 31 38; www.lesechoir.com; 125 Rue du Général Lambert) One of Réunion's venues for contemporary theatre, dance and music, as well as puppet shows, circus acts and other cultural activities. The organisers also put on open-air concerts and film shows in the area. Contact the tourist office to find out about the latest shows.

ℹ Information

Office du Tourisme (☑0262 34 63 30; www.saintleu.re; 1 Rue Le Barrelier; ☺1.30-5.30pm Mon, 9am-noon & 1.30-5.30pm Tue-Fri, 9am-noon & 2-5pm Sat; 🛜) At the north end of the main road passing through the centre of town. It has brochures galore and helpful, English-speaking staff. *Gîtes de montagne* can also be booked here. Free wi-fi.

6Bar (Rue Barrelier; per hr €1.80; ☺10am-7pm Tue-Sun; 🛜) Internet access. Doubles as a bar. Wi-fi is free if you buy a drink.

ℹ Getting There & Away

Car Jaune (p268) buses between St-Denis and St-Pierre run through the centre of St-Leu (€4.20, about 15 daily). The bus station is near the town hall. From there, Kar'Ouest minibuses have services for most villages in the Hauts.

Around St-Leu

After all that exertion in St-Leu, there's no better way to wind down than by exploring the villages that cling to the sloping hills high above the town. The zigzagging roads are scenic to boot and the atmosphere wonderfully laid-back.

◉ Sights

To the north of St-Leu, take the D12, known as Route des Colimaçons – a series of intestine-like S-curves – then veer due south on the D3 to **La Chaloupe St-Leu** before plunging back to the coast via **Piton St-Leu**, where the brightly painted **Hindu temple** is worth a gander. If you really want to get away from it all, you could continue to drive uphill from the village of **Les Colimaçons** until you reach the Route Forestière des Tamarins, which threads for 36km across the slopes from Le Tévelave to Le Maïdo – sensational. Whatever your itinerary, a good road map is essential as it's easy to get disorientated.

Conservatoire Botanique National de Mascarin
GARDENS

(☑0262 24 92 27; www.cbnm.org; 2 Rue du Père Georges, Les Colimaçons; adult/child €7/5; ☺9am-5pm Tue-Sun) On the Route des Colimaçons, on the slopes north of St-Leu, this attractive garden is in the grounds of a 19th-century Creole mansion and contains an impressive collection of native plant species, all neatly labelled, as well as many from around the Indian Ocean. Spitting distance from the

Conservatoire is the **Église du Sacré-Coeur**. This majestic church was built in 1875, using lava stones.

Stella Matutina   MUSEUM
(✆0262 34 16 24; www.stellamatutina.fr; 10 Allée des Flamboyants) About 4km south of St-Leu on the D11 to Piton St-Leu and Les Avirons, this museum is dedicated primarily to the sugar industry, but also provides fascinating insights into the history of the island and has exhibits on other products known and loved by the Réunionnais, such as vanilla, orchids, geraniums and vetiver.

Note that the museum was closed at the time of writing because of major renovation works. It should be open by the time you read this.

🛏 Sleeping & Eating

There are several peaceful villages within 10km of St-Leu that offer accommodation in a relaxed, rural setting. Many places boast bird's-eye views down to the coast.

Caz' Océane   B&B €
(✆0692 74 63 94, 0262 54 89 40; www.lacazoceane.com; 28 Chemin Mutel, Notre-Dame des Champs; s €30-40, d €40-50, incl breakfast; P🖥) Under new management since 2011, this snug B&B in the hamlet of Notre-Dame des Champs offers good value for money. No one would accuse the four rooms of being over-decorated but they are neat and spacious and guests can use a terrace with million-dollar views – perfect for an *apéro* (apéritif) after a bout of sightseeing. The owners can cook some reputedly good evening meals (€20). Excellent breakfast too, with home-made bread and jam. English is spoken.

★ Les Lataniers   APARTMENT €€
(✆0692 25 13 38, 0262 34 74 45; leslataniers.free.fr; 136ter Rue Adrien Lagourgue, Piton St-Leu; d €65-70; P🖥🏊) An excellent surprise, with tasteful decor, a fantastic garden with panoramic views and a stunning pool looking straight out to the sea. The four apartments are huge, well appointed and sun-filled. It's an ideal base for hikers as the female owner is a keen walker with lots of route information on the island. Find Les Lataniers on the southern fringes of Piton St-Leu, towards Les Avirons.

Le Balcon Créole – Chez François et Michèle Huet   B&B €€
(✆0692 67 62 54, 0262 54 76 70; www.gitehuet-reunion.fr; 202 Chemin Potier, Les Colimaçons; d incl breakfast €50-58; P🖥) The four rooms here are sparkling, fresh and colourful, but only two rooms come with a sea view. Ask for the spacious Creole-style *gîte* in the flower-filled garden if you intend to stay more than three nights. When it comes to preparing fish dishes, the Huets know their stuff. It's signposted, uphill from the botanical garden.

Bardzour – Chez Marie-Claire Vion   B&B €€
(✆0262 34 13 97; www.bardzour.com; 87 Chemin des Serres, Piton St-Leu; d incl breakfast €50-65; P🖥🏊) This is a lovely option if you're looking for a secluded, rural atmosphere, though it cops some noise from the Route des Tamarins below. The three well-equipped rooms and the cute Case Planteur set among orchards provide a very cushy landing after a hard day's driving. *Table d'hôte* (€23) meals are available twice a week. The pool is an added bonus. To find it, take the D11 towards Stella Matutina and Piton St-Leu.

Le Tévelave

POP 1500

Le Tévelave, about 10km up an impossibly twisty road in the hills above Les Avirons, is a gem of a village. It offers a real taste of rural life and is a great base for walkers. You can really feel a sense of wilderness and seclusion here, light years away from the bling and bustle of the coast. At the top of the village is the starting point for the **Route Forestière des Tamarins**. This road leads through a cryptomeria forest and emerges 36km later below Le Maïdo. Picnic sites abound along the road.

🛏 Sleeping & Eating

L'Écorce Blanc   B&B €€
(✆0692 02 16 30; 46 Rue Francis Rivière, Le Tévelave; d incl breakfast €50-70; P🖥) Perched on the side of a hill, way above town, this friendly *ferme auberge* (farm inn) is beloved by locals for its authentic home cooking (meals €22, by reservation). Sadly, the indoor dining room is about as atmospheric as a dentist's waiting room. There are also four rooms in the same building as the dining room (noisy at meal times); they have been recently spruced up and feature good bedding, flat screen TVs and sparkling bathrooms. Be warned, though: driving up the 600m-long access road to the farm inn calls for Schumacher-standard driving skills.

Domaine des Fougères INN €€
(☎0262 38 32 96; www.domainedesfougeres.com; 53 Route des Merles, Le Tévelave; s €67, d €75-85, incl breakfast; P🖤) The panoramic views and the secluded location, right at the start of the forest road, are the biggest perks to staying in this rural hotel with Creole architecture. Otherwise, the atmosphere is a bit staid with functional rooms. The more expensive Prestige rooms come with sea views and have been modernised. There's an on-site restaurant, which specialises in hearty Creole fare.

Étang-Salé-les-Bains

POP 12,000

Miles away from the hullabaloo around St-Gilles, Étang-Salé-les-Bains is a low-key resort more for locals than foreign tourists, though its superb black-sand beach is no longer a secret for in-the-know sunbathers, swimmers and surfers.

◉ Sights & Activities

Croc Parc ZOO
(☎0262 91 40 41; www.crocparc.re; Route Forestière; adult/child €8/6; ⊙10am-5pm) Wanna keep the kids happy? Take a small detour to this zoo, near Étang-Salé-les-Hauts (it's signposted). There are about 100 reptiles at the complex. Admission is steep, but worthwhile if your visit coincides with a feeding demonstration, held at 4pm on Wednesday and Sunday.

Plongée Salée DIVING
(☎0262 91 71 23; www.plongeesalee.com; 5 Rue Mottet de Narbonne; ⊙daily) Very few visitors know that diving is available at Étang-Salé-les-Bains. The sites are almost untouched. The owners of this reputable outfit take only small diving groups. Single dives start at €39. An introductory dive costs €63.

Ecole de Surf du Sud SURFING
(☎0692 63 68 95; www.ecoledesurf-dusud.com; 8 Ruelle des Roses; ⊙by reservation) Hawaii it ain't, but Étang-Salé-les-Bains has respectable waves that are suitable for beginners. Ecole de Surf du Sud runs lessons (from €30) and courses. Guided stand-up paddle board tours are also offered.

🏊 Beaches

The generous stretch of ash-coloured **beach** on the northern outskirts of town is great for sunbathing, swimming and ogling unfor-

tunate tan lines, and offers excellent sunset vistas. Most of the beach has a shallow bottom with a gradual slope. To the south, near the harbour, there's a smaller beach known as **Bassin Pirogue**, which is ideal for kids – a shallow reef close to shore makes for calm, protected waters.

🛏 Sleeping & Eating

You'll find a few *camions-snacks* along the beach.

Camping Municipal de l'Étang-Salé-les-Bains CAMPGROUND €
(☎0262 91 75 86; www.camping-reunion.com; Rue Guy Hoarau; camp site per night €22-28) Facilities are a bit worn but it's located in a shady spot a short walk back from the beach. There are plans to upgrade the ablution blocks.

Les Sables Noirs HOSTEL €
(☎0692 08 06 28, 0262 38 04 89; 88b Ave Raymond Barre; dm €15, d without bathroom €40; ❈🖤) If being near the beach isn't a must, this hostel-like venture, efficiently run by Evelyne, is manna from heaven for thrifty travellers. It shelters one eight-bed dorm, one 12-bed dorm and a few doubles, which are all squeaky clean and well appointed. It's in Étang-Salé-les-Hauts, about 4km from Étang-Salé-les-Bains, near the church. It's easy to get to the beach by bus.

★Zot Case en Natte BUNGALOW €€
(☎0692 82 33 26, 0262 26 57 73; www.zot-case-en-natte.allonslareunion.com; 3 Impasse Alamanda, Route des Canots; bungalows for 2-3 nights €268; P❈🖤) This place is a bit tricky to find, tucked away in a side street in Étang-Salé-les-Hauts, but it's well worth the detour if you're after something quirky. Picture this: a lovely Creole house that has been renovated with a happy respect for the place, sheltering three rooms with parquet flooring. The price quoted is valid for two nights on weekends and three nights weekdays.

Le Floralys (Caro Beach) & Roseaux des Sables HOTEL €€
(☎0262 91 79 79; www.hotel-floralys.com; 2 Ave de l'Océan; d €80-110; P❈🖤≋) Filling a gap in the midrange market, this well-run three-star abode is set in a 3-hectare garden beside the roundabout in the middle of town. It comprises two sections: the Floralys, with a clutch of clean-yet-unexciting bungalows, and the Roseaux des Sables, with upscale villas, at the far end of the property. The on-site restaurant prepares French-inspired

LES MAKES & LA FENÊTRE

One of Réunion's best-kept secrets, **Les Makes** boasts a wonderful bucolic atmosphere and a lovely setting. Snuggled into the seams of the Hauts, it's accessible via a tortuous secondary road from St-Louis (12km). At almost 1200m, breathing in the fresh alpine air here is enough therapy for a lifetime.

The area is ideal for stargazing. The **Observatoire astronomique** (☎0262 37 86 83; www.ilereunion.com/observatoire-makes; 18 Rue Georges Bizet, Les Makes; adult/child €9/5) offers stargazing programs from 9pm to midnight. It's best to call ahead to confirm the program is on. Horse riding is also a terrific way of exploring the surrounding forests. It can be arranged through **Centre Équestre de la Fenêtre** (☎0262 37 88 74; Route de la Fenêtre, Les Makes; per hr €18; ☉Tue-Sat by reservation).

It's a sin to visit Les Makes and not take the forest road that leads to **La Fenêtre** (The Window), another 10km further uphill. Hold on to your hat and lift your jaw off the floor as you approach the viewpoint: the view over the entire Cirque de Cilaos and the surrounding craggy summits that jab the skyline will be etched in your memory forever. La Fenêtre is also a wonderful picnic spot. Hint: arrive early, before it gets cloudy.

Should you fall under the spell of this charming area (no doubt you will), you can bunk down at the **Le Vieil Alambic – Chez Jean-Luc d'Eurveilher** (☎0262 37 82 77; www.levieilalambic.com; 55 Rue Montplaisir, Les Makes; d incl breakfast €55), an adorable B&B on the road to La Fenêtre, with four uninspiring but tidy rooms (no views) and highly respected traditional meals (from €26).

dishes with a tropical twist. The large pool is a great addition in warmer months.

Le Bambou   FRENCH, CREOLE €€
(☎0262 91 70 28; Rue Octave Bénard; mains €10-25; ☉lunch & dinner Thu-Mon) You're sure to find something to fill a gap at this lively eatery near the main roundabout. There are lots of hearty pasta dishes, grilled meats, Creole classics, salads and fish. The €10 lunch menu is brilliant value.

ℹ Information

The **office du tourisme** (☎0820 203 220; www.sud.reunion.fr; 74 Rue Octave Bénard; ☉9am-noon & 1-4.30pm Mon-Sat) is housed in the old train station on the roundabout that marks the town centre. *Gîtes de montagne* can be booked here.

St-Louis

POP 44,000

If St-Gilles and L'Hermitage are very Westernised and touristy, St-Louis, by contrast, is very Indian and falls below many travellers' radars. This is the heart of Tamil culture on the west coast, and it won't take long to feel that the city exudes an undeniably exotic atmosphere. The town doesn't have anything fantastic to offer, but it is certainly worth a stop to admire a handful of religious buildings, including a Tamil temple, a splendid mosque and the biggest church on the island.

A highlight (and a major landmark, with its big chimneys) is the **Sucrerie du Gol** (☎0262 91 05 47; www.gqf.com; Rond-Point du Gol; adult/child €6/4; ☉9.30am-7pm Tue-Sat, tours by reservation), about 1.5km west of St-Louis. You can tour this old sugar refinery, one of only two on the island still functioning, during the cane harvest (July to December). Visits take place Tuesday to Saturday with prior reservation.

Car Jaune buses between St-Denis and St-Pierre run through St-Louis (about 10 daily). Buses to Cilaos run from the bus station (€1.50, 12 daily, eight on Sunday).

Entre-Deux & Le Dimitile

POP 5170

The sweet little village of Entre-Deux, high in the hills 18km north of St-Pierre, got its name (which means 'between two') because it is situated on a ridge between two valleys – the Bras de Cilaos and the Bras de la Plaine. Entre-Deux is a delightful place to stay and get a taste of rural life.

◉ Sights & Activities

Entre-Deux boasts a wealth of *cases créoles*, traditional country cottages surrounded by well-tended and fertile gardens, many of which are being restored. There's also a strong tradition of local crafts, including natty slippers made from the leaves of an aloe-like plant called *choca*.

Opportunities for **hiking** abound. Many visitors come here for the tough hike up the slopes of iconic Le Dimitile (1837m) to a sensational view over the Cirque de Cilaos. This summit is also endowed with a strong historical significance; *marrons* (runaway slaves) took refuge in the area in the late 19th century. Just before the summit, the modest yet well-organised **Espace Culturel Muséographique Dimitile** (ECM; ☑ 0692 39 73 26; Le Dimitile; admission €2, with an audio guide €5; ☺ 9.30am-2pm) does a good job of explaining *marronage* and tracing the history of slavery in Réunion.

There are several options to reach the summit. The shortest route starts from the end of the D26 (there's a small parking area), about 10km from Entre-Deux, at an altitude of 1100m. Count on a four- to five-hour return slog. To soak up the atmosphere, it's not a bad idea to overnight at one of the *gîtes* near the summit.

The tourist office can provide information and sketch maps detailing the various routes. Feeling lazy? Join a 4WD tour. **Kreolie 4x4** (☑ 0692 86 52 26, 0262 39 50 87; www.kreolie4x4.com; 4 Impasse des Avocats) runs day trips that include Entre-Deux and the viewpoint at Le Dimitile (€100, including lunch). Guides are informative, providing interesting tidbits on the area's flora and fauna (in French).

🛏 Sleeping

Gîte Émile   GÎTE €
(☑ 0262 57 43 23, 0692 67 24 54; Le Dimitile; dm with half board €35) Up on Le Dimitile. Has basic accommodation in five- to 12-person dorms. From the *gîte* to the viewpoint, it's a 30- to 45-minute walk.

Gîte Valmyr   GÎTE €
(☑ 0692 98 34 73; Le Dimitile; dm with half board €35; ☺ Wed-Sat) Not far from the lookout that affords splendid views down into the Cirque de Cilaos, this is a great find for walkers and nature lovers.

L'Échappée Belle   B&B €€
(☑ 0692 55 55 37, 0262 22 91 31; www.lechappee-belle.com; 13 Impasse du Palmier; d incl breakfast €105; Ⓟ @ 🛜 ≋) Concealed behind high walls down a cul-de-sac near the *mairie*

(town hall), this bright, contemporary three-room B&B has a number of points in its favour – not least its leafy garden and its pool (accessible between 9am and noon, and from 3pm to 7pm) – lovely for unwinding after a day's explorations. No air-con.

Dimitile Hotel   HOTEL €€€
(☑ 0262 39 20 00; www.dimitile.eu; 30 Rue Bras Long; d incl breakfast €205; Ⓟ @ 🛜 ≋) This beautifully manicured haven is run with care by a couple from Alsace – saffron yellows on the facade, cosy beds on the floors, natural stones, a lovely pool – but it's missing something to bring it all together... something like soul. And there's no air-con. It has a well-regarded on-site **restaurant** (mains €20-24, menus €32-41; ☺ lunch Sat & Sun, dinner daily). There are often good deals available on room rates – check the website.

🍴 Eating

L'Estanco   FAST FOOD €
(☑ 0262 44 14 28; 1 Rue Payet; mains €7-12; ☺ lunch Tue-Sun, dinner Tue-Fri) The food here is unmemorable but it's super central and it's open for dinner – a rarity in Entre-Deux.

Le Longanis   CREOLE €
(☑ 0262 39 70 56; 9bis Rue du Commerce; mains €6-12; ☺ lunch Fri-Tue) This venue, right in the centre, boasts a happy buzz at lunchtime and whips up lip-smacking, dirt-cheap meals. Grab a dish from the daily specials, add a salad and you're sorted.

L'Arbre à Palabres   CREOLE, INTERNATIONAL €€
(☑ 0262 44 47 23; 29 Rue Césaire; mains €10-16; ☺ lunch Tue-Sun, dinner Sat) For a menu that strays a little off the familiar 'sausage *rougail* and chicken curry' path, try this cute eatery in a Creole house, near the tourist office. The menu changes daily, according to what's available at the market. You can also dine in the cool shade of a massive lychee tree on the terrace at the rear.

ℹ Information

The **tourist office** (☑ 0262 39 69 80; www.ot-entredeux.com; 9 Rue Fortuné Hoareau; ☺ 8am-noon & 1.30-5pm Mon-Sat) occupies a pretty *case créole* on the road into the village. Staff can arrange guided visits (adult/child €9/5; usually in French) of the village and can provide leaflets on walks in the region (including climbing Le Dimitile) and on local artisans.

❶ Getting There & Away

Car Jaune operates a bus service between Entre-Deux and the *gare routière* in St-Pierre. There are five buses a day from Monday to Saturday and two on a Sunday.

THE CIRQUES

No amount of hyperbole could ever communicate the astonishingly guileless beauty of the island's heart and soul. Knitted together like a three-leaf clover, the Cirques of Cilaos, Salazie and Mafate are different in spirit

The Cirques & Les Hautes Plaines

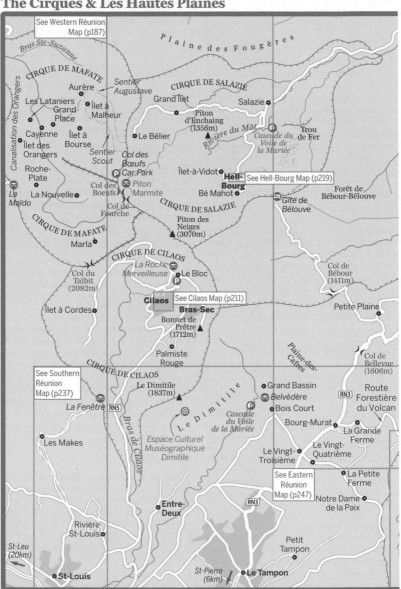

See Western Réunion Map (p187)

Plaine des Fougères

Bras Ste-Suzanne

CIRQUE DE MAFATE

Canalisation des Orangers

Aurère

Sentier Augustave

Grand Îlet

CIRQUE DE SALAZIE

Salazie

Les Lataniers
Grand Place

Îlet à Malheur

Piton d'Enchaing (1356m)

Rivière du Mât

Trou de Fer

Cayenne
Îlet des Orangers

Îlet à Bourse

Le Bélier

Cascade du Voile de la Mariée

Roche-Plate

Sentier Scout

Col des Boeufs

Car Park

Îlet-à-Vidot

Hell-Bourg

See Hell-Bourg Map (p219)

Forêt de Bébour-Bélouve

Le Maïdo

La Nouvelle

Col des Boeufs

Piton Marmite

Bé Mahot

CIRQUE DE SALAZIE

Gîte de Bélouve

Col de Fourche

Piton des Neiges (3070m)

CIRQUE DE MAFATE

Marla

CIRQUE DE CILAOS

La Roche Merveilleuse

Le Bloc

Col de Bébour (1411m)

Col du Taïbit (2082m)

Cilaos

See Cilaos Map (p211)

Bras-Sec

Îlet à Cordes

Bonnet de Prêtre (1712m)

Petite Plaine

Palmiste Rouge

CIRQUE DE CILAOS

Plaine des Cafres

Col de Bellevue (1606m)

See Southern Réunion Map (p237)

Le Dimitile (1837m)

Grand Bassin

RN3

Route Forestière du Volcan

La Fenêtre

RN5

Le Dimitile

Belvédère

Bois Court

Cascade du Voile de la Mariée

Bras de Cilaos

Bourg-Murat

La Grande Ferme

Espace Culturel Muséographique Dimitile

Le Vingt-Troisième

Le Vingt-Quatrième

Les Makes

See Eastern Réunion Map (p247)

La Petite Ferme

Entre-Deux

RN3

Notre Dame de la Paix

Rivière St-Louis

St-Leu (20km)

Petit Tampon

St-Louis

St-Pierre (6km)

Le Tampon

from the rest of the island – more inward-looking, more secretive, more austere. Quintessentially Réunionnais. The fast-paced and hedonistic coastal life seems light years away. The few roads daring to traverse the gorges and ranges are more crooked than

a politician, winding in and out of tortuous valleys.

The whole island was once the dome of a vast prehistoric shield volcano, centred on Piton des Neiges, but the collapse of subterranean lava chambers formed the starting point for the creation of the Cirques. Millions of years of rainfall and erosion did the rest, scouring out the amphitheatres that are visible today.

No prize for guessing that this rugged region is a fantastic playground for the stimulus-needy, with staggering mountain scenery, a mesh of well-marked trails and jaw-dropping canyons that beg to be explored. But if all you need is to decompress, there are also epicurean delights, including a robust cuisine scene and welcoming accommodation options where you can rejuvenate mind and body.

Nature is not the only drawcard. The Cirques are also of strong historical interest. They first began to be settled by *marrons* in the 18th century, and their descendants still inhabit some of the wild remote villages of the Cirques. The people residing here are an independent and unhurried lot, adamantly tied to their *îlet* (village) and their traditions.

Each Cirque has its own personality – try to include all three of them when planning your trip.

Cirque de Cilaos

The setting couldn't be more grandiose. Think snaggle-toothed volcanic peaks, deep ravines and forests that are straight out of a Brothers Grimm fairy tale. At times, swirling banks of cloud add a touch of the bizarre. A sweet sprinkling of secluded hamlets top off this area's indisputable 'wow!' effect.

Thrill-seekers, rejoice: the Cirque de Cilaos is the mother of all canyoning experiences on the island, with three iconic canyons that are set in some of the most impressive scenery in Réunion. Hiking is also extraordinary.

To get here, clunk in your seatbelt and take a deep breath: the RN5, which connects St-Louis with Cilaos, 37km to the north, is Réunion's premier drive (and that is saying a lot). Snaking steeply around more than 400 twists and turns along the way up into the amphitheatre, it provides vista-point junkies with a steady fix. *Bon voyage!*

RÉUNION CIRQUE DE CILAOS

THE CIRQUES & THE VOLCANO FROM ABOVE

The helicopter dilemma: you're loath to add to noise and air pollution. But your heart is set on a bird's-eye view of the magnificent Cirques and the volcano. While they aren't cheap (between €85 and €300, depending on the duration of the tour), most travellers rate such a trip as a highlight of their visit to Réunion. Ultimately you'll go with your gut (and budget). Contact **Helilagon** (☑ 0262 55 55 55; www.helilagon.fr) or **Corail Hélicop-tère** (☑ 0262 22 22 66; www.corail-helicopteres.com).

If you really want to feel the wind in your hair, several outfits offer tandem microlight flights with a qualified instructor. They run about 10 different tours around the island, starting at €40 for a gentle tour above the lagoon. Needless to say, all flights are dependent on the prevailing weather conditions. For more information, contact the following:

Felix ULM (☑ 0262 43 02 59; www.felixulm.com)

Les Passagers du Vent (☑ 0262 42 95 95; www.ulm-reunion.com)

Mascareignes Air Lines (☑ 0262 32 53 25; www.mascareignes.fr)

Papangue ULM (☑ 0692 08 85 86; www.papangue-ulm.fr)

❶ Getting There & Around

Cilaos is located 112km from St-Denis by road and 37km from the nearest coastal town, St-Louis.

Buses to Cilaos depart from St-Louis. There are about 12 buses daily, and eight on Sunday (€1.50, 1½ hours). The last service up to Cilaos leaves St-Louis at 6.30pm (5.30pm on Sunday); going down again, the last bus leaves Cilaos at 6.05pm (5.20pm on Sunday).

There are nine buses a day (four on Sunday) from Cilaos to Bras-Sec (€1) between 6am and 7pm. For Îlet à Cordes (€1) there are about nine buses daily (four on Sunday) from 5.50am to 7pm, with the last bus back at 6pm. The tourist office in Cilaos has timetables.

Another option is the minibus service offered by the **Société Cilaosienne de Transport** (☑ 0692 66 13 30, 0262 31 85 87), which costs €30 for two people for Îlet à Cordes. The same outfit provides transport from Cilaos to Le Bloc on the GR® R1 to the Piton des Neiges and Hell-Bourg (€10 for two people) and to the trailhead for the Col du Taïbit on the GR® R1/R2 to Mafate (€15 for two people), saving you at least an hour's walking time in each case.

Cilaos

POP 6000

Cilaos is ensnared by scenery so mind-blowingly dramatic it's practically Alpine. One name says it all: Piton des Neiges (3070m). The iconic peak towers over the town of Cilaos, acting like a magnet to hiking fiends. But there's no obligation to overdo it: a smattering of museums, a slew of underrated vineyards and plenty of short walks mean this incredible dose of natural magnificence can also be appreciated at a more relaxed pace.

The largest settlement in any of the Cirques, Cilaos sits 1200m above sea level. Developed as a spa resort at the end of the 19th century, the town's fortunes still rest on tourism, particularly hiking and canyoning, backed up by agriculture and the bottled mineral-water industry. The area is known for the production of lentils, embroidery and, increasingly, palatable rosé and white wines.

Cilaos fills up quickly on weekends. But despite its popularity it manages to stave off changes that would detract from its appeal as an 'ecotourism' destination – there are no massive hotels or blaring discos, only low-key, small-scale operations.

◎ Sights

Maison de la Broderie   MUSEUM
(☑ 0262 31 77 48; Rue des Écoles; admission €1; ◎ 9.30am-noon & 2-5pm Mon-Sat, 9.30am-noon Sun) The originator of Cilaos' embroidery tradition was Angèle Mac-Auliffe, the daughter of the town's first doctor of thermal medicine. Looking for a pastime to fill the long, damp days in the Cirque, Angèle established the first embroidery workshop with 20 women producing what later evolved into a distinctive Cilaos style of embroidery.

Nowadays, the Maison de la Broderie is home to an association of 30 or so local women dedicated to keeping the craft alive. They embroider and sell children's clothes, serviettes, place settings and tablecloths. It's laborious work: a single placemat takes between 12 and 15 days to complete.

Cilaos

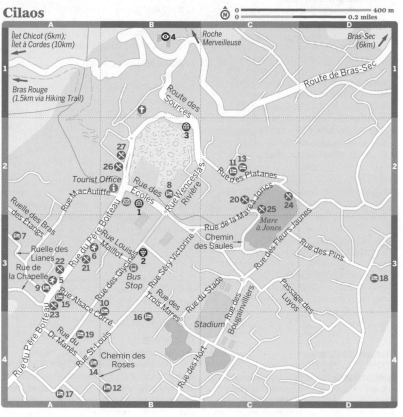

Cilaos

OFF THE BEATEN TRACK

ÎLET CHICOT

You can get a better understanding of the environment and traditional life of the Cirque de Cilaos by visiting Îlet Chicot (☑0692 72 27 17; admission €2, hut per person incl breakfast €15, with half board €40; ☺10am-3pm Tue-Sun), which can be reached by foot only. The Hoarau family aims to give you a sensitive introduction to the *vie lontan* (traditional life of yore). Their property is reached after an easy 10-minute walk from the D242, about 6km from Cilaos (look for the sign on the right). It features an organic garden with fruit-bearing trees, medicinal herbs and aromatic plants. Wanna go bush? Stay in one of the three *ti cases* (huts), which are constructed using vetiver straw. They're simple, but it's wonderful to be able to linger amid the beauty of the natural surroundings and enjoy the jaw-dropping views over Cilaos. The lack of electric lights makes for great stargazing.

Thermes de Cilaos　　　　BATHHOUSE
(☑0262 31 72 27; thermes-cilaos@cg974.fr; Route de Bras-Sec; ☺daily, by appointment) The *sources thermales* (thermal springs) of Cilaos were first brought to the attention of the outside world in 1815 by a goat hunter from St-Louis, Paulin Técher. A track into the Cirque was constructed in 1842, paving the way for the development of Cilaos as a health spa for rich colonials. The spring is heated by volcanic chambers far below the surface. It's said to relieve rheumatic pain, among other bone and muscular ailments.

The old thermal station was opened in 1896, but the spring became blocked in a cyclone that occurred in 1948. The project was revived in 1971, only to close in 1987 because of damage to the buildings caused by the chemicals in the spa water. The latest incarnation of the Cilaos spa is the Thermes de Cilaos at the north end of town. Several health treatments are offered, including a 20-minute hydromassage (€15). This is a perfect way to rejuvenate tired and sore muscles after your hike.

Maison des Vins du Chai de Cilaos　　WINE
(☑0262 31 79 69; 34 Rue des Glycines; ☺9am-noon & 2-5.30pm Mon-Sat) **FREE** You can learn

more about Cilaos wine at the Maison des Vins du Chai de Cilaos. A short film (in French) is followed by a wine tasting session. Take home a bottle from about €13.

Philippe Turpin's Studio　　　　GALLERY
(☑0692 28 03 03, 0262 31 73 64; 2 Route des Sources; ☺9am-6pm) The sculptor, painter and printmaker Philippe Turpin, who etches on copper and then rolls the prints off the inky plates, has a studio that is open to the public. Turpin captures the wonder of Réunion in a fantastical, almost medieval way; his renditions of the Cirques resemble illustrations of fairy kingdoms.

La Roche Merveilleuse　　　　LOOKOUT
(Marvellous Rock) Head to the Marvellous Rock for an eagle-eye panorama of Cilaos. It's accessible on foot or by road. From Cilaos, take the road to Bras-Sec. The turn-off to La Roche Merveilleuse is signposted on the left, after about 2km.

Bring a picnic – the setting is enchanting and there are a few kiosks (wooden shelters) to protect picnickers from any rain.

 Activities

Canyoning
Of the stellar spots for canyoning in Réunion, the Cilaos area tops the list, with three major canyons that draw action-seekers like bees to a honey pot: Canyons de Gobert, Fleurs Jaunes and Bras Rouge. All are very atmospheric; you can expect various jumps, leaps into natural pools and jaw-dropping rappelling. Access to the canyons involves a preliminary five- to 45-minute hike. The time spent in the canyon is about three to five hours. The most suitable canyons for beginners and families are Canyon de Gobert and Mini Fleurs Jaunes (which is a section of Fleurs Jaunes). All canyoning outings are led by a qualified instructor. Some of the major operators don't have offices but can be reached by phone.

Aparksa Montagne　　　　OUTDOORS
(☑0692 66 50 09; www.aparksa-montagne.com) For canyoning trips or guided walks, this outfit has good credentials. The owner, Thomas Percheron, has lived in South Africa and is fluent in English.

Bouisset Fabrice　　　　CANYONING
(☑0692 66 22 73; bouisset.fabrice@wanadoo.fr) Bouisset Fabrice is one of the many canyoning operators in the area.

Canyon Ric a Ric CANYONING
(☑0692 86 54 85; www.canyonreunion.com) Canyon Ric a Ric is one of the major canyoning operators in the area. Plan on €55 and €85 per person, depending on the duration of the outing.

Cilaos Aventure CANYONING
(☑0692 66 73 42; www.cilaosaventure.com) A reliable outlet that can arrange all kinds of canyoning trips in the area. Rates range between €45 and €85.

Run Évasion CANYONING
(☑0262 31 83 57; www.canyon-reunion.fr; 23 Rue du Père Boiteux) A well-established operator that has canyoning tours for all levels. Prices vary depending on the number of people – count on €45/80 for a half-/full-day outing.

Rock Climbing
Rock climbing is becoming increasingly popular in Cilaos. There is no shortage of awesome cliffs and gorges, particularly the stunning Fleurs Jaunes area, which is home to dozens of mind-boggling ascents, graded 4 to 8 (easy to difficult). For novices, there are also *falaise-écoles* (training cliffs that are specially equipped for beginners). Run Évasion (p213) and Cilaos Aventure (p213) employ qualified instructors. Plan on €45 per person.

Cycling
The Cirque de Cilaos, with its dramatic topography and great scenic roads, is superb cycling terrain for experienced cyclists.

Novices can ride to La Roche Merveilleuse (p212).

Tof Bike MOUNTAIN BIKING
(☑0692 01 90 80; 68 Rue du Père Boiteux; half/full day €14/19; ⊗8.30am-noon & 2.30-6pm Mon-Sat, 8.30am-noon Sun) This outfit rents out mountain bikes in tip-top condition and gives advice on various circuits.

★✰ Festivals & Events

Cilaos has two great rural fairs, the **Fête de la Vigne** (Wine Harvest Festival) in January and the **Fête des Lentilles** (Festival of Lentils) in October. The **Cross du Piton des Neiges** (running race to the Piton des Neiges) is held in October.

🛏 Sleeping

Cilaos has ample choice of accommodation options, but it can become crowded at weekends and during the tourist season.

★ La Case Bleue GÎTE €
(☑0692 65 74 96; www.gitecasebleue.com; 15 Rue Alsace Corré; dm/d €15/40) An excellent deal, this *gîte d'étape* (walkers' lodge) occupies an attractive Creole house painted in blue. Top marks go to the light-filled dorm, the back-friendly mattresses, the salubrious bathrooms and the impeccable communal kitchen. There's also a smallish double with its own entrance and bathrooms – ideal for couples, although it opens onto the dorm's terrace, which may be noisy if the *gîte* is full. Meals (breakfast €6, dinner €20) come

---

HIKING AROUND CILAOS

There are fabulous hiking options in the vicinity of Cilaos, with well-marked trails suitable for all levels of fitness. The tourist office produces a small leaflet that gives an overview of the walks in the Cirque. The most popular walks include the following:

➜ Bras Rouge – about 2½ hours return. An easy walk to the top of a waterfall.

➜ Col du Taïbit – about 4½ hours return, with 830m of altitude gain. An iconic climb to the pass that separates the Cirque de Cilaos from the Cirque de Mafate. From the pass you can walk down to Marla in the Cirque de Mafate in about 45 minutes. The starting point is signposted on the D242 (the road to Îlet-à-Cordes), 5km from Cilaos.

➜ La Chapelle – this path connects Cilaos to Îlet-à-Cordes (about four hours return). You can skip the return walk by taking the bus from Îlet-à-Cordes.

➜ La Roche Merveilleuse – about two hours return. A gentle ramble to the lookout (p212), with lofty views over Cilaos. Also accessible by car.

➜ Sentier Botanique – an easy 90-minute loop with a focus on local flora (most species are labelled). Perfectly suitable for families. It starts at La Roche Merveilleuse.

➜ Le Kervéguen – about five hours return. Offers spendid views of the Cirque. The starting point is signposted on the D241 (the road to Bras-Sec), 5km from Cilaos.

CLIMBING PITON DES NEIGES

The mind-boggling ascent to Réunion's highest point (3070m) is vigorous, but the 360-degree panorama at the summit is worth the effort. It's usually done in two days, with an overnight stay in **Gîte de la Caverne Dufour** (☑0262 51 15 26; dm €17, breakfast/dinner €5/15), reached after three hours from the start of the path at Le Bloc, between Cilaos and Bras-Sec (it's signposted). From the *gîte*, the summit is reached after about 1½ hours amid lunar landscapes. Hard-core hikers may want to complete the round trip in one day (about 10 hours).

in for warm praise and the owners are well clued up on hiking in the Cirque. There are only 10 beds, so book ahead.

Le Calbanon
GÎTE €

(☑0692 09 27 30; www.lecalbanon.fr; 9 Rue des Platanes; dm/d €15/35) This neat *gîte d'étape* in a modern building boasts a quiet location and ample views of Cilaos. It offers simple accommodation in quads, which can also be used as doubles, or in a 12-bed dorm. There's a communal kitchen, too. Dinners are available on request (€20).

La Roche Merveilleuse
GÎTE €

(☑0262 31 82 42; 1 Rue des Platanes; dm/d €16/42, d without bathroom €38; ℗) This all-wood *gîte* looks like a Canadian chalet transplanted to Cilaos. Opt for one of the four snug doubles, which feel like cosy birds' nests, but the real appeal is the panoramic view from the terrace. The hosts can provide dinners (€20) if there's a minimum of five people.

Clair de Lune – Chez Alex Clain
GÎTE €

(☑0692 82 47 13, 0692 00 57 54; 10 Rue Wenceslas Rivière; dm/d incl breakfast €18/36; ℗) Run by Alex, who knows a thing or 50 about Cilaos and adopts all guests like stray kittens, this congenial spot has rooms of varying size and shape, with three- to seven-bed dorms and one double. Bathrooms are shared. The living area is a good place to swap tales with like-minded travellers.

Le Fanal
GÎTE €

(☑0692 04 30 29, 0262 31 94 21; Chemin des Roses; dm €17; ℗) No smelly dorms in this modern *gîte* opened in 2013 – instead, think two- to

eight-bed rooms that are quiet and modern (if a little sterile) and come equipped with good mattresses and their own tiled bathrooms. Meals are available.

★ Le Bois Rouge
B&B €€

(☑0692 30 57 57, 0262 47 57 57; www.ilereunion.com/leboisrouge; 2 Route des Sources; s/d incl breakfast €70/90; ℗ 🛜) Character and charm. Somewhere between a boutique hotel and B&B, the Bois Rouge has five immaculate rooms that are uniquely decorated with works by artist Philippe Turpin and boast parquet flooring made of precious wood as well as terraces overlooking Cilaos. Bonuses: complimentary bicycles, a well-stocked DVD library, and free transfers to the start of most hiking trails near Cilaos. Discounts are available in low season.

★ Le Platane
B&B €€

(rest.leplatane@orange.fr; 46 Rue du Père Boiteau; d incl breakfast €85; 🛜) Finally Cilaos has produced a B&B with style. No rustic decor here but clean lines, muted tones, cutting-edge design, good mountain views and sparkling bathrooms. Oh, and it's super central. One quibble: it's above the eponymous restaurant (where the reception is), which means it might be a bit noisy in the evening.

Les Coeurs Bleus
B&B €€

(☑0692 60 84 60; www.lescoeursbleus.com; 4 Rue des Glycines; d incl breakfast €65-70; 🛜) Opened in 2012, this very genteel and well-done B&B-cum-hotel has sparsely furnished but spacious and light rooms (opt for one upstairs). It also runs a restaurant in an adjoining building.

Le Bois de Senteur
B&B €€

(☑0692 29 81 20, 0262 31 91 03; www.leboisdesenteur.com; 4 Chemin des Roses; d/q incl breakfast €60/80; ℗ 🛜) This trim place in a peaceful cul-de-sac is brought to life with lashings of colourful paint on the facade. Inside, the 10 rooms are modestly furnished and feel a tad compact – if available, ask for one of the upstairs rooms, which have balconies and afford dashing views of the Piton des Neiges (especially rooms 6, 7 and 10).

Les Aloès
HOTEL €€

(☑0262 31 81 00; www.hotel-aloes.com; 14 Rue St-Louis; s/d incl breakfast €58/74; ℗ 🛜) Friendly, unfussy two-star hotel on the edge of town. Bright blues, yellows and ochres colour the well-tended rooms. The upstairs ones have the best views. The owner is very knowledgeable about hiking.

Case Nyala
B&B €€

(📞0692 87 70 14, 0262 31 89 57; www.case-nyala. com; 8 Ruelle des Lianes; s €60, d €75-85, incl breakfast, bungalow d/tr €85/110; 🛜) On a quiet back street close to the centre, this little Creole place with lemon-yellow walls and green shutters harbours a clutch of diminutive but bright rooms and a well-appointed communal kitchen. The complimentary rum in the glass flasks on the shelves will help you forget that this place is a tad overpriced. Families will opt for the larger, self-contained bungalow at the rear.

Le Vieux Cep
HOTEL €€€

(📞0262 31 71 89; www.levieuxcep-reunion.com; 2 Rue des Trois Mares; s €90-105, d €95-115, incl breakfast; 🅿🛜🏊) One of Cilaos' largest establishments, Le Vieux Cep has its pros and cons – on the plus side it's welcoming and well located; it enjoys great views of Piton des Neiges; it has solid amenities, including a restaurant, a small sauna and a pool; and many rooms have been refreshed. The minuses: said rooms are cramped and lack character; it's a bit overpriced; and the attached restaurant is quite expensive. There are plans to build a new wing with 25 larger rooms.

Les Chenêts
HOTEL €€€

(📞0262 31 85 85; www.hotelleschenets.fr; Rue des Trois Mares; s €91-96, d €109-114, ste €129-191; 🅿@🛜🏊) Cilaos' biggest hotel is a colourful place with a touch of a hunting lodge about its foyer. The rooms are serviceable and crisp but the decor and furnishings are in dire need of a freshen-up. A heated pool, a sauna, a bar and a restaurant round out the offerings.

Hôtel Tsilaosa
HOTEL €€€

(📞0262 37 39 39; www.tsilaosa.com; Rue du Père Boiteau; s €91-100, d €114-124, incl breakfast; 🅿@🛜) This well-run three-star abode in a restored Creole home offers a smooth stay, with 15 rooms that are imaginatively decked out in local style; those upstairs boast mountain views (rooms 15 and 16 are the best). The owner has set up a wine cellar in the basement and offers tastings of Cilaos tipples (€5) when he's in town.

🍴 Eating

Despite the choice of eateries on offer, don't expect gastronomic thrills in Cilaos. Most places tend to rest on their laurels, with rather stodgy fare served in generic surrounds. On the bright side, Cilaos holds a few surprises up its sleeve. It's noted for its lentils, grown mainly around Îlet à Cordes, and its wines.

Self-caterers will find grocery stores along the main street.

Boulangerie
BAKERY €

(64 Rue du Père Boiteau; pastries & sandwiches from €0.80; ⏱6.30am-7pm Mon-Sat, to noon Sun) Ask a local where they go for the best *macatias* (buns) and croissants and they point to this delectable little bakery. It has a wide variety of cavity-inducing goodies, as well as excellent baguette sandwiches.

Le Cass' Dale
SANDWICHES €

(📞0262 31 84 29; Mare à Joncs; mains €5; ⏱10am-7pm) This open-air kiosk overlooking the Mare à Joncs is a great place to chill with regulars over a greasy sandwich or an equally greasy *poulet frites* (chicken with fries).

Salon de Thé de l'Hôtel Tsilaosa
TEA HOUSE €

(📞0262 37 39 39; Rue du Père Boiteau; cakes €4; ⏱3-6pm) This delightfully peaceful venue in the hotel's tea room will torment the sweet-toothed and weak-willed with homemade cakes and pies, including a *gâteau banane* (banana cake), and about 15 varieties of tea.

Chez Miko Fils
CREOLE €€

(📞0262 31 70 52; 25 Rue du Père Boiteau; mains €8-18, menus €13-20; ⏱lunch & dinner Fri-Wed) Smack dab in the centre, this informal joint is a good spot for a fast, affordable meal. Whatever you choose you can't go wrong, though it does suffer slightly from being a jack-of-all-trades. The streetside terrace allows for a dash of people-watching at lunchtime.

Le Platane
CREOLE, PIZZERIA €€

(📞0262 31 77 23; Rue du Père Boiteau; mains €7-20; ⏱lunch & dinner Thu-Tue) The most eclectic menu in town. Here you can wrap your mandibles around omelettes, salads and *carris*, but skip the unexceptional pizzas. There's a small terrace at the back.

Le Petit Randonneur
CREOLE €€

(📞0262 31 79 55; Rue du Père Boiteau; mains €10-18; ⏱lunch Sat-Thu, dinner Sat-Wed) A favourite haunt of hungry walkers, this family-run restaurant serves up hearty local dishes such as smoked sausages and chicken in a vanilla sauce, as well as moderately priced *plats du jour* (daily specials) and crêpes, best enjoyed

A TOAST IS IN ORDER

You mustn't leave Cilaos without sampling a glass (or three) of *vin de Cilaos* (Cilaos wine). Not to be deprived of their wine, the French brought vines with them to Réunion in the 17th century. They were originally grown along the west coast, but in the late 19th century settlers introduced vines into the Cirques, cultivating them on trellises outside their houses or on tiny terraces hacked out of the hillside. For years, the wines they produced were sugary sweet whites, reminiscent of sherry and tawny port. In the late 1970s, however, a few enterprising growers in Cilaos upgraded their vine stock and began producing something far more palatable. In addition to sweet and dry whites, growers now produce reds and rosés. They are not necessarily the most distinguished of wines but they're improving in quality, especially the rosés.

on the terrace, with plastic tables. At €18, the Sunday Creole buffet is a bargain.

Les Coeurs Bleus CREOLE, CHINESE €€
(✆ 0692 60 84 60; www.lescoeursbleus.com; 4 Rue des Glycines; mains €10-18; ⊙ lunch & dinner Mon-Sun) There aren't too many options at this family-run venture, but there are always flavoursome daily specials scrawled on a chalkboard. And if you can squeeze in something for dessert, how about a chocolate mousse?

Auberge Ti Bonheur CREOLE €€
(✆ 0262 28 67 54; 10 Rue de la Mare à Joncs; mains €10-19; ⊙ lunch Fri-Wed, dinner Fri-Tue) Exercise the taste buds with soul-satisfying traditional cuisine at this excellent restaurant blessed with a breezy terrace overlooking Mare à Joncs. Try the *carri pat' cochon au vin blanc de Cilaos* (pig's trotter *carri* in a local white-wine sauce), the house's signature offering.

Les Sentiers CREOLE €€
(✆ 0262 31 71 54; 63 Rue du Père Boiteau; mains €12-14; ⊙ lunch Thu-Tue, dinner Thu-Mon) Come lunch and dinner, this cute *case créole* is alive with action. Tables spill from inside out onto a breezy terrace. Food-wise, the menu features all the Creole classics, with an emphasis on Cilaos lentils as an accompaniment. The rustic decor is easy on the eye, with exposed beams and flashing laminate floors.

Chez Noë CREOLE €€
(✆ 0262 31 79 93; 40 Rue du Père Boiteau; mains €13-15, menus €26-30; ⊙ lunch Tue-Sun, dinner Tue-Sat) A longstanding institution, Chez Noë is almost a rite of passage in Cilaos. It churns out invigorating Creole favourites such as pork rib with lentils and *gratin de chouchou* (choko; a green squash-like vegetable that is served baked). Bonus: there's an enticing, shady terrace in warm weather.

Le Cottage CREOLE €€
(✆ 0262 31 04 61; 2 Chemin des Saules; mains €13-22, menus €16-22; ⊙ lunch daily, dinner Mon-Sat) The all-wood surrounds boast a kind of rustic charm and the dining room overlooks the Mare à Joncs (reserve a table near the windows). Has a good repertory of palate-pleasing Creole dishes. Downside: there's no terrace.

Les Physalis CREOLE, FRENCH €€
(✆ 0262 31 85 85; Rue des Trois Mares; mains €15-21; ⊙ lunch & dinner) A well-regarded venue, at the Les Chenêts hotel. Sadly, the sterile dining room seriously detracts from the atmosphere.

❶ Information

There are no banks in Cilaos.

Post Office (76 Rue du Père Boiteau; ⊙ 8am-4pm Mon-Fri, 8-11.30am Sat) Has an ATM that accepts Visa and MasterCard, but don't rely on it completely: it occasionally runs out of euros, especially on weekends.

Tourist Office (✆ 0820 203 220; www.sud.reunion.fr; 2bis Rue Mac Auliffe; ⊙ 8.30am-12.30pm & 1.30-5pm Mon-Sat, 9am-noon Sun) The tourism office is particularly helpful, with multilingual staff who provide reliable information about local and long-distance walks and dispense lists of accommodation, restaurants and activities. The office has pamphlets on bus schedules in the Cirque and sells walking maps. You can also book *gîtes de montagne* here.

Îlet à Cordes

POP 430

Îlet à Cordes is a marvellous stop-the-world-and-get-off place and you'll leave with reluctance. The setting is truly photogenic: wherever you look, this tiny *écart* (settlement) is cradled by soaring mountains, with major peaks looming on the horizon. Vineyards and fields where lentils are grown complete the picture.

🛏 Sleeping & Eating

Gîte d'Étape et Chambre d'Hôte de l'Îlet
GÎTE €

(☑0692 64 74 48, 0262 25 38 57; www.gite-ilet. com; 27 Chemin Terre-Fine; dm/d incl breakfast €20/50; ⚉) No typo – here the *coup de grâce* is the sparkling pool (one of only two swimming pools in the Cirques), which is even heated during the colder months! The wood-panelled rooms, which can sleep two to six, are nothing fancy but well maintained. Solange Grondin, your amenable hostess, prides herself on her farm cooking, which usually means chicken, *brèdes chouchou* (a mix of local vegetables) and homemade cakes.

Chez Hélène Payet
B&B €

(☑0692 68 49 68, 0262 35 18 13; 13 Chemin Terre-Fine; d incl breakfast €44) Madame Payet has four reassuringly Air-Wicked rooms in an alluring tropical garden. The food (dinner €23) is more poultry with homegrown vegetables than creative concoctions, but it gets rave reviews from travellers.

Le Tapacala
B&B €€€

(☑0692 69 57 50; 2c Chemin Les Orangers; d €139) This surprisingly modern venture is the pride and joy of Mickael Gonthier and his spouse, your hosts, who can speak English and are well clued up about the island. The three rooms are huge and tastefully designed, with clean lines and elegant furnishings but, despite the initial 'wow' factor, we can't help thinking that it's overpriced by Cilaos standards. Dinner costs €25.

Le Reposoir
CAFE €

(☑0692 70 08 15; Chemin Terre-Fine; ⊙7am-7pm Mon-Sat, to 1pm Sun) This modest cafe-bar serves snacks and sandwiches, and has a limited selection of goods if you're fixing your own food.

Bras-Sec

POP 600

As in Îlet à Cordes, you've reached *le bout du monde* (the end of the Earth) in Bras-Sec, about 6km from Cilaos. This is a place to just kick back and enjoy the get-away-from-it-all atmosphere. If you've got itchy feet, a recommended **hike** is the Tour du Bonnet de Prêtre, a 4½-hour loop that skirts around the bizarrely shaped peak that lies south of the village.

🛏 Sleeping

Gîte Courtois
BUNGALOWS €

(☑0692 23 31 96, 0262 25 59 44; Chemin Saül; per person €18) Four self-contained bungalows on the main street. Nothing fancy, but they get the job done.

Les Mimosas
GÎTE €

(☑0262 96 72 73; 29 Chemin Saül; dm/d incl breakfast €17/40) This is an unflashy but homey place with functional two- to six-person rooms. Dinners (€25) are ultra-copious and come in for warm praise.

L'Oiseau de Paradis
BUNGALOW €

(☑0692 16 98 18; 33 Chemin Saül; d €40) This three-room cottage on the main street is a good deal for self-caterers.

Cirque de Salazie

If you need a break from beach-bumming and want to cool off in forested mountains, head to the Cirque de Salazie. Like the Cirque de Cilaos, the Cirque de Salazie has bags of natural panache, with soaring peaks, soul-stirring vistas, thundering waterfalls, tortuous roads and a spattering of rural hamlets thrown in for good measure.

The winding mountain road that slithers into the Cirque from St-André on the northeast coast offers awesome views and is reason enough to make the trip. Yet the prize at the end of it is golden too: with its Creole colour, Hell-Bourg is the crowning glory of the Cirque.

The Cirque de Salazie is a bit 'flatter' (although 'flat' is not the first word that will spring to mind when you see it!) than the Cirque de Cilaos, but the scenery as you approach is nearly as awesome. The vegetation is incredibly lush and waterfalls tumble down the mountains, even over the road in places – Salazie is the wettest of the three Cirques.

❶ Getting There & Around

There are seven buses daily from St-André to Salazie (€1.70) between 6.10am and 5.45pm (in the opposite direction, buses run from 5.30am to 4.40pm). On Sunday buses leave St-André at 8.40am, 1.30pm and 5.45pm (8am, 12.40pm and 3.45pm from Salazie).

Buses from Salazie to Hell-Bourg run about every two hours from 6.45am to 6.20pm. In the opposite direction, there are services from 6.15am to 5.45pm. There are four buses in each direction on Sunday.

RÉUNION CIRQUE DE SALAZIE

There are eight buses a day (four on Sunday) from Salazie to Grand Îlet and Le Bélier between 6.45am (9.15am on Sunday) and 6.20pm. Heading back to Salazie services depart from Le Bélier between around 5.45am and 5pm (7am to 5.20pm on Sunday), calling at Grand Îlet 10 minutes later.

From Le Bélier to Col des Bœufs, there are two buses per day on Monday, Wednesday and Friday at 7.35am and 2.35pm, as well as two buses on Sunday (at 10am and 4.25pm). In the opposite direction, buses leave at 8.05am and 3.05pm (10.25am and 4.55pm on Sunday).

There's only one petrol station, in Salazie – fill up in St-André.

Salazie

POP 2400

The road alongside the gorge of the Rivière du Mât from St-André to Salazie, which lies at the eastern entrance to the Cirque, winds past superb waterfalls. There's not much to detain you in Salazie, though, and most visitors press on to Hell-Bourg. You'll have to change buses here if you're heading further up into the Cirque.

Further along the road to Hell-Bourg, just north of the turn-off to Grand Îlet, you'll see the **Cascade du Voile de la Mariée** (Bridal Veil Falls) on your left. These towering falls drop in several stages from the often cloud-obscured heights into the ravine at the roadside. You get an even better view from the Grand Îlet road.

Hell-Bourg

POP 2200

The town of Hell-Bourg emerges like a hamlet in a fairy tale after 9km of tight bends from Salazie. You can't but be dazzled by the fabulous backdrop – the majestic mountain walls that encase Hell-Bourg like a grandiose amphitheatre. No prize for guessing that this rugged terrain offers some fantastic hiking opportunities. It offers plenty of more sedentary opportunities as well.

Culture aficionados will get their fill in this quintessential Réunionnais town with its enchanting centre, where old Creole mansions line the streets.

Hell-Bourg takes its curious name from the former governor Amiral de Hell; the town itself is anything but! It served as a thermal resort until a landslide blocked the spring in 1948.

◉ Sights

First up, architecture and history buffs should take a look at the town's appealing **Creole buildings**, with their typical wrought-iron *lambrequins*. These buildings date back as far as the 1840s, when Hell-Bourg was a famous resort town that attracted a rather well-heeled crowd. You can go on a guided tour organised by the tourist office; it takes about an hour and costs €9 (by reservation).

Maison Folio HISTORIC BUILDING
(☑ 0262 47 80 98; 20 Rue Amiral Lacaze; admission €5; ◷ 9-11.30am & 2-5pm) One of the loveliest of Hell-Bourg's Creole houses is Maison Folio, a typical 19th-century bourgeois villa almost engulfed by its densely planted garden. The owners show you around, pointing out the amazing variety of aromatic, edible, medicinal and decorative plants, and give insights into local culture – unfortunately, only in French.

Thermal Bath RUIN
FREE Visitors can see the ruins of the old baths, which were in use until 1948. They are found in a ravine a 10-minute walk west of town (walk past Le Relais des Cimes hotel; it's signposted). It's a quiet and leafy spot.

Îlet-à-Vidot VILLAGE
(⊚) The landscape surrounding the hamlet of Îlet-à-Vidot, about 2km from Hell-Bourg, is little short of breathtaking. The iconic, flat-topped Piton d'Enchaing, covered with thick vegetation, seems to stand guard over the town.

Rivière du Mât RIVER
From Îlet-à-Vidot, the asphalted road continues for about 2km until a small parking lot. From here, a steep footpath leads in about 15 minutes to the Rivière du Mât valley. Cross the footbridge and you'll soon reach a lovely picnic site by the river.

Bé Mahot VILLAGE
About 3.5km from Hell-Bourg, Bé Mahot is a cute hamlet that's well worth visiting. With its clunky, colourful Creole houses clinging on the hillside and fantastic vistas of the Cirque, it's scenic to boot. There are several picnic sites along the road.

Activities

Canyoning

The canyoning options available in the Cirque will make your spine tingle. Get wet

Hell-Bourg

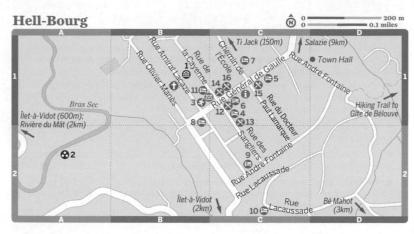

at Trou Blanc, which is said to be the most 'aquatic' canyon in Réunion, with lots of *toboggans* (plunging down water-polished chutes) and leaps. Some sections are appropriately named 'The Washing Machine', 'The Bath', 'The Aquaplaning'... Another reputable canyon is Voile de la Mariée, near Salazie, which is a more aerial circuit that includes a 50m rappel. Note that these canyons are not accessible during the rainiest months (from December to March).

Alpanes CANYONING
(☑ 0692 77 75 30; www.alpanes.com; ⊘ by reservation) Doesn't have an office in Hell-Bourg. Offers canyoning trips to Trou Blanc, Voile de la Mariée. Count on €45/65 for a half-/full-day excursion.

Austral Aventure CANYONING
(☑ 0692 87 55 50, 0262 32 40 29; www.australaventure.fr; Rue Amiral Lacaze, Hell-Bourg; ⊘ by reservation) Has canyoning trips to Trou Blanc and

Trou de Fer (from Hell-Bourg), as well as guided hikes to Forêt de Bébour-Bélouve (€50). A half-/full-day canyoning outing will set you back €50/70.

🛏 Sleeping

★ La Mandoze GÎTE €
(☑ 0692 65 65 28, 0262 47 89 65; lamandoze@hotmail.fr; Chemin de l'École; dm €18, d incl breakfast 45; ⓟ 🛜) This *gîte*, set in a Creole house, has all the hallmarks of a great deal: well-maintained (if a bit boxy) rooms that can sleep six people, well-scrubbed bathrooms, a tranquil location and a tab that won't burn a hole in your pocket. For those wanting more privacy, three adjoining doubles, with wood-panelled walls, are available. They're fairly compact and share bathrooms. The owner, Patrick Manoro, is a mine of local knowledge and occasionally plays guitar for his guests in the evening. Breakfast (€6) and dinner (€20) are available.

HIKING IN HELL-BOURG

Not surprisingly, the Hell-Bourg area is an adventure playground for hiking enthusiasts, with a good selection of day hikes. Hikers doing the Tour des Cirques (p41) route will have to pass through Hell-Bourg as they cross the Cirque de Salazie.

➡ Hell-Bourg–Gîte de Bélouve – about four hours return, with 570m of altitude gain. From Gîte de Bélouve (p230), you can continue to the Trou de Fer viewpoint (seven hours return from Hell-Bourg).

➡ Îlet-à-Vidot–Piton d'Enchaing – this soaring 1356m peak is a popular but challenging five- to six-hour hike (return), with 670m of altitude gain.

➡ Hell-Bourg–Terre Plate–Source Manouilh–Îlet-à-Vidot–Hell-Bourg – an exhilarating six-hour loop, with a net altitude gain of about 600m.

➡ Hell-Bourg–Gîte du Piton des Neiges – a pleasant alternative to Cilaos if you're planning to hike up to Piton des Neiges. Expect a tough seven-hour climb (one way), with a net altitude gain of 1470m.

★ **Ti Jack**   GÎTE €
(☎0692 19 94 73; gitetijacques@hotmail.fr; 17 Impasse des Dahlias; d without bathroom €40, incl breakfast €52; P🖥) Just a five-minute stroll from the main drag, there's smashing value to be found at this pert little B&B-style *gîte* that features four doubles in a brightly painted Creole house. They're small but cute and tidy, and there's a cosy lounge area. Ask for a room with a view of the Piton des Neiges. The owner offers lots of local information, and dinners are available.

★ **Mon Ti Caze Creol**   GÎTE €
(☎0692 61 44 60; www.monticazecreol.fr; 1 Rue de la Cayenne; s/d €25/50) This is no ordinary *gîte*. Mon Ti Caze Creol is a genuine old Creole villa with absolutely bundles of character. It shelters three rooms that share bathrooms and a spick-and-span modern kitchen. The whole house is clean as a whistle and it's super central. Nice extra: towels are provided. The whole house can be rented for €160/200 for four/six people. An excellent deal.

Le Relax   CAMPGROUND €
(☎0692 66 58 89; 21 Chemin Bras-Sec, Îlet-à-Vidot; camp site per person €11; P) Head to this homely camp site, in the hamlet of Îlet-à-Vidot, about 2km northwest of Hell-Bourg, if you're after a peaceful setting to pitch your tent within a grassy property. The ablution block is in good nick and there's a kitchen for guests' use. Laurent, the sporty owner (he's the local fireman and has run the Grand Raid race), can take you to various scenic spots in the area and provide

you with a wealth of information (alas, in French) about local plants and architecture.

Chez Madeleine Parisot   GÎTE €
(☎0262 47 83 48; 16 Rue Général de Gaulle; dm €16) This homely *gîte d'étape* on the main drag features two- to four-bed rooms in several Creole-style buildings full of nooks and crannies. Some rooms are better than others, so ask to see a few before committing. Breakfast (€3) and dinner (€18) are available.

Gîte du Piton d'Enchaing   GÎTE €
(☎0692 33 93 35; davina.olivier@yahoo.fr; Rue Général de Gaulle; dm €18) This well-run *gîte* is a secure spot to hang your rucksack, the rates are good and it's handily set on the main drag. It features four salubrious four- to six-bed rooms with well-scrubbed bathrooms and communal kitchen. Davina, your friendly host, can prepare breakfast (€6).

Chez Alice   GUESTHOUSE €
(☎0262 47 86 24; 1 Rue des Sangliers; d incl breakfast €35) Clad in more wood than a Swedish sauna, this is a good option if you're counting the pennies. The seven rooms feel a tad hanky-sized but are perfectly acceptable and have private bathrooms. It's behind the eponymous restaurant.

Le Relais des Gouverneurs   B&B €€
(☎0262 47 76 21; calouboyer@wanadoo.fr; 2bis Rue Amiral Lacaze; d incl breakfast €60-75; P🖥) Although the structure is starting to show its age, this B&B is still a reliable option. The two Superieure rooms feature four-poster beds, wooden floors and pastel-coloured walls. The cheaper Standard and Familiale

rooms are less exciting, but the densely vegetated grounds add a lot of charm. *Table d'hôte* meals (€23) are available if there's a minimum of six people.

Le Relais des Cimes
HOTEL €€
(☑0262 47 81 58; www.relaisdescimes.com; 67 Rue Général de Gaulle; s/d incl breakfast €68/78; [P][✿]) The rooms in the motel-like building lack character but they're fresh and tidy. Most upstairs rooms have mountain views. There's a second building across the street, which features four rooms that occupy two tastefully refurbished Creole houses – ask for the 'Chambres Case Créole'.

Les Jardins d'Héva
HOTEL €€
(☑0262 47 87 87; www.lesjardinsdheva.com; 16 Rue Lacaussade; d incl breakfast €98; [P][✿]) This is a wonderfully relaxing option with five handsomely designed bungalows, each with two adjoining rooms; they're all decorated differently. One glitch: they turn their back on the fantastic views of the Cirque. The real steal is the little spa featuring a hammam, a sauna and a Jacuzzi, where you can reinvigorate weary feet after a busy day's walking – access is free for guests. There's an on-site restaurant if you're feeling too lazy to travel elsewhere.

🍴 Eating

While Cilaos is known for its lentils, Hell-Bourg is synonymous with *chouchou*, a green, pear-shaped vegetable imported from Brazil in 1834. It comes in salads, gratins and as *chouchou gateau* to finish. You can stock up on basic provisions at the grocers and other food shops along the main road.

Crêperie Le Gall
CRÊPERIE €
(☑0262 47 87 48; 55 Rue Général de Gaulle; mains €3-10; ☺lunch & dinner) The only place for miles around that serves succulent pancakes. Yes, pancakes! Try the Ti Chou Chou with, you guessed it, *chouchou*. Wash it all down with a *bolée de cidre* (bowl of cider). Lovely.

P'tit Koin Kréol
CREOLE €
(☑0692 61 03 41; Rue du Général de Gaulle; mains €5-9; ☺lunch) This tiny restaurant in a cute Creole house is a good place to sample authentic Réunionnais fare prepared mammastyle. Tour your taste buds with a *gratin de chouchous* (*chouchou* with melted cheese) or a tasty curry.

La Coco Lé Là!
CREOLE, CAFETERIA €
(☑0693 80 92 56; 38 Ave du Général de Gaulle; mains €6-12; ☺9am-6pm Tue-Sun) In a courtyard back from the main drag, this is a cool place for a fruit juice or a light meal, with a short list of palate pleasers: duck Creolestyle, roasted chicken, homemade dessert. The view is serene and the ambience relaxed.

La Christophine
CREOLE €
(☑0692 52 15 46; Rue des Sangliers; mains €7-13, menu €19; ☺lunch Thu-Tue, dinner Mon, Fri & Sun) Located in a cute Creole house, this familystyle eatery serves up great cheap eats and local ambience. Excellent *carris* are served in little pots. Last orders are at 7.45pm. Takeaway meals are available (€5.50 to €6.50).

Chez Alice
CREOLE, FRENCH €€
(☑0262 47 86 24; 1 Rue des Sangliers; mains €10-18, menu €22; ☺11.45am-1.45pm Tue-Sun, 6.30-7.45pm Tue-Thu & Sat) The fare at this familyrun veteran is certainly not gourmet but has a temptingly pronounced regional flavour. Among the many winners are the Hell-Bourg trout, the *gratin de chouchou* (baked choko) and the *carri porc aux pommes de terre* (pork with potatoes), all served at affordable prices in rustic surrounds. Portions are large enough to satisfy the most voracious hiker. Takeaway is available.

Le Relais des Cimes
CREOLE, FRENCH €€
(☑0262 47 81 58; 67 Rue Général de Gaulle; mains €12-18, menus €18-22; ☺lunch & dinner) At this Hell-Bourg stalwart the eclectic food is well presented and served in rustic surrounds, with wooden ceilings and red tablecloths. Dishes worth trying include the trout with vanilla flambéed in rum and the roasted guinea fowl with peach and guava.

Ti Chou Chou
CREOLE €€
(☑0262 47 80 93; 42 Rue Général de Gaulle; mains €12-25, menus €18-26; ☺11.30am-2pm & 6.30-7.45pm Sat-Thu) This small restaurant, with its appealing colourful facade on the main drag, is run by a friendly young team. Herbivores will opt for the *assiette ti chouchou*, which offers a combination of *chouchou, cresson* and *capucine* (all local vegetables). There's a shady terrace at the back.

Les Jardins d'Héva
BUFFET €€
(☑0262 47 87 87; 16 Rue Lacaussade; buffet €15-25; ☺lunch Fri-Tue, dinner daily) Superb setting: central Hell-Bourg at your feet, the jagged peaks of the Cirques in the distance. The

RÉUNION CIRQUE DE SALAZIE

food is average, but the lunch buffet (€15) is good value.

ⓘ Information

There are no banks in Hell-Bourg, and there's only one ATM.

Office du Tourisme (☑0262 47 89 89; www. est.reunion.fr; 47 Rue Général de Gaulle; ☺8.30am-noon & 1-5.30pm; ☎) Has pamphlets on hiking options and bus schedules in the Cirque. Can also arrange bookings at *gîtes de montagne* and guided tours in English if given advance notice. Offers free wi-fi.

Post Office (Rue du Général de Gaulle; ☺8.30am-noon & 1-2.45pm Mon-Fri, 8-11am Sat) Has an ATM.

Grand Îlet & Col des Bœufs

This is a sweet, picturesque spot. About 17km west of Salazie, accessed by a scenic white-knuckle road, Grand Îlet really feels like the end of the line. The village sits at the base of the ridge separating the Cirque de Salazie and the Cirque de Mafate. Above the village are the mountain passes of Col des Bœufs and Col de Fourche, which form the main pedestrian routes between the two Cirques; access is via the village of **Le Bélier**, 3km above Grand Îlet, where you'll find the start of the tarred *route forestière* (forestry road) that leads to Col des Bœufs. The *route forestière* is dotted with a number of *kiosques* (picnic shelters) that are popular at weekends.

About 500m before the guarded car park at Col des Bœufs, there's a sign indicating the path to **Piton Marmite** on the left. Follow it and after about 10 minutes you'll reach a lookout with fabulous views of the Cirque de Salazie.

🍴 Sleeping & Eating

Chez Liliane Bonnald   B&B **€**
(☑0262 41 71 62; liliane.bonnald@wanadoo.fr; Chemin Camp-Pierrot; d incl breakfast €42; 🅿☎) In a modernish house on the road to Le Bélier, the five rooms upstairs won't be selected for a *Wallpaper* photo shoot but are kept tickety-boo and boast a few fancy touches, such as Creole ceilings and wood panelling on the walls. Liliane Bonnald, your affable host, is a good cook too. Dinner costs €22.

La Campierelle – Chez Christine Boyer   B&B **€**
(☑0262 47 70 87; Chemin Camp-Pierrot; d incl breakfast €40; 🅿) Here you'll be greeted by an old lady wearing a straw hat, Madame Boyer. She rents out four humble rooms in a small Creole house just off the road. It's no great shakes and the bathrooms feel a bit dated, but it's OK and when it comes to concocting traditional *carris* at dinner (€22), Madame Boyer knows her stuff.

Le Cimendef – Chez Noeline et Daniel Campton   B&B **€€**
(☑0262 47 73 59; www.chambresdhotecimendef. com; Route du Bélier; s/d/ste incl breakfast €45/50/85; 🅿☎) All five rooms are pleasing and are graced with ravishing views over the Cimendef (2226m), but we were smitten by the darling Prestige suite, which features a Jacuzzi, timber floor, a luminous bathroom with well-chosen tiles, Creole ceilings, flat-screen TV, teak furniture, an enticing orange colour scheme and your own terrace. You'll also eat well here; dinner costs €24.

ⓘ Getting There & Around

If you're coming here to hike and have your own car, you can leave it in the guarded car park (parking one/two days €2/10) at Le Petit Col, 6.5km up the *route forestière* and only 20 minutes' walk below the Col des Bœufs. On Saturday and during school holidays, the warden can drive you to the start of Sentier Scout or Sentier Augustave.

Cirque de Mafate

Nothing can prepare you for that first glimpse of this geologic wonder, with its dramatic scenery, shifting colours, blissful serenity (except for the occasional whirring of choppers) and unsurpassed grandeur. No cars, no towns, no stress. Just soaring mountains, jagged peaks, giddily deep ravines, thick forests and a sprinkle of tiny *écarts* where time seems to have stood still.

Apart from its grandiose topography, what sets the Cirque de Mafate apart is its relative inaccessibility, despite being very close to the coastal fleshpots. There are no roads that lead into the Cirque (although a *route forestière* runs right up to the pass at Col des Bœufs), so the villages that are scattered in this giant extinct volcano are accessible only by foot.

Unsurprisingly, the Cirque de Mafate is a walker's paradise, with a good network of paths connecting the villages.

The Cirque was named after a runaway slave, the chieftain and sorcerer Mafate, who took refuge among its ramparts. He was

FORAYS INTO THE CIRQUE DE MAFATE

If you have a day to spare, do not miss the opportunity to hike into the Cirque de Mafate. From the car park just below Col des Bœufs, it takes only two hours to descend to La Nouvelle, dubbed 'the capital of Mafate' – it makes a great half-day hike, and you can have lunch in La Nouvelle. A longer option is to take the Sentier Scout which branches off the *route forestière* (it's signposted, about 2.3km before the car park at Col des Bœufs) and leads to Aurère in Bas Mafate; you can spend the night in Aurère and walk back to the *route forestière* the next day by following the super scenic Sentier Augustave – a lovely loop.

tracked down and killed in 1751 by a hunter of runaway slaves.

⊙ Sights & Activities

Despite its remoteness and seclusion, the Cirque de Mafate is populated. In the valleys, plateaus and spurs that slice up the jaw-dropping terrain are scattered discreet little Creole settlements that retain a rough-diamond rural edge. Not much happens in these villages but it's hard not to fall under the spell of their phenomenal setting. They provide a few trappings of civilisation if you're walking through the Cirque.

The southern part of the Cirque is called Haut Mafate (Higher Mafate) and receives the bulk of visitors. It comprises peaceful **Marla**, the highest hamlet of the Cirque at an altitude of 1621m; **La Nouvelle**, dubbed the 'capital of Mafate' and one of the main gateways to the Cirque, perched on a plateau at an altitude of 1421m; and **Roche-Plate**, at the foot of the grandiose Maïdo.

The northern part of the Cirque is called Bas Mafate (Lower Mafate) and is considered even more secretive than Haut Mafate. It comprises **Îlet à Bourse**, **Îlet à Malheur**, **Aurère**, **Grand Place**, **Cayenne**, **Les Lataniers** and **Îlet des Orangers**. Aurère is perched Machu Picchu–like above the precipitous canyon of the Bras Bémale. The two tiny communities of Grand Place and Cayenne lie above the rushing Rivière des Galets near the Cirque's main outlet.

Mafate offers some of the most inspirational **hiking** trails in Réunion, so pack your sturdy shoes and delve into the Cirque – see p39 for more information. If you'd prefer to take it easy and see all this fantasyland from the air, book a helicopter or an ultralight aircraft tour (see p210).

LES HAUTES PLAINES & THE PITON DE LA FOURNAISE

Réunion's only cross-island road passes through the Plaine-des-Cafres and the Plaine-des-Palmistes, collectively known as Les Hautes Plaines. At an altitude of about 1000m, the air is refreshingly crisp and often swathed in misty fog – a blessing if you're coming from the scorching coastal cities.

These relatively large open areas actually form the saddle that separates the massif (comprising the three Cirques) from the volcano, Piton de la Fournaise. And what a volcano! It ranks as one of the most active volcanoes on Earth, playing in the same league as Hawaii. It's also one of the most accessible ones – you can trek up the caldera.

Because there's a road from the Hautes Plaines that approaches within a few kilometres of the summit of the volcano, nearly all visitors approach it from this side.

Plaine-des-Cafres & Bourg-Murat

Velvet-green hills and pastures undulating off into the horizon. Fresh air. Mist. Filled with iconic pastoral landscapes, the Plaine-des-Cafres area bears an unexpected likeness to Bavaria. It is cool, relaxing and oxygenated. Chalk that up to altitude and attitude. It sits 1200m above sea level and is regularly massaged by cool breezes. Once a refuge for runaway slaves from the coast, the Plaine-des-Cafres is a vast, gently rolling area that spreads between the Cirques and Piton de la Fournaise.

As you make the approach from the south (St-Pierre), the Plaine-des-Cafres begins shortly after the sprawling, nondescript town of Le Tampon and ends at Col de Bellevue, at the top of the winding road that plunges down to Plaine-des-Palmistes. North of Le Tampon on RN3 (the cross-island road) are numerous small settlements that are named for their distance from the sea – Le Vingt-Quatrième (24th), for example, is 24km from the ocean.

The most interesting place on the Plaine-des-Cafres from a visitor's perspective is **Bourg-Murat**, which is the obvious launch pad for the volcano. It's in this rural settlement where the Route Forestière du Volcan turns off to Piton de la Fournaise. The town and the surrounding area have a wealth of accommodation and dining choices, making it a handy base.

⊙ Sights & Activities

Maison du Volcan   MUSEUM
(☑0262 59 00 26; www.maisonduvolcan.fr; RN3, Bourg-Murat; adult/child €8/4; ⊙9.30am-5pm Tue-Sun) Everything you need to know about Piton de la Fournaise and volcanoes in general should become clear at the excellent Maison du Volcan. It was completely refurbished and modernised in 2013, so you can expect state-of-the-art facilities and animations.

OFF THE BEATEN TRACK

GRAND BASSIN – THE LOST VALLEY

The utterly picturesque valley of Grand Bassin, known as *la vallée perdue* (the lost valley) or *Mafate en miniature* (Mafate in miniature), is one of the few areas in Réunion that is only accessible on foot. Thanks to its splendid isolation, this little morsel of paradise is a dream come true for those seeking to get well and truly off the beaten track.

To get there, follow the road D70 to Bois Court from Vingt-Troisième village. At the end of the road you can look down into the valley from the **Belvédère** viewpoint. The path down to Grand Bassin begins about 800m south of the Belvédère (it's signposted). It plunges almost straight down to the river 600m below; allow 1½ hours for the descent and at least 2½ hours to get back up again. You can leave your car at a few private homes near the trailhead. It costs €3 (€10 for overnight parking).

Grand Bassin is formed by the confluence of three rivers. Near to where they join is a quiet hamlet with a handful of *gîtes*. From the hamlet, follow the river towards the west and you'll soon reach a few rock pools where you can dunk yourself – just blissful. Further west, you can descend at the base of the impressive **Cascade du Voile de la Mariée** waterfall.

Grand Bassin is a terrific place to kick off your shoes for a few days and sample authentic rural Réunionnais life. Digs are in rustic dorms or in doubles, but that's part of the fun. Day-trippers will fork out €18 to €20 for a meal, usually a wholesome *carri* made with locally grown products.

Le Randonneur (☑0692 78 04 50; www.gitelerandonneur.net; Grand-Bassin; per person with half board €40-45) A chalet-like venue with good views. A bit more expensive than other venues in Grand-Bassin, but it feels more intimate, with only three doubles and three quadruples, all tiled.

La Vieille Tonnelle (☑0262 59 20 27, 0262 27 51 02; Grand Bassin; per person with half board €38) Has two snug doubles. Luc, the friendly owner, will treat you to a wicked *rhum bois* (rum flavoured with an endemic wood). Good homemade jams.

Les Orchidées (☑0692 03 90 38, 0262 38 02 73; Grand-Bassin; per person with half board €35-40) On the eastern outskirts of the hamlet. Has two quadruples, two eight-bed dorms and two doubles. Good homemade honey.

Le Paille-en-Queue (☑0692 24 31 73, 0262 59 03 66; Grand-Bassin; per person with half board €38) Features two doubles and six- to eight-bed dorms.

Auberge de Grand-Bassin (☑0692 26 74 55, 0262 59 10 34; Grand-Bassin; per person with half board €38) Has three doubles and six- to 16-bed dorms.

Les Mimosas (☑0692 16 09 90; www.lesmimosas.re; Grand-Bassin; d with half board €156; ⓦ) This recent B&B has been beautifully built and decorated using local materials. The all-wood bungalow sits in a superb tropical garden and sports two doubles that are as cosy as a bird's nest. Great for couples or families. Vegetarian meals can be arranged.

Horse Riding

Horse riding is a fun, ecofriendly way to commune with the pastoral wilderness around Bourg-Murat. The ultimate is a two- to three-day excursion that takes in the eerie landscape around the volcano – highly recommended.

Centre Équestre Alti Merens   HORSE RIDING
(☑0692 31 47 92; www.alti-merens-reunion.com/web; 120 Rue Maurice Krafft, PK26; ⊙by reservation) On the southern edge of Bourg-Murat. You'll pay €20 for a one-hour guided trip.

Écuries du Volcan   HORSE RIDING
(☑0692 66 62 90; www.ecuriesduvolcan.e-mon-site.com; 9bis Domaine Bellevue, Bourg-Murat; ⊙daily by reservation) On the northern edge of Bourg-Murat. Reckon on €20 for a one-hour jaunt and €120 per day for a multiday trek. Also offers an interesting day trip (€140) that includes a visit to a traditional farm and a Creole lunch.

🛏 Sleeping

Gîte de Bellevue   GÎTE €
(☑0692 07 80 83, 0262 59 15 02; Domaine Bellevue, Bourg-Murat; dm €15, bungalows €50-100) A good find in a bucolic property, behind the equestrian centre Écuries du Volcan. Has two doubles and two quads, all scrubbed attentively. The all-wood bungalow is fully equipped and can sleep five. There's also a smaller bungalow for couples. Bar breakfast (€5); no other meals are provided but there are kitchen facilities.

Gîte de la Fournaise   GÎTE €
(☑0692 22 89 88, 0262 59 29 75; gitedelafournaise@wanadoo.fr; RN3, Bourg-Murat; dm/s/d €16/30/36, dinner €21; P) The three six-bed dorms downstairs are OK and come with their own bathroom, but the renovated double room upstairs really cuts the mustard, with its own terrace and views of Piton des Neiges. The French owner is extra nice and offers to pick up walkers from the GR® R2 walking trail (and drop them off the next morning), which passes a few kilometres north of Bourg-Murat.

Gîte Marmite Lontan   GÎTE €
(☑0692 60 51 38, 0262 57 46 09; www.marmite-lontan.com; Route Forestière du Volcan; s with half board €38; ⊙lunch daily) Not your average *gîte*, this little cracker is isolated on the Route Forestière du Volcan about 5km from the centre of Bourg-Murat. Entering the property, you feel as if you've stumbled onto the set of *Little House on the Prairie*. In the role of Charles Ingalls you have amiable Pilou (or his son). The five dorms are neat and can sleep two to four people. The whole place radiates a ramshackle air – from the quirky facade, which is entirely covered with thongs, to the dining room, which is a Pandora's box of *objets lontan* (utensils and other knick-knacks from the old days). It also serves *plats du jour* (daily specials) at lunchtime.

Hôtel-Auberge Le Volcan   INN €
(☑0262 27 50 91; aubvolcan@wanadoo.fr; RN3, PK27, Bourg-Murat; s/d €30/42; P☎) Features stock-standard rooms in various pavilions on a property smack-bang in the middle of Bourg-Murat. The mattresses will keep your chiropractor happy; however, its central address means it can be noisy.

Chez Alicalapa-Tenon   B&B €€
(☑0692 08 80 09, 0262 59 10 41; c.alicalapatenon@ool.fr; 154 Route du Champ de Foire, Bourg-Murat; s/d incl breakfast €40/50; P☎) This sweet B&B in a modern house is a good base to explore the area, with four simple wood-panelled rooms that are kept spick and span. Ask for a room that opens onto the garden.

La Diligence   HOTEL €€
(☑0262 59 10 10; www.ladiligence974.com; 8 Rue Paul De Peindrey, PK28, Bourg-Murat; dm €15, s/d €42/50; P☎) This low-slung building immersed in greenery harbours seven nicely laid-out rooms as well as a 14-bed dorm and a good restaurant.

La Ferme du Pêcher Gourmand   B&B €€
(☑0692 66 12 48, 0262 59 29 79; www.pechergourmand.re; RN3, PK25; s €50, d €55-65, bungalow €70, incl breakfast; P☎) This modern *auberge* is run by a friendly couple and is surrounded by a pleasant garden. The five adjoining rooms are a bit of a squeeze, but the setting more than compensates. There's also a stand-alone bungalow, which offers more privacy, and two larger *cases* (Creole-style houses) that are ideal for families. Bonus: there's a widely acclaimed on-site restaurant – it's worth opting for half board.

Les Géraniums   HOTEL €€
(☑0262 59 11 06; hotelgeranium@wanadoo.fr; RN3, PK24; s/d €58/67; P@☎) The Géraniums is a tad overrated but nonetheless of a good standard, especially if you nab a room with mountain views, especially rooms 2, 4, 6 or 8; avoid the rooms that overlook the parking lot. Precious perks include a sauna,

RÉUNION PLAINE-DES-CAFRES & BOURG-MURAT

a hammam and a well-regarded on-site **restaurant** (menus €22-30) which is a lovely place to dine on innovative regional cooking. It's in Le Vingt-Quatrième on the main road south of Bourg-Murat.

Hôtel l'Ecrin   HOTEL €€

(☑ 0262 59 02 02; www.hotel-ecrin.fr.st; RN3, PK27, Bourg-Murat; s/d incl breakfast €59/82; P ☎) A cluster of small cottages scattered amid gardens that carpet a knoll. The rooms are a tad frayed around the edges and it's overpriced but it's an acceptable fallback.

✖ Eating

Most lodgings offer half board.

★ Palais des Fromages   CHEESE €

(☑ 0262 59 27 15; Route du Volcan, Bourg-Murat; cheese & waffles €2.50-6; ⊙ 8.30am-5pm Wed-Fri, to 3pm Sat, to 6pm Sun) The aptly named 'Cheese Palace' is famous for its superb range of cheeses, including a delicious *fromage crémeux au combava* (creamy cheese flavoured with combava), best enjoyed at a picnic table in the cryptomeria forest nearby. Also concocts waffles and pancakes on weekends. Find it on the outskirts of Bourg-Murat, towards the volcano. Cash only.

Ti Resto Lontan   CREOLE €

(☑ 0262 43 90 42; RN3, PK27, Bourg-Murat; mains €9-16; ⊙ 11.30am-3.30pm & 6.30-10pm Wed-Mon) Don't let the bland building put you off – this jovial venture has won a faithful following for its value-for-money seasonal fare. Tuck into tasty *carris*, copious salads and simply cooked meat and fish dishes. Service is friendly and the laid-back atmosphere is conducive to a nice, relaxed meal.

★ Le QG   CREOLE €€

(☑ 0262 38 28 55; 60bis Rue Alfred Picard, Bourg-Murat; mains €14-20; ⊙ 7am-9.30pm Fri-Tue, to 3pm Wed; ☎) What do you get if you cross a Réunionnais chef (André), a Senegalese waiter (Abdou) and a snug dining room? The QG! If the thought of *rougaille saucisse* (sausage stew Creole-style) or *entrecôte grillée* (grilled beef ribsteak) exquisitely cooked in the hearth doesn't make you dribble then you've started pushing up daisies. If you happen to be in Bourg-Murat on Friday, you'll be treated to Senegalese specialities – *poulet yassa* (grilled chicken marinated in a thick onion and lemon sauce), anyone? Also serves breakfast. Oh, and it's the only place for miles around that offers some entertainment (think: karaoke) on Friday evening.

La Diligence   RESTAURANT €€

(☑ 0262 59 10 10; www.ladiligence974.com; 8 Rue Paul De Peindrey; set lunch €15; ⊙ lunch & dinner Tue-Sun) The restaurant at the La Diligence hotel (open to nonguests) has garnered high praise for its quality fare. The onus is on grilled meat – the *entrecôte grillée* is a good bet – but there are some excellent non-fish options. The set lunch (weekdays) is a bargain.

Hôtel-Auberge du Volcan   CREOLE, FRENCH €€

(☑ 0262 27 50 91; RN3, PK27, Bourg-Murat; mains €12-18, menu €17; ⊙ lunch Tue-Sun, dinner Tue-Sat) You'll find all the usual Creole favourites and a sprinkling of *métro* dishes served in hearty portions in this country inn in the centre of Bourg-Murat. Last orders are at 8pm.

Le Vieux Bardeau   CREOLE, FRENCH €

(☑ 0262 59 09 44; www.levieuxbardeau.fr; RN3, PK24; mains €13-20, menus €12-22; ⊙ lunch Tue-Sun, dinner Wed-Sat) Recapture the atmosphere of the colonial era in this gracefully ageing diva occupying a lemon-yellow Creole mansion beside the main road in Le Vingt-Quatrième. Come here for lunch to make the best of the great-value *menus*. You'll also find *métro* specialities à la carte.

Relais Commerson   CREOLE €€

(☑ 0692 60 05 44; 37 Bois Joly Potier, Bourg-Murat; mains €12-23, menus €15-28; ⊙ lunch Thu-Tue) A rustic dining room and a menu laden with inspired Creole dishes, which you can follow up with something from the tempting selection of desserts.

Le Panoramic   CREOLE, FRENCH €€

(☑ 0262 59 36 12; RN3, PK27, Bourg-Murat; mains €14-23, menus €15-30; ⊙ lunch Sun-Fri, dinner daily) This modern abode behind Hôtel l'Ecrin offers a carefully constructed menu built around local produce, but the food can be hit-and-miss according to local gourmands.

La Ferme du Pêcher Gourmand
CREOLE, FRENCH **€€**

(☑ 0262 59 29 79; RN3, PK25; mains €17-20, menus €20-25; ☺ lunch Sat & Sun, dinner Mon-Sat) This delightful *ferme-auberge* (farm restaurant) on the main road south of Bourg-Murat offers superb value for money and delicious, no-nonsense farmhouse food. Duck preparations and seasonal, organic vegetables are mainstays of the earthy menu. A *crème brûlée à la vanille* (cream pie with a caramelised topping and flavoured with vanilla) will finish you off sweetly.

ⓘ Information

Near the Caltex petrol station, the **tourist office** (☑ 0262 27 40 00; www.tampontourisme.re; 160 Rue Maurice Krafft, Bourg-Murat; ☺ 9am-12.30pm & 1.30-5pm Mon-Sat) does bookings for *gîtes de montagne* and has brochures and walking maps.

ⓘ Getting There & Away

There are three buses daily (two on Sunday) each way between St-Benoît and St-Pierre via Plaine-des-Cafres and Plaine-des-Palmistes. From St-Pierre to Bourg-Murat, the fare is €2.80. Coming from St-Benoît, it's €4.20.

Piton de la Fournaise (The Volcano)

The magnum opus of Mother Nature in Réunion, Piton de la Fournaise is the island's most famous natural attraction. Simply dubbed *le volcan* (the volcano) by Réunionnais, Piton de la Fournaise is not a dormant monster, but an active geological wonder that erupts with great regularity; in April 2007 the central, 900m-wide crater collapsed by 300m, and new lava fields were formed on its southeastern flanks, down to the coast. In early January 2010 a new eruption occurred, though less powerful. Scientists keep a close watch on the volcano's moods, and are poised to issue warnings if things look to be gathering steam. At the first sign of an eruption, the paths near the volcano and the road up to it will be closed.

The good news is that it's one of the world's most accessible active volcanoes, and it's possible to hike up to the crater rim (though this is subject to change depending on current conditions, so ask while you're there). You can also fly over the volcano, approach the area from the saddle of a horse or simply enjoy the scenery from a viewpoint at **Pas de Bellecombe** (2311m), the 'entrance'

Piton de la Fournaise

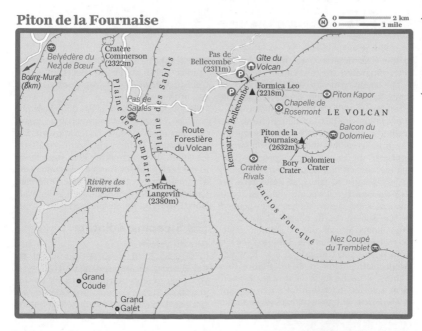

Ⓝ 0 ___ 2 km / 0 ___ 1 mile

HIKING UP PITON DE LA FOURNAISE

Réunion's iconic feature, Piton de la Fournaise is simply a must-do for walkers. From Pas de Bellecombe, it's possible to hike up to **Balcon du Dolomieu**, a viewpoint on the northeastern side of the Dolomieu Crater rim, from where you can gaze down upon the bottom of the caldera, some 350m below. Balcon du Dolomieu is a five-hour, 14km out-and-back walk. It's graded moderate and has an altitude gain of about 500m. It can get very busy, but the eerie landscape more than makes up for the crowds of people. Note that since the 2007 eruption it's no longer possible to do a circuit around the Dolomieu Crater and the Bory Crater; ignore all maps showing this circuit, as they're not up to date.

From the car park at Pas de Bellecombe, follow the path to the northeast that leads to a door (closed when the volcano is active). This is where the path starts in earnest by plunging 527 steps to the floor of the immense Enclos Fouqué, reached after about 15 minutes. You're now walking on a field of solidified lava. The route across the lava plain is marked with white paint spots. At times it can feel like you are walking on Mars, with only the dry crunch of the cinders underfoot for company. You'll first pass the very photogenic Formica Leo and, about 45 minutes from the start, a spectacular cavern in the lava known as **Chapelle de Rosemont** comes into view. From here, the path veers to the left and takes a gradual route up the eastern wall of the cone until it reaches the Balcon du Dolomieu viewpoint. Caveat! There's no guardrail, just a white line.

While the volcano walk is popular and is not technically demanding, it shouldn't be undertaken lightly. The landscape here is harsh and arid, despite the mist that can drench hikers to the skin. The chilly wind whips away moisture, leaving walkers dehydrated and breathless.

Early morning is the best time to climb the volcano, as you stand a better chance of clear views, but this is when everyone else hits the trail as well.

Since the eruption of April 2007, two new walks in the Enclos Fouqué have been established. They do not lead to Dolomieu Crater, but to **Piton Kapor** (about three hours return), a small volcanic cone north of Piton de la Fournaise, and to **Cratère Rivals** (about four hours return), in the southwestern part of the Enclos. Leaflets detailing these routes are available at the tourist office in Bourg-Murat.

Many people get a head start by staying at the Gîte du Volcan and leave at the crack of dawn, so be sure to book well in advance.

---

to the volcanic area, right on the crater's outer rim, where the road ends.

The main gateway to the volcano is Bourg-Murat. From there, a scenic, zigzagging secondary road leads to Pas de Bellecombe, about 30km southeast of Bourg-Murat. The gradual change of scenery is mind-boggling. The grassy meadows and cryptomeria forests typical of the Hautes Plaines progressively change to scrubland and Martian landscape. Be sure to pause at **Belvédère du Nez-de-Bœuf** (viewpoint), blessed with unsurpassable views over the valley gouged by the Rivière des Remparts. About 22km from Bourg-Murat, there's another fabulous viewpoint at **Pas des Sables** (2360m), from where you can gaze at a wide windswept plain, made of ashes, **Plaine des Sables**. With its lunar landscape, it could form a perfect backdrop for a new version of *Mad Max*. The road plunges down to the plain and becomes a dirt road with wicked potholes (but it's OK with a car) before continuing uphill to Pas de Bellecombe and Gîte du Volcan (p228). You've reached the end of the world.

From the viewpoint at Pas de Bellecombe you'll be rewarded with mesmerising views of the volcano and its outer crater, known as **Enclos Fouqué**. The very photogenic, small scoria cone with bizarre ochre hues you can see to the east in Enclos Fouqué is **Formica Leo**. The main crater, the 900m-wide **Dolomieu Crater**, is active; the 2632m-high, 200m-wide **Bory Crater**, to the east, is inactive.

🍽 Sleeping & Eating

Gîte du Volcan
GÎTE **€**

(☑ 0692 85 20 91; www.legiteduvolcan.com; dm €16-18, d bungalow incl breakfast €60, q €80; P) If you wish to stop overnight to soak up this grandiose scenery, the 65-bed Gîte du Volcan boasts a stunning location, a 15-minute walk from Pas de Bellecombe. Digs are in four- to 12-bed dorms. There are also two cute bungalows that come with bathrooms. Hot water is limited and is token-operated (€1.50). In principle, bookings are to be made through Centrale d'Information et de Réservation Régionale – Île de la Réunion Tourisme (p37) or through any tourist office, but the caretakers usually accept travellers who haven't reserved if the *gîte* is not full (but reservations are recommended, especially during the trekking season). The **restaurant** is open at lunch for day trippers and serves up five different dishes. The real clinchers are the picture-windows with lovely mountain views. Water is recycled. Breakfast/lunch/dinner cost €6.50/14/19. Credit cards are accepted.

Cafeteria   SANDWICHES, SWEETS €
(Pas de Bellecombe; snacks from €1; ⏰9am-5pm daily) This modest place near the parking lot at Pas de Bellecombe sells snacks and refreshments.

ⓘ Getting There & Away

There's no public transport to/from the Piton de la Fournaise.

For those with a vehicle, getting to the volcano couldn't be easier because of the all-weather Route Forestière du Volcan, which climbs 30km from Bourg-Murat all the way to Pas de Bellecombe.

Without your own car, the 5½-hour hike to the volcano from Bourg-Murat via the Sentier Josémont (GR® R2) is regarded as something of a walk for masochists, as it's easy to pick up a ride along the Route Forestière du Volcan instead.

Plaine-des-Palmistes

There were once large numbers of palm trees on the Plaine-des-Palmistes (hence the name), but as a result of heavy consumption of palm-heart salad, few now remain. The town itself is spread out along the highway and is a good base for Forêt de Bébour-Bélouve. Its only specific sight is the **Domaine des Tourelles**, a lovely 1920s Creole building just south of the town centre, which now houses a shop selling local crafts and produce.

If you want to commune with nature, be sure not to miss the walk to the **Cascade Biberon**, a 240m-high waterfall to the north of Plaine-des-Palmistes (it's signposted). It's an easy one-hour return walk along a well-marked path.

🍽 Sleeping & Eating

Gîte du Pic des Sables   GÎTE €
(📋0262 51 37 33; 2 Allée des Filaos, Plaine-des-Palmistes; dm €20, breakfast/dinner €5/20; Ⓟ) This cleanish but cramped *gîte d'étape* is on the road to Forêt de Bébour-Bélouve, about 4km from the highway (in the direction of Petite Plaine). It has mountain bikes for rent (€5 per hour) and serves hearty meals at dinner.

La Ferme du Pommeau   HOTEL, RESTAURANT €€
(📋0262 51 40 70; www.pommeau.fr; 10 Allée des Pois de Senteur; s €63, d €73-87; 🌐🏊) In a quiet location on the eastern edge of town, La Ferme du Pommeau is a rambling two-star hotel consisting of several nicely maintained buildings. Most rooms have benefitted from a touch-up and are super clean. The Superior ones are slightly dearer but offer more privacy. There's a heated pool, a farm (which you can visit) and a reliable **restaurant** (mains €15-28, menus €26-38; ⏰noon-1.30pm & 7-8pm Mon-Sat) on-site, which strives to use only local ingredients. Menu stalwarts include chicken curry, lamb cutlet and roast pork. Some English is spoken at the reception.

Les Platanes –
Chez Jean-Paul   CREOLE, CHINESE €€
(📋0262 51 31 69; 167 Rue de la République; mains €12-19, menu €17; ⏰lunch Wed-Sun) One of the best-known eateries in the area, this unfussy spot on the main drag is always full with Réunionnais families at lunch on Sunday – a good sign. The atmosphere is laid-back and the food is similarly unpretentious with the emphasis on hearty, home-cooked Creole and Chinese staples. All at very honest prices.

Le Relais des Plaines   CREOLE, FRENCH €€
(📋0262 20 00 68; 303 Rue de la République; mains €11-15, menus €15-19; ⏰lunch Thu-Tue, dinner Thu-Mon) Traditional cuisine is given a modern makeover at this restaurant occupying a tastefully restored Creole house just off the main road. The menu is short but you'll find tempting daily specials.

ⓘ Getting There & Away

Plaine-des-Palmistes is situated on the cross-island highway between St-Benoît and St-Pierre. There are three buses a day (two on Sunday) in each direction. The fare from St-Pierre is €4.20.

WORTH A TRIP

FORÊT DE BÉBOUR-BÉLOUVE

An absolute must-see, the majestic Forêt de Bébour-Bélouve could set the stage for a new version of *Jurassic Park*, with a mix of tamarind trees, huge *fanjan* (fern trees) and moss. It lies to the northwest of Plaine-des-Palmistes, and is accessible via a surfaced forest road which begins at Petite Plaine, just southwest of Plaine-des-Palmistes, and finishes 20km further on, 400m from the **Gîte de Bélouve** (☑ 0692 85 93 07; Forêt de Bébour-Bélouve; dm €16-18, d with shared bathroom €42-44, breakfast/meal €6/19; ☺ lunch Thu-Tue, dinner daily; closed lunch Feb), which is scenically wedged onto a bluff lording over the Cirque de Salazie. Digs are in six- to 12-bed dorms. There are also two cosy doubles. Bookings are essential.

Forêt de Bébour-Bélouve is a superb playground for mountain biking. You can rent a mountain bike at **Gîte du Pic des Sables** (☑ 0262 51 37 33, 0692 64 54 97; 2 Allée des Filaos, Plaine-des-Palmistes; bike rentals per hour €5) and explore the area at your leisure. Come during the week – you'll have the whole area to yourself.

You'll also find some excellent picnic spots at the beginning of the forest. It's a popular walking area, with a network of footpaths of varying levels of difficulty. The tourist office at Plaine-des-Palmistes has a leaflet on walks in the forest. Some favourites:

➡ Sentier Botanique de la Petite Plaine – a 45-minute loop with interpretative panels about flora.

➡ Sentier de la Tamarineraie – a 1½-hour loop, from the Gîte de Bélouve.

➡ Sentier du Trou de Fer – an easy 3.5km walk that leads to a lookout from where you can marvel at horseshoe-shaped falls known as the Trou de Fer, hailed as one of the most spectacular natural sights in Réunion: it has graced the covers of many books. The path starts at the Gîte de Bélouve.

➡ Tour du Piton Bébour – an easy 1¼-hour loop.

ST-PIERRE

POP 79,000

If you need to let off steam before (or after) heading off into the Cirques, you've come to the right place. St-Pierre pulses with an energy unknown elsewhere on the island, especially at weekends. Havana it ain't, but this vibrant, feisty, good-natured city knows what really counts in life: having a good time.

If St-Denis is Réunion's administrative and business capital, enchanting St-Pierre is its throbbing heart. Basking in the clear light of the southwest, the 'capital of the south' has an entirely different feel from its northern counterparts. It remains unmistakably more Creole than cosmopolitan and rather staid St-Denis.

Compact, colourful St-Pierre is easily seen in a day on foot.

◉ Sights

Centre Ville   ARCHITECTURE

You'll find a scattering of attractive colonial-era edifices scattered in the centre, including the old **Hôtel de Ville** (Place de la Mairie), which started life as a coffee warehouse

for the French East India Company during the 18th century. The old colonial-era **train station** is now occupied by the Café de la Gare – Latina Café (p235). Another must-see is the **Entrepôt Kervéguen** (Rue du Four à Chaux), which was also used as a warehouse by the French East India Company. In the same area, keep your eyes peeled for the **médiathèque Raphaël Barquisseau** (off Rue des Bons Enfants), another building dating from the thriving era of the French East India Company.

There are many other Creole mansions and houses that beg to be admired, especially along Rue Marius et Ary Leblond. One of the grandest is the **Sœurs de Saint-Joseph de Cluny** (Rue Marius et Ary Leblond) complex, which was built in the late 18th century. To the east, the neoclassical **Hôtel de la Sous-Préfecture** (Rue Augustin Archambaud) is also worthy of interest.

Culture buffs shouldn't miss St-Pierre's other architectural gems such as the **St-Pierre Church** (Rue Augustin Archambaud), the splendid **Attyaboul Massadjid mosque** (Rue François de Mahy; ☺ 9am-noon, 2-4pm) and the discreet **Chinese temple** (Rue Marius et Ary Leblond). West of the centre, the highly colourful **Tamil temple** (Shri Mahabadra Karli; Ravine Blanche) is also well worth a gander.

Terre Sainte NEIGHBOURHOOD

It's well worth exploring the Terre Sainte district, situated to the east of the centre. Though no longer the traditional fishing village it used to be, this area has its own peculiar appeal, especially along the seashore, where fishermen can be seen playing dominoes in the late afternoon.

Main Market MARKET

(Blvd Hubert-Delisle; ⊘7am-noon Sat) If you're in St-Pierre on a Saturday morning, be sure to browse around the joyous, thriving main market, which sprawls along the seafront at the west end of Blvd Hubert-Delisle – a staple of local life.

Covered Market MARKET

(Rue Victor le Vigoureux; ⊘8am-6pm Mon-Sat) Housed in a metallic structure dating from 1856, the small covered market is a great place to wander if you're after fresh fruit, vegetables, local spices and herbs, *vacoa* bags and the usual assortment of Malagasy crafts.

La Saga du Rhum MUSEUM

(☑0262 35 81 90; www.sagadurhum.fr; Chemin Fredeline; adult/child €8.50/6; ⊘10am-5pm) Those who want to understand how the ambrosia called rum starts in the sugar-cane fields and ends on their palates should come to this museum, which is set on the site of the Isautier estate, one of the oldest rum distillers on Réunion. It's about 5km northwest of Saint-Pierre (in the direction of Bois d'Olives).

Beaches

For those who love nothing better than splashing in lapis-lazuli waters or lounging on white sand, St-Pierre's **main beach** is the perfect answer. This is where you can find locals taking a quick dip on a hot day. Hint: there's a lesser-known, more intimate beach in **Terre Sainte**.

Activities

There's excellent diving off St-Pierre. See p32 for details.

Plongée Australe DIVING

(☑0692 14 01 76; www.plongeeaustrale.com; Harbour; ⊘daily) This low-key diving venture is by all accounts reputable. It specialises in small groups and offers an intimate feel to its aquatic adventures. Single dive trips cost from €47 while introductory dives are €60.

✸✸ Festivals & Events

Sakifo MUSIC

(www.sakifo.com) One of the highlights of Reunion's events calendar, Sakifo is a great music festival with an eclectic program that might include styles as diverse as *maloya*, salsa, blues and African.

⌂ Sleeping

Reservations are essential at weekends. A new three-star venture, **Lindsey Hotel** (21b Rue François Isautier; d €90-110) was going to open at the time of writing – check with the tourist office for details.

Chez Papa Daya HOSTEL €

(☑0692 12 20 12, 0262 25 64 87; www.chezpapadaya.com; 27 Rue du Four à Chaux; s €30, d €35-40, s/d without bathroom €25/30; P☀☏) Run by affable Roger, Papa Daya is a solidly reliable option, with 20 simple, scrupulously clean rooms. Overall it's more homely than its nearby competitors, with lots of greenery and jolly murals around, and facilities include a simple kitchen, a laundry and a TV lounge. Parking is available at the front, but there are only six spaces. Cash only.

Le Nathania HOSTEL €

(☑0262 25 04 57, 0692 70 87 60; www.hotelnathania.com; 12 Rue François de Mahy; d €35-45, without bathroom €30; P☀☏) Its motto is 'clean, comfy, well-priced', and frankly it would be hard to argue with that. What it lacks in style is made up for by an ace location and tidy rooms with fridge. The cheapest have shared facilities but have air-con. There's also a kitchen (for breakfast only) and laundry area. Private parking is available (five spaces only).

L'Escale Touristique HOSTEL €

(☑0692 60 58 58, 0262 35 20 95; www.hotelescaletouristique.com; 14 Rue Désiré Barquisseau; d €40, s without bathroom €30, d without bathroom €30-35; P☀☏) Don't expect dollops of atmosphere in this modern venture, but rooms are spotlessly clean and the location is great. Ask for rooms 101, 102 or 103, which come with a balcony. Air-con is only available in the more expensive rooms. Added perks include private parking, a communal kitchen (for breakfast only) and a laundry area. Prices drop by €5 if you stay two nights or more.

St-Pierre

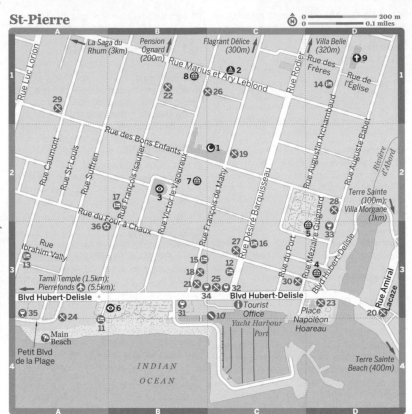

Pension Ognard

GUESTHOUSE €

(☑ 0262 25 89 72; www.pensionognard.com; 113 Rue François Isautier; d with shared bathroom €30; ⓟ 🛜) This modest venture in the pinch-a-penny category is located in a quiet street north of the centre (but within an easy stroll of the seafront). Eight humble rooms provide simple sleeping and open onto a lush tropical garden. Precious perks include a communal kitchen for guests' use, free wi-fi and private parking. No towels are provided, though. Prices drop by €2 if you stay three nights or more. Cash only.

Hôtel Cap Sud

HOTEL €€

(☑ 0262 25 75 64; www.hotel-capsud-reunion.com; 6 Rue Caumont; d €50; ⓟ 🌣 🛜) This renovated two-star venture occupies a modern building not far from the seafront. Rooms here are uncluttered, functional and forgettable. Some rooms enjoy good views, though.

Alizé Plage

HOTEL €€

(☑ 0262 35 22 21; www.alizeplage.fr; 17bis Blvd Hubert-Delisle; d €95; 🌣 🛜) Pro: its position right on the beach is peerless. Con: its location off the main boulevard cops the full brunt of the peak-hour traffic noise (and the nearby food vans in the evening). The hotel benefitted from an extension and renovation program in 2013 and now features 15 rooms, most of which overlook the beach. There's an on-site restaurant.

★ Villa Belle

BOUTIQUE B&B €€€

(☑ 0692 65 89 99; www.villabelle.net; 45 Rue Rodier; s €180-220, d €190-250, ste €370; ⓟ 🌣 🛜 🏊) Erik and Antonio are the creative energy behind this faultless, oh-so-chic *maison d'hôte* in a converted Creole mansion. Villa Belle is the epitome of a refined cocoon, revelling quietly in minimalist lines, soothing colour accents and well-thought-out decorative touches. In 2012, the owners added two

St-Pierre

RÉUNION ST-PIERRE

magnificent Creole villas at the back of the property. Like the rest of the place, the communal areas are a sensory interplay of light, wood and stone. After a day of turf pounding, relax in the stress-melting pool. Breakfast (€20-40) and dinner (€60) are available by request. Prices drop by 15% if you stay three nights or more. Gay-friendly.

Villa Morgane   BOUTIQUE B&B €€€
(☑0262 25 82 77; www.villamorgane.re; 334 Rue de L'Amiral Lacaze, Terre Sainte; d €130-145, ste €165-195; ❄☎❄) You'll go giddy over the exuberant, ever-so-slightly OTT interior of this *maison d'hôte* in a quiet street in Terre Sainte. The themed rooms and suites have been creatively designed, some with Italian flair, some with Asian touches. The Pompéi suite, complete with frescoes and ornate stucco ceilings, has to be seen to be believed (check out the website). Avoid the Venise room, which feels a tad cramped. There's a small but nicely laid-out tropical garden where guests can chill by the pool. No meals are provided except breakfast (€13 per person), but there's a restaurant across the road.

✖ Eating

The excellent Creole, French, Italian and Asian restaurants make this town as pleasing to the belly as it is to the eye; you won't want to be skipping any meals here. Many bars also double as restaurants.

★**Esprit Surf**   SEAFOOD €
(☑0692 28 64 24; 25 Rue Amiral Lacaze; mains €7-12; ☺lunch Tue-Sat; ☎) If the idea of budget seafood usually sets alarm bells ringing, think again. This welcoming hole-in-the-wall near the tourist office is one of the few places where you can feast on delicious fresh fish and still get change from €20. You won't get much variety – what's served depends on what the boats have brought it – but tasty staples usually include fish tartare and homemade fish burgers. Excellent value.

Manciet   BAKERY €
(☑0262 25 06 73; 64 Rue Victor le Vigoureux; pastries from €0.90; ☺6.30am-12.30pm & 2.30-6.30pm Tue-Sat, 6.30am-12.30pm Sun) This gourmet emporium is a veritable feast of perfectly presented pastries, cakes and chocolates. Simply divine.

Castel Glacier   ICE CREAM, CAFETERIA €
(☑0262 22 96 56; 38 Rue François de Mahy; ice creams €2-6, mains €6-12; ☺12.30-6.30pm Mon-Fri, noon-11.30pm Sat, 2.45-8pm Sun; ☎) Generous scoops and about 20 flavours are the trademarks of this drool-inducing ice-cream

parlour opposite the mosque. Also serves up snacks and light meals at lunchtime.

Restaurant des Bons Enfants   CREOLE €

(✍ 0262 25 08 27; 114 Rue des Bons Enfants; mains €5-8; ☺ lunch & dinner) Occupying a small Creole house, this simple venture earns top marks across the board for hearty Creole specialities and economical prices. That said, the decor is super dull and boring – it's best to take away.

Snack Galam Massala   INDIAN, CREOLE €

(✍ 0692 37 12 98; 5 Rue du Four à Chaux; mains €7.50-9; ☺ lunch Tue-Sat, dinner Fri) You wouldn't guess it from the humble surrounds, but this family-run place concocts tasty Indian staples, including beef or chicken curry and one vegetarian dish.

★ Le Jardin Réunionnais   CREOLE €€

(✍ 0262 91 15 28; 9 Petit Blvd de la Plage; mains €13-22, menu €14-15; ☺ lunch & dinner Tue-Sun) Dining at this inviting restaurant on the seafront is all about having a good time enjoying the finer pleasures of life. The cuisine is resolutely Creole, traditional, well prepared and well priced. Colourful paintings on the walls brighten the dining room, while various tropical plants shade the pleasant terrace.

Kaz Nature   FRENCH, CAFETERIA €€

(✍ 0262 25 30 86; 6 Rue François de Mahy; mains €8-19, lunch menus €13-15; ☺ lunch Mon-Sat, dinner Fri & Sat; ☎) This slick modern eatery speedily serves tasty wraps, crunchy salads, zesty pastas and melt-in-the-mouth tarts to a fashionable, young crowd. The dinner menu features more elaborate dishes.

Belo Horizonte   FRENCH €€

(✍ 0262 22 31 95; 10 Rue François de Mahy; mains €10-18; ☺ lunch Mon-Sat, dinner Thu-Sat) Walls saturated in cheery coloured accents and other fancy decorative touches set the tone of this zinging joint, where you can tuck into salads, hot tarts, pizzas and pasta dishes. Excellent homemade desserts, too. The sun-dappled patio garden is enticing.

Le Rétro   BRASSERIE €€

(✍ 0262 25 33 06; 34 Blvd Hubert-Delisle; mains €10-25, menus €14-26; ☺ lunch & dinner) Of all the things you might not expect to see on the seafront, an 'authentic' Parisian brasserie ranks quite highly. But that's exactly what this is, except that serveurs are less surly than in the City of Light. Pastas, salads, carris, seafood and meat dishes grace the menu.

O'Baya   FUSION €€

(✍ 0262 59 66 94; 7 Rue Auguste Babet; mains €16-21; ☺ lunch & dinner Tue-Sat) Sick of stodgy carris? Then head here for lovable fusion fare served in a strong design-led interior. The menu drips with panache and is highlighted by delectable dishes such as kangaroo with berries and speculoos crumble.

La Kaz à Léa   CREOLE €€

(✍ 0262 25 04 25; 34 Rue François Isautier; mains €17-22, lunch menu €14) Don't miss a visit to this atmospheric case (traditional house) with its shady terrace, cosy dining room and beautifully presented Creole and métro dishes. At €14, the three-course lunch menu is a steal. It also has a takeaway outlet next door that rustles up sandwiches (€3) and Creole staples (€6).

O' Flamboyant   FRENCH, CREOLE €€

(✍ 0692 62 48 35; 11 Rue Désiré Barquisseau; mains €18-26, lunch menus €16-21; ☺ lunch & dinner Thu-Tue) This atmospheric eatery prepares delectable French-inspired dishes with a tropical twist, served on the terrace in the shade of a stately flamboyant tree.

Le Cap Méchant d'Abord   BUFFET €€

(✍ 0262 91 71 99; Blvd Hubert-Delisle; buffets €20-25; ☺ lunch Tue-Sun, dinner Tue-Sat) Commanding an enviable location directly on the seafront, this large and busy restaurant is famous for one thing and one thing only: its brilliant-value all-you-can-eat buffets. Palm-heart salad is served on Tuesday, which explains why it's packed to the rafters.

Flagrant Délice   FUSION €€€

(✍ 0692 87 28 03; 115 Rue François de Mahy; mains €24-29, lunch menu €20; ☺ lunch Tue-Fri, dinner Tue-Sat) This hip eatery housed in a private villa is a gourmand's playpen, with a tempting selection of imaginative dishes. Be good to yourself with kangaroo fillet flavoured with cocoa, roasted duck in a maple syrup sauce and luscious wines. The setting is another draw – tables are arranged around a small pool in a tropical garden.

🍷 Drinking & Entertainment

Night owls, rejoice: St-Pierre has a well-established party reputation. The best buzz can be found on the seafront. Most places open from 6pm and close at around 2am or later. Most drinking spots also serve food.

Café de la Gare – Latina Café BAR
(☏0262 35 24 44; 7 Blvd Hubert-Delisle; ⊗7am-midnight; 🛜) Despite the noisy terrace on the main drag, this cafe in the old train station is one of the most atmospheric spots in town for a drink (or a light meal). In the evening it transforms into a convivial bar. There's live music on Sunday (at around 6pm). It may change location during the lifetime of this book – stay tuned.

Kahlua Bar BAR
(☏0262 32 83 86; 32 Blvd Hubert-Delisle; ⊗Tue-Sat; 🛜) A chill-out bar by day, this place heats up to club temperature at night on weekends when groovy DJs take over with deep and chill house, electronica and other beats.

Long Board Café BAR
(☏0692 82 09 95; Petit Blvd de la Plage; ⊗10am-5pm Mon, 10am-2am Tue-Fri, 5pm-2am Sat & Sun) Spiffing setting, in a Creole house with a terrace opening onto the seafront – a great place for quaffing a sunset beverage. Offers live entertainment and karaoke on selected evenings.

Les Sal' Gosses BAR
(☏0262 96 70 36; 38 Blvd Hubert-Delisle; ⊗daily) This cool den on the seafront hosts gigs from local bands – usually on Wednesday and Thursday. Good blend of jazz, soul and funk. Also has a wide-ranging menu (but the food is only so-so), tapas and billiards.

Le Toit BAR
(☏0262 35 32 45; 5 Rue Auguste Babet; ⊗Tue-Sat) Attracting mostly Zoreilles regulars, this hanky-sized bar is well worth a gander for its quirky decor, with an onslaught of postcards, posters and murals. Great value beers and cocktails are two more reasons to stay. Skip the food.

L'Africa Queen CLUB
(7 Blvd Hubert-Delisle; ⊗Fri & Sat) If there's a constant here, it's the promise that the music, whatever the style, will get you groovin'. DJs roll through salsa, hip hop, house, electro and soul but always find a way to keep the dance floor filled. Heart-start the night with a few shots at Café de la Gare, in the same building.

O Pub à Tapas LIVE MUSIC
(☏0262 34 61 94; 53 Rue du Four à Chaux; ⊗6pm-2am Tue-Sat) No rock 'n' roll and no R&B here – this popular venture is famed for the quality of its live-music sessions featuring *maloya* (traditional dance music), salsa and African sounds. And, yes, it serves tapas.

❶ Information

There are ATMs at the central post office and at most banks in the town centre. The Kahlua Bar (p235) offers wi-fi access.

Tourist Office (☏0820 220 202; www.sud.reunion.fr; Blvd Hubert-Delisle; ⊗9am-noon & 1-4.45pm Mon-Sat) Has English-speaking staff and can provide useful brochures and a town map. You can book *gîtes de montagne* here and it can also organise guided tours in English.

❶ Getting There & Away

AIR

Air Mauritius and Air Austral operate daily flights between Pierrefonds Airport (p268), 5km west of St-Pierre, and Mauritius.

Air Austral (☏0825 01 30 12; www.air-austral.com; 14 Rue Augustin Archambaud)

Air Mauritius (☏0262 96 06 00; www.airmauritius.com; 7 Rue François de Mahy)

BUS

Car Jaune (p268) has a bus stop at the long-distance bus station beside the junction of Rue Presbytère and Rue Luc Lorion, west of town. Buses to/from St-Denis (€7) run frequently along the west coast via St-Louis and St-Gilles-les-Bains or direct via the Route des Tamarins if it's a Z'éclair service. There are also two or three services a day to St-Benoît via Plaine-des-Palmistes (€7.50) and the same number around the south coast through St-Joseph and Ste-Philippe (€7). For Cilaos, change in St-Louis.

THE WILD SOUTH

Aaaah, the *Sud Sauvage* (Wild South), where the unhurried life is complemented by the splendid scenery of fecund volcanic slopes, occasional beaches, waves crashing on the rocky shoreline and country roads that twist like snakes into the Hauts. In both landscape and character, the south coast is where the real wilderness of Réunion begins to unfold. Once you've left St-Pierre, a gentle splendour and a sense of escapism become tangible. The change of scenery climaxes with the Grand Brûlé, where black lava fields slice through the forest and even reach the ocean at several points.

St-Pierre to St-Joseph

Life – and travel – becomes more sedate as one heads west through some of the south coast's delicious scenery. With only a few exceptions urban life is left behind once the road traverses **Grand Bois** and snakes its way along the coastline via **Grande Anse** and **Manapany-les-Bains**.

If you want to explore the Hauts, take the turn-off for **Petite Île**, from where a scenic road wobbles slowly up to some charming villages. Continue uphill until the junction with the D3. If you turn left, you'll reach **Mont-Vert-les-Hauts**, approximately 5km to the west (and from then it's an easy drive downhill to the coast via Mont-Vert-les-Bas); if you turn right, you will cross **Manapany-les-Hauts** before reaching **Les Lianes** for St-Joseph.

Brochures and maps are available at the **Maison du Tourisme du Sud Sauvage** (Tourist Office; ☑ 0262 37 37 11; www.sud.reunion.fr; 15 Allée du Four à Chaux, Manapany-les-Bains; ⊘ 9.30am-noon & 1-5.30pm Mon-Fri, 10am-5pm Sat; ☏) in Manapany-les-Bains. It also offers free wi-fi access.

Beaches

Beach lovers should stop at **Plage de Grande Anse**, which is framed with basaltic cliffs and features a white-sand beach, a protected **tide pool** and picnic shelters (take the D30 that branches off the RN2 and winds down for about 2km to the beach). On weekends, the beach is often swamped with locals. Note that it's not safe to swim outside the tide pool due to unpredictable currents.

A few kilometres further east, there's another lovely swimming spot at Manapany-les-Bains. There's no proper beach here (the shore is rocky) but there's a protected **tide pool** where you can splash about. It gets crowded on weekends.

Activities

L'Écurie du Relais　　　　HORSE RIDING
(☑ 0692 00 42 98, 0262 56 78 67; www.ecurie-durelais.com; 75 Chemin Léopold Lebon, Manapany-les-Hauts; 1hr/day €20/115; ⊘ by reservation Tue-Sun) Seeing the area from the saddle of a horse is a fun way to experience the visual appeal of the region, even if you're not an experienced rider. This well-established equestrian centre has guided trips in the Hauts as well as day tours to Grande Anse. The two-hour ride (€36) takes you to rarely visited points in the Hauts with stunning views of Plaine-des-Grègues.

Sleeping & Eating

Despite some signs on the road, many places are not easy to find, but that's part of the charm. Check locations on the website (if there is one) or call ahead. Of course, some words in French for directions always helps.

Mont-Vert-les-Bas

La Cour Mont Vert　　　　B&B €€
(☑ 0262 88 38 95; www.courmontvert.com; 18ter Chemin Roland Garros; d incl breakfast €70; P ☏) Your heart will lift at the dreamy views over the coast; your body will rejuvenate with the Valatchy's healthy meals (€25); your soul will find peace in the four button-cute Creole bungalows set in rural grounds awash with mangoes and lychees. Simply arrive, absorb and enjoy. Rates drop to €65 if you stay at least two nights.

Soleil Couchant　　　　HOTEL €€
(☑ 0262 31 10 10; www.hotel-reunion-soleilcouchant.com; 2 Chemin de L'Araucaria; d €68-85; P ✳ ☏ ☲) This small complex features three pavilions shaped like cubic Tetris pieces, which sit on a grassy patch of land. The nine rooms are bright and tidy, but lack character. The real draws are the ocean vistas – straight from heaven – and the gleaming pool. Rooms 1 and 2 have the best views. There's an on-site restaurant, but food is only so-so.

Grande Anse

Vérémer　　　　B&B €€
(☑ 0262 31 65 10; www.chambre-gite-veremer.com; 40 Chemin Sylvain Vitry; d incl breakfast €50-60; ✳ ☏ ☲) Three cocoon-like rooms in two neat Creole buildings nestled in a well-tended tropical garden, with superlative views and a splendid pool that guests can use in the morning and in the afternoon. Aim for the slightly dearer Mer room, which opens onto the garden and the pool. There's also an inviting TV lounge. Prices vary according to season. Grande Anse beach is 3.5km away. Gay-friendly.

Palm Hotel & Spa　　　　LUXURY HOTEL €€€
(☑ 0262 56 30 30; www.palm.re; Grande Anse; d €220-330, ste €320-390, lodges €480-580, all incl breakfast; P ✳ @ ☏ ☲) If you're really looking to push the boat out in the Wild South,

Southern Réunion

10 km
5 miles

Anse des
Cascades

St-Benoît
(30km)

Bois Blanc

Pointe du
Tremblet

Le Tremblet

Takamaka

Pointe de
la Table

Puits Arabe

Ravine Ango

I N D I A N

O C E A N

See Eastern Réunion Map (p247)

Lava
Field

RN2

Viewing
Platform of the
2007 Lava Field

Les Grand Brûlé

Sentier Botanique
de Mare Longue

St-Philippe

Mare
Longue

Le Baril

Puits des
Anglais

Le Jardin
des Parfums
et des Épices

Formica Leo
(2218m)

Piton de la
Fournaise (2632m)

Enclos Fouqué

Puy Ramond
(2108m)

Route Forestière
de Basse Vallée

D37

Matouta

Basse Vallée

Cap Méchant

Jacques-
Payet

D34

See Piton de la Fournaise Map (p227)

Plaine des
Sables

Morne Langevin
(2380m)

Forêt de
la Crête

La
Crête

Vincendo

Belvédère
du Nez
de Bœuf

Roche-
Plate

Grand
Galet

Cascade de la
Grande Ravine

Rivière Langevin

Langevin

St-
Joseph

St-Benoît
(20km)

La Grande
Ferme

RN3

Grand
Coude

Petit
Serré

Jean
Petit

D33

Rivière des Remparts

Manapany-
les-Bains

Plaine-des-Cafres

Bois
Court

Bourg-
Murat

Le Vingt-
Quatrième

La Petite
Ferme

Petit
Tampon

Plaine-des-
Grègues

D32

Les Lianes

La Croisée

Bésaves

Petite
Île

Grand
Bassin

Gîte
Émile

Le Vingt-
Troisième

See The Cirques &
Les Hautes Plaines Map (p208)

Mont-Vert-
les-Hauts

Manapany-
les-Hauts

D3

Grand
Bois

Grande
Anse

Cilaos
(15km)

Le Dimitile
(1837m)

Bras de la Plaine

D3

Mont-Vert-
les-Bas

CIRQUE DE CILAOS

RN5

Bras de Cilaos

Entre-
Deux

Le Tampon

RN1

La Dérivante

La Fenêtre

Les
Makes

Rivière St-Étienne

La Saga
du Rhum

St-Pierre

Les Ancres &
Le Tombant
aux Ancres

RN2

Bellevue

Rivière
St-Louis

RN5

RN5

Pierrefonds
Airport

RN1

St-Louis
(20km)

St-Leu
(20km)

RN1

then to be honest there's only this five-star resort. Peacefully reposed on a promontory overlooking the cerulean ocean, it sports well-furnished units that are designed with finesse but, frustratingly, only the three lodges face out towards the sea. Bask lizard-like by the turquoise pools (yes, two pools), recharge the batteries in the luxurious spa or treat yourself to a sophisticated meal at one of the two restaurants (open to nonguests by reservation). From the hotel, a steep path leads down to Plage de Grande Anse.

★ **Les Badamiers** CREOLE €€
(☑ 0262 56 97 53; 22 Chemin Neuf; mains €9-12; ☺ lunch Mon-Sat, dinner Mon-Fri) Heartily recommended by locals, this family-run eatery in a private house spins tasty *carris* and ace homemade desserts (hmm, the *crème brûlée* flavoured with local vanilla...). Everything is fresh, the atmosphere is reliably jovial and the prices incredibly good value for the area. The icing on the cake: a terrace with stupendous sea views. It's about 100m away from the beginning of the road that descends to Grande Anse. No credit cards.

Le Vacoa CREOLE, CHINESE €€
(☑ 0262 56 95 17; 25 Route de Grande Anse; mains €13-23; ☺ lunch Sat-Thu, dinner Tue-Thu, Sat & Sun) Strategically positioned on the road to Plage de Grande Anse, this modest eatery offers a full menu of familiar favourites, including Creole and Chinese dishes. Bag a seat on the breezy terrace or take away and eat on the beach.

🛏 Petite Île

Chez Maoul B&B €€
(☑0262 56 82 26; 6 Rue du Piton; d incl breakfast €60; 🕸🛜🏊) The four wood-clad rooms in this homely B&B nestled in a jungle-like garden have a cabin-in-the-woods feel but offer a fine sense of originality, as testified by the cute Do-Myel room: walls are bedecked with newspapers (as in old Creole houses). The upstairs rooms get more light. The tiny pool is an added bonus. Creole-inspired *table d'hôte* dinners (€15) can be arranged if there's a minimum of four guests; the food is great and varied, with homegrown vegetables.

🛏 Manapany-les-Bains

L'Eau Forte APARTMENT €€
(☑ 0262 56 32 84; www.eau-forte.fr; 137bis Blvd de L'Océan; d €50; 🕸🛜) Bargain! Perfect for self-caterers, this fully equipped, spick-and-span villa boasts an ace location, on a velvety emerald hillside just above Manapany's tide pool, with sublime views of the rocky coastline. Don't fancy cooking? Find a restaurant a coin's toss down the road. There's no minimum stay, but one-week stays are preferred. Cash only. Book early.

Gandalf Safari Camp GUESTHOUSE €€
(☑ 0692 40 78 39, 0262 58 45 59; www. gandalfsafaricamp.de; 87 Blvd de l'Océan; s/d incl breakfast €50/60; 🕸@🛜) Christina and Claus, the German owners, have long lived in Africa – hence the name. Their B&B with an eco bent (it's solar heated and rainwater is recycled) features five rooms that are individually designed, but feel a tad compact due to the cubicle shower plonked in the corner. Two larger rooms (pompously called 'suites') should be added by the time you read this. Perks include a kitchen for guests' use, a TV lounge and a relaxing garden, plus 4WD tours can be organised (€50). Good English is spoken. Air-con is extra (€5). Rates drop by €5 if you stay two nights. It's a five-minute stroll from the tide pool. Cash only.

Chez Jo CREOLE €
(☑ 0262 31 48 83; 143 Blvd de L'Océan; mains €10-17; ☺ lunch Thu-Tue, dinner Fri & Sat) In this buzzy eatery overlooking the tide pool in Manapany-les-Bains, you're bound to find something on the menu that takes your fancy. Treat yourself to grilled tuna, salads or homemade desserts, or just pop in for an exquisite fruit juice (€3 to €6). Good sandwiches (€3 to €4.50) and takeaway meals, too.

St-Joseph

POP 13,000

The Wild South's hub, modernish St-Joseph (say 'St-Jo' if you want to sound local) won't leap to the top of your list of preferred destinations in Réunion but it offers useful services, including supermarkets and banks with ATMs. While it oozes the kind of sunny languor you'd associate with the tropics, the bustling shopping streets at peak hours impart the energy (and stress) of a city.

If you can, plan to be in St-Jo on a Friday morning, when the streets spill over with numerous stalls.

One of the best-kept secrets in the area is a secluded cove with a splendid black-sand **beach**, at the entrance of St-Jo (coming from St-Pierre). Drive past the first roundabout, then take the first right (towards 'Déchèterie'). Follow the road for about 300m until you reach a skate park. Leave your car here and walk for about five minutes down a path to the shore...enjoy!

For a bird's-eye view of St-Jo and the coast, you can walk up to **Piton Babet**, the knoll that lies between the main road and the ocean. It shouldn't take more than 10 minutes.

🛏 Sleeping & Eating

Accommodation options are thin on the ground in St-Jo; most visitors stay in B&Bs in the Hauts or in Manapany-les-Bains.

La Case APARTMENTS €
(📞0262 56 07 50; www.case.fr; 2 Rue Jean Bart; d without bathroom €37, studio €50; P❄🛜🀄) If it weren't located on the main road, this laid-back venture set in a well-groomed garden of colourful vegetation would feel like a little oasis. The three rooms in the main house are bright and airy with minimal decor and plain, functional furniture, toilets are shared. At the back of the compound, the five impeccably maintained studios open onto a rectangular pool. There isn't much atmosphere but it's a good base to explore the area. Breakfast costs €5. On the eastern edge of town.

L'Arpège Austral B&B €€
(📞0692 70 74 12, 0262 56 36 89; arpegeaustral. minisite.fr; 53 Rue des Prunes; s/d incl breakfast €50/55; 🛜) It's wonderful to be so near St-Joseph (2.5km), yet in such a serene spot. Sylvie, your hostess, offers two light-flooded rooms with sloping ceilings. For more privacy, the adjoining bungalow, sheathed with soothing ochres and decked out with a small private terrace, fits the bill. Book in for a *table d'hôte* meal (€20) and you may sample a low-calorie *carri* on the shady terrace. It's on the road to Grand Coude (follow the D33).

Au P'tit St Jo FRENCH, BURGERS €€
(📞0262 29 53 11; 229bis Rue Raphaël Babet; mains €10-24; ⊙lunch Tue-Fri, dinner Tue, Fri & Sat; 🛜) Great food served in welcoming surrounds at honest prices: the recipe for success sounds simple but few manage it as well as this friendly, pocket-sized eatery tucked in an alley near the post office. It made its name serving succulent meat dishes and burgers, but the chef also knows his way around a fish. It's all delightfully decadent, especially as portions are encyclopaedic in size. Adding to the fun is a bustling atmosphere and live music on weekends.

🛈 Getting There & Away

St-Joseph lies on Car Jaune's coastal bus route between St-Pierre and St-Benoît. In addition to the central bus station, buses stop in Petite Île, Vincendo and Manapany-les-Bains.

Around St-Joseph

Lose yourself in the Hauts! Starting from St-Joseph you can cherry-pick an itinerary in the hinterland that takes in drowsy hamlets where locals all know each other, green-velvet mountains cloaked in layers of wispy cloud, rolling sugar-cane fields, twisting roads and panoramas to make the heart beat faster.

Follow the picturesque D3 that cuts inland before swinging northwestwards to Manapany-Les-Hauts. You'll pass **Bésaves** and **Les Lianes**. You could also drive up to **Plaine-des-Grègues** (follow the D32, which branches off the D3 in La Croisée), the highest village of the area, which crouches in a bowl of mountains. This village is famed for its plantations of curcuma and vetiver, which are both used in perfumery. Learn more about the virtues (and fragrances) of these plants at the **Maison du Curcuma** (📞0262 37 54 66; www.maisonducurcuma.fr; 14 Chemin du Rond, Plaine-des-Grègues; ⊙9am-noon & 1.30-5pm) FREE. It also sells delicious homemade marmalades and jams as well as locally grown spices.

🛏 Sleeping

Chez Nathalie Hoareau B&B €€
(📞0262 37 61 92; www.giterunsud.com; 205 Rue Edmond Albius, Bésaves; s/d incl breakfast €50/55; P) Get back to basics at this welcoming village address in the gently rolling Hauts de St-Joseph. It features three plain rooms at the back and a manicured garden. Breakfast, which is served by the super-hospitable Nathalie, is a feast of delicious homemade jams. Sadly, no dinner is offered, so you'll have to drive down to St-Joseph (7km). Prices drop by €5 if you stay three nights or more. Cash only.

St-Joseph to Grand Coude

The timeless hamlet of Grand Coude, perched on a plateau at an altitude of

OFF THE BEATEN TRACK

RIVIÈRE DES REMPARTS

If you really want to get away from it all, check out the Rivière des Remparts, an easily overlooked splendour immediately north of St-Joseph. This valley – one of the wildest in the south – is accessible on foot (or by 4WD). The classic **hike** is along the river, up to the hamlet of **Roche-Plate**, about 18km to the north, and on to **Nez de Bœuf** on the road that leads to Piton de la Fournaise (p227). Allow about four hours to reach Roche-Plate from St-Joseph, and another four hours to Nez de Bœuf.

You can break up your journey in Roche-Plate. Both the **Gîte de la Rivière des Remparts** (☑ 0692 68 35 32; Roche-Plate; dm incl half board €40) and the **Gîte Le Mahavel** (☑ 0692 76 97 23, 0692 20 76 52; Roche-Plate; dm incl half board €40) feature well-scrubbed dorms. Both are closed during the rainy season – usually between mid-December and late April. Bookings are essential.

Note that 4WD transfers from St-Joseph can be arranged by the *gîtes* (€150 return, up to 10 people), but we don't really encourage it – the best way to get a feel for the valley is to explore it on foot.

1300m, boasts a marvellous setting, with the soaring Morne Langevin (2380m) as the backdrop. Here you'll be smitten by mellow tranquillity and laid-back lifestyle.

From St-Joseph, take the narrow D33, which passes through **Jean Petit** and twists its way across splendidly rugged scenery of looming peaks and deep gorges. Pull over for a picnic at **Petit Serré**, where a narrow ridge divides two valleys – the valley of the Rivière Langevin on your right and the valley of the Rivière des Remparts on your left. At one point the ridge is little wider than the road itself – you have the feeling of driving on a razor's edge!

At the end of the D33, about 15km north of St-Joseph, **Grand Coude** appears like a mirage.

◉ Sights

Le Labyrinthe En Champ Thé　　　GARDENS
(☑ 0692 60 18 88; Grand Coude; adult/child €5/4, guided tour €8/4; ◷9am-noon, 1-5pm Mon-Sat, 9am-5pm Sun) At the entrance of Grand Coude, Le Labyrinthe En Champ Thé is worth an hour or so for anyone interested in tropical flora, with an emphasis on tea. This botanical garden is the only place in Réunion where tea is cultivated. A 50g bag costs €10.

La Maison de Laurina　　　MUSEUM
(☑ 0692 68 78 72; www.lamaisondulaurina.fr; 24 Chemin de la Croizure, Grand Coude; admission €11; ◷by reservation) Caffeine-addicts should make a beeline for La Maison de Laurina, whose owner grows a top-quality variety of coffee, the Bourbon Pointu. Price is a bit steep but it includes a visit to the plantation and tastings of various homemade delicacies flavoured with coffee (biscuits, liquor, rum). It's in Grand Coude, in the same location as the B&B L'Eucalyptus.

🛏 Sleeping & Eating

L'Eucalyptus – Chez Marie-Claude Grondin　　　B&B €
(☑ 0262 56 39 48; 24 Chemin de la Croizure, Grand Coude; s/d incl breakfast €34/44, bungalow d €40, dinner €25) Absolute peace and quiet prevail at this unfussy B&B. Choose between the dinky all-wood bungalow or one of the two simple rooms in a white-and-yellow Creole building. Unwind in the generous garden, where coffee and geranium fill the air (ask for a cup of Bourbon Pointu coffee). Excellent Creole meals are served at dinner – you'll be treated to homemade desserts and veggies from the garden.

Au Lapin d'Or　　　B&B €€
(☑ 0692 70 09 18, 0262 56 66 48; rolande.sadehe@hotmail.fr; 55bis Chemin Concession, Jean Petit; s/d incl breakfast €57/62, dinner €25) Do you like rabbit? We dare ask because the owners of this pert little B&B (which translates as 'Golden Rabbit') in Jean Petit raise rabbits, meaning you'll enjoy them prepared Creole-style at dinner. The three rooms are outfitted with cheerful pastels and super-clean bathrooms that, unfortunately, don't have proper doors, just curtains. Our favourite thing about Au Lapin d'Or is the warm welcome and the genuine smiles. Don't miss out on their homemade

rhum tisane (aromatic rum), best enjoyed under a gazebo in the garden.

La Plantation   B&B €€
(☑ 0693 92 53 01, 0262 56 08 86; www.laplanta-tion.net; 124 Route de Jean Petit, Jean Petit; d €90-100, ste €125, incl breakfast; P ❄ 🛜 🏊) This B&B nestled amid sugar-cane fields boasts a small pool, an outdoor Jacuzzi and lush tropical garden with staggering views of the coast. There are three rooms and one larger suite, all featuring handsomely designed bathrooms. Downsides: only one room comes with sea views, and *table d'hôte* meals (dinner €28) are available only on Monday, Wednesday and Friday. No credit cards. On the road to Grand Coude, about 5km from St-Joseph.

St-Joseph to St-Philippe

The coastline between St-Joseph and St-Philippe is definitely alluring: a string of rocky coves and dramatic cliffs pounded by crashing waves and backed by steep hills clad with dense forests and undulating sugar-cane fields, with a few black-sand beaches thrown in for good measure.

Inland, it's no less spectacular. Abandon your map and follow the sinuous *départementales* (secondary roads) that wiggle up to the Hauts and creep through beguiling settlements, which warrant scenic drives and boast killer views over the ocean and plunging canyons.

Rivière Langevin

About 4km east of St-Joseph, you'll reach the coastal town of **Langevin**. From the coast, the Rivière Langevin valley slithers into the mountains. A narrow road follows the wide stony bed of the river and leads to **Cascade de la Grande Ravine**, an impressive waterfall about 9km from the junction with the coastal road. If you need to cool off, there are plenty of natural pools along the river where you can dunk yourself. Our favourites include **Trou Noir** (it's signposted) and a pool that lies about 300m before the Cascade de la Grande Ravine (you can't miss it). Come prepared: this valley is extremely popular with picnicking families on Sunday.

🏃 Activities

Aquasens   ADVENTURE SPORTS
(☑ 0692 20 09 03; www.aquasens.re; outings with equipment & instructor €35-50; ☺ by reservation)

This professional adventure centre runs fantastic guided *randonnées aquatiques* (a mix of walking, sliding, swimming and some serious jumping or plunging down water-polished chutes into natural pools) along the river. They can be undertaken by participants of all ages provided they can swim. Outings last from one hour to four or five hours, depending on the circuit. Expect lots of slippery dips, exhilarating water jumps, short swims and fun scrambles in a picturesque setting – it's immensely fun!

🍴 Eating

If you haven't brought a picnic, there's a bevy of cheap and cheerful eateries along the river at the entrance to the valley. They're pretty much of a muchness and serve up Creole classics, which you can eat inside or take away.

Le Benjoin   CREOLE, CHINESE €
(☑ 0262 56 23 90; Route de la Passerelle; mains €13-20, menu €12; ☺ lunch Sat-Thu) One of a number of popular eateries along the river, this snug eatery has built a strong local reputation on the back of its copious Creole and Chinese classics. It's also famed for its *thé dansant* (tea dance) on Sunday (from 9am) – a great way to immerse yourself in local culture. There's a takeaway counter, too.

Vincendo & Les Hauts

In Vincendo, few visitors get wind of the black-sand **beach** fringed by *vacoa* trees a few kilometres south of the RN2. There are some dangerous currents at certain times of the year, so ask around before diving in. It's a great place for a picnic.

Back in the village, follow the D34 that goes uphill to the north and takes you to the hamlet of **La Crête**. From there, the D37 leads due east to another peaceful settlement, **Jacques-Payet**, before zigzagging downhill to the junction with the coastal road.

🛏 Sleeping & Eating

La Table des Randonneurs   GÎTE €
(☑ 0692 61 73 47; 17 Chemin des Barbadines, Jacques-Payet; dm/d incl breakfast €20/40, bungalow per person without breakfast €20, dinner €22-25) Way up in the hills, 'The Hikers' Table' is a safe bet, with two doubles, one quad and one six-bed room in a modern house. They're in no danger of appearing in *House Beautiful,* but everything is in immaculate

shape and functional. There are also two self-contained bungalows that can sleep four people. The menu features local delicacies like smoked duck with *vacoa*. It's about 7km northeast of Vincendo (follow the D37).

Ferme-Auberge Desprairies
B&B €

(☑0692 64 61 70, 0262 37 20 27; www.ferme-auberge-desprairies.com; 44 Route de Matouta, Matouta; d incl breakfast €40, dinner €22; ☎) One of the best things about this peaceful inn is the road to it, which travels through sugarcane fields despite being only a couple of kilometres from the coast. There are a few signs of wear and tear in the six rooms but they're kept tidy and in this location for this price, you won't hear anyone complaining. The owners also prepare delicious home-cooked meals. Follow the D37 to the east to get here.

★Rougail Mangue
GUESTHOUSE €€

(☑0262 31 55 09; www.rougailmangue.com; 12 Rue Marcel Pagnol, Vincendo; s/d/tr/q €39/49/63/76, bungalow €63; ☞⊞☎☎) You'd never guess it from the road but this 'boutique guesthouse' is as welcoming as an old friend's hug thanks to its Italian owner, Cosimo. The ground floor is occupied by a smart lounge area, one six-bed room, two squeaky-clean quads and a cheery double opening onto a well-tended garden. Air-con is extra (€10). For a higher degree of privacy, book the cute-as-can-be bungalow, with stupendous sea views. The *coup de grâce* is the glorious pool, with the ocean as a backdrop (look at the picture on the website – no Photoshopping), and the outdoor Jacuzzi (€5). Add €3 for breakfast (or €15 for a gargantuan brunch), best enjoyed alfresco under a gazebo. There's also a kitchen. It's on the main road, between Langevin and Vincendo.

La Médina du Sud
APARTMENTS €€

(☑0262 37 32 51; 23 Chemin de la Marine, Vincendo; d for 2 nights €130; ☞⊞☎) There's nothing Moorish in this modern building by the turn-off for the beach, except the owner's origins. The six flats are characterless but fully equipped, well proportioned and perfectly serviceable, with the added bonus of a pool. The owner also runs a restaurant next door.

Les Grands Monts
B&B €€€

(☑0692 17 53 42, 0262 23 60 16; 2a Impasse Sabine; d incl breakfast €110; ☞⊞☎☎) Looking for a night at some place extra special? Make a beeline for this lovely *maison d'hôte* in

a historic building made of stones. It shelters three spacious, cocoon-like rooms that ingeniously blend volcanic stones and hardwoods. However, the open bathrooms in two rooms may not be to everyone's taste. The pool in the garden is a delight. It's in a cul-de-sac about 300m north of the RN2.

Le Papangue
CREOLE, FRENCH €€

(☑0262 31 48 92; rratane@gmail.com; 2 Impasse des Vacoas, Vincendo; mains €14-23; ☺lunch Mon & Wed-Sun, dinner Thu-Sat) Housed in a lovely family villa just back from the main road, this is a charming restaurant specialising in *métro* fare (the chef has worked in France) and authentic island cuisine. Dishes such as the *poulet pays rôti façon du chef* (roasted chicken flavoured with island spices) and *andouillette* (chitterlings) will please every palate.

Basse-Vallée & Cap Méchant

The Basse-Vallée area is known for its production of baskets, bags (called *bertels*), hats and other items from *vacoa* fronds. It's also famous for its rugged coastline; head to **Cap Méchant** (it's signposted), one of the eeriest landscapes in the Wild South, with huge lava fields, windswept black cliffs, rows of *vacoa* trees and the mandatory picnic shelters. There's an excellent coastal path along the sea cliffs (bring sturdy shoes).

🛏 Sleeping & Eating

Gîte de Montagne de Basse Vallée
GÎTE €

(☑0262 37 36 25; Route Forestière, Basse-Vallée; dm €16-18, dinner €18) This simple *gîte de montagne* is about 8km above the village of Basse Vallée, along the Route Forestière de Basse Vallée. It comprises six- to eight-bed dorms. Bookings must be made through the Centrale de Réservation – Île de la Réunion (p37) or any tourist office on the island, but if you turn up without a reservation and there's space, the caretaker will probably let you in.

Ferme-Auberge Le Rond de Basse Vallée
INN €

(☑0692 69 65 51; Route Forestière, Basse-Vallée; d incl breakfast €40, dinner €22; ☞) Another great place to commune with nature, further up the Route Forestière. There are four rooms with spick-and-span bathrooms in a Creole-style building in harmony with the environment. The restaurant is across the road and

GÎTE DE THÉOPHANE ET YOLAINE

For a slice of authentic local life, make a beeline for **Gîte de Théophane et Yolaine** (☑0262 37 13 14, 0692 87 25 43; Route Forestière, Basse-Vallée; dm with half board €45). This rural paradise, lost in the middle of the forest, is accessible on foot (about 20 minutes) via a scenic *sentier forestier* (forest dirt track) or by 4WD only from the Route Forestière (signed at the junction, about 5.5km above the village of Basse-Vallée). Digs are in six-bed dorms, each with its own bathroom. At dinner the owners will treat you with the freshest island ingredients. It can't get more Wild South than this. Book early.

features regional dishes with authentic flavours, including – you guessed it – *vacoa*.

Coco Vanille   B&B €€
(☑0692 53 92 72, 0262 93 18 76; 68 Rue Labourdonnais, Basse-Vallée; d incl breakfast €60, dinner €15; 🛜🏊) This laid-back B&B is a good deal with cool rooms, small bathrooms, no decor to speak of, and a small breakfast terrace. The swimming pool in the tropical garden is a great addition when it's stifling hot. It's within walking distance of Cap Méchant.

L'Étoile de Mer   CHINESE, CREOLE €€
(☑0262 37 04 60; Cap Méchant; mains €10-18; ⏱lunch) The food here is a crowd-pleasing mix of Chinese dishes, Creole staples and *métro* classics.

Le Cap Méchant   CHINESE, CREOLE €€
(☑0692 85 39 28; Cap Méchant; mains €11-18; ⏱lunch Tue-Sun) Le Cap Méchant is mobbed at weekends but almost deserted on weekdays. It serves great *carris*, chop sueys and *porc au palmiste* (pork with palm hearts).

Le Pinpin   CHINESE, CREOLE €€
(☑0262 37 04 19; Cap Méchant; mains €12-17; ⏱lunch Thu-Tue) There's sure to be a dish on the extensive menu that suits your palate. Very popular with weekending families.

Le Baril

Le Baril is the last settlement before St-Philippe. The main attraction here is the **Puits des Anglais** (the Wells of the British), a splendid saltwater pool that has been constructed in the basaltic rock. It's mobbed at weekends but you'll have the whole place to yourself during the week.

🛏 Sleeping & Eating

Le Pinpin d'Amour   B&B €€
(☑0262 37 14 86; www.pinpindamour.com; 56 Chemin Paul Hoareau, Le Baril; d incl breakfast €60, dinner €29; 🅟) Spending a night at this original *chambre d'hôte* makes a good story to tell the folks back home. Your hosts have a passion for *vacoa* and *pinpin* (the palm's edible artichoke-like fruit), meaning you'll be guaranteed to taste them at dinner (and sometimes at breakfast), prepared in all their forms. Accommodation-wise, the six appealing, if a bit itty-bitty and sombre, rooms sport pastel-coloured walls and honey-boarded floors. It's amid the sugar-cane fields above Le Baril, about 2km from the coastal road. Alas, no sea views from the rooms. There's a 10% discount for stays of two nights and more.

★**Table Paysanne Chez Fiarda**   CREOLE €€
(☑0692 69 03 48; 21 Chemin Ceinture, Le Baril; menu €27; ⏱lunch by reservation Tue-Sun) Plenty of smiles from the owners, recipes plucked straight out of grandma's cookbook, a serene setting in the Hauts and lovely views from the terrace – if you're after an authentic Creole experience, this place is hard to beat. Here you can eat local specialities that are hard to find elsewhere, such as chicken with palm hearts. Downside: it's not a walk-in restaurant but a private home that's open by reservation only. It's signposted from the main road.

Le Puits des Anglais   CREOLE, CHINESE €€
(☑0692 68 30 33; Le Puits des Anglais, Le Baril; mains €8-14; ⏱9.30am-5pm Sat-Thu) This unfussy little eatery could hardly be better situated; it overlooks the saltwater pool at Puits des Anglais. The menu concentrates on simply prepared Creole dishes as well as appetising Chinese specialities and sandwiches (from €2.50). Also does take away.

St-Philippe

POP 5000

Vegetarians will reach Shangri-la in St-Philippe, the self-proclaimed capital of *vacoa*. No joke – no less than 5000 visitors turn

RÉUNION ST-PHILIPPE

RÉUNION FOR CRAZIES

If you want to work off any extra pounds gained in Réunion's fine restaurants, here's the solution: take part in the Grand Raid, one of the world's most challenging cross-country races. It's held every October or November. The route roughly follows the path of the GR® R2 hiking trail, which traverses the island from St-Denis to Mare Longue, near St-Philippe, taking in parts of the Mafate and Cilaos Cirques, the Plaine-des-Cafres and the lunar landscape around Piton de la Fournaise.

Covering some 150km, the Grand Raid would be a challenging race over level ground, but runners also have to negotiate a total of some 9000m of altitude change, hence the race is nicknamed La Diagonale des Fous (the 'Cross-Country for Crazies')! The pack leaders can complete this agonising run in 22 hours or less, but contestants are allowed up to 64 hours to finish.

Too difficult for you? Try the 'easier' Trail de Bourbon, which starts from Cilaos and covers about 90km, or the Mascareignes, which starts from Hell-Bourg and covers 61km.

For more information, contact the Association **Le Grand Raid** (www.grandraid-reunion.com).

---

up to join St-Philippois townsfolk for the 10-day **Fête du Vacoa** in August.

The only town of consequence in the Wild South (along with St-Joseph), St-Philippe has a wonderfully down-to-earth, unfussy ambience. Although this friendly little town is devoid of overwhelming sights, it has a slew of (good) surprises up its sleeve and is optimally placed for explorations of the coast and forays into the Hauts. Oh, and St-Philippe lies in the shadow of Piton de la Fournaise.

◉ Sights

Le Jardin des Parfums et des Épices   GARDENS
(☑ 0692 66 09 01; http://jardin.ep.fontaine.pag-esperso-orange.fr; 7 Chemin Forestier; adult/child €6.10/3.05; ☉ tours 10.30am & 2.30pm) Inland between Le Baril and St-Philippe, don't miss the 3-hectare garden, Le Jardin des Parfums et des Épices. It contains over 1500 species in a natural setting in the Mare Longue forest, 3km west of St-Philippe. Knowledgeable and enthusiastic guides present the island's history, economy and culture through the plants; tours are in French.

Sentier Botanique de Mare Longue GARDENS
A few kilometres further up from Le Jardin des Parfums et des Épices is the Sentier Botanique de Mare Longue. This pristine forest has an end-of-the-world feeling that will appeal to those in search of hush. From the car park you can tackle one of the three interpretative trails in the primary forest.

Eco-Musée de St-Philippe – Au Bon Roi Louis   MUSEUM
(☑ 0262 37 12 98; 1 Rue de la Marine; adult/child €5/2; ☉ 9am-noon & 2-4.30pm Mon-Sat) The small Eco-Musée de St-Philippe – Au Bon Roi Louis, a few doors down from St-Philippe's town hall, makes for a perfect introduction to the area's history and culture. The little Creole house is stuffed with an eclectic assortment of antiques and agricultural equipment.

Fishing Harbour   HARBOUR
With its handful of colourful fishing boats, the teensy fishing harbour is worth a peek.

🛏 Sleeping & Eating

Le Palmier   B&B €€
(☑ 0692 02 85 71, 0262 37 04 11; nicolelepalmier@yahoo.fr; 8 Rue de la Pompe; d incl breakfast €52; ❄️🛜♨️) Lacking excitement, maybe, but this friendly B&B down a little lane at the east end of St-Philippe is a safe bet. Rooms are neat, with immaculate tiles, prim bathrooms and colourful bedspreads for a dash of panache. Avoid the larger one at the back, which has obstructed views. Guests can use the pool in front of the owners' house if they stay at least two nights – a good incentive, indeed.

Au Domaine du Vacoa   B&B €€
(☑ 0692 64 89 89, 0262 37 03 12; www.domainedu-vacoa.fr; 12 Chemin Vacoa; d incl breakfast €65-70; 🅿️❄️🛜♨️) This B&B set in a pert little *case créole* features two spacious rooms enhanced with splashes of colour, back-friendly

mattresses, crisply dressed beds and spotless bathrooms. Au Domaine du Vacoa's ultimate trump card, though, is its infinity pool – which was built in 2013 – with great sea views. At dinner (€26), warm your insides with duck, *vacoa* and other vegetables from the garden – all organic, of course.

La Bicyclette Gourmande   CHINESE, CREOLE **€€**
(✆ 0693 93 71 93; 43 Rue Leconte de Lisle; mains €12.50-18; ⊙ lunch Wed-Mon, dinner Fri-Sun) Opposite the Écomusée de St-Philippe, this laid-back eatery set in a small Creole house has an agreeable terrace overlooking the main road. The eclectic menu covers enough territory to please most palates, from wood-fired pizzas (available at dinner on Friday, Saturday and Sunday) and Creole classics to mainstream Chinese and *métro* dishes. Unfortunately, it's on a busy thoroughfare and isn't very peaceful.

Marmite du Pêcheur   SEAFOOD **€€**
(✆ 0262 37 01 01; 18a Ravine Ango; mains €13-30, Sunday buffet €25; ⊙ lunch Thu-Tue) Can't stomach one more morsel of *carri poulet*? Then opt for this eatery where cuisine is predominantly fishy – crab, shrimps, fish and mussels, climaxing with a gargantuan *marmite du pêcheur* (€30), a kind of seafood stew. Downside: the dining room doesn't register even a blip on the charm radar. It's just off the main road, east of St-Philippe.

Le Grand Brûlé

The crowning glory of the Wild South, the arid, eerie landscape of Le Grand Brûlé is a 6km-wide volcanic plain formed by the main lava flow from the volcano. This is where the action goes when the volcano is erupting. The steep slopes above, known as Les Grandes Pentes, have funnelled lava down to the coast for thousands of years.

◉ Sights

Leaving St-Philippe to the east, you'll first come across **Puits Arabe** (Wells of the Arabs), a manmade hole in the basaltic rock. It's a popular picnic site, with shelters scattered amid rows of *vacoa* trees.

In 1986, the lava unusually flowed south of Le Grand Brûlé to reach the sea at **Pointe de la Table**, a few hundred metres north of Puits Arabe. Part of the magmatic flow also reached **Pointe du Tremblet**, to the north. This eruption added over 30 hectares to the island's area, and more than 450 people had to be evacuated and several homes were lost. An interpretative trail has been set up at Pointe de la Table and makes for a lovely hike on the basaltic cliffs pounded by the ocean. Previous lava flows have been colonised by various kinds of plants, including ferns and shrubs.

In April 2007, in one of the most violent eruptions ever recorded, another impressive lava flow was formed, about 2km north of Pointe du Tremblet. The road was cut off for several months. It's a primal experience to drive through the barren moonscape that is this huge expanse of solidified, pure black lava field. Six years after the eruption, some patches were still warm and belched off steam when it rained. It's forbidden to walk across the lava flow, but a **viewing platform** has been built just off the RN2.

⌦ Sleeping & Eating

A number of so-called 'restaurants' (in fact, private homes turned into casual eateries)

DON'T MISS

EXPLORING LAVA TUBES

Visitors to Réunion don't have to confine themselves to exploring the surface of its volcanic formations – at Le Grand Brûlé, it's possible to go caving inside volcanic tubes (elongated tunnels formed by the cooling and rapid hardening of lava) and walk *under* the volcano. A number of operators organise guided excursions through these lava tubes. The tunnels are generally quite tall (and there are some openings in the ceilings, which allows for superb plays of light), but be prepared to stoop or squeeze at times. Another plus is that it's suitable to all levels of difficulties – bring the kids! All you need is good shoes; torches and helmets are provided.

Prices vary between €45 and €75 for a half-day outing, depending on the length of the circuit. A few reputable operators include **Envergure Réunion** (✆ 0693 43 23 52; www.canyon-reunion.re; ⊙ by reservation), **Rougail Rando** (✆ 0692 92 14 34), **Julien Dez** (✆ 0692 11 50 13; http://juliendez.reunion.fr) and Canyon Ric a Ric (p213).

have recently sprung up along the RN2 between St-Philippe and Le Grand Brûlé.

★ Le Crabe Sous la Varangue   B&B €€
(📞0692 92 13 56, 0262 92 13 56; lacazboyer@la poste.net; 1 RN2, Le Tremblet; d incl breakfast €65-70; P@) This welcoming B&B sits in isolated splendour on the main road between St-Philippe and Le Grand Brûlé. It exudes quiet sophistication; the two individually decorated rooms in the main house have pretty painted concrete floors and colourful walls, while the third one occupies a cosy Creole house endowed with polished parquet floors. Breakfast and dinner (from €25) are served on the sweet terrace in the warmer months. The owner runs excursions to the lava tubes in Le Grand Brûlé.

Chez Moustache   CREOLE €
(📞0692 40 18 03, 0692 33 27 03; 9 RN2, Le Tremblet; mains €9-15; ⊙lunch) A welcoming family-run outfit with tables in a picturesque Creole house complete with a courtyard garden, Chez Moustache serves authentic Creole specialities at honest prices. The food is grounded in island tradition, as testified by the wood-fired oven. The menu changes nightly, and includes only four or five mains, but brevity guarantees freshness. Take away available (€5 to €6) except Sunday. It's about 4km south of the 2007 lava flow.

Le Vieux Port   CREOLE, SEAFOOD €€
(📞0692 15 79 31; RN2, Le Tremblet; mains €11-20; ⊙lunch) A fine specimen of a restaurant, Le Vieux Port is ideally situated in a tropical garden about 500m south of the 2007 lava flow. It is strictly local cuisine – albeit of a refreshingly creative nature. Locals rave about the *rougail boucané* (smoked pork ribs prepared Creole-style) and the delicious palm-heart salad. It also features a repertoire of fish dishes that you won't find elsewhere, such as maccabit (a kind of grouper). Reservations are advised on weekends. It also does take away. Cash only.

THE EAST

The east coast is everything the west coast is not: low-key, unpretentious and luxuriant (yes, it *does* get much more rain). While this coast lacks the beaches of the west, the region makes up for it with spectacular waterfalls, lush tropical vegetation and fantastic picnic spots. The main produce of the area

is sugar cane, but the region is also known for its vanilla plantations and fruit orchards, including lychees.

This coastal stretch is also considered to be 'other', partially as it's the bastion of Tamil culture in Réunion. Here you'll find a distinctive atmosphere, with numerous temples and colourful religious festivals. For visitors it's an opportunity to discover a Réunion you never imagined.

Tourism in this area remains on a humble scale, with no star attractions. However, it's worth taking a few days to explore the quiet recesses of this less-visited part of the island where you can experience Réunion from a different perspective.

Ste-Suzanne & Around

POP 20,000

The seaside town of Ste-Suzanne is usually glimpsed in passing by most tourists on the route down the coast, which is a shame because there are charming pockets in the area that beg discovery, including the splendid Rivière Ste-Suzanne, which is both a playground for outdoorsy types and a hot spot for sunbathers and picnickers.

◉ Sights

Lighthouse   LIGHTHOUSE
Next to the tourist office, the small lighthouse – the only one on the island – is worth a gander. It was built in 1845. It's no longer in operation.

Chapelle Front de Mer   TEMPLE
Notable religious buildings in Ste-Suzanne include the Chapelle Front de Mer, an ornate Tamil temple built on a pebbly beach north of town (it's unsigned).

Domaine du Grand Hazier   HISTORIC SITE
(📞0692 68 50 19, 0262 52 32 81; www.domainedu grandhazier.re; Allée Chassagne, Le Grand Hazier; tours €5; ⊙daily by reservation) Garden fans and architecture buffs will especially enjoy a visit to the classic Domaine du Grand Hazier, a superb 18th-century sugar-planter's residence 3km southwest of Ste-Suzanne. It's an official French historical monument with a 2-hectare garden planted with a variety of tropical flowers and fruit trees.

La Vanilleraie   VANILLA
(📞0262 23 07 26; www.lavanilleraie.com; Allé Chassagne, Domaine du Grand Hazier; tours adult/ child €5/3; ⊙9am-noon & 1.30-5pm Mon-Sat) At

Eastern Réunion

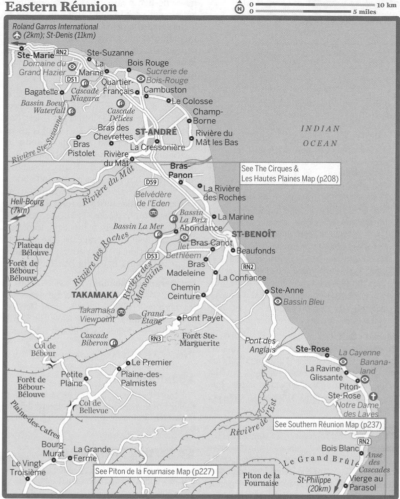

Domaine du Grand Hazier you'll also find La Vanilleraie, where you can see vanilla preparation and drying processes and also purchase vanilla pods. The manager speaks English.

Bassin Boeuf   WATERFALL

If you need to cool off, the Bassin Boeuf waterfall beckons. From Ste-Suzanne, follow the D51 in the direction of Bagatelle for about 7km until you see the signpost 'Bassin Boeuf'. Leave your car at the small parking area and walk for a few minutes down a dirt road to the Rivière Ste-Suzanne. It presents

a series of enticing natural pools fringed with stone slabs, ideal for picnicking and sunbathing. To get to the waterfall, cross the river and follow the path on the right for about five minutes.

Cascade Niagara   WATERFALL

Just beyond the church towards the southern end of town is a road signposted inland to Cascade Niagara, a 30m waterfall which is also on the Rivière Ste-Suzanne. At the end of the road, about 2km further on, you wind up at the waterfall. On weekends it's a popular picnic site.

TAMIL FESTIVALS

If you happen to be around Ste-Suzanne and St-André at certain periods of the year, you'll discover a very exotic side of the island, with lots of colourful festivals organised by the Tamil community. If you're about, be sure to join in the heady hype of these local festivals. In January, don't miss **Tamil fire-walking** ceremonies, when participants enter a meditative state and then walk over red-hot embers as a sign of devotion to various deities. Thousands of goats are slaughtered as offerings and are distributed among the participants. Another must-see is the **Cavadee festival**, which usually takes place in January or February. In October or November, make a beeline for **Divali** (aka Dipavali), the Festival of Light. Dancers and decorated floats parade through the town centre. Visitors are welcome. Contact the tourist office in St-André for specific dates.

Cascade Délices WATERFALL
(Quartier-Français) In the Quartier-Français district, Cascade Délices is another easily accessed waterfall. It's only 4m high, but the jungle-like setting will appeal to nature lovers, and you can dunk yourself in the cool water.

Activities

Niagara Vertical CLIMBING
(✔ 0692 48 55 54; www.niagara-vertical.net; adult/ couple €25/40; ☺ Wed, Sat & Sun school term, daily school holidays) If you want to see Cascade Niagara from a different perspective, this outfit has set up three via ferrata circuits of varying degrees of difficulty.

Alpanes CANYONING
(✔ 0692 77 75 30; www.alpanes.com; half-day €45; ☺ by reservation) The top spot for canyoning in the east is the spectacular Rivière Ste-Suzanne. Expect jumps, leaps in natural pools and scrambling over rocks.

Sleeping & Eating

Le Pharest GUESTHOUSE €€
(✔ 0262 98 91 10; www.pharest-reunion.com; 22 Rue Blanchet; s €32-58, d €52-86, incl breakfast; ✳ ⬤ ⬤) We're suckers for the relaxing atmosphere that prevails in this oasis of calm, near the lighthouse. The five wooden bungalows are kept in good nick and are set in a well-tended tropical garden. Added pluses include a swimming pool and a restaurant (*menus* €15-36). The kitchen features salads made with local produce and locally caught fish. Air-con is extra (€4).

La Cuisine de Clemencia B&B €€
(✔ 0692 80 01 47, 0262 47 52 78; lacuisinede clemencia@orange.fr; 18 Chemin des Galets, Bras Pistolet; d incl breakfast €75) This B&B is a winner, not least for the marvellous sense of peacefulness that wraps the property, in a secluded hamlet up in the Hauts. The stand-alone bungalow feels like a cosy doll's house and proffers ample coastal views. At the end of the day, make sure you treat yourself to a copious *table d'hôte* (€25); the delicious Creole specialities are made using local produce. From Quartier-Français, take the D46 in the direction of Deux Rives, then follow Route des Hauts, Église du Père Laval.

Les Berges du Bocage CREOLE, CHINESE €€
(✔ 0262 94 43 17; 1 Chemin du Bocage; mains €10-20, lunch buffet €12; ☺ lunch & dinner Mon-Sat) The lunch buffet, with five different Creole and Chinese dishes, is brilliant value, and the location, in a verdant property by the river, is ace. It's at the southern end of town.

ⓘ Information

The **tourist office** (✔ 0262 52 13 54; www.nord. reunion.fr; Rue du Phare; ☺ 9am-noon & 2-5pm) is near the lighthouse. *Gîtes de montagne* can be booked here.

ⓘ Getting There & Away

Ste-Suzanne is served by Car Jaune (p268) bus routes F and G running between St-Denis and St-Benoît.

St-André & Around

POP 44,000

St-André is the epicentre of Tamil culture in Réunion, and you'll see more women draped in vividly coloured saris than Zoreilles wearing designer glasses and trendy shirts. Busy streets transport you to a city somewhere in India with curry houses, sari shops and bric-a-brac traders. You'll definitely feel closer to Bombay than Paris.

The mainly Tamil population in the area is descended from indentured labourers who were brought from India to work in the sugar-cane fields and factories after slavery was abolished in 1848.

◎ Sights

St André's Indian atmosphere is most apparent in the Hindu temples dotted around the town. The most imposing are the **Temple of Colosse** (Chemin Champ-Borne) and **Temple du Petit Bazar** (Ave de l'Île de France). It's not possible to visit the interior, but guided tours can be arranged; contact the tourist office.

Maison Martin Valliamé HISTORIC BUILDING
(1590 Chemin du Centre; guided tours €3; ☺9am-12.30pm & 1.30-5pm Mon-Fri) Worth a look is Maison Martin Valliamé, a handsome colonial villa dating from 1925, northeast of the centre. Guided tours in French are available from 10am to 4pm on the hour.

Plantation de Vanille Roulof VANILLA PLANTATION
(☑0262 46 01 15; www.lavanilledelareunion.com; 470 Chemin Deschanets; guided tours €3; ☺9am-4pm Mon-Sat) If you're after Réunion's Vanille Bourbon, head to Plantation de Vanille Roulof, a small family-run operation where you can buy vanilla pods at reasonable prices (€11 for 25g). You can also find out about the technique of 'marrying' the vanilla, a delicate operation in which the flowers are fertilised by hand.

Sucrerie de Bois-Rouge DISTILLERY
(☑0262 58 59 74; www.bois-rouge.fr; 2 Chemin du Bois Rouge; guided tour adult/child €10/5, distillery €5/2.50; ☺by reservation Mon-Sat) The Sucrerie de Bois-Rouge is on the coast 3km north of St-André. During the cane harvest (July to December) visitors are shown around the huge, high-tech plant, following the process from the delivery of the cut cane to the final glittering crystals. The two-hour tour includes the neighbouring distillery, where the by-products (cane juice and molasses) are made into rum. From January to June, you can only visit the distillery. Children under seven years aren't allowed into the refinery. There's a shop, **Tafia et Galabé** (www.distilleriesavanna.com; 2 Chemin du Bois Rouge; ☺9am-6pm Mon-Sat), where you can sip (and buy) the good stuff.

★★ Festivals & Events

Cavadee RELIGIOUS
Tamil procession held in February.

Divali RELIGIOUS
(Dipavali) Tamil festival of light in late October or early November; celebrations take place in St-André and other locations.

⌁ Sleeping

Chez Véronique Savriama B&B €€
(☑0692 60 23 91, 0262 46 69 84; auberge-savriama@wanadoo.fr; 1084 Chemin Quatre-Vingt, Rivière du Mât les Bas; d incl breakfast €50; Ⓟ✳︎�🛜) This place is efficiently run but the four upstairs rooms are a tad sombre and smallish, though they come with air-con and have their own entrance. Best asset are the tasty *table d'hôte* meals, with an Indian emphasis. Pity about the very ordinary dining room. Prices drop to €45 for longer stays. It's in the district of Rivière du Mât les Bas on the coast east of St-André.

Le Domaine des Oiseaux B&B €€
(☑0692 52 25 20, 0262 92 50 22; 300 Chemin Grand Canal, Champ-Borne; d incl breakfast €75; Ⓟ✳︎🏊) This B&B occupying a massive villa not far from the seafront was undergoing major renovation works at the time of writing. It should feature nine rooms with all mod-cons, a pool and a Jacuzzi. You can expect a warm welcome from the Agenors, who are *bons viveurs* (fun loving).

✖ Eating

Ti Fred CREOLE €
(☑0692 62 57 76; 561 Chemin Colosse; mains €5-9; ☺lunch & dinner Mon-Sat) No culinary acrobatics in this few-frills haunt near the Temple of Colosse, just keep-the-faith Creole staples and pizzas at puny prices. Eat in or take away.

Le Beau Rivage CHINESE €€
(☑0262 46 08 66; Chemin Champ-Borne; mains €10-40; ☺lunch Tue-Sun, dinner Tue, Wed, Fri & Sat) True to its name ('the beautiful shore'), Le Beau Rivage boasts a fantastic location – it's on the seafront, beside the church ruins in Champ-Borne (ask for a table near the windows). The cuisine is predominantly Chinese.

ⓘ Information

You'll find banks with ATMs in the centre. The **tourist office** (☑0262 46 16 16; 1590 Chemin du Centre, Maison Martin Valliamé; ☺9am-12.30pm & 1.30-5pm Mon-Fri; 🛜) is housed in Maison Valliamé.

BELVÉDÈRE DE L'EDEN

A fabulous place to chill out is the aptly named Belvédère de l'Eden, in upcountry Bras-Panon. From Bras-Panon, take the road to St-André, then turn left onto the D59 (in the direction of Vincendo, Bellevue) for about 9km (follow the signs) until you reach a car park. From there, follow the meandering trail signed L'Eden. After about 20 minutes, you'll discover a wonderfully secluded picnic spot locals wish you hadn't. The views of the coast are incomparable.

❶ Getting There & Away

Buses from St-Denis to St-Benoît pass through St-André. If you're travelling to Salazie by bus, you will have to change here; there are seven buses daily in each direction (three on Sunday). From Salazie there are connections to Hell-Bourg.

Bras-Panon

POP 9800

Bras-Panon is Réunion's vanilla capital, and most visitors come here to see (and smell!) the fragrant vanilla-processing plant. The town is also associated with a rare sprat-like delicacy known as *bichiques*. In early summer (around November or December) these are caught at the mouth of the Rivière des Roches as they swim upriver to spawn.

◉ Sights

Provanille   VANILLA

(☑0262 51 70 12; 21 RN2; tours adult/child €5/free; ☉8.30am-noon & 1.30-5pm Mon-Sat) This working vanilla-processing plant offers an introduction to the process of producing Réunion's famous Vanille Bourbon via a 45-minute guided tour and a film on the history of vanilla cultivation. You'll find various vanilla products at the factory shop. It's worth a visit just for the dreamy smell.

Bassin La Paix & Bassin La Mer   WATERFALL

A blissful site is Bassin La Paix, in the Rivière des Roches valley, about 2.5km west from Bras-Panon (it's signposted). From the car park, a path quickly leads to a majestic waterfall tumbling into a large rock pool. Swimming is forbidden, but it's an ideal picnic spot.

For a more off-the-beaten-track experience, you can continue upstream from Bassin La Paix to Bassin La Mer, another cascading delight that can be reached on foot only. The start of the trail is signposted from the car park, and it's an enjoyable (though exposed and hot) 40-minute walk. Reward yourself with a dip in the swimming holes at the bottom of the falls.

🛏 Sleeping & Eating

La Passiflore   B&B €€

(☑0262 51 74 68; www.lapassiflore.re; 31 Rue des Baies-Roses; d incl breakfast €55; ❋🏊🅿) Run by a well-travelled *métro* couple, this B&B stands in a haven of tropical peace in a side street near Provanille. The three clinically clean rooms have their own entrance and are embellished with a few exotic bits and bobs; avoid the 'Amis' room in the owners' house. Float in the scintillating pool or bask in the sunny garden. Air-con is extra (€5).

★Chez Éva Annibal   CREOLE €€

(☑0262 51 53 76; 6 Chemin Rivière du Mât; dinner €25) Pack a hearty thirst and giant-sized appetite before venturing into this plain but feisty inn. The Full Monty feast comprises rum, *gratin de légumes* (baked vegetables), fish curry, duck with vanilla, and cakes, all clearly emblazoned with a Creole Mama stamp of approval. There are also three functional but clean rooms (doubles without bathroom including breakfast €40) with sloping ceilings and communal facilities upstairs; in warmer months, they can be stifling given the lack of air-con.

Le Bec Fin   CREOLE, CHINESE €€

(☑0262 51 52 24; 66 RN2; mains €10-25, menu €13-18; ☉lunch daily, dinner Fri & Sat) Tickle your taste buds with a slurp of *planteur* (aromatic rum), then continue your indulgence with a feisty portion of *sarcives* (a variety of sausage) or *poisson sauce piquante* (fish in spicy sauce). On weekdays it lays on an excellent buffet lunch for just €13.

❶ Getting There & Away

Car Jaune buses (lines F and G) stop outside the vanilla cooperative en route between St-André and St-Benoît.

St-Benoît & Around

POP 31,500

Sugar-cane fields, lychee and mango orchards, rice, spices, coffee... Great carpets of deep-green felt seem to have been draped over the lower hills that surround St-Benoît, a major agricultural and fishing centre.

Bar a few impressive religious buildings – a mosque, a church and a Tamil temple on the outskirts of town – no one can accuse St-Benoît of being overburdened with tourist sights. The area's best features lie elsewhere; turn your attention from the coast and plant it firmly on the cooler recesses of the hills and valleys to the west. The Rivière des Marsouins valley in particular is a delight, with its plunging waterfalls and luxuriant vegetation. Small wonder that Réunion's best white water is found here.

◉ Sights

Forêt Ste-Marguerite   FOREST
(☉9am-4pm Tue-Sun) For a complete change of pace and atmosphere, consider spending some time in the protected 159-hectare Forêt Ste-Marguerite, way up in the hills. Fans of flora will get their kicks here; there are over 150 indigenous species of plants. A network of easy walking trails snakes through the quiet forest.

Take the RN3 in the direction of Plaine-des-Palmistes until you reach a roundabout at Chemin Ceinture; Forêt Ste-Marguerite is signed on the left.

Takamaka Viewpoint   LOOKOUT
North of St-Benoît the D53 strikes southwest, following the Rivière des Marsouins 15km upstream to end beside the Takamaka viewpoint. Be prepared to fall on your knees in awe: despite a small power plant near the viewpoint, the overwhelming impression is of a wild, virtually untouched valley, its vertical walls cloaked with impenetrable forests. Here and there the dense green is broken by a silver ribbon of cascading water.

Grand Étang   LAKE
Around 12km southwest of St-Benoît along the road towards Plaine-des-Palmistes, is the 3km road to Grand Étang (Big Pond). This pretty picnic spot lies at the bottom of an almost vertical ridge separating it from the Rivière des Marsouins valley. Most people simply walk around the lake, following a well-defined path. It's muddy in places, but shouldn't take more than three hours from the car park, including a side trip to an impressive **waterfall**.

🏃 Activities

Ferme Équestre du Grand Étang   HORSE RIDING
(☑0262 50 90 03; Pont Payet; half/full day €55/130; ☉daily) Horse riding is a low-impact way to soak up the drop-dead gorgeous scenery. The Ferme Équestre du Grand Étang, just beyond the turn-off to Grand Étang, arranges half-day treks to Grand Étang; the full-day trek includes lunch. It's also possible to arrange longer excursions to Bras Canot (two days) and Takamaka (three days). One-day excursions in the area of Piton de la Fournaise – most notably in the far west-looking Plaine des Sables – are also on offer (€150; horses are transferred by van). Ask for Fanou, who can speak English.

Oasis Eaux Vives   RAFTING
(☑0692 00 16 23; www.oasisev.com) The Rivière des Marsouins and Rivière des Roches offer magical white-water experiences for both first-time runners and seasoned enthusiasts. This well-established operator runs half-day excursions (€45).

Run Aventures   RAFTING
(☑0262 64 08 22; www.runaventures.com) Specialises in rafting trips on the Rivière des Marsouins and Rivière des Roches.

🛏 Sleeping & Eating

L'Orangeraie   B&B €€
(☑0692 01 18 87, 0262 50 97 60; gite-natura. monsite-orange.fr; Pont Payet; d incl breakfast €57; P🐾) A good port of call if you want to get away from it all. The rooms, the bungalow and the *gîte* are nothing special but the setting

---

OFF THE BEATEN TRACK

ÎLET BETHLÉEM

Very few visitors have heard about Îlet Bethléem, a magical spot by the Rivière des Marsouins that locals would like to keep for themselves. Reached after a 15-minute walk from the car park, it features an old chapel (1858) – still a pilgrimage site – and a smattering of picnic shelters amid lush vegetation. It's also an excellent swimming spot, with lots of natural rock pools. Unfortunately, the area is sometimes sprinkled with rubbish. Follow the D53 in the direction of Takamaka, then turn left after about 1km (it's signposted).

RÉUNION ST-BENOÎT & AROUND

is relaxing – tropical plants everywhere – and Madame is a good cook (reckon on €25 for dinner). Much of the produce cooked up is straight from the *potager* (veggie patch). At breakfast, you can dip into several varieties of homemade jams. It's about 7km from St-Benoît along the road towards Plaine-des-Palmistes (take the RN3 in the direction of Plaine-des-Palmistes and follow the signs from the Ferme Équestre at Pont Payet).

Longanis Lodge APARTMENT €€€
(☑0692 76 84 52; www.longanilodge.com; Chemin Harmonie, Abondance; lodge d/q €100/130; ℗ 🛜)
🍃 The Longanis stuns with its design-led architecture and bucolic setting by a river shaded by majestic longani trees. The villa can accommodate up to six people, so it's a fantastic deal for friends or families. There's no restaurant nearby, but the owner can prepare meals on request (€25). It's ecofriendly (water is solar heated, ventilation is natural and rainwater is recycled). It's in Abondance, about 5km from St-Benoît (take the road to Takamaka).

★**Les Letchis** CREOLE €€
(☑0692 66 55 36; www.restaurant-les-letchis. com; 42 Îlet Danclas, Bras Canot; mains €20-35; ☺lunch) Eastern Réunion's best-kept secret, Les Letchis boasts a fantastic location in a luxuriant garden by the Rivière des Marsouins. The menu is an ode to Creole classics and 'riverfood'; standouts include *carri bichiques* and braised duck. If you want to explore new culinary territories, try *carri chevaquines* (a curry made from small freshwater prawns) or *carri anguilles* (eel curry). Reservations are advised.

Le Régal' Est FRENCH, SEAFOOD €€
(☑0262 97 04 31; 9 Place Raymond Albius, St-Benoît; mains €10-30, menu €15; ☺lunch & dinner Mon-Sat) This attractive venture located upstairs in the covered market serves a modern, creative fish and meat menu. Not all the dishes work, though. The lunchtime menu (€15) is good value.

Le Beauvallon SEAFOOD, CREOLE €€
(☑0262 50 42 92; Rue du Stade Raymond-Arnoux, Rivière des Roches; mains €12-30; ☺lunch) Le Beauvallon is well known to everyone in the area, not least for its location beside the mouth of the Rivière des Roches and its seasonal, scrumptious *carri bichiques*. On the flipside, the vast dining room doesn't contain one whit of soul or character.

❶ Getting There & Away

From St-Benoît a scenic road (the RN3) cuts across the Plaine-des-Palmistes to St-Pierre and St-Louis on the far side of the island. Alternatively, you can continue south along the coast road, passing through Ste-Anne, St-Rose, St-Philippe and St-Joseph to reach St-Pierre.

St-Benoît is a major transport hub. Bus services to and from St-Denis run approximately every half-hour. There are also two services linking St-Benoît and St-Pierre: line H follows the RN3 over the Plaine-des-Palmistes; line I takes the coast road via St-Philippe and St-Joseph. In both cases there are about four buses daily.

VANILLA UNVEILED

The vanilla orchid was introduced into Réunion from Mexico around 1820, but early attempts at cultivation failed because of the absence of the Mexican bee that pollinates the flower and triggers the development of the vanilla pod. Fortunately for custard lovers everywhere, a method of hand-pollination was discovered in Réunion in 1841 by a 12-year-old slave, Edmond Albius. Vanilla was highly prized in Europe at the time and Albius' discovery ushered in an economic boom, at least for the French 'vanilla barons'.

The vanilla bubble burst, however, when synthetic vanilla – made from coal – was invented in the late 19th century. Réunion's vanilla industry was almost wiped out, but in recent years the growing demand for natural products has led to something of a revival. You'll now find vanilla 'plantations' hidden in the forests from Ste-Suzanne south to St-Philippe.

The majority of Réunion's crop is exported (Coca-Cola is the world's single biggest buyer), but vanilla is still a firm favourite in local cuisine. It crops up in all sorts of delicacies, from cakes and pastries to coffee, liqueurs, even vanilla duck and chicken. Best of all is the sublime flavour of a vanilla-steeped *rhum arrangé* (a mixture of rum, fruit juice, cane syrup and a blend of herbs and berries).

Ste-Anne

About 5km south along the coast from St-Benoît, Ste-Anne is an unpretentious town that's noted for its visually striking church. There's no beach, but if you're in the mood for a dip, there are some enticing natural pools.

◉ Sights

Bassin Bleu   LAGOON
If you need to cool off, there's no better place than Bassin Bleu, appropriately dubbed 'the lagoon of the east', at the mouth of a river, on the southern edge of town. It's a superb swimming spot, with crystal-clear water and big boulders. Take a plunge! Note that it's mobbed at weekends.

Église   CHURCH
You can't help but be dazzled by this surprisingly extravagant church that was erected in 1857. The facade of the building is covered in stucco depictions of fruit, flowers and angels. The overall effect is flamboyant rather than tasteful, and is reminiscent of the *mestizo* architecture of the Andes in South America.

Pont des Anglais   BRIDGE
Between Ste-Anne and Ste-Rose is the graceful Pont des Anglais suspension bridge over the Rivière de l'Est, now bypassed by the main highway but open to pedestrians. It was claimed to be the longest suspension bridge in the world at the time of its construction in the late 19th century.

🛏 Sleeping & Eating

Diana Dea Lodge & Spa   BOUTIQUE HOTEL €€€
(✆0262 20 02 02; www.diana-dea-lodge.re; 94 Chemin Helvetia, Cambourg, Ste-Anne; d incl breakfast from €190; 🅿❄🛜🏊) What a surprise it is to come upon a charming boutique hotel in such a remote location – Diana Dea Lodge & Spa is set high in the hills above Ste-Anne (it's signposted) and is reached after 12km of numerous twists and turns amid cane fields. This is one of those special places that lingers in the mind for its serenity. It's also set apart by its design, which combines wood and stone. Precious perks include a heated pool, a spa, a bar and a top-notch restaurant (open to nonguests by reservation) – not to mention astounding views of the coast. Be forewarned: you may never want to leave.

Il Etait Une Fois dans l'Est   CREOLE €
(✆0692 64 60 11; 133 RN2; mains €5-11; ☺lunch Mon-Sat) It's not cutting-edge cuisine at this humble place on the main road, but the daily specials are all flawlessly cooked. Don't be put off by the location on the main road; there's a peaceful dining room with sea views at the back.

L'Auberge Créole   CHINESE, CREOLE €€
(✆0262 51 10 10; 1 Chemin Case; mains €9-34, menus €20-35; ☺lunch Tue-Sun, dinner Tue-Sat) In this respected option, the menu roves from Creole dishes and *métro* classics to pizzas (evenings only) and Chinese specialities at prices that are more sweet than sour. Pity about the drab, neon-lit interior; take your order to go and eat under *vacoa* trees at Bassin Bleu.

ℹ Information

There's a small **tourist office** (✆0262 47 05 09; www.est.reunion.fr; Rue de l'Église; ☺9am-noon & 1-5.30pm Mon-Sat; 🛜) beside the church. It has maps and brochures and does bookings for *gîtes de montagne*. Also offers wi-fi access.

ℹ Getting There & Away

Ste-Anne is a stop on the coastal bus route from St-Benoît to St-Pierre.

Ste-Rose & Around

POP 6600
South of St-Benoît, the landscape becomes more open and less populated as the road hugs the coast around Piton de la Fournaise, the volcano which regularly spews lava down its flanks. The small fishing community of Ste-Rose has its harbour at the inlet of La Marine.

South of Ste-Rose the first tongues of lava from Piton de la Fournaise start to make their appearance. Beyond Anse des Cascades, the main road continues south along the coast, climbs and then drops down to cross the 6km-wide volcanic plain known as Le Grand Brûlé (p245).

◉ Sights

At the picturesque **harbour** you'll see a **monument** to the young English commander Corbett, who was killed in 1809 during a naval battle against the French off the coast.

Further south you'll reach **La Cayenne**, which has a superb picnic area scenically perched on a cliff overlooking the ocean – well worth a pause.

Notre Dame des Laves
CHURCH

(Piton Ste-Rose) Notre Dame des Laves is in Piton Ste-Rose, 4.5km south of Ste-Rose. The lava flow from a 1977 eruption went through the village, split when it came to the church and reformed again on the other side. Many people see the church's escape as a miracle of divine intervention. A wooden log 'washed up' by the lava now forms the lectern inside the church, while the stained-glass windows depict various stages of the eruption.

Bananaland
FARM

(☑ 0262 53 49 74; 371ter RN2, Piton Ste-Rose; admission €3; ⊙ 9am-4.30pm Sun-Thu) Just north of Piton Ste-Rose is this family-run operation where you can visit a banana plantation and buy various banana products, including jam and cakes. Everything is homemade and organic.

Anse des Cascades
BAY

This super scenic *anse* (bay) is beside the sea about 3km south of Piton Ste-Rose. The water from the hills drops dramatically into the sea near a traditional little fishing harbour. The coconut grove is splendid and is a hugely popular picnic spot, and there's a popular restaurant close to the shore.

✦ Festivals

Pèlerinage à la Vierge au Parasol
RELIGIOUS

(Pilgrimage to the Virgin with the Parasol) On August 15, the site of the Vierge au Parasol – by the coastal road about 10km south of Ste-Rose – attracts hundreds of pilgrims.

⊨ Sleeping & Eating

⊨ Ste-Rose

★ Matilona
B&B €€

(☑ 0692 85 86 86; matilona.monsite-orange.fr; 84 Chemin du Petit Brûlé; s/d incl breakfast €53/58, studio s/d incl breakfast €58/63; P❋@☎☒) Formerly a supermarket, it's amazing what a renovation and an ownership change does for a place. Don't be put off by the peeling facade; push the door open and you're in another reality – simple yet inviting rooms with recently modernised bathrooms, generously sized communal areas and a seductive garden overflowing with colourful plants. And a killer pool. Dinner costs €30 and is available three days a week. Monsieur is a former chef, so you can expect to eat well. Brilliant value.

Ferme-Auberge La Cayenne
B&B €€

(☑ 0262 47 23 46; www.ferme-auberge-lacayenne. fr; 317 Ravine Glissante; d incl breakfast €55; P) This well-run guesthouse scores points for its location – it's perched above the sea in La Ravine-Glissante, 1.5km south of Ste-Rose. The six sun-soaked rooms are as neat as a pin, and the views of the swishing indigo waters from the balcony are nothing short of charming. The owner, Madame Narayanin, cooks beautifully, using mostly homegrown ingredients. Let the breeze tickle your skin while you eat authentic cuisine alfresco on the covered terrace. Dinner costs from €25.

La Fournaise
HOTEL €€

(☑ 0262 47 03 40; www.hotellafournaise.fr; 154 RN2; d €67; P❋☎☒) There's a fresh feel in this modernish venture on the main road. Spruce rooms, shiny-clean toilets, air-con, an on-site restaurant (mains €17 to €22, menu €25) and a pool are the order of the day here. The catch? It's sorely lacking in charm. Go for a room with a sea view; there's no extra charge. Note that the restaurant is open for dinner only as well as for lunch on Sunday.

Cana Suc
BUNGALOW €€

(☑ 0692 77 81 96; www.canasuc.re; 219 RN2; d incl breakfast €80) This is an adorable nest with a row of three well-designed Creole bungalows opening onto expansive lawns. Two units are *gîtes* that are rented for longer stays (three nights from €210).

Snack Chez Louiso
FAST FOOD €

(☑ 0262 47 26 57; 46 Chemin de la Marine; mains €5-10; ⊙ lunch Tue-Sun) Chez Louiso is a casual open-air eatery overlooking the harbour. The menu is limited to sandwiches and a couple of daily specials, but they're well prepared and sizzling-hot value.

⊨ Piton Ste-Rose

Le Joyau des Laves
INN €

(☑ 0262 47 34 00; www.joyaudeslaves.com; 474ter RN2, Piton Ste-Rose; d €43-70; P☎) On a headland 7km south of Ste-Rose, this friendly inn run by a delightful young couple has four unfussy rooms. The more expensive one is spacious and blessed with great sea views. Even if you're not staying, it's worth phoning ahead to eat in the restaurant (menus €10 to €28) and try local specialities such as palm hearts and *baba figues* (banana flowers) from the surrounding gardens. Breakfast is extra (€5).

Les 2 Pitons de la Fournaise CREOLE €€
(☑ 0262 47 23 16; RN2; mains €12-19; ⊙ lunch) Opposite Notre Dame des Laves church, this no-frills eatery specialises in Creole classics. The setting being bland, your best bet is to take away (mains €5) – you'll find plenty of atmospheric spots along the coast driving south of Piton Ste-Rose.

🛏 Anse des Cascades

Restaurant des Cascades CREOLE, SEAFOOD €€
(☑ 0262 47 20 42; Anse des Cascades; mains €13-27, menus €12-25; ⊙ lunch Sat-Thu) A local and tourist favourite, this beach restaurant in a lovely coconut grove bursts to the seams on weekends. It serves fresh fish and Creole dishes as well as sandwiches and a lovely palm-heart salad. The lunch buffet (€12) served on weekdays is brilliant value. Nab a seat if it's not too busy, otherwise take your order to go and enjoy it in a quieter spot near the beach.

ℹ Getting There & Away

Buses running from St-Benoît to St-Pierre make handy stops near Notre Dame des Laves and Anse des Cascades.

UNDERSTAND RÉUNION

Réunion Today

Réunion is one of the richest islands in the Indian Ocean. The standard of living is fairly high, and it's no surprise. As a French *département* (a French overseas territory), the island receives a lot of financial support from mainland France (la *métropole*). However, Réunion faces numerous challenges. The unemployment rate, for example, currently hovers around 29% (60% among people aged between 15 and 24), way above the national average (about 11% at the time of writing). It's particularly problematic for women and young people without qualifications. This situation has led to a series of riots in Le Port in February 2012 and February 2013.

Tourism, which is a major source of income, plummeted to 278,000 visitors in 2006 (down from 410,000 tourist arrivals in 2005) as a result of the chikungunya epidemic (see p325). Good news: since 2007, the sector has been picking up again (450,000 tourist arrivals in 2012) – not least because 40% of the island was designated a Natural World Heritage Site. Despite this prestigious recognition, the vast majority of visitors are French. There's a huge potential for growth, but there are a few hurdles: it's under-promoted in Anglophone markets; English is not widely spoken on the island (to say the least); and the cost of flights is still prohibitive. Local authorities also fear that the fatal shark attacks on surfers, which occurred in 2011, 2012 and 2013, might have a negative impact on tourism.

History

Réunion has a history similar to that of Mauritius. It was colonised by the French after the mid-17th century but later fell briefly under British rule. As in Mauritius, the colonisers introduced plantation crops and African slaves. Later came Indian indentured labourers and Chinese merchants, creating an ethnic diversity which is one of these islands' most distinctive characteristics. While Mauritius gained its independence in 1968, Réunion remains an overseas department of France.

Welcome to Paradise

The first visitors to the uninhabited island were probably Malay, Arab and European mariners, none of whom stayed. Then, in 1642, the French took the decision to settle the island, which at the time was called Mascarin. The first settlers arrived four years later, when the French governor of Fort Dauphin in southern Madagascar banished a dozen mutineers to the island.

On the basis of enthusiastic reports from the mutineers, King Louis XIV of France officially claimed the island in 1649 and renamed it Île Bourbon.

However appealing it seemed, there was no great rush to populate and develop the island. It was not until the beginning of the 18th century that the French East India Company and the French government took control of the island.

Coffee, Anyone?

Coffee was introduced between 1715 and 1730 and soon became the island's main cash crop. The island's economy changed dramatically. As coffee required intensive labour, African and Malagasy slaves were brought by the shipload. During this period, cereals, spices and cotton were also introduced as cash crops.

Like Mauritius, Réunion came of age under the governorship of the visionary Mahé de Labourdonnais, who served from 1735 to 1746. However, Labourdonnais treated Île de France (Mauritius) as a favoured sibling, and after the collapse of the French East India Company and the pressure of ongoing rivalry with Britain the governance of Île Bourbon passed directly to the French crown in 1764.

After the French Revolution, the island's name was changed to La Réunion (meaning 'Joining' or 'Meeting').

The British Move In...

In 1810, during the Napoleonic Wars, Napoleon Bonaparte lost the island to the *habits rouges* (redcoats). Under British rule, sugar cane was introduced to Réunion and quickly became the primary crop. The vanilla industry, introduced in 1819, also grew rapidly.

The British didn't stay long: five years later, under the Treaty of Paris, the spoils were returned to the French as Île Bourbon. The British, however, retained their grip on Mauritius, Rodrigues and the Seychelles.

...And the French Come Back to Stay

In 1848, the Second Republic was proclaimed in France, slavery was abolished and Île Bourbon again became La Réunion. Like Mauritius, Réunion immediately experienced a labour crisis and, like the British in Mauritius, the French 'solved' the problem by importing contract labourers from India, most of them Hindus, to work the sugar cane.

Réunion's golden age of trade and development lasted until 1870, with the country flourishing on the trade route between Europe, India and the Far East. Competition from Cuba and the European sugar-beet industry, combined with the opening of the Suez Canal (which short-circuited the journey around the Cape of Good Hope), resulted in an economic slump.

After WWI, in which 14,000 Réunionnais served, the sugar industry regained a bit of momentum, but it again suffered badly through the blockade of the island during WWII.

Réunion became a Département Français d'Outre-Mer (DOM; French Overseas Department) in 1946 and has representation in the French parliament. Since then there have been feeble independence movements from time to time but, unlike those in France's Pacific territories, these have never amounted to much. While the Réunionnais seemed satisfied to remain totally French, general economic and social discontent surfaced in dramatic anti-government riots in St-Denis in 1991.

In March 1998, there was a major eruption at the Piton de la Fournaise – the longest eruption of the volcano in the 20th century, with a total of 196 days of volcanic activity. In April 2007, another major eruption resulted in the RN2 expressway being closed for several months.

The turn of the century marked a new era for Réunion; the local authorities managed

---

BLACK HISTORY

The late 18th century saw a number of slave revolts, and many resourceful Malagasy and African slaves, called *marrons*, escaped from their owners and took refuge in the mountainous interior. Some of them established private utopias in inaccessible parts of the Cirques, while others grouped together and formed organised communities with democratically elected leaders. These tribal chieftains were the true pioneers of the settlement of Réunion, but most ultimately fell victim to bounty hunters who were employed to hunt them down. The scars of this period of the island's history are still fresh in the population's psyche; perhaps from a sense of shame, there's surprisingly little record of the island's Creole pioneers except the names of several peaks (Dimitile, Enchaing, Mafate, Cimendef) where they were hunted down and killed. The Espace Culturel Muséographique Dimitile (ECM) at Entre-Deux provides excellent introductions to these sensitive subjects, tracing the history of slavery and *marronage* (the act of escaping plantation life) and celebrating the achievements of these unsung heroes of the Cirques.

to sign a few agreements with the French state, which confirmed the launching of subsidised *grands chantiers* (major infrastructure works), including the expressway called the Nouvelle Route des Tamarins, the tram-train between Ste-Marie and St-Paul and the enlargement of the Route du Littoral (the expressway between St-Paul and St-Denis). These huge civil engineering works are expected to sustain growth on the island. So far, only the Route des Tamarins has been completed.

The Culture

The physical and cultural distinctions between the various ethnic groups are far less apparent in Réunion than in Mauritius. In Réunion there has been much more interracial mixing over the years. Ask the Réunionnais how they see themselves and the chances are they'll say 'Creole' – not in the narrow sense of having Afro-French ancestry, but simply meaning one of 'the people'. That is, someone who speaks Creole, was born and bred on the island and is probably – but not necessarily – of mixed ancestry. This sense of community is the gel that holds society together.

The Réunionnais are in general more reserved than the Mauritians, but within this overall pattern there are local differences: southerners are reckoned to be more relaxed and friendly, while perhaps not surprisingly the people living in the Cirques are the most introverted.

While the Réunionnais also regard themselves as French, they don't really identify with people from the mainland. There is even a slight undercurrent of resentment towards the 100,000 or so mainlanders who dominate the island's administration and economy. The locals refer to them very slightly derogatorily as Zoreilles (the Ears); the usual explanation is that they are straining to hear what's being said about them in the local patois.

Daily Life

Contemporary Réunionnais are a thoroughly 21st-century people. The vast majority of children receive a decent standard of education and all islanders have access to the national health system, either in Réunion or in France. There are traffic jams, everyone is on a mobile (cell) phone, and

> ### SUNDAY PICNIC: A RÉUNIONNAIS INSTITUTION
>
> At the weekend there's nothing the Réunionnais like better than trundling off to the seaside or the mountains for a huge family picnic – think giant-sized rice cookers replete with hearty *carris* (curries) in the company of *gramounes* (grandparents) and *marmailles* (children). To get the most sought-after picnic shelters, some members of the family sometimes arrive at 4am to reserve them! Visitors are welcome, and are usually invited to share a meal.

flashy cars are ubiquitous. But beneath this modern veneer, there are many more traditional aspects.

One of the strongest bonds unifying society, after the Creole language, is the importance placed on family life. It's particularly made evident at the *pique-nique du dimanche en famille* (Sunday family picnic). Religious occasions and public holidays are also vigorously celebrated, as are more personal family events, such as baptisms, first communions and weddings.

Though Réunion can't be mistaken for, say, Ibiza, Réunionnais share a zest for the fest. On weekends St-Gilles-les-Bains, L'Hermitage-les-Bains and St-Pierre are a magnet for Réunionnais from all over the island. The towns turn wild on those evenings as flocks of night owls arrive en masse to wiggle their hips and guzzle pints of Dodo beer and glasses of rum.

On a more mundane level, you'll quickly realise that the possession of a brand new car is a sign of wealth and respect. The 'car culture' is a dominant trait; small wonder that traffic jams are the norm on the coastal roads. Many Réunionnais spend up to two hours daily in their car going to and from work! One favourite topic of conversation is the state of the roads, especially the tricky Route du Littoral between St-Paul and St-Denis, which is sometimes closed due to fallen rocks.

Another noticeable (though less immediately so) characteristic is the importance of *la di la fé* (gossip). If you can understand a little bit of French (or Creole), tune in to **Radio Free Dom** (www.freedom.fr) – you'll soon realise that gossip is a national pastime.

RÉUNION THE CULTURE

Despite the social problems that blight any culture, on the whole it's a society that lives very easily together.

Women

There's a refreshingly liberal attitude towards women, and younger Réunionnais women especially are quite outspoken and emancipated. Divorce, abortion and childbirth outside marriage are all fairly uncontentious issues. However, it's not all rosy: women are poorly represented in local government and politics, and domestic violence is prevalent. This is closely connected to high rates of alcoholism.

Population

Cultural diversity forms an integral part of the island's social fabric. Réunion has the same population mix of Africans, Europeans, Indians and Chinese as Mauritius, but in different proportions. Cafres (people of African ancestry) are the largest ethnic group, comprising about 45% of the population. Malbars (Hindu Indians) comprise about 25% of the population, white Creoles (people of French ancestry) 15%, Europeans (who are also known as Zoreilles) 7%, Chinese 4% and Z'arabes (Muslim Indians) 4%.

The bulk of the island's population lives in coastal zones, with Malbars living predominantly in the east. The rugged interior is sparsely populated. Because the birth rate has remained quite high, a third of the population is under 20 years of age.

Réunion also sees a continual tide of would-be immigrants. With a system of generous welfare payments for the unemployed, the island is seen as a land of milk and honey by those from Mauritius, the Seychelles and some mainland African countries. In recent years there has been significant immigration from the neighbouring Comoros and Mayotte Islands.

Religion & Beliefs

An estimated 70% of the population belongs to the Catholic faith, which dominates the island's religious character. It's evidenced in the many saints' days and holidays, as well as in the names of towns and cities. Religious rituals and rites of passage play an important part in the lives of the people, and baptisms, first communions and church weddings are an integral part of social culture.

About a quarter of Réunionnais are Hindus, which is the dominant faith in the east. Traditional Hindu rites such as *teemeedee*, which features fire-walking, and *cavadee*, which for pilgrims entails piercing the cheeks with skewers, often take place. Muslims make up roughly 2% of the population; as in Mauritius, Islam tends to be fairly liberal.

Interestingly, a great deal of syncretism between Hinduism, Islam and Catholicism has evolved over the years. In fact, many of the Malbar-Réunionnais participate in both Hindu and Catholic rites and rituals.

Apart from celebrating the Chinese New Year, the Sino-Réunionnais community (making up about 3% of the population) is not very conspicuous in its religious or traditional practices.

Religious tolerance is the norm here. Mosques, churches, Hindu temples and

---

THE ODD CULT OF ST EXPÉDIT

You can't miss them. Red shrines honouring St Expédit are scattered all over the island, including on road sides. St Expédit is one of Réunion's most popular saints, though some scholars argue there never was a person called Expédit. Whatever the truth, the idea was brought to Réunion in 1931 when a local woman erected a statue of the 'saint' in St-Denis' Notre-Dame de la Délivrance church in thanks for answering her prayer to return to Réunion. Soon there were shrines all over the island, where people prayed for his help in the speedy resolution of all sorts of tricky problems.

Over the years, however, worship of the saint has taken on the sinister overtones of a voodoo cult: figurines stuck with pins are left at the saint's feet; beheaded statues of him are perhaps the result of unanswered petitions. The saint has also been adopted into the Hindu faith, which accounts for the brilliant, blood-red colour of many shrines. As a result the Catholic Church has tried to distance itself from the cult, but the number of shrines continues to grow.

pagodas can be found within a stone's throw of each other in most towns.

Arts

One of the greatest pleasures of visiting Réunion is experiencing Creole-flavoured French culture or French-flavoured Creole culture, depending on how you look at it. For news of cultural activities on the island, keep an eye on the local press and visit local tourist offices, where you can pick up flyers, theatre programs and a number of free events guides such as the monthly *Azenda* (www.azenda.re).

LITERATURE

Few Réunionnais novelists are known outside the island and none are translated into English. One of the most widely recognised and prolific contemporary authors is the journalist and historian Daniel Vaxelaire. His *Chasseurs des Noires,* an easily accessible tale of a slave-hunter's life-changing encounter with an escaped slave, is probably the best to start with.

Jean-François Sam-Long, a novelist and poet who helped relaunch Creole literature in the 1970s, also takes slavery as his theme. *Madame Desbassyns* was inspired by the remarkable life story of a sugar baroness.

Other well-established novelists to look out for are Axel Gauvin, Jules Bénard, Jean Lods and Monique Agénor.

MUSIC & DANCE

Réunion's music mixes the African rhythms of reggae, *séga* (traditional slave music) and *maloya* with French, British and American rock and folk sounds. Like *séga, maloya* is derived from the music of the slaves, but it is slower and more reflective, its rhythms and words heavy with history, somewhat like New Orleans blues; fans say it carries the true spirit of Réunion. *Maloya* songs often carry a political message and up until the 1970s the music was banned for being too subversive.

Instruments used to accompany *séga* and the *maloya* range from traditional homemade percussion pieces, such as the hide-covered *rouleur* drum and the maraca-like *kayamb*, to the accordion and modern band instruments.

The giants of the local music scene, and increasingly well known in mainland France, are Daniel Waro, Firmin Viry, Gramoun Lélé, Davy Sicard, Kaf Malbar

and the group Ziskakan. More recently, women have also emerged on the musical scene, including Christine Salem and Nathalie Nathiembé. All are superb practitioners of *maloya*. Favourite subjects for them are slavery, poverty and the search for cultural identity.

As for Creole-flavoured modern grooves, the Réunionnais leave those to their tropical cousins in Martinique and Guadeloupe, although they make popular listening in Réunion. It's all catchy stuff, and you'll hear it in bars, discos and vehicles throughout the islands of the Indian Ocean.

ARCHITECTURE

The distinctive 18th-century Creole architecture of Réunion is evident in both the grand villas built by wealthy planters and other *colons* (settlers/colonists) and in the *ti' cases,* the homes of the common folk.

Local authorities are actively striving to preserve the remaining examples of Creole architecture around the island. You can see a number of beautifully restored houses in St-Denis as well as in the towns of Cilaos, Entre-Deux, Hell-Bourg and St-Pierre, among other places. They all sport *lambrequins* (filigree-style decorations), *varangues* (verandas) and other ornamental features.

Food & Drink

Réunionnais like to eat and their food is a pleasure on the palate, with a balanced melange of French cuisine (locally known as *cuisine métro*) and Creole specialities and flavours, not to mention Indian and Chinese influences.

RÉUNION FOOD & DRINK

Réunion Classics

It's impossible to visit Réunion without coming across *carri* (curry), also spelt *cari* locally, which features on practically every single menu. The sauce comprises tomatoes, onions, garlic, ginger, thyme and saffron (or turmeric) and accompanies various kinds of meat, such as chicken *(carri poulet)*, pork *(carri porc)*, duck *(carri canard)* and guinea fowl *(carri pintade)*. Seafood *carris*, such as tuna *(carri thon)*, swordfish *(carri espadon)*, lobster *(carri langouste)* and freshwater prawn *(carri camarons)* are also excellent. Octopus *carri*, one of the best *carris* you'll eat, is called *civet zourite* in Creole. Local vegetables can also be prepared *carri*-style – try *carri baba figue* (banana-flower *carri*) and *carri ti jaque* (jackfruit *carri*) – but they incorporate fish or meat. *Carris* are invariably served with rice, grains (lentils or haricot beans), *brèdes* (local spinach) and *rougail*, a spicy chutney that mixes tomato, garlic, ginger and chillies; other preparations of *rougail* may include a mixture of green mango and citrus.

The word *rougail* is a bit confusing, though. It's also used for some variations of *carris*. *Rougail saucisses* is in fact sausages cooked in tomato sauce, while *rougail boucané* is a smoked-pork *carri* (without saffron), and *rougail morue* is cod *carri* (also without saffron). You'll also find *civet*, which is another variety of stew. A widespread Tamil stew is *cabri massalé* (goat *carri*). On top of this, you'll find excellent beef (usually imported from South Africa) prepared in all its forms (steak, sirloin, rib).

Snacks include samosas, *beignets* (fritters) and *bonbons piments* (chilli fritters). You'll also find cheap and tasty sandwiches.

Seafood

Seafood lovers will be delighted to hear that the warm waters of the Indian Ocean provide an ample net of produce: lobster, prawns, *légine* (toothfish), swordfish, marlin, tuna and shark, among others. Freshwater prawns, usually served in *carri*, are highly prized.

Breakfast

Breakfast is decidedly French: *pain-beurre-confiture* (baguette, butter and jam) served with coffee, tea or hot chocolate is the most common threesome. Added treats may include croissants, *pain au chocolat* (chocolate-filled pastry), brioches and honey.

Desserts

What about desserts? If you like carb-laden cakes and pies, you'll be happy in Réunion. Each family has its own recipe for *gâteaux maison* (homemade cakes), which come in various guises. They are usually made from vanilla, banana, sweet potato, maize, carrot, guava... One favourite is *macatia* (a variety of bun), which can also be served at breakfast.

Fruits

Fruits reign supreme in Réunion. Two iconic Réunionnais fruits are *litchis* (lychees) and *ananas Victoria* (pineapple of the Victoria variety). Local mangoes, passionfruit and papaya are also fabulously sweet. The local vanilla is said to be one of the most flavoured in the world.

Vegetarians & Vegans

Vegetarians won't go hungry. Réunionnais love vegetables, eating them in salads or in gratins (a baked dish). You'll certainly come

---

TRAVEL YOUR TASTE BUDS

If you're a gastronomic adventurer, start your culinary odyssey with *salade de palmiste*, a delectable salad made from the bud of the palmiste palm tree, known as the 'heart of palm'. The palm dies once the bud is removed, earning this wasteful salad delicacy the title 'millionaire's salad'. For something a bit more unusual, try *carri bichiques* (a sprat-like delicacy), which is dubbed *le caviar réunionnais* (Réunionnais caviar). You might need to seek out *larves de guêpes* (wasps' larvae), another local delicacy that is available from April to October. Fried and salted, they reputedly increase sexual stamina.

You may also want to learn the terms for *carri pat' cochons* (pig's trotter *carri*) and *carri anguilles* (eel *carri*) so you don't accidentally order them in a restaurant. Réunionnais also drool over *carri tang* (hedgehog *carri*), which you're not likely to find served in restaurants.

WHERE TO EAT & DRINK

There is a wondrous array of eateries in Réunion, from snack-bar-cum-cafes to high-class restaurants serving fine French cuisine, to *tables d'hôtes* (home-cooked meals served at *chambres d'hôtes*) and beach restaurants. For self-caterers, there's no shortage of very well-stocked supermarkets, not to mention numerous markets, where you can stock up on delicious, fresh ingredients. On Sunday, most Réunionnais opt for a picnic on the beach or in the Hauts.

On top of *la carte* (the menu), most restaurants have *menus* (set courses) and daily specials. You'll also find numerous roadside stalls selling fruits, especially during the lychee season from December to February.

across *chou chou* (choko; a speciality in the Cirque de Salazie), lentils (a speciality in the Cirque de Cilaos), *bois de songe* (a local vegetable that looks like a leek) and *vacoa* (a speciality in the Wild South), not to mention *bringelles* (aubergines) and *baba figue* (banana flower). Salads, rice and fruits are ubiquitous. In Chinese restaurants, menus feature vegetarian dishes, such as chop suey and noodles. Most supermarkets have vegetarian fare too, and *chambre d'hôte* owners will be happy to cook vegetarian dishes if you let them know well in advance.

Drinks

Rum, rum, rum! Up in the hills, almost everyone will have their own family recipe for *rhum arrangé*, a heady mixture of local rum and a secret blend of herbs and spices. In fact, not all are that secret. Popular concoctions include *rhum faham*, a blend of rum, sugar and flowers from the faham orchid; *rhum vanille*, made from rum, sugar and fresh vanilla pods; and *rhum bibasse*, made from rum, sugar and tasty *bibasse* (medlar fruit). The family *rhum arrangé* is a source of pride for most Creoles; if you stay in any of the rural *gîtes* or *chambres d'hôtes* you can expect the proprietor to serve up their version with more than a little ceremony.

Réunion being French territory, wine is unsurprisingly taken seriously. Along with French wines, you'll find a good choice of South African reds and whites. The island also has a small but blossoming viniculture in Cilaos, where you can do a tasting.

The local brand of beer, Bourbon (known as Dodo), is sold everywhere. It is a fairly light, very drinkable beer. Foreign beers are also available. For a refresher, nothing beats a fresh fruit juice or a glass of Cilaos, a high-quality sparkling water from Cirque de Cilaos.

The French take their coffee seriously and it's a passion that hasn't disappeared just because they're now in the Indian Ocean. A cup of coffee can take various forms but the most common is a small, black espresso called simply *un café*.

Environment

Réunion lies about 220km southwest of Mauritius, at the southernmost end of the great Mascarene volcanic chain. Réunion's volcano, Piton de la Fournaise, erupts with great regularity, spewing lava down its southern and eastern flanks.

The Land

There are two major mountainous areas on Réunion. The older of the two covers most of the western half of the island. The highest mountain is Piton des Neiges (3070m), an alpine-class peak. Surrounding it are three immense and splendid amphitheatres: the Cirques of Cilaos, Mafate and Salazie. These long, wide, deep hollows are sheer-walled canyons filled with convoluted peaks and valleys, the eroded remnants of the ancient volcanic shield that surrounded Piton des Neiges.

The smaller of the two mountainous regions lies in the southeast and continues to evolve. It comprises several extinct volcanic cones and one that is still very much alive, Piton de la Fournaise (2632m). This rumbling peak still pops its cork relatively frequently in spectacular fashion. The last major eruption occurred in 2007, when lava flows reached the sea and added another few square metres to the island. Since 1998 there have been spectacular eruptions almost every second year – attractions in their own right. No one lives in the shadow of the volcano, where lava flowing down to the shore has left a remarkable jumbled slope of cooled black volcanic rock, known as Le Grand Brûlé.

UNESCO WORLD HERITAGE SITE

Réunion's landscapes and natural riches are so unique that in 2010, Unesco designated over 40% of the island a Natural World Heritage Site under the title 'Pitons, Cirques & Remparts'. This is an exceptional recognition of the island's phenomenally appealing mountainscapes and its remarkable biodiversity. Other natural sites in the world that have been awarded such a distinction include the Galapagos islands, the Great Barrier Reef and the Grand Canyon National Park.

These two mountainous areas are separated by a region of high plains, while the coast is defined by a gently sloping plain which varies in width. Numerous rivers wind their way down from the Piton des Neiges range, through the Cirques, cutting deeply into the coastal plains to form spectacular ravines.

Wildlife

ANIMALS

The mammals which you are likely to see are introduced hares, deer, geckoes, rats and, if you're lucky, chameleons. Tenrecs (called *tang* in Creole), which resemble hedgehogs, are a species introduced from Madagascar.

The most interesting creepy crawlies are the giant millipedes – some as long as a human foot – which loll around beneath rocks in more humid areas. Other oversized creatures are the yellow-and-black *Nephila* spiders whose massive webs are a common sight. You'll also find the *Heteropoda venatoria* or huntsman spider, called *babouk* in Creole.

As far as bird life is concerned, of the original 30 species endemic to the island, only nine remain. The island's rarest birds are the *merle blanc*, or cuckoo shrike – locals call it the *tuit tuit*, for obvious reasons – and the black petrel. Probably the best chance of seeing – or, more likely, hearing – the *tuit tuit* is directly south of St-Denis, near the foot of La Roche Écrite.

Bulbuls, which resemble blackbirds (with yellow beaks and legs but grey feathers) and are locally known as *merles,* are also common. Birds native to the highlands include

the *tec-tec* or Réunion stonechat, which inhabits the tamarind forests. There's also the *papangue*, or Maillardi buzzard, a protected hawklike bird which begins life as a little brown bird and turns black and white as it grows older. It is Réunion's only surviving bird of prey and may be spotted soaring over the ravines.

The best-known sea bird is the white *paille-en-queue*, or white-tailed tropicbird, which sports two long tail plumes.

Mynahs, introduced at the end of the 18th century to keep the grasshoppers under control, are common all over the island, as are the small, red cardinal-like birds known as fodies.

The best spots to see birdlife are the Forêt de Bébour-Bélouve above Hell-Bourg, and the wilderness region of Le Grand Brûlé at the southern tip of the island.

PLANTS

Thanks to an abundant rainfall and marked differences in altitude, Réunion boasts some of the most varied plant life in the world. Parts of the island are like a grand botanical garden. Between the coast and the alpine peaks you'll find palms, screw pines (also known as pandanus or *vacoa*), casuarinas *(filaos),* vanilla, spices, other tropical fruit and vegetable crops, rainforest and alpine flora.

Réunion has no less than 700 indigenous plant species, 150 of which are trees. Unlike Mauritius, large areas of natural forest still remain. It's estimated that 30% of the island is covered by native forest.

Gnarled and twisted and sporting yellow, mimosa-like flowers, the *tamarin des Hauts* or mountain tamarind tree, is a type of acacia and is endemic to Réunion. One of the best places to see these ancient trees is in the Forêt de Bébour-Bélouve, east of the Cirque de Salazie.

At the other extreme, the lava fields around the volcano exhibit a barren, moonlike surface. Here the various stages of vegetation growth, from a bare new lava base, are evident. The first plant to appear on lava is the heather-like plant the French call *branle vert (Philippia montana).* Much later in the growth cycle come tamarind and other acacia trees.

Afforestation has been carried out mainly with the Japanese cryptomeria, *tamarin des Hauts,* casuarina and various palms.

Like any tropical island, Réunion has a wealth of flowering species, including orchid, hibiscus, bougainvillea, vetiver, geranium, frangipani and jacaranda.

National Parks

It is estimated that nearly a third of the 25km-long lagoon along the west coast from Boucan Canot south to Trois Bassins has already suffered damage from a variety of causes: sedimentation, agricultural and domestic pollution, cyclones, fishermen and swimmers. To prevent the situation deteriorating further, a marine park was set up in 1997. In addition to educating local people on the need to keep the beaches and the water clean, the **Association Parc Marin Réunion** (parcmarin.chez.com) has been working with local fishermen and various watersports operators to establish protection zones. A fully fledged nature reserve was created in 2007.

Part of the interior of the island is protected, too. The **Parc National des Hauts de la Réunion** (www.reunion-parcnational.fr) was established in early 2007, resulting in half of Réunion's total land area being now under protection. There's a tightly regulated core area of 1000 sq km, including the volcano, the mountain peaks and the areas around Mafate and Grand Bassin, surrounded by a buffer zone of some 700 sq km to encompass most of the ravines.

Environmental Issues

The central problem confronting Réunion is how to reconcile environmental preservation with a fast-growing population in need of additional housing, roads, jobs, electricity, water and recreational space.

Despite the establishment of the Parc National des Hauts de la Réunion and the Parc Marin Réunion, the island is facing major issues, all related to two massive engineering works. The 'smaller' is the Route des Tamarins, which was completed in 2009. This 34km expressway that slices across the hills above St-Gilles-les-Bains required numerous bridges over the ravines. According to local environmentalists, the road cut across the only remaining savannah habitat on the island.

The second major engineering project is a piece of technical prowess. The idea behind this herculean scheme is to transfer water from the east coast, where supply exceeds demand, to the dry and heavily populated west coast. The solution someone came up with was to drill a tunnel 30km long and 3.5m high right through the island! Tunnelling began in 1989, but needless to say they hit a few hitches along the way. It is reckoned that the project should be completed by 2015.

SURVIVAL GUIDE

❶ Directory A–Z

ACCOMMODATION

While accommodation in Réunion might not reach the stellar heights of Mauritius and the Seychelles, there is still plenty of choice. The smarter hotels tend to be concentrated around the coast and in the attractive mountain towns of Cilaos and Hell-Bourg.

In the midrange bracket, there's a smattering of small family hotels and lots of *chambres d'hôtes* (B&Bs), the best of which offer good value for money. Budget travellers will find it hard to keep costs down in St-Denis and the coastal towns around St-Gilles-les-Bains, but elsewhere *gîtes* and the cheaper *chambres d'hôtes* fit the bill.

It is wise to book well in advance, particularly in high season (the mainland France and local school holidays, particularly July, August and from mid-December to mid-January), when the best places fill up weeks, if not months, ahead. If you're planning a hiking trip in September or October, it's also imperative to book *gîtes de montagne* as early as possible, as these months are the busiest and there's only a limited number of places available.

Each year, the **Centrale d'Information et de Réservation Régionale – Île de la Réunion Tourisme** (www.reunion.fr) features updated listings of B&Bs, camp sites, *gîtes d'étapes* and hotels. Online listings are also available at www.abritel.fr, www.lareuniondecouverte.com, www.bedycasa.com and www.allonslareunion.com.

Camping

Bad news for those who want to spend their holiday under canvas: at the time of writing, there were only two official camp sites, on the southwest coast at Étang-Salé-les-Bains and L'Hermitage-les-Bains. You'll also find a couple of *camping chez l'habitant* (informal, privately run camp sites) in Entre-Deux, Îlet-à-Vidot and Bélouve. The Cirque de Mafate also features a few simple camping spots.

You can camp for free in some designated areas in the Cirques, but only for one night at a time. Setting up camp on Piton de la Fournaise (the volcano) is forbidden for obvious reasons.

ⓘ SLEEPING PRICE RANGES

Throughout this chapter, the order of accommodation listings is by price, from the least to the most expensive. Each place to stay is accompanied by one of the following symbols (the price relates to a double room with private bathroom). Prices include all government taxes.

€ less than €50

€€ €50–100

€€€ more than €100

Chambres d'Hôtes

Chambres d'hôtes are the French equivalent of B&Bs. They are normally tucked away in the hills or in scenic locations and offer a window into a more traditional way of life. Options include everything from restored Creole houses or modern buildings to rooms in family houses. On the whole, standards are high, and rooms are generally good value. B&B rates are from around €45 for a double room. Breakfast is always included.

Many *chambres d'hôtes* also offer *tables d'hôtes* (hearty evening meals) at around €17 to €30 per person (set menu), but this must be reserved in advance (usually the day before). This is a fantastic way to meet locals and sample the local cuisine.

Many *chambres d'hôtes* are members of **Gîtes de France** (www.gites-de-france-reunion.com). This organisation has a brochure listing all the *chambres d'hôtes* in Réunion; you can find it in tourist offices. They are also listed on the website. *Chambres d'hôtes* can be booked either through Gîtes de France or by phoning the owners directly.

Gîtes de Montagne

Gîtes de montagne are basic mountain cabins or lodges, operated by the local authorities through the Centrale de Réservation – Île de la Réunion. It is possible to organise a walking holiday using the *gîtes de montagne* only.

The *gîtes de montagne* in Réunion are generally in pretty good condition. Thanks to solar power, they all now have electricity, although not all get as cushy as providing warm showers. The Gîte de la Caverne Dufour at Piton des Neiges is the most basic: it has no hot water, but there are inside toilets.

Gîtes de montagne must be booked and paid for in advance, and charges are not refundable unless a cyclone or a cyclone alert prevents your arrival. In practice, you won't be denied access if you just turn up without your voucher, but you may not have a bed if it's full. Last-minute reservations may be accepted, as there are often last-minute cancellations.

You can book through the Centrale d'Information et de Réservation Régionale – Île de la Réunion Tourisme (p37) or through any tourist office on the island, including those in St-Denis, Cilaos, Salazie, Hell-Bourg, St-Gilles-les-Bains, St-Pierre, St-Leu, St-André, Ste-Anne, and Bourg-Murat. It's highly recommended that you book well in advance, especially during the busy tourist seasons. One night's accommodation without food costs €16 or €18 per person depending on season.

When staying in a *gîte de montagne,* you have to call the *gîte* at least one day ahead to book your meals (or you can ask for this to be done for you when you make the original booking). Dinner costs from €15 to €18, and usually consists of hearty *carris*. Breakfast costs around €5 and normally consists of coffee, bread and jam. Payment is made directly to the caretaker, in cash.

Sleeping arrangements usually consist of bunk beds in shared rooms, so be prepared for the communal living that this entails, although the more recent *gîtes* usually have a few private rooms. Sheets and blankets are provided, though you might want to bring a sheet sleeping bag (a sleep sheet).

It's not a bad idea to also bring along toilet paper and a torch. It can get quite chilly at night, so warm clothing will be in order. Some places will let you cook, but many kitchens are so basic – and sometimes grimy – that you probably won't bother.

On arrival and departure you must 'book' in and out with the manager, who will collect your voucher and payment for meals. In theory, you're not meant to occupy a *gîte* before 3pm or remain past 10am.

Gîtes d'Étapes

Gîtes d'étapes, sometimes simply called *gîtes*, are privately owned and work in roughly the same way as the *gîtes de montagne*, offering dorm beds and meals. Some places even have doubles. One main difference is that you can book these places directly with the owners. There are numerous *gîtes d'étapes* in the Cirque de Mafate, and others dotted around the island; most are in the vicinity of walking trails. The host will often offer meals or cooking facilities.

Local tourist offices can provide lists of *gîtes d'étapes* in their area. Also check out the website www.reunion.fr.

Meublés de Tourisme & Gîtes Ruraux

Gîtes ruraux and *meublés de tourisme* are private houses and lodges that families and groups can rent for self-catering holidays, normally by the week or weekend. There are dozens of *gîtes ruraux* scattered all over the island.

Most offer lodging for four or more people, with facilities of varying standards. Costs vary from around €300 to €600 per week and from €100 to €250 for a weekend (note that not all offer bookings for just a weekend). If you average out the per-person, per-week price and factor in cooking several meals in the house, *gîte* stays can actually be quite economical. Plus, the *gîte* owner often lives nearby and can be a mine of local information.

Contact Gîtes de France, local tourist offices or check out the websites www.reunion.fr and www.iha.fr. *Gîtes ruraux* and *Meublés de Tourisme* can be booked by phoning the owners directly. A deposit of some sort is usually required in advance.

Hotels

If you're after serious cosseting and ultraposh digs, you might be looking at the wrong place. Most hotels on the island are rated as one-, two- or three-star, and lots are unclassified. There is only a sprinkling of four- and five-star hotels.

Hotels are found in St-Denis and around the beach resorts of the west coast, though you'll also find some scattered in the interior.

CHILDREN

➡ Réunion is an eminently suitable destination if you're travelling with the kids in tow. With its abundance of beaches, picnic spots and outdoor activities, plus its healthy food, it offers plenty to do for travellers of all ages in a generally hazard-free setting.

➡ Most locals have a number of children themselves and will not be troubled by a screaming child at the next table.

➡ Few hotels offer kids' clubs but many places provide cots for free and additional beds for children at a small extra cost. Most *chambres d'hôtes* welcome children.

➡ Many restaurants have children's menus with significantly lower prices.

➡ There are excellent medical facilities in the main cities.

CONSULATES

Since Réunion isn't independent, only a few countries have diplomatic representation:

Belgium Consulate (✆0262 97 99 10; chatel@groupechatel.com; 80 Rue Adolphe Pegoud, Ste-Marie)

German Consulate (✆0692 73 68 98; st-denis@hk-diplo.de; 64 Ave Eudoxie Nonge, Ste-Clotilde)

Madagascar Consulate (✆0262 72 07 30; consulat-madrun@wanadoo.fr; 29 Rue St Joseph Ouvrier, St-Denis)

Seychelles Consulate (✆0262 57 26 38; hrop@wanadoo.fr; 67 Chemin Kerveguen, Le Tampon)

Swiss Consulate (✆0692 60 25 36, 0262 52 56 41; reunion@honrep.ch; 3bis Impasse Tapioca, Bois Rouge)

CUSTOMS REGULATIONS

➡ The following items can be brought into Réunion duty-free: 200 cigarettes, 50 cigars, 1L of strong liquor or 2L of liquor that is less than 22% alcohol by volume, 2L of wine, 50mL of perfume and 250mL of *eau de toilette*, and other goods up to the value of €880. Anything over the limit must be declared on arrival.

➡ There are restrictions on importing plants and animals, for which import permits are required.

➡ With regards to currency, anyone entering or leaving the island must declare sums in excess of €10,000.

GAY & LESBIAN TRAVELLERS

French laws concerning homosexuality prevail in Réunion, which means there is no legal discrimination against homosexual activity and homophobia is relatively uncommon. People are fairly tolerant, though by no means as liberal as in mainland France; open displays of affection may be regarded with disdain, especially outside St-Denis.

Throughout the island, but particularly on the west coast, there are restaurants, bars, operators and accommodation places that make a point of welcoming gays and lesbians. Certain areas are the focus of the gay and lesbian communities, among them St-Denis, St-Pierre and La Saline-les-Bains. You'll find some gay-friendly accommodation options on www.gay-sejour.com.

INTERNET ACCESS

➡ Many midrange and all top-end hotels offer wi-fi access, as do B&Bs, many cafes and most tourist offices, usually without a charge. In hotels, coverage may be restricted to public areas.

➡ Internet cafes can be found only in bigger towns and resort areas such as St-Denis, St-Gilles-les-Bains and St-Pierre. The connection is generally good and rates are fairly standard at around €9 per hour.

MAPS

➡ Find maps at tourist offices and bookshops. The website fr.mappy.com has online maps and a journey planner, including petrol costs.

➡ For most purposes the **IGN** (Institut Géographique National; www.ign.fr) *Carte Touristique La Réunion* map, at a scale of 1:100,000 (1cm = 1km), which covers the island in one sheet, is perfectly adequate.

➡ The most detailed and accurate maps for hiking are the six-sheet 1:25,000 series published by IGN.

MONEY

As in France, the unit of currency is the euro (€), which is divided into 100 cents. Euro coins come in denominations of one, two, five, 10, 20 and 50 cents and one and two euros. Banknotes are issued in denominations of five, 10, 20, 50 and 100 euros.

ATMs

➺ ATMs are the easiest way to access funds while in Réunion, but banks charge foreign-transaction fees plus a per-use ATM charge.

➺ Most banks and post offices have an ATM (known as a *guichet automatique de banque* or *gabier*).

➺ Visa and MasterCard are the most widely accepted.

➺ Check with your bank before you leave home to ensure that the card you plan to use to withdraw cash doesn't have a low daily or weekly limit.

➺ If you're heading off into the Cirques, it's wise to stock up with euros beforehand – Cilaos and Hell-Bourg have only one ATM each.

Credit Cards

Credit cards will prove the cheapest and easiest way to pay for major purchases in Réunion. Visa (Carte Bleue) and MasterCard (Eurocard) are the cards most widely accepted by hotels, restaurants, supermarkets, adventure centres, major petrol stations and stores. Credit cards are mandatory if you want to rent a car, as they'll be used as a form of *caution* (deposit). Smaller places, however, sometimes refuse cards for small amounts (typically under €15) and it's rare for *chambres d'hôtes* and *gîtes d'étapes* to take credit cards.

It's a good idea to check with your credit-card company before leaving home about charges on international transactions.

Moneychangers

➺ All banks in Réunion have dropped their foreign-exchange facilities in favour or ATMs.

ⓘ EATING PRICE RANGES

The service charge is included in the bill. Throughout this chapter we have used the following price ranges for a standard main course. For information on the kind of food you're likely to come across in Réunion, see p259.

€ under €10

€€ €10 to €20

€€€ over €20

➺ There's only one bureau de change on the island – it's outside Roland Garros International Airport.

➺ As a general strategy, it's sensible to bring a fair supply of euros with you and to top up from the ATMs.

Tipping

Tipping is not necessary in Réunion.

OPENING HOURS

Banks Usually open from 8am to 4pm, Monday to Friday or Tuesday to Saturday.

Bars and clubs Normally serve from late morning until the last customers leave (late); nightclubs generally go from 10pm into the wee hours on Friday and Saturday.

Government offices Open from 8.30am to noon and 2pm to 5pm Monday to Thursday, to 3pm Friday.

Restaurants Open for lunch between 11.30am or noon and 2pm and for dinner from 7pm; they are often closed on one or two days of the week.

Shops and businesses Usually from 8.30am to 5pm or 6pm Monday to Saturday, often with a break from noon to 1pm or 2pm. Some shops close on Monday.

PUBLIC HOLIDAYS

Most of Réunion's offices, museums and shops are closed during *jours fériés* (public holidays).

New Year's Day 1 January

Easter Monday March/April

Labour Day 1 May

Victory Day 1945 8 May

Ascension Day late May or June

Bastille Day (National Day) 14 July

Assumption Day 15 August

All Saints' Day 1 November

Armistice Day 1918 11 November

Abolition of Slavery Day 20 December

Christmas Day 25 December

SAFE TRAVEL

Overall, Réunion is relatively safe compared with most Western countries, but occasional robberies do occur. Don't leave anything of value in a rental car or on the beach.

Violence is rarely a problem, and muggings are almost unheard of. Intoxicated people are the most likely troublemakers.

Driving

Unfortunately Réunion has a bad record when it comes to road safety, which means that you must drive defensively at all times. Potential dangers include drunk drivers, excessive speed, twisting roads and blind bends.

Swimming

Swimmers should always be aware of currents and riptides. Drowning is a major cause of accidental death for visitors. If you're not familiar with water conditions, ask around. It's best not to swim alone in unfamiliar places.

Recent years have seen a significant increase in attacks by *les dents de la mer* (sharks) on surfers. This is no reason to be paranoid, though; the risks are statistically low. The locals know their ocean, so it's best to seek their advice before entering the water.

TELEPHONE

➡ All telephone numbers throughout Réunion consist of 10 digits; landline numbers start with 🗾 0262, and mobile-phone numbers start with 🗾 0692 or 🗾 0693. If calling a Réunion landline or mobile number from abroad (bar France), you'll need to dial your country's international-access code, Réunion's country code (🗾 262), then the local number minus the initial 0. Calling abroad from Réunion, dial 🗾 00 for international access, then country code, then area code and local number.

➡ For mobile phones, Réunion uses the GSM 900/1800 system, which is compatible with Europe and Australia, but incompatible with North American GSM 1900. The network covers most towns and villages throughout the island, including the Cirque de Mafate.

➡ If your GSM phone has been 'unlocked', it is also possible to buy a SIM card with either of the two local network operators: **Orange** (www. orange.re) and **SFR** (www.sfr.re). Recharge cards are readily available.

➡ There are various prepaid calling cards (available at newsagents) that require you to dial a free number and enter a personal identity number (PIN) before you place your call.

➡ There are no area codes in Réunion.

TOURIST INFORMATION

➡ There are generally *offices du tourisme* (tourist offices) in most main towns across the island. Most of them have at least one staff member who speaks English.

➡ Tourist-office staff provide maps, brochures and the twice-yearly magazine *Guide RUN*, which is a useful directory of hotels, restaurants, discos and other places of interest to visitors.

➡ The **Centrale d'Information et de Réservation Régionale – Île de la Réunion Tourisme** (www.reunion.fr) is Réunion's regional tourist office.

➡ You can also contact the French tourist office in your home country; these are listed on www. franceguide.com.

PRACTICALITIES

➡ **Electricity** 220V, 50Hz AC; plugs have two round pins.

➡ **Newspapers** Daily regional newspapers include *Journal de l'Île de la Réunion* (www.clicanoo.re) and *Le Quotidien* (www.lequotidien.re), both good for features and events listings.

➡ **Radio** Tune in to **Réunion 1re** (www. reunion.la1ere.fr/radio), **Kreol FM** (www. radiokreol.com) or **Radio Free Dom** (www.freedom.fr) for local news (in French and Creole).

➡ **TV** One government channel, Réunion 1re, as well as the independent Antenne Réunion and Canal + Réunion; most programming comes from mainland France.

➡ **Weights & Measures** Metric.

TRAVELLERS WITH DISABILITIES

Independent travel is difficult for anyone who has mobility problems in Réunion. Only the newest of newly remodeled businesses have features that are specifically suited to wheelchair use.

Negotiating the streets of most towns in a wheelchair is frustrating given the lack of adequate equipment, and most outdoor attractions and historic places don't have trails suited to wheelchair use. Two notable exceptions are Kelonia in St-Leu, and the renovated Maison du Volcan in Bourg-Murat.

VISAS

Though Réunion is a French department, it's not part of the Schengen treaty. The visa requirements for entry to Réunion are almost the same as for France, bar a few exceptions. For EU nationals, a national ID or a passport suffices. Citizens of a number of other Western countries, including Australia, the USA, Canada and New Zealand, do not need visas to visit Réunion as tourists for up to three months; they need only a passport.

Other nationals should check with the French embassy or consulate nearest your home address to find out if you need a visa. For example, Brazilian citizens do not need a visa to enter mainland France but do require a visa for Réunion. For up-to-date information on visa requirements see www.diplomatie.gouv.fr.

WOMEN TRAVELLERS

➡ The sight of women travelling, be it in a group or alone, is not met with too much surprise or curiosity, and women travelling by themselves should encounter no difficulties, as long as sensible precautions observed in most Western countries are adhered to.

➡ Women can enter most bars alone, but there are still a few places where this may attract unwanted attention – you'll get a pretty good idea when you enter.

➡ It's not advisable to walk alone on the trails in the interior.

❶ Getting There & Away

AIR

➡ Réunion has two international airports. The vast majority of flights come into **Roland Garros International Airport** (☑ 0262 28 16 16; www.reunion.aeroport.fr) about 10km east of St-Denis. For details on getting to St-Denis from the airport see p176. Coming from Mauritius, you have the option of landing at **Pierrefonds Airport** (☑ 0262 96 77 66; www.grandsudreunion.org), in the south of the island near St-Pierre.

➡ The main international carriers are Air France (p185), Air Austral (p185) and Corsair (p185), which offer direct daily flights to France.

➡ Air Austral also operates regular flights to Antananarivo (Madagascar), Bangkok (Thailand), Chennai (India), Johannesburg (South Africa), Mahé (Seychelles), Mauritius, Mayotte and Moroni (Comoros).

➡ Other airlines include Air Mauritius (p185), which flies three to four times a day to Mauritius, Air Madagascar (p185), which serves various destinations in Madagascar, including Antananarivo, Diego Suarez, Fort Dauphin, Île Ste-Marie, Tamatave and Tulear, and **XL Airways** (☑ +33 322 192 504; www.xlairways.fr), with weekly flights to Marseille (France).

➡ All airlines have offices in St-Denis and/or at the airport. Some airlines are also represented in St-Pierre.

➡ If you're coming from North America, your best bet is to fly to Paris and find an onward connection to Réunion. From Australasia, fly to Mauritius and then continue to Réunion with Air Austral or Air Mauritius.

SEA

The Mauritius Shipping Corporation operates two boats, the *Mauritius Trochetia* and the *Mauritius Pride*, between Réunion and Mauritius, with at least one sailing per week in low season, and up to two sailings per week in high season. The one-way journey takes about 11 hours. The return fare from Réunion in low/high season starts at roughly €160/173 for a berth in a 2nd-class cabin.

Tickets and information are available through travel agents or direct from the Mauritius Shipping Corporation representative **SCOAM** (☑ 0262 42 19 45; passagers@scoam.fr; 4 av. du 14-Juillet-1789, Le Port).

❶ Getting Around

BICYCLE

The traffic, the haste of most motorists and the steep and precarious nature of the mountain roads means that those considering cycling as a form of transport in Réunion should be prepared for some hair-raising and potentially dangerous situations.

BUS

Réunion's major towns and many of the little ones in between are linked by bus. The island's bus service is knows as **Car Jaune** (☑ 0810 123 974; www.cg974.fr/index.php/Horaires-des-Cars-jaunes.html) and has distinctive yellow buses. The main *gare routière* (bus station) is on Blvd Lancastel on the St-Denis seafront.

Buses on most routes run between about 6am and 7pm, with a limited number of services on Sunday. You can pay the driver as you board. To get the bus to stop, you ring the bell or clap your hands twice loudly.

Car Jaune provides regional minibus services for several areas on the island; they run from St-Benoît, St-Joseph, Ste-Rose, St-Leu and St-Paul. These convoluted local routes can be fairly confusing, particularly if you don't speak much French. Of most use to travellers are the buses from St-André to Salazie, Salazie to Hell-Bourg, Grand Îlet and Le Bélier, and the buses from St-Louis to Cilaos, Îlet à Cordes and Bras-Sec.

CAR

➡ With most attractions located in the hills, we strongly recommend hiring a vehicle.

➡ The road system on the island is excellent and well signposted. Inaugurated in June 2009 after six years of work, the Route des Tamarins is a four-lane expressway that connects Saint-Paul to Étang-Salé (34km) and branches onto the existing RN1. It creates a direct route between the two biggest cities, St-Denis in the north and St-Pierre in the south.

➡ Routes *départementales*, whose names begin with the letter D (or RD), are tertiary local roads, many of them very tortuous (use your horn!)

➡ There are some gorgeous runs, cruising along the island's dramatic roads; heading into the mountains via the Cirques roads is a magnificent experience. The superbly engineered roads snake through hairpin bends, up steep slopes and along sheer drops, surrounded all the while by glorious scenery.

• Be prepared for traffic jams near the main cities.

• Petrol stations are very easy to come by. A litre of unleaded cost €1.66 at the time of writing. Most stations accept credit cards.

Hire

• Good news: *location de voitures* (car hire) is extremely popular in Réunion, and rates are very reasonable. Rates start at €35 per day (including third-party liability insurance and unlimited mileage) and can drop as low as €25 per day or €20 if you rent for several weeks. Most companies require a credit card, primarily so that you can leave a *caution* (deposit).

• Most companies stipulate that the driver must be at least 21 (sometimes 23) years of age, have held a driving licence for at least a year, and have a passport or some other form of identification. EU citizens can drive on their national driving licence; from elsewhere, you'll need an international driving licence.

• Collision-damage waivers (CDW, or *assurance tous risques*) are not included and vary greatly from company to company. The *franchise* (excess) for a small car is usually around €800. You can reduce it to zero (or at least to a half) by paying a daily insurance supplement of around €10.

• Arranging your car rental before you leave home is usually cheaper than a walk-in rental. Deals can be found on the internet through online hire companies like **DriveAway Holidays** (www.driveaway.com.au) in Australia, **Holiday Autos** (www.holidayautos.co.uk) in the UK, **Auto Europe** (www.autoeurope.com) in the US and **Location de Voiture** (www.elocationdevoitures.fr) in France.

→ All major firms have a desk at the airports.

→ There are also plenty of independent operators around the island. They are cheaper than international companies but their rental cars are usually older. Most offer delivery to the airport for a surcharge. Reputable ones include the following:

Cool Location (☎0693 10 10 11, 0692 19 26 00; cool.location@orange.fr; St-Denis)

Degrif' Loc – Bonne Route (☎0262 26 29 44, 0692 05 18 32; www.degrifloc.re; St-Louis)

ITC Tropicar (☎0262 24 01 01; www.itc-tropicar.com) Has offices in St-Denis, St-Pierre, St-Gilles-les-Bains and at the airport.

Location Saint-Leusienne (☎0262 34 77 12, 0692 86 44 90; www.locationsaint-leusienne.com; St-Leu)

Mik Location (☎0262 35 30 63; www.mik-location.re) Offices in St-Denis and St-Pierre.

Multi Auto (☎0262 29 01 66, 0692 70 37 03; www.multiauto.re) In Ste-Clotilde and St-André.

Road Rules

Like mainland France, Réunion keeps to the right side of the road. Speed limits are clearly indicated and vary from 50km/h in towns to 110km/h on dual carriageways. Drivers and passengers are required to wear seat belts. The alcohol limit is 0.5g/L.

RÉUNION GETTING AROUND

Seychelles

Best Places to Eat

➡ La Plage (p283)

➡ Les Lauriers (p301)

➡ Café des Arts (p301)

➡ Domaine de L'Orangeraie Resort & Spa – Le Combava (p309)

➡ Loutier Coco (p309)

Best Places to Stay

➡ Beau Séjour (p275)

➡ Chalets d'Anse Forban (p287)

➡ Anse Takamaka View (p289)

➡ Château de Feuilles (p298)

➡ Bird Island Lodge (p311)

Why Go?

Close your eyes. And just imagine. You're lazing on a talcum-powder beach lapped by topaz waters and backed by lush hills and big glacis boulders. Brochure material? No, just routine in the Seychelles. With such a dreamlike setting, the Seychelles is unsurprisingly a choice place for newlyweds. But for those looking for more than a suntan or romance, this archipelago offers a number of high-energy distractions. There are jungle and coastal walks, boat excursions, and diving and snorkelling to keep you buzzing. Ecotourism is big – there are marine parks and natural reserves filled with endemic species that are easy to approach.

The Seychelles is more affordable than you think. On top of ultra-luxurious options, the country has plenty of self-catering facilities and family-run guesthouses that offer local colour. So if you are suffering from visions of tropical paradise, here is your medicine.

When to Go

➡ From December to March, the trade winds bring warmer, wetter air streams from the northwest. From June to September the southeast trades usher in cooler, drier weather but the winds whip up the waves and you'll want to find protected beaches.

➡ The turnaround periods (April to May and October to November), which are normally calm and windless, are ideal.

➡ The rainfall varies considerably from island to island and from year to year. Mahé and Silhouette, the most mountainous islands, get the highest rainfall.

➡ The Seychelles lies outside the cyclone zone.

➡ Temperatures range between 24°C and 32°C throughout the year.

➡ Accommodation can be hard to find during the peak seasons from December to January and July to August.

Arriving in the Seychelles

Most visitors fly into the Seychelles' only international airport, which is located on Mahé. Big hotels provide transport to and from the airport. Taxis from just outside the airport cost from Rs 500 to Beau Vallon. Regular ferries and planes connect Mahé with Praslin.

ESSENTIAL FOOD & DRINK

Meat lovers, come prepared: the cuisine of the Seychelles is heavily influenced by the surrounding ocean, with fish appearing as the main ingredient in many dishes. Cultural influences are also distinctive, with a blend of European (mostly French and Italian) and African gastronomic delights.

The real beauty of Seychellois cuisine is its freshness and simplicity. After all, what could be better than the fish of the day with rice or the bright flavours of a smoked fish salad? Throw in views of lush hills and azure sea, some fine local beer or a freshly squeezed juice and you are looking at a great culinary experience – simple but great.

You'll find various types of eateries, from takeaway outlets to refined restaurants serving more elaborate dishes.

Many visitors to the Seychelles opt for packages that include breakfast and dinner at their hotel. If you'd prefer to sample local specialities, enjoy the Seychelles' many fine eateries, feast on views, and share a beach picnic with the locals, you'll find that a bed and breakfast will allow you more flexibility.

Keeping Costs Down

➡ Buy simple Creole dishes at takeaway outlets or at the market in Victoria. You can also self-cater on the three main islands

➡ Catch the cargo ship between Mahé and La Digue instead of getting around by ferry or by plane

➡ Get around Mahé and Praslin by public bus

➡ Opt for family-run guesthouses or medium-sized, locally owned hotels

➡ Look for promotional deals on hotel websites

AT A GLANCE

➡ **Currency**
Seychellois rupee (Rs)

➡ **Languages** English, French, Creole

➡ **Mobile phones** GSM network through Cable & Wireless and Airtel; international roaming and local SIM cards available

➡ **Money** ATMs on Mahé, Praslin and La Digue; credit cards widely accepted

➡ **Visas** Not required for most countries for three-month stays

Fast Facts

➡ **Capital** Port Louis

➡ **Country code** ☎ 230

➡ **Population** 1.322 million

➡ **Time** GMT + four hours

Exchange Rates

For current exchange rates see www.xe.com.

A$1	Rs 10.2
C$1	Rs 10.8
€1	Rs 15.1
¥100	Rs 11.6
NZ$1	Rs 9
UK£1	Rs 17.7
US$1	Rs 11.3

Resources

➡ **Lonely Planet** (www.lonelyplanet.com/seychelles)

➡ **Seychelles Travel** (www.seychelles.travel)

➡ **Nature Seychelles** (www.natureseychelles.org)

SEYCHELLES

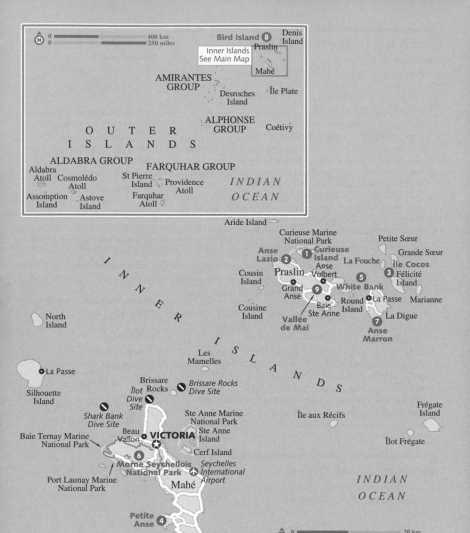

Seychelles Highlights

1 Scratch the leathery neck of a giant tortoise on **Curieuse Island** (p299)

2 Splash around in the jewelled waters of **Anse Lazio** (p293)

3 Snorkel over colourful fish and coral off **Île Cocos** (p306)

4 Unwind on blissful **Petite Anse** (p288)

5 Dive **White Bank** (p306), a thrilling site noted for its dense fish life

6 Look for the smallest frog on earth while exploring **Morne Seychellois National Park** (p284)

7 Take an unforgettable coastal hike to **Anse Marron** (p306)

8 Live out that stranded-on-a-desert-island fantasy on secluded **Bird Island** (p311)

9 Hear yourself screaming 'Oh, these coconuts are so sexy!' in the **Vallée de Mai** (p292)

MAHÉ

When it comes to wishing for the archetypal idyllic island, it's impossible to think past the glorious bays caressed by the gorgeously multi-hued waters of Mahé. To the northeast, a range of granite peaks, including Mahé's highest point, Morne Seychellois (905m), adds to this vivid panorama.

By far the largest and most developed of the Seychelles islands, Mahé (named by the French in honour of the 18th-century governor of Mauritius, Mahé de Labourdonnais) is home to the country's capital, Victoria, and to about 90% of the Seychelles' population. Small wonder that it has excellent vacation and adventure opportunities, from exploring the mountainous jungle of the interior to diving pristine sites and snorkelling with whale sharks. Or just do nothing at all and flake out on porcelain-sand beaches. Wherever you're based, paradise lies close at hand – a bus or car ride of no more than 20 minutes will bring you to fabulous natural attractions.

Victoria

POP 25,300

Victoria may be the country's main economic, political and commercial hub, but peak hour here lasts an unbearable 10 minutes! It is home to about a third of the Seychelles' population, but even so Victoria retains the air of a provincial town. While it may not fulfil all fantasies about tropical paradise, the city still has a little charm and a little promise when you scratch beneath the surface. There's a bustling market, manicured botanical gardens and a fistful of attractive old colonial buildings sidling up alongside modern structures and shopping plazas. It's also a good place to grab last-minute gifts before heading home.

Oh, and there's the setting. Victoria is set against an impressive backdrop of hills that seem to tumble into the turquoise sea.

◉ Sights

Market   MARKET
(Market St; ⊙ 5.30am-5pm Mon-Fri, to noon Sat) No trip to Victoria would be complete without a wander through the covered market. It's very small by African standards, but it's a bustling, colourful place nonetheless. Alongside fresh fruit and vegetables, stalls sell souvenirs such as local spices and herbs, as well as the usual assortment of *pareos* (sarongs) and shirts. Early morning is the best time to come, when fishmongers display an astonishing variety of seafood, from parrot fish to barracuda. It's at its liveliest on Saturday.

Clock Tower   MONUMENT
(cnr Francis Rachel St & Independence Ave) The focal point of the city centre is this downsized replica of the clock tower on London's Vauxhall Bridge. The replica was brought to Victoria in 1903 when the Seychelles became a crown colony.

Old Courthouse   HISTORIC BUILDING
(Francis Rachel St, Supreme Court) The old courthouse beside the clock tower will appeal to fans of Creole architecture, as will the colonial buildings that are scattered along Francis Rachel and Albert Sts.

Kanti House   HISTORIC BUILDING
(Albert St) Make a beeline for this atmospheric shop that has been restored. It specialises in clothing.

Botanical Gardens   GARDENS
(☑ 4670500; admission Rs 100; ⊙ 8am-5pm) For respite, the manicured botanical gardens, full of streams and birdsong, are about 10 minutes' walk south of the centre. Star attractions are the coco de mer palms lining the main alley. There's also a spice grove, a pen of giant tortoises, a patch of rainforest complete with fruit bats, and a cafeteria.

Anglican Church   CHURCH
(Albert St) Taking pride of place in the centre of town is the Anglican church, with its renovated facade and elegant tower.

**Sheikh Mohamed bin
Khalifa Mosque**   MOSQUE
(Francis Rachel St) Tucked away from the main drag is this modern mosque, which is a popular spot for the prayers of Victoria's small Muslim community, especially on Friday morning.

**Arul Mihu Navasakthi
Vinyagar Temple**   HINDU
(Quincy St) With its brightly painted decor, Victoria's small but eye-catching Hindu temple stands out among a row of nondescript buildings. It's used by the city's Indian community.

Cathedral of the Immaculate Conception
CHURCH

(Olivier Marandan St) This imposing cathedral is noteworthy for its elegant portal and colonnaded facade. The building to the left of the cathedral is the **Domus** – it's the priest's residence and a national monument.

Natural History Museum
MUSEUM

(☏4321333; Independence Ave; admission Rs 15; ◷8.30am-4.30pm Mon-Thu, to noon Fri & Sat) The Natural History Museum is worth a quick visit to learn about the islands' geology, fauna and flora. The upstairs section is devoted to marine life.

Mahé

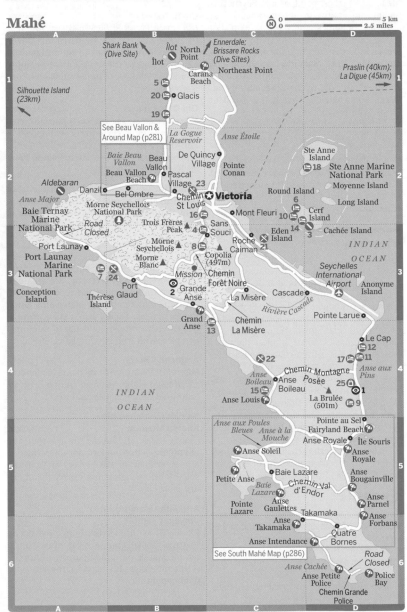

✼ Festivals & Events

Carnaval International de Victoria CARNIVAL
The biggest party in the country is usually held in late April. Three days of street parties and various performances, with a costume parade among its highlights.

FetAfrik CULTURAL FESTIVAL
The Seychelles celebrates its African origins with a weekend of music and dance in late May.

Festival Kreol CULTURAL FESTIVAL
(www.festival-kreol.sc) Week-long festival of Creole culture; last week of October.

SUBIOS Underwater Festival FILM & PHOTOGRAPHY
(www.subios.com) Three-day-long underwater-photography competition at Beau Vallon held in October or November.

🛏 Sleeping

Victoria's range of accommodation is disappointingly slim, especially considering it's the capital, so it does make sense to stay elsewhere, for instance in nearby Beau Vallon, and visit the town on day trips.

★ **Beau Séjour** GUESTHOUSE €€
(beausejourhotel_sey@yahoo.com; Curio Rd, Bel Air; s/d incl breakfast €75/100; P☀🛜) A guesthouse with style, Beau Séjour is a lovely place to dawdle in and soak up the tranquil charm. Digs are in a villa perched on a hillside, at the foot of the Trois Frères – the lo-

cation is one of the best in northern Mahé. It's sparkling clean and it even has that rare thing – character, in abundance. Shame that only rooms No 1 and 5 come with a view of Victoria and Ste Anne Marine National Park (other rooms are at the back). Meals can be arranged on request.

Mountain Rise HOTEL €€
(📞2716717, 4225308; mountainrise@seychelles.net; Sans Souci Rd; s/d incl breakfast €85/110; P🛜🛁) Up on the road to Sans Souci (but an easy bus ride from the centre), Mountain Rise is in an atmospheric, airy heritage home that offers five unadorned yet spacious rooms. There's also a good Creole restaurant and a swimming pool. No air-con, but the location benefits from cooling breezes.

🍴 Eating

★ **Lai Lam Food Shop** TAKEAWAY €
(Benezet St; mains Rs 20-50; ☺lunch Mon-Sat) Order roast chicken, beef curry or other wholesome Creole staples at this crazily popular takeaway outlet smack dab in the centre. Perfect to fill up on the cheap and take in the vibe from Victoria's working crowd.

Hot Spot Take Away TAKEAWAY €
(Quincy St; mains Rs 30-50; ☺lunch Mon-Sat) Frills are sparse, but servings are anything but stingy in this hole-in-the-wall next door to the Hindu temple. Expect salted pork, yellowfin tuna steak, fried rice and fish 'n' chips.

SEYCHELLES VICTORIA

Mahé

Double Click
CAFETERIA **€**

(☑ 4224796; Palm St; mains Rs 50-90; ⊙ 8am-9pm Mon-Sat, 9am-8pm Sun) This buzzy eatery popular with students rustles up light meals, including salads, soups and sandwiches. It's nothing to write home about but prices are competitive. Keep your fluids up with a zesty smoothie or a juice concoction.

News Café
CAFETERIA **€€**

(☑ 4322999; Albert St, Trinity House; mains Rs 70-190; ⊙ 8.30am-5pm Mon-Fri, to 3pm Sat) This cheerful cafe-bar overlooking the main drag is an excellent venue to devour a comforting breakfast (muesli!) and read the daily news-papers, or to take a lunchtime break from town.

Pirates Arms
INTERNATIONAL **€€**

(☑ 4225001; Independence Ave; mains Rs 110-260; ⊙ 9am-11pm Mon-Sat, noon-11pm Sun) Despite its old-fashioned decor and faded furniture, this central cafe-restaurant is *the* meeting point in Victoria and veritably thrums the minute it opens its doors for breakfast (served until 11am). The menu is as long as your arm and runs from salads and sand-wiches to pizzas and meat or fish dishes, all well prepared and well priced.

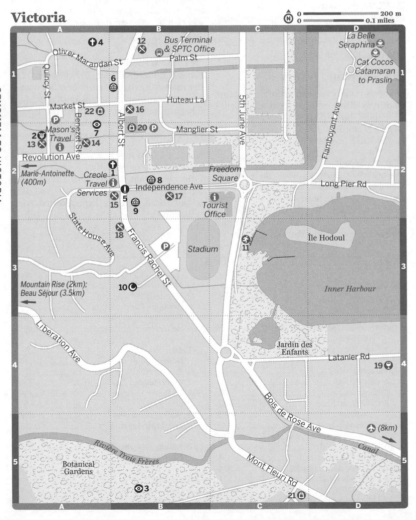

Victoria

Restaurant du Marché
SEAFOOD, EUROPEAN €€
(☑4225451; Market St; mains Rs 125-220; ⊙breakfast & lunch Mon-Sat) The food is fresh and tasty at this unpretentious yet appealing eatery within the market (upstairs). Typical dishes include smoked fish salad, tuna steak and fish fillet in coconut milk. It's a good place to catch local vibes and enjoy plenty of local colour.

Bravo
INTERNATIONAL €€
(☑4346020; Eden Island; mains Rs 180-500; ⊙noon-late Mon-Sat) A few kilometres south of town, this open-air restaurant overlooking the marina at Eden Island provides an enchanting dining experience with delectable food. Everything's pretty good, but if you want a recommendation, go for the Mega Burger or the seared tuna salad. Save some room for an ice cream with chocolate sauce.

Sam's Pizzeria
PIZZERIA €€
(☑4322499; Francis Rachel St; mains Rs 160-250; ⊙lunch & dinner) Step into this cool spot for an escape from the busy street. Walls are adorned with paintings by local artist George Camille, which gives the place a splash of style. Get things going with pizzas cooked in a wood-fired oven, salads, pasta or grilled fish and meat. And yes, it's open on Sunday – a rarity in Victoria. Take away is available.

Marie-Antoinette
CREOLE €€
(☑4266222; Serret Rd; menu Rs 265; ⊙lunch & dinner Mon-Sat) Marie-Antoinette isn't just a restaurant, it's an experience, especially at dinner. It occupies a beautiful wood-and-iron colonial Seychellois mansion. Bring an empty tum – the set *menu* includes fish and aubergine fritters, grilled fish, chicken curry, fish stew, rice and salad, though to be fair you do probably come here more for the sense of history than for the food. It's on the road to Beau Vallon.

Le Rendez Vous
INTERNATIONAL €€€
(☑4323556; Francis Rachel St; mains Rs 230-460; ⊙9am-10pm Mon-Sat) The Balinese-meets-Amazonian decor of this 1st-floor eatery overlooking the clock tower is easy on the eye, with darkwood furnishings, tropical plants and candlelit tables. The extensive menu takes in fish, meat, salads, pizzas and ice creams, but the quality of the food is a bit hit-and-miss.

🍸 Drinking & Nightlife

Pirates Arms
BAR
(Independence Ave; ⊙8am-9pm Mon-Sat, 9am-8pm Sun) Ask anyone of any age where to go for a drink in Victoria and this is always the enthusiastic answer. It's no wonder. With a reliable mix of tourists and locals, well-priced drinks and live music (a crooner with a guitar) on Friday evening, it's the most fun place in town.

Level Three Bar
BAR
(Latanier Rd; ⊙5pm-late Mon-Fri) Despite the odd location, in a nondescript building near the harbour, Level Three Bar is worth considering for its affordable cocktails (Rs 120) and its cool atmosphere. There's karaoke on Friday evening.

SEYCHELLES VICTORIA

Victoria

SEXY COCONUTS

This must be the sexiest fruit on earth. The *coco fesse* (the fruit of the coco de mer palm) looks like, ahem, buttocks with a female sex. It has been the source of many legends and erotic lore, given its peculiar shape. Now you can understand why these strange, sensual fruits excited the 17th-century sailors who first stumbled upon them after months at sea. Before 1768 the coconuts, which were occasionally found floating in the Indian Ocean, were believed to grow in a magic garden at the bottom of the sea. This rare palm grows naturally only in the Seychelles.

Only female trees produce the erotically shaped nuts, which can weigh over 30kg. The male tree possesses a decidedly phallic flower stem of 1m or longer, adding to the coco de mer's steamy reputation.

Harvesting the nuts is strictly controlled by the Seychelles Island Foundation (p278), an NGO that manages the Vallée de Mai on behalf of the government.

Boardwalk BAR
(Eden Island; ⌚11am-late) More a chilled-out bar than a restaurant, the Boardwalk is at the marina on Eden Island, a few kilometres south of town. Nab a seat on the wooden terrace, order a cocktail (from Rs 120) and ogle yachts you wished you owned. If you've got the munchies, salads, burgers and sandwiches are available.

Shopping

Camion Hall ARTS & CRAFTS
(Albert St; ⌚9am-5pm Mon-Sat) Head to this small shopping mall right in the centre for creative and interesting locally made arts and crafts.

Antik Colony Shop FASHION
(☎4321700; Independence Ave, Pirates Arms Bldg; ⌚9am-5pm Mon-Fri, 9am-1pm Sat) Antik Colony is a souvenir shop worth browsing for its quality garments, bags and T-shirts designed by the Italian owner. Essential oils are also available.

Sunstroke GALLERY
(☎4224767; Market St; ⌚9am-5pm Mon-Fri, 9.30am-1pm Sat) George Camille's lovely paintings can be found at this art gallery.

Seychelles Island Foundation COCONUTS
(SIF; ☎4321735; www.sif.sc; Mont Fleuri Rd, Victoria; ⌚9am-4pm Mon-Fri) If you want to buy a *coco fesse* (the fruit of the coco de mer palm), head to the Seychelles Island Foundation, which has some stock and will issue you the required export permit. Be prepared to fork out about €200.

Information

Barclays Bank (Albert St; ⌚8.30am-2.30pm Mon-Fri, to 11.30am Sat)

Barclays Bank (Independence Ave; ⌚8.30am-2.30pm Mon-Fri, to 11am Sat) Changes cash and has two ATMs.

Cable & Wireless (www.cwseychelles.com; Francis Rachel St; per hr Rs 40; ⌚7.30am-4.30pm Mon-Fri, 8am-noon Sat) Internet access. Also sells prepaid SIM cards.

Creole Travel Services (☎2297000; www.creoletravelservices.com; Albert St; ⌚8am-4.40pm Mon-Fri, to noon Sat) This reputable travel agency offers the full range of services, including ticketing, car hire and tours around Mahé and to other islands. Also shelters a bureau de change.

Double Click (☎4610590; Palm St; per hr Rs 40; ⌚8am-9pm Mon-Sat, 9am-8pm Sun; 📶) Internet cafe and money changer. Also offers wi-fi.

Mason's Travel (☎4288888; www.masonstravel.com; Revolution Ave; ⌚8am-4.30pm Mon-Fri, to noon Sat) A well-established travel agency. Offers a wide array of tours around Mahé and to other islands.

Tourist Office (☎4610804; www.seychelles.travel; Independence Ave; ⌚8am-4.30pm Mon-Fri, 9am-noon Sat) Has a few brochures and decent maps of Mahé, Praslin and La Digue.

Victoria Hospital (☎4388000; www.moh.gov.sc; Mont Fleuri) The country's main hospital.

Getting There & Around

Victoria is the main hub for buses around Mahé and for boats to Praslin and La Digue.

Coming from the airport, a taxi into town costs around Rs 400. Alternatively, cross the road and pick up any bus heading north.

All airlines have offices in Mahé. For further information regarding air travel, see p321.

Ste Anne Marine National Park

Ste Anne Marine National Park, off Victoria, consists of six islands. Of these, day-trippers are permitted to land on **Cerf Island** and **Moyenne Island**. Moyenne was owned by Brendon Grimshaw, an English newspaper editor, who passed away in 2012. He had spent 40 years hacking back the jungle to create his own tropical paradise. The largest of the six islands, and only 4km east of Victoria, is **Ste Anne Island**, which boasts ravishing beaches. **Round Island** was once home to a leper colony, but these days it's better known for the offshore snorkelling. A 10-villa luxury resort was under construction at the time of writing. As with Moyenne and Ste Anne Islands, the beaches are seriously alluring. **Long Island** has long been home to the prison but should welcome a new type of inmate with the opening of a swish hotel in 2014 or 2015. The smallest island of the lot, **Cachée**, lies southeast of Cerf. It's uninhabited.

Activities

The park is fantastic for **swimming** and **snorkelling**, although the coral is no longer as awesome as it was. Silting from construction works in the bay has led to significant coral damage, compounded by several episodes of coral 'bleaching'. There are superb **beaches** lapped by emerald waters, but expect some algae at certain times of the year.

The park is primarily visited on glass-bottomed **boat tours** offered by the main travel agencies in Victoria and some boat operators based in Beau Vallon. The cost of a full day's outing including snorkelling and lunch starts at €85/50 per adult/child. You can also contact the **Marine Charter Association** (MCA; 4322126; 5th June Ave, Victoria) which charges only €70/40 per adult/child. And yes, there's also **diving** in the park! There are about 10 dive sites, scattered off the various islands. Contact **Cerf Island Explorer** (2570043; palblanchard@hotmail.com; Cerf Island; Mon-Sat by reservation), a small outfit run by Marseillais Philippe Blanchard, who provides personalised service at affordable prices (€60/70 for a single/introductory dive). Dedicated snorkelling trips cost €30 (two people minimum). If you're not staying in the park, he can arrange pick-ups from Eden Island.

Note that the park authorities charge a fee of €10 per person (free for children under 12 years) to enter the marine park. Tour operators usually include this in their prices.

Sleeping & Eating

★ **Fairy Tern Chalet** APARTMENTS €€€
(4321733; www.fairyternchalet.sc; Cerf Island; d €147; ❄☎) Run by an affable South African couple, this is a great place to get away from it all. Digs are in two squeaky-clean, spacious bungalows overlooking the beach. If you don't fancy cooking, the restaurant at L'Habitation Cerf Island is a five-minute walk away. Free canoes.

L'Habitation Cerf Island HOTEL €€€
(2781311, 4323111; habicerf@seychelles.net; Cerf Island; d with half board from €210; ❄☎☒) This comfortable little colonial-style hotel is right on the beach, and just a 10-minute boat ride from Victoria. It has a tranquil, convivial and homey atmosphere with 12 sunny rooms, two villas and lovely gardens (but not much shade). The restaurant serves super-fresh seafood. Prices drop for stays longer than three nights.

Cerf Island Resort RESORT €€€
(4294500; www.cerf-resort.com; Cerf Island; d with half board from €475; ❄☎☒) This venture strikes a perfect balance between luxury, seclusion and privacy (there are only 24 villas), on a hillside. This is a romantic resort, extremely quiet and popular with honeymooners. Facilities include a small pool and a spa. One grumble: the beach lacks the wow factor.

Ste Anne Resort & Spa RESORT €€€
(4292000; www.sainteanne-resort.com; Ste Anne Island; d with half board from €975; ❄☎☒) Spread over 220 hectares of private land, the sprawling Ste Anne features a host of facilities and amenities, including an infinity pool, five restaurants, a handful of bars, a well-respected spa, a gym, a watersports centre, a kids club, tennis courts and gift shops. It comprises 87 villas (some with their own pool) scattered amid well-tended gardens and coconut palms. The icing on the cake: three beaches, all with different orientations. It's appropriate for couples and families alike. One quibble, though: part of the resort faces west towards Victoria harbour.

Beau Vallon & the North Coast

Beau Vallon (on Mahé's northwest coast, 3km from Victoria) is overbuilt by Seychellois standards, but you'll find it remarkably low-key and quiet if you have experienced other tropical destinations. The seaside ambience, with fishermen selling fresh fish late in the afternoon in the shade of takamaka trees, adds a dash of real life to the area.

Beau Vallon is the main destination on the northwest coast because of its beach and tourist infrastructure, but there's also some great scenery north, up the coast to **Glacis** and **North Point**. With your own wheels, it's a scenic drive on a narrow road that hugs the coastline, with intermittent, lovely views over secluded coves at the foot of the cliffs.

From Northeast Point, you can head down to Victoria via **Anse Étoile**.

West of Beau Vallon, the coastal road goes past **Bel Ombre**, which has a few good accommodation options and a little fishing harbour, and ends at **Danzil**, where La Scala restaurant lies. From there, you can walk to Anse Major. Ah, Anse Major...

Beaches

A long, brilliant-white arc of sand laced by palms and takamaka trees, **Beau Vallon beach** is the most popular in Mahé. Here the water is deep enough for swimming, but watch out for large swells between June and November. There's usually a lifeguard on duty.

If you're after a more intimate, more secluded strip of sand, head to the lovely **beach** just beside the Sunset Beach Hotel – no, it's not private. Going north, drive past

---

WORTH A TRIP

CARANA BEACH

Here's a secret, only known to locals (whisper it softly): Carana Beach. This tiny, dreamlike cove lapped by lapis lazuli waters offers a small patch of sand framed by big boulders, with a couple of palm trees leaning over the shore. It's at Northeast Point; look for a cement road on the left, in a high gradient descent of the road, or ask locals.

---

the hotel and after 150m look for a little cement path on the left, amid the vegetation.

Activities

Diving

There's plenty of great diving within the bay of Beau Vallon, including a few wrecks, as well as some top-notch dive sites well outside the bay. See p33 for more information.

Big Blue Divers   DIVING
(☑4261106; www.bigbluedivers.net; Beau Vallon; ⊙Mon-Sat) North of Beau Vallon, this small PADI outfit has introductory dives (€95), single dives (from €50), dive packages and certification courses.

Blue Sea Divers   DIVING
(☑2526051; www.blueseadivers.com; Beau Vallon; ⊙daily) This French-run operation offers the full slate of diving adventures, including introductory dives (from €95), single dives (from €50), certification courses and various dive packages. It also runs cruises around the Seychelles aboard the splendid live-aboard dive boat *Galatea* (www.divingcruises.com), which started operating in June 2013.

Underwater Centre/Dive Seychelles   DIVING
(☑4247165, 4345445; www.diveseychelles.com.sc; Beau Vallon; ⊙daily) This English-run, well-oiled PADI five-star dive centre is in the Berjaya Resort. Walk-in prices are from €52 per dive with full gear and €99 for an introductory dive. Certification courses and dive packages are available.

Snorkelling & Boat Tours

The bay of Beau Vallon also hosts a few good snorkelling spots, especially along the rocky shore up the coast to North Point. It's also the main launching pad for **boat excursions** and snorkelling trips to Baie Ternay at the northwestern tip of the island, where the reefs are healthy and marine life plentiful. Full-day excursions include entry fees to the park, barbecue lunch and snorkelling gear. The best season is from April to October. A group of four to six persons is required. Contact a recommended operator (or ask your hotel or guesthouse to do it for you).

At the Berjaya Resort, Underwater Centre/Dive Seychelles (p280) fits snorkelling (€20 to €30) in during its dive outings to L'Îlot, Baie Ternay Marine National Park and the lighthouse. It also rents snorkelling gear (€10 per day).

Beau Vallon & Around

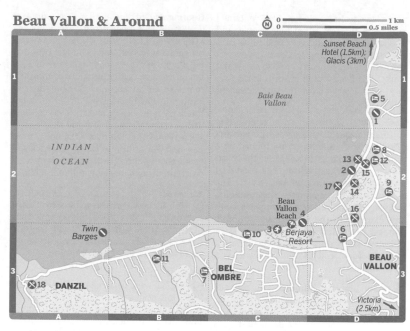

Dolphin Nemo Glass Bottom Boat
BOAT TOUR

(✆4261068, 2596922; Beau Vallon; full-day trip €80; ☺by reservation) Does the standard tours to Ste Anne Marine National Park and Baie Ternay. It has a small kiosk on the beach, just in front of the Berjaya Resort.

Jimmy Mancienne
BOAT TOUR

(✆2510269; full-day trip €85; ☺by reservation) A reputable operator. Specialises in tours to Baie Ternay but can also arrange trips to Ste Anne Marine National Park. All trips include swimming and snorkelling stops.

Teddy's Glass Bottom Boat
BOAT TOUR

(✆2511125, 2511198; half-/full-day trip €50/85; ☺by reservation) Good credentials. Runs glass-bottom trips to Baie Ternay and Ste Anne Marine National Park that include swimming and snorkelling stops.

Whale-Shark Spotting

Between August and October it's common to see whale sharks offshore from Mahé's north and west coasts. Underwater Centre/Dive Seychelles (p280) runs dedicated snorkelling trips focusing on whale sharks in September and October (€135 to €150). It also runs whale-shark monitoring programs.

Beau Vallon & Around

🛏 Sleeping

Beau Vallon Residence
APARTMENT €

(✆2516067; www.beauvallonresidence.sc; Beau Vallon; s/d/q €50/60/80; P ❋ 🛜) This one is easy to review: it has only one self-contained apartment that can sleep four people, and it's very well kept and very well priced. It's not on the beach and there's no view, but you're in a quiet property, close to shops and banks. And Beau Vallon beach is just a five-to 10-minute stroll down the road. Excellent value. Book early.

Casadani
APARTMENTS €€

(🖉 2511081, 4248481; Bel Ombre; s/d incl breakfast €70/80; 🅿 ❋ 🛜) Soothingly positioned on a velvety emerald hillside just above the coastal road, this popular venture is a good deal if you can score a room with a sea view. The 25 rooms are well-appointed yet utilitarian, but you'll be too busy soaking up the fabulous views from the vast terrace to mind. The restaurant (half-board is available) specialises in seafood that comes fresh straight from the sea – it helps that the owner is a fisherman.

★ Ocean View Guesthouse
APARTMENTS €€

(🖉 2522010; www.choicevilla.sc; Bel Ombre; d incl breakfast €75-85; 🅿 ❋) A great-value port of call. Above the road in Bel Ombre, this jolly good villa shelters four immaculate rooms with balcony. The upstairs ones proffer splendid views of the bay. The cheaper Vakwa room, at the back, has no view. It's a 20-minute walk to Beau Vallon beach.

★ Diver's Lodge Guesthouse
GUESTHOUSE €€

(🖉 4261222; www.diverslodge.sc; Glacis; d incl breakfast €90-125; 🅿 ❋ 🛜) Just above the main coast road, next to a dive centre, these four rooms in a modern villa are large, pathologically clean and equipped to a high standard. The ones upstairs are significantly dearer but offer fleeting glimpses of the ocean through the foliage of exotic trees. The owner's husband runs Teddy's Glass Bottom Boat (p281) – convenient if you plan to arrange a boat trip. Dinner can be arranged on request.

Beach House
APARTMENTS €€

(🖉 2522010; www.choicevilla.sc; Beau Vallon; s/d incl breakfast €60/80; ❋ 🛜) In an area where economical options are on the verge of extinction, the Beach House deserves a pat on the back for quoting reasonable rates. The four functional and spacious rooms ensure a decent, if unmemorable, night's sleep for guests keen to roll out of bed and onto Beau Vallon beach, just across the road. Evening meals (€13) are available on request.

Georgina's Cottage
GUESTHOUSE €€

(🖉 4247016; www.georginascottage.sc; Beau Vallon; s €80, d €85-93, incl breakfast; ❋ 🛜) This friendly operation has catered to budget travellers for years. After a serious makeover in 2012, it now features dearer but more comfortable rooms in an attractive Creole building. Its location is hard to beat – it's a 20m Frisbee throw from the beach, and it's also very close to dive centres, restaurants and shops. Light sleepers may find the road a tad noisy in the morning. For optimum views, request a sea-facing room on the 1st floor; there's no extra cost. Eddy, the manager, is full of local info.

Yarrabee
APARTMENTS €€

(🖉 4261248; www.seychelles-yarrabee.com; Glacis; studios €80-160; ❋ 🛜) Two fully equipped studios and a three-bedroom unit with heavenly views of the bay. It's near a tiny beach and a small supermarket. Excellent value.

Romance Bungalows
APARTMENTS €€

(🖉 4247732; www.romance-bungalows.com; Beau Vallon; s/d incl breakfast €105/116; 🅿 ❋ 🛜) We could tell you that the 'Romance Bungalows' live up to their name and are suitable for a cuddle with your sweetheart, but we won't. At least they provide all the home comforts, assuming you live in a spacious, well-appointed flat with a spotless kitchen (but no maid). The beach is only steps away and all amenities are within easy reach.

Hanneman Holiday Residence
APARTMENTS €€€

(🖉 4425000; www.hanneman-holidays.com; Beau Vallon; s/d €145/175; ❋ 🛜 ⛱) This muscular villa was certainly not conceived by the most inspired architect on the island but inside it's much more welcoming, with six impeccable apartments equipped to a very high standard. There's also a cheaper, smaller studio for two people (€142). Bathrooms are so meticulous you could eat off the floor. There's a nifty pool, too. Discounts are available when it's slack. It's a five-minute jog to the beach. Wi-fi is extra.

Bliss
BOUTIQUE HOTEL €€€

(🖉 4261369, 2711187; www.bliss-hotel.net; Glacis; d €180-250, ste €400, incl breakfast; 🅿 ❋ 🛜 ⛱) This place is a real heartbreaker. The Seaside building shelters eight rooms that are decorated with natural materials and enjoy ocean views that will leave you speechless. The Hillside rooms, which are in a building across the road, are much less inspiring, despite the lush tropical garden. Amenities include a pool, a little spa and a great wooden sundeck with direct access to a small (rocky) beach. Alas, prices are very high for what you get and we've heard a few complaints about poor service.

Le Méridien Fisherman's Cove   RESORT €€€
(☑ 4677000; www.lemeridienfishermanscove.com; Bel Ombre; d incl breakfast from €300; P ✳ 🛜 🏊) A reliable resort with a staggering bow-shaped lobby and 70 stylish rooms with a modern design – the bathrooms are not separate from the bedrooms. Rooms are tightly packed together but face the sea and are buffered by lush gardens. The atmosphere is more convivial than intimate. Facilities include two restaurants, a bar, a spa and a pool. One minus: the beach is disappointingly thin.

Sunset Beach Hotel   HOTEL €€€
(☑ 4261111; www.sunset-beach.com; Glacis; d incl breakfast €330-700; P ✳ @ 🛜 🏊) This sunset-friendly seducer boasts an ace location on a little headland. The 28 units, divided into three categories, hide coolly among rocks and trees. Rooms vary in shape, size and quality (the best ones are the Junior suites) and would need a freshen up, but after one sundowner in the bar overlooking the ocean all will be forgiven. Best of all, there's direct beach access and excellent snorkelling options just offshore. There's a minimum stay of four nights.

🍴 Eating

You'll find convenience stores supplying basic foodstuffs and other necessities on the beach road and around the junction with the Bel Ombre road.

Baobab Pizzeria   PIZZERIA €
(☑ 4247167; Beau Vallon; mains Rs 95-140; ⊙ lunch & dinner) Madame Michel presides over this unpretentious, sand-floored eatery right on the beach. After a morning spent in the waves, re-energise with a piping-hot pizza, a plate of spag or fish and chips.

★ Boat House   BUFFET, SEAFOOD €€
(☑ 4247898; www.boathouse.sc; Beau Vallon; lunch menu Rs 130-200, buffet dinner Rs 400; ⊙ lunch & dinner) Having benefitted from a refurbishment, this longstanding venture is a great place for a slap-up meal. Its buffet dinner should satisfy all but the hungriest visitors, with about 20 different dishes on offer, including Creole curries, salads and barbecued fish (usually tuna and, if you're lucky,

red snapper). It also has a limited but tasty selection of fish dishes at lunchtime. The open-sided dining areas let in the marina breezes to keep things cool.

Banana Leaf   INTERNATIONAL, SEAFOOD €€
(☑ 4261369; Glacis; mains Rs 120-290; ⊙ lunch & dinner) The in-house restaurant of the Bliss hotel has that perfect balance of laid-back and chic, and the setting is ravishing – there are daybeds, it's candlelit at dinner and the views of the ocean will take your breath away. The menu is concise and tempting – here's your chance to dine at sunset on fresh fish, burgers and top-notch salads.

La Fontaine   EUROPEAN, SEAFOOD €€
(☑ 4422288; Beau Vallon; mains Rs 120-400; ⊙ noon-10pm Mon-Sat) You're sure to find something to fill a gap at this unpretentious eatery across the road from the beach (no sea views). The menu is a mixture of French, Italian and island influences, with seafood at the fore. Try the smoked fish salad or the crab with ginger.

★ La Plage   FUSION €€€
(☑ 4620240; Beau Vallon; mains Rs 200-500; ⊙ noon-10pm Thu-Tue) Belgian chef Christelle Verheyden infuses her cooking with a panoply of flavours...think Thai casserole, roasted duck with foie gras, dim sum or *waterzooi* (a Belgian stew). Presentation is impeccable, decor is enticing, with large, well-spaced tables and high ceilings, and the place fills up reliably. Plus it has the added bonus of offering absolute waterside tables and chairs. It has a can't-go-wrong wine list – treat yourself to a Chablis Premier Cru (a French white).

La Perle Noire   ITALIAN, SEAFOOD €€€
(☑ 4620220; Bel Ombre; mains Rs 230-380; ⊙ dinner Mon-Sat) The 'Black Pearl' scores high on atmosphere, with an eye-catching nautical theme and seafaring paraphernalia liberally scattered around the dining rooms (can we borrow your superb model ships?). The food – mostly fish and meat dishes with an Italian twist – doesn't quite live up to the promise of the surrounds, though.

La Scala   ITALIAN, SEAFOOD €€€
(☑ 4247535; Danzil; mains Rs 160-500; ⊙ dinner Mon-Sat) An old favourite of visitors and locals alike, this restaurant specialises in Italian cooking. It might feel weird to sit down to *gnocchi della casa* and breaded veal on a tropical Indian Ocean island, but go with the flow – the low-lit ambience on the

DON'T MISS

BAZAR LABRIN

On Wednesday evening don't miss Bazar Labrin, which injects a bit of vitality and excitement into the neighbourhood. Numerous food and craft stalls take positions along the seafront, with impromptu live bands or sound systems. It's popular with local families and flirting youngsters. For tourists, it's a great opportunity to catch local vibes.

breezy terrace overlooking the sea is suitably romantic despite the dated decor. The *tiramisu* will finish you off sweetly. At the end of the coast road near Danzil.

Lounge 8 FUSION €€€

(☑ 2746808; Glacis; menus Rs 670-915; ☺ dinner) It seems that everybody goes gaga for the surprise three- or five-course *menus* concocted at this hip eatery with a strong design-led decor. The food is imaginatively prepared and beautifully presented, but we found the prices somewhat inflated.

Drinking & Nightlife

Beau Vallon is the most 'happening' (by Seychellois standards, which isn't saying much) area on Mahé. The bars at Le Méridien Fisherman's Cove and Sunset Beach Hotel are great for a sunset cocktail.

ℹ Information

In Beau Vallon village, where the road from Victoria forks west to Bel Ombre and northeast to Glacis, there is a petrol station, two ATMs, a couple of bureaux de change, the police station and **Skynet** (Bel Ombre; per hr Rs 30; ☺ 9.30am-8pm Mon-Sat, 10.30am-7pm Sun), which shelters an internet cafe, a call centre and a bureau de change.

ℹ Getting There & Away

Buses leave regularly from Victoria for Beau Vallon, either straight over the hill via St Louis, or the long way round via Glacis. The last bus to Victoria leaves around 7.30pm; it's a Rs 200 taxi ride if you miss it.

Morne Seychellois National Park

While the dazzling coastline of Mahé is undoubtedly the main attraction, it's crucial

that you take the time to explore the island's mountainous interior. One of Mahé's highlights, the splendid Morne Seychellois National Park encompasses an impressive 20% of the land area of Mahé and contains a wide variety of habitats, from coastal mangrove forests up to the country's highest peak, the Morne Seychellois (905m). Choked in thick forest formation, the enigmatic, central part of the park is virtually deserted and can only be reached by walking trails; you don't have to go very far before the outside world starts to feel a long, long way away.

The road over the mountains from Victoria to Port Glaud (take the Bel Air Rd, which branches off Liberation Ave, and continue on Sans Souci Rd), which cuts through the Morne Seychellois National Park, is a stunning scenic drive. At **Mission** you can see the ruins of a school that was built by the London Missionary Society in 1875. There's also a superb **lookout** with spectacular views of central Mahé and the west coast.

Tea lovers will pause at the working **tea factory** (☑ 4378221; Sans Souci Rd; admission Rs 25; ☺ 7am-4pm Mon-Fri), about 3km above Port Glaud. Free 20-minute tours showing the tea-making process are conducted during opening hours, but it's best to visit before noon, when you can see the whole process from drying to packing. There's also a gift shop where you can sample and purchase the fragrant SeyTé and *citronnelle*.

🛏 Sleeping & Eating

Copolia Lodge B&B €€€

(☑ 2761498; www.copolialodge.com; Bel Air, Sans Souci; d incl breakfast €145-165; ⓟ ✳ 🛜 🏊) Copolia Lodge is magical, if you don't mind the sense of isolation – it's a 15-minute drive uphill from Victoria. Poised on a greenery-shrouded promontory, this very well run villa proffers cracking views of the coastal plain and Ste Anne Marine National Park. It sports six bright, immaculate rooms with clean lines, ample space and lots of amenities, including a superb pool. Excellent meals (€30) are available on request. It's just across the road from the Copolia trailhead.

East Coast

Let's face it: much of the east coast is given over to housing, so there are only a few spots that fit the picture-postcard ideal. And swimming is not *that* tempting, with

DON'T MISS

TOP NATURE WALKS IN MORNE SEYCHELLOIS NATIONAL PARK

If you've got itchy feet, there are excellent walks in the Morne Seychellois National Park, with a number of hiking trails through the jungle-clad hills. These are detailed in a series of leaflets that are available at the botanical gardens in Victoria (p273). The trails are poorly signed, though, and muggings have been reported, so it's not a bad idea to hire a guide, who will also provide natural and cultural insights. **Jacques Barreau** (☑ 2579191) and **Basile Beaudoin** (☑ 2514972) lead hiking and bird-watching trips into the Mahé back country and charge between €50 and €80 for an informative day's walk with picnic and transport (between €40 and €60 for a half-day). You can also contact **Terence Belle** (☑ 2722492), who charges between €30 and €40 for a half-day, but he only works on Saturday and Sunday. Bring plenty of water. Following is a selection of inspirational hikes.

Danzil to Anse Major

The walk to this secluded beach takes you along a coast fringed by impressive glacis rock formations. The path starts at the end of the road heading west from Beau Vallon, a few hundred metres further up from La Scala restaurant. It's a fairly easy one-hour romp, but most of the path is exposed to the sun. Before descending to the beach, the path goes past a lookout that affords fantastic vistas of Anse Major. The beach is blissfully quiet, and is good for swimming, though there can be strong currents. You'll have to return by the same route.

Tea Factory to Morne Blanc

The imposing white bulk of Morne Blanc (667m) and its almost sheer 500m face make a great hiking destination. Although the track is only 600m long, it is quite steep – climbing 270m from start to finish. Plan on roughly an hour for the ascent. The reward is a tremendous view over the west coast. The path starts 250m up the road from the tea factory (p284) on the cross-island road from Victoria to Port Glaud. You have to descend the same way.

Copolia

This is the most popular walk on Mahé, and possibly the easiest. It also has a pleasant Indiana Jones feel – you walk almost all the way amid a thick jungle, with lots of interesting fauna and flora. Now is your chance to spot leaf insects and the *Sooglossus gardineri*, the smallest frog on earth. The trail starts on the cross-island Chemin Forêt Noire about 5km above Victoria. It's only just over 1km to the granite platform of Copolia (497m), but the final section is quite steep; allow roughly two hours there and back. The views of Victoria and Ste Anne Marine National Park are sensational.

Trois Frères

Trois Frères (Three Brothers) refers to the three cliffs that tower over Victoria. The path is signed from the Sans Souci forest station on the Chemin Forêt Noire, about 4km from Victoria. The first part of the walk, until a kiosk from which you get ample views, is fairly easy and can be covered in about one hour. The second leg, to the cross on the summit (699m), is tricky to follow and involves some scrambling. Still game? Allow an extra two hours to reach the summit. You have to descend the same way.

very shallow waters and a profusion of algae – hardcore beach-hounds may be disappointed. This is not to say the east coast isn't a worthwhile place to visit. South of the airport are a number of small enclaves and undeveloped areas, where travellers looking for peace and isolation will find both in no short supply.

⊙ Sights

Le Jardin du Roi GARDENS
(☑ 4371313; Enfoncement, Anse Royale; adult/child Rs 110/55; ⊗ 10am-5pm) Located 2km up in the hills above Anse Royale, this lush spice garden owes its existence to Pierre Poivre, the French spice entrepreneur. There is a self-guided walk around the 35-hectare

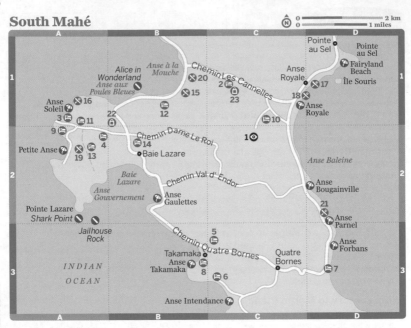

South Mahé

orchard-crossed-with-forest. The planter's house contains a one-room **museum** and there's a pleasant cafe-restaurant with smashing views down to the coast. Homemade jams, marmalade and spices are available at the gift shop.

Takamaka Bay   DISTILLERY
(☎4372010; www.takamaka.sc; Le Cap; guided tours Rs 200; ⊙10am-4pm Mon-Fri) On this popular tour you learn the colourful story behind the island's main distillery and about the rummaking process. The one-hour tour runs at 11.30am and 1.30pm and concludes with a tasting and an opportunity to purchase

bottles of rum at factory prices. It also features a well-regarded bar-restaurant.

Beaches

The oft-overlooked, little-known **Fairyland Beach** offers shimmering waters and great snorkelling around tiny **Île Souris**, just offshore. Other good strips of sand are found at **Anse Royale**, **Anse Bougainville**, **Anse Parnel** and **Anse Forbans**, further south.

🛏 Sleeping

The east coast may not be the sexiest part of the island, but we've unearthed a smattering of excellent-value (by Seychellois standards), family-run ventures from where you can easily reach the western coast, by bus or by car.

★ Devon Residence   APARTMENTS €€

(☑2512721; www.devon.sc; Pointe au Sel; villas €87-113; P❋☎) No, you're not hallucinating, the view is real. Poised on a greenery-shrouded hillside, the five villas overlook Anse Royale – full frame. They're extremely well appointed, spacious, bright and immaculate. A flotilla of perks, including free transfers to/from the airport, daily cleaning service, free wi-fi, TV and washing machine make this one of the best-value stays you'll have. Bonus: the owner rents cars at unbeatable rates (you'll need wheels to stay here).

Lalla Panzi Beach Guesthouse   GUESTHOUSE €€

(☑4376411; lpb@seychelles.sc; Le Cap; s/d incl breakfast €45/60; ❋) Lalla Panzi is not the beachfront paradise you were dreaming of, but it's a neat property leading down to the sea. This friendly guesthouse offers four scrupulously clean rooms arranged around a cosy lounge; rooms 2 and 3 have sea views. Furnishings are slightly dated and the decor is a tad kitsch but that's part of the charm. Though on the main road, it's quiet enough at night.

Résidence Charlette   APARTMENTS €€

(☑2715746; d_charlette@yahoo.com; Le Cap; s €45, d €65-70; P❋☎) An unfussy abode with an unpretentious appeal. The dual attractions here are the affordable rates and the spotlessness of the two self-catering apartments. They are set on grassy garden areas. Bonuses: free transfers to/from the airport, free laundry service, and a Creole dinner for stays of one week or more. No meals, but there are a few stores nearby.

Jamelah Apartments   APARTMENTS €€

(☑4410819, 2523923; jamelah@intelvision.net; Le Cap; d €60, apt €85-95, incl breakfast; P❋☎) This reliable option is run by Florie, who has a great insight into the needs of the budget traveller. The two serviceable rooms (each with a balcony and sea views) are a cast-iron bargain. If you're travelling with the kids in tow, opt for the four self-contained apartments in a separate building. They face a small 'beach', which is just adequate for a waist-high dip at high tide. The nearest stores and takeaway counters are just a 15-minute walk away. Meals can also be prepared by prior arrangement.

Koko Grove Chalets   BUNGALOWS €€

(☑2585986; www.kokogrove.nl; Anse Royale; chalets €95-150; P❋✿) If you're after hush and seclusion, then these three timbered chalets, outstandingly positioned in the velvety emerald hills above Anse Royale, are the answer. The three units are self-contained, with cosy living areas and private verandahs overlooking the tiny swimming pool, with the ocean as a backdrop. Air-con is an extra €5 per day. If you're preparing your own food, there's a store 400m down the road. If you don't fancy cooking, the maid can prepare excellent Creole meals. It's 400m before Le Jardin du Roi. No wi-fi.

★ Chalets d'Anse Forban   BUNGALOWS €€€

(☑4366111; www.forbans.com; Anse Forbans; d €150, q €210-240; P❋☎) 'Tranquillity; 12 sparklingly clean, fully equipped bungalows that are well spaced out; recent furniture and mattresses; expansive lawns; family-friendly; lovely beach with good swimming; fishermen selling their catch on the beach in the afternoon' – this is what we scribbled on our notepad when we visited. Add a few sun-loungers and the proximity of a store, and you have a great deal. There's a minimum stay of three nights.

🍴 Eating

Le Jardin du Roi   SEAFOOD, EUROPEAN €€

(☑4371313; Anse Royale; mains Rs 110-250; ☺10am-4.30pm) The setting is wonderful at this cafe-restaurant way up the hills at the spice garden (p285), and it puts you in the mood for a fruit juice or a crunchy salad as soon as you sit down. Seafood and sandwiches also feature on the menu. Save a cranny for ice creams: they are confected fresh on the premises with fruits from the garden. The Sunday *planteur* buffet (Rs 400)

SEYCHELLES EAST COAST

is a popular weekly event. A beer costs a whopping Rs 70.

Les Dauphins Heureux
Café-Restaurant   CREOLE, CAFE €€
(☑ 4430100; www.lesdauphinsheureux.com; Anse Royale; mains Rs 130-300; ☺ lunch daily, dinner Mon-Sat) A classic beachfront setting with a shady terrace and a tropical garden characterises this eatery with a modernish feel. Chow down on subtly flavoured fish, seafood, curries and meat from an elaborate menu. Head here on Sundays for the Creole buffet (RS 400) served at lunchtime.

Surfers Beach Restaurant   CREOLE €€
(☑ 2783703; Anse Parnel; mains Rs 140-350; ☺ noon-9.30pm) In a sublime location overlooking the seductive beach at Anse Parnel, Surfers Beach is a heart-stealing, open-air joint. Linger over salads, grilled fish, mussels, crab or chicken while enjoying the caress of the breeze on your face.

Kaz Kreol   SEAFOOD, PIZZERIA €€
(☑ 4371680; Anse Royale; mains Rs 150-450; ☺ 11am-9.30pm) Right on the beach at Anse Royale, this venue with a casual atmosphere and a ramshackle charm is great for the indecisive – the menu strikes a good balance between seafood, wood-fired pizzas and meat, not to mention a wide choice of Chinese specialities. Don't expect swift service, though.

La Plaine St André   INTERNATIONAL, BAR €€€
(☑ 4372010; www.laplaine.sc; Le Cap; mains Rs 230-300; ☺ lunch & dinner Mon-Fri) At Takamaka Bay distillery (p286), you couldn't ask for a more atmospheric setting – think a lovely old colonial house, creaky parquet flooring and Creole furnishings throughout, and an enticing menu featuring a small selection of fish and meat dishes. Lunch is a more casual affair, with burgers and light meals (from Rs 160). The terrace at the back opens onto a tropical garden. Lovely.

🛍 Shopping

Domaine de Val des Prés   ARTS & CRAFTS
(Anse aux Pins; ☺ 9.30am-5pm) The Domaine de Val des Prés at Anse aux Pins consists of a cluster of craft shops grouped around an old plantation house with a few bits of memorabilia. The rather motley assortment of crafts on offer includes model boats, pottery, paintings, clothing and products fashioned from the hugely versatile coconut tree.

❶ Getting There & Away

Buses leave regularly from Victoria for the east coast. The last bus to Victoria leaves Anse Royale around 7.30pm.

West Coast

The west coast is exquisite on the eyes. There are one or two sights to aim for, but it's the beaches and coastal scenery that are the star attractions. Wilder than the east, this is the part of Mahé where green hills tumble past coconut-strewn jungles before sliding gently into translucent waters.

There's only a handful of settlements, including the fishing villages of **Anse Boileau**, **Grande Anse** and **Port Glaud.** If it really is isolation you're after, continue north on the narrow coastal road to **Baie Ternay**, which is as far as you can go at present.

The west coast is easily accessed from the east coast via several scenic roads that cut through the mountainous interior.

🏖 Beaches

Anse Petite Police & Police Bay   BEACH
From the village of Quatre Bornes, a road leads to Police Bay, a splendid, blissfully isolated spot at the southern tip of the island. Sadly, the currents are too dangerous for swimming, but the beaches are great places to watch the surf (bring a picnic).

Anse Intendance   BEACH
A top-end resort lines the northern portion of this high-profile beach. The southern end is almost deserted and offers good swimming and snorkelling. From the police station at Quatre Bornes, take the 1.7km concrete road that leads down to Anse Intendance.

Anse Takamaka   BEACH
The gently curving Anse Takamaka is a gorgeous strand for walking unfettered on white sand and gaping at sunsets. Facilities include Batista's bar-restaurant (p291).

Petite Anse   BEACH
This pristine curve of white sand is accessible via the Four Seasons hotel (p290). Wait at the gate, and a buggy will take you down to the beach. Come late afternoon – as the sun-low sky deepens to orange, this beach just might be heaven, despite the fact that it has been partly privatised by the hotel. Visitors can use the hotel's beach restaurant for food and drink.

Anse Soleil
BEACH

The idyllic little beach of Anse Soleil is a pocket-sized paradise where you can pause for lunch; there's a beach restaurant (p291). It's accessible via a secondary road (it's signposted).

Anse Louis
BEACH

To the north of Anse à la Mouche the coast is a bit less glam but appealing nonetheless. If you can find access to Anse Louis, where the super-swish Maia resort (p291) lies, you'll be rewarded with a superlative beach you never knew existed.

Grande Anse
BEACH

Grande Anse is an immense swath of sand that glimmers with a fierce but utterly enchanting beauty. No other beach provides the same opportunities for long, solitary walks. It's not suitable for swimming, though, due to strong currents.

🏃 Activities

Dive Resort Seychelles
DIVING

(☎ 2717272, 4372057; www.seychellesdiving.net; Anse à la Mouche; ☺ Mon-Sat) This esteemed venture takes beginners and experienced divers to some truly impressive dive sites off the southwestern coast. An introductory/single dive costs €90/55.

Underwater Centre/
Dive Seychelles
WHALE SHARK SPOTTING

(☎ 4345445, 4247165; www.diveseychelles.com.sc; Beau Vallon) In conjunction with MCSS (www.mcss.sc), this dive outfit based in Beau Vallon organises whale-shark spotting off Mahé's west coast in September and October.

🛏 Sleeping

La Rocaille
BUNGALOW €

(☎ 2524238; lelarocaille@gmail.com; Anse Gouvernement Rd, Anse Soleil; d €60; P) This is a pleasant find, but there's only one unit, on the hill that separates Anse Gouvernement from Anse Soleil. It's very simple but well kept, and the grounds are nice enough, with lots of vegetation and birdsong. The friendly owners, who live next door, offer fruits to guests and are happy to drive them to the nearest village to stock up on food supplies (it's self-catering), but you'll need a car if you're staying here. The nearest beach is at Anse Gouvernement, about 400m down the hill. No air-con.

La Residence
APARTMENTS €€

(☎ 4371733; www.laresidence.sc; Anse à la Mouche; d €75-90, q €155-200; P ☀ ☎) Perched on a hillside, the five fully equipped studios and three villas are roomy, straightforwad and tidy, if a bit old-fashioned. The buildings are functional rather than whimsical but there are good views from the terrace (despite the odd power line). Breakfast costs €5 and dinner is €16.

Chez Batista's
BUNGALOWS €€

(☎ 4366300; www.chezbatista.com; Anse Takamaka; d €80-100, villas from €150, incl breakfast; P ☀ ☎) Your only concern here: whether to frolic on the beach *now* or first sip a cocktail at the restaurant. This longstanding venue on Takamaka beach features 11 bland but acceptable rooms (no sea views) as well as two villas that are right on the beach. The whole property feels a bit compact and we've heard reports of irregular service but, to be honest, it's the idyllic location that's the pull here.

Anse Soleil Resort
APARTMENTS €€

(☎ 4361090; www.ansesoleil.sc; Anse Soleil; d/q incl breakfast €92/138; P ☀ ☎) Run by a hospitable family, this discreet number has just four self-catering apartments; the Kitouz is the best, but all are well equipped, nicely laid out and spacious, and come with a large terrace from where you can soak up the view over Anse à la Mouche (if you can ignore the power lines). We can hear you: 'Where's the nearest beach, darling?' – Anse Soleil is 1.6km down the road. Meals (€15) are available on request.

⭐ Anse Takamaka View
APARTMENTS €€

(☎ 2510007; www.atv.sc; Takamaka; d €90-130, q €170; P ☀ ☎ ⊠) No photo retouching on the website – we guarantee that the views from the terrace are *that* terrific, the pool (complete with a pool bar) *that* scintillating, and the three villas *that* roomy and comfortable. Run by a Seychellois–German couple, this wonderfully peaceful property is a winner. Meals (€18) are available twice a week. The minimum stay is three nights. It's secluded and not on the beach, so you'll need your own wheels to stay here. Free pick-up at the airport.

⭐ La Maison Soleil
APARTMENTS €€

(☎ 2516523, 2712677; www.maisonsoleil.info; Anse Soleil Rd; d or tr incl breakfast €108-170; P ☀ ☎) Seeking a relaxing cocoon with homey qualities without the exorbitant price tag? Run by artist Andrew Gee, whose gallery is just

SEYCHELLES WEST COAST

next door, this champ of a self-catering option has all the key ingredients, with three tastefully done apartments, prim bathrooms and a colourful garden. Anse Soleil is within walking distance. There's a minimum stay of three nights. Check the website for last-minute deals.

Angel Heights
APARTMENT €€

(☎2714599; Chemin Les Cannelles; villa €100; P ☀ @) A recent three-bedroom villa with all mod-cons for just €100? Yes, it's possible. This modern house just off the cross-island road is a great deal for friends or families.

Blue Lagoon Chalets
APARTMENT €€€

(☎4371197; www.seychelles.net/blagoon; Anse à la Mouche; d €125; P ☀) The friendly owner here offers four well-cared-for holiday units that are peppered across a well-tended park, a hop from the sea shore. They sleep up to four people and are fully equipped. Air-con is extra (€10). No wi-fi, but there's an internet café down the road.

Anse Soleil Beachcomber
HOTEL €€€

(☎4361461; www.beachcomber.sc; Anse Soleil; d incl breakfast €140-200; P ☀ ☎) Location, location, location: this family-run hotel, among rocks on the idyllic cove of Anse Soleil, has the location thing sorted. The rooms, which are clean and simple with private terraces, are less exciting than the views (and location) but the flowery grounds add a lot of charm. Rooms 6, 7 and 8 open onto the sea shore, but the more recent Premier rooms, which are slightly set back from the shore, are much larger. Half board is available. Free canoes. Anse Soleil Café is next door.

Valmer Resort
BUNGALOWS €€€

(☎4381555; www.valmerresort.com; Baie Lazare; d from €200; P ☀ ☎ ☎) A cluster of well-organised villas cascades down a hillside cloaked in green, each enjoying stupendous ocean views. Apart from the four ordinary 'garden studios', which are just off the main road, the 17 units are sun-filled, capacious and tastefully done out. A real hit is the pool, built at the foot of a big granite boulder. There's an onsite restaurant (by the pool) and an art gallery where you can marvel at (and buy) works by local painter Gerard Devoud. One weak point: the walk up to the bungalows may leave the terminally unfit short of breath. You will need a car to get around from here. Minimum three nights.

Le Méridien Barbarons
RESORT €€€

(☎4673000; www.lemeridien.com/barbarons; Barbarons; d incl breakfast €200-550; P ☀ ☎ ☎ ☎) The '80s-style exterior could use a facelift, but it's one of the least expensive resorts you'll find for a beachfront stay on Mahé. While there is nothing very remarkable about the flimsy motel-like structure, the 124 rooms are OK and amenities include a small spa, a pool and tennis courts, as well as B-level restaurants and grounds. This is an acceptable deal if you can get internet specials (when we last checked, rooms cost €194) and like to socialise.

Constance Ephelia
RESORT €€€

(☎4395000; www.epheliaresort.com; Port Launay; d with half board from €370; ☀ ☎ ☎ ☎) High on ambition, but low on atmosphere, this sprawling resort is not a bad option if you can get online promos. Its public facilities are its strength: two beaches with a full array of free water sports, tennis courts, two pools, a fitness centre, five restaurants, a kids club... Due to its position on the northwest corner of the island, it gets plenty of natural light from sunrise to sunset. With its varied accommodations it's appropriate for couples and families alike.

Four Seasons Resort
RESORT €€€

(☎4393000; www.fourseasons.com/seychelles; Petite Anse; d incl breakfast from €850; P ☀ ☎ ☎) With its stadium-sized villas perched on a hillside, swoony ocean views, sense of privacy and lovely spa, this five-star bigwig, opened in 2009, is a fab place for honeymooners and loved-up couples, but it's a shame that it has partly privatised Petite Anse beach. The bedrooms and bathrooms are massive and both masterpieces of understatement despite including luxuries such as works of art adorning the walls, teak furnishings, high-quality linen and king-size beds.

Banyan Tree
RESORT €€€

(☎4383500; www.banyantree.com; Anse Intendance; d incl breakfast from €750; P ☀ ☎ ☎) The Banyan Tree has everything the finicky glam jet-set patron would expect. Two highlights: the spa, possibly the most attractive on Mahé (and that's saying a lot), and a fabulous location on a greenery-shrouded hillside with heavenly views of the sea. Due to its position, its 54 wonderfully roomy villas get plenty of sunshine, even in late afternoon.

Maia Luxury Resort & Spa   RESORT €€€
(☑ 4390000; www.maia.com.sc; Anse Louis; d incl
breakfast from €1720; P ❋ 🛰 ☒) Easily Mahé's
most exclusive hotel, the Maia is a bubble
of exclusivity that will render you speechless
and never wanting to leave the premises.
Overlooking glorious Anse Louis, it's truly
beautiful, with great expanses of white beach,
palm-shaded landscaped grounds, a splendid infinity pool and 30 gorgeous villas –
each with its own pool. You get the feeling
nothing is too much trouble for the obliging
staff here. With such a dreamlike setting, it's
unsurprisingly a honeymooners' choice.

✗ Eating

Most luxury hotels welcome outside guests
at their restaurants (by reservation).

Sundown Restaurant   CREOLE, EUROPEAN €€
(☑ 4378352; Port Glaud; mains Rs 180-270;
☺ noon-9pm) This venture overlooking the
water was being refurbished at the time of
research. It should feature a nicely laid-out
dining room and an extensive menu.

Maria's Rock Cafeteria   CAFETERIA €€
(☑ 4361812; Anse Gouvernement Rd, Anse Soleil;
mains Rs 150-300; ☺ 10am-9pm Wed-Mon) Maria,
the Seychellois spouse of artist Antonio Filippin, runs this quirky restaurant beside her
husband's studio. The cavernous interior is
discombobulating, with granite tabletops
and concrete walls sprayed with paint. Food-
wise, it majors on fish and meat dishes,
grilled on a metal plate. Skip the pancakes,
which taste like plastic.

★ Anse Soleil Café   SEAFOOD, CHINESE €€€
(☑ 4361700; Anse Soleil; mains Rs 200-350;
☺ noon-8pm) Everyone adores this unpretentious little eatery ideally positioned right
on the beach at Anse Soleil. The menu is
short and concentrates on simply prepared
seafood and various chop sueys served in
generous portions. Grilled bat (yes, fruit bat
is a local delicacy) is also available. Digest
all this over a drink afterwards. Note that it
doesn't take reservations and there are only
a few tables – come at noon sharp or after
1.30pm.

Chez Plume   FRENCH, SEAFOOD €€€
(☑ 4355050; www.aubergenseboileau.com; Anse
Boileau; mains Rs 190-300; ☺ dinner Mon-Sat)
The granddaddy of West Coast dining, Chez
Plume can still cut it. On top of fish specialities, it serves a mix of adventurous dishes –
terrine of fruit bat, anyone? – and innocuous

French classics. The decor is romantic, in an
old-fashioned way.

Opera   SEAFOOD, INTERNATIONAL €€€
(☑ 4371171; www.opera-mahe.com; Anse à la Mouche;
mains Rs 230-350; ☺ 11am-8.30pm Tue-Sun) Across
the road from the beach (but no views to
speak of), this modern eatery is an acceptable plan B. The food is rated as 'average' by
most visitors and service is sloooow.

Chez Batista's   SEAFOOD, BUFFET €€€
(☑ 4366300; Anse Takamaka; mains Rs 170-400;
☺ lunch Tue-Sun) The impressive thatched
canopy, the sand floor and the endless turquoise bay that spreads out in front of you
help you switch to 'relax' mode. This is a
great place for seafood, fish dishes or just a
drink, but we met some tourists who found
the place touristy and overrated. The eclectic lunch buffet (Rs 400) is a good option on
Sunday. It's wise to book on weekends.

★ Anchor Café –
Islander Restaurant   INTERNATIONAL €€€
(☑ 4371289; Anse à la Mouche; mains Rs 300-350;
☺ 4-9pm Mon-Sat; 🛰) This appreciated, family-
run restaurant takes its cooking seriously.
Its champion dishes include the blackened
fish, the grilled red snapper, plus the obligatory catch of the day. But everything is good
here, ranging from the steaks to the grilled
pork chops. A few vegetarian options also
grace the menu. Eat alfresco near a huge
anchor in the garden and enjoy the amazing sunsets over the bay. There's wi-fi access
(Rs 30 per hour).

🛍 Shopping

The glorious southwest seems to be an endless source of inspiration for a number of
artists.

Michael Adams' Studio   GALLERY
(☑ 4361006; www.michaeladamsart.com; Anse à
la Mouche; ☺ by reservation) Visit Michael Adams' studio, where silkscreen prints burst
with the vivid life of the forests. They are
irresistible and highly collectable, so bring
plenty of rupees if you're thinking of buying.

Tom Bowers   SCULPTURES
(☑ 4371518; artworks@seychelles.net; Chemin Les
Cannelles; ☺ by reservation) Creates some truly
amazing bronze sculptures.

Art Arc   WOODCARVINGS
(☑ 2510977; Baie Lazare; ☺ 10am-8pm Wed-Sat
& Mon) Antonio Filippin's somewhat risqué

SEYCHELLES WEST COAST

woodcarvings and quirky studio, Art Arc, is perched on a hill between Anse Gouvernement and Anse Soleil.

Gerard Devoud's Studio
GALLERY

(✏ 4381515; Baie Lazare; ⏱ by reservation) Gerard Devoud's eye-goggling paintings are also sure to enliven your bedroom. His studio is at Valmer Resort.

ℹ Getting There & Away

Buses leave regularly from Victoria for the west coast. The last bus to Victoria leaves Quatre Bornes around 7.30pm.

PRASLIN

A wicked seductress, Praslin has lots of temptations: stylish lodgings, tangled velvet jungle, curving hills dropping down to gin-clear seas, gorgeous stretches of silky sand edged with palm trees and a slow-motion ambience. No, you're not dreaming!

Lying about 45km northeast of Mahé, the second-largest island in the Seychelles falls somewhere between the relative hustle and bustle of Mahé and the sleepiness of La Digue. Like Mahé, Praslin is a granite island, with a ridge of small mountains running east–west along the centre. The island is 12km long and 5km across at its widest point. The 5500 inhabitants of Praslin are scattered around the coast in a series of small settlements. The most important from a visitor's perspective are Anse Volbert (also known as Côte d'Or) and Grand Anse. At the southeast tip of the island is Baie Ste Anne, Praslin's main port.

Praslin has all you need to decompress. But if playing sardines on the strand ceases to do it for you, another world beckons at the Vallée de Mai, one of the most peculiar attractions in the Seychelles. Scuba diving, snorkelling and boat excursions to nearby islands famed for their bird life will also keep you buzzing.

◉ Sights

Vallée de Mai
FOREST

(adult/child under 12 €20/free; ⏱ 8am-5.30pm) Praslin's World Heritage–listed Vallée de Mai is one of only two places in the world where you can see the rare coco de mer palms growing in their natural state (the other being nearby Curieuse Island) – not to mention more than 50 other indigenous plants and trees. If the entry price seems steep, remember this is a unique chance to

---

THE SEYCHELLES' BEST BEACHES

It's gruelling work investigating which beaches qualify as the best of Seychelles. Here are a few of our favourites:

➡ Beau Vallon (Mahé; p280) – Mahé's longest and most popular beach has sweeping blonde sand backed by takamaka trees. The best all-round choice for everyone, from singles to couples to families with kids

➡ Petite Anse (Mahé; p288) – this beach, with almost lagoon-still waters, is a fabulous spot to work your tan

➡ Anse Intendance (Mahé; p288) – famous for its hypnotically dramatic sunset; as the sun-low sky deepens to orange, the big granite boulders that frame the beach glow with muted copper tones and form a perfect backdrop for a romantic stroll

➡ Anse Takamaka (Mahé; p288) – Mahé's sexiest beach is the perfect place for sunbathing

➡ Anse Lazio (Praslin; p293) – excellent for sunbathing and snorkelling, and famous for its beach restaurants

➡ Anse Georgette (Praslin; p297) – an intimate paradise, accessible by boat or on foot

➡ Anse Source d'Argent (La Digue; p305) – crystalline, glossy and framed with glacis boulders, this is the most photogenic of all the Seychelles' beaches

➡ Grand Anse (La Digue; p305) – idyllic stretch of sand, excellent for frolicking in the crashing surf

➡ Anse Marron (La Digue; p306) – a hidden gem on the isolated south coast, this virgin swath of flaxen sand framed by ochre boulders is only accessible on foot

experience a slice of Eden. Five **hiking** trails lead through this primeval, emerald-tinged forest, which remained totally untouched until the 1930s. The shortest is about 1km and the longest is 2km – perfect for families. As you walk amid the forest, the atmosphere is eerie, with the monstrous leaves of the coco de mer soaring 30m to a sombre canopy of huge fronds. Signs indicate some of the other endemic trees to look out for, including several varieties of pandanus (screw pines) and latanier palms. Bird-watchers also rate Vallée de Mai as a top birding hot spot. Keep your eyes peeled for endemic species, including the Seychelles bulbul, the blue pigeon, the Seychelles warbler and the elusive black parrot, of which there are perhaps less than 100 left.

Beaches

Anse Lazio BEACH
Anse Lazio, on the northwest tip of the island, is picture-postcard everywhere you look. Here, the long, broad pale-sand beach has lapis lazuli waters on one side and a thick fringe of palm and takamaka trees on the other, and it's framed by a series of granite boulders at each extremity. You won't find a better place for sunbathing, and there is some good snorkelling among the rocks along the arms of the bay. Amenities include two restaurants. The beach's charms are no secret, but it never feels crowded. Watch your valuables here.

Anse Volbert BEACH
This long, gently arching beach is the most popular strand on the island. It's great for safe swimming and sunbathing, and it's also good for watersports. There are plenty of facilities, including restaurants and hotels. A small islet – Chauve-Souris – that you can swim to for snorkelling floats offshore.

Anse La Blague BEACH
Head to Anse La Blague on the east coast if you're after a secluded picnic spot. Very few tourists make it to this isolated beach, which feels like the world's end. It has no facilities, other than shady takamaka trees to hang your towel on. You might come across a few fishermen with their catch of *cordonnier* (job-fish).

Anse Marie-Louise BEACH
At the island's southern tip, Anse Marie-Louise is a pretty spot. There are no facilities and no parking lot; just pull over at the side of the road and *voilà* – you're at the beach. Continuing along the coastal road to the west, you'll find numerous coves and other beaches, including **Anse Consolation**.

Grand Anse BEACH
Grand Anse has a long beach, but swimming is only average, with shallow waters and a profusion of algae.

Activities

Diving & Snorkelling
Whether you're an experienced diver or a novice slapping on fins for the first time, you'll find superb dive sites off Praslin.

The best snorkelling spots can be found at Anse Lazio, around St Pierre Islet and off Baie Laraie on Curieuse. For more information on dive sites, see p33.

Lémuria Dive Centre DIVING
(☑4281281; lemuriaresort.constancehotels.com; Anse Kerlan; ☉daily) This luxurious diving school is inside the Constance Lémuria Resort (p297) but is open to nonguests (by reservation). It runs the full gamut of courses for beginners as well as diving trips. An introductory dive costs a whopping €150. Single dives are €90.

Octopus Dive Centre DIVING
(☑2512350, 4232350; www.octopusdiver.com; Anse Volbert; ☉daily) This dive school is very experienced after over a decade running dives around the island. An introductory dive is only €70. A standard dive runs upwards of €35. Also offers dive packages, certification courses and snorkelling trips.

White Tip Dive Centre DIVING
(☑2514282, 4232282; www.whitetipdivers.com; Anse Volbert; ☉daily) At the eastern end of Paradise Sun Hotel (p300). This small, professional outfit has years of experience diving the sites around Praslin and La Digue and charges very reasonable rates (by Seychellois standards); an introductory dive is €80 while single dives cost from €45. Packages, certification courses and snorkelling trips are also available.

Kayaking
It's not a bad idea to rent a kayak and explore Anse Volbert at your leisure and paddle round Chauve Souris Island. Sagittarius Taxi Boat (p299) handles rentals (from €10 per hour).

Praslin

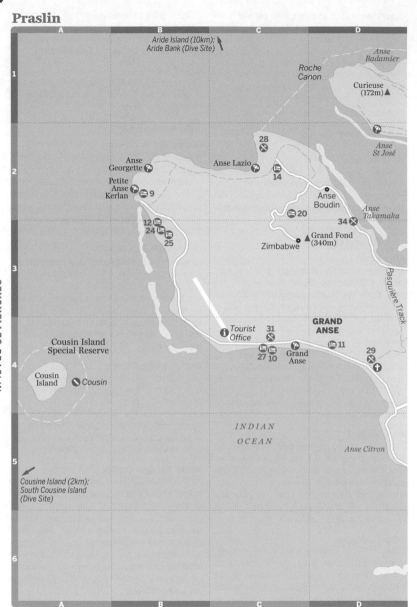

Aride Island (10km);
Aride Bank (Dive Site)

Anse
Badamier

Roche
Canon

Curieuse
(172m)▲

Anse
St José

28

Anse
Georgette

Anse Lazio

14

Petite
Anse
Kerlan

9

Anse
Boudin

Anse
Takamaka

20

34

12
24

25

Grand Fond
(340m)

Zimbabwe

Pasquière Track

GRAND
ANSE

Tourist
Office

31

11

27 10

Grand
Anse

29

Cousin Island
Special Reserve

Cousin
Island

Cousin

INDIAN
OCEAN

Anse Citron

Cousine Island (2km);
South Cousine Island
(Dive Site)

🛏 Sleeping

Demand for accommodation is high in Praslin. To avoid disappointment, particularly in high season, book your accommodation well in advance.

Anse Volbert, with its restaurants and other tourist facilities, makes a good base. Grand Anse is busier and less attractive, but less touristy, and there are some decent options within walking distance of the Baie Ste Anne jetty.

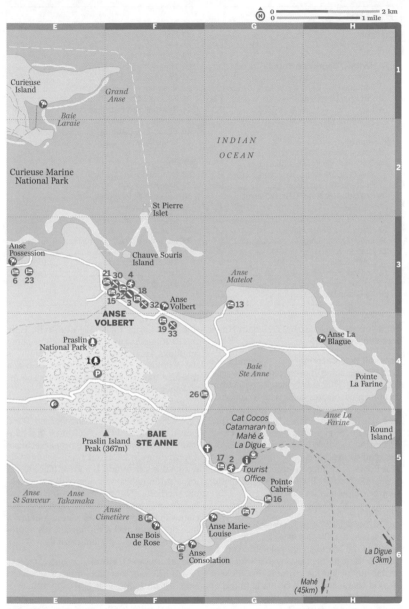

🛏 Grand Anse & Anse Kerlan

★ **Sunset Cove Villa**   APARTMENTS €
(📞 2513048; www.sunset-cove-villa.com; Anse Ker-

lan; d €60-75; P ❄) Pinch yourself – you're just steps from the sea. OK, there's no proper beach here because of erosion, but the setting is truly appealing. Digs are in two comfortable, well-equipped and light-filled houses. No meal service, but there's a

Praslin

small supermarket nearby. The main house doesn't have air-con.

Seashell Self Catering   APARTMENTS €€
(☑ 2513764; csetheve@hotmail.com; Anse Kerlan; d €60; P ✳ 🛜) This sturdy house, built from granite stones, scores goals with a combination of affordable rates and a handy position – the sea is just 100m away. Keep in mind that the beach here is not that great because of erosion and seaweed. The two large, spotless studios are pleasantly furnished, with tiled floors, sparkling bathrooms, good bedding and a terrace. Both have a kitchenette. There's a supermarket close by.

Islander's   APARTMENTS €€
(☑ 2781224, 4233224; www.islander-seychelles.com; Anse Kerlan; d €100-120; P ✳ 🛜) The good people at the Islanders are not setting out to win any 'best in its class' awards with their establishment but the virtue is that it's kept in good shape and you'll be made to feel at home. The four bungalows (eight rooms in total) are unpretentious but clean and the property opens onto Anse Kerlan. There's an onsite restaurant. Air-con is extra (€8).

Villas de Mer   HOTEL €€€
(☑ 4233972; Grand Anse; d incl breakfast from €189; P ✳ 🛜 ⊠) Villas de Mer is a great midrange option with good accommoda-

tion for its price following a full refit. Here the 10 rooms occupy two rows of low-slung buildings facing each other. A highlight is the restaurant, which has a fabulous beach frontage and serves fresh seafood. The atmosphere is relaxed and friendly.

Indian Ocean Lodge   RESORT €€€
(☑ 4283838; www.indianoceanlodge.com; Grand Anse; d incl breakfast from €260; P ✳ 🛜 ⊠) Indian Ocean Lodge has gone upmarket since a freshen-up in 2011, but it has retained its reasonable prices and is a great place to enjoy a midrange-style resort without breaking the bank. The rooms combine classical luxury and elegant simplicity, and have balconies that afford good sea views. Amenities include a pool and a restaurant. It's appropriate for couples and families alike.

Dhevatara Beach Hotel   BOUTIQUE HOTEL €€€
(☑ 4237333; www.dhevatara-seychelles.com; Grand Anse; d from €480; P ✳ 🛜 ⊠) Dhevatara is sleek and imaginative, a boutique-ish luxury venture loaded with more cool than any other on the island. With only 10 rooms divided in two categories (garden views and ocean views), it's a great choice for couples. Rooms are not huge but are individually designed; the ones upstairs get more natural light. The romantic restaurant, near the pool, specialises in *haute cuisine* and is a

ANSE GEORGETTE

Bad news: Anse Georgette, which is an indescribably lovely stretch of white sand at the northwestern tip of the island, has been engulfed by the sprawling Constance Lémuria resort. Good news: it remains a public beach that is accessible to anybody. In order not to be turned back at the gate of the Lémuria, call the reception beforehand – they will inform the guards. Once inside the property, you can get to Anse Georgette on foot or take the hourly 'shuttle' (a buggy) operated by the resort – isn't it cute? You can also get there by taxi boat from Anse Volbert; Sagittarius Taxi Boat (p299) can arrange drop-offs and pick-ups (€30 per person).

Anse Georgette could hardly be more tranquil. The seas here are fairly calm, the bay is safe, and the vista of the surrounding green hills is dramatic. There are no amenities but you'll find everything you need at the resort, which lies in the adjacent bay to the south.

great place for a cocktail. Facilities include a spa.

Constance Lémuria RESORT €€€
(☑4281281; lemuriaresort.constancehotels.com; Anse Kerlan; d incl breakfast from €550; P✳@ 🛜✈) Praslin's top-drawer establishment occupies the whole northwest tip of the island. If you're not bowled over by features such as the voluminous foyer and the marvellous spa, you certainly will be by the three-tiered infinity pool, the three gorgeous beaches and the expansive grounds in which the villas blend in among the rocks and water features. Facilities include three restaurants, a kids club and a magnificent 18-hole **golf course** (open to nonguests). One blemish: the property has engulfed the idyllic Anse Georgette, which is now a de facto part of the hotel, though it's a public beach by law. Overall, Constance Lémuria caters to a wide variety of interests and budget levels – it's a big resort but it's not crowded and has retained its friendly feel.

🛏 Anse Consolation Area

Bonnen Kare Beach Villa APARTMENT €€
(☑4322457; www.bonnenkare.com; Anse Consolation; d/q €130/230) A lovely option for a group of friends or a family, this secluded four-room villa opening onto an idyllic sandy cove really fulfils the dreams of a private beach getaway. Don't fancy cooking? The maid can prepare meals on request. No air-con.

**Coco de Mer Hotel &
Black Parrot Suites** RESORT €€€
(☑4290555; www.cocodemer.com; Anse Bois de Rose; d/ste from €260/395, incl breakfast;

P✳🛜✈) Choose the exclusive Black Parrot Suites, perched on a headland with fantastic ocean views, if you want some serious cosseting and a hideaway; the 12 sublimely stylish suites and the adjoining spa appeal to couples who come to enjoy a low-key and tranquil honeymoon (no children under 14). Along the shore, the Coco de Mer, with 40 refurbished rooms, a gym, tennis court, two restaurants, shops and a bar, has more of a resort feel. The beach is average – it's shallow and tides can cause a build-up of seaweed between May and October – but you can cool off in the pool in the shape of a *coco fesse*. All in all, a great recommendation for unpretentious and low-key luxury.

🛏 Baie Ste Anne & Pointe Cabris

Susan Self-Catering GUESTHOUSE €
(☑2595569, 4232124; Baie Ste Anne; s/d incl breakfast €30/60; P✳) Run by an elderly woman, this is a homey pick with a laid-back vibe, on the northern fringes of Baie Ste Anne. There's just one room; it's small and furnishings are a bit dated, but they get the job done. Although the setting is nothing special, it's clean, the welcome is warm, the garden is blossoming with colours and the food (dinner €15) has a good reputation.

Le Port Guest House GUESTHOUSE €
(☑4232262; mapool.leport@gmail.com; Baie Ste Anne; d/q €60/100; ✳) Not far from the jetty, this friendly guesthouse has three comfortable, fuss-free rooms, two of which enjoy partial sea views. The area doesn't scream 'vacation' but Anse Volbert is easy to reach by bus. Good value.

ℹ️ SHUTTLES TO ANSE LAZIO

Given that the beach at Grand Anse is only so-so, most accommodation options in the area offer their guests a free shuttle to Anse Lazio several times per week.

Le Grand Bleu APARTMENTS €

(📞 4232437; gbleu@seychelles.net; Pointe Cabris; d €50; P ❄️ 🛜) Bargain! Le Grand Bleu features two well-appointed villas nestled in a flowery garden. Each unit has two rooms with bathrooms, a terrace with gorgeous sea views (it's on a hillside), and its own kitchenette. No meal service, but you can head to Chalets Côté Mer & Le Colibri, which is on the same property (same family). Air-con is optional (€10).

Chalets Côté Mer & Le Colibri BUNGALOWS €€

(📞4294200; www.chaletcotemer.com; Pointe Cabris; d incl breakfast €95-140; P ❄️ 🛜 ♒) A good deal at the southeastern tip of Baie Ste Anne. Features a clutch of A-framed bungalows and villas perched on a hillside cloaked in green, with glorious views over La Digue. The Colibri bungalows are slightly hipper than the no-frills Chalets Côté Mer. Aim for the Colibri, Magpie, Fairytern, Katiti or Kato, which are the best laid out. Note that the cheaper units are fan-cooled. Lovers of fine food will enjoy the cooking here – the French owner, René Parmentier, has made a name as an adept chef (half board from €130 for two). There's no beach but snorkelling is excellent along the rocky shore. Minimum three nights.

★Château de Feuilles LUXURY HOTEL €€€

(📞4290000; www.chateaudefeuilles.com; Pointe Cabris; d incl breakfast from €571; P ❄️ 🛜 ♒) Paradise awaits you in this bijou hideaway sitting on an unfathomably beautiful headland near Baie Ste Anne. Nine luxurious villas are ingeniously deployed over several acres of tropical gardens. A serene symphony of earth tones and natural textures, elegant furnishings, sensational views, high-class amenities (including a complimentary car), an uber-romantic poolside restaurant – every detail is spot-on. The hotel's ultimate trump card, though, is its nifty hilltop Jacuzzi. There's a three-night minimum stay.

🛏️ Anse Volbert Area

L'Hirondelle APARTMENTS €€

(📞4232243; www.seychelles.net/hirondelle; Anse Volbert; d €95) The four rooms, although they won't knock your socks off, are comfortable and come fully equipped, and each has a balcony or a terrace that commands a blue-green lagoon vista. Downsides: it's not shielded from the noise of the coast road, and there's no air-con. Breakfast is €10.

Rosemary's Guest House GUESTHOUSE €€

(📞4232176; www.ile-tropicale.com/rosemary; Anse Volbert; s €50-90, d €80-125, incl breakfast; ❄️ 🛜) Yes, you read those prices right (we asked twice). Relaxed and friendly, this homey place features two types of rooms. The four fan-cooled rooms in the two older buildings feel a bit tired but are tidy, while the four ones with air-con occupy a modern building overlooking the beach. Despite the fact that the property feels a tad compact, the location is ace; you can bask lizard-like in the garden within earshot of the waves. Meals are available on request (€15).

Les Lauriers BUNGALOWS €€€

(📞4232241; www.laurier-seychelles.com; Anse Volbert; s €95-125, d €120-145, incl breakfast; P ❄️ 🛜) A pleasant oasis, despite the lack of sea views and the odd landscaping of the compound. Run by friendly Edwin and Sybille, it features six uncomplicated and smallish but neat rooms as well as eight spacious bungalows. The woodcarved posts on the terrace are a nice touch. It's well worth opting for half board (from €165 for two), given the attached high-quality restaurant.

★Le Duc de Praslin HOTEL €€€

(📞4232252; www.leduc-seychelles.com; Anse Volbert; s/d from €225/270, incl breakfast; P ❄️ 🛜 ♒) This little island of subdued glamour, a *coco fesse* throw from the beach, ranks as one of the most solid options on Praslin. The generous-sized, sensitively furnished rooms come with all mod cons and orbit around an alluring pool and a nicely laid-out tropical garden. Another plus is the onsite restaurant – a range of good-value meal plans are available. For more privacy, book one of the four colonial-style rooms that are just beside the main property. If only it had ocean views, life would be perfect.

BOAT EXCURSIONS TO NEARBY ISLANDS

Praslin is the obvious launching pad for the nearby islets.

Curieuse

Curieuse Island is a granite island 1.5km off Praslin's north coast and was a leper colony from 1833 until 1965. Today, Curieuse is used as a breeding centre for giant Aldabra tortoises. The wardens at the **giant tortoise farm** show visitors round the pens, after which you're free to explore the rest of the island. Nearby **Baie Laraie** is a fantastic place for swimming and snorkelling. From Baie Laraie, a path leads to **Anse José**, where you can visit the **doctor's house**, which contains a small historical museum. If you fancy a dip after your picnic, the **beach** is lovely: a stretch of pristine pale golden sand fringed with lofty palm trees and framed by massive granite bouldes.

Most visitors to Curieuse Island arrive on an organised tour, usually in combination with Cousin and St Pierre Islet. Tours are arranged through Praslin's hotels or any tour operator. Day trips cost around €115/55 for an adult/child including lunch, landing fees and the marine-park entry fee. The alternative is to charter your own boat from Anse Volbert. **Sagittarius Taxi Boat** (☑ 2512137, 4232234; Anse Volbert; ⊘ 9am-5pm), on the beach beside the Paradise Sun Hotel, charges €35 for Curieuse, including fees; Curieuse with St Pierre costs €40. You'll also find taxi boats at Anse Possession.

Cousin

About 2km southwest of Praslin, Cousin Island is run as a nature reserve by **Nature Seychelles** (www.natureseychelles.org). Seven species of sea birds nest here, including fairy terns, white-tailed tropicbirds and shearwaters. The bird population is estimated to exceed 300,000 on an island measuring just 1km in diameter. It's an amazing experience to walk through thick forest with birds seemingly nesting on every branch. Cousin is also home to five species of endemic land birds, including the Seychelles warbler and the magpie robin. The island is also an important nesting ground for hawksbill turtles. Between October and April, as many as 100 individuals crawl ashore to lay their eggs in the island's fringing circlet of sand. At any time of the year you're bound to see lizards: Cousin boasts one of the highest densities of lizards in the world. Well over a hundred giant tortoises also live on the island, some of which have reached truly enormous sizes, measuring more than a metre long.

Cousin can only be visited as part of an organised tour from Monday to Friday, usually in combination with Curieuse and St Pierre Islet. Day trips can be arranged through Praslin's hotels and tour operators for around €115/55 per adult/child. The adult price includes a €35 landing fee, which goes towards conservation efforts, a 90-minute guided tour led by a conservationist, and a barbecued lunch on Curieuse.

St Pierre Islet

The glassy waters around St Pierre Islet, off Anse Volbert, are excellent for snorkelling and sloshing around. Boat trips to St Pierre organised by hotels and private operators are usually offered in combination with Curieuse and Cousin. Or you can charter your own boat from Anse Volbert. Contact Sagittarius Taxi Boat (€30 including fees).

Aride

The most northerly of the granite islands, this nature reserve lies 10km north of Praslin and supports the greatest concentration of sea birds in the area, including large colonies of noddies, terns and frigate birds, as well as lizards. From the summit (134m), the views are sensational. It also boasts a fantastic **beach** that's primo for sun, sand and swimming, though not snorkelling.

Aride can be reached by boat between September and May only, as landing can be difficult at other times. During the season, the island is open to visitors three days a week. Tours can be arranged through travel agencies, hotels and guesthouses in Praslin. A day trip costs about €115/55 per adult/child, including lunch and a guided tour of the island.

L'Archipel
RESORT €€€

(☑4284700; www.larchipel.com; Anse Gouvernement; d incl breakfast from €318; P✸@🖘🏊) This resort occupies a large, nicely landscaped plot by the beach, at Anse Gouvernement (the eastern tip of Anse Volbert). Squeezed in between the spacious, standalone, split-level units are a swimming pool and a restaurant. The walk up to the highest bungalows may leave the terminally unfit short of breath. Naturally, you'll find all the usual resort facilities onsite. The beach isn't the best here, somewhat narrow at high tide and fairly shallow.

Paradise Sun Hotel
RESORT €€€

(☑4293293; www.paradisesun.com; Anse Volbert; d with half board from €490; P✸🖘🏊) If you're looking for the classic Seychelles setting, complete with shady palms, lagoon views and a splendid china-white stretch of sand just steps from your door, then this resort-style operation won't disappoint. It offers 80 comfy rooms with dark-wood fixtures and granite bricks, ample space and heaps of amenities, including a dive centre and a watersports centre. Rooms are in two-storey blocks. The focus of the resort is on the swimming pool and bar-restaurant area. Note that half-board is compulsory. It's kid-friendly. All in all, Paradise Sun is a well-run resort with a lively, sociable atmosphere.

🛏 Anse Possession

Approximately halfway between Anse Lazio and Anse Volbert, Anse Possession is convenient to both. It's also a good, quiet base. There's a thin strip of sand but it can't rival the beaches at Anse Lazio or Anse Volbert.

Chalets Anse Possession
APARTMENTS €€

(☑4232180; chesca2207@hotmail.com; Anse Possession; d €80, q €100-130, incl breakfast; P✸🖘) Four two-bedroom villas are set in lush greenery off the coast road. Although not the height of luxury, they're clean, comfy, roomy and serviceable – perfect for the traveller who's not fussy. Meals (from €10) can be served on request. The owners can pick you up at the jetty. Excellent value. If it's full, the owners' daughter has newer apartments in a modern building at the front of the property, but prices are significantly higher.

Sea View Lodge
APARTMENTS €€

(☑2780001; www.kokonet.sc/seaviewlodge; Anse Possession; d €95-120, q €150-165; P✸🖘) This place has four units, including two villas that are perched on a hillside. Needless to say the verandahs have stunning views over the bay and Curieuse Island. The smaller 'Banana' bungalows feel like cosy bird's nests and will appeal to couples on a tighter budget (€95), while the larger house closer to the coastal road is great for families. All are fully equipped and super clean. Breakfast is €8 and dinner costs €15.

🛏 Zimbabwe

★ Maison du Soleil
BUNGALOWS €

(☑2562780, 2576315; jeanlouis@seychelles.net; Zimbabwe; d €50-75, q €120) Almost too good to be true. A location scout's dream, this self-catering villa perched on a hilltop offers million-dollar views of Curieuse and Praslin's northern coastline. There's a second villa, a bit further down the hill. OK, both are very modestly furnished, there's no air-con (and no wi-fi) and you need wheels to stay here, but those are the only gripes. The property is secluded and slightly hard to find, off the *very* steep road to Zimbabwe. The owner can arrange 4WD rental (reckon on €40 per day) and evening meals (€15).

🛏 Anse Lazio

Le Chevalier
APARTMENTS €€€

(☑4232322; chevalierbay@seychelles.sc; Anse Lazio; d with half board €185; P✸) Finally, Anse Lazio has produced a place to stay. The owners of the eponymous restaurant rent eight rooms in two seperate buildings – the best ones occupy the modern house at the back. They're a bit sterile, but the location is fantastic – you're a stone's throw from one of the most famous beaches in the world. Alas, no sea views because of the foliage of takamaka trees.

🍴 Eating

🍴 Grand Anse & Anse Kerlan

Breeze Garden
CAFETERIA, EUROPEAN €€

(☑4237000; Grand Anse; mains Rs 140-260; ☺lunch & dinner) In a verdant property near the church. Sit back, relax in these lovely surroundings and enjoy fine dining, salads, curries, pasta dishes, pizzas, grilled beef or simply a piece of fish cooked just right. Take away is available.

Café Le Monde
SEAFOOD, PIZZERIA €€

(Grand Anse; mains Rs 140-400; ☺ lunch & dinner) Considered one of the best restaurants in Grand Anse, the snazzy Café Le Monde concocts Creole classics, copious sandwiches as well as tasty pizzas that you can enjoy in an atmospheric garden terrace complete with wrought-iron furnishings. Also does take away. If only it had beach frontage, life would be perfect.

Capricorn
SEAFOOD €€€

(☑ 4233224; Anse Kerlan; mains Rs 250-390; ☺ lunch & dinner Mon-Sat) At Anse Kerlan, the Islander's (p296) has a good onsite restaurant, Capricorn. It's famous for its 'octopus Patrick-style' (octopus in a saffron sauce) and homemade desserts.

✕ Anse Volbert Area

★ PK's @ Pasquière
INTERNATIONAL €€

(☑ 4236242; Anse Boudin; mains Rs 200-350; ☺ 9am-9pm Mon-Sat, to 4pm Sun) You can spot this place from the coastal road thanks to its distinctive position – it's set in a wonderfully secluded property on a hillside. Needless to say the views of the coast are stunning. Tables are widely spaced and the menu has a lightness of touch missing from many of its peers – perfect for a *tête à tête*. Any of the meat or seafood dishes can be heartily recommended, but we have a soft spot for the seared tuna steak. Great value.

La Goulue
EUROPEAN €€

(☑ 4232223; Anse Volbert; mains Rs 140-250; ☺ noon-9.30pm Tue-Sun) This little eatery doesn't have beach frontage but the terrace catches some breeze. The menu features Creole staples and various filling snacks.

Gelateria de Luca
ICE CREAM, PIZZERIA €€

(Anse Volbert; mains Rs 100-480; ☺ 11am-9pm) Praslin's prime ice-cream parlour will leave you a drooling mess. Order a *coppa tropicale*, and you'll see why. It also whips up pasta dishes, pizzas and various snacks at lunchtime, while dinner is a more formal affair, with deeply satisfying dishes like grilled lamb chop, pork spare ribs and fish fillet. It's

across the road from the beach, but there's no view because of the thick foliage.

★ Les Lauriers
BUFFET €€€

(☑ 4232241; Anse Volbert; buffet Rs 520; ☺ dinner Thu-Tue) Charismatic Edwin and his Belgian spouse prepare a spectacular buffet at dinner. Rejoicing begins with lip-smacking hors d'oeuvre displayed on a boat-shaped table (the avocado salad is to die for), followed by sizzling meat and expertly grilled fish morsels (usually red snapper, jack and job). The dining room is atmospheric and convivial. Make sure you reserve a table.

★ Café des Arts
INTERNATIONAL €€€

(☑ 4232170; www.cafe.sc; Anse Volbert; mains Rs 450-800; ☺ lunch & dinner Tue-Sun) Praslin's most stylish restaurant is perfect for a *tête-à-tête*. Flickering candles, colourful paintings on the walls, swaying palms, a breezy terrace and the sound of waves washing the beach will rekindle the faintest romantic flame. The food is suitably refined; flavourful Seychellois favourites are whipped into eye-pleasing concoctions (think red snapper fillet in passion fruit sauce or marinated chicken with tropical fruits). It's more casual at lunchtime. The complex also shelters a reputable **art gallery**.

La Pirogue
INTERNATIONAL €€€

(☑ 4236677; Anse Volbert; mains Rs 240-450; ☺ breakfast, lunch & dinner) This cheerful cafe-restaurant serves simple but well-prepared meals, including salads you can tuck into without hesitation. There is also a good selection of fish and meat dishes, as well as vegetarian options and sandwiches.

✕ Anse Lazio

Le Chevalier
INTERNATIONAL, SEAFOOD €€€

(☑ 4232322; Anse Lazio; mains Rs 200-300, menus Rs 400-850; ☺ 8am-3.30pm, dinner by reservation) OK, Le Chevalier is not right on the beach and the setting is frustratingly bland (think a vast, tiled, open-air room on the ground floor of a modern villa), but the menu offers

---

❶ EATING OUT ON PRASLIN

Since most people eat in their hotels or guesthouses, there are relatively few independent restaurants on Praslin. Most hotels have excellent restaurants that are open to all comers (by reservation).

SEYCHELLES PRASLIN

SAILING AROUND THE SEYCHELLES

Experienced sailors and novices can charter sailboats, yachts and cruisers by the day or week. Charters can be arranged by calling a local charter company or a tour agent. Most companies offer boats with a skipper and crew, as well as 'bareboat' vessels on which you're your own skipper. The best months for cruising are April and October; the worst are January, July and August. Prices start at around €1200 per person for a week-long trip. Contact **Angel Fish Yacht Charter** (www.seychelles-charter.com; Eden Island, Mahé), **Dream Yacht Charter** (www. dreamyachtcharter.com) and **Silhouette Cruises** (www.seychelles-cruises.com). For a mix of diving and sailing, **Galatea** (www.diving-cruises.com) is your best bet.

lots of variety and includes salads, burgers and fish dishes. Breakfast is served until 10.30am.

Bonbon Plume   SEAFOOD €€€
(☑4232136; Anse Lazio; mains Rs 280-800, menu Rs 400; ☺9am-4pm) Is it a tourist trap or a seafood mecca? Both, perhaps. With such a location – the palm-thatched canopy is right on the beach – tables are unsurprisingly in high demand. Anything from grilled crab in coconut sauce to the catch of the day, this is a simple seafood delight. For grilled lobster or *cigale de mer* (squill fish), you'll be looking at Rs 800.

❶ Information

You'll find several banks and bureaux de change in Grand Anse, Baie Ste Anne and Anse Volbert. All banks have ATMs and exchange facilities.
Breeze Garden – Double Click (Grand Anse; per hr Rs 40; ☺8am-10pm) Internet access as well as printing services. Also houses a bureau de change.
D&B Medianet Services (Anse Volbert; per hr Rs 120; ☺9.30am-1pm & 2-8.30pm; ☏) Internet cafe. Also has wi-fi access (same rates).
Tourist Office (☑4232669, 4233346; stbpras lin@seychelles.net; airport; ☺8am-4pm Mon-Fri, 8am-noon Sat) Can provide maps and basic information, and help with accommodation, car hire and excursion bookings. Also has a branch in Baie Ste Anne (Baie Ste Anne jetty).

❶ Getting There & Away

Praslin airport is 3km from Grand Anse and has numerous flights to/from Mahé.

You can also take the **Cat Cocos** (www.cat-cocos.com; Baie Ste Anne; ☺ticket office 7am-5.30pm) catamaran from Victoria. For La Digue, the Cat Rose catamaran operated by Inter-Island Ferry Pty (p322) runs about seven times daily and takes about 15 minutes to cross. See p322 for schedules and prices.

❶ Getting Around

Praslin has a decent bus service (Rs 5) as well as the usual taxis. A taxi ride from the Baie Ste Anne jetty to Anse Volbert or Grand Anse will set you back Rs 200.

A car is a great way to see the island. For car hire, you can negotiate directly with car-rental companies – the tourist office has a list. **Aventure Car Hire** (☑2527291, 4233805; aventure@ seychelles.net) charges about €40 per day. Most hotels and guesthouses can also assist you in organising car hire. Cars can be delivered to your hotel, the airport or the jetty.

You can hire bikes through your accommodation or from **Maki Shop** (☑277711; Anse Volbert; ☺9am-6pm) for Rs 150 per day.

Hopping around the small islands off Praslin is done by chartered boat; trips are usually organised through the hotels or tour operators.

LA DIGUE

Remember that tropical paradise that appears in countless adverts and glossy travel brochures? Here it's the real thing, with jade-green waters, bewitching bays studded with heart-palpitatingly gorgeous beaches, and green hills cloaked with tangled jungle and tall trees. As if that wasn't enough, La Digue is ideally situated as a springboard to surrounding islands, including Félicité, Grande Sœur and the fairytale Île Cocos.

Despite its lush beauty, La Digue has managed to escape the somewhat rampant tourist development that affects Mahé and Praslin. Sure, it's certainly not undiscovered, but La Digue has a more laid-back feel than the other main islands, with only a few surfaced roads and virtually no cars – just the odd ox cart. The place is definitely more of a back-to-nature than a jet-set-tourist kind of haven, making it possible to find that deserted *anse* (bay) where you really feel as though you've been stranded in paradise.

GOING BEYOND THE BEACH

If your muscles are starting to shrivel after one too many days of beachbasking, take the time to explore the island's recesses that can only be reached by walking paths – you'll discover plenty of secret spots known only to locals. Tracks are not well defined and are difficult to find and to follow; it's advisable to go with a guide. Walking guides include Robert Agnes, whose company, **Sunny Trail Guide** (☑ 2525357; www.sunnytrailguide.net; La Passe; ⊙ by reservation), had good credentials at the time of research; **Roland Sultan** (☑ 2547859, 2567147; La Passe; ⊙ by reservation), who is very knowledgeable about flora; and **Rhondy Payet** (☑ 2590368; La Passe; ⊙ by reservation). Reckon on €30 to €40 per person, depending on the walk. Fruits and sandwiches are included.

Nid d'Aigle

Ready to huff and puff? Tackle Nid d'Aigle (Eagle's Nest), the highest point on La Digue (333m), which commands sensational views. From La Passe, follow the inland concrete road that leads up to Snack Bellevue (it's signposted), then take the narrow path that starts behind the *snack*. After about 15 minutes, you'll reach an intersection on a ridge; turn right and follow the path until you reach Nid d'Aigle (no sign) after another 10 minutes. From Nid d'Aigle, it's possible to descend to Anse Cocos (add another 90 minutes), but a guide is mandatory as the path is overgrown.

Grand Anse to Anse Cocos

From Loutier Coco (p309) restaurant, it's an easy 15-minute walk to Petite Anse on a fairly well-defined path. From Petite Anse, it takes another 20 minutes to reach Anse Cocos, but the path is not clear – it's best to go with a guide.

Grand Anse to Anse Marron

If you have time for only one walk, this is the most scenic. The coastline between Grand Anse and Anse Marron is extremely alluring: a string of hard-to-reach inlets lapped by azure waters, with the mandatory idyllic beach fringing the shore, and vast expanses of chaotic granite boulders. From Loutier Coco, it takes roughly 1¼ hours to reach Anse Marron (p306), a gem of solitude. It's poorly marked, so you'll definitely need a guide. From Anse Marron, you can continue as far as Anse Source d'Argent at low tide, but there's a short section where you'll have to walk knee-deep in the water.

Anse Source d'Argent to Anse Marron

From Anse Source d'Argent, a memorable adventure consists of climbing up the granite hills that loom above the southwest coast before getting down to **Anse Pierrot**, from where you can continue along the shore to **Anse aux Cèdres** and **Anse Bonnet Kare** (and back to Anse Source d'Argent along the shore). The beauty of these stunning swaths of sand lies in the fact that they're totally secluded and there's no road here.

It's an arduous climb to reach the top of the granite hills but the panoramic views will be etched in your memory forever. It's a half-day excursion. It's also possible to continue as far as Anse Marron and up to Grand Anse.

Transport to La Digue is absurdly easy. It's only about 5km from Praslin, and getting by boat from one island to the other is simplicity itself, so you've no excuse not to spend a day or two at the very least on this island.

If money's a factor, La Digue has a growing number of quaint family guesthouses and self-catering apartments in which to rest your head.

⊙ Sights

La Passe   VILLAGE

A visit to tiny La Passe almost feels like stepping back in time, so perfectly does it capture the image of a sleepy tropical port. Virtually no cars clog the streets. Men and women talk shop on the jetty while waiting for the ferry to arrive. Children ride bicycles on the tree-lined roads. Come Saturday

La Digue

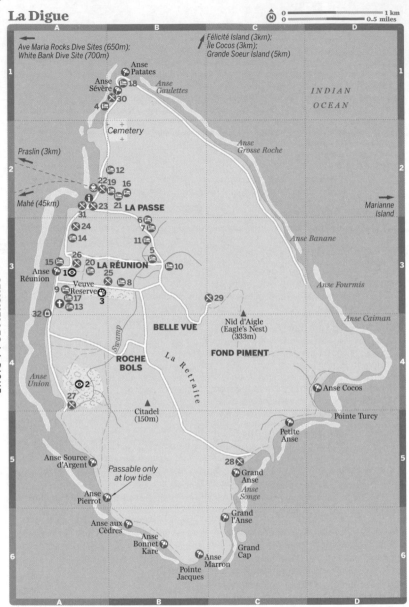

night, most islanders head to Tarosa for some serious dancing and drinking.

Check out the few souvenir shops near the jetty, sign up for a boat excursion or hire a bicycle and just peddle around a bit.

L'Union Estate & Copra Factory HISTORIC SITE (admission Rs 100 or €10) At one time, the main industry on La Digue was coconut farming, centred on L'Union Estate coconut plantation south of La Passe. These days L'Union Estate is run as an informal 'theme park',

La Digue

with demonstrations of extracting oil from copra (dried coconut flesh). Also in the grounds are the Old Plantation House, a colonial-era graveyard, a boatyard and the obligatory pen of giant tortoises.

Veuve Reserve WILDLIFE RESERVE
(📞 2783114; La Passe; ⊙ information centre 8am-noon & 1-4pm Mon-Fri) **FREE** La Digue is the last refuge of the black paradise flycatcher, which locals call the *veuve* (widow). This small forest reserve has been set aside to protect its natural habitat. At the time of writing there were 20 pairs within the reserve. The male has long black tail feathers. The ranger, Josiana, claims that sightings are guaranteed if she goes on a small tour with you – we confirm. Other species include terrapins, fruit bats and moorhens. Several walking trails punctuated with interpretive panels about flora have been set up. There's also a small information centre.

🏖 Beaches

Anse Source d'Argent BEACH
Most new arrivals head straight for the beach at Anse Source d'Argent, and we don't blame them. *This* is the tropical paradise we've all been daydreaming about all winter: a dazzling white-sand beach backed by naturally sculpted granite boulders that would have made Henry Moore proud.

Alas, don't expect a Robinson Crusoe experience – it can get pretty crowded here, especially at high tide when the beach virtually disappears. Another downside: Anse Source d'Argent is scenic, but not that great for swimming due to the shallow water.

Take note that the path down to Anse Source d'Argent runs through the old L'Union Estate coconut plantation. In other words, you'll have to pay the Rs 100 or €10 entry fee (valid for a day) to access the beach.

Grand Anse BEACH
On the southeast coast, Grand Anse is a stunning beach to sun yourself on, and it sees fewer visitors because of the effort required to get there (though you can easily walk or cycle the 4km or so from La Passe). One caveat: swimming may be dangerous because of the strong offshore currents during the southeast monsoon, from April to October.

Petite Anse BEACH
North of Grand Anse, the wonderfully dramatic crescent of Petite Anse is accessible on foot only. Strong riptides make it dangerous for swimming but the peace you find sitting here under a coconut palm may be as good as it gets on La Digue.

Anse Cocos
BEACH

From Petite Anse, you can also take your beach towel further north to the equally scenic Anse Cocos, which is reached by a rather vague track at the north end of Petite Anse. The bay here is dazzling to behold – a salt-white strip of sand lapped by turquoise waters. Backed by casuarina trees and craning palms, it's a gorgeous place to sun yourself. Because of rip currents, Anse Cocos isn't good for swimming; for a dip, head to the northern tip of the beach, which has protected pools.

Anse Marron
BEACH

At the southern tip of the island, little-known Anse Marron is a hidden morsel of tranquillity. The fact that this fantastically wild beach can only be reached on foot adds to its wonderful sense of remoteness.

Anse Réunion
BEACH

True, Anse Réunion, south of La Passe, hardly compares to Grand Anse or Anse Source d'Argent – there is usually algae drifting along the shore – but it's an easy walk from town and a pretty place to watch the sun set.

Anse Patates
BEACH

At the northern tip of the island, this beach is alluring but lacks the wow factor. It's a great place for a picnic, though, and has some good snorkelling.

Anse Sévère
BEACH

On the north coast, this beach is not the most photogenic, but is great for snorkelling.

⚡ Activities

Boat Excursions

Taking a boat excursion to nearby Île Cocos, Félicité and Grande Sœur will be one of the main highlights of your visit to the Seychelles and it's well worth the expense. Full-day tours typically stop to snorkel off Île Cocos and Félicité and picnic on Grande Sœur. The best snorkelling spots can be found off the iconic Île Cocos.

Most lodgings and travel agencies on La Digue can arrange such trips. Prices are about €110, including a barbecued fish lunch. Half-day tours can also be organised (€55).

Diving & Snorkelling

La Digue features a range of excellent dive sites, including the iconic White Bank. Snorkelling is also top notch. Sweet spots around the island include Anse Sévère and Anse Patates. Île Cocos and Félicité seem to be tailored to the expectations of avid snorkellers, with glassy turquoise waters and a smattering of healthy coral gardens around. All boat tours include snorkelling stops.

Azzurra Pro-Dive
DIVING

(☑4292535; www.ladigue.sc; Anse Réunion; ⊘daily) This PADI-certified dive centre organises a variety of dive trips and certification courses. Based at La Digue Island Lodge.

🛏 Sleeping

Most places offer half-board options. The cheapest ones don't accept credit cards.

La Passe Guest House
GUESTHOUSE €€

(☑4234391; La Passe; s/d incl breakfast €35/65; ✳) Unfussy, low-key and priced a hair lower than the competition – a bonanza for budget-conscious visitors. The three fan-cooled rooms (plus one which has air-con and costs an extra €10) won't have you writing 'wish you were here' postcards, but you can save the postage for sampling the good Creole dinners (€12) prepared by Marie-Anne, the friendly owner. A stand-alone bungalow should also be available by the time you read this, and there are plans to install air-con in all of the rooms (which will drive up prices by €10).

Buisson Guesthouse
GUESTHOUSE €€

(☑2592959; www.buissonladigue.jimdo.com; La Passe; s/d incl breakfast €45/70; ✳🛜) Down a dirt road south of the harbourfront you'll find this cute house in a proudly maintained and flowered little property. It shelters two simple, neat rooms – opt for the larger one, which has a lounge (same price). Substantial breakfasts and dinners (on request) are other pluses.

Veronic Guesthouse
GUESTHOUSE €€

(☑2592463, 4234743; seyladigue@yahoo.com; La Passe; s/d/q €40/75/140) Embedded in a manicured tropical garden, this venture is a good option for budgeteers, with three comfortable if rather unloved rooms.

Pension Hibiscus
APARTMENTS €€

(☑2575896, 4234029; hibiscus@email.sc; La Passe; s/d €60/80; ✳🛜) Bargain! Tucked away in the interior of La Passe, this pension features two three-bedroom houses with self-catering facilities. Nothing is fancy but it all feels very proper and immaculate, in a chilled-out setting. The owner, Jeanita, is a helpful gem and can prepare breakfast (€10) and dinner (€15) on request.

Oceane's Self Catering
APARTMENTS €€

(📞2511818; www.oceane.sc; La Passe; d €85; ❄️📶🍴) Yes, the apartments in this modern villa are a bit cramped, have no views and don't have much local flavour, but we won't hold this against them because otherwise they're well equipped and serviceable, and the place offers some little extras such as gazebos and a Jacuzzi in the garden, which turns an average place to stay into a great place to stay. It's family-run and friendly. You can order breakfast (€10) and dinner (€20).

⭐ Anse Sévère Bungalow
BUNGALOW €€

(📞4247354; clemco@seychelles.net; Anse Sévère; d €115-120) An atmosphere of dreamlike tranquillity characterises this self-catering, two-bedroom house with a fab sea frontage. Your biggest quandary here: a bout of snorkelling (or swimming) or a snooze on the white-sand beach? If you don't fancy cooking, Agnelle, the maid, can prepare hearty Creole meals for about Rs 250. There's no air-con, but the location benefits from cooling sea breezes. Ideal for families. Book early.

⭐Chalets d'Anse Réunion – Chez Nora
BUNGALOWS €€

(📞2515018, 4235165; www.chaletsdansereunion.com; La Passe; d €120; ❄️) The three bungalows, with their tiled floors, sunset-friendly balconies, sparkling bathrooms and generously sized rooms with a mezzanine, are light and well equipped, and the lovely natural surroundings, warm welcome and spectacular rates make this a real winner. The food is local and quite delicious (breakfast/dinner €9/18). Brilliant vlaue.

Calou Guest House
BUNGALOWS €€

(📞2781327, 4234083; www.calou.de; La Passe; s/d incl breakfast €73/105; ❄️📶) While the five bungalows with private terrace are far from fancy – think simple furnishings, old-style curtains and bedcovers, fake thatched roofs – the setting is the real draw, with an Eden-like garden replete with exotic fruit trees and soaring jungle-clad hills as the backdrop. The food is reputedly good, too. A *biergarten* (the owner, Klaus, is German) and a minuscule freshwater pool round out the fun. There are plans to smarten up the rooms.

Cocotier du Rocher
BUNGALOWS €€

(📞2514889, 4234489; www.cocotierdurocher.com; La Passe; d €100-110; ❄️📶) This charming venture has three bungalows that spread out on grassy grounds surrounded by blooming tropical gardens. They're well-appointed, prettily decorated and kept scrupulously clean. Verena and her son Stéphane, your courteous hosts, go above and beyond to ensure you enjoy your stay. Breakfast (€5) and dinner (€20) are available on request.

Bois d'Amour
APARTMENTS €€

(📞2529290, 4234490; www.boisdamour.de; La Passe; d €85-130) Three all-wood, fully equipped chalets in a garden overflowing with blossoming tropical flowers. They're amply sized and well spaced out, and may remind you of the little house on a Swiss cuckoo clock. The Kokoleo, at the far end of the property, is the best. Evening meals (€15) can be arranged on request. Minuses: no aircon and no wi-fi access.

Fleur de Lys
BUNGALOWS €€

(📞4234459; fleurdelysey@yahoo.com; La Passe; d €120; ❄️📶) A chilled universe is created here by a lazy-day garden and a clutch of trim, Creole-style bungalows with spotless bathrooms and kitchenettes. Breakfast is an extra (€10).

Casa de Leela
APARTMENTS €€

(📞2512223, 4234193; www.casa-de-leela.bplaced.net; La Passe; d/q from €120/180; ❄️🍴) Three well-designed bungalows and four apartments with all mod cons as well as a swimming pool set in a tropical garden. Breakfast (€10) and dinner (€25) on request.

Domaine Les Rochers
APARTMENTS €€

(www.domainelesrochers.com; La Passe; d €120-150; ❄️📶) This Italian-run place offers large and well-thought-out apartments with separate bedrooms and well-equipped kitchens, but what really makes this place special are the verdant gardens and sense of privacy.

La Digue Island Lodge
RESORT €€€

(📞4292525; www.ladigue.sc; Anse Réunion; d incl breakfast from €140; ❄️📶🍴) This hodge-podge of a resort comprises A-frame chalets packed rather close together as well as an atmospheric plantation house and standard rooms, some with sea views. They're all showing their age a tad but enjoy a privileged position – they're set on exotic garden areas overlooking Anse Réunion. Sunbathing is top-notch but swimming is not that enthralling, with very shallow waters and algae. Amenities are solid, with two restaurants, two bars, a dive centre and a pool.

Château St Cloud
HOTEL €€€

(☑ 4234346; www.seychelles.net/stcloud; La Passe; d incl breakfast from €165; ❋❄☀) Choose your accommodation wisely and this agreeable place set in a former colonial estate can be a sweet deal. What to pick: one of the superior rooms that are dotted on a forest-clad hillside or a deluxe room, which marries modern and Creole design influences. What to avoid: a smallish, utilitarian standard room. Facilities include a pool and a restaurant.

Le Repaire
BOUTIQUE HOTEL €€€

(www.lerepaireseychelles.com; La Passe; d incl breakfast €190-230; ❋❄☀) This nearly-but-not-quite boutique hotel will appeal to design-savvy travellers, with stylish furniture, soothing tones, a lovely garden and a spiffing seaside location (but the shore is no good for swimming). Be sure to score a sea-facing Superior room, rather than a darker standard room.

L'Océan Hotel
HOTEL €€€

(☑ 4234180; www.hotelocean.info; Anse Patates; s/d incl breakfast €165/200; ❋) A safe bet, with an oceanfront location. The hotel's total capacity is eight, making it wonderfully intimate. Every bedroom boasts stupendous views of the sea and is decorated with driftwood, shells and paintings by local artist George Camille. Hint: aim for the Petite Sœur and Grande Sœur rooms. There's no beach but snorkelling is excellent just offshore. There's an onsite restaurant. For the price you'd expect wi-fi.

★ Domaine de L'Orangeraie Resort & Spa
LUXURY HOTEL €€€

(☑ 4299999; www.orangeraie.sc; Anse Sévère; d incl breakfast from €300; ❋❄☀) Tropical luxury at its best. Dramatically deployed on hilly grounds in a sea of spruce greenery, Domaine de L'Orangeraie feels like heaven. No expense has been spared in dousing guests in sassy swank – creatively landscaped grounds, natural materials and high-class amenities (including a superb spa and two restaurants). Each villa is furnished in muted earth tones with subtle Asian accents. Step inside and let the Zen-like tranquillity envelop you. One weak point: the artificial beach, next to the restaurant, is nothing special.

✖ Eating

Other options worthy of interest include the hotel restaurants: L'Océan Hotel, Château St Cloud and La Digue Island Lodge all welcome visitors in their enchanting settings.

Bakery
BAKERY €

(La Passe; ☉ 9am-7pm Mon-Sat) This small bakery near the pier sells fresh bread and cakes. Come early; by 10am the cakes are sold out.

Gregoire's Store
SUPERMARKET €

(☑ 4234024; La Passe; ☉ 7.30am-7pm Mon-Sat, to 1pm Sun) For self-caterers, Gregoire's Store is the best-stocked supermarket on the island.

Bor Lanmer Takeaway
TAKEAWAY €

(La Passe; mains Rs 50; ☉ lunch & dinner) If you're looking for a quick food fix at unbeateable prices, check out the options at this cheap-and-cheerful eatery near the jetty. Servings are well sized and the food's tasty. It has a few outdoor tables.

Gala Takeaway
TAKEAWAY €

(☑ 2525951; La Passe; mains Rs 50-55; ☉ lunch & dinner Mon-Sat) This friendly, hole-in-the-wall place dishes up excellent *barquettes* (cartons) of fried rice, chicken with vegetables, fish and other Creole staples at puny prices. Near Veuve Reserve. Take away is available.

Takamaka Kiosk
SANDWICHES €

(Anse Sévère; sandwiches Rs 50-100; ☉ 9am-4pm) Recharge the batteries with a fresh fruit platter or a copious sandwich at this shack nudging pleasingly up Anse Sévère.

Snack Bellevue
CAFETERIA €

(Belle Vue; mains Rs 80-120; ☉ 11am-6pm) It's a hell of a hike or ride to get to this eagle's eyrie, but you'll be amply rewarded with cardiac-arresting views from the terrace. It serves up the usual suspects at very reasonable prices (not a mean feat, given the location).

★ Lanbousir
SEAFOOD €€

(Anse Union; mains Rs 130-175; ☉ 12.30-3.30pm) This sand-floored eatery run by three affable ladies is an ideal spot for a filling lunch after (or before) working your tan at nearby Anse Source d'Argent. Start things off with smoked fish salad, move on to a meltingly tender fish fillet, then finish off with a rich banana pancake. Wash it all down with a lemon juice or a chilled coconut. A traveller's life is hard, isn't it?

★**Loutier Coco** BUFFET €€
(📞2514762; Grand Anse; buffet Rs 320; ⊕12.30-3.30pm) Feel the sand in your toes at this oasis of a place on Grand Anse beach, but be prepared to share the experience with a raft of day-trippers here to enjoy the lavish buffet at lunchtime. The spread on offer includes grilled fish, traditional Creole curries and salads, fruit and coffee.

Tarosa CAFETERIA €€
(📞4234407; La Passe; mains Rs 120-220; ⊕breakfast, lunch & dinner) This is La Digue's social hub, on the jetty. There's a little of everything for everyone, from satisfying breakfasts to sandwiches and fish dishes, but the food is only so-so. It features DJs on Saturday evening.

Chez Marston EUROPEAN €€
(📞4234023; La Passe; mains Rs 120-260; ⊕lunch & dinner) To be totally honest the food here isn't all that great, but the atmosphere is relaxed and the menu covers most tastes with salads, sandwiches, prawns, fish or crab curries, pizzas and burgers. Desserts include pancakes and ice creams.

★**Domaine de**
L'Orangeraie Resort
& Spa – Le Combava INTERNATIONAL €€€
(📞4299999; Anse Sévère; mains Rs 400-800; ⊕lunch & dinner daily) Ah, Le Combava. This elegant restaurant within the Domaine de L'Orangeraie Resort & Spa offers the intoxicating mix of fine dining, romantic atmosphere, cool setting and attentive service. The sleek dining room is by the hotel's swimming pool and is particularly magical in the evening. If nothing else, come for the suave desserts (from Rs 200) – the moist chocolate cake with vanilla ice cream is unforgettable.

Le Repaire ITALIAN €€€
(📞4234332; www.lerepaireseychelles.com; mains Rs 250-500; ⊕lunch Wed-Mon, dinner daily) Le Repaire stands apart by cooking Italian classics that will rock your world. Generous portions of fish and meat mains and creative pasta dishes are served in a sophisticated yet casual room that opens onto a flourishing tropical garden. There's a range of exemplary desserts, including an addictive tiramisu.

 Drinking

The restaurant-meets-bar **Tarosa** (La Passe; ⊕9am-late) is the most 'happening' spot in

 GETTING AROUND AFTER DARK

If eating out in the evening, remember to take a torch (flashlight) with you as there are few street lights, and note that most restaurants close around 9pm.

town and transforms itself into an open-air club on Saturday evening. This is your chance to rub shoulders with La Digue's movers and shakers and relive *Saturday Night Fever* island style!

If it's just the setting you want to absorb, check out the bars at the largest hotels.

🛍 **Shopping**

You'll find various souvenir shops in La Passe, near the jetty.

Barbara Jenson Studio GALLERY
(📞4234406; www.barbarajensonstudio.com; Anse Réunion; ⊕9.30am-6pm Mon-Sat) Barbara's work reflects the unique landscape and ethnically diverse people of the Seychelles.

ℹ **Information**

In La Passe, you'll find banks with ATMs as well as a couple of bureaux de change.

La Digue Video & Internet Café (per hr Rs 120; ⊕9am-9pm Mon-Sat, 4-8pm Sun; 🛜) Near the seafront. Also has wi-fi access (same rates).

Tourist Office (📞4234393; ⊕8am-4.30pm Mon-Fri, 9am-noon Sat) Provides basic information and helps organise tours.

ℹ **Getting There & Around**

There's no airstrip on La Digue. The island is easily reached by boat from both Mahé and Praslin; see p322 for details.

There are a few surfaced roads on the island. Given that it is less than 5km from north to south, by far the best – and most enjoyable – way to get around is on foot or bicycle. There are loads of bikes to rent. Operators have outlets near the pier, or you can book through your hotel. Most places charge around Rs 150 per day.

Ox carts used to be a popular mode of transport but are gradually being replaced by open-sided trucks.

There are only a handful of taxis on La Digue, as most people get around on bicycle or on foot. A one-way ride from the pier to Grand Anse costs around Rs 150.

SEYCHELLES LA DIGUE

OTHER INNER ISLANDS

If you want to live out that stranded-on-a-deserted-island fantasy, consider staying at a private island resort. Rack rates are sky-high, but look out for internet deals.

Apart from the sense of exclusivity, what makes these hideaways so special is their green ethos. They're all involved in pioneering conservation projects and are sanctuaries for various rare species.

Transport is handled directly by the hotels on the islands.

Silhouette

Silhouette is the pyramid-shaped island you see looming on the horizon from Beau Vallon on Mahé. With steep forested mountain peaks rising from the ocean above stunning palm-shaded beaches, Silhouette is a truly magnificent island hideaway, though only 20km north of Mahé. The highest point is Mt Dauban (740m), and there are some truly wild stretches of beach at **Anse Mondon**, **Anse Lascar**, **Anse Patate** and **Grand Barbe**. Silhouette is famed for its biological diversity and it's home to a variety of unique habitats and ecosystems. There's a small research station based in the village of **La Passe** that focuses on the conservation of giant tortoises and terrapins. Volunteers and tourists are welcome.

🛏 Sleeping & Eating

La Belle Tortue   APARTMENTS €€€
(📞4325435; www.labelletortue.com; d incl breakfast from €280; ❄🛜⚹) This venue offers something different, with nine rooms in a modern villa near the village. They are roomy, light-filled and beautifully attired, with elegant furnishings, solid amenities and a private balcony. Food is a highlight here. The nearby beach is not the best on the island, but you can walk to some paradisiacal spots. Fishing and diving trips can be arranged.

**Hilton Seychelles Labriz
Resort & Spa**   RESORT €€€
(📞4293949; www.hiltonseychelleslabriz.com; Silhouette; d incl breakfast from €300; ❄🛜⚹) Possibly the most affordable private-island resort in the Seychelles, the five-star Hilton Seychelles Labriz comprises 110 opulent villas spread along a narrow sandy area east of the island, near La Passe. The list of facilities is prolific, with five restaurants, a wonderful spa and a state-of-the-art diving centre. Nature walks are available. One minus: the beach is no great shakes – it's too thin and too shallow at low tide – but you can take a tour to splendid Anse Mondon.

North

About 6km north of Silhouette, North Island is the last word in exclusivity and its hotel is generally lauded as a milestone in the 'couture castaway' Indian Ocean experience. The arrival by helicopter says it all: laid-back indulgence and James Bond glamour in a *Bounty*-licious paradise.

🛏 Sleeping & Eating

North Island   RESORT €€€
(📞4293100; www.north-island.com; North; d with full board €3900; ❄@🛜⚹) 🖋 Look at the website. Yes, it's really like this. Dazwhite beaches? Tick. Award-winning spa and gourmet dining? Tick. A top-notch dive centre to take you to some memorable dive sites? Tick. Your own butler to attend to your every whim? Tick. Shoes? Nah – the 11-ultra-luxurious suites, which blend wood, glass and stone, define the term 'barefoot chic'. There's a green ethos; natural habitats are being restored for the reintroduction of critically endangered species, and the resident ecologist takes guests on guided walks where they can witness sea turtles nesting on the beach. It's the kind of place where you expect to see corporate moguls and movie stars here to chill out.

Silhouette
0 ——— 1 km
0 ——— 0.5 miles

North Island
(6km)

Anse
Mondon
Mt Pot
à Eau
(671m)

Hilton
Seychelles
Labriz
Resort & Spa

Mahé
(20km)

Mt Dauban
(740m)

La Belle
Tortue

Jetty
La Passe

Anse
Lascar
Pointe
Ramasse

Grand
Barbe
Anse
Patate

INDIAN
OCEAN

Denis

You land on a strip of coral by the sea. There's a white-sand beach lapped by luxuriously warm waters; a shimmering lagoon with every hue from lapis lazuli to turquoise; palm and casuarina trees leaning over the shore. Welcome to Denis, a coral island that lies about 95km northeast of Mahé.

If working your suntan ceases to do it for you, there are nature walks along scenic pathways as well as fishing, snorkelling and diving trips that will keep you active. Wildlife lovers will enjoy it here, too; although Denis is small – barely 1.3km in length and 1.75km at its widest point – it's a sanctuary for a variety of species, including giant tortoises, magpie robins, paradise flycatchers and Seychelles warblers. From July to December you'll see turtles laying eggs on the beach.

🛏 Sleeping & Eating

Denis Private Island   RESORT €€€

(☑ 4295999; www.denisisland.com; d with full board from €1250; ❀ @ ☒) 🕭 Impressive Denis Private Island is essentially Swiss Family Robinson meets stylish travel magazine. The 25 villas, which have been recently modernised, are just steps from the dazzling white beach. They have a gorgeous feel, with the use of lots of wood, quality furnishings and elegant showers – not to mention the outdoor bathroom. Food is organic and is prepared from produce grown on the island farm. Diving and fishing are catered for amply, and the entire place feels eerily empty even at full capacity. The international clientele is mainly made up of couples, but families are also welcome. All guests get around by bicycle or on foot. There's no spa, but in-room massages can be arranged. One weak point? The pool is a bit small.

Bird

Bird is the ultimate in ecotourism and birdlife viewing. Hundreds of thousands of sooty terns, fairy terns and common noddies descend en masse between May and October to nest on this coral island that lies 95km north of Mahé. Now is your chance to relive a scene from Alfred Hitchcock's *The Birds*! You just have to sit on your veranda and birds will come to land on your head. Hawksbill turtles breed on the island's beaches between October and February,

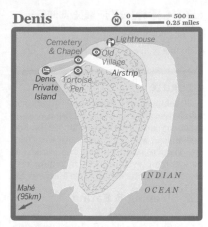

Denis

while their land-bound relatives lumber around the interior. Pay your respects to Esmeralda, the largest tortoise in the world – a 300kg, two-century-old monster of a specimen. He's still sexually active!

🛏 Sleeping & Eating

Bird Island Lodge   LODGE €€€

(☑ 4224925, 4323322; www.birdislandseychelles.com; d with full board from €455) 🕭 No phones. No TV. No air-con. No human pressures on the environment. Just you, masses of birds, 28 giant turtles, the inky blue ocean and sensational beaches. Enjoy this slice of untouched paradise in one of the 24 simple yet genuinely ecofriendly and agreeably designed chalets. They rest in a leafy plot, a thong's throw from the beach. A host of activities are available. Why not take a dolphin-spotting cruise? Or snorkel over sensational

Bird

SEYCHELLES DENIS

reefs just offshore? Or simply chill out on a secluded beach? Food is a definite plus, with copious meals using local ingredients, including (you guessed it) sooty tern eggs.

Frégate

A 30-minute flight from Mahé brings you to fairytale Frégate, which is both a wildlife sanctuary and a hideaway for celebs and millionaires who find serenity in the exclusive Fregate Island Private. The island has no less than seven beaches, including awesome **Anse Victorin** and **Anse Maquereau**.

🛏 Sleeping & Eating

Fregate Island Private   RESORT €€€
(📞 +49 6151 734 75 144 in Germany; www.fregate.com; d incl full board from €2900; ✳@🛜🏊)
🏊 Anything, anytime, anywhere – this is the mantra at this exclusive retreat that takes barefoot luxury into another realm. Perched on a hillside, the 16 seafacing villas – featuring the largest four-poster beds we've ever come across, a private pool and an open-air Jacuzzi – are reached by alleys that wind through the lush vegetation. Of course, you've got your own butler, who caters to all your needs. Swim in the jewelled waters of Anse Macquereau, enjoy breakfast in the Treehouse (a dinky platform perched in the canopy), take a diving trip or stroll hand in hand with your beloved at Anse Victorin – it's a tough life at Fregate Island. You can also book in for a beauty treatment in the serene spa, which uses only local, edible products. Don't leave without taking a guided walk with the resident conservationist, who'll show you the organic farm, the hatchery for giant tortoises, the rare magpie robin and a giant tenebrionid beetle, a 4cm-long insect that's apparently found nowhere else on earth.

OUTER ISLANDS

The majority of the Seychelles islands are scattered over hundreds of kilometres to the southwest of the main Mahé group. Sadly, most of these islands are accessible only to yachtsmen and those who can afford to stay at the extremely exclusive resorts.

The **Amirantes Group** lies about 250km southwest of Mahé. Its main island is **Desroches**, the only island that offers tourist infrastructure. Another 200km further south, the **Alphonse Group** is another cluster of coral islands that provides some of the best saltwater fly-fishing in the world. The largest of the group is the 1.2km-wide **Alphonse Island**.

The **Aldabra Group** is the most remote and most interesting of the outer-island groups. It includes **Aldabra Atoll**, the world's largest raised coral atoll, which is a Unesco World Heritage Site and nature reserve and lies more than 1000km from Mahé. Aldabra Atoll is home to about 150,000 giant tortoises, and flocks of migratory birds fly in and out in their thousands. Aldabra is managed by the Seychelles Island Foundation (p278) in Victoria. Until now the islands have only really been accessible to scientists, volunteers and a very small number of tourists.

Unfortunately, the Aldabra Group was off-limits to foreigners at the time of writing, due to the presence of Somali pirates in the area. Check with the Seychelles Island Foundation for the latest information.

🛏 Sleeping & Eating

Desroches Island Resort   RESORT €€€
(📞 4376750; www.desroches-island.com; d with full board from €1200; ✳@🛜🏊) This is a great private island resort with a heavy focus on sportfishing enthusiasts and divers (there's an onsite dive centre), but families and honeymooners will also feel welcome here. Digs are in 20 sumptuous seafacing beach chalets as well as stadium-sized luxurious villas complete with their own private pools. The spa is a killer, and world-class guided fly-fishing trips are available. The island

Frégate

SEYCHELLES FRÉGATE

itself is lovely, with dazzling white beaches almost all the way around it, as well as a turtle hatchery, a copra plantation, a tiny chapel, an old lighthouse and a small village of around 70 people. Desroches is only 6km long and barely 1km across – the stuff of castaway dreams.

The flight from Mahé takes about 45 minutes and is arranged directly through the resort.

UNDERSTAND SEYCHELLES

Seychelles Today

Economically, the Seychelles is in pretty good shape. In a climate of global recession, the 4% growth of the country's economy in 2012 (and an estimated 5% in 2013) is a respectable figure. Tourism, which is the mainstay of the economy, has been picking up in recent years and the number of arrivals to the Seychelles is on the increase, with more than 208,000 visitors in 2012 (160,000 in 2009). Most airlines based in the Gulf, including Emirates and Etihad, have launched frequent, well-priced services to the Seychelles from their respective hubs, and offer excellent connections with all major capitals in the world.

The other pillar of the economy is industrial fishing, which is one of the country's biggest foreign-exchange earners.

Nevertheless, the economy remains vulnerable to external events. Despite attempts to strengthen its agricultural base and use more locally manufactured products, the Seychelles continues to import 90% of its needs. As a result, even a slight dip in export earnings causes major ructions in the economy.

Politically, the situation has barely evolved in 35 years. The ruling party, the Seychelles People's Progressive Front (SPPF), led by President James Michel, has been governing the country since 1977. James Michel was re-elected in May 2011. The Seychellois aspire to *sanzman* (change) and more democracy, but freedom of the press is still quite limited. The next presidential elections are due in 2016.

With the increase in acts of piracy in the entire Western Indian Ocean, the Seychelles has found itself exposed to attacks led by Somali pirates. Strict measures have been taken to control the Seychellois territorial waters with the assistance of the international community – navy vessels patrol the area, which is carefully monitored. The Outer Islands were still off-limits to foreigners at the time of writing.

History

Until the 18th century the Seychelles was uninhabited. The islands were first spotted by Portuguese explorers, but the first recorded landing was by a British East India Company ship in 1609. Pirates and privateers used the Seychelles as a temporary base during lulls in their marauding.

The Colonial Period

In 1742, Mahé de Labourdonnais, the governor of what is now Mauritius, sent Captain Lazare Picault to investigate the islands. Picault named the main island after his employer (and the bay where he landed after himself) and laid the way for the French to claim possession of the islands 12 years later.

It took a while for the French to do anything with their possession. It wasn't until 1770 that the first batch of 21 settlers and seven slaves arrived on Ste Anne Island. After a few false starts, the settlers began growing spices, cassava, sugar cane and maize.

In the 18th century, the British began taking an interest in the Seychelles. The French were not willing to die for their colony and didn't resist British attacks, and the Seychelles became a British dependency in 1814. The British did little to develop the islands except increase the number of slaves. After abolition in 1835, freed slaves from around the region were also brought here. Because few British settled, however, the French language and culture remained dominant.

Over the years the islands have been used as a holding pen for numerous political prisoners and exiles.

In 1903 the Seychelles became a crown colony administered from London. It promptly went into the political and economic doldrums until 1964, when two political parties were formed. France Albert René, a young lawyer, founded the Seychelles People's United Party (SPUP). A fellow lawyer, James Mancham, led the new Seychelles Democratic Party (SDP).

Independence

Mancham's SDP, made up of businesspeople and planters, won the elections in 1966 and 1970. René's SPUP fought on a socialist and independence ticket. In June 1975 a coalition of the two parties gave the appearance of unity in the lead-up to independence, which was granted a year later. Mancham became the first president of the Republic of Seychelles and René the prime minister.

The flamboyant Sir Jim (as James Mancham was known) – poet and playboy – placed all his eggs in one basket: tourism. He jet-setted around the world with a beautiful socialite on each arm, and he put the Seychelles on the map.

The rich and famous poured in for holidays and to party, party, party. Adnan Khashoggi and other Arab millionaires bought large tracts of land, while film stars and celebrities came to enhance their romantic, glamorous images.

According to René and the SPUP, however, the wealth was not being spread evenly and the country was no more than a rich person's playground. René stated that poor Creoles were little better off than slaves.

The Long Road To Democracy

In June 1977, barely a year after independence, René and a team of Tanzanian-trained rebels carried out an almost bloodless coup while Mancham was in London attending a Commonwealth Conference. In the following years, René consolidated his position by deporting many supporters of the outlawed SDP. Opposed to René's one-party socialist state, these *grands blancs* (white landowners) set up 'resistance movements' in Britain, South Africa and Australia.

The country fell into disarray as the tourist trade dried to a trickle. The 1980s saw a campaign of civil disruption by supporters of the SDP, two army mutinies and more foiled coup attempts.

Finally, facing growing international criticism and the threatened withdrawal of foreign aid, René pulled a political about-face in the early 1990s; he abandoned one-party rule and announced the return to a multiparty democracy.

Elections were held in 1992 under the watchful eye of Commonwealth observers. René and his renamed Seychelles People's Progressive Front won 58.4% of the votes; Mancham, who had returned to the Seychelles, fielded 33.7% for his SDP and claimed the results were rigged.

René maintained his grip on power, while the SDP's star continued to wane. Even Mancham himself abandoned the SDP in favour of the centrist Seychelles National Party (SNP) in 1999. In the 2002 elections, the SNP, led by Wavel Ramkalawan, an Anglican priest, confirmed its stand as the main opposition party by winning over 42% of the vote.

In April 2004, René finally relinquished the presidency to the former vice-president, James Michel, who had stood by René through thick and thin. After a close race with Wavel Ramkalawan, the opposition leader, Michel won the 2006 presidential election, gaining 53.5% of the vote.

Michel doesn't seem willing to cede his power to any of his opponents; he prematurely dissolved the National Assembly in March 2007, following the boycott of assembly proceedings by the opposition party, and the general elections in May 2007 returned 18 SPPF members as against seven members of the SNP opposition party led by Wavel Ramkalawan (exactly the same numbers as before the dissolution). Though these elections were held democratically, the opposition claimed that the government bought votes.

On the economic front, in 2008 the highly indebted country was forced to turn to the IMF for assistance. A package of reforms was passed, including the free floating of the rupee, the abolition of all exchange restrictions and massive cuts in public spending. Debt was frozen and the economy quickly rebounded.

The Culture

Thanks to the islands' close links with Europe, the contemporary face of the Seychelles is surprisingly modern. The main island of Mahé is a rather sophisticated place, characterised as much by Western-style clothing, brand-new cars, mobile phones and modern houses as by any overt signs of traditional Creole culture. But beneath this strongly Westernised veneer, many aspects of traditional Creole culture survive. They live on in dance, music, hospitality, ancient beliefs, the language, the care-free attitude, and in many other day-to-day ways of doing things.

The society continues to be largely male dominated. Fortunately for women, the tourism industry is regarded as an equal-opportunity employer.

Most Seychellois are Catholic, but marriage is an unpopular institution. The reasons cited are that not marrying is a relic of slavery, when marriages simply didn't take place, and that marriage is expensive. As a result an estimated 75% of children are born out of wedlock. There's no taboo about illegitimacy, however.

For visitors, there are few rules and regulations to be followed, beyond respecting local attitudes towards nudity and visiting places of religious worship.

People of Seychelles

The population of the Seychelles is more strongly African than in Mauritius or Réunion, but even so you'll see almost every shade of skin and hair imaginable, arising from a mixture of largely French and African genes, together with infusions of Indian, Chinese and Arab blood. Distinct Indian and Chinese communities make up only a tiny proportion of the ethnic mix, however, the rest being Creole. As for the *grands blancs*, most were dispossessed in the wake of the 1977 coup.

As in Mauritius and Réunion, it is the Creole language, cuisine and culture that helps bind the Seychelles society. Over 90% of the population speak Creole as their first language, though most also speak English – the language of government and business – and French.

About 90% of Seychellois live on Mahé and nearly a third of these are concentrated in and around the capital. Most of the remaining 10% live on Praslin and La Digue, while the other islands are either uninhabited or home to tiny communities.

Religion

Nearly 90% of Seychellois are Roman Catholic, 7% are Anglican and 2.5% belong to the rapidly expanding evangelical churches. The remainder belong to the tiny Hindu, Muslim and Chinese communities largely based in Victoria.

Most people are avid churchgoers. On a Sunday, Victoria's Catholic and Anglican cathedrals, as well as the smaller churches scattered around the main islands, are full to bursting.

There is also a widespread belief in the supernatural and in the old magic of spirits known as *gris gris*. Sorcery was outlawed in 1958, but a few *bonhommes* and *bonnefemmes di bois* (medicine men and women) still practise their cures and curses and concoct potions for love, luck and revenge.

Arts

MUSIC

The Indian, European, Chinese and Arabic backgrounds of the Seychellois are reflected in their music. Patrick Victor and Jean-Marc Volcy are two of the Seychelles' best-known musicians, playing Creole pop and folk music. Other local stars are Emmanuel Marie and the late Raymond Lebon, whose daughter Sheila Paul made it into the local charts with an updated rendering of her father's romantic ballads.

VISUAL ARTS

Over recent decades, more and more artists have settled in the Seychelles and spawned a local industry catering to souvenir-hungry tourists. While shops are full of stereotypical scenes of palm trees and sunsets, there are also some innovative and talented artists around.

Michael Adams is the best-known and most distinctive contemporary artist. George Camille is another highly regarded artist who takes his inspiration from nature. Other notable artists are Barbara Jenson, who has a studio on La Digue, Gerard Devoud at Baie Lazare and Nigel Henry at Beau Vallon.

Look out, too, for works by Leon Radegonde, who produces innovative abstract collages; Andrew Gee, who specialises in silk paintings and watercolours of fish; and the sun-drenched paintings of Christine Harter. The painter and sculptor Egbert Marday produces powerful sketches of fisherfolk and plantation workers, but is perhaps best known for the statue of a man with a walking cane, situated outside the courthouse on Victoria's Independence Ave. Lorenzo Appiani produced the sculptures on the roundabouts at each end of 5th June Ave in Victoria.

Food & Drink

Staples & Specialities

Fish, fish, FISH! And rice. This is the most common combination (*pwason ek diri* in

SEYCHELLES FOOD & DRINK

Creole patois) in the Seychelles, and we won't complain – fish is guaranteed to be served ultra-fresh and literally melts in your mouth. You'll devour *bourgeois, capitaine,* shark, *job,* parrotfish, caranx, grouper and tuna, among others. To bring variety, they are cooked in innumerable guises: grilled, steamed, minced, smoked, stewed, salted, baked, wrapped in a banana leaf; the list goes on and on.

Seafood lovers will have found their spiritual home in the Seychelles; lobster, crab, shellfish and octopus are widely available.

The Seychelles is dripping with tropical fruit, including mango, banana, breadfruit, papaya, coconut, grapefruit, pineapple and carambole. Mixed with spices, they make wonderful accompaniments, such as the flavourful *chatini* (chutney). Vanilla, cinnamon and nutmeg are used to flavour stews and other preparations.

Gastronauts might consider trying *civet de chauve souris* (bat curry), which is considered a delicacy. You'll also find meat, mostly beef and chicken, but it's imported.

Drinks

Freshly squeezed juices and coconut water are the most natural and thirst-quenching drinks around. If you want to put some wobble in your step, Seybrew, the local brand of beer, is sold everywhere. Eku, another locally produced beer, is a bit harder to find. Wine is available at most restaurants.

Where to Eat & Drink

There's a full gamut of restaurant types, from funky shacks and burger joints to ritzy restaurants. Larger hotels have a choice of restaurants, with one always serving buffets (usually Creole or seafood). There is not a vast selection of street snacks to choose from in the Seychelles, but street vendors sell fresh fruit and fish – a good option if you're self-catering. Grocery stores are also widely available. The Victoria market is another good place to stock up on fresh food.

Vegetarians & Vegans

Restaurant menus in the Seychelles are dominated by fish, seafood and meat dishes, though there are actually a few salad and pasta dishes that are meat-free. If you're self-catering, you'll have much more choice, with a good selection of fruits and vegetables.

Environment

The Seychelles is a haven for wildlife, particularly birds and tropical fish. Because of the islands' isolation and the comparatively late arrival of humans, many species are endemic to the Seychelles.

The Land

The Seychelles lies about 1600km off the east coast of Africa and just south of the equator. It is made up of 115 islands, of which the central islands (including Mahé, Praslin and La Digue) are granite and the outlying islands are coral atolls. The granite islands, which do not share the volcanic nature of Réunion and Mauritius, appear to be peaks of a huge submerged plateau that was torn away from Africa when the continental plates shifted about 65 million years ago.

Wildlife

ANIMALS

Common mammals and reptiles include the fruit bat or flying fox, the gecko, the skink and the *tenrec* (a hedgehog-like mammal imported from Madagascar). There are also some small snakes, but they are not dangerous.

More noteworthy is the fact that giant tortoises, which feature on the Seychelles coat of arms, are now found only in the Seychelles and the Galápagos Islands, off Ecuador. The French and English wiped out the giant tortoises from all the Seychelles islands except Aldabra, where happily more than 100,000 still survive. Many have been brought to the central islands, where they munch their way around hotel gardens, and there is a free-roaming colony on Curieuse Island.

Almost every island seems to have some rare species of bird: on Frégate, Cousin, Cousine and Aride there are magpie robins (known as *pie chanteuse* in Creole); on Cousin, Cousine and Aride you'll find the Seychelles warbler; La Digue and Denis have the *veuve* (paradise flycatcher); and Praslin has the black parrot. The bare-legged scops owl and the Seychelles kestrel live on Mahé, and Bird Island is home to millions of sooty terns.

PLANTS

The coconut palm and the casuarina are the Seychelles' most common trees. There are a few banyans and you're also likely to see screw pines, bamboo and tortoise trees (so named because the fruit looks like the tortoises that eat it).

There are about 80 endemic plant species. Virgin forest now exists only on the higher parts of Silhouette Island and Mahé, and in the Vallée de Mai on Praslin, which is one of only two places in the world where the giant coco de mer palm grows wild. The other is nearby Curieuse Island.

In the high, remote parts of Mahé and Silhouette Island, you may come across the insect-eating pitcher plant, which either clings to trees or bushes or sprawls along the ground.

National Parks

The Seychelles currently boasts two national parks and seven marine national parks, as well as several other protected areas under government and NGO management. In all, about 46% of the country's total land mass

is now protected as well as some 45 sq km of ocean.

Environmental Issues

Overall the Seychelles has a pretty good record for protecting its natural environment. As early as 1968, Birdlife International set the ball rolling when it bought Cousin Island and began studying some of the country's critically endangered species. This was followed in the 1970s with legislation to establish national parks and marine reserves.

Not that the government's record is entirely unblemished. In 1998 it authorised a vast land-reclamation project on Mahé's northeast coast to provide much-needed space for housing. More recently, the construction of Eden Island, an artificial island with luxury properties off Mahé's east coast, has also raised concerns. Both projects have caused widespread silting, marring the natural beauty of this coast indefinitely, though

SEYCHELLES' NATIONAL PARKS

PARK	FEATURES	ACTIVITIES	BEST TIME TO VISIT
Aldabra Marine Reserve	raised coral atoll, tidal lagoon, birdlife, marine turtles, giant tortoises	diving, snorkelling, scientific study	Nov, Dec & mid-Mar– mid-May
Aride Island Marine Nature Reserve	granite island, coral reef, sea birds, fish life, marine turtles	birdwatching, snorkelling	Sep-May
Cousin Island Special Reserve	granite island, natural vegetation, hawksbill turtles, sea birds, lizards	birdwatching	year-round
Curieuse Marine National Park	granite island, coral reefs, coco de mer palms, giant tortoises, mangrove swamps, marine turtles, fish life	diving, snorkelling, walking	year-round
Morne Seychellois National Park	forested peaks, mangroves, glacis habitats	hiking, botany, birdwatching	May-Sep
Port Launay Marine National Park & Baie Ternay	mangrove swamps, fish life, coral reefs	diving, snorkelling	year-round
Praslin National Park (Vallée de Mai)	native forest, coco de mer palms, other endemic palms, black parrots	botany, birdwatching, walking	year-round
Ste Anne Marine National Park	marine ecosystems, marine turtles	glass-bottomed boat trips, snorkelling, diving	year-round

the alternative was to clear large tracts of forest. A difficult choice.

Tourism has had a similarly mixed impact. Every year, more resort hotels and lodges pop up, most notably on formerly pristine beaches or secluded islands. Sure, they have nothing on the concrete-and-glass horrors of, say, Hawaii or Cancun, but they still necessitate additional support systems, including roads and numerous vehicle trips, not to mention cutting down vegetation. Recent examples include Constance Ephelia Resort at Port Launay and Four Seasons at Petite Anse on Mahé, as well as the Raffles at Anse Possession (Praslin). On the other hand, tourist dollars provide much-needed revenue for funding conservation projects. Local attitudes have also changed as people have learned to value their environment.

Further impetus for change is coming from NGOs operating at both community and government levels. They have notched up some spectacular successes, such as the Magpie Robin Recovery Program, funded by the Royal Society for the Protection of Birds and Birdlife International. From just 23 magpie robins languishing on Frégate Island in 1990, there are now nearly 200 living on Frégate, Cousin, Denis and Cousine Islands. Similar results have been achieved with the Seychelles warbler on Cousin, Cousine and Aride Islands.

As part of these projects, a number of islands have been painstakingly restored to their original habitat by replacing alien plant and animal species with native varieties. Several islands have also been developed for ecotourism, notably Frégate, Bird, Denis, North, Silhouette and Desroches Islands. The visitors not only help fund conservation work, but it is also easier to protect the islands from poachers and predators if they are inhabited. With any luck, this marriage of conservation and tourism will point the way to the future.

SURVIVAL GUIDE

ℹ Directory A–Z

ACCOMMODATION

Glossy brochures focus on ultra-swish resorts but the Seychelles actually has a pretty wide range of accommodation options.

Check out www.seychelles.travel for a list of accommodation options. Other useful websites include www.seychelles-resa.com, www.seychellesbonplans.com, www.holidays-direct-seychelles.com, www.agoda.com and www.seyvillas.com.

Camping is forbidden anywhere on the islands.

Virtually all the hotels charge higher rates during peak periods (Christmas to New Year and Easter). Book well ahead.

Guesthouses & Self-Catering Accommodation

No, you don't need to remortgage the house to visit the Seychelles if you stay in one of the cheaper guesthouses or self-catering establishments that are burgeoning on Mahé, Praslin and La Digue. Self-catering options are private homes, villas, residences, studios or apartments that are fully equipped and can be rented by the night. The distinction between self-catering options and guesthouses is slim. Typically, rooms in guesthouses don't come equipped with a kitchen, and breakfast is usually offered. That said, at most self-catering ventures, breakfast and dinner are available on request. Standards are high – even in the cheapest guesthouse you can expect to get a room with a private bathroom and air-con, as well as a daily cleaning service. Both options are generally excellent value, especially for families or a group of friends. Most cost between €80 and €180. Many offer discounts for extended stays.

They also offer good opportunities for cultural immersion; they're mostly family-run operations and provide much more personal, idiosyncratic experiences than hotels.

TOP 10 ANIMALS TO WATCH FOR

➡ Whale sharks – Mahé

➡ Magpie robins – Cousin, Cousine, Aride, Denis

➡ Giant tortoises – All islands

➡ Flycatchers – La Digue

➡ Sooglossus sardinei frogs – Morne Seychellois National Park, Mahé

➡ Black parrots – Vallée de Mai, Praslin

➡ Fruit bats – Mahé, Praslin, La Digue

➡ Sooty terns – Bird Island

➡ Sea turtles – Bird, Cousin, Fregate, North, Aldabra

➡ Sharks – Off most islands

Throughout this chapter, the order of accommodation listings is by price, from the least to the most expensive. Each place to stay is accompanied by one of the following symbols (the price relates to a double room with private bathroom). Prices include all government taxes.

€ less than €50

€€ €50–100

€€€ more than €100

Resorts & Hotels

For those whose wallets overfloweth, there's no shortage of ultra-swish options. They're straight from the pages of a glossy, designer magazine, with luxurious villas that ooze style and class, and fabulously lavish spas in gorgeous settings.

For those whose budget won't stretch quite this far, there are also a few good-value, moderate-range affairs around Mahé, Praslin and La Digue, with prices around €180 for a double. Note that hotels commonly offer internet specials well below the advertised 'rack rates'.

All-inclusive, full-blown resorts featuring a wide range of recreational facilities and entertainment programs are quite rare in the Seychelles.

Private Island Resorts

If you want to combine escapism with luxury, the Seychelles offers a clutch of ultra-exclusive hideaways that almost defy description. They include Bird, Desroches, Silhouette, North, Frégate and Denis Islands. This is where you really are buying into the dream. They offer every modern convenience but still preserve that perfect tropical-island ambience – the Robinson Crusoe factor – and feature an atmosphere of romance, rejuvenation and exotic sensuality. Each private-island resort has its own personality and devotees. There's minimal contact with the local people, though.

Expect to pay between a cool €450 to a whopping €3900 a night, full board.

CHILDREN

The Seychelles is a very child- and family-friendly place. Most hotels cater for all age groups, offering baby-sitting services, kids clubs and activities especially for teenagers. While children will happily spend all day splashing around in the lagoon, boat trips around the islands should also appeal. Communing with giant tortoises is a sure-fire hit and visiting some of the nature reserves can be fun. Finding special foods and other baby products can be difficult, especially outside Victoria, so you might want to bring your favourite items with you.

EMBASSIES & CONSULATES

Countries with diplomatic representation in the Seychelles include the following:

British High Commission (☑4283666; bhcvictoria@fco.gov.uk; Francis Rachel St, Oliaji Trade Centre, Victoria)

French Embassy (☑4382500; www. ambafrance-sc.org; Immeuble La Ciotat, Mont Fleuri Rd, Victoria)

German Honorary Consulate (☑4601100; germanconsul@natureseychelles.org; Nature Seychelles, Roche Caiman, PO Box 1310, Mahé)

GAY & LESBIAN TRAVELLERS

The Seychellois are generally tolerant of gay and lesbian relationships as long as couples don't flaunt their sexuality, but there is no open gay or lesbian scene in the Seychelles. For gay and lesbian travellers there's little to worry about. We've never heard of any problems arising from same-sex couples sharing rooms during their holidays. That said, open displays of affection between gay or lesbian couples could raise eyebrows.

INSURANCE

A travel-insurance policy to cover theft, loss and medical problems is a good idea. Some policies specifically exclude dangerous activities, which can include scuba diving. If you plan on diving, we strongly recommend purchasing dive-specific insurance with **DAN** (www.diversalertnetwork.org).

Worldwide travel insurance is available at www.lonelyplanet.com/travel_services. You can buy, extend and claim online anytime – even if you're already on the road.

INTERNET ACCESS

➜ There are a couple of internet cafes in Victoria. Outside the capital, internet cafes are harder to find. Expect to pay around Rs 40 for an hour's access. Connection is still fairly slow by Western standards.

➜ Wi-fi is increasingly available – most often wi-fi access is restricted to public areas and is not free of charge.

➜ Establishments with wireless are identified in this book with a 🛜 icon.

➜ If you will be in Seychelles for a while, consider buying a USB stick ('dongle') from Cable & Wireless (the local mobile provider; see p278), which you can then load with airtime and plug into your laptop.

MONEY

➜ The unit of currency is the Seychelles rupee (Rs), which is divided into 100 cents (¢). Bank notes come in denominations of Rs 10, Rs 25,

> **ⓘ EATING PRICE RANGES**
>
> The following price ranges are used in this guide and refer to a standard main course. Service charges and taxes are included in the price. For information about the gastronomy of the Seychelles, see p315.
>
> **€** under Rs 100
>
> **€€** Rs 100–200
>
> **€€€** over Rs 200

Rs 50, Rs 100 and Rs 500; there are coins of Rs 1, Rs 5, 1¢, 5¢, 10¢ and 25¢.

➡ Euros are the best currency to carry. Prices for most tourist services, including accommodation, excursions, diving, car hire and transport are quoted in euros and can be paid in euros (and less frequently in US dollars), either in cash or by credit card. But you can also pay in rupees. In restaurants, prices are quoted in rupees but you can also pay in euros.

➡ The four main banks are Barclays Bank, Seychelles Savings Bank, Nouvobanq and Mauritius Commercial Bank (MCB). They have branches on Mahé, Praslin and La Digue. You'll also find numerous money-changers. There's no commission for changing cash. Don't lose time shopping around; rates are almost the same everywhere.

➡ There are ATMs, which accept major international cards, at the airport and at all the major banks in Victoria. You'll also find ATMs at Beau Vallon and Anse Royale on Mahé and on Praslin and La Digue. Remember that bank fees can apply.

➡ Major credit cards, including Visa and MasterCard, are accepted in most hotels, restaurants and tourist shops. Many guesthouses will still expect payment in cash. A few places add on an extra fee, typically 3%, to the bill to cover 'bank charges'.

OPENING HOURS

Banks Usually open from 8.30am to 2pm Monday to Friday, and 8.30am to 11am on Saturday.

Government offices Open from 8am to 4pm or 5pm Monday to Friday.

Restaurants Open between 11am and 2pm or 3pm and 6pm to 9pm daily.

Shops and businesses Typically 8am to 5pm Monday to Friday, and 8am to noon on Saturday.

PUBLIC HOLIDAYS

New Year 1 and 2 January
Good Friday March/April
Easter Day March/April
Labour Day 1 May
Liberation Day 5 June
Corpus Christi 10 June
National Day 18 June
Independence Day 29 June
Assumption 15 August
All Saints' Day 1 November
Immaculate Conception 8 December
Christmas Day 25 December

SAFE TRAVEL

Beaches in the Seychelles may be true beauties but some are certainly moody, changing dramatically with the seasons. They can be tranquil and flat as a lake at certain times of the year, then savage with incredible surf and mean rip currents at other periods. Most beaches are not supervised.

The Seychelles is a very safe destination, but never leave your valuables unattended on the beach or in your car.

TELEPHONE

➡ The telephone system is efficient and reliable. Telephone cards are available from Cable & Wireless (p278) and **Airtel** (☑ 4610615; Huteau Lane, Victoria; ⊙ 8.30am-4pm Mon-Fri, 8.30am-noon Sat) offices and from most retail outlets. Local calls within and between the main islands cost around Rs 2 per minute. For an idea of international rates, calls to North America, Australia and the UK with Cable & Wireless cost roughly Rs 3 per minute.

➡ Many foreign mobile services have coverage in the Seychelles, but roaming fees are high. If you have a GSM phone and it has been 'unlocked', you can use a local SIM card (Rs 50) purchased from either Cable & Wireless or Airtel. Top-up cards are widely available. There is mobile reception on Mahé, Praslin, La Digue and Silhouette.

➡ When phoning the Seychelles from abroad, you'll need to dial the international code for the Seychelles (☑ 248), followed by the seven-digit local number. There are no area codes.

TIME

The Seychelles is GMT plus four hours. When it's noon in Victoria, it's 8am in London, 3am in New York and 6pm in Sydney.

TOURIST INFORMATION

The very well-organised **Seychelles Tourism Bureau** (STB; www.seychelles.travel) is the only tourist information body in the Seychelles. The head office is in Victoria. It has two offices on Praslin and one office on La Digue.

TRAVELLERS WITH DISABILITIES

Most luxury hotels conform to international standards for disabled access, and it's usually possible to hire an assistant if you want to take an excursion. Apart from that, special facilities for travellers with disabilities are few and far between in the Seychelles, and no beach is equipped with wheelchair access.

VISAS

➡ Nationals of most Western countries don't need a visa to enter the Seychelles, just a valid passport.

➡ Initial entry is granted for a maximum of three months and proof of a planned and paid-for departure is required, although not always asked for. Immigration officers will also require that you mention the name, address and phone number of the place where you are staying in the Seychelles (if you don't know just give them the name of any large hotel).

VOLUNTEERING

Wanna get involved in turtle tagging, whale-shark monitoring or researching certain animal species? **Nature Seychelles** (www.nature-seychelles.org), Seychelles Island Foundation (p278) and **Marine Conservation Society Seychelles** (MCSS; www.mcss.sc) all have volunteer programs.

WOMEN TRAVELLERS

Generally speaking, women travellers should have few problems getting around solo in the Seychelles. As in any country, however, women should use their common sense when going to isolated stretches of beach and inland areas alone.

ⓘ Getting There & Away

AIR

➡ The **Seychelles international airport** (☑ 4384400; www.seychelles-airport.com), about 8km south of Victoria, is the only international airport in the Seychelles.

➡ The main international carriers are **Emirates** (☑ 4292700; www.emirates.com; 5th June Ave; ⊗ 8.30am-4pm Mon-Fri, 8.30am-noon Sat) and **Etihad Airways** (www.etihadairways.com; Independence Ave, Air Seychelles; ⊗ 8am-4pm Mon-Fri, 8am-noon Sat), which offer daily flights to Dubai (UAE) and Abu Dhabi (UAE) respectively and connecting flights to the rest of the world. Note that Etihad Airways has a code-share agreement with Air Seychelles.

➡ **Condor** (☑ 4288888; www.condor.com; Revolution Ave, Victoria, Mason's Travel; ⊗ 8am-4.30pm Mon-Fri, 8am-noon Sat) is the only airline that offers direct flights to/from Europe, with a weekly service from Frankfurt (Germany).

➡ **Air Seychelles** (☑ 4381000; www.airseychelles.com; Independence Ave, Victoria; ⊗ 8am-4pm Mon-Fri, 8am-noon Sat), the

national carrier, has regular flights to Abu Dhabi (UAE; in code-share with Etihad Airways), Hong Kong, Johannesburg (South Africa) and Mauritius.

➡ Other major airlines include **Air Austral** (☑ 4321044, 4323129; www.air-austral.com; Independence Ave; ⊗ 8.30am-4pm Mon-Fri, 8.30am-noon Sat), with weekly flights to Réunion, and **Kenya Airways** (☑ 4322989; www.kenya-airways.com; Independence Ave, Kingsgate House; ⊗ 8.30am-4.30pm Mon-Fri, 8.30am-12.30pm Sat), which flies three times a week to Nairobi (Kenya).

ⓘ Getting Around

AIR

Air Seychelles (p321) takes care of all inter-island flights, whether scheduled or chartered. The only scheduled services are between Mahé and Praslin, with around 25 flights per day in each direction. The fare for the 15-minute hop starts from €53 (return from €106). The luggage limit is only 15kg. Air Seychelles also flies to Bird, Denis, Desroches, Frégate and North Islands, but on a charter basis – these flights are handled directly by the hotels on the island.

Note that Mahé is the only hub for flights within the Seychelles.

For information on getting into town from the airport, see p271.

PRACTICALITIES

➡ **Currency** Seychelles rupee (Rs).

➡ **Weights and measures** Metric.

➡ **Electricity** 220V, 50Hz AC; plugs in general use have square pins and three points.

➡ **Local newspapers** The government-controlled daily *Seychelles Nation* (www.nation.sc) and weekly *People* (www.thepeople.sc), also the *Le Nouveau Seychelles Weekly* (www.seychellesweekly.com).

➡ **TV** Seychelles Broadcasting Corporation (www.sbc.com) broadcasts 6am to midnight in English, French and Creole. The news in English is at 6pm. BBC World, France 24 and CNN on satellite.

➡ **Radio** SBC runs the main radio station and 24-hour music station, Paradise FM. BBC World Service and Radio France International (RFI) available in Mahé.

BICYCLE

Bicycles are the principal form of transport on La Digue. On Praslin you can rent bikes at Anse Volbert (p293) or through your accommodation. Mahé is a bit hilly for casual cyclists and most visitors rent cars, so bike rental is hard to find there.

BOAT

Travel by boat is very easy between Mahé, Praslin and La Digue, with regular and efficient ferry services. For all other islands you have to charter a boat or take a tour.

Mahé to Praslin

The **Cat Cocos** (✆4324844, 4324842; www. catcocos.com) catamaran makes two to three return trips daily between Mahé and Praslin. Departing from Victoria, the journey takes about one hour (not that much longer than the plane, if you include check-in time) and the fare is €50 one way (€65 in the 'business' lounge); children under 12 pay half fare. In high season, it's advisable to book your ticket at least a day in advance with the ferry company or through a travel agent. Note that the company provides a free shuttle service between the jetty and the airport.

Mahé to La Digue

Not afraid of seasickness? The schooner **La Belle Seraphina** (✆2566028) is for you. This cargo boat runs between Mahé and La Digue from Monday to Friday and carries passengers if there is room. If you don't mind a bit of discomfort, it's a fun and cheap way to travel. The boat generally departs around 11.30am from Mahé, and around 5am from La Digue, but check when making the booking. The three-hour crossing costs just €15.

The Cat Cocos (p322) runs a daily service to La Digue from Mahé (€63) – it makes a brief stop in Praslin before continuing to La Digue.

Praslin to La Digue

The **Inter-Island Ferry Pty** (✆4232394, 4232329) operates a catamaran service between Praslin and La Digue. There are about seven departures daily between 7am and 5.15pm (5.45pm on Friday, Saturday and Sunday) from Praslin and between 7.30am and 5.45pm (6.15pm on Friday, Saturday and Sunday) from La Digue. The crossing takes about about 15 minutes.

The one-way/return fare is €13/25 per adult. Children under eight pay half price.

BUS

Good news: if you've got time, you don't really need to rent a car to visit the islands.

Mahé

An extensive bus service operates throughout Mahé. Destinations and routes are usually marked on the front of the buses. There is a flat rate of Rs 5 whatever the length of journey; pay the driver as you board. Bus stops have signs and shelters and there are also markings on the road.

Timetables and maps of each route are posted at the terminus in Victoria, where you can also pick up photocopied timetables (Rs 5) at the **SPTC office** (Seychelles Public Transport Corporation; ✆4280227; www.sptc.sc; Victoria; ☺8am-4pm Mon-Fri). All parts of the island are serviced. There's a bus roughly each hour on most routes from around 5.30am until 6.30pm (slightly later heading into Victoria).

Praslin

Praslin also boasts an efficient bus service. The basic route is from Anse Boudin to Mont Plaisir (for Anse Kerlan) via Anse Volbert, Baie Ste Anne, Vallée de Mai, Grand Anse and the airport. Buses run in each direction every hour (every half-hour between Baie St Anne and Mont Plaisir) from 6am to 6pm. Anse Consolation and Anse La Blague are also serviced. For Anse Lazio, get off at Anse Boudin and walk to the beach (about 20 minutes; 1km). Timetables are available at the two tourist offices. There is a flat fare of Rs 5.

CAR

If you want to be controller of your own destiny, your best bet is to rent a car. Most of the road network on Mahé and Praslin is sealed and in good shape. More of a worry are the narrow bends and the speed at which some drivers, especially bus drivers, take them.

Drive on the left, and beware of drivers with fast cars and drowsy brains – especially late on Friday and Saturday nights. The speed limit is supposed to be 40km/h in built-up areas, 65km/h outside towns, and 80km/h on the dual carriageway between Victoria and the airport. On Praslin the limit is 40km/h throughout the island.

Rental

There are any number of car-rental companies on Mahé and quite a few on Praslin. Due to healthy competition, the cheapest you're likely to get on Mahé is about €35 to €40 a day for a small hatchback. Rates on Praslin are about €5 to €10 more expensive. You can book through your hotel or guesthouse. Most apartment and guesthouse owners have negotiated discounts with car-rental outlets for their clients. A number of companies also have offices at the airport.

Drivers must be over 23 years old and have held a driving licence for at least a year. Most companies accept a national licence.

TAXI

Taxis operate on Mahé and Praslin and there are even a handful on La Digue. Agree on a fare before departure.

Survival Guide

Health

As long as you stay up to date with your vaccinations and take some basic preventive measures, you'd have to be pretty unlucky to succumb to most of the health hazards covered here. Mauritius, and to a lesser extent Réunion and the Seychelles, certainly have a fair selection of tropical diseases on offer, but you're much more likely to get a bout of diarrhoea or a sprained ankle than an exotic disease. One recent subject of concern in Mauritius and Réunion has been the chikungunya epidemic of early 2006, which, while having returned to normal at the time of writing, is still something you should be aware of and a situation you should monitor.

BEFORE YOU GO

A little planning before departure, particularly for pre-existing illnesses, will save you a lot of trouble later. Before a long trip, get a check-up from your dentist and from your doctor if you require regular medication or have a chronic illness, eg high blood pressure or asthma. You should also organise spare contact lenses and glasses (and take your optical prescription with you); get a first-aid and medical kit together; and arrange necessary vaccinations.

Travellers can register with the **International Association for Medical Advice to Travellers** (IAMAT; www.iamat.org). Its website can help travellers find a doctor who has recognised training. You might also like to consider doing a first-aid course (contact the Red Cross or St John's Ambulance) or attending a remote medicine first-aid course, such as that offered by the **Royal Geographical Society** (www.wildernessmedicaltraining.co.uk).

If you are bringing medications with you, carry them in their original containers, clearly labelled. A signed and dated letter from your physician describing all medical conditions and medications, including generic names, is also a good idea. If carrying syringes or needles, be sure to have a physician's letter documenting their medical necessity.

Insurance

Find out in advance whether your insurance plan will make payments directly to providers or will reimburse you later for health expenditures (in many countries doctors expect payment in cash). It is vital to ensure that your travel insurance will cover the emergency transport required to get you to a good hospital, or all the way home, by air and with a medical attendant if necessary. Not all insurance policies cover this, so be sure to check the contract carefully. If you need medical care, your insurance company may be able to help locate the nearest hospital or clinic, or ask at your hotel. In an emergency, contact your embassy or consulate.

Medical Checklist

It is a very good idea to carry a medical and first-aid kit with you, to help yourself in the case of minor illness or injury. Following is a list of

RECOMMENDED VACCINATIONS

The **World Health Organization** (www.who.int/en) recommends that all travellers be adequately covered for diphtheria, tetanus, measles, mumps, rubella and polio, as well as for hepatitis B, regardless of their travel destination.

Although no vaccinations are officially required, many doctors recommend hepatitis A and B immunisations just to be sure; a yellow fever certificate is an entry requirement if travelling from an infected region.

items you should consider packing.

→ antidiarrhoeal drugs (eg loperamide)

→ acetaminophen (paracetamol) or aspirin

→ anti-inflammatory drugs (eg ibuprofen)

→ antihistamines (for hay fever and allergic reactions)

→ antibacterial ointment (eg Bactroban) for cuts and abrasions (prescription only)

→ steroid cream or hydrocortisone cream (for allergic rashes)

→ bandages, gauze, gauze rolls

→ adhesive or paper tape

→ scissors, safety pins, tweezers

→ thermometer

→ pocket knife

→ DEET-containing insect repellent for the skin

→ sunblock

→ oral rehydration salts

→ iodine tablets (for water purification)

→ syringes and sterile needles (if travelling to remote areas)

Websites

There is a wealth of travel-health advice available on the internet – www.lonelyplanet.com is a good place to start. The World Health Organization publishes a superb book called *International Travel and Health*, which is revised annually and is available online at no cost at www.who.int/ith. Other health-related websites of general interest are **MD Travel Health** (www.mdtravelhealth.com), the **Centers for Disease Control and Prevention** (www.cdc.gov) and **Fit for Travel** (www.fitfortravel.scot.nhs.uk).

You may also like to consult your government's travel-health website, if one is available:

→ **Australia** (www.dfat.gov.au/travel)

→ **Canada** (www.hc-sc.gc.ca/pphb-dgspsp/tmp-pmv/pub_e.html)

→ **UK** (www.doh.gov.uk)

→ **USA** (www.cdc.gov/travel)

IN MAURITIUS, RÉUNION & SEYCHELLES

Availability & Cost of Health Care

Health care in Mauritius and Réunion is generally excellent; the Seychelles is pretty good by African standards, but some travellers have been critical of the standard of the public health system. Generally, public hospitals offer the cheapest service, but may not have the most up-to-date equipment and medications; private hospitals and clinics are more expensive but tend to have more advanced drugs and equipment and better trained medical staff.

Infectious Diseases

It's a formidable list but, as we say, a few precautions go a long way.

Chikungunya

This viral infection transmitted by certain mosquito bites was traditionally rare in the Indian Ocean until 2005 when an epidemic hit Réunion, Mauritius and Seychelles. Chikungunya (the unusual name means 'that which bends up' in the East African language of Makonde, a reference to the joint pain and physical distortions it creates in sufferers) is rarely fatal, but it can be, and it's always unpleasant. Symptoms are often flu-like, with joint pain, high fever and

body rashes being the most common.

It's important not to confuse it with dengue fever, but if you're diagnosed with chikungunya expect to be down for at least a week, possibly longer. The joint pain can be horrendous and there is no treatment; those infected need simply to rest inside (preferably under a mosquito net to prevent reinfection), taking gentle exercise to avoid joints stiffening unbearably. Over 200 people died in Réunion from chikungunya in 2005 to 2006, but at the time of writing the epidemic was over and should not be considered a major threat. Still, the best way to avoid it is to avoid mosquito bites, so bring plenty of repellent, use the anti-mosquito plug-ins wherever you can and bring a mosquito net if you're really thorough.

Hepatitis A

Hepatitis A is spread through contaminated food (particularly shellfish) and water. It causes jaundice and, although it is rarely fatal, it can cause prolonged lethargy and delayed recovery. If you've had hepatitis A, you shouldn't drink alcohol for up to six months afterwards, but once you've recovered, there won't be any long-term problems. The first symptoms include dark urine and a yellow colour to the whites of the eyes. Sometimes a fever and abdominal pain might be present. Hepatitis A vaccine (Avaxim, VAQTA, Havrix) is given as an injection: a single dose will give protection for up to a year, and a booster after a year gives 10-year protection. Hepatitis A and typhoid vaccines can also be given as a single-dose vaccine (Hepatyrix or Viatim).

Hepatitis B

Hepatitis B is spread through infected blood, contaminated needles and sexual intercourse. It can also be passed from an infected mother to the baby during childbirth. It affects the liver, causing jaundice and occasionally liver failure. Most people recover completely, but some people might be chronic carriers of the virus, which could lead eventually to cirrhosis or liver cancer. Those visiting high-risk areas for extended periods or those with increased social or occupational risk should be immunised. Many countries now routinely give hepatitis B as part of routine childhood vaccinations. It is given singly or can be given at the same time as hepatitis A (Hepatyrix). A course will give protection for at least five years. It can be given over four weeks or six months.

HIV

Human immunodeficiency virus (HIV), the virus that causes acquired immune deficiency syndrome (AIDS), is an enormous problem throughout Africa, but is most acutely felt in sub-Saharan Africa. The virus is spread through infected blood and blood products, by sexual intercourse with an infected partner and from an infected mother to her baby during childbirth and breast-feeding. It can be spread through 'blood to blood' contacts, such as with contaminated instruments during medical, dental, acupuncture and other body-piercing procedures, and through sharing used intravenous needles.

At present there is no cure; medication that might keep the disease under control is available, but these drugs are too expensive for the overwhelming majority of Africans, and are not readily available for travellers either. If you think you might have been infected with HIV, a blood test is necessary; a three-month gap after exposure and before testing is required to allow antibodies to appear in the blood.

Leptospirosis

Cases of leptospirosis have been reported in Réunion. It spreads through the excreta of infected rodents, especially rats. It can cause hepatitis and renal failure, which might be fatal. Symptoms include flu-like fever, headaches, muscle aches and red eyes, among others. Avoid swimming or walking in stagnant waters.

Malaria

The risk of malaria in Mauritius and Réunion is extremely low; there is no risk in the Seychelles.

Rabies

Rabies is spread by receiving the bites or licks of an infected animal on broken skin. In Mauritius, Réunion and Seychelles the risk is mainly from dogs. It is always fatal once the clinical symptoms start (which might be up to several months after an infected bite), so post-bite vaccination should be given as soon as possible. Post-bite vaccination (whether or not you've been vaccinated before the bite) prevents the virus from spreading to the central nervous system. Three preventive injections are needed over a month. If you have not been vaccinated, you will need a course of five injections starting 24 hours after being bitten or as soon as possible after the injury. If you have been vaccinated, you will need fewer post-bite injections, and have more time to seek medical help.

Travellers' Diarrhoea

Although it's not inevitable that you will get diarrhoea while travelling in the region, it's certainly possible. Sometimes dietary changes, such as increased spices or oils, are the cause. To avoid diarrhoea, only eat fresh fruits or vegetables if cooked or peeled, and be wary of dairy products that might contain unpasteurised milk. Although

freshly cooked food can often be a safe option, plates or serving utensils might be dirty, so you should be highly selective when eating food from street vendors (make sure that cooked food is piping hot all the way through).

If you develop diarrhoea, be sure to drink plenty of fluids, preferably an oral rehydration solution containing water (lots), and some salt and sugar. A few loose stools don't require treatment, but if you start having more than four or five stools a day, you should start taking an antibiotic (usually a quinoline drug, such as ciprofloxacin or norfloxacin) and an antidiarrhoeal agent (such as loperamide) if you are not within easy reach of a toilet. However, if diarrhoea is bloody, persists for more than 72 hours or is accompanied by fever, shaking chills or severe abdominal pain, you should seek medical attention.

Yellow Fever

Although not a problem in Mauritius, Réunion or the Seychelles, travellers should still carry a certificate as evidence of vaccination if they have recently been in an infected country. For a list of these countries visit the **World Health Organization** (www.who.int/en) website or the **Centers for Disease Control and Prevention** (www.cdc.gov) website. A traveller without a legally required, up-to-date certificate may be vaccinated and detained in isolation at the port of arrival for up to 10 days or possibly repatriated.

Diving Health & Safety

Health Requirements

Officially, a doctor should check you over before you do a course, and fill out a form full of diving health questions. In practice, most dive schools will let you dive or do a course if you complete a medical questionnaire, but the check-up is still a good idea. This is especially so if you have any problem at all with your breathing, ears or sinuses. If you are an asthmatic, have any other chronic breathing difficulties or any inner-ear problems, you shouldn't do any scuba diving.

A simple medical certificate is compulsory for diving in Réunion (but not for introductory dives). You can get one from your doctor in your home country or have it emailed to the dive centre. Otherwise, you can get one from any doctor in Réunion.

Decompression Sickness

This is a very serious condition – usually, though not always, associated with diver error. The most common symptoms are unusual fatigue or weakness; skin itch; pain in the arms, legs (joints or mid-limbs) or torso; dizziness and vertigo; local numbness, tingling or paralysis; and shortness of breath.

The most common causes of decompression sickness (or the 'bends' as it is commonly known) are diving too deep, staying at depth for too long or ascending too quickly. This results in nitrogen coming out of solution in the blood and forming bubbles, most commonly in the bones and particularly in the joints or in weak spots such as healed fractured sites.

Avoid flying after diving, as it causes nitrogen to come out of blood even faster than it would at sea level.

The only treatment for decompression sickness is to put the patient into a recompression chamber. There are recompression chambers in Mauritius, Réunion and Seychelles.

Insurance

In addition to normal travel insurance, it's a very good idea to take out specific diving cover, which will pay for evac-uation to a recompression facility and the cost of hyperbaric treatment in a chamber. **Divers Alert Network** (DAN; www.diversalertnetwork.org) is a nonprofit diving-safety organisation. It provides a policy that covers evacuation and recompression.

Environmental Hazards

Heat Exhaustion

This condition occurs following heavy sweating and excessive fluid loss with inadequate replacement of fluids and salt, and is particularly common in hot climates when taking unaccustomed exercise before full acclimatisation. Symptoms include headache, dizziness and tiredness. Dehydration is already happening by the time you feel thirsty – aim to drink sufficient water to produce pale, diluted urine. Self-treatment is by fluid replacement with water and/or fruit juice, and cooling by cold water and fans. The treatment of the salt-loss component consists of consuming salty fluids as in soup, and adding a little more table salt to foods than usual.

Heatstroke

Heat exhaustion is a precursor to the much more serious condition of heatstroke. In this case there is damage to the sweating mechanism, with an excessive rise in body temperature; irrational and hyperactive behaviour; and eventually loss of consciousness and death. Rapid cooling by spraying the body with water and fanning is ideal. Emergency fluid and electrolyte replacement is usually also required by intravenous drip.

Insect Bites & Stings

Mosquitoes in the region rarely carry chikungunya and dengue fever, but they (and other insects) can cause irritation and infected bites. To avoid these, take the same precautions as you would for avoiding malaria, including wearing long pants and long-sleeved shirts, using mosquito repellents, avoiding highly scented perfumes or aftershaves etc. Bee and wasp stings cause major problems only to those who have a severe allergy to the stings (anaphylaxis), in which case carry an adrenaline (epinephrine) injection.

Leeches may be present in damp rainforest conditions; they attach themselves to your skin to suck your blood. Salt or a lighted cigarette end will make them fall off. Ticks can cause skin infections and other more serious diseases. If a tick is found attached, press down around the tick's head with tweezers, grab the head and gently pull upwards.

Marine Life

A number of Indian Ocean species are poisonous or may sting or bite. Watch out above all for sea urchins. Other far rarer creatures

---

TAP WATER

It's not safe to drink the tap water in Rodrigues; stick with bottled water if you visit the island. As a general rule, the tap water in Réunion, the Seychelles and the rest of Mauritius is safe to drink, but always take care immediately after a cyclone or cyclonic storm as mains water supplies can become contaminated by dead animals and other debris washed into the system. Never drink from streams as it might put you at risk of waterborne diseases.

to look out for include the gaudy lion fish with its poisonous spined fins, and the cleverly camouflaged – and exceptionally poisonous – stonefish, which lives camouflaged amid coral formations. Some shells, such as the cone shell, can fire out a deadly poisonous barb. The species of fire coral, which looks like yellowish brush-like coral growths, packs a powerful sting if touched.

Shark attacks on surfers have been an issue in Réunion in recent years, especially off Boucan-Canot, St-Gilles-les-Bains and Trois-Bassins. Check with surf life-saving groups about local risks. In the Seychelles, two fatal shark attacks on swimmers were reported in 2011; both occurred at Anse Lazio.

Language

Along with the local Creoles, French is spoken (and official) in all three destinations included in this book. You'll find that menus on the islands are mostly in French, with English variations in some cases.

CREOLES

The Creoles spoken in Mauritius, Réunion and Seychelles are a blend of French and an assortment of African languages, with some regional variations. Seychelles Creole is similar to that of Mauritius, but differs significantly from the Creole spoken in Réunion. Note also that the Creole spoken in Mauritius and Seychelles is more comprehensible to French people than that of Réunion, even though Réunion itself is thoroughly French.

Mauritius

The official languages of Mauritius are English and French. English is used mainly in government and business. French is the spoken language in educated and cultural circles, and is used in newspapers and magazines. You'll probably find that most people will first speak to you in French and only switch to English once they realise you're an English speaker. Most Indo-Mauritians speak Bhojpuri, derived from a Bihari dialect of Hindi.

There are major differences between the pronunciation and usage of Creole and standard French. Here are some basic phrases you may find handy.

WANT MORE?

For in-depth language information and handy phrases, check out Lonely Planet's French Phrasebook. You'll find it at **shop.lonelyplanet.com**, or you can buy Lonely Planet's iPhone phrasebooks at the Apple App Store.

How are you?	*Ki manière?*
Fine, thanks.	*Mon byen, mersi.*
I don't understand.	*Mo pas comprend.*
OK.	*Correc.*
Not OK.	*Pas correc.*
he/she/it	*li*
Do you have ...?	*Ou éna ...?*
I'd like ...	*Mo oulé ...*
I'm thirsty.	*Mo soif.*
Cheers!	*Tapeta!*
Great!	*Formidabe!*

Réunion

French is the official language of Réunion, but Creole is the most widely spoken language. Few people speak English.

Keep in mind that a word that means one thing in French can mean something completely different in Creole, and where a word does have the same meaning, it's usually pronounced differently in Creole. Creole also has a number of *bons mots* and charming idioms, which are often the result of Hindi, Arab and Malagasy influences or misinterpretations of the original French word. For example, *bonbon la fesse* (bum toffee) is a suppository, *conserves* (preserves) are sunglasses, and *cœur d'amant* (lover's heart) is a cardamom seed. *Coco* is your head, *caze* is your house, *marmaille* is your child, *baba* is your baby, *band* means 'family', *le fait noir* means 'night', and *mi aime jou* means 'I love you'.

There are two basic rules of Creole pronunciation: r is generally not pronounced (when it is, it's pronounced lightly), and the soft j and ch sounds of French are pronounced as 'z' and 's' respectively. For example, *manzay* is the Creole equivalent of French 'manger' (to eat), *zamais* is used for 'jamais' (never), and you'll hear *sontay* instead of 'chanter' (to sing).

Seychelles

English and French are the official languages of the Seychelles. Most people speak both, although French Creole (known as Kreol Seselwa) is the lingua franca. Kreol Seselwa was 'rehabilitated' and made semi-official in 1981, and is increasingly used in newspapers and literature. These days, most Seychellois will use English when speaking to tourists, French when conducting business, and Creole in the home.

Seychelles Creole is similar to that of Mauritius and Martinique, but differs remarkably from that of Réunion. The soft pronunciation of certain French consonants is hardened and some syllables are dropped completely. The soft j becomes 'z', for example. The following Creole phrases can get you started:

Good morning./ Good afternoon.	Bonzour.
How are you?	Comman sava?
Fine, thanks.	Mon byen, mersi.
What's your name?	Ki mannyer ou appel?
My name is ...	Mon appel ...
Where do you live?	Koté ou resté?
I don't understand.	Mon pas konpran.
I like it.	Mon kontan.
Where is ...?	Ol i ...?
How much is that?	Kombyen sa?
I'm thirsty.	Mon soif.
Can I have a beer, please?	Mon kapa ganny en labyer silvouplé?

FRENCH

The pronunciation of French is pretty straightforward for English speakers as the sounds used in spoken French can almost all be found in English. There are just a couple of exceptions: nasal vowels (represented in our pronunciation guides by o or u followed by an almost inaudible nasal consonant sound m, n or ng), the 'funny' u (ew in our guides) and the deep-in-the-throat r. Bearing these few points in mind and reading our pronunciation guides as if they were English, you'll be understood just fine.

In the following phrases we have included masculine and femine forms where necessary, separated by a slash and indicated with the abbreviations 'm/f'.

Basics

Hello.	Bonjour.	bon·zhoor
Goodbye.	Au revoir.	o·rer·vwa
Excuse me.	Excusez-moi.	ek·skew·zay·mwa
Sorry.	Pardon.	par·don
Yes./No.	Oui./Non.	wee/non
Please.	S'il vous plaît.	seel voo play
Thank you.	Merci.	mair·see
You're welcome.	De rien.	der ree·en

How are you?
Comment allez-vous?   ko·mon ta·lay·voo

Fine, and you?
Bien, merci. Et vous?   byun mair·see ay voo

My name is ...
Je m'appelle ...   zher ma·pel ...

What's your name?
Comment vous appelez-vous?   ko·mon voo· za·play voo

Do you speak English?
Parlez-vous anglais?   par·lay·voo ong·glay

I don't understand.
Je ne comprends pas.   zher ner kom·pron pa

Accommodation

Do you have any rooms available?
Est-ce que vous avez des chambres libres?   es·ker voo za·vay day shom·brer lee·brer

How much is it per night/person?
Quel est le prix par nuit/personne?   kel ay ler pree par nwee/per·son

Is breakfast included?
Est-ce que le petit déjeuner est inclus?   es·ker ler per·tee day·zher·nay ayt en·klew

campsite	camping	kom·peeng
dorm	dortoir	dor·twar
guesthouse	pension	pon·syon
hotel	hôtel	o·tel
youth hostel	auberge de jeunesse	o·berzh der zher·nes
a ... room	une chambre ...	ewn shom·brer ...
single	à un lit	a un lee
double	avec un grand lit	a·vek un gron lee
twin	avec des lits jumeaux	a·vek day lee zhew·mo
with (a) ...	avec ...	a·vek ...
air-con	climatiseur	klee·ma·tee·zer
bathroom	une salle de bains	ewn sal der bun
window	fenêtre	fer·nay·trer

Directions

Where's ...?
Où est ...? — oo ay ...

What's the address?
Quelle est l'adresse? — kel ay la·dres

Could you write the address, please?
Est-ce que vous pourriez — es·ker voo poo·ryay
écrire l'adresse, — ay·kreer la·dres
s'il vous plaît? — seel voo play

Can you show me (on the map)?
Pouvez-vous m'indiquer — poo·vay·voo mun·dee·kay
(sur la carte)? — (sewr la kart)

at the corner	*au coin*	o kwun
at the traffic lights	*aux feux*	o fer
behind	*derrière*	dair·ryair
in front of	*devant*	der·von
far (from)	*loin (de)*	lwun (der)
left	*gauche*	gosh
near (to)	*près (de)*	pray (der)
opposite ...	*en face de ...*	on fas der ...
right	*droite*	drwat
straight ahead	*tout droit*	too drwa

Eating & Drinking

What would you recommend?
Qu'est-ce que vous — kes·ker voo
conseillez? — kon·say·yay

What's in that dish?
Quels sont les — kel son lay
ingrédients? — zun·gray·dyon

I'm a vegetarian.
Je suis — zher swee
végétarien/ — vay·zhay·ta·ryun/
végétarienne. — vay·zhay·ta·ryen (m/f)

I don't eat ...
Je ne mange pas ... — zher ner monzh pa ...

Cheers!
Santé! — son·tay

That was delicious.
C'était délicieux! — say·tay day·lee·syer

Please bring the bill.
Apportez-moi — a·por·tay·mwa
l'addition, s'il vous plaît. — la·dee·syon seel voo play

I'd like to reserve a table for ...	*Je voudrais réserver une table pour ...*	zher voo·dray ray·zair·vay ewn ta·bler poor ...
(eight) o'clock	*(vingt) heures*	(vungt) er
(two) people	*(deux) personnes*	(der) pair·son

Key Words

appetiser	*entrée*	on·tray
bottle	*bouteille*	boo·tay
breakfast	*petit déjeuner*	per·tee day·zher·nay
children's menu	*menu pour enfants*	mer·new poor on·fon
cold	*froid*	frwa
delicatessen	*traiteur*	tray·ter
dinner	*dîner*	dee·nay
dish	*plat*	pla
food	*nourriture*	noo·ree·tewr
fork	*fourchette*	foor·shet
glass	*verre*	vair
grocery store	*épicerie*	ay·pees·ree
highchair	*chaise haute*	shay zot

hot	chaud	sho
knife	couteau	koo·to
local speciality	spécialité locale	spay·sya·lee·tay lo·kal
lunch	déjeuner	day·zher·nay
main course	plat principal	pla prun·see·pal
market	marché	mar·shay
menu (in English)	carte (en anglais)	kart (on ong·glay)
plate	assiette	a·syet
spoon	cuillère	kwee·yair
wine list	carte des vins	kart day vun
with/without	avec/sans	a·vek/son

Meat & Fish

beef	bœuf	berf
chicken	poulet	poo·lay
crab	crabe	krab
lamb	agneau	a·nyo
oyster	huître	wee·trer
pork	porc	por
snail	escargot	es·kar·go
squid	calmar	kal·mar
turkey	dinde	dund
veal	veau	vo

Fruit & Vegetables

apple	pomme	pom
apricot	abricot	ab·ree·ko
asparagus	asperge	a·spairzh
beans	haricots	a·ree·ko
beetroot	betterave	be·trav
cabbage	chou	shoo
cherry	cerise	ser·reez
corn	maïs	ma·ees
cucumber	concombre	kong·kom·brer
grape	raisin	ray·zun

lemon	citron	see·tron
lettuce	laitue	lay·tew
mushroom	champignon	shom·pee·nyon
peach	pêche	pesh
peas	petit pois	per·tee pwa
(red/green) pepper	poivron (rouge/vert)	pwa·vron (roozh/vair)
pineapple	ananas	a·na·nas
plum	prune	prewn
potato	pomme de terre	pom der tair
prune	pruneau	prew·no
pumpkin	citrouille	see·troo·yer
shallot	échalote	eh·sha·lot
spinach	épinards	eh·pee·nar
strawberry	fraise	frez
tomato	tomate	to·mat
vegetable	légume	lay·gewm

Other

bread	pain	pun
butter	beurre	ber
cheese	fromage	fro·mazh
egg	œuf	erf
honey	miel	myel
jam	confiture	kon·fee·tewr
lentils	lentilles	lon·tee·yer
pasta/noodles	pâtes	pat
pepper	poivre	pwa·vrer
rice	riz	ree
salt	sel	sel
sugar	sucre	sew·krer
vinegar	vinaigre	vee·nay·grer

Drinks

beer	bière	bee·yair
coffee	café	ka·fay
(orange) juice	jus (d'orange)	zhew (do·ronzh)
milk	lait	lay
red wine	vin rouge	vun roozh
tea	thé	tay
(mineral) water	eau (minérale)	o (mee·nay·ral)
white wine	vin blanc	vun blong

Signs

Entrée	Entrance
Femmes	Women
Fermé	Closed
Hommes	Men
Interdit	Prohibited
Ouvert	Open
Renseignements	Information
Sortie	Exit
Toilettes/WC	Toilets

Emergencies

Help!
Au secours!   o skoor

Leave me alone!
Fichez-moi la paix!   fee·shay·mwa la pay

I'm lost.
Je suis perdu/perdue.   zhe swee·pair·dew (m/f)

Call a doctor.
Appelez un médecin.   a·play un mayd·sun

Call the police.
Appelez la police.   a·play la po·lees

I'm ill.
Je suis malade.   zher swee ma·lad

It hurts here.
J'ai une douleur ici.   zhay ewn doo·ler ee·see

I'm allergic to ...
Je suis allergique ...   zher swee za·lair·zheek ...

Where are the toilets?
Où sont les toilettes?   oo son ley twa·let

Shopping & Services

I'd like to buy ...
Je voudrais acheter ...   zher voo·dray ash·tay ...

Can I look at it?
Est-ce que je   es·ker zher
peux le voir?   per ler vwar

I'm just looking.
Je regarde.   zher rer·gard

I don't like it.
Cela ne me plaît pas.   ser·la ner mer play pa

How much is it?
C'est combien?   say kom·byun

It's too expensive.
C'est trop cher.   say tro shair

Can you lower the price?
Vous pouvez baisser   voo poo·vay bay·say
le prix?   ler pree

There's a mistake in the bill.
Il y a une erreur dans   eel ya ewn ay·rer don
la note.   la not

ATM	*guichet*	gee·shay
	automatique	o·to·ma·teek
	de banque	der bonk
credit card	*carte de crédit*	kart der kray·dee
internet cafe	*cybercafé*	see·bair·ka·fay
post office	*bureau de poste*	bew·ro der post
tourist office	*office de*	o·fees der
	tourisme	too·rees·mer

Time & Dates

What time is it?
Quelle heure est-il?   kel er ay til

It's (eight) o'clock.
Il est (huit) heures.   il ay (weet) er

It's half past (10).
Il est (dix) heures   il ay (deez) er
et demie.   ay day·mee

Question Words		
How?	*Comment?*	ko·mon
What?	*Quoi?*	kwa
When?	*Quand?*	kon
Where?	*Où?*	oo
Who?	*Qui?*	kee
Why?	*Pourquoi?*	poor·kwa

morning	*matin*	ma·tun
afternoon	*après-midi*	a·pray·mee·dee
evening	*soir*	swar
yesterday	*hier*	yair
today	*aujourd'hui*	o·zhoor·dwee
tomorrow	*demain*	der·mun
Monday	*lundi*	lun·dee
Tuesday	*mardi*	mar·dee
Wednesday	*mercredi*	mair·krer·dee
Thursday	*jeudi*	zher·dee
Friday	*vendredi*	von·drer·dee
Saturday	*samedi*	sam·dee
Sunday	*dimanche*	dee·monsh
January	*janvier*	zhon·vyay
February	*février*	fayv·ryay
March	*mars*	mars
April	*avril*	a·vreel
May	*mai*	may
June	*juin*	zhwun
July	*juillet*	zhwee·yay
August	*août*	oot
September	*septembre*	sep·tom·brer
October	*octobre*	ok·to·brer
November	*novembre*	no·vom·brer
December	*décembre*	day·som·brer

Transport

boat	*bateau*	ba·to
bus	*bus*	bews
plane	*avion*	a·vyon
train	*train*	trun
first	*premier*	prer·myay
last	*dernier*	dair·nyay
next	*prochain*	pro·shun

Numbers

1	*un*	un
2	*deux*	der
3	*trois*	trwa
4	*quatre*	ka·trer
5	*cinq*	sungk
6	*six*	sees
7	*sept*	set
8	*huit*	weet
9	*neuf*	nerf
10	*dix*	dees
20	*vingt*	vung
30	*trente*	tront
40	*quarante*	ka·ront
50	*cinquante*	sung·kont
60	*soixante*	swa·sont
70	*soixante-dix*	swa·son·dees
80	*quatre-vingts*	ka·trer·vung
90	*quatre-vingt-dix*	ka·trer·vung·dees
100	*cent*	son
1000	*mille*	meel

I want to go to ...
Je voudrais aller à ...   zher voo·dray a·lay a ...

Does it stop at ...?
Est-ce qu'il s'arrête à ...?   es·kil sa·ret a ...

At what time does it leave/arrive?
À quelle heure est-ce   a kel er es
qu'il part/arrive?   kil par/a·reev

Can you tell me when we get to ...?
Pouvez-vous me   poo·vay·voo mer
dire quand   deer kon
nous arrivons à ...?   noo za·ree·von a ...

I want to get off here.
Je veux descendre   zher ver day·son·drer
ici.   ee·see

a ... ticket	*un billet ...*	un bee·yay ...
1st-class	*de première classe*	der prem·yair klas
2nd-class	*de deuxième classe*	der der·zyem las
one-way	*simple*	sum·pler
return	*aller et retour*	a·lay ay rer·toor

aisle seat	*côté couloir*	ko·tay kool·war
delayed	*en retard*	on rer·tar
cancelled	*annulé*	a·new·lay
platform	*quai*	kay
ticket office	*guichet*	gee·shay
timetable	*horaire*	o·rair
train station	*gare*	gar
window seat	*côté fenêtre*	ko·tay fe·ne·trer

I'd like to hire a ...	*Je voudrais louer ...*	zher voo·dray loo·way ...
4WD	*un quatre-quatre*	un kat·kat
car	*une voiture*	ewn vwa·tewr
bicycle	*un vélo*	un vay·lo
motorcycle	*une moto*	ewn mo·to

child seat	*siège-enfant*	syezh·on·fon
diesel	*diesel*	dyay·zel
helmet	*casque*	kask
mechanic	*mécanicien*	may·ka·nee·syun
petrol/gas	*essence*	ay·sons
service station	*station-service*	sta·syon·ser·vees

Is this the road to ...?
C'est la route pour ...?   say la root poor ...

(How long) Can I park here?
(Combien de temps)   (kom·byun der tom)
Est-ce que je peux   es·ker zher per
stationner ici?   sta·syo·nay ee·see

The car/motorbike has broken down (at ...).
La voiture/moto est   la vwa·tewr/mo·to ay
tombée en panne (à ...).   tom·bay on pan (a ...)

I have a flat tyre.
Mon pneu est à plat.   mom pner ay ta pla

I've run out of petrol.
Je suis en panne   zher swee zon pan
d'essence.   day·sons

I've lost my car keys.
J'ai perdu les clés de   zhay per·dew lay klay der
ma voiture.   ma vwa·tewr

GLOSSARY

anse – bay
auberge – farm inn

baba figue – the blossom of the banana tree
baie – bay
bassin – small lake

Cafre – person whose ancestors are black
case créole – traditional Creole house
cavadee – Hindu festival featuring self-mutilating devotees
cerfs – stags
chambre d'hôte – family-run B&B
cirque – steep-sided hollow formed by glacial erosion
CMAS – Confédération Mondiale des Activités Subaquatiques

écart – settlement

ferme-auberge – farm restaurant
filaos – casuarina trees
forêt – forest

GAB – guichet automatique de banque
gare routière – bus station
gîte – self-catering accommodation
gîte d'étape – walkers lodge
gîte de montagne – mountain lodge

grand(e) – large
grands blancs – rich white people
gris gris – black magic
guichet automatique de banque – automatic teller machine (ATM)

hauts – highlands
hôtel de ville – town hall; see also mairie

île – island
îlet – hamlet, in Réunion
îlot – island

lambrequins – ornamental window and door borders
lontan – of yore

mairie – town hall
maloya – traditional dance music of Réunion
Malbar – persons of Tamil origin, in Réunion
marmite – traditional cooking pot
marrons – slaves who escaped from their owners
Mascarene Islands – the collective term for the group of volcanic islands in the West Indian Ocean consisting of Réunion, Mauritius and Rodrigues
menu/menu du jour – set menu of the day
métro/métropole – mainland France as known in Réunion

MWF – Mauritian Wildlife Foundation

office du tourisme – tourist office

PADI – Professional Association of Diving Instructors
petit – small
pirogue – a canoe made from a tree trunk
piton – peak

route forestière – forestry road

séga – dance of African origin
seggae – combination of reggae and traditional séga music
sentier botanique – nature trail
SSI – Scuba Schools International
sud sauvage – wild south (southern part of Réunion island)

table d'hôte – meal served at a chambre d'hôte
teemeedee – Hindu/Tamil fire-walking ceremony honouring the gods

vacoa – screw pines; also known as pandanus
varangue – verandah

Zoreilles – name used in Réunion for people from mainland France (literally 'the ears')

Behind the Scenes

SEND US YOUR FEEDBACK

We love to hear from travellers – your comments keep us on our toes and help make our books better. Our well-travelled team reads every word on what you loved or loathed about this book. Although we cannot reply individually to postal submissions, we always guarantee that your feedback goes straight to the appropriate authors, in time for the next edition. Each person who sends us information is thanked in the next edition – the most useful submissions are rewarded with a selection of digital PDF chapters.

Visit **lonelyplanet.com/contact** to submit your updates and suggestions or to ask for help. Our award-winning website also features inspirational travel stories, news and discussions.

Note: We may edit, reproduce and incorporate your comments in Lonely Planet products such as guidebooks, websites and digital products, so let us know if you don't want your comments reproduced or your name acknowledged. For a copy of our privacy policy visit lonelyplanet.com/privacy.

OUR READERS

Many thanks to the travellers who used the last edition and wrote to us with helpful hints, useful advice and interesting anecdotes:
Sarah Clarke, Anna Donaghy, Veronique M d'Unienville, Frank Gloor, Jose Guichard, Angie Juttner-Hart, Peter Levin, Joyce Mcmahon, Carly Reeves, Dave Simpson, Didier Zurwerra

AUTHOR THANKS

Jean-Bernard Carillet

Thanks to Glenn van der Knijff for his support and dedication, and to the production team, especially Brigitte, Barbara and the carto team. Special thanks to Jean-Paul, Axelle and the kids in St-Paul for their help with logistics and camaraderie. I'm also grateful to Anais, Emilie, Mavreen and Ravinia Larue. And to Chris and Eva – *un gros bisou.*

Anthony Ham

Thanks to Glenn van der Knijff for sending me here, and to David Andrew for bird-watching tips. Special thanks to Dr Vikash Tatayah of the Mauritian Wildlife Foundation, Diane Laboucherie and Raj Somma (Île aux Aigrettes), Veronique and Stefanie (Blue Bay), Amanda Waterstone (Rodrigues) and Veronique and Guillaume (Rodrigues). Thanks to Ron and Jan for welcoming us back home so warmly. And to Marina, Carlota and Valentina – *os quiero, os quiero, os quiero.*

ACKNOWLEDGMENTS

Climate map data adapted from Peel MC, Finlayson BL & McMahon TA (2007) 'Updated World Map of the Köppen-Geiger Climate Classification', Hydrology and Earth System Sciences, 11, 1633¬44.

Cover photograph: Boats at Tamarin, Mauritius, AMK/Getty Images

THIS BOOK

This 8th edition of Lonely Planet's *Mauritius, Réunion & Seychelles* guidebook was researched and written by Jean-Bernard Carillet and Anthony Ham. The previous edition was written by Jean-Bernard Carillet and Brandon Presser, while the 6th edition was written by Tom Masters and Jean-Bernard Carillet. This guidebook was commissioned in Lonely Planet's Melbourne office, and produced by the following:

Commissioning Editors Will Gourlay, Suzannah Shwer, Glenn van der Knijff

Coordinating Editors Carolyn Boicos, Monique Perrin

Senior Cartographer Corey Hutchison

Coordinating Layout Designer Joseph Spanti

Managing Editor Brigitte Ellemor

Senior Editors Catherine Naghten, Karyn Noble

Managing Cartographer Adrian Persoglia

Managing Layout Designer Chris Girdler

Assisting Editors Judith Bamber, Paul Harding

Cover Research Naomi Parker

Internal Image Research Kylie McLaughlin

Language Content Branislava Vladisavljevic

Thanks to Ryan Evans, Larissa Frost, Bronwyn Hicks, Genesys India, Jouve India, Andi Jones, Trent Paton, Kerrianne Southway, Samantha Tyson, Gerard Walker

Index

INDEX C–E

Map Legend

Sights

- Beach
- Bird Sanctuary
- Buddhist
- Castle/Palace
- Christian
- Confucian
- Hindu
- Islamic
- Jain
- Jewish
- Monument
- Museum/Gallery/Historic Building
- Ruin
- Sento Hot Baths/Onsen
- Shinto
- Sikh
- Taoist
- Winery/Vineyard
- Zoo/Wildlife Sanctuary
- Other Sight

Activities, Courses & Tours

- Bodysurfing
- Diving/Snorkelling
- Canoeing/Kayaking
- Course/Tour
- Skiing
- Snorkelling
- Surfing
- Swimming/Pool
- Walking
- Windsurfing
- Other Activity

Sleeping

- Sleeping
- Camping

Eating

- Eating

Drinking & Nightlife

- Drinking & Nightlife
- Cafe

Entertainment

- Entertainment

Shopping

- Shopping

Information

- Bank
- Embassy/Consulate
- Hospital/Medical
- Internet
- Police
- Post Office
- Telephone
- Toilet
- Tourist Information
- Other Information

Geographic

- Beach
- Hut/Shelter
- Lighthouse
- Lookout
- Mountain/Volcano
- Oasis
- Park
- Pass
- Picnic Area
- Waterfall

Population

- Capital (National)
- Capital (State/Province)
- City/Large Town
- Town/Village

Transport

- Airport
- Border crossing
- Bus
- Cable car/Funicular
- Cycling
- Ferry
- Metro station
- Monorail
- Parking
- Petrol station
- Subway station
- Taxi
- Train station/Railway
- Tram
- Underground station
- Other Transport

Note: Not all symbols displayed above appear on the maps in this book

Routes

- Tollway
- Freeway
- Primary
- Secondary
- Tertiary
- Lane
- Unsealed road
- Road under construction
- Plaza/Mall
- Steps
- Tunnel
- Pedestrian overpass
- Walking Tour
- Walking Tour detour
- Path/Walking Trail

Boundaries

- International
- State/Province
- Disputed
- Regional/Suburb
- Marine Park
- Cliff
- Wall

Hydrography

- River, Creek
- Intermittent River
- Canal
- Water
- Dry/Salt/Intermittent Lake
- Reef

Areas

- Airport/Runway
- Beach/Desert
- Cemetery (Christian)
- Cemetery (Other)
- Glacier
- Mudflat
- Park/Forest
- Sight (Building)
- Sportsground
- Swamp/Mangrove

OUR STORY

A beat-up old car, a few dollars in the pocket and a sense of adventure. In 1972 that's all Tony and Maureen Wheeler needed for the trip of a lifetime – across Europe and Asia overland to Australia. It took several months, and at the end – broke but inspired – they sat at their kitchen table writing and stapling together their first travel guide, *Across Asia on the Cheap*. Within a week they'd sold 1500 copies. Lonely Planet was born.

Today, Lonely Planet has offices in Melbourne, London and Oakland, with more than 600 staff and writers. We share Tony's belief that 'a great guidebook should do three things: inform, educate and amuse'.

OUR WRITERS

Jean-Bernard Carillet

Coordinating Author, Réunion, Seychelles Paris-based journalist and photographer Jean-Bernard has clocked up numerous trips to the Indian Ocean and written extensively about Réunion and the Seychelles. A diving instructor and a fan of all things outdoorsy, he never misses an opportunity to explore these islands in more depth. In Réunion he tackled paragliding, hiking, horse riding, diving and canyoning. In the Seychelles he examined every burg, shore and cove while searching for the perfect beach, the best dinner buffet, the best-value hotels and the most sensational panoramas. As an incorrigible Frenchman and foodie, he confesses a pronounced penchant for the delicious Creole cuisine (hmm, those hearty curries). Jean-Bernard's wanderlust has taken him to six continents, inspiring numerous articles and his writing of some 30 Lonely Planet guidebooks.

Jean-Bernard also wrote the Welcome to, Need to Know, Islands at a Glance, Diving, Hiking in Réunion, A Glimpse of Paradise and Health chapters.

Anthony Ham

Mauritius, Rodrigues Anthony has spent much of his adult life writing and photographing his way around the world, particularly Europe, the Middle East and all corners of Africa. His passions are wildlife, wilderness and wild places, and it was these that gave him particular pleasure in Mauritius (where he found himself drawn to Île aux Aigrettes, Black River Gorges and the wild eastern coast) and deliciously remote Rodrigues. After 10 years living in Madrid he recently returned to Australia, where he lives with his wife and two daughters.

Anthony also wrote the Top 17, If You Like..., Month by Month and Itineraries chapters.

Read more about Anthony at
lonelyplanet.com/members/anthony_ham

Published by Lonely Planet Publications Pty Ltd
ABN 36 005 607 983
8th edition – Dec 2013
ISBN 978 1 74220 045 3
© Lonely Planet 2013   Photographs © as indicated 2013
10 9 8 7 6 5 4 3 2 1
Printed in China

Although the authors and Lonely Planet have taken all reasonable care in preparing this book, we make no warranty about the accuracy or completeness of its content and, to the maximum extent permitted, disclaim all liability arising from its use.